# Lecture Notes in Computer Science

*Commenced Publication in 1973*
Founding and Former Series Editors:
Gerhard Goos, Juris Hartmanis, and Jan van Leeuwen

Stamatis Vassiliadis   Mladen Bereković
Timo D. Hämäläinen (Eds.)

# Embedded Computer Systems: Architectures, Modeling, and Simulation

7th International Workshop, SAMOS 2007
Samos, Greece, July 16-19, 2007
Proceedings

 Springer

Volume Editors

Stamatis Vassiliadis
Mladen Bereković
Delft University of Technology
Mekelweg 4, 2628 CD Delft,The Netherlands
E-mail: {s.vassiliadis, m.berekovic}@ewi.tudelft.nl

Timo D. Hämäläinen
Tampere University of Technology
P.O.Box 553, 33101 Tampere, Finland
E-mail: timo.hamalainen@tut.fi

Library of Congress Control Number: 2007930610


CR Subject Classification (1998): C, B


LNCS Sublibrary: SL 1 – Theoretical Computer Science and General Issues

ISSN      0302-9743
ISBN-10   3-540-73622-0 Springer Berlin Heidelberg New York
ISBN-13   978-3-540-73622-6 Springer Berlin Heidelberg New York

Springer is a part of Springer Science+Business Media

springer.com

© Springer-Verlag Berlin Heidelberg 2007
Printed in Germany

Typesetting: Camera-ready by author, data conversion by Scientific Publishing Services, Chennai, India
Printed on acid-free paper      SPIN: 12090457      06/3180      5 4 3 2 1 0

# In Memoriam Stamatis Vassiliadis (1951 - 2007)

Stamatis Vassiliadis

Professor at Delft University of Technology
IEEE Fellow - ACM Fellow
Member of the Dutch Academy of Sciences - KNAW

passed away on April 7th, 2007.

He was an outstanding computer scientist and due to his vivid and hearty
manner he was a good friend to all of us.
Born in Manolates on Samos (Greece) he established in 2001 the successful
series of SAMOS conferences and workshops.
These series will not be the same without him.
We will keep him in our hearts and we are with his family in these
mournful days.

In Memoriam Stamatis Vassiliadis (1951 - 2007)

# Preface

Stamatis Vassiliadis established the SAMOS workshop in the year 2001—an event which combines his devotion to computer engineering and his pride for Samos, the island where he was born. The quiet and inspiring northern mountainside of this Mediterranean island together with his enthusiasm and warmth created a unique atmosphere that made this event so successful. Stamatis Vassiliadis passed away on Saturday, April 7, 2007. The research community wants to express its gratitude to him for the creation of the SAMOS workshop, which will not be the same without him. We would like to dedicate this proceedings volume to the memory of Stamatis Vassiliadis.

The SAMOS workshop is an international gathering of highly qualified researchers from academia and industry, sharing their ideas during a 3-day lively discussion. The workshop meeting is one of two colocated events—the other event being the IC-SAMOS. The workshop is unique in the sense that not only solved research problems are presented and discussed but also (partly) unsolved problems and in-depth topical reviews can be unleashed in the scientific arena. Consequently, the workshop provides the participants with an environment where collaboration rather than competition is fostered.

SAMOS VII followed the series of workshops started in 2001 in a new expanded program. This year there were also two parallel sessions for current and foreseen topics. The SAMOS VII workshop attracted a total of 116 papers. We are grateful to all authors who submitted their papers. They came from 27 countries and regions: Austria(1), Belgium(4), Brazil(5), Canada(2), China(4), Croatia(1), Czech Republic(3), Finland(11), France(2), Germany(7), Greece(2), Hong Kong(1), India(4), Ireland(3), Italy(2), Japan(2), The Netherlands(9), Portugal(1), Republic of Korea(21), Republic of Singapore(2), Romania(1), Spain(7), Sweden(2), Taiwan(1), Turkey(5), UK(2), and USA(9).

All papers went through a rigorous reviewing process and each paper received at least three individual reviews, with an average of four reviews per paper. Due to time constraints in the workshop program and the high quality of the submitted papers, the selection process was very competitive and many qualified papers could not be accepted. Only 44 out of the 116 submissions could be accepted, which results in an acceptance rate of 38%. The program also included two keynote speeches by Willie Anderson, VP DSP Qualcomm, and Jos Huisken from Silicon Hive, The Netherlands.

A workshop like this cannot be organized without the help of many other people. Therefore, we thank the members of the Steering and Program Committees and the external referees for their dedication and diligence in selecting the technical presentations. The investment of their time and insight is very much appreciated. We would like to express our sincere gratitude to Sebastian Isaza and Elena Moscu Panainte for maintaining the Web site and paper submission system, and Arjan van Genderen and Carlo Galuzzi for preparing the workshop proceedings. We thank Lidwina Tromp and Karin Vassiliadis for their support in organizing the workshop.

We hope that the attendees enjoyed the SAMOS VII workshop in all its aspects, including many informal discussions and gatherings.

June 2007                                                                  Mladen Berekovic
                                                                           Timo D. Hämäläinen

# Organization

The SAMOS VII workshop took place during July 16 − 19, 2007 at the Research and Teaching Institute of East Aegean (INEAG) in Agios Konstantinos on the island of Samos, Greece.

## Workshop Chairs

Timo D. Hämäläinen          Tampere University of Technology, Finland

## Program Chair

Mladen Berekovic           Delft University of Technology,
                           The Netherlands

## Proceedings Chair

Arjan van Genderen         Delft University of Technology,
                           The Netherlands

## Publicity and Financial Chair

Stephan Wong               Delft University of Technology,
                           The Netherlands

## Symposium Board

Shuvra Bhattacharyya       University of Maryland, USA
John Glossner              Sandbridge Technologies, USA
Andy Pimentel              University of Amsterdam, The Netherlands
Jarmo Takala               Tampere University of Technology, Finland
Stamatis Vassiliadis       Delft University of Technology,
                           The Netherlands

## Steering Committee

Luigi Carro                Federal U. Rio Grande do Sul, Brazil
Ed Deprettere              Leiden University, The Netherlands
Georgi N. Gaydadjiev       TU Delft, The Netherlands
Timo D. Hämäläinen         Tampere University of Technology, Finland

# Program Committee

| | |
|---|---|
| Aneesh Aggarwal | Binghamton University, USA |
| Piergiovanni Bazzana | ATMEL, Italy |
| Jürgen Becker | Universität Karlsruhe, Germany |
| Koen Bertels | Delft University of Technology, The Netherlands |
| Bruno Bougard | IMEC, Belgium |
| Samarjit Chakraborty | University of Singapore, Singapore |
| Nikitas Dimopoulos | University of Victoria, Canada |
| Lieven Eeckhout | Ghent University, Belgium |
| Paraskevas Evripidou | University of Cyprus, Cyprus |
| Fabrizio Ferrandi | Politecnico di Milano, Italy |
| Gerhard Fettweis | Technische Universität Dresden, Germany |
| Paddy French | TU Delft, The Netherlands |
| Jason Fritts | University of Saint Louis, USA |
| Daniel Gajski | UC Irvine, USA |
| Kees Goossens | NxP, The Netherlands |
| David Guevorkian | Nokia Research Center, Finland |
| Timo D. Hännikäinen | Tampere University of Technology, Finland |
| Victor Iordanov | Philips, The Netherlands |
| Bernard Jakoby | Linz University, Austria |
| Hartwig Jeschke | Hannover University, Germany |
| Chris Jesshope | University of Amsterdam, The Netherlands |
| Wolfgang Karl | University of Karlsruhe, Germany |
| Andreas Koch | TU Darmstadt, Germany |
| Krzysztof Kuchcinski | Lund University, Sweden |
| Johan Lilius | Ado Akademi University, Finland |
| Wayne Luk | Imperial College, UK |
| Kofi Makinwa | TU Delft, The Netherlands |
| John McAllister | Queen's University of Belfast, UK |
| Guy Meynants | IMEC-NL, The Netherlands |
| Alex Milenkovic | University of Utah, USA |
| Nacho Navarro | UPC, Spain |
| Alex Orailoglu | UCSD, USA |
| Bernard Pottier | Université de Bretagne Occidentale, France |
| Hartmut Schröder | Universität Dortmund, Germany |
| Peter-Michael Seidel | SMU University, USA |
| Mihai Sima | University of Victoria, Canada |
| Leonel Sousa | TU Lisbon, Portugal |
| Juürgen Teich | University of Erlangen, Germany |
| George Theodoridis | Aristotle University of Thessaloniki, Greece |
| Dimitrios Velenis | IIT, USA |
| Jan-Willem Van De Waerdt | NxP, USA |
| Wayne Wolf | Princeton University, USA |
| Stephan Wong | TU Delft, The Netherlands |

# Local Organizers

Lidwina Tromp          Delft University of Technology,
                       The Netherlands
Karin Vassiliadis      Delft University of Technology,
                       The Netherlands
Yiasmin Kioulafa       Research and Training Institute of East
                       Aegean, Greece

# Referees

| | | |
|---|---|---|
| Agarwal, N. | Eeckhout, L. | Kühnle, M. |
| Aggarwal, A. | Erbas, C. | Kakarountas, A. |
| Ahmadi, M. | Falcão, G. | Karl, W. |
| Aho, E. | Ferrandi, F. | Kastensmidt, F. L. |
| Akesson, B. | Fettweis, G. | Klussmann, H. |
| Al-Ars, Z. | Filho, A. C. S. B. | Koch, A. |
| Angermeier, J. | Flügel, S. | Koenig, R. |
| Ashby, T. | Flatt, H. | Kozanitis, C. |
| Ayoub, R. | Fossati, L. | Kuchcinski, K. |
| Azevedo, A. | French, P. | Kulmala, A. |
| Bazzana, P. | Fritts, J. | Kumar, S. |
| Becker, J. | Gaderer, G. | Lafond, S. |
| Becker, T. | Gadkari, A. | Langerwerf, J. M. |
| Berekovic, M. | Gaydadjiev, G. N. | Lattuada, M. |
| Bertels, K. | Gelado, I. | Lee, K. |
| Bhattacharyya, S. S. | Germano, J. | Lilius, J. |
| Bougard, B. | Glossner, J. | Loschmidt, P. |
| Braun, L. | Goossens, K. | Ludovici, D. |
| Brisolara, L. | Gruian, F. | Luk, W. |
| Brito, A. | Guevorkian, D. | Mäkelä, R. |
| Buchty, R. | Hämäläinen, T. D. | Mak, T. |
| Calderon, H. | Hännikäinen, M. | Marconi, T. |
| Cappelle, H. | Hansson, A. | Mattos, J. |
| Carro, L. | Hasan, L. | McAllister, J. |
| Chakraborty, S. | Heikkinen, J. | McKeown, S. |
| Chang, Z. | Hur, J. Y. | McLoone, M. |
| Chaves, R. | Iordanov, V. | Meena, A. |
| Cheung, R. | Isaza, S. | Meynants, G. |
| Coenen, M. | Jääskeläinen, P. | Milenkovic, A. |
| Cope, B. | Jain, P. | Milenkovic, M. |
| Deprettere, E. | Jakoby, B. | Momcilovic, S. |
| Derudder, V. | Jayachandran, V. K. | Monchiero, M. |
| Dimopoulos, N. | Jeschke, H. | Morra, C. |
| Duarte, F. | Jesshope, C. | Mudge, T. |

Nachtnebel, H.
Naeem, M. M.
Navarro, N.
Nawaz, Z.
Ng, A.
Nikolaidis, S.
Novo, D.
Obsborne, W.
Orailoglu, A.
Orsila, H.
Palermo, G.
Parekh, V.
Paulsson, K.
Pimentel, A. D.
Pitkänen, T.
Pottier, B.
Pujara, P.
Raghavan, P.
Raman, B.
Ruckdeschel, H.
Säntti, T.
Sabeghi, M.

Salminen, E.
Schlichter, T.
Schröder, H.
Seidel, P.
Septinus, K.
Shabbir, A.
Sigdel, K.
Sima, M.
Sima, M.
Simon-Klar, C.
Sohail, H.
Somisetty, R. K.
Sourdis, I.
Sousa, L.
Specht, E.
Strydis, C.
Suri, T.
Syed, S.
Takala, J.
Tang, H.
Teich, J.
Theodoridis, G.

Thompson, M.
Todman, T.
Treytl, A.
Tumeo, A.
Vainio, O.
van de Waerdt, J.
van Genderen, A.
Vanne, J.
Vassiliadis, N.
Vayá, G. P.
Velenis, D.
Vidyasagar, V.
Weijers, J.
Westermann, P.
Wojcieszak, L.
Wolf, W.
Wong, S.
Yang, C.
Yankova, Y.
Yi, L.
Zhang, Z.

# Table of Contents

## Scheduling & Programming Models

## Multi-processor Architectures

## Reconfigurable Architectures

## Design Space Exploration

## Processor Components

## Embedded Processors

## SoC for SDR

## Wireless Sensors

# Software Is the Answer But What Is the Question?

Willie Anderson

Vice President, Engineering for Qualcomm CDMA Technologies

**Abstract.** Consumer electronics and communications products typically comprise embedded systems whose complexity dwarfs the supercomputer center of two decades ago. Along with this embedded hardware capability have come equally complex applications, such as digitally encoded video and advanced wireless modulation and protocols, which not only have to function in a world-wide network, but which must also do so while using miniscule amounts of energy. The primary constraint for the deployment of these systems is the availability of the software which enables them. I will present some of the issues which challenge developers of such software and the embedded systems themselves, and will examine some pragmatic approaches to the solution of these engineering problems.

S. Vassiliadis, M. Berekovic, T.D. Hämäläinen (Eds.): SAMOS 2007, LNCS 4599, p. 1, 2007.
© Springer-Verlag Berlin Heidelberg 2007

# Integrating VLIW Processors with a Network on Chip

Jos Huisken

Silicon Hive

**Abstract.** Networks are a becoming a necessity to easily integrate multiple processors on a single chip. A crucial question here is whether it is good enough to reason about statistical performance as opposed to hard real-time performance constraints. Today's processors often do not allow software design for hard real-time systems, caused by the design of the bus- and/or memory interfaces, thereby necessitating elaborate performance analysis through simulation.

In this presentation I will indicate what options a processor designer has, using Silicon Hive processor design tools, in specifying the interfaces and local memory sub-system in a processor. It allows a multitude of communication options to build either type of system: statistically bound or hard real-time bound performance.

Additionaly I will describe the multi-processor simulation and prototyping environment and touching on the processor design methodology.

S. Vassiliadis, M. Berekovic, T.D. Hämäläinen (Eds.): SAMOS 2007, LNCS 4599, p. 2, 2007.
© Springer-Verlag Berlin Heidelberg 2007

# Communication Architecture Simulation on the Virtual Synchronization Framework*

Taewook Oh[1], Youngmin Yi[2], and Soonhoi Ha[3]

[1] Embedded Systems Solution Lab, Samsung Advanced Institute of Technology,
Mt. 14-1, Nongseo-dong, Giheung-gu, Yongin-si Gyunggi-do, 446-712 South Korea
taewook.oh@samsung.com
[2] Embedded software institute, Korea University,
5 Ga, Anam-Dong, Seongbuk-Gu, Seoul, 136-701 South Korea
ymyi@korea.ac.kr
[3] School of EECS, Seoul National University,
San 56-1, Sinlim-dong, Gwanak-gu, Seoul, 151-744 South Korea
my.sha@iris.snu.ac.kr

**Abstract.** As multi-processor system-on-chip (MPSoC) has become an effective solution to ever-increasing design complexity of modern embedded systems, fast and accurate HW/SW cosimulation of such system becomes more important to explore wide design space of communication architecture. Recently we have proposed the trace-driven virtual synchronization technique to boost the cosimulation speed while accuracy is almost preserved, where simulation of communication architectures is separated from simulation of the processing components. This paper proposes two methods of simulation modeling of communication architectures in the trace-driven virtual synchronization framework: SystemC modeling and C modeling. SystemC modeling gives better extensibility and accuracy but lower performance than C modeling as confirmed by experimental results. Fast reconfiguration of communication architecture is available in both methods to enable efficient design space exploration.

## 1 Introduction

System-on-chip (SoC) designers are dealing with ever increasing design complexity. Moreover, as multi-processor system-on-chip (MPSoC) architecture becomes more and more popular, SoC designers encounters the challenge of finding the optimal communication architecture for the target platform. Since faster validation of the system performance promises wider design space exploration, fast and accurate cosimulation has been a major focus in HW/SW codesign research.

Trace-driven virtual synchronization [2] has been proposed as a cosimulation technique that increases cosimulation speed by reducing the synchronization

---

* This work was supported by Brain Korea 21 project, SystemIC 2010 project funded by Korean MOCIE, and Samsung Electronics. This work was also partly sponsored by ETRI SoC Industry Promotion Center, Human Resource Development Project for IT SoC Architect. The ICT and ISRC at Seoul National University and IDEC provide research facilities for this study.

S. Vassiliadis et al. (Eds.): SAMOS 2007, LNCS 4599, pp. 3–12, 2007.

overhead between component simulators to almost zero and by removing the unnecessary simulation of idle period in the processing components. The main characteristic of the virtual synchronization technique is to separate simulation of processing components and communication architecture unlike conventional cosimulation approaches where the communication architecture is modeled with other hardware components.

In the trace-driven virtual synchronization, component simulators generate event traces and the cosimulation kernel aligns them and performs trace-driven architecture simulation. This characteristic makes virtual synchronization technique useful for fast design space exploration of communication architectures. In the conventional cosimulation approaches, cosimulation of the entire system is needed for each architecture candidate since simulation of processing components and communication architecture is tightly coupled. However, in the virtual synchronization cosimulation, traces obtained from a single execution of component simulator can be reused to simulation of various communication architectures.

This paper proposes two methods of simulation modeling of communication architectures in the trace-driven virtual synchronization framework: One is to use SystemC modeling of communication architecture and to integrate SystemC [3] simulation kernel to the cosimulation kernel of the proposed cosimulation framework. The other is to use cycle-accurate transaction level C model(hereafter, we call it 'C model' in this paper) in the cosimulation kernel of the framework. SystemC modeling has advantages on extensibility and accuracy by reusing the pre-verified communication IPs in SystemC. On the other hand, C modeling enables much faster cosimulation speed with a little degradation on accuracy. Experimental results reveal such trade-offs and proves the usefulness of the proposed technique.

This paper is organized as follows. In the next section, we overview some related work. Section 3 briefly reviews the trace-driven virtual synchronization technique. In section 4 we present the first approach of SystemC modeling and SystemC simulation of communication architecture in the virtual synchronization framework. Section 5 explains the second approach of using cycle accurate transaction level C model in the cosimulation kernel. Experimental results and conclusions will follow in section 6 and 7 respectively.

## 2   Related Work

Performance analysis method for communication architecture proposed by Lahiri et al.[4] has a similarity with our study in that trace-driven simulation is used. However, this approach has a limitation on accuracy since it only uses transaction level architecture specification described in C for performance estimation. On the contrary, we provide both BCA (Bus Cycle Accurate) SystemC model and transaction-level C model considering transaction order inversion caused by bridge delay, which was not considered in Lahiri's method.

Baghdadi et al. [5] modeled communication overhead with a simple linear equation : $T_{comm}(n) = \lambda T_{StartUp} + T_{Trans}(n) + T_{Synch}$. $T_{StartUp}$, $T_{Trans}(n)$, and $T_{Synch}$ represent interface initialization time, data transmission time, and synchronization time respectively. $\lambda$ is set to 0 or 1 depending on the type of communication. This formula is too simple to estimate the communication overhead so their approach is not accurate enough for reliable design space exploration.

Recently novel techniques of abstracion level modeling have been proposed for faster simulation. Pasricha et al. [6] and Schirner et al. [7] proposed new abstraction level for communication architecture named CCATB (Cycle Count Accurate at Transaction Boundaries) and ROM (Result Oriented Modeling), respectively. Both of them focus on preserving timing accuracy of BCA model while achieving the speed of TLM (Transaction Level Model) simulation. In order to do so, they abstract out detailed signal modeling inside each transaction and only provide accurate timing information at the transaction boundaries. Our proposed C model is similar to their approaches in principle. Since we do not need external simulation engine like SystemC or SpecC, however, we achieve better performance. CCATB or ROM model is complementary to our SystemC based approach to increase the simulation speed.

## 3   Virtual Synchronization Technique

The core of virtual synchronization technique is that it does not synchronize component simulators for every single cycle unlike conventional cosimulation approaches. It synchronizes component simulators only when synchronization is necessary to maintain the accuracy: start and end times of the task, and data exchange between tasks. They are global events, shortly events, that affect the other components. This synchronization overhead reduction induces significant improvement on cosimulation speed. As simulation speed of component simulator itself increases, effect of synchronization reduction becomes more evident. Moreover, with virtual synchronization technique, component simulators do not have to advance its local clock merely in order to synchronize with the global clock during the idle period. This also increases the cosimulation performance significantly.

In the trace-driven virtual synchronization, events occurred by component simulators are represented as a form of trace. Conventional trace-driven simulation consists of trace collection and trace processing, and these steps are separated and performed without any feedback in most cases [1]. It saves traces generated from initial cosimulation in a file, and executes trace-driven simulation. As a result, it suffers from performance overhead of file I/O, requiring huge storage, and inaccurate modeling of dynamic behavior like OS scheduling. However, in the trace-driven virtual synchronization, traces are saved in the memory and the accumulated traces are consumed when synchronizing the component simulators. So it solves those problems.

Fig.1(a) shows structure of cosimulation environment that adapts trace-driven virtual synchronization technique. It consists of two parts. The first part is trace generation part in which traces are generated by component simulators. As shown in the upper side of Fig.1(a), each component simulator is connected

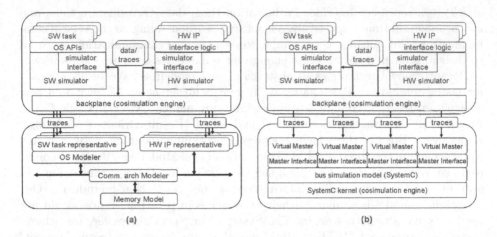

**Fig. 1.** Trace-driven virtual synchronization framework (a) previous framework (b) combined with SystemC

to the cosimulation kernel (backplane) with the simulation interface. The simulation interface is in charge of communication between a component simulator and the cosimulation kernel.

In the second part of simulation, cosimulation kernel reconstructs the global time information of each event that comes from component simulators and advances the global clock performing trace-driven architecture simulation. Trace-driven architecture simulation concerns not only communication architecture of the target platform but also OS behavior. It simulates the communication architecture considering latency and resource contention using the transaction level architecture model. Since the previous transaction level model assumes simple communication architecture as a single shared bus or does not account for the dynamic behavior such as transaction order inversion, we propose more general methods of communication modeling in the context of virtual synchronization framework in this paper.

## 4　Communication Architecture Simulation Using SystemC with Virtual Synchronization

We propose to replace the architecture simulation part in the virtual synchronization cosimulation kernel with SystemC based simulation. While a SystemC based simulation environment is in charge of communication architecture simulation, each processing component simulator is still attached to virtual synchronization cosimulation kernel. Therefore, only communication architecture modules are needed in the SystemC simulation environment. And a new wrapper module, called a 'virtual master module' is added between the SystemC simulation kernel and the cosimulation kernel. The virtual master module gets traces from virtual synchronization cosimulation kernel and triggers simulation of communication architecture module associated with these traces.

Fig.1(b) shows the modified framework of the proposed cosimulation environment that combines SystemC simulation kernel with the virtual synchronization cosimulation kernel through virtual master modules. There exists a one-to-one mapping between virtual master modules and component simulators attached to cosimulation kernel, so each virtual master module gets traces from its corresponding component simulator.

In the previous cosimulation framework the cosimulation kernel itself is in charge of communication architecture simulation. However, in the modified framework, the cosimulation kernel delivers traces generated from the component simulators to virtual master modules, and the SystemC simulation kernel actually performs communication architecture simulation.

The behavior of a virtual master module consists of the following four steps;

First, the virtual master module translates address information in the trace to target address by referencing the address map of the communication architecture. The address map is provided separately by the designer.

Second, the virtual master module determines the type of transaction and calls the corresponding transaction start function that is defined in the master interface module. If the target platform uses the different type of communication architecture, the designer only needs to modify the transaction start function for the new target communication architecture.

Third, after simulating the communication architecture module, it determines the time difference between the current trace and the next trace. A virtual master module uses wait() function defined in SystemC library to reflect this time difference in the next invocation of the module.

Fourth and the last, it may resume the blocked tasks after memory trace simulation. For example, if a write transaction to the memory causes the resuming of a blocked task, the virtual master module simulates this behavior.

The role of virtual master module is only to call a transaction start function and to resume blocked tasks if any and it does not simulate any internal processing of a component at all. Therefore, it is much simpler than the processing component module that had been attached to a conventional SystemC simulation environment. So SystemC based simulation part in the proposed framework gives faster simulation speed than the other SystemC simulation frameworks.

## 5   Communication Architecture Simulation Using C Model with Virtual Synchronization

While the SystemC modeling technique induces extensible and accurate cosimulation, it suffers from low performance of SystemC simulation kernel as the BCA model of communication architecture becomes more complex. So, we propose another modeling technique of the communication architecture: C modeling. Compared with other C modeling approaches, the proposed C model increases accuracy by providing more accurate architecture models while not sacrificing the simulation speed much. For accurate simulation of architecture, we let the designer specify the communication architecture details in a textual form, an XML file, which will be read by the model. The XML file has information about the list of components in the target platform, attributes of each component, the address map, and the topology that how components are connected. By analyzing the XML file, the simulation model can determine which components are involved in the current transaction: First it reads the address in the transaction, and finds out the component it is trying to access referencing the address maps. Then, it figures out the path from the requesting component to the destination component analyzing the topology information given in the XML file. Finally, by adding the time consumed on each communication component that is involved in the transaction, the total communication time is obtained. Since the cosimulation kernel manages all outstanding transactions and the status of all communication components, it can find out the precise location of the contention between the transactions and simulates the contention related timing accurately.

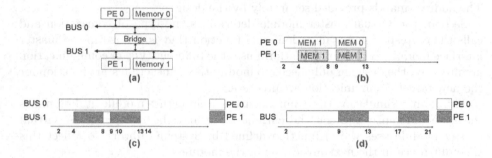

**Fig. 2.** Scenario of transaction order inversion

The proposed simulated model handles the transaction order inversion correctly while the abstraction level is maintained at transaction level. In a conventional transaction level model, a new transaction begins only after the previous transaction is completed. This scheme works correctly only for a simple architecture such as a single shared bus. Fig.2 is an example that shows a scenario of transaction order inversion. We assume that the target platform is as shown in Fig.2(a) where there are two buses connected to each other via a bus bridge. Fig.2(b) describes the start time and the target memory of the transactions requested by two processing components assuming an ideal communication architecture : PE0 makes two transactions at global times 2 and 9 with target memory 1 and memory 0, respectively. PE 1 also makes two transactions at global times 4 and 9, and both of them take memory 1 as their target memory.

Fig.2(c) shows the granted master of each data bus during the transactions in case of transactions are accurately simulated. The first transaction made by PE 0 at time 2 should go through both bus 0 and bus 1 to access memory 1. Since it has to cross the bridge to get bus 1, the bridge delay is experienced. Because of the bridge delay, the arbiter of the bus 1 gives grant to PE 1 before PE 0, even though PE 0's transaction starts earlier than PE 1's transaction. However, if each transaction is simulated atomically as shown in Fig.2(d), such transaction order inversion may not be observed in bus 1.

In order to solve this problem, the proposed model maintains a trace queue for each bus. It changes the granularity of atomicity from processing component trace to bus level trace. If a transaction described in a processing component trace goes through multiple buses, the transaction is split into multiple bus level traces. Each bus level trace has information about the transaction start time on the bus considering the bridge delay. Changing the granularity of atomic simulation enables more accurate simulation of grant order for each bus, which results in the accurate simulation of parallel transactions in a complex architecture. Since the overhead of splitting a transaction into bus-level traces is not significant, the proposed method does not give burden to the cosimulation kernel while it enhances the accuracy of communication architecture models.

# 6  Experimental Results

In this section, we present the experimental results and demonstrate the accuracy and efficiency of the proposed methods. In the first set of experiments, it is shown that combing the virtual synchronization framework with a SystemC cosimulation environment improves cosimulation performance significantly compared with conventional SystemC simulation environments. Next, by comparing the cosimulation results of the SystemC model simulation and the C model simulation, we demonstrate that the C model gives much faster simulation speed with about 3% accuracy loss.

## 6.1  Comparing Lock-Step Approach and Virtual Synchronization Technique Applied to SystemC Based Simulation Environment

The objective of this experiment is to examine the performance comparison between virtual synchronization framework with SystemC model of communication architecture and a conventional SystemC-based TLM simulation, where the communication architecture is modeled at the BCA level. This conventional framework provides the maximum accuracy at the TLM level since it conservatively synchronizes at every cycle by using lock-step approace.

In the experiment, the target platform consists of two processors and one shared bus. We disabled cache memory and used a JPEG decoder as the target application for both processors, in order to examine the simulation capability in case of extensive contention on the communication architecture. Table 1 shows the experimental results.

As shown in table 1, applying virtual synchronization technique does not deteriorate simulation accuracy at all while improving the simulation performance by 75%. Table 2 shows the partition of the simulation times between the component simulators and the communication architecture simulators. As shown in the table, since SystemC model is made at the BCA level, it becomes the simulation

**Table 1.** Comparing Lock-step approach and Virtual Synchonization method

| Configuration | Lock-step + SystemC | Virtual Sync. + SystemC |
|---|---|---|
| Simulated Cycles | 34,724,826 | 34,724,826 |
| Simulation Time(sec.) | 1551.402 | 886.99 |
| Error Rate | 0% | 0% |
| Performance Improvement | 1 | 1.75 |

**Table 2.** Comparing the portion of component simulator and SystemC simulator in total simulation time

| | Lock-step + SystemC | | Virtual Sync. + SystemC | |
|---|---|---|---|---|
| | Time(sec.) | Portion(%) | Time(sec.) | Portion(%) |
| Component Simulator | 419.54 | 27.04 | 40.57 | 4.58 |
| SystemC Simulator | 1131.86 | 72.96 | 846.42 | 95.42 |
| Total | 1551.402 | 100.00 | 886.99 | 100.00 |

bottleneck in the proposed framework. If we implement the SystemC module at a higher level of abstraction, simulation speed enhancement will be increased. It motivates the use of C model in the virtual synchronization framework.

## 6.2   Comparing C Model and SystemC Model for Communication Architecture Simulation

The second set of experiments compares the simulation speed and the accuracy of the proposed C model with those with the SystemC model. The experiment is divided into two parts. First, we show that the C model provides high degree of accuracy. Second, C model shows much faster simulation speed than SystemC model with real-life multimedia applications.

To confirm the accuracy of the C model, we have performed two experiments. First, we assumed that the target architecture consists of four processors and a single shared bus. As the number of processors running a JPEG decoder application increased from one to four, we observed the increase of contention delay on the proposed simulation environment. We disabled the cache memory of processors to see the contention effect more clearly. Table 3 shows the result of experiment.

**Table 3.** Result of experiment on contention modeling accuracy

| Number of Master(s) | SystemC Model | C Model | |
|---|---|---|---|
| | Cycles | Cycles | Error Rate(%) |
| 1 | 20,997,500 | 20,531,185 | 2.22 |
| 2 | 26,008,700 | 26,136,879 | 0.49 |
| 3 | 37,808,400 | 37,868,814 | 0.16 |
| 4 | 49,286,200 | 50,514,368 | 2.49 |

The result shows that the proposed C model has error rate of less than 3%, compared to the SystemC model(error rate is defined as (simulated cycles[C model] - simulated cycles[SystemC model])/simulated cycles[SystemC model]). The result also shows that the total simulation time due to contention on the bus increases as the number of processors increases.

In addition, we set up the experiments that may have transaction order inversion between concurrent transactions on multiple buses. We make four processors to execute the identical JPEG decoder application and make three different configurations on the communication architecture. In the first configuration, a single shared bus and a single memory are shared by four processors. In the second configuration, a pair of processors shares a bus and a memory so that there are two buses and two memory components in the platform. In the third configuration, each processor has their own memory through dedicated bus. We also disabled the cache memory for this experiment. The experimental results are shown in Table 4.

**Table 4.** Result of experiment on split bus modeling accuracy

| Number of Bus(es) | SystemC Model | C Model | |
|---|---|---|---|
| | Cycles | Cycles | Error Rate(%) |
| 1 | 49,286,200 | 50,514,368 | 2.49 |
| 2 | 25,460,800 | 26,102,775 | 2.52 |
| 4 | 20,531,300 | 21,085,048 | 2.49 |

The simulation result demonstrates that the proposed C model correctly reflects the reduction of the contention between transactions by bus splitting. The error rate of experiment was also less than 3%, and it means that decrease of accuracy caused by using a higher abstracted model is not that serious.

Second, we carried out an experiment to measure the performance improvement by using C model instead of SystemC model for communication architecture simulation. We enabled cache memory for this experiment, since the performance improvement should be measured on a more realistic situation.

We used two applications for this experiment. One is a JPEG decoder and four processors execute the identical JPEG decoder application on the platform with a single shared bus. The other is an H.263 decoder, and we partitioned and mapped DCT and Dequantization of U, V frame to two processors and the other processors took charge of the other tasks. Table 5 shows the results.

**Table 5.** Comparing simulation performance of SystemC model and C model

| Application | H.263 Decoder | | JPEG Decoder | |
|---|---|---|---|---|
| Architecture Model | SystemC | C Model | SystemC | C Model |
| Simulated Cycles | 19,725,900 | 19,749,850 | 5,220,570 | 5,220,525 |
| Simulation Time(Sec.) | 332.129 | 20.359 | 92.438 | 14.26 |
| Error Rate(%) | 0.00 | 0.12 | 0.00 | 0.00 |
| Performance Improvement | 1.00 | 16.31 | 1.00 | 6.48 |

Table 5 shows that using C model for communication architecture simulation improves simulation performance drastically while maintaining the error rate less than 0.2%. Therefore, communication architecture simulation using C model is useful for exploring wide design space with reasonable accuracy.

# 7   Conclusion

This paper proposes two communication architecture simulation methods in the virtual synchronization cosimulation framework. We proposed two methods: SystemC modeling and C modeling. The former method has an advantage for extensibility and accuracy by reusing the already verified simulation models, commercial SystemC simulation environment. The latter method is advantageous when exploring wider range of design space since it induces faster simulation speed.

Since the current implementation of C model only supports AMBA AHB bus, future research will be focused on the modeling of other communication architectures including bus matrix and network-on-chip architecture. We also need to simulate various peripheral devices like interrupt or memory controllers in the proposed framework.

# References

1. Uhlig, R., Mudge, T.: Trace-Driven Memory Simulation: A Survey. ACM Computing Surveys 29(2) (1997)
2. Kim, D., Yi, Y., Ha, S.: Trace-Driven HW/SW cosimulation using virtual synchronization technique. In: DAC. Proc. Design Automation Conference (2005)
3. SystemC initiative, http://www.systemc.org
4. Lahiri, K., Raghunathan, A., Dey, S.: System-level performance analysis for designing on-chip communication architectures. IEEE Transactions on CAD of Integrated Circuits and Systems 20(6), 768–783 (2001)
5. Baghdadi, A., Zergainoh, N., Cesario, W.O., Jerraya, A.A.: Combining a performance estimation methodology with a hardware/software codesign flow supporting multiprocessor systems. IEEE Transactions on Software Engineering 28(9), 822–831 (2002)
6. Pasricha, S., Dutt, N., Ben-Romdhane, M.: Fast exploration of bus-based on-chip communication architectures. CODES+ISSS (2004)
7. Schirner, G., Dömer, R.: Accurate yet fast modeling of real-time communication. CODES+ISSS (2006)

# A Model-Driven Automatically-Retargetable Debug Tool for Embedded Systems

Max R. de O. Schultz, Alexandre K.I. Mendonça, Felipe G. Carvalho,
Olinto J.V. Furtado, and Luiz C.V. Santos

Federal University of Santa Catarina, Computer Science Department,
Florianópolis, SC, Brazil
{max, mendonca, fgcarval, olinto, santos}@inf.ufsc.br

**Abstract.** Contemporary SoC designs ask for system-level debugging tools suitable to heterogeneous platforms. Such tools will have to rely on some low-level model-driven debugging engine that must be retargetable, since embedded code may run on distinct processors within the same platform. This paper describes a technique for automatically retargeting debugging tools for embedded code inspection. The technique relies on two key ideas: automatic extraction of machine-dependent information from a formal model of the processor and reuse of a conventional binary utility package as implementation infrastructure. The retargetability of the technique was experimentally validated for targets MIPS, SPARC, PowerPC and i8051.

## 1 Introduction

Modern embedded systems are often implemented as *systems-on-chip* (SoCs) whose optimization requires design space exploration. Alternative CPUs may be explored so as to minimize code size and power consumption, while ensuring enough performance to fulfill real-time constraints. Therefore, design space exploration requires the generation, inspection and evaluation of embedded code for distinct target processors. Besides, contemporary SoC designs ask for *system-level debugging* tools suitable to heterogeneous platforms. Such tools will have to rely on some low-level model-driven debugging engine that must be retargetable, since embedded code may run on distinct processors within the same platform.

As manually retargeting is unacceptable under the time-to-market pressure, automatically retargetable tools are mandatory. Retargetable tools [1] automatically extract machine-dependent information from a processor model, usually written in some *architecture description language* (ADL).

To prevent the tools from being tied to a given ADL, an abstract processor model could be envisaged. To be practical, such a model should be synthesizable from a description written in some ADL. Figure 1 describes a typical model-driven tool chain. It summarizes distinct classes of information flow (tool generation, code generation, code inspection and code evaluation). Exploration consists of four major steps, as follows.

First, given a target processor model, code generation tools (compiler backend, assembler and link editor), code inspection tools (dissassembler and debugger) and an instruction-set simulator are automatically generated.

S. Vassiliadis et al. (Eds.): SAMOS 2007, LNCS 4599, pp. 13–23, 2007.

14      M.R. de O. Schultz et al.

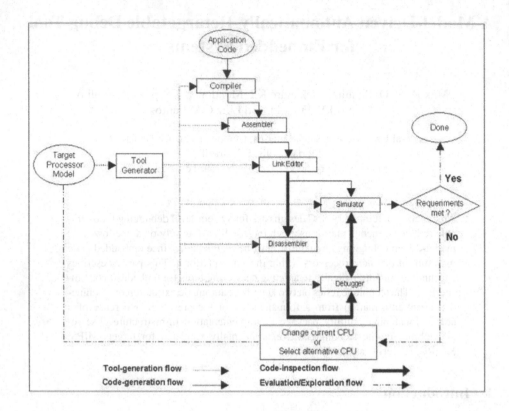

**Fig. 1.** Model-driven tool flows

Then, the application source code can be compiled, assembled and linked, resulting in executable code.

In a third step, the executable code can be run on the instruction-set simulator and its functionality can be observed with the help of disassembling and debugging tools. These tools allow the code to be executed incrementally (step) or to be stopped at certain code locations (breakpoints) so as to monitor program values (watchpoints).

Finally, as soon as proper functionality is guaranteed by removing existent bugs, continuous execution on the simulator allows the evaluation of code quality with respect to design requirements. If some requirement isn't met, an alternative *instruction set-architecture* (ISA) may be envisaged to induce a new solution. If the current processor is an *application-specific instruction-set processor* (ASIP), its ISA may deserve further customization. Otherwise, a new candidate processor may be selected.

This paper focuses on a technique for generating debugging tools from an arbitrary processor model. The technique relies on two key ideas. First, ISA-dependent information is automatically extracted from the model of the target processor. Second, the well-known GNU Binutils [2] and GNU debugger [3] packages are employed as implementation infrastructure: ISA-independent libraries are reused, while target-specific libraries are automatically generated.

The remainder of this paper is organized as follows. Section 2 briefly reviews related work. Section 3 formalizes the processor model that drives tool retargeting. Section 4 discusses implementation aspects. Experimental results are provided in Section 5. In Section 6, we draw our conclusions and comment on future work.

## 2  Related Work

### 2.1  Manually Retargetable Tools

Manually retargetable binary utilities are available within the popular GNU Binutils package [2]: assembler (gas), linker (ld), debugger (gdb) [3] and disassembler (obj-dump). Essentially, the Binutils package consists of an invariant ISA-independent core library and a few ISA-dependent libraries that must be rewritten for each new target CPU. Among the ISA-dependent libraries, there are two main libraries, namely Opcodes and BFD, which require retargeting.

The Opcodes library describes the ISA of a CPU (instruction encoding, register encoding, assembly syntax). Unfortunately, there is no standard for ISA description within this library.

The BFD library provides a format-independent (ELF, COFF, A.OUT, etc.) object file manipulation interface. It is split into two blocks: a front-end, which is the library's abstract interface with the application and a back-end, which implements that abstract interface for distinct object file formats.

### 2.2  Automatically Retargetable Tools

A great deal of contemporary retargetable tools rely on automatic generation from a CPU model, written in some ADL, such as nML [4], ISDL [5], and LISA [6].

Although disassembler and debugger are available for most ADLs, it is unclear to which extent they are automatically generated or simply hand-retargeted. For instance, once a simulator is generated in the LISA tool chain, it can be linked to a debugging graphical user interface, but there is no clue on how the underlying mechanism actually works.

It has been acknowledged that novel assembly-level optimization approaches, like SALTO [7] and PROPAN [8], deserve further investigation [1]. Such techniques allow conventional compiler infrastructure to be reused by enabling post-compiling machine-dependent optimizations to further improve code quality.

Although such post-compiling optimizations are promising, they may inadvertently introduce flaws. Code inspection tools could loose track of breakpoints and watchpoints due to optimizations not connected to the source code (in face of new locations and distinct register usage). Therefore, conventional debuggers are likely to overlook flaws introduced by post-compiling optimizations.

A technique for retargeting assemblers and linkers to the GNU package was presented in [9]. It relies on a formal notation to describe both the target ISA and its relocation information. Although the formalism is solid, experimental results are scarce. Besides, it is not possible to foresee if the proposed framework is able to address retargetable debugging tools.

Two facts motivated the work described in this paper: first, the lack of information reporting how code inspection tools are made retargetable and at which extent this is performed automatically; second, the scanty experimental results providing evidence of proper retargetability.

Although we pragmatically reuse a conventional binary-utility package as implementation infrastructure (like in [9]), we rely on an ADL-independent processor model.

## 3   Processor Model

This section formalizes the ISA aspects of the processor model in the well-known BNF notation. To ease its interpretation, an example is also provided. Figure 2 specifies the formal structure for the information typically available in processor manuals, which relies on the notions of instruction, operand and modifiers.

A modifier is a function that transforms the value of a given operand. It is written in C language and it has four pre-defined variables to specify the transformation: input is the original operand value, address represents the instruction location, parm is a parameter that may contain an auxiliary value (such as required for evaluating the target address for PC-relative branches), output returns the transformed operand value.

An operand type oper-type specifies the nature of an instruction field and it is tied to a binary value encoded within a given field. Examples of operand types are imm for immediate values, addr for symbolic addresses and exp for expressions involving immediate values and symbols.

Figure 3 shows an illustrative example of the processor model, according to the specified syntax. Lines 1 to 5 describe the mapping for the operand reg, where the symbols $0, $1, ..., $90 are mapped to the values 0, 1, ..., 90. Note that many-to-one mappings are allowed. For instance, the symbols $sp $fp, $pc and $ra are mapped to values already mapped in line 1. Lines 7 to 8 define the modifier R, which defines a function to be applied for PC-relative transformations. The modifier's results (output) is evaluated by adding the current location (address) to the operand value (input) and to an offset (parm). Lines 10 to 15 define the instruction beq. Line 11 defines its instruction format as a list of fields and its associated bit sizes. Line 12 defines its assembly syntax: reg, reg and exp are tied to instruction fields rs, rt and imm (beq is the instruction mnemonic). The modifier R (whose offset is 2) is applied to operand type imm, thereby specifying that the resulting value is PC-relative and shifted 2 bits to the left. Finally, in line 14, the constant value 0x04 is assigned to the instruction's op field.

From the processor model, a table of instructions is generated as a starting point for the retargeting algorithms. Each table entry is a tuple defined as follows:

```
table-entry = (mnemonic, opinfo, image, mask, pseudo, format-id)
```

Let's illustrate the meaning of its elements by means of an example. From the model in Figure 3, the following table entry would be generated for the instruction beq:

```
{"beq", "%reg:1:,%reg:2:,%exp:3:", 0x10000000, 0xFC000000, 0, Type_I}
```

The first element is the instruction's mnemonic (beq). The second stores information like type (reg, reg, exp) and instruction field location (1, 2, 3). The third element stores the partial binary image of the instruction (0x10000000). The fourth element stores a

```
<isa-def> ::= <list-operand> <list-modifier> <list-instruction>

<list-operand> ::= <operand-def> <list-operand> | <operand-def>

<operand-def> ::= operand oper-id { "mapping definition" }

<list-modifier> ::= <modifier-def> <list-modifier> | empty

<modifier-def> ::= modifier modifier-id { "modifier code" }

<list-instruction> ::= <instruction-def> <list-instruction>
                     | <instruction-def>

<instruction-def> ::= instruction insn-id { <format-desc> ; (<syntax-desc>) :
                      ( <operand-decoding> ) ; <opcode-decoding> }

<format-desc> ::= field-id : constant , <format-desc> | field-id : constant

<syntax-desc> ::= mnemonic-id <oper-type-list>

<oper-type-list> ::= <qualifier> <oper-type> , <oper-type-list>
                   | <qualifier> <oper-type>

<oper-type> ::= oper-id | imm | addr <modifier> | exp <modifier>

<modifier> ::= << modifier-id ( constant ) | empty

<operand-decoding> ::= field-id , <operand-decoding> | field-id

<opcode-decoding> ::= field-id = constant , <opcode-decoding>
                    | field-id = constant

<qualifier> ::= # | $ | empty
```

**Fig. 2.** Processor model specification

```
 1. operand reg { $[0..90] = [0..90];
 2.               $sp = 29;
 3.               $fp = 30;
 4.               $ra = 31;
 5.               $pc = 37; }
 6.
 7. modifier R { output = input + address + parm; }
 8.
 9. instruction beq {
10.    op:6, rs:5, rt:5, imm:16,
11.    (beq reg, reg, exp << R(2)) : (rs, rt, imm);
12.    op=0x04
13. }
```

**Fig. 3.** A segment of the MIPS model

mask (0xFC000000) to be used by the dissassembling algorithm in order to identify the instruction. The fifth element specifies whether the entry refers to a pseudo-instruction or not (0 = not). Finally, the last element stores the instruction format identifier (Type_I, in this case).

## 4   Implementation

Our generation technique reuses the GNU Binutils and the GNU gdb packages as much as possible. The structure of the disassembling and debugging tools is depicted in Figure 4, where the generated machine-dependent libraries are marked with an asterisk.

Observe that both tools share the BFD and Opcodes libraries. Besides, note that each tool consists of a target-specific library and a machine-independent core library. Therefore, the key to automatic tool retargeting is to generate both libraries and both target-specific libraries automatically, as will be described in the next subsections. The ISA-dependent information is automatically extracted from the model of the target CPU.

Note that a retargeted tool is obtained by simply compiling the generated target-specific libraries together with the respective core library. Each generated library consists of a few files, whose organization is summarized in Figure 5, where [arch] represents a given ISA. The remaining of this section focuses on the main generated files.

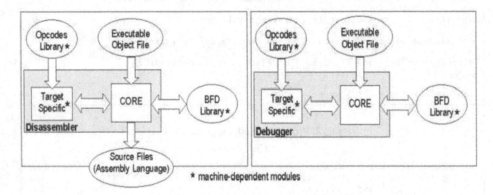

**Fig. 4.** Tools structure

### 4.1   Generation of Library Opcodes

The file include/opcodes/[arch].h declares three data structures supporting instruction decoding and encoding, the mapping between register names and actual encodings, and pseudo-instruction manipulation. (It should be noted that disassembling doesn't make use of pseudo-instructions to avoid ambiguity).

The corresponding opcodes/[arch]-opc.c file contains the above mentioned data structures, which are fed with the information extracted from the processor model.

### 4.2   Generation of Library BFD

ISA attributes extracted from the processor model are encoded within this library. Since we have adopted the ELF format, only the ELF-related files are generated. Among them, the most important file is bfd/cpu-[arch].c, which contains information such as architecture name, word length and address lenght.

```
- binutils                // GNU Binutils
  - bfd                   // library BFD
    . cpu-[arq].c
    . elf32-[arq].c
  - opcodes               // library Opcodes
    . [arq]-opc.c
    . [arq]-dis.c
  - include               // general files include
    - elf
      . [arq].h
    - opcode
      . [arq].h
- gdb                     // GNU Debugger
  - bfd                   // library BFD
    . cpu-[arq].c
    . elf32-[arq].c
  - opcodes               // library Opcodes
    . [arq]-opc.c
    . [arq]-dis.c
  - include               // general files include
    - elf
      . [arq].h
    - opcode
      . [arq].h
  - gdb                   // files of debugger
    . [arq]-tdep.c
    - config
      - [arq]
        . [arq].mt
```

**Fig. 5.** Generated file tree

### 4.3 Target-Specific Disassembler Library

The main file for the disassembling process is opcodes/[arch]-dis.c. It manipulates the data structures mentioned in Section 4.1 and invokes BFD interface methods to read object files.

### 4.4 Target-Specific Debugger Library

Within this library, the most important file is gdb/[arch]-tdep.c. It contains functions handling subroutine calls and giving access to general-purpose and specific registers (e.g. program counter, stack pointer and frame pointer), so as to allow breakpoint control and value watching.

## 5 Experimental Results

For the sake of tool validation, we have adopted the well-known Mibench [10] benchmark. In order to validate our tool generators, conventional manually-retargeted tools were used to set reference files and values. Then, we compared results produced by the generated tools with the reference values obtained from conventional tools.

Tool validation is achieved, not only by observing proper functionality of the generated tools, but also by observing the retargetability of the generating tool. To check for retargetability, the validation procedures described in the following subsections were repeated for four distinct targets: PowerPC, MIPS, SPARC and i8051.

### 5.1   Validation of Disassembling Tools

To validate generated disassembling tools, we employed the following key idea: given a reference object file, if it is disassembled and then re-assembled, the resulting file should match the reference file. Figure 6 shows the adopted validation flow. Rectangles represent tools and ellipses denote files. The procedure starts from a reference object file, which is fed to the generated disassembler (to be validated), giving rise to an output assembly file. Then, this file is submitted to an assembler, resulting in an object output file. In the end, the input file (reference) and output file (under validation) are compared to check whether they matched or not.

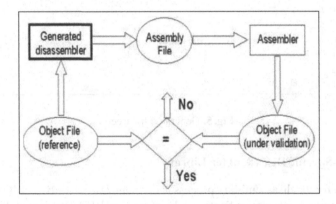

**Fig. 6.** Validation flow for disassembling

It could be argued that such a validation procedure should compare assembly codes, instead of object codes. However, the direct comparison of assembly codes is hampered by the presence of pseudo-instructions or instructions admitting multiple assembly syntaxes. For instance, the MIPS instruction "jump at register" can be written in two different ways: "jr 1"or"j1". That's why reversed matching was used instead of direct matching, without loss of generality. We repeated the validation procedure for each target CPU and for every benchmark program. As a result, all the comparisons matched, therefore providing evidence of proper functionality.

### 5.2   Validation of Debugging Tools

To validate generated debugging tools, we defined a set of breakpoints and watchpoints for a given executable file and observed the resulting values and control for both conventional and generated debuggers. Figure 7 shows the adopted validation flow. Rectangles represent tools, while ellipses represent either a file or a set of observed values. The

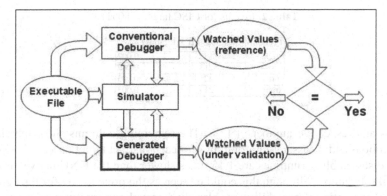

**Fig. 7.** Validation flow for debugging

procedure starts from a given executable file, which is run on an instruction-set simulator of the target CPU. First, breakpoints and watchpoints are inserted in the code by a conventional debugger. As a result of running the instrumented code, watch point values are set as a reference. Then, a generated debugger was used to repeat the procedure for exactly the same breakpoints and watch points. In the end, the values under validation were compared to the reference values.

We repeated the validation procedure for each target CPU and for every benchmark program. Since all comparisons matched, they indicate that the generated debuggers are equivalent to their manually retargeted counterparts.

### 5.3  Tool Efficiency

We provide some quantitative evidence of tool efficiency by showing the relation between program size and runtime for the disassembling tool. Since the debugging tool intensively invokes the disassembling engine, those results serve to assess the efficiency of both tools.

To check for proper retargetability of the generating tool, the procedure above was repeated for RISC (PowerPC, MIPS, SPARC) and CISC (i8051) targets, whose results are shown in Tables 1 and 2, respectively. The first two columns show the benchmark

**Table 1.** Results for RISC targets

| Program | Files | Size [Kb] | | |
|---|---|---|---|---|
| | | Runtime [s] (our \| objdump) | | |
| | | MIPS | SPARC | PowerPC |
| typeset | 1 | 29.7 | 32.6 | 25.3 |
| | | 0.049\| 0.035 | 0.071\| 0.031 | 0.050\| 0.039 |
| bitcount | 9 | 4.9 | 4.1 | 4.1 |
| | | 0.010\| 0.006 | 0.010\| 0.009 | 0.009\| 0.008 |
| susan | 1 | 64.7 | 59.4 | 52.7 |
| | | 0.099\| 0.074 | 0.139\| 0.057 | 0.104\| 0.095 |
| jpeg | 60 | 284.8 | 239.8 | 228.2 |
| | | 0.442\| 0.317 | 0.537\| 0.219 | 0.437\| 0.406 |
| fft | 3 | 5.9 | 5.5 | 5.3 |
| | | 0.010\| 0.007 | 0.014\| 0.010 | 0.012\| 0.012 |

**Table 2.** Results for CISC target ( i8051)

| Program | Files | Size [b] | Runtime [s] |
|---------|-------|----------|-------------|
| int2bin | 1 | 188 | 0.002 |
| cast | 1 | 213 | 0.002 |
| sort | 1 | 425 | 0.003 |
| xram | 1 | 214 | 0.003 |

programs and respective number of files. The remaining columns show the sizes of ".text" sections and disassembling runtimes for each distinct target processor. On average, our disassembling runtimes are 1.15 times slower than the GNU native disassembling tool (objdump). Although this could be seen as the price to pay for the benefit of achieving automatic retargetability, we already detected opportunities to optimize the prototype tool so as to reduce our runtimes.

## 6  Conclusions

The relevance of the proposed technique lies in the tracks opened by promising assembly-level post-compiling optimizations and by the need of contemporary system-level debugging tools in heterogeneous platforms. The proposed technique fits in a pragmatic approach for automatic tool retargeting. Its underlying mechanism was clearly described, as opposed to related work.

Experimental validation gives evidence of proper functionality and actual retargetability for all tested cases. In particular, our technique was able to generate a disassembling tool for a processor with no pre-existent GNU porting (the i8051).

We first intend to improve the code of the prototype tool so as to reduce runtimes and then perform experiments with new targets like Motorola ColdFire and Altera Nios2. As future work, we intend to elaborate an API to the retargeting engine so as to enable tool generation from an arbitrary ADL. Also, we want to address mechanisms to tie the retargetable debugger to a system-level debugging tool.

## References

1. Leupers, R., Marwedel, P.: Retargetable Compiler Technology for Embedded Systems - Tools and Applications. Kluwer Academic Publishers, Dordrecht (2001)
2. Pesch, R.H., Osier, J.M.: The GNU binary utilities. Free Software Foundation, Inc. (1993)
3. GNU: The GNU Project Debugger, http://www.gnu.org/software/gdb
4. Hartoog, M.R., Rowson, J.A., Reddy, P.D., Desai, S., Dunlop, D.D., Harcourt, E.A., Khullar, N.: Generation of software tools from processor descriptions for hardware/software codesign. In: Proceedings of the 34th Annual Conference on Design Automation, pp. 303–306. ACM Press, New York (1997)
5. Hadjiyiannis, G., Hanono, S., Devadas, S.: ISDL: an instruction set description language for retargetability. In: Proceedings of the 34th Annual Conference on Design Automation, pp. 299–302. ACM Press, New York (1997)
6. Pees, S., Hoffmann, A., Zivojnovic, V., Meyr, H.: LISA – machine description language for cycle-accurate models of programmable DSP architectures. In: Proceedings of the 36th ACM/IEEE Conference on Design Automation, pp. 933–938. ACM Press, New York (1999)

7. SALTO Project, http://www.irisa.fr/caps/projects/Salto
8. Kästner, D.: Propan: A retargetable system for postpass optimizations and analyses. In: Proceedings of the ACM SIGPLAN Workshop on Languages, Compilers, and Tools for Embedded Systems, pp. 63–80. ACM Press, New York (2000)
9. Abbaspour, M., Zhu, J.: Retargetable binary utilities. In: Proceedings of the 39th Conference on Design Automation, pp. 331–336. ACM Press, New York (2002)
10. Guthaus, M.R., Ringenberg, J.S., Ernst, D., Austin, T.M., Mudge, T., Brown, R.B: A free, commercially representative embedded benchmark suite. In: Proceedings of the 4th Annual IEEE Workshop on Workload Characterization, pp. 3–14 (2001)

# Performance Evaluation of Memory Management Configurations in Linux for an OS-Level Design Space Exploration

Sangsoo Park[1] and Heonshik Shin[2]

[1] University of Michigan, Department of Electrical Engineering and Computer Science
2260 Hayward St., Ann Arbor, MI 48109 USA
ssoopark@eecs.umich.edu
[2] Seoul National University, School of Computer Science and Engineering
San 56-1, Sinlim, Gwanak, Seoul 151744 Korea
shinhs@snu.ac.kr

**Abstract.** The objective of this paper is to analyze how the memory management configuration in Linux influences run-time performance of embedded systems. Extensive experiments confirm that the configuration of the memory management subsystem significantly affects the overall execution time, the memory performance, and the system call overhead. Our quantitative experimental results will help embedded systems designers to understand the effect of memory management configurations on the applications within a system, and contribute to the design of more efficient systems with an OS-level design space exploration.

## 1 Introduction

For many years, the majority of small-scale embedded systems have been implemented without an operating system (OS). Traditionally, such embedded systems have performed multitasking using various programming techniques such as a polled loop, co-routines, and interrupt-driven scheduling. As embedded systems grow in size and complexity, however, an OS has become essential to simplify their design. Today, any serious embedded software employs a real-time multitasking executive, or a fully fledged OS such as embedded Linux. The OS provides an effective development and execution environment for application programmers, enabling them to develop target systems with ease and efficiency.

During the design of an embedded system, small variations in a few parameters may exert significant effects on its performance and cost. It is therefore important to explore the design space carefully, and to examine different implementation choices, in order to determine appropriate trade-offs among conflicting objectives [1].

Most modern computer systems now support virtual memory, which provides a distinct virtual address space for each process and also offers hardware-assisted memory protection for multi-programming. A virtual memory system is maintained by the memory management subsystem of the OS, and requires hardware support from an MMU (memory management unit) in the CPU. The presence of the MMU greatly helps the OS to control memory use at run-time, which improves functionality, productivity, and

S. Vassiliadis et al. (Eds.): SAMOS 2007, LNCS 4599, pp. 24–33, 2007.

maintainability [2]. However, a significant increase in computational overhead is inevitable with an MMU, as resources are required to manage the virtual memory system as well as the MMU hardware, which of course also consumes power and incurs manufacturing cost. In this sense, how to configure the memory management subsystem in an OS becomes one of the important design parameters for embedded systems.

In this paper, we investigate how the memory management configuration influences its performance at run-time. We will do this by quantitatively evaluating the performance of various embedded applications running under different memory management configurations in embedded Linux. We will define four memory management configurations that are adopted and developed for the evaluations and describe the pros and cons of their architectures. Experimental results for various embedded applications, such as execution time, memory performance, and system call overhead will be presented and their effect on performance analyzed.

The rest of this paper is organized as follows: Section 2 introduces the four memory management configurations. Section 3 describes our methodology, experimental environments, the experimental results and their analysis. Section 4 concludes this paper.

## 2  Memory Management Configurations

### 2.1  VM (Virtual Memory)

In general, the introduction of virtual memory has made many tasks simpler, and this is also true for embedded systems. Benefits include memory protection and the provision of distinct virtual address spaces for the kernel and for each user process. However, there is an inevitable computational overhead in managing the virtual memory system.

Translating virtual to physical address requires one or more memory accesses from the page tables which are managed by the memory management subsystem. But most modern CPUs include a TLB (translation lookaside buffer) to cache recently used translations to speed up the process [3]. But the TLB contains a fixed number of entries. When it cannot supply the required translation, additional memory accesses by the memory management subsystem of the OS are required to translate the address and then to load it into the TLB. The TLB miss ratio is a measure of the frequency of this event, and is therefore an important criterion for assessing the performance overhead incurred by a virtual memory system. This will be evaluated in Section 3.3.

### 2.2  VM+KMT (VM & Kernel-Mode Thread)

A simple but effective approach to reduce the overhead of virtual address translation is to modify the memory management configuration so as to share the virtual address space between the kernel and the process, by running a program as a *KMT* (kernel-mode thread) [2], as shown in Fig. 1. By sharing address space, the burden of memory management is reduced. For instance, separate page tables for kernel and process are merged into one page table. To support sharing address space, we have modified the C library to run in the kernel-mode thread by replacing all the system calls, and the glue code with corresponding function calls in the kernel. The idea of running a program as

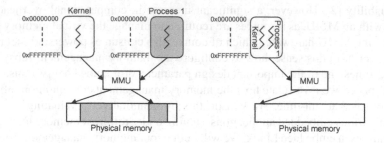

**Fig. 1.** Kernel-mode thread comparisons

a kernel thread is not new. Many researchers have been using this approach in various applications to improve performance [4]. However, previous work has focused on just one of its side-effects, the reduced overhead for system call. But there are actually three major side-effects of adopting *VM+KMT*, as follows.

1. System call overhead - It is well known that system calls are a significant overhead for user processes. The software trap and context switch are known to involve a severe performance penalty [5]. But the overhead for processing OS services is minimized by the *VM+KMT*, because both the kernel and the user process run in kernel mode because system calls are replaced with function calls. We will evaluate the overhead of a system call in Section 3.4.
2. Memory performance - Most microprocessors with an MMU use virtual addressing for the cache tag. This is because virtual addressing eliminates address translation after a cache hit. However, a context switch implies a change to the virtual address mappings in the page tables; thus, all the TLB and cache entries have to be flushed to make sure that they do not contain stale data after the switch [6]. Therefore, frequent context switches are necessarily incurring high overheads and leading to poor cache performance. It seems reasonable to expect that the cache hit ratio could be improved by minimization of the context switching that occurs with the *VM+KMT*, and this possibility will be evaluated in Section 3.3.
3. Memory protection - In the *VM+KMT*, the kernel and the user program share the virtual address space in kernel mode. This raises a memory protection problem because the MMU, which is responsible for memory protection, can no longer differentiate between references by the kernel and by the user program. The *VM+KMT* has sacrificed automatic memory protection to reduce the overhead of system calls and to improve cache performance.

### 2.3  FM (Flat Memory)

The *VM+KMT* requires a virtual memory system and therefore a hardware MMU must be in place. Many small embedded systems have severe restrictions on their power consumption or manufacturing cost, making the inclusion of an MMU infeasible. The *FM* shares physical addresses between the kernel and user processes, like the *VM+KMT*, but *FM* does not require an MMU. The differences between the two configuratons are in the cache tags and in the use of system call. Using the *FM*, cache entries are indexed by their physical addresses. The effect on memory performance of physical and virtual addressing in cache tags will be evaluated in Section 3.3. The *FM* also needs to use system calls, and therefore incurs the overhead of context switching, because user programs are running as user-level processes.

In a system without an MMU, the memory management subsystem of the OS has the advantage that it does not need to handle per-process page tables (or TLB misses) and the associated protection required by the virtual memory system. But this introduces restrictions on the use of some APIs such as the *fork()* system call, and on handling memory-related features. Application programmers are still able to allocate non-overlapping memory regions to the application, but with caution, because implicit restrictions are placed on memory usage as depicted in Fig. 2 [7]. For example, the programmer must define the stack size carefully in order to avoid an overflow. Overwriting the stack with data or code will also lead to a system crash.

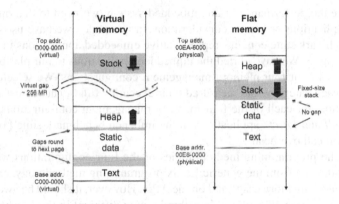

**Fig. 2.** Virtual memory vs. flat memory

## 2.4   FM+KMT (FM & Kernel-Mode Thread)

Changing from either the *VM* or the *VM+KMT* to the *FM* simplifies memory management but requires more stringent discipline in using memory. Any comparison between the *FM* and *VM+KMT* must be skewed, because the *FM* suffers from the overhead of system calls, whereas the *VM+KMT* can call OS services much more efficiently when it is implemented as a function. We will now apply the kernel-mode thread to the *FM*, and the resulting *FM+KMT* can be more fairly compared with *VM+KMT*.

## 3   Performance Evaluation

### 3.1   Experimental Environment

In order to experiment with varying hardware design parameters, we used the ARM926EJ-S as the CPU with an MMU, and the ARM946E-S without [8]. We used the ARMulator, a highly configurable system simulator, which can not only simulate various CPU cores but can also model different types of memory, a range of cache architectures, and also external hardware. We configured the ARMulator with the minimum set of components that are required to run an OS which includes an interrupt controller and a timer together with a CPU and RAM. Also, we configured the cache as follows: 32KB size data and instruction cache with 4-way associative and 32-byte line. We have ported Linux to ARMulator and used it to run the embedded applications. Table 1 summarizes the experimental environment.

**Table 1.** Summary of the experimental environment

| CPU | MMU | Kernel | Library | Compiler |
|-----|-----|--------|---------|----------|
| ARM926EJ-S | Yes | linux-2.4.21-rmk1 | uClibc-0.9.19 | gcc-2.95.3 (-Os) |
| ARM946E-S | No | linux2.4.21-uc0 | uClibc-0.9.19 | gcc-2.95.3 (-Os) |

To evaluate the performance of an embedded system, we need to determine which embedded applications are under consideration. In this paper, we have used MiBench [9]. This benchmark suite contains representative embedded applications in seven categories as in Fig. 3. We have ported the embedded applications to our platform so that they will run with our four memory management configurations. We selected two applications in each category, and measured their execution times, cache miss ratios, and TLB miss ratios, for each of the four memory management configurations. Also, we used *lat_syscall* and *lat_ctx* applications in the lmbench benchmark suite [10] to measure the system call overhead.

Note that the programming methodologies of the four configurations we have selected do not deviate from the generic Linux programming methodology, except for a few restrictions on memory usage and on the APIs. However, it should be aware that the DSA (dynamic storage allocation) algorithm is quite different in the *VM* and the *FM*. That is because DSA relies on the *sbrk()* system call, which utilizes the virtual mapping features provided by the MMU in the *VM*, but which is implemented in *FM* through the *mmap()* [7]. We would expect the execution time and memory performance of an embedded application to be affected by these changes to the DSA. In order to identify its impact, we measured the proportion of the execution time used by the DSA for each application in *VM* as shown in Fig. 3.

### 3.2  Execution Time

The experimental execution times are shown in Fig. 4. For the purposes of comparison, the results for the *VM+KMT*, *FM*, and *FM+KMT* are presented as percentage reductions compared with the execution time for the *VM*. As shown in Fig. 4, the reduction in execution time varies between 0.10% (adpcm.decode under *VM+KMT*) and 23% (rijndael.decode under *FM+KML*) depending on the application and the memory management configuration.

We observe that the execution times for each configuraton obey the inequalities, VM > FM, VM > VM+KMT, FM > FM+KMT. However, when *VM+KMT* is compared with *FM*, the results for some applications (qsort, tiff2rgba, patricia, ispell, and

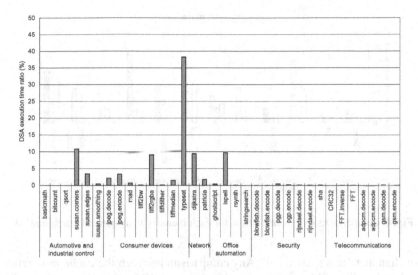

**Fig. 3.** Execution time ratio for dynamic storage allocation in MiBench applications

gsm decode) are characterized by $VM+KMT < FM$, although the rest of the applications show the more general tendency $VM+KMT > FM$. This variation occurs because the trade-off between the overhead of system calls and that of managing the MMU differs from application to application. However, in general, the experimental results indicate that the performance of these benchmark embedded applications improves as we simplify the memory management configuration. This is obvious, however, such quantitative results would be useful for determining the configuration while exploring design space. On the basis of these results, we are now going to identify and characterize opportunities for improving the design of embedded operating systems in terms of memory performance and related OS services.

### 3.3 Memory Performance

Table 2 summarizes the memory performance; instruction cache miss ratio, data cache miss ratio, and TLB miss ratio for each experiment. These results suggest that the TLB miss ratio decreases substantially, as described in Section 2.2, when the memory management configuration is changed from $VM$ to $VM+KMT$. The absence of an overhead for managing the virtual memory system is apparent in the results for the $FM$.

Using the $VM+KMT$, the memory management subsystem manages one common page table, instead of separate tables for kernel and process. The number of context switches, which change the virtual address mapping in the page tables and TLB, and the frequency of cache flushing, are minimized by $VM+KMT$. As a result, the cache miss ratios for the $VM+KMT$ are less than those for the $VM$. But this observation cannot be extended to a comparison between the $FM$ and $FM+KMT$. The cache miss ratio is higher using the $FM+KMT$ than it is with the $FM$, for applications such as tiff2rgba, adpcm.decode, and gsm.decode. However, $FM+KMT$ gains because fewer memory references are required, since the CPU instructions required for a function call is much

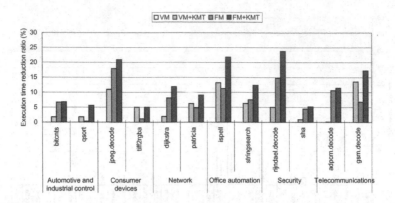

**Fig. 4.** Comparisons of execution time for each memory management configuration

smaller than that for a system call. Any comparison between the cache miss ratios for physical addressing (*FM*) and for virtual addressing (*VM*) of the cache tags is highly dependent on the application.

All these experimental results are affected by memory references incurred by the kernel and by the user process. To identify the extent to which the kernel affects the performance, further results were obtained to characterize the behavior of the OS and the way that its impact varies between applications with the results reported elsewhere [11]. The experimental results shows that a significant number of memory references are made by the kernel, especially when compared with the number of instructions executed. We deduce that the OS kernel has a poor memory performance in these benchmark applications. This implies that the OS has a significant impact on overall performance [12], a fact which we cannot ignore in our evaluation.

### 3.4 System Call Overhead

To identify the extent to which *KMT* actually contributes to the improved performance in Section 3.2, we used the *lat_syscall* benchmark, which measures the latency of system calls for certain OS services.

The results of this test are presented in Fig. 5. They show that the latency for processing OS services is significantly reduced by adopting *KMT*. For example, the latency of the simplest system call, *getpid()*, is reduced by between 72% and 75%. We can also see that the absence of an MMU reduces the latency by between 12% and 26%, which is due to the reduced overhead of context switching. This suggests that there is potential for significant performance improvements in applications which frequently request OS services.

On the other hand, the benchmark *lat_ctx* measures the context switching time for different numbers of processes and sizes of processes, i.e. size of local memory region for computation. Using more and larger processes leads to a more realistic measure of latency, because a large number of data accesses cause cache misses. As shown in Fig. 6, the latencies of context switching for the *FM* are shorter than those for the *VM*

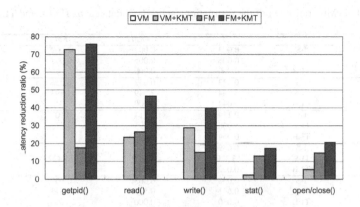

**Fig. 5.** Comparison of system call latency for each memory management configuration

when the size of processes is 0KB and thus the number of data accesses to local memory region which in turn generate memory bus traffic is negligible. But, if the size of the processes is increased to 32KB, the latencies of context switching for the *FM* are longer than those for the *VM*, when there are more than six processes.

To delve more deeply into these results, we conducted additional experiments to measure the data cache miss ratio for the cases identified by dotted lines in Fig. 6. If the average size of a process multiplied by the number of processes exceeds the 32KB cache size, a context switch is triggered and the cache is flushed, regardless of the memory management configuration. With 32KB processes, the cache miss ratio is higher for *FM* than for *VM*, which causes longer latencies during context switching, as shown in Table 3.

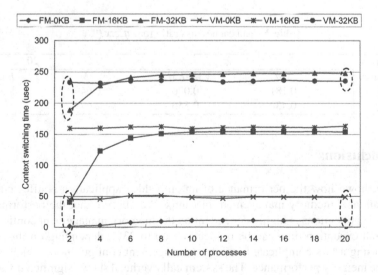

**Fig. 6.** Latency of context switching

**Table 2.** Miss ratio (%) of the instruction cache (I-$), data cache (D-$), and TLB

|  |  | VM | VM+KMT | FM | FM+KMT |
|---|---|---|---|---|---|
| bitcount | I-$ | 0.003 | 0.002 | 0.002 | 0.002 |
|  | D-$ | 0.006 | 0.006 | 0.007 | 0.003 |
|  | TLB | 0.000 | 0.000 |  |  |
| qsort | I-$ | 0.033 | 0.032 | 0.056 | 0.009 |
|  | D-$ | 3.534 | 2.949 | 2.593 | 2.408 |
|  | TLB | 0.044 | 0.000 |  |  |
| jpeg.decode | I-$ | 0.119 | 0.114 | 0.107 | 0.088 |
|  | D-$ | 5.936 | 4.595 | 4.771 | 4.472 |
|  | TLB | 0.064 | 0.000 |  |  |
| tiff2rgba | I-$ | 0.039 | 0.025 | 0.038 | 0.040 |
|  | D-$ | 15.370 | 13.809 | 15.477 | 13.355 |
|  | TLB | 0.022 | 0.004 |  |  |
| dijkstra | I-$ | 0.008 | 0.003 | 0.004 | 0.004 |
|  | D-$ | 0.621 | 0.578 | 0.573 | 0.563 |
|  | TLB | 0.030 | 0.000 |  |  |
| patricia | I-$ | 0.083 | 0.064 | 0.079 | 0.070 |
|  | D-$ | 0.278 | 0.176 | 0.254 | 0.174 |
|  | TLB | 0.023 | 0.000 |  |  |
| ispell | I-$ | 0.167 | 0.156 | 0.051 | 0.041 |
|  | D-$ | 11.057 | 8.580 | 10.008 | 8.300 |
|  | TLB | 0.592 | 0.125 |  |  |
| stringsearch | I-$ | 0.142 | 0.052 | 0.055 | 0.050 |
|  | D-$ | 4.373 | 3.693 | 3.634 | 3.845 |
|  | TLB | 0.034 | 0.000 |  |  |
| rijndael.decode | I-$ | 0.202 | 0.105 | 0.074 | 0.043 |
|  | D-$ | 1.829 | 1.559 | 1.547 | 1.505 |
|  | TLB | 0.215 | 0.000 |  |  |
| sha | I-$ | 0.019 | 0.016 | 0.016 | 0.011 |
|  | D-$ | 3.439 | 3.256 | 3.064 | 3.018 |
|  | TLB | 0.002 | 0.000 |  |  |
| adpcm.decode | I-$ | 0.099 | 0.086 | 0.044 | 0.033 |
|  | D-$ | 7.152 | 7.070 | 6.877 | 6.918 |
|  | TLB | 0.010 | 0.000 |  |  |
| gsm.decode | I-$ | 0.038 | 0.034 | 0.038 | 0.030 |
|  | D-$ | 0.758 | 0.756 | 0.435 | 0.608 |
|  | TLB | 0.019 | 0.000 |  |  |

**Table 3.** Data cache miss ratio for *lat_ctx* (%)

| Num. of proc. | 2 | | 20 | |
|---|---|---|---|---|
| Size of proc. | VM | VM+KMT | FM | FM+KMT |
| 0KB | 0.181 | 0.076 | 0.649 | 0.393 |
| 32KB | 0.438 | 0.556 | 2.679 | 3.190 |

## 4  Conclusions

We have shown how the performance of an embedded application is affected by the configuration of memory management in Linux. We observe that the performance of embedded applications is highly dependent on the memory management configuration. The overall execution time can be reduced by up to 23%, depending on the application, by using a less complicated memory management configuration, which also improves the memory performance. The system call overhead shows significant variations as well, depending on the OS services. However, the OS would no longer provide the rigorous memory management such as automatic memory protection and extendable stack which may require additional verifications of memory usage in the design time. By providing data that quantifies the effect of the memory management subsystem on the overall performance, the application-specific configuration of the memory management subsystem in Linux will contribute to the design of more efficient systems by enabling an OS-level design space exploration.

## Acknowledgement

This work was supported by the Korea Research Foundation Grant funded by the Korean Government(MOEHRD). (KRF-2006-214-D00127)

## References

1. Rosa, A.L., Lavagno, L., Passerone, C.: Hardware/software design space exploration for a reconfigurable processor. In: Proceedings of IEEE Design, Automation and Test in Europe, March 2003, pp. 570–575. IEEE Computer Society Press, Los Alamitos (2003)
2. Crowley, C.: Operating Systems: A Design-Oriented Approach. Irwin (1997)
3. Stallings, W.: Operating Systems: Internals and Design Principles. Prentice-Hall, Englewood Cliffs (2001)
4. King, R., Neves, R., Russinovich, M., Tracey, J.M.: High-performance memory-based web servers: kernel and user-space performance. In: Proceedings of USENIX Annual Technical Conference, June 2001, pp. 175–188 (2001)
5. Maeda, T.: Safe execution of user programs in kernel mode using typed assembly language. Master's thesis, University of Tokyo (2002)
6. Hennessy, J.L., Patterson, D.A.: Computer Architecture: A Quantitative Approach. Morgan Kaufmann, San Francisco (1996)
7. de Blanquier, J.: Supporting new hardware environment with uclinux. Journal of Linux Technology 1(3), 20–28 (2000)
8. Furber, S.: ARM System-on-Chip Architecture. Addison-Wesley, Reading (2000)
9. Guthaus, M.R., Ringenberg, J.S., Ernst, D., Austin, T.M., Mudge, T., Brown, R.B.: Mibench: A free, commercially representative embedded benchmark suite. In: Proceedings of IEEE Annual Workship on Workload Characterization, December 2001, IEEE Computer Society Press, Los Alamitos (2001)
10. McVoy, L., Staelin, C.: lmbench: portable tools for performance analysis. In: Proceedings of USENIX Technical Conference, January 1996, pp. 279–295 (1996)
11. Park, S.: Operating system performance and its effect on embedded systems. Technical report Available at http://cslab.snu.ac.kr/~sspark/paper/tr-osmp.pdf
12. Park, S., Lee, Y., Shin, H.: An experimental analysis of the effect of the operating system on memory performance in embedded multimedia computing. In: Proceedings of ACM International Conference on Embedded Software, September 2004, pp. 26–33 (2004)

# SC2SCFL: Automated SystemC to $SystemC^{FL}$ Translation

Ka Lok Man[1], Andrea Fedeli[2], Michele Mercaldi[3], Menouer Boubekeur[1],
and Michel Schellekens[1]

[1] Centre for Efficiency-Oriented Languages (CEOL), Department of Computer Science,
University College Cork (UCC), Cork, Ireland
SystemCFL@gmail.com, m.boubekeur@cs.ucc.ie, m.schellekens@cs.ucc.ie
[2] STMicroelectronics, Agrate (Milan), Italy
andrea.fedeli@st.com
[3] M.O.S.T., Turin, Italy
michele.mercaldi@most.it

**Abstract.** $SystemC^{FL}$ is the formalisation of a reasonable subset of SystemC based on classical process algebras. During the last few years, $SystemC^{FL}$ has been successfully used to give formal specifications of SystemC designs. For formal analysis purposes, so far, users have been required to transform manually their SystemC codes into corresponding $SystemC^{FL}$ specifications. To verify some desired properties of $SystemC^{FL}$ specifications using existing formal verification tools (e.g. NuSMV and SPIN), similarly, manual translations have been needed for turning $SystemC^{FL}$ specifications into corresponding terms of the input language (e.g. SMV and PROMELA) of the selected formal verification tool. Since manual transformation and translations between SystemC codes, $SystemC^{FL}$ specifications, and various formalisms are quite laborious and therefore error-prone, these translations have to be made as much automatic as possible. The first step of the research in these directions is to automate the transformation from SystemC codes to $SystemC^{FL}$ specifications. In this paper, we present SC2SCFL (an automatic translation tool), which converts SystemC codes into corresponding $SystemC^{FL}$ specifications.

## 1 Introduction

SystemC [1] is a modelling language consisting of C++ class library and a simulation kernel for HDL designs, encompassing system-level behavioural descriptions down to *Register Transfer Level* (RTL) representations. Nowadays, SystemC is becoming the de-facto standard for system level modelling and design. Although SystemC has been successfully applied in many different industrial areas, and some attempts to apply formal methods to verify SystemC descriptions have been made, it still does miss the possibility of *formal reasoning* of descriptions.

$SystemC^{FL}$ (SCFL in ASCII format) [2,3,4] is the formalisation of a reasonable subset of SystemC based on the classical process algebras *Algebra of Communicating Processes* (ACP) [5] and *A Timed Process Algebra for Specifying Real-Time Systems* (ATP) [6]. The semantics of $SystemC^{FL}$ has been defined by means of deduction rules in a

S. Vassiliadis et al. (Eds.): SAMOS 2007, LNCS 4599, pp. 34–45, 2007.
© Springer-Verlag Berlin Heidelberg 2007

*Structured Operational Semantics* (SOS) [7] style that associates a time transition system (TTS) with a $SystemC^{FL}$ process. The introduction of $SystemC^{FL}$ (since three years ago) initiated an attempt to extend the knowledge and experience collected in the field of process algebras to system level modelling and design.

$SystemC^{FL}$ is aimed at giving formal specifications of SystemC designs and to perform formal analysis of SystemC processes. Furthermore, $SystemC^{FL}$ is a single formalism that can be used for specifying concurrent systems, finite state systems and real-time systems (as in SystemC). Desired properties of these systems specified in $SystemC^{FL}$ can be verified with existing formal verification tools by translating them into different formats that are the input languages of formal verification tools. Hence, $SystemC^{FL}$ can be purportedly used for formal verification of SystemC designs. For instance, safety properties of concurrent systems specified in $SystemC^{FL}$ can be verified (see [8]) by translating those systems to PROMELA [9], which is the input language of the SPIN Model Checker [9]. Similarly, [10] reported that some desired properties of finite state systems specified in $SystemC^{FL}$ can be fed into the SMV Model Checker [11] to verify them. Furthermore, a formal translation was defined in [12] from $SystemC^{FL}$ to a variant (with very general settings) of timed automata [13]. The practical benefit of the formal translation from a $SystemC^{FL}$ specification (describing real-time systems) to a timed automaton is to enable verification of timing properties of the $SystemC^{FL}$ specifications using existing verification tools for timed automata, such as UPPAAL [14].

During the last few years, $SystemC^{FL}$ has been successfully used to give formal specifications of SystemC designs (see also [3,4,15]). For formal analysis purposes, so far, users have been required to manually transform their SystemC codes into corresponding $SystemC^{FL}$ specifications. To verify some desired properties of $SystemC^{FL}$ specifications using existing formal verification tools (see also [8,10,12]), similarly, manual translations have been needed for turning $SystemC^{FL}$ specifications into corresponding terms of the input language of the selected formal verification tool. Since manual transformation and translations between SystemC codes, $SystemC^{FL}$ specifications and various formalisms are quite laborious and therefore error-prone, these translations have to be automated.

For the sake of simplicity, our first goal (of the research in these directions as already reported in [16]) is to develop an automatic translation tool which converts SystemC codes (mainly untimed) into corresponding $SystemC^{FL}$ specifications that can be further mapped to the input languages of several formal verification tools (e.g. SPIN and NuSMV). SC2SCFL is such an automatic translation tool.

Over the years, automatic translation tools from SystemC to other description languages have been developed (e.g. [17]). To our knowledge, this is the first article to report an automatic translation tool from SystemC to a formal language (i.e. $SystemC^{FL}$).

This paper is organised as follows. In Section 2, we give a brief overview of a subset of $SystemC^{FL}$ formalism that is relevant for the use in this paper. Section 3 captures the main ideas of our proposed translation from SystemC to $SystemC^{FL}$. Section 4 describes the architectures of the automatic translation tool SC2SCFL. A translation example of using SC2SCFL is given in Section 5. We also illustrate our practical interest of verification of $SystemC^{FL}$ specifications, in Section 6, by translating the $SystemC^{FL}$ specification shown in Section 5 to the equivalent NuSMV [18] specification which is further validated by the NuSMV Model Checker [18]. Finally, concluding remarks are made in Section 7 and the direction of future work is pointed out in the same section.

## 2   SystemC$^{\mathbb{FL}}$

An overview of SystemC is not given in this paper. Some familiarity with SystemC is required. The desirable background can, for example, be found in [1]. In this section we give, just for illustration purposes, an overview of a small subset of SystemC$^{\mathbb{FL}}$ (that is relevant for the use of this paper); a more extensive treatment can be found in [3] and [4].

### 2.1   Data Types

To define the semantics of SystemC$^{\mathbb{FL}}$ processes, we need to make some assumptions about the data types. Let *Var* denote the set of all variables $(x_0, \ldots, x_n)$, and *Value* denote the set of all possible values $(v_0, \ldots, v_m)$ that contains at least $\mathbb{B}$ (booleans) and $\mathbb{R}$ (reals). A valuation is a partial function from variables to values (e.g. $x_0 \mapsto v_0$). The set of all valuations is denoted by $\Sigma$. The set *Ch* of all channels and the set $S$ of all sensitivity lists with clocks may be used in SystemC$^{\mathbb{FL}}$ processes that are assumed. Notice that the above proposed data types are the fundamental ones. Several extensions of data types (e.g. "*sc_bit*" and "*sc_logic*") were already introduced in [15].

### 2.2   Syntax

To ease the handling of SystemC$^{\mathbb{FL}}$ specifications, the syntax of SystemC$^{\mathbb{FL}}$ is now given, in ASCII format, (see [3] and [4] for the same syntax in LATEXversion). P denotes the sets of process terms in SystemC$^{\mathbb{FL}}$ and p ∈ P are the core elements of SystemC$^{\mathbb{FL}}$. Notice that the syntax of the equality, relational and logical operators of SystemC$^{\mathbb{FL}}$ (in ASCII format) is defined in an exact way as such operators in SystemC. We also choose, in ASCII format, the following symbols:

```
->, {}, ?
```

to represent mapping ($\mapsto$, i.e. pair correspondence in the relation graph), empty element and the undefinedness respectively. The formal language SystemC$^{\mathbb{FL}}$ is defined according to the following grammar for process term p ∈ P:

```
p ::= deadlock | skip | x := e | cond(b) p p | b watch p | p ; p
    | p ``|'' p | rep p | p merge p
```

The operators are listed in descending order of their binding strength as follows : {watch, ;, rep},{cond, |, merge}. The operators inside the braces have equal binding strength. In addition, operators of equal binding strength associate to the left, and parentheses may be used to group expressions. SystemC$^{\mathbb{FL}}$ has the following syntax:

- the *deadlock* process term "deadlock" is introduced as a constant, which represents no behaviour;
- the *skip* process term "skip" performs the internal action "tau";

- the *assignment* process term "x:=e", which assigns the value of expression "e" to "x" (modelling a SystemC assignment statement);
- the *conditional composition* "cond(b) p q" operates as a SystemC if_then_else statement, where "b" denotes a boolean expression; and "p" and "q" are process terms;
- the *watch* process term "b watch p" is used to model a SystemC construct of event control;
- the *sequential composition* "p ; q" models the process term that behaves as "p", and upon termination of "p", continues to behave as process term "q";
- the *alternative composition* "p | q" models a non-deterministic choice between process terms "p" and "q";
- the *repetition* process term "rep p" (modelling a SystemC loop construct) executes "p" zero or more times;
- the *parallel composition* "p merge q" is used to express parallelism.

## 2.3  Formal Semantics

A *SystemC*$^{\mathbb{FL}}$ process is a quintuple [p,gb,gc,s,m], where $p \in P$ is a process term; gb,gc $\in \Sigma$ are valuations; $s \in S$ is a sensitivity list with clocks; and $m \in Ch$ is a channel. We give a formal semantics for *SystemC*$^{\mathbb{FL}}$ processes (see [3] and [4] for details) in terms of a TTS. Three kinds of transition relations are defined for *SystemC*$^{\mathbb{FL}}$ processes. They can be explained as follows:

1. An action transition [p,gb,gc,s,m] -a- [p',gc,ga,s,m] is that the process [p,gb,gc,s,m] executes a (discrete) action "a" starting with the current valuation gc (at the moment of the transition taking place) and by this execution p evolves into p'; notice that gb represents the previous accompanying valuation of the process, and ga represents the accompanying valuation of the process after the action "a" is executed.
2. Similarly, a termination [p,gb,gc,s,m] -a- [@,gc,ga,s,m] is that the process executes the action "a" followed by termination, where @ is used to indicate a successful termination, and @ is not a process term.
3. A time transition [p,gb,gc,s,m] -d- [p',gc,ga,s,m] is that the process [p,gb,gc,s,m] may idle during a time d and then behaves like [p',gc,ga,s,m].

The above transition relations are defined through deduction rules in a SOS style. These rules (of the form $\frac{premises}{conclusions}$) have two parts: on the top of the bar we put *premises* of the rule, and below them the *conclusions*. If the premises hold, then we infer that the conclusions hold as well. Rules for operational semantics, congruence result and the set of properties of *SystemC*$^{\mathbb{FL}}$ are not given in this paper; see [3,4] for more details.

## 3  SystemC to *SystemC*$^{\mathbb{FL}}$ Translation

In this section, due to reasons of space, we briefly outline the main concepts and ideas of the translation from a reasonable subset of SystemC to *SystemC*$^{\mathbb{FL}}$ (that is relevant for the use in this paper). A more detailed account of such a translation can be found in [19].

## 3.1 Simplifications and Restrictions

In order to simplify the implementation of SC2SCFL, we make the following simplifications/restrictions:

- Since the translation of a SystemC design to the corresponding $SystemC^{FL}$ process is only relevant for the development of $SystemC^{FL}$ simulator and other translation tools like SCFL2NuSMV, SCFL2SPIN and SCFL2UPP as reported in [16], simulator and different verification tools have different data type restriction. The development of SC2SCFL is just our first step. It is not our intention to include all possible data type conversion between SystemC, $SystemC^{FL}$ and other formalisms in such a tool. Hence, no data type conversion is implemented in SC2SCFL. This also leads to the conversion of the data types of variables from SystemC to $SystemC^{FL}$ becoming irrelevant.
- Due to the above mentioned facts that SC2SCFL purely focuses on the translation at the syntactical level from SystemC modules to the corresponding $SystemC^{FL}$ process terms without any consideration of data type conversion.
- Also, we can write a SystemC module in many different ways, for the sake of simplicity, we restrict ourselves to use only the construct of a SystemC module as shown in Subsection 3.2. This is not a strong restriction, since most of SystemC modules are usually written using this kind of construct, as we have seen in all SystemC User's Guides (e.g. [20]).
- At this moment, SC2SCFL does not support the translation of the synchronisation and communication mechanism between SystemC concurrent processes to the corresponding $SystemC^{FL}$ processes in a parallel context.

## 3.2 SystemC Module

The following construct of the SystemC module (illustrated by means of a simple example: a synchronous D flip-flop) is supported by SC2SCFL:

```
SC_MODULE(dff) {
 sc_in<bool> din;
 sc_in<bool> clock;
 sc_out<bool> dout;
 void doit() {
  dout = din;
 };
 SC_CTOR(dff) {
   SC_METHOD(doit);
  sensitive_pos << clock;
 }
};
```

## 3.3 Translation Procedure

Based on the SystemC module given in Subsection 3.2, the translation procedure is implemented in SC2SCFL as follows:

1. Each method process is translated to the corresponding $SystemC^{FL}$ sub-process term in which renaming mechanism is applied (if necessary) to the local variables of the method process in such a way that name conflict problem is avoided (i.e. the local variables of method processes are unique after the translation).
2. The elements in the sensitivity list of a SystemC module are placed in the set of the sensitivity list with clocks associating to the corresponding $SystemC^{FL}$ process term (of the SystemC module).
3. The SystemC constructor of a SystemC module is translated to the corresponding watch process term in a specified way as indicated in Subsection 3.5.
4. Following the above mentioned procedures and translating each method process of a SystemC module to the corresponding $SystemC^{FL}$ sub-process term according to the translation rules and the translation of $SystemC^{FL}$ constructor as defined in Subsection 3.4 and Subsection 3.5, respectively, then the corresponding $SystemC^{FL}$ process term of the SystemC module is generated.
5. When more than one SystemC module is translated, the parallel composition operator of $SystemC^{FL}$ is applied to connect the corresponding $SystemC^{FL}$ process terms (of the SystemC modules translated) together.

### 3.4   Translation Rules

The following translation rules define the functionality of SC2SCFL for some gb, gc and s, where gb and gc are valuations, and o is a sensitivity list with clocks. For simplicity and for the use in this paper, we illustrate several translation rules by means of examples. A more detailed set of translation rules for SC2SCFL can be found in [19]. The syntax of the equality, relational and logical operators of $SystemC^{FL}$ is defined in an exact way as such operators in SystemC. Hence, the translation rules of the equality, relational and logical operators are omitted.

| trans. | SystemC | SCFL |
|--------|---------|------|
| assig. | x = 3 | x := 3 |
| seq. | x = 3; y = 7 | x := 3 ; y := 7 |
| if | if (x == 3) {x = 1;} | cond (x == 3) x := 1 deadlock |
| i_t_e | if (y <= 3) {y = 1;} else {y = 7;} | cond (y <=3) y := 1 y := 7 |
| while | while (true) {y = 1; x = 5;} | true watch rep (y := 1 ; x := 5) |
| for | for (int i = 0; i <= 8; i++) {x = y;} | i := 0 ; (i <= 8 watch (rep (x := y ; i := i + 1))) |

### 3.5   $SystemC^{FL}$ Constructor

```
SystemC:
void f1() {
  x = y;
};

SC_CTOR(f1) {
  SC_METHOD(f1);
  sensitive << s1;
  sensitive_pos << clk1;
```

```
}

SCFL:
SEN(s1) || SEN_p(clk1) watch x := y
```

SEN(s1) is defined as a function that returns a boolean expression "true" if the valuation of s1 in gc has changed with respect to the valuation in gb. In a similar way, SEN_p(clk1) is defined as a function that returns a boolean expression "true" if a positive edge occurs on the clock clk1. The formal definitions of these auxiliary functions used for the watch process term can be found in [3]. Also, || is used to represent the logical operator "OR".

## 4    Architectures of SC2SCFL

SC2SCFL is an automatic translator which converts a reasonable subset of SystemC to $SystemC^{FL}$. It is entirely developed in the Java language (jdk 1.5.0) using JavaCC 4.0 as a parser generator. JavaCC enables one to extract the structures of SystemC files with a comprehensive interpretation of general C++ constructs. The choice of using the Java language and JavaCC as a parser generator is immaterial and other programming language and parser may be used as well.

The input format of SC2SCFL is a file of SystemC codes. In the current release of SC2SCFL, only one SystemC module can be declared in each input file. The translation process is divided into three steps:

1. According to the grammar rules used by JavaCC to build the parser, the input file is first divided in tokens and then parsed.
2. In order to generalise the translation process, an *Abstract Syntax Tree* (AST) is created (as a preprocessing step for the translation). In the future version of SC2SCFL, the AST could be dumped to have an abstract representation of $SystemC^{FL}$ constructs. This will be also useful for the development of other translation tools (e.g. SCFL2NuSMV).
3. The last step implements the visit of the AST and produces $SystemC^{FL}$ specifications according to the translation rules as defined in [19].

## 5    Case Study: Scalable Synchronous Bus Arbiter

In this section we show by means of a case study the use of $SystemC^{FL}$ to verify the correctness of a digital circuit written in SystemC. We transform a SystemC design into the corresponding $SystemC^{FL}$ specification and then further translate it to the equivalent NuSMV specification.

For this purpose we choose a synchronous scalable $n$-cells bus arbiter controlling the access to n-clients deciding which of them gets access grants to the shared resource. It has request inputs and acknowledgements, and no restriction is applied to inputs, hence at any clock cycle any possible subset of the requests can be high (i.e. their logical values are "1"). The task of the arbiter is to set at most one of the corresponding acknowledgements high. This circuit has been already used for formal verification exemplification,

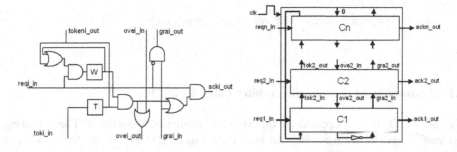

**Fig. 1.** Single arbiter cell and the interconnection between cells

as in [11] and [21]. Figure 1 shows a single arbiter cell and the interconnection of arbiter cells.

The SystemC code for one cell of the arbiter is given below. Based on the interconnection diagram, we can build such an arbiter with multiple inputs using positional connection.

```
#include "systemc.h"
SC_MODULE(Cell)
{
  sc_in<bool> clk;
  sc_in<bool> req_in, tok_in, gra_in, ove_in;
  sc_out<bool> ack_out, gra_out, tok_out, ove_out;
  sc_signal<bool> persistent;

  void calc_token() {
    tok_out = tok_in;
    cout << "@end calc_token " << tok_out << endl;
  }

  void calc_persistent() {
    persistent = (persistent || tok_out) && req_in;
    cout << "@end calc_persistent " << persistent << endl;
  }

  void comb() {
    ove_out = (persistent && tok_out) || ove_in;
    gra_out = !req_in && gra_in;
    ack_out = req_in && (persistent && tok_out || gra_in);
    cout << "@end Cell " << req_in << ack_out << endl;
  }

  SC_CTOR(Cell) {
    SC_METHOD(calc_token);
    sensitive << clk.pos();
    SC_METHOD(calc_persistent);
    sensitive << clk.pos();
```

```
SC_METHOD(comb);
sensitive << persistent << tok_out << ove_in << req_in << gra_in;
}
};
```

## 5.1  Translation of the Scalable Arbiter Using SC2SCFL

The SC2SCFL tool is applied on the SystemC design of the arbiter. The following
$SystemC^{\mathbb{FL}}$ specification is obtained after executing SC2SCFL on the SystemC code
of the one-cell arbiter. We can easily observe the correspondences between them (also
with some initial conditions of variables that are assumed for illustration purposes).

```
[(SEN_p(clk) watch tok_out := tok_in)
merge
   (SEN_p(clk) watch persistent := (persistent || tok_out) && req_in)
merge
  ove_out = (persistent && tok_out) || ove_in;
  gra_out = !req_in && gra_in;
  ack_out = req_in && (persistent && (tok_out || gra_in)),

{req_in->?, gra_in->?, ove_in->?, tok_in->?,
persistent->?, ack_out->?, gra_out->?, ove_out->?,
tok_out->?, clk->true},

{req_in->?, gra_in->?, ove_in->?, tok_in->?,
persistent->false, ack_out->?, gra_out->?, ove_out->?,
tok_out->true, clk->false},

{clk}, {}]
```

## 6  Verification of $SystemC^{\mathbb{FL}}$ Specification Using NuSMV

In order to proceed to the formal verification phase, the obtained $SystemC^{\mathbb{FL}}$ specification is translated into the equivalent NuSMV specification. As the $SystemC^{\mathbb{FL}} \rightarrow$
NUSMV translator is not available yet, we manually translated the single arbiter cell
from the original SystemC code, taking into account the translation rules defined above
for SystemC$\rightarrow SystemC^{\mathbb{FL}}$.

For the composition of two arbiter cells, each of which would be an instance of the
SC2SCFL-produced specification, we write according to the translation rules the following NuSMV specification. Due to reasons of space, we only give parts of the specification.

```
MODULE arbiter_cell(
  req_in, ack_out, tok_in, tok_out,
  ove_in, ove_out, gra_in, gra_out, init_token
)
```

```
VAR
  persistent : boolean;

SCFLpt_1 : SCFLpt_1(tok_out, tok_in);
SCFLpt_2 : SCFLpt_2(persistent, tok_out, req_in);
SCFLpt_3 : SCFLpt_3(
  ove_out, persistent, tok_out, ove_in,
  gra_out, req_in, gra_in, ack_out
);

ASSIGN
  init(persistent):=0;

MODULE SCFLpt_1(tok_out, tok_in)
ASSIGN
  next(tok_out):=tok_in;

MODULE SCFLpt_2(persistent, tok_out, req_in)
ASSIGN
  next(persistent):=(persistent | tok_out) & req_in;

MODULE SCFLpt_3(
  ove_out, persistent, tok_out, ove_in, gra_out, req_in, gra_in, ack_out)
ASSIGN
  ove_out := (persistent & tok_out) | ove_in;
  gra_out := !req_in & gra_in;
  ack_out := req_in & (persistent & (tok_out | gra_in));

// Manually added to represent the whole verification context

MODULE main
VAR
  req1_in: boolean; req2_in: boolean;
  ack1_out: boolean; ack2_out: boolean;
  g1:    boolean; g2:    boolean;
  o0:    boolean; o1:    boolean;
  t1:    boolean; t2:    boolean;

  e1 : arbiter_cell(req1_in, ack1_out, t2, t1, o1, o0,!o0, g1, 1);
  e2 : arbiter_cell(req2_in, ack2_out, t1, t2, 0, o1, g1, g2, 0);

ASSIGN
  init(t1):=!t2;

ASSIGN
  next(req1_in):=case
    req1_in & !ack1_out : req1_in;
    1: {0,1};
  esac;
```

```
next(req2_in):=case
  req2_in & !ack2_out : req2_in;
  1: {0,1};
esac;

SPEC AG (req1_in -> AF(ack1_out))
SPEC AG !(ack1_out & ack2_out)
```

We have verified a liveness and a safety property of the above NuSMV specification using the NuSMV Model Checker. As a liveness property, the arbiter satisfied the following CTL formula: $AG\ (req1\_in \rightarrow AF\ (ack1\_out))$. Such a property states that if the request ($req1\_in$) is continuously held high, eventually there will be an acknowledgement ($ack1\_out$). The safety property that was also satisfied by the arbiter is as follows (described in CTL): $AG\ !(ack1\_out\ \&\ ack2\_out)$. It expresses the mutual exclusion between the acknowledgements. The above-mentioned properties were also verified for 2 and 3-cells arbiters.

## 7 Conclusions and Future Work

In this paper, we presented an automatic tool SC2SCFL which converts a reasonable subset of SystemC to $SystemC^{\mathbb{FL}}$. The main features of SC2SCFL were explained and illustrative examples for the use of SC2SCFL were given. To show our practical interest of verification of $SystemC^{\mathbb{FL}}$ specifications, we also translated a $SystemC^{\mathbb{FL}}$ specification to the equivalent NuSMV specification, which was further validated by the NuSMV Model Checker.

SC2SCFL is in a continuous improving process by adding new features and correcting bugs. New features and improvements will be included in the next release of SC2SCFL are as follows: instantiation of SystemC modules, positional connections in SystemC and support for more C++ constructors. Furthermore, we also plan to have a prototype SCFL2NuSMV, which translates a significant subset of $SystemC^{\mathbb{FL}}$ to NuSMV, working before the end of 2007.

## Acknowledgements

Ka Lok Man wishes to thank Jos Baeten, Bert van Beek, MohammadReza Mousavi, Koos Rooda, Ramon Schiffelers, Pieter Cuijpers, Michel Reniers, Kees Middelburg, Uzma Khadim and Muck van Weerdenburg for many stimulating and helpful discussions (focusing on process algebras for distinct systems) in the past few years.

## References

1. IEEE: IEEE Standard for SystemC Language Reference Manual (IEEE STD 1666TM-2005). IEEE. (2005)
2. $SystemC^{\mathbb{FL}}$: $SystemC^{\mathbb{FL}}$ homepage http://digilander.libero.it/systemcfl/.

3.  Man, K.L.: $SystemC^{FL}$: Formalization of SystemC. In: the 12th Mediterranean Electrotechnical Conference MELECON, Dubrovnik, Croatia, IEEE (2004)
4.  Man, K.L.: Formal communication semantics of $SystemC^{FL}$. In: the 8th Euromicro Conference on Digital System Design DSD, Porto, Portugal, IEEE (2005)
5.  Baeten, J.C.M., Weijland, W.P.: Process Algebra. Volume 18 of Cambridge Tracts in Theoretical Computer Science. Cambridge University Press, Cambridge, United Kingdom (1990)
6.  Nicollin, X., Sifakis, J.: The algebra of timed processes, ATP: Theory and application. Information and Computation **114** (1994) 131–178
7.  Plotkin, G.D.: A structural approach to operational semantics. Technical Report DAIMI FN-19, Computer Science Department, Aarhus University (1981)
8.  Man, K.L.: Formal verification of $SystemC^{FL}$ specifications using SPIN. In: the 5th WSEAS International Conference on Microelectronics, Nanoelectronics and Optoelectronics MINO, Prague, Czech Republic, WSEAS (2006)
9.  Holzmann, G.J.: The SPIN Model Checker: Primer and Reference Manual. Addison Wesley Professional, Boston (2003)
10. Man, K.L.: Verifying $SystemC^{FL}$ designs using the SMV model checker. In: the 8th IEEE Workshop on Design and Diagnostics of Electronic Circuits and Systems DDECS, Sopron, Hungary (2005)
11. McMillan, K.L.: Symbolic Model Checking. Kluwer Academic Publisher (1993)
12. Man, K.L.: Analyzing $SystemC^{FL}$ designs using timed automata. In: the 9th IEEE Baltic Electronics Conference BEC, Tallinn, Estonia (2004)
13. Alur, R., Dill, D.: A theory of timed automata. Theoretical Computer Science 126 (1994) 183–236
14. Larsen, K.G., Pettersson, P., Yi, W.: UPPAAL in a Nutshell. Int. Journal on Software Tools for Technology Transfer 1(1–2) (1997) 134–152
15. Man, K.L.: Modeling with the formal language of SystemC: Case studies. In: the 11th IEEE International Conference Mixed Design of Integrated Circuits and Systems MIXDES, Szczecin, Poland (2004)
16. Man, K.L., Fedeli, A., Mercaldi, M., Schellekens, M.P.: $SystemC^{FL}$: An infrastructure for a tlm formal verification proposal (with an overview on a tool set for practical formal verification of systemc descriptions). In: the 2nd East-West Design & Test Workshop EWDTW, Sochi, Russia, IEEE (2006)
17. J. Castillo, J., Huerta, P., Martnez, J.: An open-source tool for SystemC to Verilog automatic translation. Journal of Latin American Applied Research (2007) accepted for publication.
18. NuSMV: NuSMV Model Checker User Manual. (2006) http://nusmv.irst.itc.it/.
19. Man, K.L.: An overview on sc2scfl. Draft paper (2007) http://digilander.libero.it/systemcfl/.
20. SystemC: SystemC Users Guide and SystemC Language Reference Manual (Version 2.0). http://www.systemc.org.
21. Drechsler, R., Große, D.: Formal verification of ltl formulas for SystemC designs. In: Int. Symposium on Circuits and Systems ISCAS, Bangkok, Thailand, IEEE (2003)

# Model and Validation of Block Cleaning Cost for Flash Memory*,**

Seungjae Baek[1], Jongmoo Choi[1], Donghee Lee[2], and Sam H. Noh[3]

[1] Division of Information and Computer Science, Dankook University, Korea,
Hannam-Dong, Yongsan-Gu, Seoul, 140-714 Korea
{ibanez1383,choijm}@dankook.ac.kr
[2] Department of Computer Science, University of Seoul, Korea,
Jeonnong-Dong, Dongdaemun-Gu, Seoul, 130-743 Korea
dhlee@venus.uos.ac.kr
[3] School of Computer and Information Engineering, Hongik University, Korea,
Sangsu-Dong, Mapo-Gu, Seoul, 121-791, Korea
samhnoh@hongik.ac.kr

**Abstract.** Flash memory is a storage medium that is becoming more and more popular. Though not yet fully embraced in traditional computing systems, Flash memory is prevalent in embedded systems, materialized as commodity appliances such as the digital camera and the MP3 player that we are enjoying in our everyday lives. The cost of block cleaning is an important factor that strongly influences Flash memory file system performance analogous to the seek time in disk storage based systems. We show that three performance parameters, namely, utilization, invalidity, and uniformity characteristics of Flash memory strongly effect this block cleaning cost and present a model for the block cleaning cost based on these parameters. We validate this model using synthetic workloads on commercial Flash memory products.

**Keywords:** Flash memory, model, validation, block cleaning.

## 1 Introduction

Recent developments in Flash memory technology have brought about numerous products that make use of Flash memory. While still controversial, optimists envision Flash memory will replace much of the territory that disk storage has been occupying. Whether this will happen or not will have to be seen [1]. However, one sure thing is that Flash memory is a storage medium that is being more and more widely used in everyday commodity embedded systems and is bringing about significant changes to the computing environment.

In view of these developments, in this paper, we explore and identify the characteristics of Flash memory and analyze how they influence the latency of data

---

* This work was supported in part by grant No. R01-2004-000-10188-0 from the Basic Research Program of the Korea Science & Engineering Foundation.
** This work was supported in part by MIC & IITA through IT Leading R&D Support Project.

S. Vassiliadis et al. (Eds.): SAMOS 2007, LNCS 4599, pp. 46–54, 2007.
© Springer-Verlag Berlin Heidelberg 2007

access. We identify the cost of block cleaning as the key characteristic that influences latency. A performance model for analyzing the cost of block cleaning is presented based on three parameters that we derive, namely, utilization, invalidity, and uniformity, which we define clearly later. We find that the cost of block cleaning is strongly influenced by uniformity just like seek is a strong influence for disk based storage.

The rest of the paper is organized as follows. In Section 2, we elaborate on the characteristics of Flash memory and on block cleaning, in particular. Then, we present the block cleaning cost model in Section 3. In Section 4, we present the experimental setting and results that are used to validate the model. We briefly discuss related works in Section 5 and conclude in Section 6.

## 2  Flash Memory and Block Cleaning

Flash memory that is most widely used today is either of the NOR type or the NAND type. Other types of Flash memory such as OR type or AND type do exist, but are not popular. One key difference between NOR and NAND Flash memory is the access granularity. NOR Flash memory supports word-level random access, while NAND Flash memory supports page-level random access. Hence, in embedded systems, NOR Flash memory is usually used to store code, while NAND Flash memory is used as storage for the file system. NOR and NAND Flash memory also differ in density, operational time, and bad block marking mechanisms.

Flash memory is organized as a set of blocks, each block consisting of a set of pages. According to the block size, NAND Flash memory is further divided into two classes, that is, small block NAND and large block NAND. In small block NAND Flash memory, each block has 32 pages, where the page size is 528 bytes. A 512-byte portion of these bytes is the data area used to store data, while the remaining 16-byte portion is called the spare area, which is generally used to store ECC and/or bookkeeping information. In large block NAND Flash memory, each block has 64 pages of 2112 bytes (2048 bytes for data area and 64 bytes for spare area).

Flash memory as a storage medium has characteristics that are different from traditional disk storage. These characteristics can be summarized as follows [2].

1. Access time in Flash memory is location independent similar to RAM. There is no "seek time" involved.
2. Overwrite is not possible in Flash memory. Flash memory is a form of EEPROM (Electrically Erasable Programmable Read Only Memory), so it needs to be erased before new data can be overwritten.
3. Execution time for the basic operations in Flash memory is asymmetric. Traditionally, three basic operations, namely, read, write, and erase, are supported. An erase operation is used to clean a used page so that the page may be written to again. In general, a write operation takes an order of magnitude longer than a read operation, while an erase operation takes another order or more magnitudes longer than a write operation.
4. The unit of operation is also different for the basic operations. While the erase operation is performed in block units, read/write operations are performed in page units.

5.  The number of erasures possible on each block is limited, typically, to 100,000 or 1,000,000 times.

Let us now consider the specific operations used in Flash memory. Reading data from Flash memory is simply like reading from disk. The distinction from a disk is that all reads take a constant amount of time. For a write operation, a distinction has to be made between a new write and a write that is modifying existing data. When totally new data is being written, this is almost identical to a disk write, that is, a page is allocated and written to. However, there are occasions when no free pages are available to be written to. In such a case, an erase operation must precede the write operation. This will result in considerable delay in writing out the data.

For writes that update existing data, the story is totally different. As overwrite to the updated page is not possible, various mechanisms for non-in-place update have been developed [3,4,5,6]. Though specific details differ, the basic mechanism is to allocate a new page, write the updated data onto the new page, and then, invalidate the original page that holds the (now obsolete) original data. The original page now becomes a dead or invalid page. Likewise, in this situation, an erase operation may have to precede the write operation.

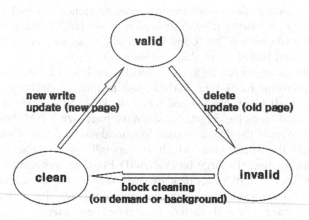

**Fig. 1.** Page state transition diagram

Note that from the above discussions that a page can be in three different states. A page holding legitimate data is in a valid state. If the page is deleted or updated, the page becomes an invalid page and transitions into an invalid state. Note that a page in this state cannot be written to until the block it resides in is first erased. Finally, if the page has not been written to in the first place or the block in which the page resides has just been erased, then the page is clean, and this page is in a clean state. Figure 1 shows the state transition diagram of pages in Flash memory.

Note from the tri-state characteristics that the number of clean pages diminishes not only as new data is written, but also as existing data is updated. In order to store more data and even to make updates to existing data, it is imperative that invalid pages be continually cleaned. Since, cleaning is done via erase operation, which is done in block units, valid pages in the block to be erased must be copied to a clean block. This exacerbates the already large erase overhead needed for cleaning a block.

# 3   Block Cleaning Cost Model

In this section, we identify the parameters that affect the cost of block cleaning. We formulate a cost model based on these parameters and analyze their effects on the cost.

## 3.1   Performance Parameters

Two types of block cleaning are possible in Flash memory. The first is when valid and invalid pages coexist within the block that is to be cleaned. Here, the valid pages must first be copied to a clean page in a different block before the erase operation on the block can happen. We shall refer to this type of cleaning as 'copy-erase cleaning'. The other kind of cleaning is where no valid page exists in the block to be erased. All pages in this block are either invalid or clean. This cleaning imposes only a single erase operation, and we shall refer to this type of cleaning as 'erase-only cleaning'.

Observe that for copy-erase cleaning the number of valid pages is a key factor that affects the cost of cleaning as all the valid pages need to be moved to another block before cleaning may happen. For erase-only cleaning, the way in which the invalid pages are distributed plays a key role. From these observations, we identify three parameters that affect the cost of block cleaning. They are defined as follows:

- **Utilization** ($u$): the fraction of valid pages in Flash memory
- **Invalidity** ($i$):  the fraction of invalid pages in Flash memory
- **Uniformity** ($p$): the fraction of uniform blocks in Flash memory,

where a uniform block is a block that does *not* contain both valid and invalid blocks simultaneously.

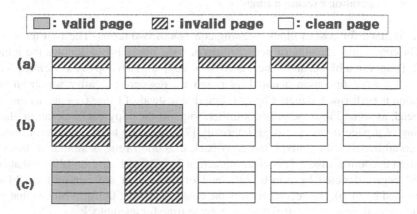

**Fig. 2.** Situation where utilization ($u$=0.2) and invalidity ($i$=0.2) remains unchanged, while uniformity ($p$) changes (a) $p = 0.2$ (b) $p = 0.6$ (c) $p = 1$

Figure 2 shows three page allocation situations where utilization and invalidity are the same, but uniformity is different. Since there are four valid pages and four invalid pages among the 20 pages for all three cases utilization and invalidity are both 0.2. However, there are one, three, and five uniform blocks in Figure 2(a), (b), and (c), hence uniformity is 0.2, 0.6, and 1, respectively.

Utilization determines, on average, the number of valid pages that need to be copied for copy-erase cleaning. Invalidity determines the number of blocks that are candidates for cleaning. Finally, uniformity refers to the fraction of uniform blocks. A uniform block is a block with zero or more clean pages and the remainder of the pages in the block are uniformly valid or uniformly invalid pages. Another definition of uniformity would be "1 – the fraction of blocks that have both valid and invalid pages." Of all the uniform blocks, only those blocks containing invalid pages are candidates for erase-only cleaning.

From these observations, we can formulate the cost of block cleaning as follows:

### Cost of Block Cleaning

= Cost of copy-erase cleaning + Cost of erase-only cleaning

$$= ((1\text{-}p)\cdot\min(B, i\cdot P))\cdot((r_t + w_t)\cdot(P/B\cdot u)+e_t)) + ((p\cdot B\cdot i)\cdot e_t)$$

where
u: utilization ($0 \leq u \leq 1$)
i : invalidity ($0 \leq i \leq 1\text{-} u$)
p: uniformity ($0 \leq p \leq 1$)
P: number of pages in Flash memory
(P=capacity/size of page)
B: number of blocks in Flash memory
(P/B: # of pages in a block)
$r_t$ : read operation execution time
$w_t$: write operation execution time
$e_t$ : erase operation execution time

The formula for cost of block cleaning consists of two terms. The first term is the cost for copy-erase cleaning of non-uniform blocks, where $P/B\cdot u$ denotes the number of valid pages in a block, and hence, need to be copied. Each copy is associated with a read and a write operation denoted by $r_t$ and $w_t$, respectively, after which an erase operation is performed, denoted by $e_t$. (Note that instead of using $(r_t + w_t)$ as the copy overhead, as some Flash memory controllers support the copy-back operation, that is, copying of a page to another page internally [7], this copy-back operation execution time could be used. In general, the copy-back execution time is similar to the write operation execution time.) This cleaning action is executed only on blocks that have invalid pages, denoted by $\min(B, i\cdot P)$, and of those, that are non-uniform blocks, represented by $(1\text{-}p)$.The second term is the cost of cleaning uniform blocks that have invalid pages denoted by $(p\cdot B\cdot i)$ costing $e_t$ erase time for each block.

# 4 Model Validation

In this section, we discuss the experimental environment used to validate the model and also present the validation results.

## 4.1 Platform and Workload

We use an embedded hardware platform to validate the block cleaning cost model. Hardware components of the system include a 400MHz XScale PXA CPU, 64MB SDRAM, 0.5MB NOR Flash memory, and embedded controllers. A small block 64MB NAND Flash memory that has 128K pages and 4096 blocks is used for Flash memory [7]. Table 1 summarizes the hardware components and their specifications [8].

**Table 1.** Hardware component and specification

| Hardware Components | Specification |
|---|---|
| CPU | 400MHz XScale PXA 255 |
| RAM | 64MB SDRAM |
| Flash | 64MB NAND, 0.5MB NOR |
| Interface | CS8900, USB, RS232, JTAG |

The Linux kernel 2.4.19 was ported on the hardware platform and YAFFS is used to manage the NAND Flash memory [3]. YAFFS uses the open(), read(), write() interface provided by the VFS layer. Below the YAFFS layer, the MTD layer uses the *readchunkfromnand()*, *writechunktonand()*, and *eraseblockinnand()* interface to actually access and control Flash memory [3].

The workload that we use in the experiments is the Postmark benchmark. This is a popular benchmark widely used for measuring file system performance [18,19]. This benchmark creates a large number of randomly sized files. It then executes read, write, delete, and append transactions on these files. We create 500 files (the default number) and perform 500 transactions (again, the default value) for our experiments.

To measure the block cleaning cost, we developed a tool that sets the state of Flash memory based on the three parameter values, which may be manually designated. Based on these settings, block cleaning is performed. Another tool that we developed is used to measure the actual cost of block cleaning. Both tools are implemented within YAFFS to validate our model. For space reasons, we do not elaborate on the details of these tools.

Another issue that must be clarified is the level at which the model is to be validated. In the model, the read, write, and erase times are used to estimate the block cleaning cost. The times used for these operations will drastically influence the model estimation time. The simplest way to determine these values is by using the data sheet provided by the Flash memory chip vendor. However, through experiments we observe that the values reported in the datasheet and the actual time seen at various levels of the system differ considerably. Figure 3 shows these results. The results shows that while the datasheet reports read, write, and erase times of 0.01ms, 0.2ms,

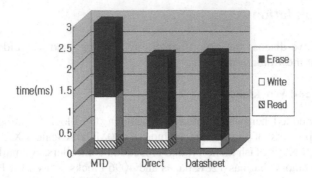

**Fig. 3.** Execution time at each level

and 2ms, respectively, for the Flash memory used in our experiments, the times observed for directly accessing Flash memory at the device driver level is 0.19ms, 0.3ms, and 1.7ms, respectively. Furthermore, when observed just above the MTD layer, the read, write, and erase times are 0.2ms, 1.03ms, and 1.74ms, respectively. Which values are used in the model will drastically influence the accuracy of the model. In our study, we use the observations made just above the MTD layer as this level is where the block cleaning cost is measured.

## 4.2 Validation Results

Figure 4 compares the measured block cleaning cost and the cost estimated by the model. In each figure, the initial values of the three parameters are all set to 0.5. Then, we decrease utilization in Figure 4(a), increase uniformity in Figure 4(b), and decrease invalidity in Figure 4(c). The measured values and the estimated values show similar results as well as similar trends. The results indicate that the block cleaning model that we derived is fairly accurate.

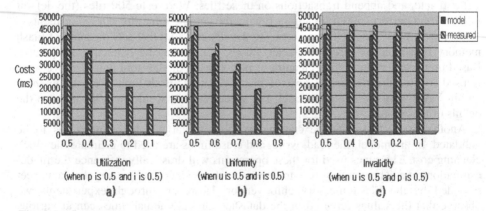

**Fig. 4.** Performance comparison of block cleaning cost model and experimental measurements

Also, from these figures, we find that the impact of utilization and uniformity on block cleaning cost is higher than that of invalidity. Since utilization is not controllable by the system, this implies that to keep cleaning cost down, keeping uniformity high may be a better approach.

## 5  Related Works

The issue of block cleaning has been considered for both Flash memory and disk based systems. For disk based systems, segment cleaning in the Log-structured File System (LFS) is closely related to block cleaning for Flash memory. LFS writes data to a clean segment and performs segment cleaning to reclaim space occupied by obsolete data [9,10,11,12,13].

In the Flash memory arena, studies related to block cleaning have been conducted in many studies [4,14,15,16,17]. Among these Kawaguchi et al. propose using two separate segments for cleaning: one for newly written data and the other for data to be copied during cleaning [4]. Wu and Zwaenepoel present a hybrid cleaning scheme that combines the FIFO algorithm for uniform access and locality gathering algorithm for highly skewed access distribution [16].

These works, however, generally take an algorithmic approach to improve block cleaning. The focus of this paper is in identifying and modeling the key ingredients that affect block cleaning cost in Flash memory.

## 6  Conclusion

In this paper, we identify three performance parameters from features of Flash memory and derive a performance model for block cleaning cost based on these parameters. We validate the model through experimental measurements of block cleaning cost of a 64MB NAND Flash memory chip on an embedded board. The results show that the model that we propose accurately captures the block cleaning cost observed at the MTD layer.

Using this model, we are able to observe the factors that strongly influence block cleaning cost. These observations form the basis for our next step, which is to develop a new page allocation scheme. The new page allocation scheme should take into consideration the factor that most strongly influences block cleaning, namely, the uniformity factor.

## References

1. Goldstein, H.: Too little, too soon [solid state flash memories]. IEEE Spectrum 43(1), 30–31 (2006)
2. Sharma, A.K.: Advanced Semiconductor Memories: Architectures, Designs, and Applications, WILEY Interscience (2003)
3. Aleph One, YAFFS: Yet another Flash file system, www.aleph1.co.uk/yaffs/
4. Kawaguchi, A., Nishioka, S., Motoda, H.: A Flash-memory based file system. In: Proceedings of the 1995 USENIX Annual Technical Conference, pp. 155–164 (1995)

5. Gal, E., Toledo, S.: A transactional Flash file system for microcontrollers. In: Proceedings of the 2005 USENIX Annual Technical Conference, pp. 89–104 (2005)
6. Woodhouse, D.: JFFS: The journaling Flash file system, Ottawa Linux Symposium (2001), http://source.redhat.com/jffs2/jffs2.pdf
7. Samsung Electronics, NAND Flash Data Sheet, http://www.samsung.com/Products/Semiconductor/NANDFlash
8. EZ-X5, www.falinux.com/zproducts
9. Rosenblum, M., Ousterhout, J.K.: The design and implementation of a log-structured file system. ACM Transactions on Computer Systems 10(1), 26–52 (1992)
10. Blackwell, T., Harris, J., Seltzer, M.: Heuristic cleaning algorithms in log-structured file systems. In: Proceedings of the 1995 Annual Technical Conference, pp. 277–288 (1993)
11. Matthews, J., Roselli, D., Costello, A., Wang, R., Anderson, T.: Improving the performance of log-structured file systems with adaptive methods. In: ACM Symposiums on Operating System Principles (SOSP), pp. 238–251 (1997)
12. Wang, J., Hu, Y.: WOLF - a novel reordering write buffer to boost the performance of log-structured file systems. In: Proceedings of the USENIX Conference on File and Storage Technologies (FAST), pp. 46–60 (2002)
13. Wang, W., Zhao, Y., Bunt, R.: HyLog: A High Performance Approach to Managing Disk Layout. In: Proceedings of the USENIX Conference on File and Storage Technologies (FAST), pp. 145–158 (2004)
14. Gal, E., Toledo, S.: Algorithms and Data Structures for Flash Memories. ACM Computing Surveys 37(2), 138–163 (2005)
15. Chiang, M-L., Lee, P.C.H., Chang, R-C.: Using data clustering to improve cleaning performance for Flash memory. Software: Practice and Experience 29(3), 267–290 (1999)
16. Wu, M., Zwaenepoel, W.: eNVy: a non-volatile, main memory storage system. In: Proceeding of the 6th International Conference on Architectural Support for Programming Languages and Operation Systems (ASPLOS), pp. 86–97 (1994)
17. Chang, L.P., Kuo, T.W., Lo, S.W.: Real-time garbage collection for Flash memory storage systems of real time embedded systems. ACM Transactions on Embedded Computing Systems 3(4), 837–863 (2004)
18. PostMark, http://www.netapp.com/ftp/postmark-1_5.c
19. Katcher, J.: PostMark: A New File System Benchmark. Technical Report TR3022, Network Appliance Inc. (1997)

# VLSI Architecture for MRF Based Stereo Matching

Sungchan Park, Chao Chen, and Hong Jeong

Pohang University of Science and Technology
Electronic amd Electrical Engineering
Pohang, Kyungbuk, 790-784, South Korea

**Abstract.** As a step towards real-time stereo on 2D markov random field (MRF), we will present fast belief propagation (FBP) VLSI architecture for stereo matching, which has a parallel, distributed and memory-efficient structure and lowest error rates among the real-time systems. FBP can reduce memory complexities by 17 times smaller than belief propagation (BP) and output 320x240 disparity image of 32 levels with 320 parallel processors on 2 Xilinx FPGAs at 30 frames/s. Multiple chips can be cascaded to increase computation speed due to its linear array architecture. Our structure is more adequate for high resolution and real-time applications like 3D video conference, multi-view coding and 3D modelling.

## 1 Introduction

In the real-time systems, computation speed, memory size and data bus bandwidth are important factors in addition to output precision. The iteration algorithms like BP need the effective trade-off between good approximation results and small iteration times in the viewpoint of the computational efficiency. Here, we will present our paper from this real-time perspective.

Stereo vision is the process of recreating depth or distance information from a pair of images from the same scene. Its methods fall into two broad categories. One is the local method, like block matching and feature matching technique, which uses local constraints within small pixel windows. The other is the global method, like BP [5], [6] and graph which uses global constraints over several scan-lines or the whole image. Many real time systems [2] are realized by local methods. Although it has low computational complexities, there are some local problems where it may fall into mismatch, due to occlusions, uniform texture, ambiguity of low texture and etc. The global methods can solve these local problems but suffer from time and memory complexities. BP has to calculate on the 2D MRF nodes and access a huge number of message memories iteratively, which is not apt for parallel structure due to the bandwidth limitations of data bus. To solve this problem, we will introduce an efficient linear array architecture, which can avoid accessing each message on the MRF network iteratively and sequentially. It scans the MRF network only one time and meanwhile shows the same result as the iteration technique. FBP requires the least memory resource and achieves high-speed parallel processing architecture. Its arrays are highly regular, consisting of identical and simple processing elements (PEs). Hence, it is possible to construct a real-time stereo vision chip which can output disparity images with high depth resolution.

S. Vassiliadis et al. (Eds.): SAMOS 2007, LNCS 4599, pp. 55–64, 2007.

## 2 Background

Given $M$x$N$ left and right images $g^l$, $g^r$ and parameters $C_d$, $C_v$, $K_d$, $K_v$ [5], pair wise MRF energy model of stereo matching can be represented as follows.

$$E(d) = \sum_{p,q \in N^2} V(d_p, d_q) + \sum_{p \in P} D_p(d_p), \tag{1}$$

$$m_{pq}^t(d_q) = \min_{d_p} \left( V(d_p, d_q) + D_p(d_p) + \sum_{s \in N_b(p) \backslash q} \left( m_{sp}^{t-1}(d_p) - \alpha \right) \right), \tag{2}$$

$$\hat{d}_p = \arg\min_{d_p} \left( D_p(d_p) + \sum_{s \in N(p)} m_{qp}^T(d_p) \right), \tag{3}$$

$$D_p(d_p) = \min(C_d|g^r(d_p) - g^l(p)|, K_d), \tag{4}$$

$$V(d_p, d_q) = \min \left( C_v|d_p - d_q|, K_v \right), \alpha = \sum_{d_p} m_{sp}^{t-1}(d_p), \tag{5}$$

where $D_p(d_p)$ is the data cost of the label $d_p$ at the pixel $p$ in the image $P$, $V(d_p, d_q)$ is the discontinuity cost between $d_p$ and its neighbor $d_q$, $N_b(p) \backslash q$ denotes the neighbors of p other than q, and $\alpha$ is the normalization value. $m_{pq}^t(d_q)$ is the message calculated at iteration t and sent from the node p to the neighbour node q using Eq. (2). After T iterations, the $\hat{d}_p$ at each node is decided using Eq. (3). The message memory complexity of BP is $O(SN^2)$ given the state number $S$. The time complexity is $O(STN^2)$.

## 3 Fast Belief Propagation Structure

Hierarchical BP [5] uses matching costs from coarse-to-fine scale level and has fast convergence within fewer and fixed iterations.

When the iterations in BP structure are considered as layers, it can be viewed as a dynamic bayesian network with upward propagation as in Fig. 1(c). Here, we will present a method to show the results that are equivalent to [5] while the MRF network is scanned through FBP structure as in Fig. 2. Here, we denote the MRF axes as $p = (p_0, p_1)$, the level index as $k$, the iteration layer index as $l^k$ and node index as $p^k$. To clarify the layer structure, we can align nodes vertically by the layer transform on the $p_0$ axis as in Fig. 1(b). Node indexes are transformed from $p_0^k$ to $p_0^k - l^k$.

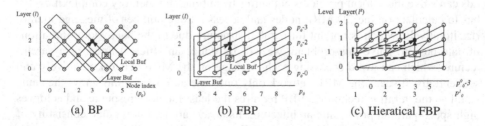

(a) BP        (b) FBP        (c) Hieratical FBP

**Fig. 1.** Layer transform of Hieratical FBP

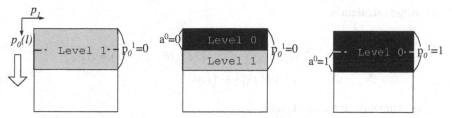

(a) Current step to scan each $g_0$   (b) Next step to scan each $g_0$   (c) Next step to scan each $g_1$

**Fig. 2.** Scanning sequence of Hierarchical FBP

Given local nodes $h$ and $s \in N_b(h)$ in the group, we can represent the message as $M_{hs}^k(d_h, l^k)$, which corresponds to $m_{p^k N(p^k)}(d_{p^k})$ in the MRF. It is calculated by the parallel processor $h$ at each layer in the group. The MAP state $\hat{d}_{p(L)}$ is outputted at the last layer $L$ and then the next neighbor group on the $p_0$ axis is processed. In the group, the higher coarse level group is scanned at first and the next lower fine level groups are processed within the higher coarse level group range. Given the parallel processor size $H^k$, processor index $h$, group index $g$, and group size $G^0 = N/(H_0 2^{K-1})$, $C^k = H_0 2^{K-1}/(2^k H^k)$, the algorithm to calculate messages $M_{hs}(d_h, l)$ is shown as follows.

*Algorithm:*(Hieratical FBP)
    for each group $g^0$ from 0 to $G^0 - 1$,
      for each level $k$ from $K - 1$ to 0,
      Message_scaling_between_level($k$).
      for each group $g^k$ from 0 to $G^k - 1$,
        for each layer $l^k$ from 1 to $L^k$,
        Message_update_within_level($k,l^k$).

1. Message_scaling_between_level($k$).
for each parallel processor $h \in [(0,0), (H_0 2^{K-1-k}, N/2^k - 1)]$,

$$M_{hs}^k(d_h, 0) = \begin{cases} 0, & \text{if } k = K - 1, \\ M_{(h')(s')}^{k+1}(d_{h'}, L^{k+1}), & \text{otherwise}, \end{cases} \tag{6}$$

$$(s \in N_b(h), h' = h/2, s' = (s - h) + h') . \tag{7}$$

2. Message_update_within_level($k,l^k$).
for each parallel processor $h \in [(0,0), (H^k - 1, N/2^k - 1)]$,

$$p_0^k = \begin{cases} h - l^k, & \text{if } k = K - 1, \\ h + H^k * g^k - (l^k + L(k+1)), & \text{otherwise}, \end{cases} \tag{8}$$

$$p_1^k = h_1, s \in N_b(h), L(k+1) = \sum_{j=K-1}^{k+1} L^j 2^{j-k} . \tag{9}$$

3. Message calculation.

$$M_{hs}^k(d_s, l^k) = \min_{d_h} \left( \begin{array}{c} V(d_h, d_s) + D_{p^k}(d_h) \\ + \sum_{u \in N_h} \left( M_{uh}^k(d_h, l^k - 1) - \alpha \right) \end{array} \right),$$ (10)

$$N_h = N_b(h - (1,0)^T) \backslash (s - (1,0)^T).$$ (11)

4. State estimation at the last layer L.

$$\hat{d}_{p(L)} = \arg \min_{d_h} \left( \begin{array}{c} D_{p(L)} d_h \\ + \sum_{s \in N(h)} M_{sh}^0(d_h, L^0) \end{array} \right)$$ (12)

$$(L = \sum_{k=0}^{K-1} L^k 2^k).$$ (13)

$N_b(p) \backslash q$ in Eq. (2) is modified to $N_h$ in Eq. (10) by the layer transform on the $p_0$ axis. $u_0 \in (h_0 + a_0)$ of $-2 \le a_0 \le 0$, In Fig. 2, the processed area is represented as the gray intensity area, and the layer buffer($b^k$) where the messages need to be stored is denoted as the thick line. If $u_0 < 0$, that is, it is not in the group, then $M_{uh}(d_h, l - 1)$ is loaded from the layer buffer saved by the previous group. Otherwise, the message is read from the local buffer of the previous layer. The updated messages $M_{hs}^k(d_s, l)$ of $h_0 \ge H^k - 2$ refresh the layer buffer for the next group processing.

The function of the Message_scaling_between_level ($k$) changes message scales between different levels. The Message_update_within_level ($k, l^k$) calculates the messages within one group in parallel. The node $p^k$ on the k level's MRF is calculated by the local node $h$, the layer $l^k + L(k + 1)$, and the group location $H^k * g^k$. The iteration layer number $L^k$ at each level is decided by the environment such as the image size.

# 4 Architecture

## 4.1 Array Architecture

The VLSI logic includes two parts: multi-scale-level data cost calculation and FBP PE array structure.

Fig. 3 shows the architecture for calculating data costs from level 0 to level 3. In block A, the left and right scan lines are loaded to the registers and then the scan line of right image pixels are shifted by disparity $d$. The level 0 matching cost is calculated by the absolute difference of the left and right pixel values at each state. Block B shows how to calculate higher level matching cost. At level k, two neighbor level k-1 matching cost is summed up and then accumulated over $2^k$ scan lines. This is equivalent to applying the summation over $2^k$ x $2^k$ window. All data costs are saved in the data cost Block RAM, which will be used by PEs at each level's the first layer.

Fig. 4 shows the architecture of the PE group which includes 8 PEs. Totally, 40 PE group arrays are implemented for a pair of 320 x 240 images as shown in Fig. 6.

Fig. 5 represents the local and layer buffer assignment for each PE in the PE group, where the usage of PE is not equal at each level. As shown in Fig. 3 and Fig. 5, each different level's data costs that are computed in data cost module, are processed and

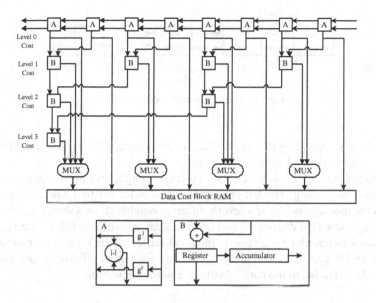

**Fig. 3.** Architecture for data cost calculation

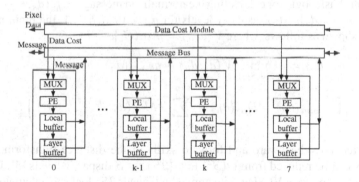

**Fig. 4.** Architecture of PE group

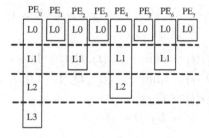

**Fig. 5.** Buffer assignment in PE group

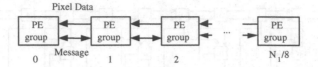

Pixel Data

**Fig. 6.** Linear array architecture of FBP

saved in the corresponding PEs and buffers. For example, $PE_0$ is used at all the levels, but $PE_3$ is only operated at the finest level 0.

The multiplexer (MUX) is to select the corresponding level's messages and data costs at each level processing. The left and right messages have 4-to-1 MUX which is used to access the message buffer of 4 level's different neighborhoods shown in Fig. 5.

Fig. 6 represents the distributed and systolic array structure of FBP, which calculates the messages in parallel by accessing the local buffer or the layer buffer messages in the neighbor PE group. The memory resource is consumed efficiently and can obtain high-speed results due to the parallel structure at the same time.

### 4.2 Architecture of Processing Element (PE)

The PE is the basic logic for calculating the normalized message $M_{hs}^k(d_s, l^k) - \alpha$, which is denoted as $m_o(d_s)$. At $S$ disparity levels for $d_s = 0, ..., S - 1$, the main numerical formula is shown as follows, where $V(d, k) = min(C_v|d - k|, K_v)$.

$$m_o(d_s) = \min_{d_h \in [0, S-1]} V(d_s, d_h) + m_{sum}(d_h)$$

$$\left( m_{sum}(d_h) = D_{\boldsymbol{p}^k}(d_h) + \sum_{u \in N_h} \left( M_{uh}^k(d_h, l^k - 1) - \alpha \right) \right).$$

By the recursive backward and forward skills of the distance transform, the time complexity can be reduced from $O(S^2)$ to $O(2S)$ for $S$ disparity levels [5]. Upon this transform, we propose a VLSI architecture which needs 3S clocks to calculate the message $m_o(d_s)$.

Forward process:
    Initialize $D_1(-1) = B$, $D_2(-1) = B$ ($B$ is as big as possible).
    For $t = 0, ..., S - 1$,

$$D_1(t) = min(m_{sum}(t), D_1(t - 1) + C_v), \qquad (14)$$

$$D_2(t) = min(m_{sum}(t), D_2(t - 1)), \qquad (15)$$

$$m_f(t) = D_1(t), \qquad (16)$$

$$m_f(-1) = D_2(D - 1) + K_v. \qquad (17)$$

Backward process:
    Initialize $D_3(-1) = B$, $D_4(-1) = 0$.

For  $t = 0, ..., S - 1,$

$$D_3(t) = \min(m_f(S - 1 - t), D_3(t - 1) + C_v),\qquad(18)$$
$$m_b(t) = \min(D_3(t), m_f(-1)),\qquad(19)$$
$$D_4(t) = m_b(t) + D_4(t - 1),\qquad(20)$$
$$m_b(-1) = D_4(S - 1)/S.\qquad(21)$$

Normalization:
  For  $t = 0, ..., S - 1,$

$$m_o(t) = m_b(t) - m_b(-1).\qquad(22)$$

The following VLSI architecture will be explained along with this algorithm. Fig. 7 shows the PE internal structure. The forward PE reads the messages and data costs, outputs the forward cost $m_f(t)$ and saves it to the stack. Then the backward PE reads it from the stack and calculates $m_b(t)$, which is then normalized.

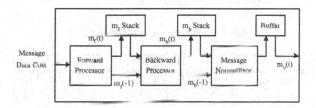

**Fig. 7.** Internal pipeline structure of PE

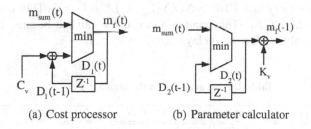

(a) Cost processor            (b) Parameter calculator

**Fig. 8.** Forward processor

In the forward processor architecture, Fig. 8(a) and Eq. (14) show the cost processor and sequences that output the minimum value between $m_{sum}(t)$ and $D_1(t - 1) + C_v$ once the neighbor messages are summed together with the data cost $D(t)$ to calculate $m_{sum}(t)$. Fig. 8(b) and Eq. (15) prepare the parameter for backward process.

In the backward processor architecture, Fig. 9(a), Eq. (18) and Eq. (19) show the cost processor that reads the $m_f(D - 1 - t)$ from the stack, calculates the minimum value $D_3(t)$, and outputs the minimum value between $D_3(t)$ and the parameter $m_f(-1)$. In Fig. 9(b), Eq. (20) and Eq. (21), messages $m_b(t)$ are summed up and then divided by the disparity level $S$. If the disparity level is 2's exponent, then the divider can be replaced by a bit shifter. This normalization parameter will be used in the normalization process.

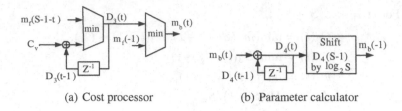

(a) Cost processor                    (b) Parameter calculator

**Fig. 9.** Backward processor

### 4.3 Memory and Time Complexities

Given iteration layer $L^k$, state number $S$, and $B$ bit cost, the local buffer size is calculated as ( 4 messages + 1 data cost ) x group size $N_1^k$ x $SB$. The layer buffer size is calculated as ( 4 messages + 1 data cost ) x group size $N_1^k$ x layer number $L^k$ x $SB$. The total buffer size is $\sum_{k=0}^{K-1} 5SB(L^k + 1)N_1^k$.

**Table 1.** Comparisons of HBP and FBP

|  | HBP | FBP |
|---|---|---|
| memory | $5SBN_1N_0$ | $\sum_{k=0}^{K-1} 5SBL^kN_1^k$ |
| time complexity | $O(\sum_{k=0}^{K-1} SL^kN_1^kN_0^k)$ | $O(\sum_{k=0}^{K-1} SL^kN_0^k)$ |
| PE | 1 | $N_1$ |

FBP uses less memory than HBP by $N_0/\sum_{k=0}^{K-1}((L^k + 1)/2^k)$. Thus our algorithm takes effect when $L^k \ll N_0$. This condition is usually satisfied because hierarchical structure requires only small iteration layer $L^k, k = 0, ..., K - 1$.

**Table 2.** Resource used in the architecture

| level $k$ | layer No. $L^k$ | local buffer (bit) | PE No. $N_1^k = N_1/2^k$ | layer buffer (bit) |
|---|---|---|---|---|
| 3 | 5 | 5x40x32x10 | 40 | 5x40x5x32x10 |
| 2 | 5 | 5x80x32x10 | 80 | 5x80x5x32x10 |
| 1 | 10 | 5x160x32x10 | 160 | 5x160x10x32x10 |
| 0 | 5 | 5x320x32x10 | 320 | 5x320x5x32x10 |
| total | 25 | 960,000 | 320 | 6,080,000 |

Table. 2 shows the resources used for each level. The total memory size is 960+6,080 = 7,040 kbits at 32 disparity levels, 10 bit message and 320x240 image, which is smaller than hierarchical BP's $5SBN_1N_0 = 122,880$ kbits by $N_0/\sum_{k=0}^{3}(L^k/2^k) \approx 17$ times.

The time complexity is $O(\sum_{k=0}^{K-1} SL^kN_1^kN_0^k/N_1^k) = O(\sum_{k=0}^{K-1} SL^kN_0^k)$ which is reduced from HBP's complexity by $N_1^k$ parallel processors at each level. Approximately, it is faster than HBP by $N_1$.

$$T_{HBP}/T_{FBP} = N_1 \left( \sum_{k=0}^{K-1} L^k/2^{2k} \right) / \left( \sum_{k=0}^{K-1} L^k/2^k \right) \approx N_1 \qquad (23)$$

## 5  Experimental Results

Table. 3 shows the software performance using Middlebury data set. The error rate here represents the amount of unoccluded pixels whose disparities are different from the truth map. Our method shows the lowest error rate among real-time methods. Fig. 10 shows the quality of our method on the Tukuba image and real image.

**Table 3.** Disparity error comparison of several methods(%)

| Image | Tsukuba | Map | Venus | Sawtooth |
|---|---|---|---|---|
| Real-time DP [4] | 2.85 | 6.45 | 6.42 | 6.25 |
| Real-time GPU [1] | 2.05 | NA | 1.92 | NA |
| Real-time BP [3] | 1.5 | NA | 0.8 | NA |
| Our method | 1.9 | 0.3 | 0.8 | 0.8 |

(a) Tsukuba left image    (b) Real left image        (c) Resulting depth map

**Fig. 10.** Depth maps results of our method

**Table 4.** Comparisons of computation time

| Spec | Image | Levels | fps |
|---|---|---|---|
| Real-time DP [4] | 320x240 | 100 | 26.7 |
| Real-time GPU [1] | 320x240 | 48 | 18.5 |
| Real-time BP [3] | 320x240 | 16 | 16 |
| Our chip | 320x240 | 32 | 30 |

Table. 4 shows the computational time performance. Due to the fully parallel VLSI structure, our algorithm can achieve superior real-time processing which has 2 times higher depth resolution and 2 times faster frame rate than real-time BP.

Our architecture was implemented on 2 Xilinx FPGAs. The implemented stereo matching board incorporates 320 PEs working at 25MHz. Its detailed spec. is described in Table. 5. We spent 2 times more Block RAM (14.4Mbits) than the expected FBP memory(7.04M kbits) due to the Xilinx FPGA optimization. But, still, it used less memory than HBP by 9 times. We can cascade chips to process higher resolution image.

**Table 5.** Hardware spec

|                              | Spec.(Resource usage percentage) |
|------------------------------|----------------------------------|
| FPGA                         | Xilinx Virtex II pro-100         |
| Clock Speed                  | 25MHz(Max.=79MHz)                |
| Number of FPGA               | 2                                |
| Number of Block RAM(18kbit)  | 800(90%)                         |
| Number of Multiplier         | 0                                |
| Number of Divider            | 0                                |
| Number of Slice Flip Flops   | 55,712(31%)                      |
| Number of 4 input LUTs       | 94,014(53%)                      |

# 6   Conclusions

In this paper, new VLSI techniques for finding a approximated global solution on the 2D MRF are presented. We changed the iteration structure of BP to the memory efficient FBP structure. Due to the small and distributed memory requirement and fully parallel structure, our VLSI chip can process the 2D MRF global energy minimization in real-time. We implemented it on 2 Xilinx FPGAs, which can provide 32 disparity levels' real-time stereo matching for the 320 x 240 images at 30 frames/s.

# References

1. Wang, L., et al.: High-quality real-time stereo using adaptive cost aggregation and dynamic programming. In: 3DPVT (2006)
2. Hariyama, M., et al.: Architecture of a stereo matching vlsi processor based on hierarchically parallel memory access. In: The 2004 47th Midwest Symposium on Cir-cuits and Systems, number 2, pp. II245 – II247 (2004)
3. Yang, Q. et al.: Real-time global stereo matching using hierarchical belief propagation. In: The British Machine Vision Conference (2006)
4. Forstmann, S., et al.: Real-time stereo by using dynamic programming. In: CVPR, Workshop on real-time 3D sensors and their use (2004)
5. Felzenszwalb, P.F., Huttenlocher, D.R.: Efficient belief propagation for early vision. In: Proceedings of the 2004 IEEE Computer Society Conference on Computer Vision and Pattern Recognition, (1), pp. I261–I268 (2004)
6. Zheng, N.N., Sun, J., Shum, H.Y.: Stereo matching using belief propagation. IEEE Transactions on Pattern Analysis and Machine Intelligence 25(7), 787–800 (2003)

# Low-Power Twiddle Factor Unit for FFT Computation

Teemu Pitkänen, Tero Partanen, and Jarmo Takala

Tampere University of Technology, P.O. Box 553, FIN-33101 Tampere, Finland
{teemu.pitkanen, tero.partanen, jarmo.takala}@tut.fi

**Abstract.** An integral part of FFT computation are the twiddle factors, which, in software implementations, are typically stored into RAM memory implying large memory footprint and power consumption. In this paper, we propose a novel twiddle factor generator based on reduced ROM tables. The unit supports both radix-4 and mixed-radix-4/2 FFT algorithms and several transform lengths. The unit operates at a rate of one factor per clock cycle.

## 1  Introduction

Fast Fourier transform (FFT) has gained popularity lately due to the fact that OFDM has been used in several wireless and wireline communication systems, e.g., IEEE 802.11a/g, 802.16, VDSL, and DVB. An integral part of the FFT computation are the twiddle factors, which, in software implementations, are typically stored into RAM memory implying large memory footprint. The twiddle factors can be generated at run-time. A traditional method is to use CORDIC as described, e.g., in [1]. The sine and cosine values are needed in direct digital frequency synthesizers and often the generation is based on polynomials, e.g., in [2]. An other approach is to use a function generator based on recursive feedback difference equation [3,4]. Typically these approaches result in smaller area than memory based approaches. However, since the computation is done at run-time, there is a huge amount of transistor switching implying higher power consumption in CMOS implementations.

Another approach is to store the twiddle factors into a ROM table. In an $N$-point FFT, there are $N/2$ different twiddle factors and an approach exploiting this property has been reported in [5]. Methods requiring only $N/4$ coefficients to be stored into a table are described in [6,7]. There is, however, even more redundancy since the real and imaginary parts of the factors are sine values and $N/8 + 1$ complex coefficients are needed to reconstruct all the factors for an $N$-point FFT [8]. In [9], a coefficient manipulation method is presented where only $N/8 + 1$ coefficients are needed to generate the twiddle factors. However, the previous methods are designed only for radix-2 algorithms containing more arithmetic operations than radix-4 algorithms.

A twiddle factor generator unit could be used as a special function unit in an application-specific instruction-set processor (ASIP) but it may not increase the performance of the software implementation. Often several instructions are needed to compute the correct index to the unit. Considerable performance increase can be expected, if the unit can also perform the index modifications to avoid additional instructions. However, the indexing of the twiddle factors varies depending on the FFT variant. More detailed discussion on twiddle factor indexing can be found from [10].

S. Vassiliadis et al. (Eds.): SAMOS 2007, LNCS 4599, pp. 65–74, 2007.

In this paper, we propose a low-power twiddle factor unit based on a ROM table. The proposed work differs from the related work such that the proposed unit a) supports radix-4 and mixed-radix-4/2 FFT algorithms, b) supports several transform sizes (power-of-two), and c) integrates index manipulation. By supporting radix-4 algorithms, the performance of FFT computation is increased significantly compared to radix-2 algorithms. In addition, the overhead of address manipulation in software implementation is omitted, which increases the performance even more. The unit can generate factors at a rate of one factor per clock cycle. The proposed unit has already been used in the FFT implementations described in our previous work [11,12] but here the twiddle factor generation is described in detail.

## 2  FFT Algorithms

In this work, we have used the traditional in-place radix-4 decimation-in-time (DIT) radix FFT algorithm with in-order-input, permuted output as given, e.g., in [13]. In this work, we would like to expose the different permutations, thus we formulate the traditional algorithm in the following fashion:

$$F_{2^{2n}} = R_{2^{2n}} \left[ \prod_{s=n-1}^{0} [O_{2^{2n}}^s]^T (I_{2^{(2n-2)}} \otimes F_4) A_{2^{2n}}^s O_{2^{2n}}^s \right] ; \qquad (1)$$

$$F_4 = \begin{pmatrix} 1 & 1 & 1 & 1 \\ 1 & -j & -1 & j \\ 1 & -1 & 1 & -1 \\ 1 & j & -1 & -j \end{pmatrix} ; \qquad (2)$$

$$R_{2^{2n}} = \prod_{k=2}^{n} I_{2^{(2n-2k)}} \otimes P_{2^{2k},4} ; \qquad (3)$$

$$O_{2^m}^s = I_{4^s} \otimes P_{2^{(m-2s)},2^{(m-2s-2)}} \qquad (4)$$

where $j$ is the imaginary unit, $I_n$ is an identity matrix of order $n$, and the permutation matrices $R_N$ and $O_N$ are based on stride-by-$S$ permutation matrices [14] $P_{N,S}$ defined as

$$[P_{N,S}]_{mn} = \begin{cases} 1, & \text{iff } n = (mS \bmod N) + \lfloor mS/N \rfloor \\ 0, & \text{otherwise} \end{cases} , \quad m,n = 0,1,\ldots,N-1 \qquad (5)$$

The matrix $A_N^s$ contains $N$ twiddle factors $W_K^k = e^{j2\pi k/K}$ as follows

$$A_N^s = Q_N^s \left[ \bigoplus_{b=0}^{N/4-1} \text{diag}\left( W_{4s+1}^0, W_{4s+1}^{\lfloor \frac{b4^{s+1}}{N} \rfloor}, W_{4s+1}^{2\lfloor \frac{b4^{s+1}}{N} \rfloor}, W_{4s+1}^{3\lfloor \frac{b4^{s+1}}{N} \rfloor} \right) \right] ; \qquad (6)$$

$$Q_N^s = \prod_{l=0}^{s} P_{4^{(s-l)},4} \otimes I_{N/4^{(s-l)}} . \qquad (7)$$

Examples of signal flow graphs of this algorithm are depicted in Fig. 1a) and 1c).

As the Fig. 1 shows the output data is not in order, thus to give it in order, input permutation is needed at each column and it complicates the index modifications in the coefficient generator.

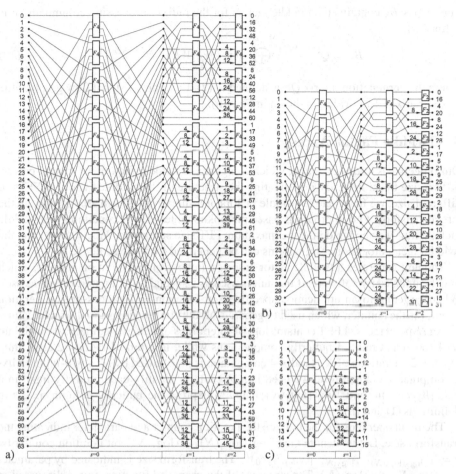

**Fig. 1.** Signal flow graph of a) 64-point radix-4, b) 32-point mixed-radix, and c) 16-point radix-4 FFT. A constant $k$ in the signal flow graph represents a twiddle factor $W_{64}^k$.

The radix-4 algorithms can be used only when the FFT size is a power-of-four. Power-of-two transforms can be supported by using mixed-radix approach and a mixed-radix-4/2 FFT consists of radix-4 processing columns followed by a single radix-2 column as follows

$$F_{2^{2n+1}} = S_{2(2n+1)}\left(I_{4^n} \otimes F_2\right) B_{2(2n+1)} \cdot$$

$$\left[\prod_{s=n-1}^{0} [O_{2(2n+1)}^s]^T \left(I_{2(2n-1)} \otimes F_4\right) A_{2(2n+1)}^s O_{2(2n+1)}^s\right]; F_2 = \begin{pmatrix} 1 & 1 \\ 1 & -1 \end{pmatrix} \quad (8)$$

where the matrices $O_N^s$ and $A_N^s$ are defined in (4) and (6), respectively. The matrix $S_N$ is a permutation matrix given as

$$S_N = (I_2 \otimes R_{4^n}) P_{N,2}, N = 2^{2n+1}. \quad (9)$$

The matrix $B_N$ contains the twiddle factors for the radix-2 processing column and it is defined as

$$B_N = Q_N^{\log_4(N/2)} \bigoplus_{b=0}^{N/2-1} \text{diag}\left(W_N^0, W_N^b\right), N = 2^{2n+1} \tag{10}$$

where the permutation matrix $Q_N^s$ is defined in (7). Example of signal flow graph of the mixed-radix-4/2 algorithm is shown in Fig. 1b).

## 3  Twiddle Factor Access

Our objective is to design a unit, which can generate twiddle factors for several power-of-two size transforms. By investigating the structure of the twiddle factors in FFTs of different size, we find that the twiddle factors of a shorter transform are included in the larger transform. Our approach is based on lookup tables (LUT) containing the twiddle factors, thus we need to define the maximum FFT size supported, $N_{max} = 2^{n_{max}}$, and the twiddle factors for shorter transforms can be generated from the same LUT.

The unit generates a twiddle factor based on index from an iteration counter, which may be updated by software, if the unit is used as a special function unit in a processor. When targeting to an application-specific fixed-function FFT processor, the iteration counter is the counter, which used to generate all the control signals in the architecture.

An $N$-point radix-4 FFT contains $\log_4(N)$ iterations of butterfly columns divided into $N/4$ four-input radix-4 butterfly computations while, in a mixed-radix-4/2 algorithm, $\log_4(N/2)$ iterations of $N/4$ radix-4 computations is followed by $N/2$ two-input radix-2 computations. Therefore, we need $\log_2(N)$ bits to identify each butterfly input in a butterfly column and $\lceil \log_2(\log_4(N)) \rceil$ bits to express the butterfly column, i.e., $s$ in definitions (1) and (8).

The input operands for the unit are the iteration counter and parameter indicating the transform size. Let us denote the $(\lceil \log_2(\log_4(N)) \rceil + \log_2(N))$-bit iteration counter by $c = (c_{\lceil \log_2(\log_4(N)) \rceil + \log_2(N)-1}, \ldots, c_1, c_0)^T$. The transform size is indicated by parameter $f = \log_2(N_{max}) - \log_2(N)$. The structure of the proposed function unit is discussed in the following sections with an example design supporting FFT sizes of 16, 32, and 64. In this example case, the input parameter $f$ can have values 0, 1, or 2 to indicate FFT sizes 64, 32, or 16, respectively. A 5-bit iteration counter $c$ is used when FFT size is 16 and, for a 64-point FFT, an 8-bit counter is needed. The block diagram of the example design is illustrated in Fig. 2. The input parameters are written into registers $f$ and $c$ and the final twiddle factor is obtained from the output registers.

### 3.1  Scaling

In order to minimize the bit-level shifts due to different transform sizes, we first shift the iteration counter $c$ to the left by the number of bits indicated by the parameter $f$. This implies that after the shift we obtain a bit-field where the $\lceil \log_2(\log_4(N_{max})) \rceil + \log_2(N_{max})$ bits indicate the butterfly column $s$ and the $\log_2(N_{max}) = n_{max}$ least significant bits contain the index of the twiddle factor in the column to be generated. Let us denote this part by $d = (d_{n_{max}-1}, \ldots, d_0)^T$. However, the actual index is in the most significant bits index and $d$ contains $(n_{max} - \log_2(N))$ zeros in the least significant bits. The rest of the operation is based on operands $s$ and $d$.

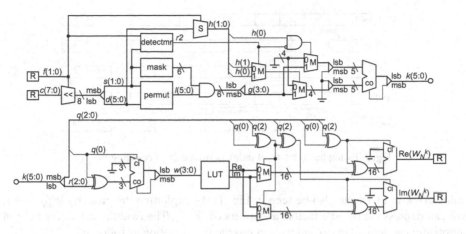

**Fig. 2.** Block diagram of twiddle factor generator supporting transform sizes of 16, 32, and 64. R: register. M: multiplexor. co: carry out. ci: carry in. <<: left shifter.

## 3.2 Permutation

The order of twiddle factors depends on the FFT algorithm and, in this work, we concentrate on the in-order input, permuted output FFTs given in (1) and (8). In these particular cases, we need to consider the implementation of matrices $A_N^s$ and $B_N^s$ defined in (6) and (10), respectively.

Our approach is based on index modifications, thus first we need to perform the permutation $Q_N^s$ in (7). The the permutation can be investigated by considering the bit-level rotations as discussed in [15,16]. This shows that the permutation is actually the traditional bit-reversed permutation but here 2-bit fields are used instead of a single bit. It should also be noted that the permutation varies according to the butterfly column $s$. The permutation in our case is actually independent on the transform size, since we have shifter the index earlier, thus the permuted index, $l = (l_{\log_2(N)}, \dots, l_1, l_0)$, of an $N$-point FFT can be expressed in bit-level in matrix form as follows

$$l = \begin{pmatrix} \bar{I}_s \otimes I_2 & \\ & I_{n_{max}-2s} \end{pmatrix} d \; ; \; \bar{I}_s = \begin{pmatrix} & & 1 \\ & \cdot & \\ & \cdot & \\ 1 & & \end{pmatrix} \tag{11}$$

where $\bar{I}_m$ is an antidiagonal matrix of order $m$. The bit-level permutations in a general case are illustrated in Fig. 3. In our example case, the permutations are performed in the block "permut" and the first two, i.e. the maximum butterfly column $s$ is 2, permutations from Fig. 3 are needed.

## 3.3 Lookup Table Index

Our approach is to store the twiddle factors to a lookup table and the indexing into the table is based on the exponent $k$ in the twiddle factor $W_N^k$ as defined in (6). Different

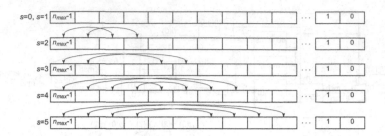

**Fig. 3.** Examples of bit-level index permutations according to (11)

values of $k$ in FFTs can also be seen in Fig. 1. By exploiting the property $W_{aN}^a = W_N$, we can express the twiddle factors as powers of $W_{N_{max}}$. The twiddle factors for radix-4 algorithm are defined in (6) and we can rewrite this equation as follows:

$$A_N^s = Q_N^s \bigoplus_{b=0}^{N} W_{N_{max}}^{(b \bmod 4)\lfloor \frac{\lfloor b/4 \rfloor 4^{s+1}}{N} \rfloor \frac{N_{max}}{4^{s+1}}} \tag{12}$$

where mod is the modulus operation. Here we need an equation for the exponent $k$ for factor $W_{N_{max}}^k$, which can be found from the previous. In addition, we have used a shifted index and, therefore, the index $b$ can be replaced with the permuted index $l$ from (11) by the relation $l = bN_{max}/N$, thus we obtain

$$k = (b \bmod 4)\lfloor \frac{\lfloor b/4 \rfloor 4^{s+1}}{N} \rfloor \frac{N_{max}}{4^{s+1}} = \left[\lfloor \frac{lN}{N_{max}} \rfloor \bmod 4\right]\left[\lfloor \frac{\lfloor l/4 \rfloor 4^{s+1}}{N_{max}} \rfloor \frac{N_{max}}{4^{s+1}}\right]. \tag{13}$$

We may denote the first term as $h$ and the second as $g$. Then the operation at bit-level representation can defined as follows:

$$k = hg \; ; \; g = \begin{pmatrix} I_{2s} \\ 0_{n_{max}-2s-2, n_{max}-2s} \end{pmatrix} l \; ; \; h = (0_{2,n_{max}-f-2}, I_2, 0_{2,f}) l \tag{14}$$

where $0_{n,m}$ is an $n \times m$ matrix containing zeros and $f$ is the input operand defining the index shift, $f = n_{max} - \log_2(N)$. In the example case in Fig. 2, the block "mask" generates a 6-bit mask, where the $2s$ most significant bits are ones and the rest are zeros. This is used to mask the 6-bit permuted index $l$. Then the two least significant bits are omitted and the 4-bit result is passed to multiplication with $h$. Since $h$ is a 2-bit variable, a simple solution is to us adder, where the same operand is fed but the second one is shifted one bit to right, i.e., multiplied by two. Multiplexers can be used to feed either the operand or zero to the adder and these multiplexers are controlled by the multiplicand $h$.

The 2-bit variable $h$ needs to be extracted from $l$ with the aid of multiplexer controlled with $f$. Figure 2 indicates that $h$ can be extracted also from $d$, which shortens the critical path. The block "S" performs the extraction, i.e., $h = (h_1, h_0)^T = (d_{f+1}, d_f)^T$.

In the last butterfly column of mixed-radix-4/2 algorithm, the twiddle factors have a bit different form and by using the fact that, in the last column, $s = \log_4(N/2)$ we may rewrite (10) as follows:

$$B_N = Q_N^s \bigoplus_{b=0}^{N} W_{N_{max}}^{(b \bmod 2) \lfloor \frac{\lfloor b/2 \rfloor 4^{(s+1)}}{N} \rfloor \frac{N_{max}}{4^{(s+1)}}}. \tag{15}$$

By following the procedure used to define the exponent $k$ in radix-4 case, we can define $k$ in this case as follows

$$k = (b \bmod 2) \lfloor \frac{\lfloor b/2 \rfloor 4^{s+1}}{N} \rfloor \frac{N_{max}}{4^{s+1}} = \left[ \lfloor \frac{lN}{N_{max}} \rfloor \bmod 2 \right] \left[ \lfloor \frac{\lfloor \frac{l}{2} \rfloor 4^{s+1}}{N_{max}} \rfloor \frac{N_{max}}{4^{s+1}} \right]. \tag{16}$$

By comparing this equation to (13), we find that there is a scaling difference in the second term and, if the same hardware is used to generate exponent for both radix-4 and mixed-radix-4/2 twiddle factors, this needs to be compensated. In bit-level representation, this can be defined as

$$k = 2hg \; ; \; h = (0_{1,n_{max}-f-1}, 1, 0_{1,f}) l \tag{17}$$

where $g$ is obtained as in (14). The example case in Fig. 2 shows a block "detectmr", which is used to detect when mixed-radix algorithm is used and the twiddle factors are for the last butterfly column consisting of the radix-2 butterflies. In this case, the least significant bit of $f$ can be used to detect the mixed-radix transform and the detection of the last butterfly column is detected with the aid of hard-coded detection. Signal "r2" is active-high, which masks the signal "h(1)" since $h$ is only a 1 bit parameter. In addition, the operand $g$ is directed to the lower input of the adder, where the operand is shifted one bit to the left, thus the additional multiplication by two is realized.

### 3.4 Memory Reduction

Here we propose a method to reconstruct twiddle factors for radix-4 and mixed-radix-4/2 FFT from a ROM table containing $N/8 + 1$ coefficients. The twiddle factors in 64-point radix-4 FFT are shown in Table 1 and it can be seen that by reordering the coefficients into six blocks, $B0 \ldots B5$, all the twiddle factors can be retrieved from coefficients in block $B0$ containing nine complex coefficients. Since we need to support several transform sizes up to an $N_{max}$-point FFT, we store $(N_{max}/8 + 1)$ complex-valued coefficients into a table, $M = (M_0, M_1, \ldots, M_{N/8}) \mid M_k = W_{N_{max}}^k$. The rest of the twiddle factors can be obtained from the table $M$ as follows:

$$W_{N_{max}}^k = \begin{cases} M_k , & k \leq \frac{N_{max}}{8} \\ -jM_{\frac{N_{max}}{4}-k} , & \frac{N_{max}}{8} < k \leq \frac{N_{max}}{4} \\ -jM_{k-\frac{N_{max}}{4}}^* , & \frac{N_{max}}{4} < k \leq \frac{3N_{max}}{8} \\ -M_{\frac{N_{max}}{2}-k}^* , & \frac{3N_{max}}{8} < k \leq \frac{N_{max}}{2} \\ -M_{k-\frac{N_{max}}{2}} , & \frac{N_{max}}{2} < k \leq \frac{5N_{max}}{8} \\ jM_{\frac{3N_{max}}{4}-k}^* , & \frac{5N_{max}}{8} < k \end{cases} \tag{18}$$

where $M_k^*$ is the complex conjugate of $M_k$.

**Table 1.** Twiddle factors in 64-point radix-4 FFT. The decimal value is shown as (real,imaginary).

| B0 | B1 | B2 | B3 | B4 | B5 |
|---|---|---|---|---|---|
| $W_{64}^{0}$ (1.0,0.0) | $W_{64}^{16}$ (.00,-1.0) | | | | |
| $W_{64}^{1}$ (1.0,-.10) | $W_{64}^{15}$ (.10,-1.0) | | | $W_{64}^{33}$ (-1.0,.10) | |
| $W_{64}^{2}$ (.98,-.20) | $W_{64}^{14}$ (.20,-.98) | $W_{64}^{18}$ (-.20,-.98) | $W_{64}^{30}$ (-.98,-.20) | | |
| $W_{64}^{3}$ (.96,-.29) | $W_{64}^{13}$ (.29,-.96) | | | | $W_{64}^{45}$ (-.29,.96) |
| $W_{64}^{4}$ (.92,-.38) | $W_{64}^{12}$ (.38,-.92) | $W_{64}^{20}$ (-.38,-.92) | $W_{64}^{28}$ (-.92,-.38) | $W_{64}^{36}$ (-.92,.38) | |
| $W_{64}^{5}$ (.88,-.47) | $W_{64}^{11}$ (.47,-.88) | $W_{64}^{21}$ (-.47,-.88) | $W_{64}^{27}$ (-.88,-.47) | | |
| $W_{64}^{6}$ (.83,-.56) | $W_{64}^{10}$ (.56,-.83) | $W_{64}^{22}$ (-.56,-.83) | $W_{64}^{26}$ (-.83,-.56) | | $W_{64}^{42}$ (-.56,.83) |
| $W_{64}^{7}$ (.77,-.63) | $W_{64}^{9}$ (.63,-.77) | | | $W_{64}^{39}$ (-.77,.63) | |
| $W_{64}^{8}$ (.71,-.71) | | $W_{64}^{24}$ (-.71,-.71) | | | |

In order to generate correct twiddle factor $W_N^k$ for the given exponent $k$ defined earlier, we need to create an index to the table $M$. Such a method can be obtained by noting the fact that the twiddle factors are defined by vectors with equal spaced angles along a unit circle, thus when starting from zero angle the indices to the table $M$ increase by one until $k = N/8$. Then the indices decrease until $k = N/4$ and they start to increase again. This behavior results in six regions as shown in Table 1.

In bit-level, we may generate the index to lookup table by dividing the bit-field $k$ into two parts; the three most significant bits of $k$ are denoted as $q = (k_{n_{max}-1}, k_{n_{max}-2}, k_{n_{max}-3})^T$ and the least significant bits by $r = (k_{n_{max}-4}, \ldots, k_1, k_0)^T$. The index to the lookup table is obtained as follows

$$w = \begin{cases} r & \text{, if } q_0 = 0 \\ \sim r + 1 & \text{, otherwise} \end{cases} \tag{19}$$

where $\sim r$ denotes inversion of bits in $r$. This can be seen in the lower part in Fig. 2. The index $w$ is used to access the lookup table $M$ ("LUT" in Fig. 2) and the obtained complex value $M_w$ needs to be modified according to (18), which shows that the correct twiddle factor can be obtained as follows

$$W_{N_{max}}^k = \begin{cases} (-1)^{q_0 \triangledown q_2} \Re(M_w) + j(-1)^{q_0 \triangledown q_1 \triangledown q_2} \Im(M_w) & \text{, if } q_0 \triangledown q_1 = 0 \\ (-1)^{q_0 \triangledown q_2} \Im(M_w) + j(-1)^{q_0 \triangledown q_1 \triangledown q_2} \Re(M_w) & \text{, otherwise} \end{cases} \tag{20}$$

where $\triangledown$ denotes bitwise exclusive-OR operation and $\Re(x)$ and $\Im(x)$ denote real and imaginary part of $x$, respectively. Figure 2 shows that this modification requires two multiplexors and two real adders with XOR-gates in inputs.

## 4  Experiments

We have described the proposed twiddle factor unit in VHDL language such that $N_{max} = 2^{14}$, i.e., the unit supports power-of-two FFTs up to 16K, thus lookup table contains 2049 complex-valued coefficients. The inputs to the unit are 17-bit $c$ register and 4-bit

**Table 2.** Power dissipation and area of twiddle factor unit designs: proposed unit, pipelined (two stages) and non-pipelined, and unit based on ROM table [5]

|        | pipelined@250MHz | | non-pipelined@140MHz | | ROM table [5]@250MHz | |
|--------|------------------|--------------|---------------------|--------------|---------------------|--------------|
|        | Power [mW] | Area [kgates] | Power [mW] | Area [kgates] | Power [mW] | Area [kgates] |
| LUT    | 1.50 | 12  | 2.24 | 15.8 | 43.00 | 20.5 |
| Pipeline | 0.95 | 0.3 | | | | |
| Total  | 3.70 | 14.3 | 4.11 | 18.4 | 43.00 | 20.5 |

$f$ register. The lookup table contains complex-valued coefficients with 16-bit real and imaginary parts, i.e., word width of lookup table is 32 bits.

The design has been synthesized with Synopsys tools onto a 130 nm standard cell technology. Then power estimates have been obtained with Synopsys tools with aid of gate level simulations. The analysis results are listed in Table 2.

The analysis results show that the critical path limits the clock frequency to 140 MHz when no pipelining is exploited. When two pipeline stages are used, the maximum clock frequency is 275 MHz. The lookup table has been designed with hard-wired logic for reducing the power consumption. If the lookup table was implemented as a ROM memory, the power consumption would have been eight times higher, although the area had been half smaller.

For comparison, we have also implemented a unit based on the traditional ROM table approach where $N_{max}/2 = 8192$ coefficients are stored ("ROM table" in Table 2). The method in [9] is not compared since it does not support radix-4 algorithms.

We have also the twiddle factor unit in an ASIP tailored for FFT computations [12] and, in this 32-bit processor containing, e.g., complex multiplier and adder, the twiddle factor unit uses about 23% of the core area (instruction and data memories not included), while the power consumption is only 7% of the total power consumption of the core. However, the unit improved significantly the performance of the FFT software implementation; the unit provides twiddle factor once per instruction cycle without additional address manipulation instructions.

## 5  Conclusions

In this paper, we have described a twiddle factor unit supporting radix-4 and mixed-radix-4/2 FFT algorithms and several power-of-two FFT sizes. The unit can be used as a special unit in an ASIP architecture or a coefficient generator in application-specific FFT processors. The unit shows significant power savings compared to the popular approach where the twiddle factors are stored into a ROM table.

## Acknowledgement

This work has been supported in part by the Academy of Finland under project 205743 and the Finnish Funding Agency for Technology and Innovation under research funding decision 40441/05.

# References

1. Wu, C.S., Wu, A.Y.: Modified vector rotational CORDIC(MVR-CORDIC algorithm and its application to fft. In: Proc. IEEE ISCAS, Geneva, Switzerland, vol. 4, pp. 529–532 (2000)
2. Xiu, L., You, Z.: A new frequency synthesis method based on flying-adder architecture. IEEE Trans. Circuits Syst. 50(3), 130–134 (2003)
3. Fliege, N.J., Wintermantel, J.: Complex digital oscillator and FSK modulators. IEEE Trans. Signal Processing 40(2), 333–342 (1992)
4. Chi, J.C., Chen, S.G.: An efficient FFT twiddle factor generator. In: Proc. European Signal Process. Conf., Vienna, Austria, pp. 1533–1536 (2004)
5. Cohen, D.: Simplified control of FFT hardware. IEEE Trans. Acoust., Speech, Signal Processing 24(6), 577–579 (1976)
6. Chang, Y., Parhi, K.K.: Efficient FFT implementation using digit-serial arithmetic. In: Proc. IEEE Workshop Signal Process. Syst., Taipei, Taiwan, pp. 645–653. IEEE Computer Society Press, Los Alamitos (1999)
7. Ma, Y., Wanhammar, L.: A hardware efficient control of memory addressing for high-performance FFT processors. IEEE Trans. Signal Processing 48(3), 917–921 (2000)
8. Wanhammar, L.: DSP Integrated Circuits. Academic Press, San Diego, CA (1999)
9. Hasan, M., Arslan, T.: FFT coefficient memory reduction technique for OFDM applications. In: Proc. IEEE ICASSP, Orlando, FL, vol. 1, pp. 1085–1088 (2002)
10. Chu, E., George, A.: Inside the FFT Black Box: Serial and Parallel Fast Fourier Transform Algorithms. CRC Press, Boca Raton, FL (2000)
11. Pitkänen, T., Mäkinen, R., Heikkinen, J., Partanen, T., Takala, J.: Low-power, high-performance TTA processor for 1024-point fast Fourier transform. In: Vassiliadis, S., Wong, S., Hämäläinen, T.D. (eds.) SAMOS 2006. LNCS, vol. 4017, pp. 227–236. Springer, Heidelberg (2006)
12. Pitkänen, T., Mäkinen, R., Heikkinen, J., Partanen, T., Takala, J.: Transport triggered architecture processor for mixed-radix FFT. In: Proc. Asilomar Conf. Signals, Systems, and Computers, Pacific Grove, CA (2006)
13. Rabiner, L.R., Gold, B.: Theory and Application of Digital Signal Processing. Prentice Hall, Englewood Cliffs (1975)
14. Granata, J., Conner, M., Tolimieri, R.: Recursive fast algorithms and the role of the tensor product. IEEE Trans. Signal Processing 40(12), 2921–2930 (1992)
15. Akopian, D., Takala, J., Astola, J., Saarinen, J.: Multistage interconnection networks for parallel Viterbi decoders. IEEE Trans. Commun. 51(9), 1536–1545 (2003)
16. Bóo, M., Argüello, F., Bruguera, J., Doallo, R., Zapata, E.: High-performance VLSI architecture for the Viterbi algorithm. IEEE Trans. Commun. 45(2), 168–176 (1997)

# Trade-Offs Between Voltage Scaling and Processor Shutdown for Low-Energy Embedded Multiprocessors*

Pepijn de Langen and Ben Juurlink

Delft University of Technology, Computer Engineering Lab.
Mekelweg 4, 2628 CD Delft, The Netherlands
{pepijn,benj}@ce.et.tudelft.nl

**Abstract.** When peak performance is unnecessary, Dynamic Voltage Scaling (DVS) can be used to reduce the dynamic power consumption of embedded multiprocessors. In future technologies, however, static power consumption is expected to increase significantly. Then it will be more effective to limit the number of employed processors, and use a combination of DVS and processor shutdown. Scheduling heuristics are presented that determine the best trade-off between these three techniques: DVS, processor shutdown, and finding the optimal number of processors. Experimental results show that our approach reduces the total energy consumption by up to 25% for tight deadlines and by up to 37% for loose deadlines compared to DVS. We also compare the energy consumed by our scheduling algorithm to two lower bounds, and show that our best approach leaves little room for improvement.

## 1 Introduction

Recently, (single-chip) multiprocessors such as the IBM/Sony/Toshiba Cell architecture [1] and Philips Wasabi [2] have been introduced or announced for the high-performance embedded market. For such systems, the energy consumption is an important design consideration. The power consumption of a processor consists of a dynamic part (due to switching activity) and a static part (due to leakage current). In past technologies, the dynamic power has been much larger than the static power. With each technology generation, however, the leakage current is predicted to increase by a factor of five [3] and is predicted to surpass the dynamic power consumption [4].

In this paper we consider the problem of scheduling tasks on a multiprocessor system to minimize the total energy consumption. When the dynamic power dominates the static power, an effective technique to reduce the energy is to schedule the tasks on as many processors as possible to reduce the makespan of the schedule. Thereafter, the remaining time before the deadline (the *slack*) is used to scale down the supply voltages and operating frequencies. We refer to this technique as *Schedule-and-Stretch* (S&S).

When the static and dynamic power are comparable, however, S&S is no longer effective because it increases the amount of leakage current by using more processors than necessary and by lengthening the time it takes to complete the computation. In previous work [5] we have proposed LAMPS (Leakage-Aware MultiProcessor Scheduling).

---

* This research was supported in part by the Netherlands Organisation for Scientific Research (NWO).

S. Vassiliadis et al. (Eds.): SAMOS 2007, LNCS 4599, pp. 75–85, 2007.
© Springer-Verlag Berlin Heidelberg 2007

LAMPS does not employ as many processors as possible to maximize the amount of slack, but determines an optimal balance between the number of processors that should be used and the level of frequency/voltage scaling.

In this work, we extend both S&S and LAMPS in the following ways. First, we assume discrete voltage levels, while in [5] we have assumed that any voltage/frequency level can be used. Second, we extend both heuristics with the option to shut down processors temporarily. Third, we include two lower bounds, one for the case where only a single frequency is used for all tasks, and one for the case where processors can run at different frequencies and these frequencies may change over time.

Experimental results show that our best approach reduces the total energy consumption by up to 25% for tight deadlines (1.5x the critical path length) and by up to 57% for loose deadlines (8x the critical path length) compared to S&S and by up to 14% respectively 11% compared to LAMPS. Comparing these results to the theoretical bounds indicates there is little room left for improvement. More specifically, for fairly coarse-grain task graphs LAMPS+PS attains over 94% of the possible savings, provided the frequency is the same for all active processors and is constant throughout the schedule.

This paper is organized as follows. Section 2 contains an overview of related work. The power model employed in this work, dynamic voltage scaling, and processor shutdown are explained in Section 3. Section 4 reviews S&S and LAMPS and presents our novel scheduling heuristics that extend S&S and LAMPS with the possibility to shut down processors for a period of time. Experimental results are provided in Section 5. In Section 6, conclusions are drawn and some directions for future research are given.

## 2  Related Work

Applying DVS to multiprocessor scheduling has been investigated by a significant number of researchers. An overview is provided by Jha [6]. As described in Section 1, one approach is to use an existing scheduling algorithm, such as list scheduling with earliest deadline first (EDF), to finish the tasks as early as possible and use the remaining slack before the deadline to lower the supply voltage. This technique has been proposed by several authors [7,8] using different names and, therefore, we refer to it as *Schedule and Stretch* (S&S). Leakage current was not included in their energy calculations, however.

Jejurikar et al. [9] showed that there is an optimal operating point, called the critical speed, at which the total energy consumption is minimized. Lowering the supply voltage below this point increases the energy consumption. They combined this knowledge with processor shutdown and DVS and used it for real-time scheduling. A similar approach was followed by [10], who employed a fixed priority instead of EDF. However, these works assumed that the tasks are independent and focussed on single-processor scheduling. The same model is assumed in [11] and [12]. In addition, the first did not consider DVS, and the second assumed a continuous voltage range.

In other work [13], the scheduling is done in a way to optimize the possibilities for selecting different voltages. Varatkar et al. [14] tried to execute part of the code on a lower supply voltage while minimizing communication. Some researchers have proposed to improve DVS by also adjusting the threshold voltage when scaling the supply voltage [15,16,17,18]. None of these works, however, attempted to determine the number of processors that yields the least energy consumption.

Xu et al. [19] proposed to minimize energy consumption by both using a combination of DVS and choosing the correct number of employed processors. Their work, however, targets embedded clusters in which the nodes provide the same type of service in a client-server model. Furthermore, these authors do not consider static scheduling but instead propose an online algorithm similar to [8].

Our work differs in the following ways. First, we focus on static multiprocessor scheduling, where others mainly focussed on single-processor or real-time multiprocessor scheduling. Second, we use a detailed power model and limit the voltage to discrete steps. Third, we consider DVS as well as processor shutdown and finding the correct number of processors. Fourth, we use a publicly available set of task graphs, where most others have used randomly generated graphs.

## 3  Preliminaries

In this section we describe the employed models, as well as two primary ways to reduce power dissipation: dynamic voltage scaling and processor shutdown.

**System and Application Model.** We assume a shared memory multiprocessor system running parallel applications, for which the scheduling and mapping are statically determined. The applications are represented as weighted directed acyclic graphs (DAGs), where nodes correspond to tasks, edges to task dependences, and node weights to task processing times. We furthermore assume that this system is CPU bound. As explained by Liberato et al. [20], real-time applications with periodic tasks can be translated to DAGs using the *frame-based scheduling* paradigm.

Another common application model is Kahn Process Networks [21], where a group of processes are connected by communication channels to form a network of processes. Each process is in principle infinite and receives data over its input channels, processes it, and sends the results over the output channels. Here there is not a single deadline but a certain throughput must be guaranteed. This model can be converted to DAGs by making several copies of the KPN, by adding an edge from each node in the $i$th copy to the corresponding node in the $(i+1)$st copy, and by assigning the output nodes of the first copy an arbitrary but reasonable deadline. The deadline of the output nodes of each successive copy is set to the deadline of the corresponding node in the previous copy plus the reciprocal of the throughput. A simple example is depicted in Fig. 1.

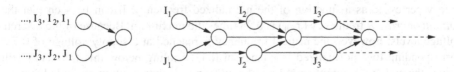

**Fig. 1.** Simple example for translating KPNs into DAGs

Mainly due to unpredictable behavior in the memory system, the execution time of a task does not solely depend on the clock frequency. However, since reducing the frequency will make memory accesses relatively less costly, it is safe to assume that executing a task on $1/N^{th}$ of the frequency will take at most $N$ times as much time.

**Power Model.** In this work, we use the power model described in [9], which in turn is based on the model and parameters given in [16], where it has been verified with SPICE simulations. In this model, the power consumption of a processor is given by:

$$P = P_{AC} + P_{DC} + P_{on},$$

where $P_{AC}$ is the dynamic power consumption (due to switching activity), $P_{DC}$ is the static power consumption (due to leakage current), and $P_{on}$ is the intrinsic power consumption needed to keep the processor on. Like [9], we assume $P_{on}$ is $0.1W$. The dynamic and static power are given by:

$$P_{AC} = C_{eff}V_{dd}^2 f \quad \text{and} \quad P_{DC} = V_{dd}I_{subn} + |V_{bs}|I_j,$$

where $C_{eff}$ is the effective switching capacitance, $V_{dd}$ is the supply voltage, $f$ is the operating frequency, $I_{subn}$ is the sub-threshold leakage current, $V_{bs}$ is the voltage applied between body and source, and $I_j$ is the reverse bias junction current. The sub-threshold leakage current and the threshold voltage are given by:

$$I_{subn} = K_3 e^{K_4 V_{dd}} e^{K_5 V_{bs}} \quad \text{and} \quad V_{th} = V_{th1} - K_1 V_{dd} - K_2 V_{bs},$$

where $K_1 \dots K_5$ and $V_{th1}$ are constants. Finally, the relation between operating frequency, supply voltage, and threshold voltage is:

$$f = (V_{dd} - V_{th})^\alpha / L_d K_6,$$

where $L_d$ represents the logic depth and $K_6$ and $\alpha$ are constants for a certain technology. We use the same constants for $70nm$ technology as [9,16], which are omitted due to space constraints. The maximum frequency of this processor is $3.1GHz$, which requires a supply voltage of $1V$. Figures 2(a) and 2(b) depict the resulting power consumption and energy per cycle as a function of the normalized operating frequency.

**Dynamic Voltage Scaling.** DVS mainly reduces the dynamic power consumption, which increases quadratically with the supply voltage. The static component, although having a exponential relation with supply voltage, does not decrease as much with decreasing supply voltage as the dynamic component, as is depicted in Fig. 2(a).

Since energy equals power times time, the energy consumption will actually start to increase if the frequency is decreased below a certain point. Fig. 2(b) depicts the energy per cycle as a function of the normalized frequency. It can be seen that the *optimal* or *critical* frequency ($f_{crit}$) is 0.38 times the maximum. Because of the discrete voltage levels, however, the critical frequency is reached at a supply voltage of 0.7V, corresponding to a normalized frequency of 0.41. Scaling below this frequency will reduce the power consumption but not the total energy consumption, provided that the processors can be shut down for the remaining time. When there is no sleep/shutdown mode, scaling below $f_{crit}$ will, in fact, reduce the total energy consumption, since the processors also consume energy for the remaining time.

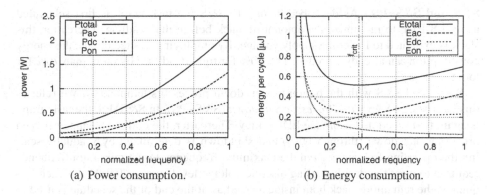

(a) Power consumption.  (b) Energy consumption.

**Fig. 2.** Power and energy consumption as a function of the normalized frequency

**Processor Shutdown.** The second technique to reduce the energy consumption of a multiprocessor system is to put idle processors temporarily in a deep sleep or shutdown mode. The advantage of this technique over DVS is that it reduces all terms of the total power consumption, not only the dynamic part. When shutting down a processor, however, the contents of, e.g., caches and branch predictors are lost. When a processor is switched back on, they have to be warmed up again, which causes additional delay and consumes extra energy. We use the estimates of Jejurikar et al. [9], who estimated that a processor in sleep state consumes about $50\mu W$ of power and that shutting down and resuming a processor incurs an energy overhead of $483\mu J$. This overhead includes the supply voltage switching as well as the energy spent to warm up caches and predictors. The additional delay incurred by powering down can be hidden by waking up the processor a short time before the end of the idle period.

Processor shutdown is only beneficial if a processor is idle for a sufficiently long period. Since in most cases applications with rather fine-grain tasks will have relatively short idle periods (unless the task graph is very unbalanced), such applications will in general not benefit from to shutting down processors temporarily between the execution of two tasks. However, it might still be energy efficient to shut down at the end of the schedule, provided the deadline is relatively long.

## 4 Scheduling for Energy Minimization

In this section we review S&S and LAMPS and enhance both scheduling approaches with the option to shut down processors temporarily. In the schedules produced by these approaches, all processors run at the same operating frequency and this frequency is constant throughout the whole schedule. Both S&S and LAMPS employ list scheduling with earliest deadline first (LS-EDF) to perform the actual scheduling. EDF does not necessarily produce the best schedule, however. To investigate if other scheduling algorithms could result in additional energy gains, we also present an ideal model in which idle processors are assumed to consume no energy. Furthermore, we also show the improvements that could be attained if the frequency could vary among processors and over time.

**S&S and S&S+PS.** As described before, in S&S the task graph is first scheduled using LS-EDF to maximize the amount of slack before the deadline. Thereafter, this slack is exploited to lower the supply voltage. By employing this technique, the energy consumption can already be reduced by 30% for tight deadlines by more than 70% for loose ones [5].

We extend S&S with the option to shut down processors temporarily. We refer to this heuristic as *S&S with Processor Shutdown* (S&S+PS). In S&S+PS, the task graph is again first scheduled using the EDF policy. Thereafter, the optimal balance between processor slowdown (through DVS) and shutdown is determined by gradually scaling the operating frequency from the maximum frequency to the minimum frequency required to meet the deadline using discrete voltage level steps of 0.05V. For each frequency, the remaining slack both inside as well as at the end of the schedule is used to shut down processors, provided the idle period is greater than the minimum idle period to result in energy savings. In other words, the slack is only used to shut down a processor if it is large enough to make up for the additional energy consumption due to loss of state.

**LAMPS and LAMPS+PS.** In LAMPS, a trade-off is made between the number of processors that should be employed and the amount of voltage scaling. The remaining processors are turned off. The number of processors that minimizes the energy is found by calculating the energy consumption of the schedule produced by S&S for $N_{min}$, $N_{min} + 1$, ..., $N_{max}$ processors, where $N_{min}$ is the number of processors needed to finish before the deadline and $N_{max}$ is the number of processors that can be used to reduce the makespan of the schedule.

We also enhance the LAMPS heuristic with the option to shut down processors and refer to the resulting heuristic as LAMPS+PS. As in LAMPS, the number of processors that minimizes the total energy consumption is determined by calculating the energy consumption for $N_{min}$, $N_{min} + 1$, ..., $N_{max}$ processors, where $N_{min}$ is the minimal number of processors needed to meet the deadline and $N_{max}$ is the number of processors that can be employed efficiently. For each number of processors, we then determine the balance between DVS and processor shutdown by scaling the frequency from the maximum to the minimum frequency required to meet the deadline. For each frequency, we then use the available slack to shut down processors, similar to the S&S+PS heuristic.

**LIMIT-SF & LIMIT-MF.** In the approaches described above, the schedule is always produced by EDF. It is known, however, that EDF is suboptimal for multiprocessor scheduling. Furthermore, in the approaches the frequency is always constant throughout the entire schedule. To investigate if additional energy can be saved by employing a different scheduling algorithm or by allowing different frequencies, we also include two lower bounds, one for the case with a single frequency (LIMIT-SF) and one for the case where multiple frequencies are allowed (LIMIT-MF).

LIMIT-SF has the following characteristics. First, idle processors are assumed to consume no energy at all. In other words, only active cycles are considered when calculating the energy consumption and, consequently, there is no benefit from or penalty for shutting down processors. Second, the number of processors is equal to the number of tasks. Since idle processors consume no energy, using fewer processors will not reduce the energy. Third, the frequency is scaled down to the optimal frequency if possible to meet the deadline, or otherwise as much as possible. No schedule can consume less energy than this ideal model, provided that the frequency is the same for all active processors and is constant throughout the schedule.

The difference between LIMIT-MF and LIMIT-SF is that in LIMIT-MF all tasks are scheduled at the critical frequency. Because of this and since idle processors are assumed to consume no energy, LIMIT-MF is an absolute lower bound, even for the case where processors can run at different speeds and where the frequency may change over time. We note, however, that it may happen that the schedule produced by LIMIT-MF does not meet the deadline.

Since both LIMIT-SF and LIMIT-MF do not depend on any particular scheduling algorithm, this implies that these results cannot be improved by employing a different scheduling algorithm than EDF.

## 5   Experimental Evaluation

In this section, we present and compare the results of the different scheduling approaches discussed in Section 4. We use the same power model as used by [16] and [9], as explained in Section 3. We again emphasize that a processor in sleep state consumes $50\mu W$ and that switching a processor off and on requires $483\mu J$ of energy.

**Experimental Setup.** Table 1 lists the benchmarks that have been used, as well as the number of nodes and edges, the critical path length, and the sum of all node weights (total work). These benchmarks have been taken from the *Standard Task Graph Set* [22]. The first three have been derived from real applications, while the other three have been randomly generated. We note that most previous works have used only randomly generated task graphs to validate their approaches.

Table 1. Employed benchmarks and their main characteristics

| name | number of nodes | number of edges | critical path | total work |
|------|-----------------|-----------------|---------------|------------|
| fpppp | 334 | 1196 | 1062 | 7113 |
| robot | 88 | 130 | 545 | 2459 |
| sparse | 96 | 128 | 122 | 1920 |
| proto001 | 273 | 1688 | 167 | 4711 |
| proto003 | 164 | 646 | 556 | 1599 |
| proto279 | 1342 | 16762 | 735 | 13302 |

Since the Standard Task Graph Set does not provide deadlines, we have used deadlines of 1.5, 2, 4, and 8 times the critical path length (CPL) when running at the maximum frequency of 3.1GHz. It also does not define the unit of the task weights. Instead, the weights are given as integers in the range from 1 to 300. Therefore, two different scenarios are considered. In the first scenario, corresponding to rather coarse-grain tasks, a weight of 1 in a task graph implies an execution time of $3.1 \cdot 10^6$ cycles, which is 1 millisecond when running at the maximum frequency of 3.1GHz. In the second scenario, corresponding to relatively fine-grain tasks, the same weight implies an execution time of $3.1 \cdot 10^4$ cycles, which at maximum frequency takes 10 microseconds.

**Experimental Results.** Figs. 3 and 4 depict the results for coarse grain and fine grain tasks, respectively. For each scenario, we show the energy consumption for deadlines of 1.5, 2, 4, and 8 times the CPL. Each figure shows the results of the four different approaches explained in Section 4, as well as the theoretical limits. Throughout this section, S&S is used as the baseline against which we compare the other heuristics.

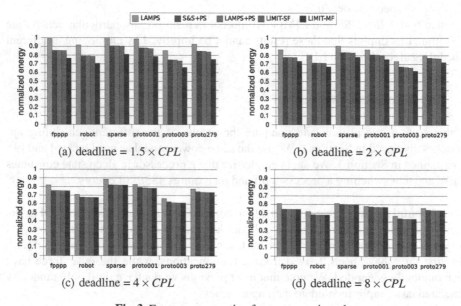

Fig. 3. Energy consumption for coarse-grain tasks

First we compare the energy consumption of the schedules produced by LAMPS to the energy consumption of the schedules generated by S&S. Figs. 3 and 4 show that LAMPS improves upon S&S mainly for less strict deadlines. This can be expected because for tight deadlines (1.5x the CPL), LAMPS requires the same or nearly the same number of processors as S&S to meet the deadline, and therefore consumes the same or nearly the same amount of energy as S&S. In other words, if the deadline is tight, there is less opportunity to turn off processors. For loose deadlines (8x the CPL), on the other hand, LAMPS consumes significantly less energy than S&S, simply because it can employ fewer processors. In this case LAMPS reduces the total energy consumption by 45% on average compared to S&S with a maximum of 53%. For fine-grain tasks, depicted in Fig. 4, the relative differences between S&S and LAMPS are the same as with coarse-grain tasks, since both heuristics do not shut down processors. Compared to [5] the energy savings are generally slightly smaller because there a continuous voltage range was assumed while in this work discrete voltage levels are assumed.

We now compare S&S+PS to S&S. Because S&S employs a large number of processors, it consumes a significant amount of static power. Therefore, S&S+PS improves

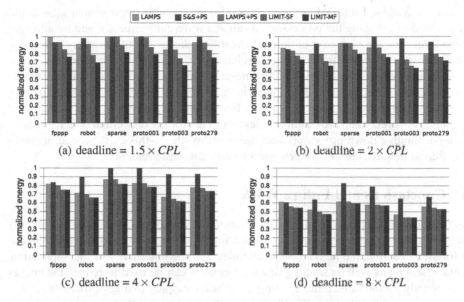

Fig. 4. Energy consumption for fine-grain tasks

upon S&S significantly, by shutting down idle processors temporarily. The gains, in this case, are considerably larger for coarse-grain tasks (30% on average) than for fine-grain tasks (12% on average), because in the latter case the slack is often not large enough to make shutdown beneficial.

LAMPS+PS improves upon LAMPS mostly for coarse-grain tasks. Again, the main reason for this is that for fine-grain tasks, the slack is often not large enough to make shutting down worthwhile. With coarse grain tasks, however, a significant amount of energy can be saved by shutting processors down temporarily. The improvement of LAMPS+PS over LAMPS is typically less than the improvement of S&S+PS over S&S. This is because in LAMPS the static dissipation is already reduced by using a smaller number of processors compared to S&S. For coarse-grain tasks, the maximum improvements by LAMPS+PS upon LAMPS are 14% and 11%, for deadlines of 1.5× and 8× the CPL respectively.

For coarse-grain tasks, the total improvement by LAMPS+PS upon S&S is 29% on average, with a maximum of 25% for deadlines of 1.5× the CPL and a maximum of 57% for deadlines of 8× the CPL. For fine-grain tasks, LAMPS+PS improves upon S&S by 25% on average, with a maximum of 15% for deadlines of 1.5× the CPL and a maximum of 57% for deadlines of 8× the CPL.

LIMIT-SF in Figs. 3 and 4 gives an upper limit on the energy savings using our current single-frequency model. Using S&S as the baseline and LIMIT-SF as the maximum, it shows that LAMPS+PS attains more than 94% of the possible energy reduction with coarse-grain tasks, for all combinations of benchmarks and deadlines. For fine-grain tasks and strict deadlines (1.5× the CPL), LAMPS+PS achieves more than 41% of the potential savings on 4 out of the 6 benchmarks. With less strict deadlines, LAMPS+PS attains more than 50% of the possible savings on all benchmarks.

In Figs. 3 and 4, Limit-MF is an indication for the possible improvements that could be attained by allowing the processors to run at a different frequency, and by allowing these frequencies to change over time. The results indicate that there is very little room for improvements when the deadline is relatively loose. For stricter deadlines, some savings may be attained, but mostly for fine-grain tasks. In the case of fine-grain tasks with strict deadlines, the periods of inactivity are often too small to make shutting down worthwhile. In this case, allowing varying frequencies might result in some additional savings. However, when the deadline is less strict and/or the task graph is fairly coarse-grained, shutting down processors becomes worthwhile. In this case, scheduling tasks at different frequencies will not provide a significant improvement.

## 6    Conclusions and Future Work

As feature sizes keep decreasing, the contribution of leakage current to the total energy consumption is expected to increase. Depending on the amount of slack that remains before the deadline, the amount of parallelism, and the granularity of the application, voltage scaling as well as shutting down processors can be used to reduce the energy significantly. At the same time, it is important not to employ to many processors.

We have shown that LAMPS+PS reduces the total energy by up to 25% for tight deadlines and up to 57% for loose ones compared to the S&S algorithm. For coarse-grain tasks and a single frequency, LAMPS+PS attains more than 94% of the possible energy reduction, i.e., the energy reduction achieved by LIMIT-SF compared to S&S. Since LIMIT-SF is independent of the scheduling algorithm, this implies that there is almost no room left for improvement by using other scheduling algorithms than EDF.

Even when multiple frequencies are allowed, LAMPS+PS reduces the energy consumption close to the theoretical limit (LIMIT-MF). For loose deadlines ($4\times$ or $8\times$ the critical path length), LIMIT-MF consumes the same amount of energy as LIMIT-SF, and so LAMPS+PS again attains over 94% of the potential savings with coarse-grain tasks. Averaged over all tested deadlines, our best approach still attains over 84% of the possible savings. As a result, it will be nearly impossible to reduce the overall energy consumption further by using other scheduling algorithms that produce schedules in which different processors can run at different frequencies and in which the frequency can change over time. Applications consisting of relatively fine-grain tasks, on the other hand, might benefit from using other scheduling approaches. However, since LIMIT-MF does not take the deadline into account, real scheduling approaches will probably not reach this limit. Consequently, the actual benefit from having multiple frequencies will probably be much less. We intend to investigate the impact of multiple frequencies and other scheduling algorithms in future research.

## References

1. Hofstee, H.: Power Efficient Processor Architecture and the Cell Processor. In: Proc. Int. Symp. on High-Performance Computer Architecture, pp. 258–262 (2005)
2. Stravers, P., Hoogerbrugge, J.: Homogeneous Multiprocessing and the Future of Silicon Design Paradigms. In: Proc. Int. Symp. on VLSI Technology, Systems, and Applications, pp. 184–187 (2001)

3. Borkar, S.: Design Challenges of Technology Scaling. IEEE Micro 19(4), 23–29 (1999)
4. Duarte, D., Vijaykrishnan, N., Irwin, M., Tsai, Y.: Impact of Technology Scaling and Packaging on Dynamic Voltage Scaling Techniques. In: Proc. IEEE Int. ASIC/SOC Conf, IEEE Computer Society Press, Los Alamitos (2002)
5. de Langen, P., Juurlink, B.: Leakage-Aware Multiprocessor Scheduling for Low Power. In: Proc. Int. Parallel and Distributed Processing Symp. (2006)
6. Jha, N.: Low-Power System Scheduling, Synthesis and Displays. IEE Proc. on Computers and Digital Techniques 152(3), 344–352 (2005)
7. Gruian, F., Kuchcinski, K.: LEneS: Task Scheduling for Low-Energy Systems Using Variable Supply Voltage Processors. In: Proc. Conf. on Asia South Pacific Design Automation, pp. 449–455 (2001)
8. Zhu, D., Melhem, R., Childers, B.: Scheduling with Dynamic Voltage/Speed Adjustment Using Slack Reclamation in Multiprocessor Real-Time Systems. IEEE Trans. on Parallel and Distributed Systems 14(7), 686–700 (2003)
9. Jejurikar, R., Pereira, C., Gupta, R.: Leakage Aware Dynamic Voltage Scaling for Real-Time Embedded Systems. In: Proc. Conf. on Design Automation, pp. 275–280 (2004)
10. Quan, G., Niu, L., Hu, X.S., Mochocki, B.: Fixed Priority Scheduling for Reducing Overall Energy on Variable Voltage Processors. In: Proc. Int. Real-Time System Symposium, pp. 309–318 (2004)
11. Lee, Y., Reddy, K., Krishna, C.: Scheduling Techniques for Reducing Leakage Power in Hard Real-Time Systems. In: Proc. Euromicro Conf. on Real Time Systems, pp. 105–112 (2003)
12. Irani, S., Shukla, S., Gupta, R.: Algorithms for Power Savings. In: ACM-SIAM Symp. on Discrete Algorithms, pp. 37–46 (2003)
13. Zhang, Y., Hu, X.S., Chen, D.Z.: Task Scheduling and Voltage Selection for Energy Minimization. In: Proc. Conf. on Design Automation, pp. 183–188 (2002)
14. Varatkar, G., Marculescu, R.: Communication Aware Task Scheduling and Voltage Selection for Total Systems Energy Minimization. In: Proc. Int. Conf. on Computer-Aided Design, pp. 510–517 (2003)
15. Gonzalez, R., Gordon, B., Horowitz, M.: Supply and Threshold Voltage Scaling for Low Power CMOS. IEEE Journal of Solid-State Circuits 32(8), 1210–1216 (1997)
16. Martin, S., Flautner, K., Mudge, T., Blaauw, D.: Combined Dynamic Voltage Scaling and Adaptive Body Biasing for Lower Power Microprocessors under Dynamic Workloads. In: Proc. Int. Conf. on Computer-Aided Design, pp. 721–725 (2002)
17. Andrei, A., Schmitz, M., Eles, P., Peng, Z., Al-Hashimi, B.M.: Overhead-Conscious Voltage Selection for Dynamic and Leakage Energy Reduction of Time-Constrained Systems. In: Proc. Conf. on Design, Automation and Test in Europe, pp. 518–525 (2004)
18. Yan, L., Luo, J., Jha, N.K.: Combined Dynamic Voltage Scaling and Adaptive Body Biasing for Heterogeneous Distributed Real-time Embedded Systems. In: Proc. Int. Conf. on Computer-Aided Design, pp. 30–37 (2003)
19. Xu, R., Zhu, D., Rusu, C., Melhem, R., Moss, D.: Energy-Efficient Policies for Embedded Clusters. In: Proc. ACM SIGPLAN/SIGBED Conf. on Languages, Compilers, and Tools for Embedded Systems. pp. 1–10 (2005)
20. Liberato, F., Lauzac, S., Melhem, R., Moss, D.: Fault Tolerant Real-Time Global Scheduling on Multiprocessors. In: Proc. Euromicro Conf. on Real-Time Systems. (1999) 252–259
21. Kahn, G.: The Semantics of a Simple Language for Parallel Programming. In: Information Processing, pp. 471–475 (1974)
22. Kasahara, H., Tobita, T., Matsuzawa, T., Sakaida, S.: Standard Task Graph Set, http://www.kasahara.elec.waseda.ac.jp/schedule/

# An Automatically-Retargetable Time-Constraint-Driven Instruction Scheduler for Post-compiling Optimization of Embedded Code

José O. Carlomagno F., Luiz F.P. Santos, and Luiz C.V. dos Santos

Federal University of Santa Catarina - Computer Science Department
Florianópolis, SC, Brazil,
{jocf, penkal, santos}@inf.ufsc.br

**Abstract.** Although SoC design space exploration requires retargetable tools and real-time constraint awareness, conventional compiler infrastructure barely provides both. This paper proposes a novel, automatically retargetable, time-constraint aware instruction scheduler to fulfill both needs. The tool is based upon a unified representation of instruction precedence and timing constraints. It relies on a formal model of the target processor, written in an architecture description language. Experimental results show that the technique not only handles time-constraint analysis efficiently, but also exploits them successfully to guide code optimization. To give proper evidence of retargetability, we present results for the processors MIPS, PowerPC and SPARC. We obtained speed-ups of 1.18 to 1.23 over pre-optimized code.

## 1 Introduction

The increasing complexity of systems-on-chip (SoCs) gave rise to the platform-based design paradigm [1]. Later, the need to launch embedded software development as early as possible asked for higher level platform descriptions, such as the transaction-level modeling (TLM) [2].

To minimize code size and power consumption, while ensuring enough performance to fulfill real-time constraints, SoC design space exploration has to consider alternative target processors. Often, SoCs are heterogeneous multiprocessor architectures that may contain processors ranging from general-purpose processors and digital signal processors to application-specific instruction-set processors (ASIPs). Such variety of processors requires *retargetable tools*.

TLM descriptions are growing in importance in contemporary system design flows, since they allow the early development of hardware-dependent software. For efficiency reasons, such design flows start with an untimed TLM description (cycle-accurate models are too time consuming to begin with). Later, timing is annotated to the model, leading to timed TLM models (called TLM+T [2]). Such annotation imposes time-constraints to pre-compiled code. Therefore *post-compiling time-constraint driven tools* are welcome.

Acceptable average performance levels are likely to be obtained with state-of-the-art instruction scheduling techniques built in classical compilers. However, since conventional schedulers aim at optimizing average performance, they are unable to determine

S. Vassiliadis et al. (Eds.): SAMOS 2007, LNCS 4599, pp. 86–95, 2007.

the worst-case execution time of a code segment. Therefore, under real-time constraints, a conventional scheduler is prone to trial-and-error. The tighter the time constraint, the larger the number of trials.

As stated in [3], it would be desirable that a compiler could switch to heavier optimization techniques when dealing with code hot spots (such as time-critical loops). Since this is not observed in practical compilers, a developer would be forced either to manually improve a critical code segment at the source level or to hand-optimize compiled code. However, if repeated for several processor targets, such a makeshift would become unacceptable under time-to-market pressure. That's why a retargetable, time-constraint aware optimizing engine can be envisaged as a pragmatic way to preserve classical compiler infrastructure by automatically analyzing and optimizing time-critical code at the assembly level.

This paper describes an automatically retargetable technique that combines time-constraint analysis and assembly code scheduling. The technique relies on the automatic extraction of processor-dependent information from a formal description of an arbitrary target processor (to gain retargetability), and on the encoding of precedence and time constraints on a unified graph representation (to provide grounds for time-constraint analysis).

The remainder of this paper is organized as follows. Section 2 reviews related work. The unified representation of constraints is formalized in Section 3. Section 4 describes the proposed post-compiling scheduling engine. Experimental results are summarized in Section 5, while our conclusions are drawn in Section 6.

# 2  Related Work

## 2.1  Time-Constraint Analysis

In the compiler domain, scheduling algorithms barely address time-constraint feasibility since they focus on average performance. However, the time-constrained scheduling problem has been addressed in the domains of behavioral synthesis and code generation for in-house DSP processors.

A weighted sequencing graph was proposed in [4] to unify the representation of time-constraints and data dependencies. Such a modeling allows an elegant formulation for time-constrained scheduling by casting it as a longest-path problem. Therefore, a schedule can be found by means of classical algorithms such as Bellman-Ford's [5].

An extension of that modeling was suggested in [6], where all constraints (timing, precedence, resources) are modeled on a same graph. If two operations compete for a same resource, their conflict will be avoided by inserting an edge between them (weighted with the resource's delay). An edge is inserted for each new scheduled operation. A constraint analyzer is invoked after each new operation is scheduled, keeping track of time-constraint feasibility while the scheduler seeks for a suitable ordering. Since edge insertion reduces the scheduler search space, the analyzer speeds up the convergence to a feasible schedule. Since the approach in [6] assumes a VLIW DSP target architecture, it is not suitable for general core exploration in SoC design.

## 2.2  Automatically Retargetable Tools

Most contemporary retargetable compilers are based upon Architecture Description
Languages (ADLs). For instance, AVIV [7] relies on ISDL [8] and EXPRESS [9] in
EXPRESSION [10].

Instruction scheduler generation from LISA [11] was reported in [12]. The approach
focused on the automatic generation of a structural hazard description, but it didn't
address automatic instruction latency extraction from LISA descriptions.

Assembly-level optimization techniques like SALTO [13] and PROPAN [14] allow
existing compilers to be reused, while machine-dependent optimizations can be added
to improve code quality.

A comprehensive review of retargetable techniques can be found in [3].

## 2.3  Bridging the Gap

In summary, while ADL-based tools grant retargetability, but don't address time-
constraint feasibility properly, behavioral synthesis and some DSP code generation approaches properly deal with time constraints, but are inherently not retargetable, as they
are driven towards an application-specific target architecture.

We propose a technique to bridge this gap by providing a retargetable time-constraint
aware scheduling engine. To our knowledge, no ADL-based retargetable technique published so far has properly addressed time-constraint analysis as a driver for optimization.
Despite its novelty, the proposed technique doesn't require a new framework, fitting in a
pragmatic approach: the resort to a post-compiling scheduler tailored to deal with time-
constraints, while preserving conventional compiler infrastructure (as will be shown in
Section 4).

Our technique relies on a well-defined graph-based modeling, as summarized in the
next section.

## 3   Unified Modeling of Constraints

The technique described in this paper adopts the constraint representation proposed in
[4], as summarized below.

**Definition 1.** A **weighted precedence graph** WPG(V, E, W) is a directed weighted
graph where each vertex $v_i$ represents an instruction, each edge $(v_i, v_j)$ represents a
precedence constraint and the weight $w_{ij} \in Z$ represents the relative delay between the
start times of instructions $v_i$ and $v_j$. The poles $v_0$ and $v_n$ are called **source** and **sink**,
respectively.

**Definition 2.** Given a WPG(V, E, W) and a number $k \in Z^+$, a **minimum delay** of k
cycles between the start times of instructions $v_i$ and $v_j$ is represented by an edge $(v_i, v_j)$
with weight $w_{ik} = +k$, thereby constraining instruction $v_j$ to start its execution at least k
cycles after operation $v_i$ has started execution.

**Definition 3.** Given a WPG(V, E, W) and a number $k \in Z+$, a **maximum delay** of k
cycles between the start times of instructions $v_i$ and $v_j$ is represented by an edge $(v_i, v_i)$

with weight $w_{ji} = -k$, thereby constraining instruction $v_j$ to start its execution at most k cycles after operation $v_i$ has started execution.

**Definition 4.** Given a WPG(V, E, W) and a number $k \in Z+$, an **exact delay** of k cycles between the start times of instructions $v_i$ and $v_j$ is represented by an edge $(v_i, v_j)$ with weight $w_{ij} = +k$ and an edge $(v_j, v_i)$ with weight $w_{ji} = -k$, thereby constraining instruction $v_j$ to start its execution at exactly k cycles after operation $v_i$ has started execution.

**Definition 5.** Let $\tau(v_i, t)$ be a function that binds each instruction $v_i$ at time t to a resource type required for its execution. Let $a_r$ be the number of resources of type r in the target processor. A function called **schedule** $\varphi : V \to N$ maps each instruction $v_i$ to a start time $\varphi(v_i)$ such that:
- $\forall(v_i, v_j) \in E: \varphi(v_j) \geq \varphi(v_i) + w_{ij}$ ;
- $\forall t$ in $[\varphi(v_i), \varphi(v_i) + w_{ij}] : |\{v_k \in V : [\tau(v_k,t) = r] \wedge [t = \varphi(v_k)]\}| \leq a_r$ .

It has been shown that a longest-path algorithm such as Bellman-Ford's [5] can induce a schedule $\varphi$ provided that resource constraint is properly encoded in the graph model [6]. It was proven [4] [5] that when the Bellman-Ford algorithm doesn't converge within a limited number of iterations, then the set of constraints is infeasible. This is the key to feasibility analysis, as will be shown in Section 4.

# 4   The Retargetable Scheduling Engine

This section first describes the structure of our retargetable tool and the main underlying algorithms.

## 4.1   Engine Structure

Figure 1 depicts the structure of our retargetable scheduling engine. Ellipses denote distinct code representations. Rectangles represent tool components. Solid arrows indicate the flow of code transformations, while dashed arrows show how target-dependent information is fed to the proper components.

From a processor model, written in an ADL, a model parser extracts target-specific information such as assembly syntax, instruction latency and the specification of the set of general-purpose registers.

The input code consists of raw assembly generated by a conventional compiler. As a conventional compiler doesn't capture time-constraints, an editor is employed to insert them into the code. A pair of pseudo instructions is used to enclose the code fragment affected by a time-constraint. For instance, the pair [MIN k, label] and [/MIN label] represents a minimum delay of k cycles imposed to the enclosed code fragment. Similarly, the pair [MAX k, label] and [/MAX label] represents a maximum delay, whereas the pair [EXACT k, label] and [/EXACT label] represents an exact delay. This process results in is instrumented assembly code.

The instrumented code is parsed, giving rise to a weighted precedence graph (WPG). In order to remove false dependences and therefore expose more parallelism to the scheduler, registers are renamed such that every produced value is stored on a distinct symbolic register. For every instruction whose destination symbolic register is the

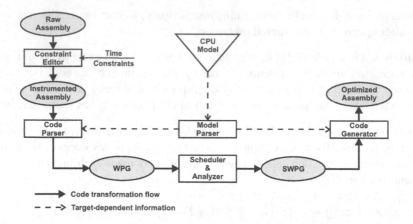

**Fig. 1.** Code optimization flow

source for another instruction, the code parser inserts an edge in the WPG. The weight of that edge is the consumer's latency to the producer, whose value is extracted from the processor model. Moreover, every time-constraint pseudo instruction results in the insertion of weighted edges according to Definitions 2, 3 and 4.

The engine works on the WPG so as to find a feasible time-constrained schedule, as described in the next subsection. Essentially, the original WPG is modified by inserting a pair of new edges for each scheduled instruction, producing a scheduled weighted precedence graph (SWPG). Its set of weighted edges induces a linear ordering of instructions.

In the end, each SWPG vertex (instruction) is visited in the induced order while optimized assembly code is generated. Register allocation takes place during such code generation so as to map the symbolic registers into the finite set of real registers.

Since target-dependent information is automatically extracted from the ADL description and the WPG is target-independent, our optimizing tool is granted automatic retargetability.

## 4.2  Algorithms

The scheduler and the analyzer are tightly coupled engines whose main procedures are defined by Algorithm 1.

For simplicity, two auxiliary procedures invoked in Algorithm 1 are informally described as follows. Given a time step t, procedure FindAvailableInstructions returns the set of instructions whose operands are ready to be consumed at time t. Procedure SelectInstruction returns the instruction with highest priority within that set. Although the selection of instructions resembles the list scheduling mechanism, our engine provides a generic function for inducing priority and it can capture distinct scheduling heuristics.

Given a WPG, when the well-known Bellman-Ford algorithm returns false, meaning that the set of edge weights (which represent timing constraints) is inconsistent, procedure Infeasible returns true.

**Algorithm 1.** Main scheduler procedures

```
Procedure: Infeasible(WPG(V, E, W))
1: return (¬ BellmanFord(WPG(V, E, W)));
Procedure: ScheduleStep(t, A)
2:   v_i = SelectInstruction(A);
3:   while v_i ≠ none do
4:       E = E (v_0, v_i);
5:       w_0i = +t;
6:       E = E (v_i, v_0);
7:       w_i0 = -t;
8:       if Infeasible(WPG(V, E, W)) == TRUE then
9:           return (FALSE);
10:      end if
11:      v_i = SelectInstruction(A);
12:  end while
13:  return TRUE;
Procedure: Schedule( )
14:  t = 0;
15:  W = BellmanFord(WPG(V, E, W)); // Weight initialization
16:  A = FindAvailableInstructions (t);
17:  while A ≠ ∅ do
18:      if ScheduleStep(t, A) == FALSE then
19:          return(∞);
20:      end if
21:      t = t + 1;
22:      A = FindAvailableInstructions (L);
23:  end while
24:  return (t);
```

Procedure ScheduleStep assigns as many available instructions as possible to time step t. Once an instruction $v_i$ is selected, two edges $(v_0, v_i)$ and $(v_i, v_0)$ are inserted in the WPG. Their weights are set according to Definition 4, meaning that instruction $v_i$ must start execution exactly t cycles after the initial time reference (represented by the source node $v_0$).

Finally, procedure Schedule invokes ScheduleStep for successive time steps until all instructions are scheduled according to Definition 5 or infeasibility is detected.

# 5  Experimental Results

To implement a prototype tool, we had to adopt an ADL and build the respective model parser. Due to its availability under general-public license, we adopted the ADL ArchC [15]. We have selected code segments from the well-known Mibench benchmark suite [16]. Basic blocks belonging to inner loops and highly probable traces were preferred, since they have higher impact on the global cycle budget. To give evidences of proper retargetability, three target processors were adopted: MIPS R2000, PowerPC 405 and SPARCV8. GNU gcc was the adopted compiler. The computer configuration used in the experiments was a Pentium 4 running at 3GHz with 1GB main memory.

To isolate the impact of exploiting time constraints from the impact of a specific scheduling heuristic that might be chosen for our scheduler, we deliberately set the priority function to keep the original instruction order whenever ties must be broken.

Table 1 shows our benchmark characterization. The first column shows code segment names, while the second indicates the programs from which they were extracted. For

**Table 1.** Benchmark characterization

| Segment | Benchmark | MIPS | | PowerPC | | SPARC | |
|---------|-----------|------|------|------|------|------|------|
| | | $\lvert V \rvert$ | $\lvert E \rvert$ | $\lvert V \rvert$ | $\lvert E \rvert$ | $\lvert V \rvert$ | $\lvert E \rvert$ |
| Isqrt | basicmath | 22 | 52 | 20 | 63 | 21 | 51 |
| Bitarray | bitcount | 12 | 29 | 26 | 70 | 25 | 67 |
| Bitstrng | bitcount | 20 | 54 | 22 | 64 | 19 | 55 |
| Qsort | qsort | 67 | 137 | 43 | 97 | 70 | 154 |
| Jdcolor1 | jpeg | 86 | 197 | 52 | 130 | 83 | 198 |
| Jdcolor2 | jpeg | 58 | 126 | 58 | 150 | 51 | 122 |
| Rdbmp1 | jpeg | 35 | 90 | 36 | 95 | 36 | 93 |
| Rdbmp2 | jpeg | 83 | 185 | 110 | 340 | 110 | 278 |
| SHA | sha | 41 | 98 | 37 | 94 | 41 | 96 |
| Timing | adpcm | 19 | 42 | 12 | 28 | 22 | 53 |

a given target processor, a pair of columns displays the size of the resulting WPG in terms of number of vertices ($\lvert V \rvert$) and edges ($\lvert E \rvert$).

### 5.1   Time-Constraint Feasibility Analysis

To provide evidence that the scheduler handles time-constraints effectively, we submitted each code segment to distinct time constraints and computed the percentage of feasible solutions among all benchmarks. To generate such constraints, we set a baseline time constraint for each code segment and then progressively relaxed it. The baseline, denoted by ε, assumes that each instruction would execute within one clock cycle, making sure that the experiment starts with tight time constraints.

In Fig. 2, we show the percentage of solutions that turned out to be feasible under maximum delay constraints of $\lfloor 1.1 \rfloor \varepsilon$, $\lfloor 1.2 \rfloor \varepsilon$, and $\lfloor 1.3 \rfloor \varepsilon$.

Note that only for a deviation of 30% with respect to ε all code segments satisfy time constraints, showing. This is an evidence of the difficulty in meeting constraints without a time-constraint aware scheduler.

### 5.2   Runtime Efficiency

Since our scheduler invokes a longest-path algorithm for each scheduled instruction, the overhead of time-constraint analysis should be properly assessed.

Figure 3 displays scheduler runtime (expressed in seconds on the right-side scale) in correlation with WPG size (expressed in number of vertices and edges on the left-side scale) for the MIPS, PowerPC and SPARC processors.

Observe that, on average, the runtime is bounded to the number of vertices for all target processors. This is an evidence that our time-constraint analysis has low overhead.

### 5.3   The Impact of the Optimization

As opposed to conventional compilers, our technique exploits time-constraints to guide optimizations. Optimizations possibly overlooked by a conventional compiler are enforced to ensure time-constraint compliance for critical code segments.

In order to assess to which extent time-constraints are actually exploited, we compared the schedule length of a given (time-unconstrained) raw code segment with that

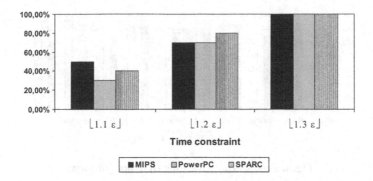

**Fig. 2.** Percentage of feasible solutions

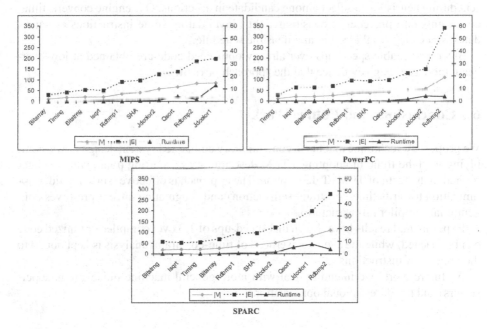

**Fig. 3.** WPG size and runtime correlation

of the equivalent optimized code segment obtained under tight time constraints. In the experiments, a maximum delay of $\lfloor 1.3 \rfloor \varepsilon$ was imposed to each code segment.

Figure 4 plots the ratio between the schedule lengths of raw and optimized code for every target processor. The benchmarks are displayed in order of increasing size from left to right.

The average speed-up was 1.18 for the five smallest segments and 1.23 for the five largest, due to the more abundant optimization opportunities within larger basic blocks. Notice that, since raw assembly is actually the output of a conventional but optimizing compiler, the speed up was measured relatively to *pre-optimized* code. Therefore, the experimental results indicate that the compiler actually overlooked some optimization

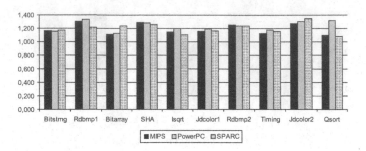

**Fig. 4.** Code speed-up resulting from optimization

opportunities. Being unaware of time-constraints, the compiler might have relied on its scheduling heuristics to select among candidate instructions. Our engine converts time-constraints into precedence constraints, thus invalidating some instructions as candidates, since they would lead to an infeasible schedule.

Since reasonable speed-ups over already optimized code are obtained at low overhead, there is enough evidence that the approach pays off.

## 6   Conclusions and Future Work

We proposed a technique that fits in contemporary embedded system design flows, complying with the trend of adopting a TLM description as a starting point, which is later refined in the form of TLM+T description. The approach is effective (since it guides optimization towards time-constraint satisfaction) and pragmatic (since it preserves conventional compiler infrastructure).

Experimental results have shown that speed-ups of 1.3 over compiler-optimized code can be reached, while the average overhead of time-constraint analysis is kept bound to the number of instructions.

As future work, we intend to deal with more general machine models (e.g. super-scalars) and to address global optimizations.

## References

1. Vincentelli, A.S.: Defining platform-based design. EEDesign of EETimes (February 2002)
2. Ghenassia, F.: Transaction-level Modeling with SystemC - TLM Concepts and Applications for Embedded Systems. LNCS. Springer, Heidelberg (2005)
3. Leupers, R., Marwedel, P.: Retargetable Compiler Technology for Embedded Systems: Tools and Applications. Kluwer Academic Publishers, Norwell, MA (2001)
4. Micheli, G.D.: Synthesis and Optimization of Digital Circuits. McGraw-Hill, New York (1994)
5. Cormen, T.H., Leiserson, C.E., Rivest, R.L.: Introduction to Algorithms. McGraw-Hill, New York (1990)
6. Mesman, B., Strik, M.T.J., Timmer, A.H., van Meerbergen, J.L., Jess, J.A.G.: Constraint analysis for DSP code generation. In: ISSS 97, pp. 33–40 (1997)

7. Hanono, S., Devadas, S.: Instruction selection, resource allocation, and scheduling in the AVIV retargetable code generator. In: 35th DAC, June 1998, pp. 510–515. ACM Press, New York (1998)
8. Hadjiyiannis, G., Hanono, S., Devadas, S.: ISDL: An instruction set description language for retargetability. In: 34th DAC, June 1998, pp. 299–302. ACM Press, New York (1997)
9. Halambi, A., Shrivastava, A., Dutt, N., Nicolau, A.: A customizable compiler framework for embedded systems. In: International Workshop on Software and Compilers for Embedded Processors (March 2001)
10. Halambi, A., Grun, P., Ganesh, V., Khare, A., Dutt, N., Nicolau, A.: EXPRESSION: A language for architecture exploration through compiler/simulator retargetability. In: Design, Automation and Test in Europe March 1999, pp. 485–490 (1999)
11. Pees, S., Hoffmann, A., Zivojnovic, V., Meyr, H.: LISA — machine description language for cycle-accurate models of programmable DSP architectures. In: 36th DAC, pp. 933–938 (1999)
12. Wahlen, O., Hohenauer, M., Leupers, R., Meyr, H.: Instruction scheduler generation for retargetable compilation. IEEE Design and Test of Computers 20(1), 34–41 (2003)
13. Salto: The Salto Project (2006), http://www.irisa.fr/caps/projects/Salto/
14. Kstner, D.: PROPAN: A retargetable system for postpass optimizations and analyses. In: Davidson, J., Min, S.L. (eds.) LCTES 2000. LNCS, vol. 1985, pp. 63–80. Springer, Heidelberg (2001)
15. ArchC: The ArchC ADL (2005), http://www.archc.org
16. MiBench: Mibench benchmark suite (2006), http://www.eecs.umich.edu/mibench/

# Improving TriMedia Cache Performance by Profile Guided Code Reordering

Norbert Esser[1], Renga Sundararajan[1], and Joachim Trescher[2]

[1] NXP Semiconductors, San Jose, CA, USA
[2] NXP Research, Eindhoven, The Netherlands
{norbert.c.esser, renga.sundararajan, joachim.trescher}@nxp.com

**Abstract.** There is an ever-increasing gap between memory and processor performance. As a result, exploiting the cache becomes increasingly important, especially for embedded systems where cache sizes are much smaller than that of general purpose processors. The fine-tuning of an application with respect to cache behavior is now largely dependent on the skill of the application programmer. Given the difficulty of predicting cache behavior, this is, even when great skill is applied, a cumbersome task. A wide range of approaches, in hardware as well as in software, can be used to relieve the programmer's burden. On the hardware side, we can experiment, for example, with cache sizes, line sizes, replacement policies, and cache organization. On the software side, we can use various optimization techniques like software pipelining, branch prediction, and code reordering. The research described in this paper focussed on improving performance by using code reordering techniques.

This paper reports on the work that we have done to reduce the number of line-fetches in the instruction cache. We have extended the functionality of the linker in the TriMedia compiler chain, such that the number of fetches during program execution is reduced. By reordering the code, we ensure that hot code stays in the cache and the cache is not polluted with cold code. Because fewer fetches are needed we expect a performance increase. By analyzing and profiling code, we obtain execution statistics that can help us find better code-allocations.

**Keywords:** cache, code layout, profiling.

## 1   Introduction

Like other processors, the TriMedia uses an instruction cache to speed up program execution. Code that is executed frequently is termed "hot code" and code that is rarely executed is "cold code". Since cache lines are a finite resource, lines may be victimized and later fetched again. Two aspects affect the number of fetches during program execution. A victimized line may contain hot code and a fetched line may contain cold code, both of which need to be avoided for better I-cache performance.

These aspects bear similarity to register-allocation in compilation. One big difference between register-allocation and cache-line allocation is that cache-line allocation and victimization is performed by a fixed hardware algorithm and can only be influenced indirectly via the layout of the code.

S. Vassiliadis et al. (Eds.): SAMOS 2007, LNCS 4599, pp. 96–106, 2007.

By extending the TriMedia linker with the functionality to reorder code according to linker maps, we are able to investigate various code-reordering algorithms. The linker maps are constructed by using algorithms based on those described by Friedman [1] and Pettis and Hansen [2]. For reference, we also implemented a more basic algorithm that places the most frequently used code fragments consecutively in memory.

There are some unique differentiating aspects of our work compared to previous work. One is that we study code reordering for a VLIW machine. The "code blocks" of VLIW machines are larger than basic blocks of traditional machines which may have influence on the chosen algorithms. We investigate code reordering of decision trees (dtrees)[3], aka, treegions, [4][5]. Our research extends prior work by investigating reordering of both functions and decision trees.

Further, the results for the TriMedia TM3271 [6] show the usefulness of code reordering techniques in an embedded, multi-media context.

## 2   Previous Work

McFarling [7] proposes one of the earliest approaches to improve performance by remapping machine instructions. The approach specifically targets direct mapped instruction caches. Using profiling information, a tree is built with labels that correspond to basic blocks. Labeled blocks should be added to the cache, unlabeled blocks can be excluded from the cache. All instructions with the same label and all instructions with descendant labels are positioned so that they will not interfere in the cache.

Hwu and Chang [8] propose a similar approach to improve the efficiency of caching in the instruction memory hierarchy. They aim at maximizing the sequential and spatial localities by grouping, for each function, the basic blocks that tend to be executed in sequence. Functions are then placed in a sequential order, where each time the most important descendent function is placed after its ancestor.

Pettis and Hansen [2] proposed constructing an undirected edge-weighted call graph, in which nodes correspond to either procedures or basic blocks and the edges respectively correspond to calls between the procedures or to the blocks following each other directly in sequential execution. The edges are weighted by the number of times the call or execution takes place. Nodes joined by an edge with a large weight are merged using a "closest is best" strategy. By minimizing the overlap in cache lines between nodes with a high edge weight, they were able to gain performance improvements of 8 to 10 percent on average. They also conclude that the gain is predominantly due to repositioning basic blocks rather than on reordering procedures.

Friedman [1] proposes an approach similar to that of Pettis and Hansen. He uses a sequence graph instead of a call graph. His algorithm does not use a "closest is best" strategy when merging nodes. Friedman first generates a function call trace. The sequence graph is built up by sectioning of a "window" of this trace and increasing the weight on the arcs between all functions that are together in the window. The complete sequence graph is constructed by then sliding the window over the trace, until the end is reached.

Hashemi et al. [9] improve upon the work of Pettis and Hansen by applying graph-colouring techniques to map cache lines to procedures. Procedures are placed such that the cache lines of a procedure do not overlap with the cache lines of its parents and children in the call graph.

A number of approaches, e.g., those proposed by Gloy et al. [10], Kirovski et al. [11], and Brown et al. [12], have been proposed to further improve on the algorithms mentioned by adding more information to the control flow graph, mostly resulting in a better notion of the temporal correlation between nodes in the graph. More recent optimization approaches, as the ones described by Luk et al. [13], employ similar techniques.

Instead of using dynamic profiling information, some approaches use static estimation techniques, such as those proposed by Hashemi et al. [14] and Mendlson et al. [15].

We do not give an in-depth comparison between these various approaches and our work. Some of the approaches are very different from ours, making comparison difficult. We further consider some aspects future work, see also Section 8

## 3    TriMedia TM3271

This section gives a global overview of the architecture of the TM3271. Since we focus on reducing the instruction cache line fetches, we will focus in particular on the instruction cache architecture.

### 3.1    TM3271 Architecture

The TM3271 is the latest TriMedia VLIW-based media-processor, which is backward source code compatible with other processors in the TriMedia family [16]. Typically, the TM3271 is used as an embedded processor in a System-on-a-Chip (SoC). Table 1 gives an overview of the main architectural features of the TM3271.

### 3.2    TM3271 Instruction Cache Architecture

The instruction cache size of the TM3271 is configurable. The available instruction cache size configurations are: 8, 16, 32, and 64 Kbytes, all with a 128-byte block size. Each block has an own address tag. The cache is 8-way set-associative. A TM3271 with an instruction cache size of 64 KB would therefore have 512 blocks and there would be 64 sets, each containing 8 tags. Each block has a single valid bit, which means that a block and its associated address tag are either entirely valid or invalid. This means that on a cache miss all the 128 bytes are read from memory to make the entire block valid. The instruction cache architecture of the TM3271 is identical to that of the TM3270, which is described in detail in [17].

Instruction addresses are mapped onto the cache as shown in Figure 1. An instruction address consists out of three fields. The set field selects one of the sets in the cache. The offset field indicates the byte offset within the set. The tag field is the instruction's address tag, which is compared against the address tags of the set members. The TM3271 implements a full least-recently-used (LRU) replacement policy. When a cache miss occurs, the instruction cache starts filling the requested block from the beginning of the block.

**Table 1.** TM3271 Architecture

| Architectural feature | Quantity |
|---|---|
| Architecture | 5 issue slot VLIW<br>guarded RISC-like operations |
| Address width | 32 bits |
| Data width | 32 bits |
| Register-file | Unified, 128 32-bit registers |
| Functional units | 41 |
| IEEE-754 floating point | yes |
| SIMD capabilities | 1 x 32-bit, 2 x 16-bit, 4 x 8-bit |
| Instruction cache | 8, 16, 32, or 64 Kbytes, 128-byte lines,<br>8 way set-associative,<br>LRU replacement policy |
| Data cache | 8, 16, 32, 64, or 128 Kbytes,<br>128-byte lines, 4 way set-associative,<br>LRU replacement policy,<br>Allocate-on-write miss policy |

**Fig. 1.** Instruction address for 64 KB instruction cache

# 4   Algorithms

This section describes the algorithms that we have implemented. All the algorithms described here focus on reducing the number of incurred instruction cache misses by reordering functions or dtrees. We will explain the algorithms using dtrees, but the case for functions is fully analogous. "A decision tree is defined as a portion of code with one entry point and potentially many exit points. Decision trees can also contain control flow constructs such as if-then-else or select-or. Because a function call involves returning to the instruction after the function was called, a function call will end that path of the decision tree" [3]. We choose to reorder dtrees because they correspond to the smallest relocatable objects in the TriMedia linker. Further, the linker could be easily extended to add the functionality to relocate dtrees. We can relocate a function by relocating all its corresponding dtrees.

## 4.1   Execution Count

We start out with a basic algorithm. For each dtree we derive statistics of how often it is executed. We use the execution count as a measure to identify hot code. The higher the execution count, the hotter the code. We can reduce the number of instruction cache misses by ensuring that the hottest dtrees do not conflict with each other in the cache. We observe that by placing two pieces of code directly after each other in memory they will not compete for the same set in the cache. The basic algorithm is based on this. It sorts the dtrees by execution count and places them in the resulting order.

## 4.2 Sequential Locality

The basic algorithm of Section 4.1 does not consider any locality. For example the two dtrees with the highest execution count may be executed in completely different parts of the program and may therefore not compete with each other in the cache anyway. To improve our algorithm we introduce a notion of sequential locality. Two dtrees have a high degree of sequential locality if they tend to be executed in a sequential order. We want to prevent that pairs of dtrees that have a high sequential locality and are often executed compete with each other in the cache. If we do not prevent this, then we run the risk of a high degree of cache thrashing.

We determine sequential locality by using dynamic control flow graphs. A dynamic control flow graph gives an overview of the control flow during execution of an application. In our case, the nodes in the graph correspond to dtrees and the edges correspond to control flow passing from one dtree to another. We annotate the edges with the number of times the edge is taken during execution. We derive our dynamic control flow graphs from execution traces. For example, the dynamic control flow graph presented in Figure 3 corresponds to the execution trace shown in Figure 2. Node A has a higher degree of sequential locality with node B than with nodes C and D, which by definition means that control flows more often between nodes A and B than between nodes A and C and nodes A and D. Our dynamic control flow graph are essentially the same as the sequence graphs described by Friedman [1], where we take the window on the execution trace to be of size 2.

After we build up a dynamic control flow graph, we can order the dtrees using the algorithm as described by Friedman [1]. The algorithm repeatedly selects the edge with the highest count and merges the nodes it connects. Merging two nodes corresponds to placing the related dtrees consecutively in memory. This ensures that they do not compete with each other in the cache.

If we execute the algorithm on our example dynamic control flow graph, depicted in Figure 3, then it starts with randomly choosing either the edge between A and B or the edge between C and D, since these two edges have the highest count. Let us assume the algorithm chooses the edge between A and B first. The nodes A and B are merged and the edge counts are updated. Figure 4 depicts the graph after the first iteration of the algorithm.

In the second iteration the edge between C and D is chosen. Again the nodes are merged, and edge counts are updated. Figure 5 shows the resulting graph.

Finally the edge between AB and CD is chosen and the nodes are merged, resulting in the ordering ABCD.

## 4.3 Closest Is Best

The algorithm described in Section 4.2 merges nodes through simple concatenation. We can extend this algorithm by a smarter placement of the nodes that are being merged.

A D A C D C D C D A B A B C A B A

**Fig. 2.** Example execution trace

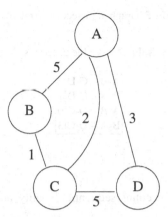

**Fig. 3.** Example dynamic control flow graph

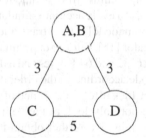

**Fig. 4.** Graph after first iteration

Pettis and Hansen [2] present an algorithm that uses a "closest is best" strategy to determine the relative placement. The main idea is that if control frequently flows from one node to another, then these nodes need to be placed close together. The described algorithm adopts the same approach as described in 4.2, but the actual merging of the nodes differs. The original graph is used to determine mutual relationships between nodes and this is used to choose the actual ordering.

In our case, when merging nodes, we use the original dynamic control flow graph to choose the ordering by determining which dtrees have the strongest relationship. See for example Figure 5. The next step is to merge nodes AB and CD. Instead of simply concatenating CD after AB when merging these nodes, we can also try to determine which ordering is best. We identify four possible orderings, as reverse orderings can be considered identical. Table 2 shows the possible orderings and the mutual edge weights from the original graph in Figure 3.

We observe that in the original graph A and D have the strongest relationship (edge with weight 3) and we therefore choose the fourth ordering, being BADC.

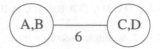

**Fig. 5.** Graph after second iteration

**Table 2.** Possible orderings

| A-B – C-D | 2 |
| B-A – C-D | 1 |
| A-B – D-C | 0 |
| B-A – D-C | 3 |

## 5    Methodology

We implemented the execution count, sequential locality, and closest is best reordering algorithms.

We obtain the execution count statistics and the function and dtree execution traces, which we use as input to our algorithms, from a functional simulator. For the actual performance measurements we use a cycle accurate simulator, which is derived from the original hardware design by automatic RTL-to-C translation. The RTL-to-C translation is done using the free tool Verilator [18]. For our experiments we simulate the TM3271 with instruction cache sizes of 16, 32 and 64 Kbytes and a data cache size of 128 Kbytes.

The TriMedia linker links code according to the order of the object files on the command line. The order of object files effects the order of code and therefore possibly the performance. We therefore not only look at the "out-of-the-box" object ordering but also 20 random object orderings. We further obtain the results of linking with 20 random dtree orderings. We finally compare the performance using the implemented algorithms to the best performance obtained from all the random orderings and the "out-of-the-box" ordering.

We chose a number of typical TriMedia Media applications: an MPEG2 video decoder, an 8/10-bit up-converter, a 10-bit halo-reduced up-converter, a motion estimator, and an H.264 CABAC decoder. For reference we also looked at Spec95 Compress, being a non-media application.

All applications were compiled with the TriMedia Compilation System (TCS) 5.01 compiler and with only the default compiler options. The reordering algorithms are applicable with any set of compiler options, however, choosing different compiler options can have both a positive and a negative effect on the performance of the algorithms. We chose the default compiler options since those are the options that most users use.

## 6    Results

We first show the effect of reordering using the existing TriMedia linker. Figure 6 shows the results of linking with the original, "out-of-the-box" object order and 20 random object orderings. The minimum and maximum number of cache misses obtained over the

| | | I-cache size | | |
|---|---|---|---|---|
| | | 16 | 32 | 64 |
| Media | Min | 395002 | 8896 | 2232 |
| | Max | 488764 | 48060 | 2378 |
| | Mean | 434759 | 22832 | 2285 |
| | Median | 437941 | 19817 | 2276 |
| | StDev | 22311 | 9704 | 36 |
| Compress | Min | 3164 | 413 | 248 |
| | Max | 3404 | 590 | 252 |
| | Mean | 3368 | 563 | 249 |
| | Median | 3404 | 590 | 248 |
| | StDev | 88 | 65 | 1 |

**Fig. 6.** I-cache misses: random reordering of object files

| | | I-cache size | | |
|---|---|---|---|---|
| | | 16 | 32 | 64 |
| Media | Min | 501454 | 67488 | 2496 |
| | Max | 719822 | 151334 | 12047 |
| | Mean | 613349 | 106783 | 3676 |
| | Median | 623093 | 108896 | 2975 |
| | StDev | 51928 | 26546 | 2261 |
| Compress | Min | 3952 | 441 | 252 |
| | Max | 9361 | 1754 | 312 |
| | Mean | 6725 | 1024 | 278 |
| | Median | 6853 | 976 | 280 |
| | StDev | 1331 | 436 | 19 |

**Fig. 7.** I-cache misses: random reordering of dtrees

various orderings shows the potential effect of code ordering on performance, especially with smaller cache sizes.

Figure 7 shows the results of linking with 20 random dtree orderings. Again the effect that the order of code can have on performance is very clear. We also note that the performance of randomly reordering dtrees is worse than randomly reordering object files. This is not surprising, since only reordering object files still maintains code locality, which is completely lost when randomly reordering dtrees.

Figure 8 shows the results for function and dtree reordering on the TM3271 for various instruction cache sizes, using execution count (EC), sequential locality (SL) and closest is best (CB) approaches to reordering applied to functions or dtrees. The figure shows the number of instruction cache misses, when using the various algorithms, in percentages of the number of instruction cache misses in the original executable (denoted as Org). As mentioned in Section 5 the numbers for the original executable are obtained by taking the best performance from all the random orderings and the "out-of-the-box" ordering. Note that this provides a favorable base for the "original" ordering.

If we look at dtree reordering we see a consistent improvement for all benchmarks across the various instruction cache sizes. In all cases we outperform the best random ordering. As discussed in Section 4, the execution count, sequential locality, and closest

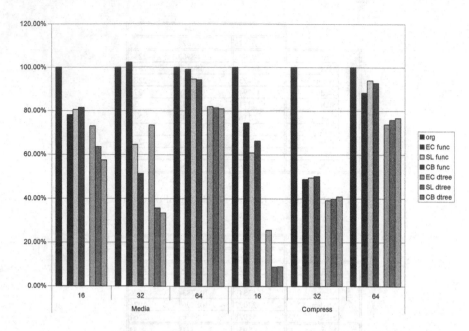

**Fig. 8.** Reduction in I-cache misses due to reordering

is best algorithms are increasingly more sophisticated than the previous one. In general the more sophisticated algorithms outperform the simpler ones. With a relatively large instruction cache size we see however that the difference in performance between the various algorithms is small. This is not surprising since it is more likely that the application's working set will fit in the cache. This of course means that there will be less instruction cache misses to start off with and therefore also less to optimize.

If we look at the function reordering we again see a consistent improvement for all benchmarks across the various instruction cache sizes. In the case of function reordering it seems harder to predict which algorithm will perform best and in a lot of cases the simplest algorithm (using only execution count statistics) even performs best. It is clear that in all cases dtree reordering outperforms function reordering, especially with smaller cache sizes. On average we see that dtree reordering outperforms function reordering by at least a factor 2. This is to be expected, since functions tend to have both "hot code" and "cold" code and as a result reordering at function level is therefore often too coarse grained.

Finally it is interesting to note that the cache sizes have an influence on the performance of the algorithms. In general: the smaller the cache, the larger the initial amount of cache misses will be, and the more room for improvement. On the other hand, if the cache size is smaller than the working set of the application, there will be an inherent number of cache misses. An example of this is seen with the Media benchmarks (see Figures 6, 7, and 8) where the reordering algorithms perform best with a 32 Kbyte cache. With a 16Kbyte cache the cache is smaller than the working set of some of the applications and although the reordering algorithms can still significantly reduce the number of cache misses they are not as effective as when using a larger cache. When using a 64Kbyte cache the initial number of cache misses is low to begin with, so there is less improvement to be gotten and therefore the algorithms are less effective.

# 7    Conclusions

We have shown that function and dtree reordering using profile information can give a substantial reduction in instruction cache misses on TriMedia. We have further shown that dtree reordering on average gives twice as much reduction in instruction cache misses as function reordering. We have also shown that especially for smaller cache size the "closest is best" algorithm performs the best, while at larger cache sizes the performance difference between the algorithms is very small.

# 8    Future Work

For newer multimedia algorithms (like H.264, and WMV9) the instruction cache performance is becoming increasingly important, while the data cache performance remains dominant. Our work can be extended by including data cache performance optimizations, e.g. as described by Luk et al. [13]. This can be further extended by studying how our algorithms can steer the software and combined software/hardware data prefetching in the TriMedia.

Another extension consists of investigating how our algorithms can steer the cache-locking mechanisms available on the TriMedia.

Current work used execution traces to derive (dynamic) control flow graphs. We plan to investigate the usefulness of static control flow graphs in future, to eliminate the need for a separate profiling run. Approaches using static estimation techniques, for example as proposed by Hashemi et al. [14] and Mendlson et al. [15], have shown promising results.

Other promising future improvements include adding more information to the control flow graphs, such as a better notion of temporal correlation between the nodes in the graph, or excluding certain nodes (say, those of interrupt service routines).

# Acknowledgments

We thank all members of the TriMedia compiler team at NXP Research for their help and valuable feedback. We also thank Jan Hoogerbrugge at NXP Research and Paul Gorissen, Wil Michiels and Henk Schepers at Philips Research for all their advice and guidance. Finally, we would like to thank the anonymous reviewers for their constructive comments and suggestions.

# References

1. Friedman, N.: GNU Rope–a subroutine position optimizer (1998)
2. Pettis, K., Hansen, R.C.: Profile guided code positioning. In: PLDI '90. Proceedings of the ACM SIGPLAN 1990 conference on Programming language design and implementation, pp. 16–27. ACM Press, New York (1990)

3. Philips Semiconductors: TriMedia™ Compilation System 5.01 User Manuals, vol. 3, Ch. 8, pp. 173–184 (2006)
4. Banerjia, S., Havanki, W.A., Conte, T.M.: Treegion scheduling for highly parallel processors. In: Lengauer, C., Griebl, M., Gorlatch, S. (eds.) Euro-Par 1997. LNCS, vol. 1300, pp. 1074–1078. Springer, Heidelberg (1997)
5. Havanki, W., Banerjia, S., Conte, T.: Treegion scheduling for wide issue processors. In: HPCA '98. Proceedings of the 4th International Symposium on High-Performance Computer Architecture, Washington, DC, 266. IEEE Computer Society Press, Los Alamitos (1998)
6. van de Waerdt, J.W., Vassiliadis, S., Das, S., Mirolo, S., Yen, C., Zhong, B., Basto, C., van Itegem, J.P., Amirtharaj, D., Kalra, K., Rodriguez, P., van Antwerpen, H.: The tm3270 media-processor. In: MICRO 38. Proceedings of the 38th annual IEEE/ACM International Symposium on Microarchitecture, Washington, DC, pp. 331–342. IEEE Computer Society Press, Los Alamitos (2005)
7. McFarling, S.: Program optimization for instruction caches. In: ASPLOS-III. Proceedings of the third international conference on Architectural support for programming languages and operating systems, pp. 183–191. ACM Press, New York (1989)
8. Hwu, W.W., Chang, P.P.: Achieving high instruction cache performance with an optimizing compiler. In: ISCA '89. Proceedings of the 16th annual international symposium on Computer architecture, pp. 242–251. ACM Press, New York (1989)
9. Hashemi, A.H., Kaeli, D.R., Calder, B.: Efficient procedure mapping using cache line coloring. In: PLDI '97. Proceedings of the ACM SIGPLAN 1997 conference on Programming language design and implementation, pp. 171–182. ACM Press, New York (1997)
10. Gloy, N., Blackwell, T., Smith, M.D., Calder, B.: Procedure placement using temporal ordering information. In: MICRO 30. Proceedings of the 30th annual ACM/IEEE international symposium on Microarchitecture, Washington, DC, pp. 303–313. IEEE Computer Society Press, Los Alamitos (1997)
11. Kirovski, D., Lee, C., Potkonjak, M., Mangione-Smith, W.H.: Synthesis of power efficient systems-on-silicon. In: Asia and South Pacific Design Automation Conference, pp. 557–562 (1998)
12. Brown, S.S., Asher, J., Mangione-Smith, W.H.: Offline program re-mapping to improve branch prediction efficiency in embedded systems. In: ASP-DAC '00. Proceedings of the 2000 conference on Asia South Pacific design automation, pp. 111–116. ACM Press, New York (2000)
13. Luk, C.K., Muth, R., Patil, H., Cohn, R., Lowney, G.: Ispike: A post-link optimizer for the Intel® Itanium® architecture. In: CGO '04. Proceedings of the international symposium on Code generation and optimization, Washington, DC, USA, p. 15. IEEE Computer Society Press, Los Alamitos (2004)
14. Hashemi, A., Kaeli, D., Calder, B.: Procedure mapping using static call graph estimation. In: Proceedings of the Workshop on Interaction between Compiler and Computer Architecture (1997)
15. Mendlson, A., Pinter, S.S., Shtokhamer, R.: Compile time instruction cache optimizations. SIGARCH Comput. Archit. News 22, 44–51 (1994)
16. Rathnam, S., Slavenburg, G.: An architectural overview of the programmable multimedia processor, TM-1. In: COMPCON '96. Proceedings of the 41st IEEE International Computer Conference, Washington, DC, 319. IEEE Computer Society Press, Los Alamitos (1996)
17. van de Waerdt, J.: The TM3270 Media-processor. PhD thesis, Delft University of Technology (2006)
18. Snyder, W.: Verilator-3.631 (2007)

# A Streaming Machine Description and Programming Model

Paul Carpenter, David Rodenas, Xavier Martorell,
Alex Ramirez, and Eduard Ayguadé

Barcelona Supercomputing Center, Barcelona, Spain
Universitat Politècnica de Catalunya, Barcelona, Spain
HiPEAC European Network of Excellence

**Abstract.** In this paper we present the initial development of a streaming environment based on a programming model and machine description. The stream programming model consists of an extension to the C language and it's translation towards a streaming machine. The extensions will be a set of OpenMP-like directives. We show how a serial application can be converted into a streaming parallel application using the proposed annotations. We also show how the machine description can be used to parametrize a cost-model simulator to predict the performance of the stream program. The cost model allows the compiler to determine the best task partitioning and scheduling for each architecture.

## 1 Introduction

A stream programming model is most likely to be adopted by the mainstream if it is possible to incrementally modify an existing sequential application into a streaming one. We do not expect the programmer to learn a whole new language before any benefit can be seen, nor do we assume that the compiler can automatically extract a stream program from the original code without modifications. We propose a new streaming environment[1] consisting in a Stream Programming Model (SPM), implemented as an annotated version of the C programming language, and an Abstract Streaming Machine (ASM), implemented as a cost-model simulator. The SPM and ASM should cooperate to make the same code with the same annotations suitable for many different architectures.

We have developed a runtime to experiment with the SPM and their possible interpretations. We have manually applied transformations to a small set of benchmarks. We have collected traces showing the state and communications of each application. The cost-model simulator evaluates costs for a prototype compiler to guide the partitioning and scheduling of the stream program onto the hardware. It uses a machine description and either the application description and its proposed mapping onto the hardware or a previously generated trace in which all communication between tasks is visible. All results and studies are visualized using Paraver[2] traces, which allow us to see what is happening at each timestamp with a minimum overhead.

S. Vassiliadis et al. (Eds.): SAMOS 2007, LNCS 4599, pp. 107–116, 2007.

The rest of the paper is structured as follows: Section 2 presents the Stream Programming Model, Section 3 presents the Abstract Streaming Machine, and Section 4 describes our initial experiments. Section 5 compares our approach to related work and Section 6 concludes the paper.

## 2    Stream Programming Model

The SPM describes an application as multiple tasks connected via point-to-point streams. Each task may be viewed as an independent process, with all its data private. Communication and synchronization of tasks happens only via streams. A stream is directed, and we refer to its ends, *stream-ends*, from the point of view of the task, so that the producer has an output stream and the consumer has an input stream; the two ends are permanently connected together, and cannot be moved during execution.

### 2.1    Directives

We have defined SPM as a set of directives in the same style as OpenMP[3]. The OpenMP directives allow one to start with an existing serial application and parallelize it incrementally, checking at each step that the program still works. This allows nonexpert users to obtain immediate benefit and learn more about it only as further knowledge is required.

SPM directives define how the application is converted into a stream program, by defining the tasks and the streams between them. The outermost directive is the #pragma taskgroup, which defines the region in which the tasks exist. It initializes all its tasks, starts them, executes the body of the outer *control-task*, finally waiting for all of the tasks to finish; i.e. it defines an implicit barrier. The #pragma task directive defines a task, and must be lexically inside the #pragma taskgroup; any statements not enclosed by a #pragma task belong to the control-task. It is possible to nest task and taskgroup definitions. The pragma task directive may have two clauses: input and output, both taking a list of variables. The input(v1,v2,...,vn) clause defines n input streams that receive the values of v1,v2,...,vn. The output(w1,w2,...,wm) clause defines m output streams that send the values of w1,w2,...,wm produced by the task. The body specified by the task directive will be executed as many times as it has inputs available.

Figure 1 shows an example program, tolower, which defines a taskgroup region that contains the whole loop, and two explicit task definitions, each containing a single line of code. In total, there are therefore three tasks, the first is the control-task (referred to as *fread*), and the other two are the first #pragma task (referred to as *tolower*) and the second #pragma task (referred to as *fwrite*). There are three visible stream-ends and two streams. The resulting graph is shown at Figure 2 a).

```
int main(int argc, char **argv)
{
  FILE *in, *out;
  char c,x,y;
  in = fopen(argv[1], "r");
  out = fopen(argv[2], "w");
  fread(&c, sizeof(char), 1, in);
  #pragma taskgroup /* fread */
  while (!feof(in))
  {
    #pragma task input(c) output(x)   /* tolower */
    if ('A' <= c && c <= 'Z')
        x = c - 'A' + 'a';
    else
        x = c;

    #pragma task input(x)  /* fwrite */
    fwrite(&x, sizeof(char), 1, out);

    fread(&c, sizeof(char), 1, in);
  }
  fclose(in);
  fclose(out);
  return 0;
}
```

**Fig. 1.** Annotated C code for tolower example

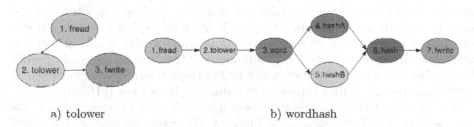

a) tolower                                    b) wordhash

**Fig. 2.** Example communication-graphs

## 2.2  Graph Optimization

As we have seen in the previous example we need some kind of graph analysis
in order to connect the two ends of each stream together. If the compiler is not
able to do this optimization it is always possible to send the data via a common
outer task.

We suggest to use data flow analysis to detect stream connections. Automatic
dependence analysis in the compiler can take place either when building the
graph of stream tasks, or when transforming the intermediate representation.
The former is at the original source level. The compiler will obtain the positions
where data is consumed (...=v) and where data is produced (v=...) and will
consider them as stream-ends. The latter is at transformed intermediate representation level. In that point compiler has created a large number of non-efficient
stream connections translated as special push and pop instructions. Pushes have
to be performed as soon as possible, and Pops as late as possible. If a value, x,

popped from one stream is immediately pushed, without modification, onto another stream, then it is usually preferable to replace the outgoing stream with a direct one from the source of x to its destination. If x is not otherwise consumed by the intermediate task, then the incoming stream may be removed.

In case the resulting graph does not contain cycles, the compiler can apply blocking to allow the unrolling of the task control-loop and also its vectorization.

# 3   Abstract Streaming Machine

The ASM description is defined in three parts: the program, machine and system. The program description defines the application, its tasks and its streams. The machine description defines the available processors, buses and communications properties. The system description is the glue that maps the program into the machine.

## 3.1   Program Description

For the purposes of the cost-model simulator, a streaming program is a directed graph of *tasks* and *streams*. Each stream carries a sequence of homogeneous values between tasks. Each task has, as the elementary unit of work, a work function, which consists of three distinct stages: a *pop* stage, in which a fixed number of elements are popped from each input stream, a *processing* stage, in which a fixed amount of work is performed, and a *push* stage, in which a fixed number of elements are pushed onto each output stream. Pops and pushes block when the stream becomes empty or full respectively. This definition of a streaming program is thus similar to Synchronous Data Flow (SDF)[4].

The program description specifies the graph topology, data rates, and processing costs; see the tolower example in Figure 3. The execution time of each kernel is currently constant, and estimated by the compiler, although it could come from a statistical model, with parameters estimated by the compiler.

It is possible that the producer and consumer tasks do not push and pop the same number of elements per iteration, in which case the producer and consumer

```
# Define program
def setup_program():

    # Streams
    #                      num name elemSize
    streams = [ Stream ( 1, 'c', 1 ),
                Stream ( 2, 'x', 1 ) ]

    # Tasks
    #               num   name      inputs         outputs       cpu_time
    tasks = [ Task ( 1, 'fread',   [],            [('c',1,2)],  5 ),
              Task ( 2, 'tolower', [('c',1,2)],   [('x',1,2)],  5 ),
              Task ( 3, 'fwrite',  [('x',1,2)],   [],           5 ) ]

    return Program ( tasks, streams )
```

**Fig. 3.** Program description for tolower example

execute at different rates. The stream constructor has an optional argument giving the number of elements to prequeue onto the stream, as required for feedback loops.

The program description defines the default length of queue for each stream, normally set to a value large enough to prevent deadlock. For example, setting the queue length to be smaller than the number of elements pushed by the producer at each iteration would cause it to immediately deadlock. The system mapping file can override these values as necessary to get good performance.

## 3.2   Machine Description

The machine description defines the platform on which a streaming program may be executed, and is represented by a hypergraph of *processors* connected via communication hardware *links*, each joining two or more processors. Each communications link has a single unbounded queue to hold the messages ready to be transmitted, and one or more *channels* on which to transmit them. The reason for having two levels: channels and links, rather than just one, is that it allows the choice of channel within a link to be deferred until run time.

Communication links are not executed directly, instead corresponding to shared state and parameters for the channels. *Threads* and *edges* are used to model the compiled *binary* (see next section), but here it is useful to know that when a stream is statically mapped onto the available links in the hardware, it is divided into edges, each of which corresponds to one hop in the route.

When a processor is connected to a link with more than one channel, we assume that it is not possible for the same processor to transmit onto more than one channel in the same link simultaneously; similarly for receive. The interface between the processor and link may be configured as either full-duplex or half-duplex, depending whether it is possible to transmit and receive on different channels at the same time.

Figure 4 shows a simplified model of the Cell processor [5]. Following Girona et al.[6] we approximate the four rings of the EIB using a set of buses (in this example four buses). The interface of each processor to the EIB has bandwidth equal to a single channel of the EIB, so it can be represented using the model of the interface, as presented above (in full-duplex mode). We are currently in the process of validating our approach and determining the optimal values of the parameters.

## 3.3   System Description

The system description references the program and machine descriptions, and maps the former onto the latter to provide the binary. Together, the *program*, *platform* and *binary* form the executable system to be simulated. The binary is comprised of threads, each of which executes a list of tasks on a particular processor, and edges, each of which is part of a stream statically routed onto a fixed link.

```
# Define platform
def setup_platform( ):

    # define processors
    processors = [ Processor ( 1, 'PPE'),
                   Processor ( 2, 'SPE0'), Processor ( 3, 'SPE1'),
                   Processor ( 4, 'SPE2'), Processor ( 5, 'SPE3'),
                   Processor ( 6, 'SPE4'), Processor ( 7, 'SPE5'),
                   Processor ( 8, 'SPE6'), Processor ( 9, 'SPE7') ]

    # Model EIB as four buses; although it's actually four rings

    # All processors are on the bus
    processorsOnBus = [ proc.name for proc in processors ]

    # Define bus
    #                 num name       processors     start bandwidth gap
    links = [ Link ( 1, 'EIB', processorsOnBus, 159, 8, 2, numChannels=4) ]

    return Platform ( processors, links )
```

**Fig. 4.** Simplified platform description for Cell

The simulator will automatically generate a route for each stream, assuming one exists, using the minimum number of hops. It does not however attempt to balance the total communication load across the network. Local communication within a processor is not normally modelled by the simulator, so is effectively zero latency and infinite bandwidth. In all cases it is possible to override the routing decisions in the system description file.

Each message is transferred using a single (unidirectional) transfer on the bus, which carries both the data and the necessary control.

Figure 5 shows a potential mapping of the tolower program onto a CPU plus accelerator. It is assumed that the accelerator does not have the ability to perform I/O, so the fread and fwrite tasks have both been mapped to the CPU, in different threads to allow concurrency. Note that the system description only deals with issues of partitioning and scheduling. Compiler optimizations such as loop transformations or blocking should be represented at the program level.

```
# Define binary
def setup_binary( program ):

    # Threads
    # num name proc tasks
    threads = [ Thread ( 1, 'A', 'CPU', [ 'fread' ] ),
                Thread ( 2, 'B', 'Accelerator', [ 'tolower' ] ),
                Thread ( 3, 'C', 'CPU', [ 'fwrite' ] ) ]

    return Binary( threads )
```

**Fig. 5.** Mapping file for tolower program on CPU plus accelerator

Figure 6 shows a Paraver trace for the simulation of the tolower program, as defined by the Figure 3. Each row corresponds to a thread, but it is possible,

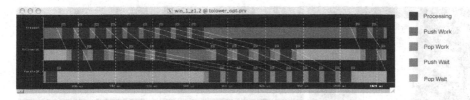

**Fig. 6.** Tolower simulation on Cell Paraver trace

using the Visualizer module of Paraver, to plot processors or tasks instead from the same trace.

## 4   Experiments

We have manually transformed two example applications, tolower and word-hash, using the shown directives. Both are graph optimized and we have applied blocking of 128 elements.

The translated source code uses the *acolib* runtime, and has been tested on Intel, PowerPC and OpenPower platforms. Each task has its own dedicated processor. We present traces for the tolower example on a two-processor dual core PowerPC970MP (total 4 cores), and the wordhash example on a two-processor dual core dual thread Power5 (total 8 threads).

Figure 7 shows a trace for the tolower example. The color of the line represents the state of the task at any given time. Cyan represents idle state, blue represents computing state, and yellow are the communication lines. The trace shows the communication latencies and the computation time of each task. Because we are executing in shared memory the latency is negligible. The trace shows that input task takes more time than tolower and fwrite tasks together. The ASM should predict this, and the compiler may use this information to merge the tolower and fwrite tasks.

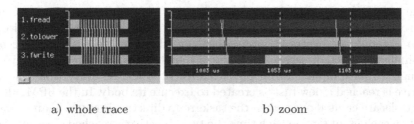

a) whole trace                              b) zoom

**Fig. 7.** Paraver trace for the tolower example

The wordhash example, shown in Figure 2 b), has two main characteristics: it sends complex data structures through streams (an array of five elements), and it has conditional data flow. Figure 8 shows a trace for this example. We can observe that tasks 4 through 7 are executed once every five iterations. This

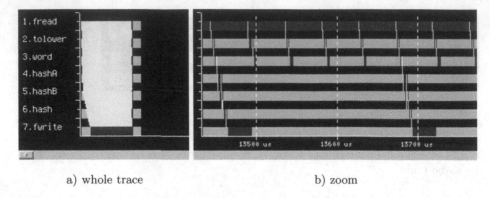

a) whole trace                                    b) zoom

**Fig. 8.** Paraver trace for the wordhash example

is because their tasks are defined inside a conditional statement that is only satisfied every five iterations.

## 5   Related Work

There are some other models similar to the SPM; for example StreamIt[7], and GNU Radio[8]. StreamIt is a whole infrastructure with its own language: a mix between C and Java oriented to filters, and a compiler able to deal with the filters and interconnections. There are some limitations: each filter has exactly one input and output stream, and streams can only carry values from a small set of primitive types. GNU Radio is a framework developed in C++ and Python. The graph of filters and connections is described using Python, and the filters are constructed as C++ classes. GNU Radio has its own scheduler and the system can be deployed on multiple architectures, even including FPGA. GNU Radio provides more than 100 blocks. Both StreamIt and GNU Radio are designed for signal processing applications, and require the program to be written specifically in terms of streaming blocks.

The proposal for OpenMP 3.0[9] supports task parallelism using the new taskgroup and task directives. The task directive specifies that the serial code within it should be executed by another thread inside the taskgroup's scope. The similarly named directives in the SPM intentionally have similar behaviour, although we have input and output streams. In OpenMP every time the task directive is reached a new task is created to execute its body. In the SPM, all the inner tasks are created once when the taskgroup directive is reached, and a value is sent on each input stream each time the task directive is reached. This is a form of synchronization that does not exist in the OpenMP 3.0 proposal. However, there are other proposals for OpenMP that add synchronization between threads. Gonzalez et al. [10][11] propose three new directives: PRED, SUCC and NAME. The NAME directive labels a worksharing, and this label can be used by PRED and SUCC directives, which specify synchronization. Another approach using annotated C is Cell superscalar[12], which uses a task directive to mark the inputs and outputs of a function. Each time the function is called, new tasks and dependencies between them are tracked using the information about the inputs and outputs.

Dimemas[13] is a simulator designed to predict the performance of an application running on a different system configuration. It takes as input a Paraver trace and the system parameters, generating a new trace for the target system. The cost model simulator is able to use a Paraver input trace in a similar manner.

# 6   Conclusions

As far as we know this is the first attempt to define a streaming language that allows an existing serial application to be converted into a streaming program using only pragma-style directives. This approach allows a nonexpert programmer to modify the application step by step. We have proposed a small set of basic directives, which have easy to understand and predictable behaviour; in the future we will extend our set of directives as necessary.

We have presented some very simple benchmarks, which we have used to test the algorithm and experiment with the cost model. We can see how simple applications can be converted automatically into stream programs with minimal programmer effort. We expect to extend our set of directives to handle new cases; for example tasks defined outside the lexical scope of the taskgroup. We have modelled these benchmarks using a simple cost-model simulator, visualizing the execution using Paraver, and have seen behaviour similar to that on the real hardware. We expect to integrate the work into a real compiler that takes a serial application with minimal markup, automatically partitioning and scheduling the tasks for optimal performance on a given architecture.

# Acknowledgements

We would like to acknowledge our partners in the Acotes project for the insightful discussions on the topics presented in this paper. This research is supported by the Spanish Government under contract CICYT TIN200407739C0201, and the IST program of the European Community under contract IST034869 (Acotes Project).

# References

1. Carpenter, P., Rodenas, D., Martorell, X., Ramirez, A., Ayguade, E.: Code generation for streaming applications based on an abstract machine description. Technical Report UPC-DAC-RR-CAP-2007-3, Universitat Politecnica de Catalunya (April 2007)
2. CEPBA: Paraver performance visualization and analysis tool,
   http://www.cepba.upc.edu/paraver/
3. OpenMP: OpenMP Application Program Interface, http://www.openmp.org/

4. Lee, E., Messerschmitt, D.: Synchronous data flow. Proceedings of the IEEE 75(9), 1235–1245 (1987)
5. Chen, T., Raghavan, R., Dale, J., Iwata, E.: Cell Broadband Engine Architecture and its first implementation. IBM developerWorks (2005)
6. Girona, S., Labarta, J., Badia, R.: Validation of Dimemas communication model for MPI collective operations. In: Proc. EuroPVM/MPI (2000)
7. Gordon, M., Thies, W., Amarasinghe, S.: Exploiting coarse-grained task, data, and pipeline parallelism in stream programs. In: Proceedings of the 12th international conference on Architectural support for programming languages and operating systems, pp. 151–162 (2006)
8. Blossom, E.: GNU radio: tools for exploring the radio frequency spectrum. Linux Journal 2004, 122 (2004)
9. Eduard, A., Copty, N., Duran, A., Hoeflinger, J., Lin, Y., Federico, M., Su, E., Unnikrishnan, P., Guansong, Z.: A proposal for task parallelism in OpenMP. Submitted to IWOMP2007 (2007)
10. Gonzalez, M., Ayguade, E., Martorell, X., Labarta, J.: Complex Pipelined Executions in OpenMP Parallel Applications. International Conference on Parallel Processing (ICPP'2001) (to appear)
11. Gonzalez, M., Ayguade, E., Martorell, X., Labarta, J.: Exploiting pipelined executions in OpenMP. Parallel Processing 2003. In: Proceedings. 2003 International Conference on pp. 153–160 (2003)
12. Bellens, P., Perez, J., Badia, R., Labarta, J., Center, B., II, U., Girona, J.: CellSs: a Programming Model for the Cell BE Architecture. In: Proceedings of the 2006 ACM/IEEE Conference on Supercomputing (2006)
13. CEPBA: Dimemas performance analysis tool, http://www.cepba.upc.edu/dimemas/

# Mapping and Performance Evaluation for Heterogeneous MP-SoCs Via Packing

Bastian Ristau and Gerhard Fettweis

TU Dresden, Vodafone Chair Mobile Communications Systems
01062 Dresden, Germany
{ristau, fettweis}@ifn.et.tu-dresden.de

**Abstract.** The computational demand of signal processing algorithms is rising continuously. Heterogeneous embedded multiprocessor systems-on-chips are one solution to tackle this demand. But to be able to take advantage of the benefits of these systems, new strategies are required how to map applications to such a system and how to evaluate the system's performance at a very early design stage. We will present a static, analytical, bottom-up methodology for temporal and spatial mapping of applications to MP-SoCs based on packing. Furthermore we will demonstrate how the result can be used for performance evaluation and system improvement without the need for simulations.

## 1 Introduction

The computational demand of signal processing algorithms is rising continuously. Heterogeneous embedded systems-on-chip are one solution to tackle this demand. Though ASIC centered single chip solutions are usually smaller and more energy efficient [1], flexibility and reusability of MP-SoC components is comparatively higher. This is important especially in signal processing, since it enables to react to future changes in signal processing algorithms or even to implement new algorithms without changing the hardware. But to take advantage of this flexibility new strategies are required to determine how to map applications to such a system and to evaluate the system's performance at a very early design stage.

We will present a static, analytical, bottom-up methodology for mapping applications spatial and temporal to a given architecture following the Y-Chart approach [2]. The basic idea of the Y-Chart approach is to model applications and architecture separately, to perform a mapping of application to architecture and to iterate over different mappings, architectures and application descriptions until the desired architecture and mapping is found. In our proposed methodology the iterations over different mappings is done automatically. Furthermore the resulting static mapping can be utilized for performance evaluation and system improvement without the need for simulations. For determining an initial system there already exist works (e.g. [3,4]) using linear or multi-objective optimization (MOO). These can be used easily in interaction with our method.

In this paper we will concentrate on mapping for minimal execution time, although the methodology is not restricted to this. In a lot of signal processing applications we have to face semi-hard real-time constraints. Thus, it is important to know in the first place, if the chosen system can meet the given timing constraints. If not, the system

S. Vassiliadis et al. (Eds.): SAMOS 2007, LNCS 4599, pp. 117–126, 2007.
© Springer-Verlag Berlin Heidelberg 2007

has to be modified. We think of this of a starting point for further optimizations, if the timing requirements are met. This can be done by modifying some constraints and the objective in our methodology, but also by applying other approaches, e.g. [5,6,7,8].

We rejected the use of MOO in the first performance evaluation step, because there are two major downsides. Firstly, MOO produces a set of pareto-optimal solutions, from which the preferred one has to be chosen manually. Secondly, the existence of more than one solution prevents solvers from efficiently making use of branch&bound or equivalent techniques. Thus, relevant details usually have to be neglected in the model to get acceptable solving times. The result of these methods has to be checked with simulations afterwards [3].

## 2 Methodology

In this section we will give a short overview of the setup of our methodology followed by a more detailed description, how the mapping problem can be regarded as and solved via solving packing problems.

But first we want to give a short description about the methodology we used for modeling applications and architectures. For modeling there is a variety of languages, which can roughly be divided into process-network based and control & data-flow graph (CDFG) based approaches. We have chosen a CDFG based kind of view, because in comparison to process networks the complete parallelism of the application is exposed explicitly. We use YML [9], which was designed to deal with Kahn-Process-Networks derived from Compaan [10], but is suitable for CDFGs as well. Another advantage of YML is, that it can be used to model the architecture as well in the same way.

As mentioned, our methodology is a single objective, bottom-up, analytical approach. We favored an analytical over a simulation based approach, because in this way each corner-case does not have to be identified and simulated individually, but is considered within the model. However, this – as well as the fact that our methodology is static – limits our approach to applications that can be scheduled statically. The methodology is designed bottom-up due to fact, that implementation and performance figures are available usually at very low abstraction levels – or at least can be estimated more precise. Multiple abstraction levels are included by finding mappings on the lowest abstraction levels, inserting the gained results into higher abstraction levels and in this way reaching the top-level step-by-step.

To find a mapping and evaluate the performance of the given system, we propose the methodology depicted in Fig. 1. First we do a fast optimization to check, if the chosen system can meet the required timing constraints without resource constraints. This problem can be solved exact in polynomial time for example via shortest path algorithms from the field of graph theory. Since the algorithms are well-known, we neglect the details in this paper.

If the timing constraints can be met disregarding resource constraints, we perform a 3-step mapping algorithm, which is described in detail in the following subsections. The three steps can be seen as a stepwise refinement of the mapping. After each step the mapping process is stopped, if the timing constraints cannot be met. In the first step the tasks are mapped onto the system. Second, the variables are mapped to suitable

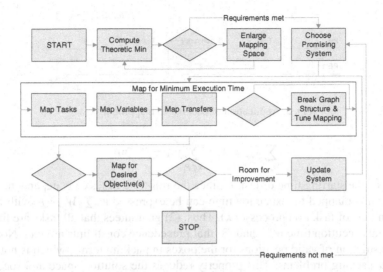

**Fig. 1.** Block diagram of the presented methodology and the possible steps beyond

memories of the system and memory addresses. This step also determines, if the chosen memory capacity is sufficient. After that transfers are taken care of.

We are aware of the fact, that there have been efforts treating individual phases – just to name [11,12] as prominent examples. Our approach differs in putting all of these problems down to the class of packing problems. Another advantage esp. in memory allocation is the fact, that not two, but an arbitrary number of memories can be handled simultaneously. In addition, we keep the graph structure of the application throughout the whole mapping process, which can be useful for further optimizations.

After the 3-step mapping algorithm an optional refinement step can be performed, which breaks up the graph structure. If the timing constraints can be met, further optimizations can be executed utilizing the results of the mapping result.

## 2.1 Mapping Tasks and Transfers

The problem of mapping tasks temporal and spatial can be interpreted as 2-dimensional strip-packing problem [13]. In strip-packing, boxes of fixed length and width have to be arranged into a strip of fixed width in such a manner, that total height is minimized. Figure 2 illustrates the application of packing to mapping tasks.

Applied to mapping tasks the boxes to be packed represent the tasks. The length of these boxes is defined by the execution time of the tasks. The width of the strip is the total execution time and height represents the available processing elements in discrete unified steps. Thus, not the height but the width of the strip $w^{\min}$ is minimized, when optimization of total execution time is desired.

Let $P_i$ be the set of processors capable of processing task $i$ and $y_{i,k} := 1$, if task $i$ is mapped to processor $k$. First, we have to ensure that each task $i$ is mapped onto a processor $k$ capable of processing this task. This is done by (1).

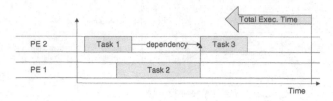

**Fig. 2.** Application of packing to mapping tasks

$$\sum_{k \in P_i} y_{i,k} = 1, \quad \sum_{k \notin P_i} y_{i,k} = 0 \quad \forall i \tag{1}$$

Let $x_i$ be the starting time of task $i$. Since the run-time of task $i$ is dependent on the processor it is mapped to, execution time can be expressed as $\sum_k W_{i,k} y_{i,k}$ (with $W_{i,k} :=$ execution time of task $i$ on processor $k$). Thus, (2) guarantees that all tasks are finished before total execution time $w^{\min}$ and (3) that precedence constraints are met. Note that (3) is a restriction of valid positions for the boxes in packing terms, which is not given in regular packing problems. This property reduces the solution space and speeds up solution time. The solution space can be reduced even more by considering ALAP and ASAP times for the tasks, which we did not implement yet.

$$x_i + \sum_k W_{i,k} y_{i,k} \le w^{\min} \quad \forall i \tag{2}$$

$$x_i + \sum_k W_{i,k} y_{i,k} \le x_j \quad \forall i, j : j \text{ depends on } i \tag{3}$$

Next, we have to obey machine restrictions. Let be $i, j$ tasks and $k, l$ the indices of the assigned processors. Let be $u_{i,j} := 1$, if $k \le l$, and $b_{i,j} := 1$, if $i$ is executed before task $j$ (0 otherwise). Since DSPs and ASICs usually do not support multi-threading, tasks cannot be executed in parallel on the same processor. Equations (4) – (8) provide this non-overlapping in packing terms and are stated for each interfering task-pair $(i, j)$ with $P_i \cap P_j \neq \emptyset$. In this context two tasks do not interfere, if there exists a path between $i$ and $j$ in the CDFG or if they are belonging to different case-blocks of a switch-case-construct. In the latter case, the tasks may be mapped onto the same processor at the same time, because only one of the tasks will be executed in reality. By including this property into our methodology, each possible branch that can be realized in the CDFG is considered automatically.

$$x_i + \sum_k W'_{i,k} y_{i,k} - W^{\max} + W^{\max} b_{i,j} \le x_j \tag{4}$$

$$\sum_k k y_{i,k} + 1 - H^{\max} + H^{\max} u_{i,j} \le \sum_k k y_{j,k} \tag{5}$$

$$b_{j,i} + b_{i,j} \le 1 \tag{6}$$

$$u_{j,i} + u_{i,j} \le 1 \tag{7}$$

$$u_{j,i} + u_{i,j} + b_{j,i} + b_{i,j} \ge 1 \quad \forall \text{ interfering } i, j \tag{8}$$

Note, that not run-time but the earliest starting time of the next task on the same processor is relevant to ensure a valid temporal mapping. The earliest starting time for subsequent tasks after the start of task $i$ on processor $k$ is denoted by $W'_{i,k}$. Constants $W^{\max} := \sum_{i,k} W_{i,k}$ and $H^{\max} := |\bigcup_i P_i|$ make sure, that (4) and (5) are redundant with $x_j \geq 0$ and $\sum_k k y_{j,k} \geq 0$ in case of $b_{i,j} = 0$ and $u_{i,j} = 0$, respectively.

Finally we need an objective that minimizes total execution time $w^{\min}$. The sum term in (9) (with $A :=$ adjacency matrix) additionally minimizes the time between two adjacent tasks and therefore liveness of variables. The objective can be refined by adding additional terms, e.g. trying to put adjacent tasks onto the same processor for reducing needed transfers.

$$W^{\min} + \left( \sum_{i,j} \frac{A_{i,j}(x_j - x_i - \sum_k W_{i,k} y_{i,k})}{W^{\max}} \right) \to \min \qquad (9)$$

For mapping transfers, the same methodology can be applied, because the transfers have to be performed by some components of the system. But since the components involved in these transfers are determined by the memory allocation, this has to be done after the mapping of variables and cannot be integrated into the mapping of tasks.

### 2.2 Mapping Variables

The results of the task mapping are now used for mapping variables. Since the set of valid memories depends on the processor, the related task is mapped to, the mapping of variables has to take place after the tasks are mapped.

Mapping variables in heterogeneous MP-SoCs is similar to register allocation in compiler construction. A well known solution for this problem is Chaitin's graph coloring algorithm [12]. But in opposite to register allocation there are usually more than the two memories (register and global memory) in MP-SoCs, like local, shared and global memories or vector and scalar memories. Thus not each memory is suitable for storing a variable. But the concept of interference can be utilized and extended.

In our methodology two variables interfere, if they *can* share the same memory and *can* be live simultaneously. Since we keep the graph structure throughout the whole mapping process instead of looking at sequential code, the possibility rather than the fact of being live simultaneously is important.

The problem of mapping variables can now be seen as shelf-packing problem as follows: Each shelf represents a memory $k$ of the system, whose height is defined by the capacity $C_k$. The variables $i$ to be mapped represent the boxes to be packed into the shelves, whose heights $h_i$ matches the size of the variables.

Let $M_i$ be the set of memories suitable for storing variable $i$ and $x_{i,k} := 1$, if variable $i$ is stored in memory $k$ (0 otherwise). First, we have to select a valid memory (shelf) for each variable (10).

$$\sum_{k \in M_i} x_{i,k} = 1, \quad \sum_{k \notin M_i} x_{i,k} = 0 \quad \forall i \qquad (10)$$

Let $y_i$ be the starting address of variable $i$ in the memory. Eq. (11) takes care, that the variable is stored in a valid memory address.

$$y_i + h_i \leq \sum_k C_k x_{i,k} \quad \forall i \qquad (11)$$

Let $H_k^{\text{offset}}$ be the shelf height of memory $k$ and $H^{\max} \geq \max_k \{H_k^{\text{offset}} + C_k\}$ a constant denoting the height of the rack. To make certain that two variables are not stored in the same memory at the same address, we introduce non-overlapping constraints (12) & (13) for all interfering variables $i, j$.

$$y_i + h_i + \sum_k H_k^{\text{offset}} x_{i,k} - H^{\max} + H^{\max} u_{j,i} \leq y_j + \sum_k H_k^{\text{offset}} x_{j,k} \qquad (12)$$

$$u_{j,i} + u_{i,j} = 1 \quad \forall \text{ interfering } i, j \qquad (13)$$

Since each memory $k$ has different access times denoted by $W_k$, we minimize not only needed memory resources, but also force the allocation of variables into fast memories. This is done by (15), where the required resource amounts for memory $k$ are denoted with $y_k^{\min}$ and constraint by (14).

$$y_i + h_i + H^{\max} x_{i,k} - H^{\max} \leq y_k^{\text{mem}} \quad \forall i, k \qquad (14)$$

$$\sum_{i,k} W_k x_{i,k} + \sum_k y_k^{\text{mem}} C_k^{-1} \rightarrow \min \qquad (15)$$

## 3   Results

In this section we will apply the proposed method to a case study. For the case study we considered a processor core [14] based on Synchronous Transfer Architecture (STA) as a MP-SoC. The intermediate representations our test bench applications generated by the MOUSE [15] compiler front-end served as sample applications.

STA is the concept of loosely coupled functional units and different memory types connected by an interconnection network. Thus, these functional units can be considered as processors in the MP-SoC. In our case study we selected a STA core with 21 functional units. As an important property for legitimating this architecture for the MP-SoC case study there are some operations that have to be executed on a dedicated functional unit of the architecture and some operations, that can be mapped to an element of a subset of functional units of the STA core. In addition, each of these units has output registers. This characteristic is used to model the behavior of keeping data in local memory as rather than having to write it back to shared or global memory.

The advantage of this abstract example is, that we have on the one hand well-known execution times for the instructions and on the other hand a set of test benches, that suit as complex examples (up to 135 nodes per basic block) to demonstrate the potentials and limits of our methodology.

### 3.1   Results for Mapping Tasks

After transferring the STA core as well as the applications into our internal YML-based data structure, we applied the methodology described in Sect. 2 to our test benches. We compared the performance of our methodology with the results from our compiler and the theoretic minimum which is defined as the minimal number of VLIWs required

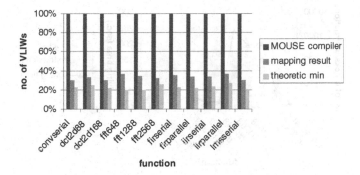

**Fig. 3.** Comparison of the quality of the task mapping methodology with the MOUSE Compiler and the theoretic min without resource constraints

without resource constraints. Figure 3 shows an improvement of about 75% in average compared to the existing MOUSE compiler. But even more important is the comparision with the theoretic optimum without resource constraints on the same kind of architecture. As Fig. 3 shows, we are within a factor of 1.45 of this minimun in average.

Solving was done by passing the problem to CPLEX 10.1. Although it was not possible to compute the optimal mapping in acceptable time for applications with a large number of nodes, first solutions were found fast. Therefore we implemented a time limit for finding a better solution of 10 seconds after an improvement of a solution was found. To get an indicator about the quality of these solutions, we ran the CPLEX solver for one block of an application for more than six hours, which showed improvement of about 10% over the solution found after less than a minute.

Figure 4 shows the times required for mapping tasks. We think the denoted running times up to 250 sec. are worth to be spend at an early design stage, since no additional simulations are required. Moreover, note that the solving time can be accelerated by reducing the time specified for finding a better solution during progress.

### 3.2 Results for Mapping Variables

We applied the shelf-packing methodology for mapping variables to the test benches. As mentioned, the functional units can hold data in their output registers, which is used in the case study for modeling the behavior of keeping data in local memory as rather than having to write it back to shared or global memory. The results of our methodology applied to the test benches showed that this is an important property to be considered in the mapping process. It significantly reduced not only required memory resources to 10% in average but also communication overhead.

### 3.3 Utilizing Results for Performance Evaluation and System Refinement

As mentioned in Sect. 1, the methodology is designed for performance analysis of an existing MP-SoC in the first place. But the results can be utilized to guide the designer

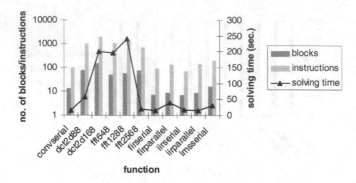

**Fig. 4.** Number of blocks and instructions to be mapped and the resulting solving times

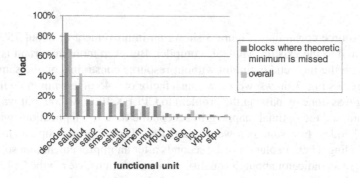

**Fig. 5.** Load analysis of the task mapping result for all test benches

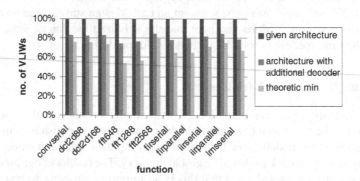

**Fig. 6.** Improvement gained by adding a second decoder unit to the given architecture as result of the load analysis

in the process of modifying the system to improve metrics as performance, for example. Since we have a static mapping, we can derive some performance figures like processor loads or memory requirements very easily. Figure 5 shows, that the load of the decoder is very high in comparison to the other functional units.

Thus, we modeled a system with two decoders and did the mapping for this modified system. Figure 6 shows the improvement compared to the original system. With this quite simple analysis of the loads of the functional units and the derived modification of the system we were able to reduce the gap between the theoretic minimum without resource constraints and our mapping result from about 45% to under 20%.

# 4  Conclusion

We have shown that mapping of applications to a given heterogeneous MP-SoC can be regarded as packing problem. These packing problems can be solved efficiently by existing optimization software. Furthermore the results of our static, analytical methodology can be utilized to guide the system designer, how to refine the given system.

# Acknowledgement

This research is supported by NXP Semiconductors Dresden within the project MxMobile Multi-Standard Mobile Platform of the German Federal Ministry of Education and Research (BMBF).

# References

1. Blume, H., Feldkämper, H.T., Noll, T.G.: Model-based exploration of the design space for heterogeneous systems on chip. J. VLSI Signal Process. Syst. 40, 19–34 (2005)
2. Kienhuis, B., Deprettere, E., Vissers, K., van der Wolf, P.: An approach for quantitative analysis of application-specific dataflow architectures. In: ASAP '97. Proceedings of the IEEE International Conference on Application-Specific Systems, Architectures and Processors, pp. 338–349. IEEE Computer Society Press, Los Alamitos (1997)
3. Erbas, C., Erbas, S.C., Pimentel, A.D.: A multiobjective optimization model for exploring multiprocessor mappings of process networks. In: CODES+ISSS '03. Proceedings of the 1st IEEE/ACM/IFIP International Conference on Hardware/Software Codesign and System Synthesis, pp. 182–187 (2003)
4. Schwiegershausen, M., Pirsch, P.: A formal approach for the optimization of heterogeneous multiprocessors for complex image processing schemes. In: EURO-DAC '95/EURO-VHDL '95. Proceedings of the Conference on European Design Automation, pp. 8–13 (1995)
5. Pimentel, A.D., Erbas, C., Polstra, S.: A systematic approach to exploring embedded system architectures at multiple abstraction levels. IEEE Transactions on Computers 55, 99–112 (2006)
6. Bakshi, A., Prasanna, V.K., Ledeczi, A.: MILAN: A model based integrated simulation framework for design of embedded systems. In: LCTES '01. Proceedings of the ACM SIGPLAN Workshop on Languages, Compilers and Tools for Embedded Systems, pp. 82–93. ACM Press, New York (2001)
7. Govindarajan, R., Gao, G., Desai, P.: Minimizing memory requirements in rate-optimal schedules. In: ASAP '94. Proceedings of the International Conference on Application Specific Array Processors, pp. 75–86 (1994)
8. Ristau, B., Fettweis, G.: An optimization methodology for memory allocation and task scheduling in SoCs via linear programming. In: Vassiliadis, S., Wong, S., Hämäläinen, T.D. (eds.) SAMOS 2006. LNCS, vol. 4017, pp. 89–98. Springer, Heidelberg (2006)

9. Coffland, J.E., Pimentel, A.D.: A software framework for efficient system-level performance evaluation of embedded systems. In: Matsui, M., Zuccherato, R.J. (eds.) SAC 2003. LNCS, vol. 3006, pp. 666–671. Springer, Heidelberg (2004)
10. Turjan, A., Kienhuis, B., Deprettere, E.: Translating affine nested-loop programs to process networks. In: CASES '04. Proceedings of the 2004 International Conference on Compilers, Architecture, and Synthesis for Embedded Systems, pp. 220–229 (2004)
11. Liu, C.L., Layland, J.W.: Scheduling algorithms for multiprogramming in a hard-real-time environment. J. ACM 20, 46–61 (1973)
12. Chaitin, G.J., Auslander, M.A., Chandra, A.K., Cocke, J., Hopkins, M.E., Markstein, P.W.: Register allocation via coloring. Computer Languages 6, 47–57 (1981)
13. Belov, G., Chiglintsev, A.V., Filippova, A.S., Mukhacheva, E., Scheithauer, G., Shirgazin, R.: The two-dimensional strip packing problem: A numerical experiment with waste-free instances using algorithms with block structure. Preprint MATH-NM-01-2005 TU Dresden (2005)
14. Matus, E., Seidel, H., Limberg, T., Robelly, P., Fettweis, G.: A GFLOPS Vector-DSP for broadband wireless applications. In: CICC '06. Proceedings of the IEEE Custom Integrated Circuits Conference, pp. 543–546. IEEE Computer Society Press, Los Alamitos (2006)
15. Cichon, G., Fettweis, G.: MOUSE: A shortcut from matlab source to SIMD DSP assembly code. In: SAMOS '03. Proceedings of the International Workshop on Systems, Architectures, MOdeling, and Simulation, pp. 159–167 (2003)

# Strategies for Compiling μTC to Novel Chip Multiprocessors

Thomas A.M. Bernard, Chris R. Jesshope, and Peter M.W. Knijnenburg

Computer Systems Architecture group, Informatics Institute
University of Amsterdam, The Netherlands
tbernard@science.uva.nl, jesshope@science.uva.nl,
peterk@science.uva.nl

**Abstract.** Microthreaded C also called *μTC* is a concurrent language based on the C language which allows the programmer to code concurrency-oriented applications for targeting chip multiprocessors. *μTC* source code contains fine-grained concurrent control structures, where the concurrency is explicitly written via new keywords. This language is used as an interface for defining dynamic concurrency and as an intermediate language to capture concurrency from data-parallel languages such as Single-Assignment C, or as the target for parallelizing compilers for sequential languages such as C. This paper presents an overview of *μTC* language, emphasizing the aspects of memory synchronization and concurrent control structures. In order to understand the properties and scopes of the language, we also present the outlines of the architectures after discussing the global concepts of the microthreading model. Finally we show the toolchain we are currently developing to support the model, focusing on compiler strategies.

## 1 Introduction

Microthreading is an approach to parallel computing for on-chip concurrency in order to improve performance.

Until the recent past, the classic improvements of CPU designs are obtained either by increasing the clock speed or by increasing the number of instructions issued per cycle. In order to exploit a different approach and avoid the classic problem of power consumptions and heat dissipations, chip designers often look to other CPU features like cache size and number of cores. Recently, Intel has pledged up to 80 cores on a chip within the next five years. Intel has built an 80-cores-on-chip processor prototype, which might be able to perform a trillion floating-point operations per second. Nevertheless these new features dramatically increase the complexity of the chip for the programmers. Important issues such as the existence of proper languages to exploit all the new features of the chip might be a problem.

The Microgrid Project is a research effort to design a chip multiprocessor with a tool suite which comprises a chip simulator and compilation tools based on the Microthreading model of concurrency [1]. In order to improve the parallelization of computations, the Microthreading [1] model proposes a new self-similar approach to concurrency,

S. Vassiliadis et al. (Eds.): SAMOS 2007, LNCS 4599, pp. 127–138, 2007.

from ILP to user tasks. This approach is based on massive thread-level parallelism augmented by two forms of synchronization, namely, bulk synchronization between concurrent sections and fine-grain synchronization within concurrent sections. This model is captured in the language $\mu TC$, which represents this explicit concurrency in the code by using high-level structures that are implemented as instructions in a microthreaded ISA. The $\mu TC$ language is an extension to the C language, and provides concurrency control structures which can represent all forms of concurrency from units which are a single instruction up to complete programs. Our microthreaded architecture is a chip multiprocessor [2]. More precisely, it is a reconfigurable pool of processors, which can be connected by ring networks for executing concurrent sections. Each portion of code or microthread is created dynamically with a collection of registers or a *context* in the fine-grain synchronizing memory allocated to it. $\mu TC$ captures the concept of fine-grain synchronization between concurrent computations, as well as bulk synchronization in non-synchronized memory. Concurrency control structures in the code are directly mapped to low-level operations by using new ISA instructions [2].

There is related work on parallel languages in the current literature. OpenMP [3] is similar in some aspects to $\mu TC$, though there are significant differences. The major difference is that OpenMP uses pragmas to annotate the code and $\mu TC$ uses concurrent control structures which can be issued. The other point is that $\mu TC$ assumes a synchronizing memory. This captures dependencies between threads allowing sequence to be transformed into concurrency, where any dependencies are managed transparently in a data-driven manner. Similar to $\mu TC$, UPC [4] is another language which is an extension of C. It uses new keywords and pragmas to specify concurrency in C code. The major difference is that $\mu TC$ does not have any notion of mapping threads to the hardware (except to manage resource deadlock), since this is managed by the architecture.

This paper presents the main definition of the language with code examples and demonstrates how it allows a programmer to code an application directly in a concurrency-oriented manner using this language. We are currently at an early stage of the project where the $\mu TC$ language can be used by the programmer or as an interface language with other projects. Eventually, the $\mu TC$ language will be only internal, which means that the programmer will only have to code in standard C. The compiler suite will take care of the aspects of concurrency described in this paper. To understand the properties and scopes of the $\mu TC$ language, we present first the outlines of our architecture after explaining the global concepts of the Microthreading model.

## 2   Problem and Motivation

The motivation of this work is to provide a deterministic method of programming large scale concurrency. New developments in microprocessor design will force even the commodity market, currently dominated by out-of-order issue processors, to adopt explicit concurrency as multi-core chips become the norm. A recent paper by Edward Lee [5] warns of the danger of exposing a thread-based programming model to the vagaries of non-deterministic scheduling in a multi-processor environment. His own carefully managed software developments threw up bugs that had lain dormant in the code for years when exposed to a multi-core environment.

Our thesis is that the only sensible way to program multi-core devices is by using ordinary sequential code that is compiled to parallel code. However, years of research and development in parallelizing compilers has not yet yielded any significant solutions. This is despite the fact that discovering some forms of concurrency in sequential code is easy. Data dependence analysis can expose much concurrency in a unit of code. What is difficult, however, is scheduling that concurrency onto current microprocessors where there is little or no support for synchronization. This results in non-optimal schedules being generated statically by the compiler using coarse-grain units of concurrency. Coarse granularity is a necessity imposed by the inefficiency of software scheduling methods used by the operating system or the language run-time support.

Our approach is to expose all of this concurrency to the hardware but to insist that the hardware supports *synchronization* and *efficient scheduling*. Dataflow models (e.g., [6]) can execute the data-dependence graph directly. However, these models are inefficient in managing the contextualisation of the code (e.g. managing different iterations on a loop or different calls to a function). Our approach is to retain the data driven semantics but to embed this in a conventional RISC architecture. Close to the processor, synchronization is managed by the processors registers, just like an out-of-order processor. This means that a microthread's execution will be blocked if any of the data required by the current instruction is not available. It would be expensive to implement this form synchronization universally on all memory locations and so we also adopt a dynamic model of concurrency creation, with barrier synchronization between concurrent sections and this is used to manage synchronization in the slower main memory.

This separation of concerns, namely, exposing concurrency in the compiler and managing concurrency in the microprocessor, allows us to achieve our goal of programming multi-core chips, but only provided that the cores adopt the dynamic RISC approach defined by microthreaded execution.

## 3   The Microthreading Model

Our Microthreading model aims to increase the concurrency of computations on the chip [1]. Code is split into fragments , which are called *microthreads*, and those code fragments are executed on several processors, as shown in Figure 1. Code fragments can be identified as loops or function bodies or even sub-divisions of basic blocks. A microthread is issued independently on a processor. Microthreads are created as families (for instance, a loop represents a family of microthreads) of indexed microthreads. The model adds just a few new instructions to an existing ISA to implement explicit concurrency controls which are recursively applied to define parametric sets (families) of concurrent code fragments, which are scheduled dynamically on multiple processors, as explained in section 4. Concurrency in Microthreading is parametric and its schedules are dynamic, thus allowing the same binary code to be run on an arbitrary number of processors. This allows dynamic management of resources. These new ISA instructions [2] also handle data dependencies between microthreads.

Our Microthreading model supports a shared-register model of data using blocking reads. The model also provides the programmer the opportunity to explicitly capture concurrency in the code by means of this new language, as explained in section 5.

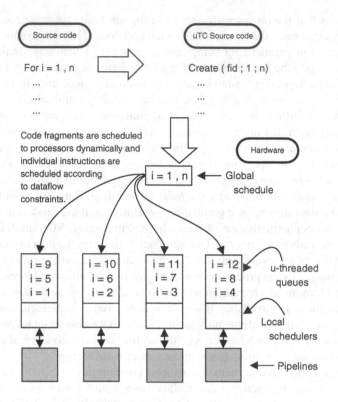

**Fig. 1.** Illustration of Microthreaded Scheduling

## 4 Microthreaded Architecture

### 4.1 Overview

A microthreaded architecture is a chip multiprocessor which in principle can comprise a very large number of processors. It does not matter how many processors execute the code as the same code will run on any number of processors, bounded only by the loop limit. A global schedule determines the distribution of the microthreads over the processors when created by the ISA instruction **create**.

As shown in Figure 2, each processor consists of

- a local scheduler which manages the families of microthreads,
- a local pipeline which executes instructions,
- a large local register file providing memory for contexts. Each context is divided in four classes: local, global, shared and dependent,
- links to the bus and a ring network (for communication with the others processors).

Each microthread can access a set of local registers, a set of read only registers, and global registers which can be accessed by all microthreads. We support communication between adjacent threads in a family by defining some registers of the local context

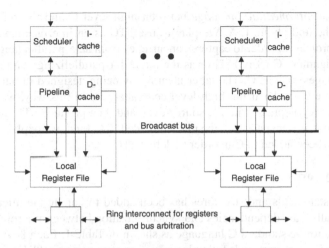

**Fig. 2.** Microthreaded Architecture

as shared. In this way, the processors can exchange data in the shared registers for dependencies between microthreads by a ring network, as shown in Figure 2. Each microthread has its own set of local registers for local data. Global registers contain global values which are accessible to all microthreads of the family. Global values are derived from local values in the creating thread and cannot be modified by the microthreads so as to maintain determinism.

### 4.2   Synchronizing Memory: Hardware Perspective

Each thread created has a context of local registers which store scalar variables and which are dynamically allocated to it. These registers have special state bits that indicate whether or not the register contains a value that is written by the source of a dependency. They are used to synchronize between dependent threads. The collection of all these registers is called the *synchronizing memory*. These registers are initialized to the empty state on creation of a thread and are garbage collected when the thread completes. The only exception is the index variable that is set to the corresponding value of the iteration. These variables provide synchronization on data from non-synchronizing memory and on data from other threads if the variables are declared as shared. Reading an empty variable in synchronizing memory will block the thread reading it until the value has been set (the thread is suspended and can no longer proceed until the data is available). Synchronizing memory is dynamic (like ordinary registers) and data created by a thread must be shared with another thread or written to non-synchronizing memory before the thread terminates. Otherwise it will be lost.

## 5   $\mu$TC Language

### 5.1   Introduction to the Language

The $\mu$TC language is an extension of the C language. However, we should emphasize that $\mu$TC is not meant to be a language that should be used by a programmer. Instead, we use it as an *intermediate language* between high level C and the microthreaded extension of the underlying ISA. We plan to use $\mu$TC as an interface language to be used in other projects in order to capture concurrency from data-parallel languages such as Single-Assignment C (SAC) [7] or as the target for parallelizing compilers for sequential languages such as C. The latter is currently being designed in our group as a source-to-source compiler using high-level code analysis. In this way, we can detect where concurrency is present in a C source code and then produce $\mu$TC code. Subsequently, this code is translated into the microthreaded ISA. First, we explain which new keywords have been added to C in order to define $\mu$TC.

## 5.2 New Keywords

A set of new statements and structures has been added to handle the microthreading model, especially data dependencies and synchronization between microthreads. $\mu$TC adds keywords to the standard C language as shown in Table 1. Each keyword can be used anywhere in a C source code following a number of restrictions [8]. For instance, the **create** statement has to follow syntax rules such as the braces and semantic rules such as no function call inside the body or definitions of the parameters (integer or expression).

**Table 1.** Concurrency-control keywords

| Keywords | Semantics |
|---|---|
| create | control structure used to create a family of microthreads |
| thread | type specifier to indicate the functions that define the microthreads |
| squeezable | function qualifier identifying threads that propagate a squeeze signal to subordinate families |
| shared | type qualifier of variables shared between microthreads |
| index | type of the index variable of a family of microthreads |
| family | type used to specify a variable that identifies a family of threads |
| place | type used to specify a variable that identifies a place at which to execute a family of threads |
| sync | construct that waits for the termination of a specified family |
| break | construct that terminates a family from one of its threads |
| kill | construct that terminates a specified family externally |
| squeeze | construct that preempts the execution of a specified family so that it may restarted without loss of state |

A $\mu$TC source file contains explicit statements to define code fragments. For example, the **create** statement is a concurrent control structure which produces a family of microthreads. Its semantics resembles a **for** construct in ordinary C. In the example below, each iteration is a microthread which can be created and managed from one to n processors.

```
...
create (fid; ; 0; m-1; ; ; )
{
        index i;
```

```
        sum[i]=i+1;
    }
    printf ("fid %d", fid);
    foo (fid);
    ...
    sync (fid);
```

For handling synchronization, the **sync** statement blocks until the family of microthreads specified by *fid* has completed and then completes its execution. The creating thread can continue until it needs to sync, as shown the example above. This example has the same behaviour as a **for** loop statement with *m* iterations, but here each iteration is executed concurrently. The programmer can also explicitly specify structures which can be microthreaded by means of the **thread** function specifier, as follows.

```
thread sumint(shared int sum, int array[])
{
    index idx;
    sum = sum + array[idx];
}

    ...
int main(void)
{
    int *a;
    int fid, s=0, n=10;
    create(fid; ; 0; n-1; ; ; )
        sumint(s, *a);
    sync(fid);
    return 0;
}
```

In order to notify the compiler of a dependency between threads in a concurrent control structure, the **shared** keyword is used. In the following example, a variable is shared between the iterations as well as the example above. The initialization is exposed to the creating environment and depends on the scoping of variables. In the example above, the shared variable is used as parameter. In the example below, the shared variable located within a microthreaded structure needs to be initialized by an outer variable.

```
    int s_init=0;
    create (fid; ; 0; m-1; ; ; )
    {
        index i;
        shared int s=s_init;
        s=s+a[i];
    }
    sync (fid);
```

This has a similar semantics to a scalar in a loop, as each thread shares its shared variable with the next thread in index sequence. Finally, another type qualifier, called

**index**, identifies an index within the family of microthreads. **index i** gets a value corresponding to the iteration numbered by the hardware. This value **index** is set by the processor for each thread created by the create instruction/control. These executable constructs added, (i.e. with the exception of the thread, index and shared type qualifiers) all correspond to machine instructions added to an ISA to support microthreading.

### 5.3   Synchronizing Memory: Language Perspective

Communicating between threads in the same family must use synchronizing memory by using a variable declared as **shared**. Such variables have a unique location in each thread and define a dependency chain through all threads. To initialize this chain of neighbours, the first thread reads a variable of the same name from the creating environment (not declared as **shared**) or in the case of a named thread, a binding is made to a variable in the creating environment such as in the example below, the variable **s** is initialized by a variable in the creating environment. Following the termination of the family (i.e., after a **sync** statement), a read of the initialising variable in the creating environment will yield the value written to the shared variable by the last thread created.

```
int *a, s_init=0;
create (fid; ; 0; 99; ; ; )
{
      index i;
      shared int s = s_init;
      s=s+1;
      a[i]=s;
}
sync (fid);
```

From the previous example, the variable **s** is shared with the following 'iteration'. Its first value is initialized to **0** during the first read. After the synchronization **sync (fid)**, the value of **s** would be the last value written which is **101**.

## 6   $\mu$TC Compiler Strategies

We plan to have a compiler suite which comprises three main tools: two source-to-source compilers (bold-line rectangles) and one core compiler (rounded-corners rectangle), which is shown in Figure 3.

All of those tools are still in development and require testing suite experiments for checking the quality of code, the performance, the use of memory, etc. For the purpose of building a working core compiler ($\mu$TC-to-assembly) as soon as possible, the compilation and the code analysis have been split up. However in the future we plan to merge all the tools into the same system. The second reason is that we collaborate with different partners within a project called AETHER [9]. We use the $\mu$TC language as a language interface with two other source-to-source compilers under development at the University of Hertfordshire: from Single-Assignment C to $\mu$TC, and from SNET to $\mu$TC.

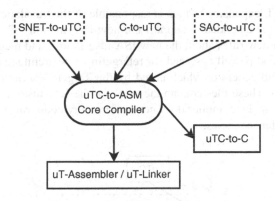

**Fig. 3.** $\mu$T-Compiler chain

At the University of Amsterdam, we use two different frameworks for our compilers. We currently use the gcc 4.1 core release as the framework of our core compiler. And the CoSy [10] system from Ace is used as the C-to-$\mu TC$ parellizing compiler. In this section we are going to focus on the design of the core compiler.

The $\mu TC$-to-C source-to-source compiler has the behaviour of a code checker / translator. This tool translates directly the microthreaded code to a classic sequential C source code by using line-by-line replacements and keywords detections.

The strategy of the C-to-$\mu TC$ compiler is to work on a high-level representation of the code in order to detect which portions of code can be transformed (e.g. loops) to a microthreaded code. The tool handles the data dependencies of the code and synchronization by using the $\mu TC$ keywords. This compiler will also be extended with transformation strategies to extract more parallelism from the original program following the microthreading model. The CoSy [10] system is used for the development of this source-to-source compiler. It uses a convenient system of engines which works on a centralized representation (CCMIR) of the program. $\mu TC$ does not contain any scheduling information, this is done at the hardware level. This compiler needs only to discover the parallelism within a C source code.

The gcc 4.1 compiler is built in three main parts: the front-end which handles the input languages (like C or Java) and the middle-end which manages most of the optimizations (language- and target-independent) and then the back-end which generates the assembly code and does some target-dependent optimizations. The main goal is to port the gcc compiler to this new language and the targeted architecture. For that purpose, our strategy is to extend the C front-end with our new keywords and concurrent structures. The lexical, syntax and semantic analysis need to be extended as well in order to support the new rules and semantics of the language. As shown in Figure 4, the gcc 4.1 compiler has three internal representations from high-level (GIMPLE, tree-based), optimization-level (SSA) until low-level (RTL, list of objects). To support the mapping from high-level structures to low-level operations, we have to extend all of them during all the stages of the compilation. The 'gimplification' produces the GIMPLE form and needs to be updated with new structures to represent the new statements. The 'out-of-SSA' stage needs to be extended to support the new statements from the

GIMPLE. The 'RTL expansion' which is responsible of the translation from the GIM-
PLE to RTL nodes is extended to support the new information. 'Code generation' is
also extended with new rules about the new ISA instructions and memory description.
The gcc 4.1 back end is well designed for retargeting new architecture. The back-end
works as a back-end generator which is fed by the Target Description Files (TDF as
shown in Figure 4). These files contain the rules for the 'expansion' and for the 'code
generation'. For now the compiler does not perform any code transformation or code
analysis like data dependencies.

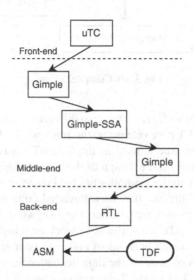

**Fig. 4.** Intermediate Representations of gcc 4.1

## 7    Challenges for Compiling $\mu TC$

Besides adding new concepts within the compiler via new keywords and new structures, $\mu TC$ has other complex challenges for compiler architecture. It is common know
that register allocation is most important challenge for compiler architects. Normally the
register allocation works at the late stages of compilation and follows a specific description of the memory features of the targeted architecture. The register allocation basically
starts analyzing from the low-level internal representation which uses an infinite number
of registers called pseudo registers. The Target Description Files (TDF as shown in Figure 4) explain for instance what kind of registers are used for a specific type of operations
such as arithmetic operations or pointers operations. The numbers of those registers are
fixed for a specific target and are real hardware registers. They are called hard registers
in the literature. After the register allocation passes and algorithms passes for memory
optimizations, all the used registers are hard registers in pseudo-assembly code of the
initial program. In our case, the register allocator occurs differently than classic register
allocations. Firstly, because of the memory features of the microthreaded architecture,
we use four classes of register which have been explained previously. The global amount

of registers is 31, nevertheless, there are not a fixed number for each class of register. Our register allocator should perform a dynamic allocation after analyzing the needs of the source code. To summarize the amount of registers of each class is different depending on the source program and can differ from one program and another. Classic register allocations work on a static amount of registers and known before compile-time. However for our model, at compile-time we have to perform memory and data analysis in order to determine the needs for each class of register.

Furthermore, the former challenge brings a new one which is the data information. The data structure indeed is part of our model which introduces classes of variables: global, local, shared and dependent. Keeping track of data information all along the compilation stages is a big issue in compiler architecture. The amount of data information which are discovered during code analysis can be large. Because of storage issues and loses between compilation stages, this information can be lost. By using new memory types in μTC, the language explicitly specifies data information which are needed for an efficient register allocation.

The dragon book [11] presents a chapter about the issues in the design of a code generator. Finally these two challenges introduce the need of useful and complete intermediate representations (three within gcc 4.1) in order to keep track of all information (such as new statements from the μTC language, scopes of variables) from the high level to the low-level representation.

## 8  Initial Results

The μTC compiler is still in development but the front-end supports most of the μTC language. Source code can be parsed and the compiler is able to display syntax errors such as misspelled keyword or invalid parameter. It is also capable of basic semantics checks such as variable declaration for a parameter of a keyword. In the near future we plan to make more efficient semantic checks for a source program. For instance a sync statement would have to refer to a valid create statement. One other point is the break statement has to be used only within a microthreaded code (body of a create statement or body of thread statement) such as the break from the C language which has to be used within a loop or if-then-else statement or a switch statement).

From source code, the μTC compiler produces an intermediate tree representation of the program. In oder to support the new specifications of the language and also for overcoming the challenges explained before, this representation has been updated. Moreover we plan to have some analysis on the tree representation in order to make some experiments about some potential optimizations.

## 9  Conclusions and Further Research

This paper has shown how the μTC language allows to capture thread-based concurrency in the code and the strategies to compile it. We are currently developing the core compiler based on gcc 4.1 which compiles μTC to assembly code. Secondly one of our objective is to be able to extract concurrency from sequential code and for this we are expanding our field of research to include the area of source-to-source compilation and code analysis. We are looking at a parallel source-to-source compiler which has to discover concurrency in *C* code and produce $\mu TC$ code. A $\mu TC$-*to*-*C* translator has been already implemented and creates a sequential *C* source code.

In the future, we plan to do experiments and benchmarks to determine the efficiency of the code and the performance at run-time by using the $\mu T$ simulator. Depending on the results of the experiments, we also plan to make some appropriate code optimizations in the $\mu TC$ compiler in order to improve the code for our architecture.

# References

1. Jesshope, C.: Microthreading - a distributed paradigm for instruction-level concurrency. Parallel Processing Letters. In: Proc. of IFIP 10.3 Workshop 2003 (2006) (to be published)
2. Bousias, K., Hasasneh, N., Jesshope, C.: Instruction-Level Parallelism through Microthreading - a scalable Approach to Chip Multiprocessors. Computer Journal 49(2), 211–233 (2006)
3. OpenMP: OpenMP Version 2.5 Specification (accessed 16/4/2006) (2005), http://www.openmp.org/drupal/mp-documents/draft_spec25.pdf
4. Carlson, W., Draper, J., Cullera, D., Brooks, K.Y.E., Warren, K.: Introduction to UPC and Language Specification. Technical Report CCS-TR-99-157 (May 13, 1999)
5. Lee, E.A: The Problem With Threads. IEEE Computer 36(5), 33–42 (2006)
6. Swanson, S., Schwerin, A., Mercaldi, M., Petersen, A., Putnam, A., Michelson, K., Oskin, M., Eggers, S.: The WaveScalar Architecture. Accepted by Transactions on Computer Systems (TOCS) (to appear, 2006)
7. Scholz, S.B.: Single Assignment C - Efficient Support for High-Level Array Operations in a Functional Setting. Journal of Functional Programming 13(6), 1005–1053 (2003)
8. Jesshope, C.: $\mu TC$ - an intermediate language for programming chip multiprocessors. In: Proceedings Asia-Pacific Computer Systems Architecture 2006, ACSAC06 (2006) (to be published)
9. AETHER: Self-adaptive computing, http://www.aether-ist.org/
10. ACE: CoSy Compiler Development System, http://www.ace.nl/compiler/cosy.html
11. Aho, A.V., Sethi, R., Ullman, J.D.: Compilers: Principles, Techniques, and Tools, pp. 514–519. Addison-Wesley, Reading (1986)

# Image Quantisation on a Massively Parallel Embedded Processor

Jan Jacobs[1], Leroy van Engelen[2], Jan Kuper[2], and Gerard J.M. Smit[2]

[1] Océ Technologies BV, P.O. Box 101,
5900MA Venlo, The Netherlands
jan.wm.jacobs@oce.com
[2] University of Twente, P.O. Box 217,
7500AE Enschede, The Netherlands

**Abstract.** Recent advances in embedded processing architectures allow for new powerful algorithms, which exploit the intrinsic parallelism present in image processing applications. This paper describes the results of the mapping process of stochastic image quantisation on a massively parallel processor. The problem can be modeled in a parallel way. Despite the fact that the implementation is IO bound, good speedups are achieved ($16\times$ compared to a standard image processing package running on a Pentium processor).

## 1 Introduction

Océ Technologies develops document systems for the office as well as for the design engineering market. Sample products are: printers, copiers, and scanners, which support professionals in their daily work. In order to maintain competitiveness Océ is interested in new algorithms and embedded architectures that raise quality and/or reduce development effort. In this paper, we focus on a parallel architecture and a relatively new algorithm in the context of *business graphics*. Business graphics are characterised by large areas filled with a single colour. This type of information, such as presentation sheets and charts (Fig. 1), is often scanned in an office environment. During scanning the image is sampled, which leads to distortion. One of the possible distortions is blurring, a kind of smearing, with the effect that more colours are introduced in a scan than necessary (Fig. 1, rightmost image). Reducing the number of colours in such scans is essential for image quality and can be useful as a first step in image compression. This process is called *colour quantisation*. Popular quantisation algorithms include median cut and octree algorithms [1]. These algorithms use a statistical approach: they count the occurrences of each colour and try to assign quantised colours using only this (frequency) information. The quality can be improved by including spatial (interpixel) relationships. In this paper we use one of the most recent image processing models, Markov Random Field (MRF) [2]. *Simulated Annealing*[3], which is an efficient stochastic procedure to solve combinatorial optimisation problems, is used to execute the MRF model in an iterative way till convergence is reached. Their combined advantage comes from the little a priori information on the world model and their suitability for parallel processing.

S. Vassiliadis et al. (Eds.): SAMOS 2007, LNCS 4599, pp. 139–148, 2007.

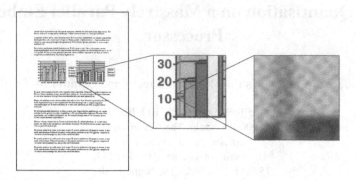

**Fig. 1.** Typical office scan containing text and charts. Scanning introduces image degradation: the number of unique grey-values increases from 10 to 229.

Present practice, however, makes such algorithms unusable since they are far too inefficient when run on sequential machines. It is our intention to find an embedded solution with a good performance-cost ratio, therefore we turn to massively parallel computing to implement these powerful algorithms. In our case we address the performance issues with the Aspex Linedancer processing array[4].

These considerations lead to the following research question:

*How to map image quantisation, based on Simulated Annealing and using an MRF image model, on a Linedancer massively parallel processing array?*

This study will be presented here in the following manner. In Section 2 we introduce the theoretical concepts that lie at the base of our quantisation algorithm, we give a mathematical description of our image model and we briefly describe Simulated Annealing. The processor used in this research is also introduced. Next, Section 3 describes the parallel model and the related complexity estimates. Then the implementation is described in Section 4, followed by the results in Section 5. Finally, conclusions and recommendations are given in Section 6.

## 2 Background

### 2.1 Image Model for Quantisation

The basic problem is to recover a limited set of colours from a scanned business graphics original. The process, which reduces the number of colours by assigning them to a limited number of *classes* in an image, is called quantisation. For simplicity we restrict ourselves in this study to grey-value images since this does not alter the essence of both algorithm and mapping. See Fig. 2 for a result of a state of the art quantisation algorithm. To better observe quantisation artifacts, the quantised image is visualised in false colours, see Fig. 2(b). A false colour image is an image that depicts a subject in colours that magnifies the differences between values that are almost equal and, as a consequence, is good visible for human perception. Note for example the ringing around edges and the various speckles in Fig. 2(b), showing the substructure in the light and dark parts barely visible in Fig. 2(c). This false colouring can be steered by a grey-value

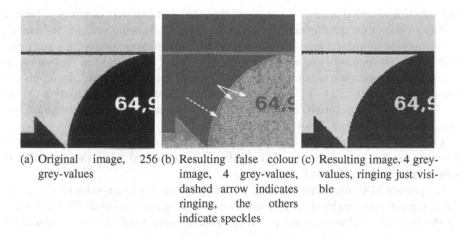

(a) Original image, 256 grey-values

(b) Resulting false colour image, 4 grey-values, dashed arrow indicates ringing, the others indicate speckles

(c) Resulting image, 4 grey-values, ringing just visible

**Fig. 2.** Example of state of the art quantisation algorithm

histogram, which can reveal such a situation. See for example the two adjacent peaks as depicted by the upper diagram in Fig. 3. *The problem we want to solve here is to raise the quality of the quantisation by a postprocessing step in an efficient way.*

First, we introduce some basic concepts, followed by two specific image models and conclude with a general image model based on the theory of MRF. The theory is described extensively in [2], the image model itself is taken from [5].

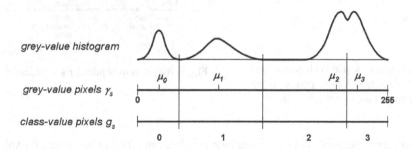

**Fig. 3.** Estimation of classes with associated class means

A pixel $s_{i,j}$ is denoted as a tuple $(i,j)$, with $i \in H = \{0,\dots,h-1\}$, $j \in W = \{0,\dots, w-1\}$ in which $w$ and $h$ are the width and height of an image. We define $\mathcal{N}_{i,j} = \{(k,l)|\sqrt{(k-i)^2+(l-j)^2} \leq \delta, (k,l) \neq (i,j)\}$ as the *neighbourhood* $\mathcal{N}_{i,j}$ of pixel $s_{i,j}$. Thus, $\mathcal{N}_{i,j}$ contains all pixels within distance $\delta$ from $s_{i,j}$, except $s_{i,j}$ itself. See Fig. 4 for a neighbourhood with radius $\delta = 2$.

An image is defined on a grid of pixels $S = \{s_{i,j}|i \in H, j \in W\}$. The scanning process produces grey-values that are assigned to pixels and denoted by $\gamma_s \in \{0,\dots,255\}$. A desired property of quantisation is that it resembles the colour or grey-value of the original. This so called *fidelity*, is optimised when the distance between grey-value and the mean value of the quantisation class (e.g. $\mu_{0...3}$ in Fig. 3) is minimal for all pixels.

The purpose of quantisation is to determine the optimal quantisation class per pixel. Each class corresponds to an ordered sub-set of $\gamma_s$ (e.g. $\{30\cdots40\}$) and this sub-set is represented by their class means $\mu_{g_s}$ (e.g. 36). These classes are identified by *labels* and denoted by $g_s \in \{0,\ldots,L-1\}$, where $L$ represents the number of quantisation classes $1 \leq L \ll 256$. $L$ is determined by inspecting the dominant peaks in the histogram, see for example Fig. 3 where $L = 4$.

A desired property of business graphics is the occurence of large planes with a single colour or label. This property, called *regularity*, is optimised when the dissimilarity between neighbouring labels is minimised.

The general MRF image model combines both the fidelity (grey-value) and the regularity (spatial relation) by simply minimising their weighted sum over all pixels. Finding **the** optimal label assignment is computationally very hard. However, reasonably

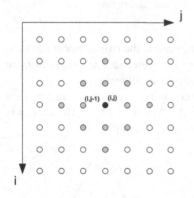

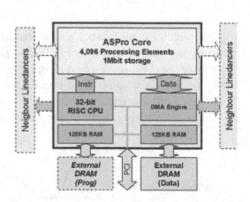

**Fig. 4.** Pixels in a grid with neighbourhood. The grey coloured pixels are all neighbours of the central pixel $(i, j)$.

**Fig. 5.** Aspex Semiconductor's Linedancer

good solutions can be found by *Simulated Annealing*, an efficient procedure for solving combinatorial optimisation problems [3]. The algorithm repetitively executes the MRF model and searches a *state* (class-values or labels of all pixels in an image) where the weighted sum, or *energy*, is minimal. Each iteration the label of a single pixel is randomly chosen and its effect on the energy is computed. States which do decrease energy are always accepted (*deterministic acceptance*), but occasionally also slight increases are accepted in order to escape from local minima (*probabilistic acceptance*). In general the combination of MRF and Simulated Annealing is considered a powerful generic framework that can be used whenever an optimisation model can be constructed of a problem. See for example half-toning in [6], a more complex application than quantisation. For our purposes, however, the main advantage of this approach is that the algorithm can be run in parallel for all pixels, as will be shown in Section 3.

## 2.2   Associative Processing

Traditional computers rely on a memory that stores and retrieves data by its address rather than by its content. In such an organisation (von Neumann architecture), every accessed data word must travel individually between the processing unit and the memory. The simplicity of this retrieval-by-address approach has ensured its success, but has also produced some inherent disadvantages. One is the von Neumann bottleneck, where the memory-access path becomes the limiting factor for system performance. A related disadvantage is the inability to proportionally increase the bandwidth between the memory and the processor as the size of the memory scales up. Associative memory, in contrast, provides a naturally parallel and scalable form of data retrieval for both structured data (e.g. sets, arrays, tables, trees and graphs) and unstructured data (raw text and digitised signals). An associative memory can be extended to process the retrieved data in place, thus becoming an associative processor. This extension is merely the capability of writing a value in parallel into selected cells [4]. Applications range from handheld gaming, multi-media, wireless base stations, on-line transaction processing to heavy image processing, pattern recognition and data mining [4,7].

Aspex's Linedancer is an implementation of a parallel associative processor. The approach taken by Aspex Semiconductor is to use many simple associative processors in a SIMD arrangement (ASProCore). Each of the 4096 processing elements (PEs) on the Linedancer device has about 200 bits of memory (of which 64 bits are fully associative) and a single bit ALU, which can perform a 1 bit operation in 1 clock cycle. Operations on larger data types take multiple clock cycles. The aggregate processing power of the Linedancer depends entirely on parallel processing. For example: a 32-bit add will take many more clock cycles compared to a high-end scalar processor, but due to the parallelism 4096 additions can be performed in parallel. Multiple Linedancer devices can be connected together to create an even wider SIMD array.

The Linedancer device (shown in Fig. 5) includes an intelligent DMA controller, to ensure that data is moved in and out of the ASProCore concurrently with data processing, and a RISC processor (Sparc), to issue high level commands to the ASProCore and to set-up the DMA controller. All parts of the device run at the same clock frequency, which can be up to 400 MHz.

A Linedancer is programmed in an extended version of C, with additional syntax for controlling the ASProCore.

The reason Linedancer was chosen for this application is its scalable property towards the number of labels that can be processed by using its associative functionality (as opposed to other solutions, e.g. CNN [5]). Other reasons are scalable performance and its attractive performance-cost ratio.

## 3   Specification of the Algorithm

The flow of the system is depicted in Fig. 6. The module denoted by MRF and Simulated Annealing is the topic of this paper. To accelerate the Simulated Annealing procedure we follow the Modified Metropolis Dynamics (MMD) approach as described extensively in [5]. Contrary to MRF with its global energy, MMD strives for minimising a

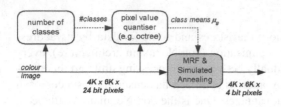

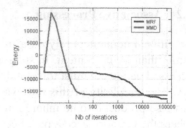

**Fig. 6.** Context of the quantisation module

**Fig. 7.** The energy decrease of MRF and MMD

local energy $\mathcal{E}_s$ per pixel in parallel and therefore converges much faster when running on a parallel architecture. Although the MRF is in the long run somewhat better in quality (i.e. lower energy), MMD offers a better "quantisation result/compute time" ratio[5]. Fig. 7 illustrates the convergence power of MMD. Let $\gamma_s$ be the observed grey-value image of pixel $s$, $g_s$ be the quantisation class or label of pixel $s$, and $g_r$ be the label of a pixel in the neighbourhood of $s$, then the energy of pixel $s$ for the MMD approach is given by:

$$\mathcal{E}_s = \underbrace{(\gamma_s - \mu_{g_s})^2}_{\text{fidelity}} + \underbrace{\sum_{r \in \mathcal{N}_s} \beta \delta(g_s, g_r)}_{\text{regularity}}, \tag{1}$$

where

$$\delta(g_s, g_r) = \begin{cases} -1 & \text{if } g_s = g_r, \\ +1 & \text{if } g_s \neq g_r \end{cases} \tag{2}$$

Minimising the energy $\mathcal{E}$ will raise the quality of the quantisation. The fidelity term depends on the class means $\mu_{g_s}$, which are constant, initialised by a previously executed module in the pipeline, see Fig. 6. The regularity term prefers neighbours having same labels (2), and $\beta$ is a positive model parameter controlling the homogeneity of the regions of the image.

The Simulated Annealing procedure is coded in Algorithm 1. Here $g$ represents the complete state of all pixels in an image and $\hat{g}$ represents a randomly chosen state of all pixels. An essential control variable in this algorithm is $T$ or *Temperature*, named after related concepts in Physics [3]. A desired property of this procedure is the controlled and slow transition from a pseudo-stochastic to a deterministic phase. This transition corresponds to the transition from a broad search for global minima to the homing in on one –hopefully the best– minimum. Because $T$ is high in the beginning, the system is able to jump to states that do (not too excessively) increase the energy (line 8), allowing escape from local minima. With $T$ getting lower the system will behave more deterministic and fewer states that increase energy are accepted (lines 6 and 8). The threshold $\alpha$ controls the degree of probabilistic acceptance. The procedure can start off with an arbitrary state.

The values of parameters $\alpha$, $\beta$ and initial temperature $T_0$ are obtained from literature or based on preliminary computational experience. Typical values for these parameters are: threshold $\alpha \in [0.01, 1)$, regularity weighting $\beta \in [1, 100]$, temperature $T_0 \in [0, 16]$,

```
1:  g ← initialisation state
2:  for T ← T_0, T_0 · C, ..., T_0 · C^{n-1} do
3:      ĝ ← randomly chosen quantisation state g
4:      for all s ∈ S do
5:          ΔE_s ← E(ĝ_s) − E(g_s)
6:          if ΔE_s ≤ 0 then {Deterministic acceptance}
7:              g_s ← ĝ_s
8:          else if ΔE_s ≤ T · − ln α then {Probabilistic acceptance}
9:              g_s ← ĝ_s
10:         end if
11:     end for
12: end for
```

**Algorithm 1.** Modified Metropolis Dynamics

cooling factor $C \in [0.95, 1)$ and the number of iterations $n \in [50, 200]$. The typical dynamic behaviour of MMD versus MRF is illustrated by Fig. 7. In contrast to MRF, MMD settles around 100 iterations, independent of image size.

The complexity analysis of the sequential implementation of MRF is $O(n \cdot w \cdot h)$. Here $w$ and $h$ stand for the width and height of an image, respectively. The complexity analysis of the parallel implementation of MMD is $O\left(\frac{n \cdot w \cdot h}{\#PEs}\right)$, where $\#PEs$ stands for the number of Processing Elements.

## 4  Implementation Restrictions and Choices

To map this quantisation scheme on a Linedancer several implementation concerns have to be considered. Four of them: Look Up Table (LUT), tiling, bit-width of variables, and random number generation, are described below.

For most fine grain SIMD systems the size of the local memory is limited. In order to really be scalable in the number of labels, one must be able to retrieve the class means $\mu_{g_s}$ in an efficient way. The associative functionality of the Linedancer is very suitable in providing lookup functionality for all PEs.

Choosing a pixel-per-PE scheme means that a single Linedancer can host a $64 \times 64$ tile of pixels. To process larger images we use *tiling*, i.e. we divide the image in small chunks (of $64 \times 64$ pixels) that fit on the Linedancer. When running each tile, one after another for all $n$ iterations, without providing for inter-tile communication, maximum speedup will be achieved but quality might be compromised. In order to counter this loss of quality a multi-pass scheme is used. In this way tiles are fetched multiple times, using overlapped fetch, effectively allowing for inter-tile communication.

The Linedancer does not support floating point arithmetic. For the various variables an accuracy analysis is made for determining the necessary bit-width in an integer arithmetic scheme. For the energy computation (1), the fidelity term takes the largest bit budget because of the square operation of a subtraction of two 8-bit values. The energy field is dimensioned to a 20-bit number representation, sufficient for storing the addition result of both the fidelity and regularity terms.

For every iteration a new state ($\hat{g}$) has to be generated in a random fashion. Pseudo random generators based on Linear Feedback Shift Register (LFSR) have low memory footprint and only need simple bit operations: XOR and Shift [8]. A 10 bit LFSR with only two tap points generates a pseudo random number sequence with cycle length $2^{10} - 1 = 1023$, which is sufficient.

## 5   Results and Discussion

Table 1 summarises the timing results of three distinct implementations for $L = 16$ quantisation classes. Two of them implement the MMD scheme, one executed on a 2 GHz Pentium Xeon with 1 GB RAM and one on the Linedancer. For comparison also a state of the art quantisation algorithm Octree[1] is used, which is part of the image processing package ImageMagick. The current Linedancer implementation is 16 times faster than Octree running on the above mentioned Pentium processor (and $128\times$ faster compared to MMD on a Pentium).

**Table 1.** Execution times of quantisation for $L = 16$ classes: Octree and the MMD version both on a Pentium, and MMD on the Linedancer. All MMD processing is performed with $n = 100$ iterations.

| # Pixels | Time (ms) | | |
|---|---|---|---|
| | Octree on Pentium | MMD on Pentium | MMD on Linedancer |
| 10000 | 108 | 517 | 5.95 |
| 40000 | 343 | 2070 | 23.1 |
| 160000 | 1171 | 8420 | 80.3 |
| 640000 | 4406 | 34600 | 280 |
| 2560000 | 16796 | 138000 | 1080 |

To give an idea how many cycles the different parts of the algorithm take, we measured the number of cycles taken for different stages of the algorithm. The results can be seen in Table 2. For the "For each neighbour"-parts, which take 3592 cycles each, 3200 (estimate based on a communication model) are spent on communication per part. This is approximately 73% of a total of 8754 cycles for each iteration per tile. However, clever reuse in communicating the neighbourhood could reduce this overhead, provided some memory space is available for storing intermediate results. Then 55% of a reduced total of 5207 cycles is spent in communication, yielding a speedup of 1.7.

A further improvement can be obtained by extending the Linedancer's synchronous inter-PE communication with a chordal ring, e.g. with an extra link for each PE with distance 64. This would yield a total speedup of 3.0 and would turn this realisation into a processing bound solution; only 20% of a reduced total of 2935 cycles is then spent in communication.

In quality terms the improvement w.r.t. state of the art quantisation algorithms is difficult to judge. The ringing at the edges and the speckles have disappeared when comparing the image in Fig. 2(b) and the image of Fig. 8(a). But the redistribution of classes lead to larger inhomogeneous areas and further study is needed to reduce this

**Table 2.** Number of measured cycles used for each iteration per tile of the algorithm. Nesting indicates loops, bold numbers indicate accumulated results.

| Activity | # Cycles |
|---|---|
| Preparation | 70 |
| Processing one tile | |
|   Calculate a new random labeling | 44 |
|   For each label | **352** |
|     $y - \mu_{g_s}$        (16×) | 22 |
|     Square | 164 |
|   For each neighbour | **3592** |
|     Add or subtract β (avg)    (12×) | 299.3 |
|   Load $y$ | 16 |
|   For each label | **352** |
|     $y - \mu_{g_s}$        (16×) | 22 |
|     Square | 164 |
|   For each neighbour | **3592** |
|     Add or subtract β (avg)    (12×) | 299.3 |
|   Subtract energies, threshold values and update | 70 |
| Dump result | 338 |
| Total | **8754** |

side-effect. The MMD implementation is single pass, i.e. process each tile just once. However, single-pass results in annoying artifacts as can be seen in Fig. 8(a). To counter this, each tile can be processed multiple times, effectively allowing neighbouring tiles to communicate their regularity information, see image in Fig. 8(b). This can be done without performance degradation because on the Linedancer the dumping of the result of a previous tile and the loading of the next one can be completely hidden in the processing of the current tile.

## 6  Conclusions and Recommendations

An MMD implementation on the Linedancer has a high performance gain w.r.t. a state of the art sequential algorithm (speedup 16×), even in the case of a multi-pass approach. Careful engineering of the inter-PE communication could increase the speed by an extra factor of 1.7. When the processing array is extended with a chordal ring interconnection structure, with extra chords connecting PEs at distance 64, then a total speedup of approximately 3.0 can be obtained.

Though not the focus of this study some conclusions may be drawn on quality. First of all MMD promotes the redistribution of classes to larger uniform areas than the conventional method, as shown in the false coloured visualisations. The speckles and ringing effects at edges have disappeared. However, the redistribution of classes leads to larger inhomogeneous areas and further study is needed to reduce this side-effect.

From an architectural point of view we recommended an improvement in the inter-PE communication of the Linedancer.

148     J. Jacobs et al.

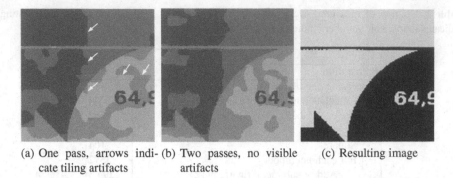

(a) One pass, arrows indi-  (b) Two passes, no visible     (c) Resulting image
cate tiling artifacts            artifacts

**Fig. 8.** Quantisation by MMD on an image of 128 x 128 pixels, processed in chunks of 64 x 64 tiles

# References

1. Freisleben, B., Schrader, A.: An evolutionary approach to color image quantization. In: Proceedings of 1997 IEEE International Conference on Evolutionary Computation (ICEC 97), Indianapolis, IN, USA pp. 459–464 (1997)
2. Kato, Z.: Modelisations markoviennes multiresolutions en vision par ordinateur. Application a la segmentation d'images SPOT. PhD thesis, University of Nice, [English translation] (1994)
3. Duda, R.O., Hart, P.E., Stork, D.G.: Pattern Classification, 2nd edn. John Wiley & Sons, Inc. Chichester (2001)
4. Aspex Semiconductor Ltd: Linedancer - overview (2005), http://www.aspex-semi.com/pages/products/products_linedancer_overview.shtml
5. Sziranyi, T., Zerubia, J., Czuni, L., Geldreich, D., Kato, Z.: Image segmentation using Markov random field model in fully parallel cellular network architectures. Real-Time Imaging 6, 195–221 (2000)
6. Geist, R., Reynolds, R., Suggs, D.: A markovian framework for digital halftoning. ACM Trans. Graph. 12(2), 136–159 (1993)
7. Krikelis, A., Weems, C.: Associative Processing and Processors, 1st edn. IEEE Computer Society Press, Los Alamitos (1997)
8. Golomb, S.W., Golomb, S.: Shift Register Sequences. Aegean Park Press, Laguna Hills, CA, USA (1981)

# Stream Image Processing on a Dual-Core Embedded System

Michael G. Benjamin and David Kaeli

Northeastern University, Computer Architecture Research Laboratory
409 Dana Research Center, 360 Huntington Ave, Boston, MA 02115, USA
{mbenjami,kaeli}@ece.neu.edu

**Abstract.** Effective memory utilization is critical to reap the benefits of the multi-core processors emerging on embedded systems. In this paper we explore the use of a stream model to effectively utilize memory hierarchies. We target image processing algorithms running on the Analog Devices Blackfin BF561 fixed-point, dual-core DSP. Using optimized assembly to effectively use cores reduces runtime, but also underscores the need to mitigate the memory bottleneck. Like other embedded processors, the Blackfin BF561 has L2 SRAM available. Applying the stream model allows us to effectively make full use of both cores and the L2 SRAM. We achieve almost a 10X speedup in execution time compared to non-optimized C code.

## 1 Introduction

Convergent, embedded architectures combine multiple instruction sets and allow traditional digital-signal processing (DSP) platforms to also run micro-controller (MCU) code. To develop applications for these platforms, developers should try to leverage open source image and video processing libraries to drastically reduce development time of embedded computer vision applications. By utilizing DSP and other special-purpose hardware available on the processor, the performance of these applications can be greatly improved. But with highly compute-optimized code, the memory bottleneck becomes even more apparent.

The growing gap between processor and memory speeds has long been acknowledged [1] and has been attacked using on-chip caches. But image and video applications exhibit characteristics not well-suited for conventional caches. Images have 2D spatial locality, while caches capture only one dimension [2,3]. Image processing shows little temporal data reuse, causing cache pollution. Cache lines corresponding to processed data are not reused and must be replaced often. This characteristic of image-based processing need cache structures that can accomodate both types of locality [4,5]. An alternative use of the on-chip memory is as scratch-pad memory, with data communication controlled explicitly by the programmer [6].

The stream model of computation has recently been proposed to address memory bottlenecks. In short, the stream paradigm decouples computation and memory accesses to ensure parallelism and locality. We examine the use of the stream paradigm in conjunction with assembly optimizations on a representative set of image processing algorithms, running on the Blackfin embedded processor from Analog Devices, Inc. (ADI) - a good example of a convergent architecture.

S. Vassiliadis et al. (Eds.): SAMOS 2007, LNCS 4599, pp. 149–158, 2007.

Section 2 discusses the stream model in further detail. Section 3 discusses the convergent architecture of the dual-core Blackfin BF561 processor. Section 4 describes the main target application discussed in this paper, an edge detection program. We also discuss our scheme to produce optimized execution on the convergent Blackfin DSP architecture. Section 5 presents our results and section 6 concludes the paper.

## 2    Stream Computing Paradigm

The goal of the stream paradigm is to maximize data locality while exposing parallelism. Stream applications decouple two aspects of computing: performing computations, and data communication required to feed the computations. Streams are sets of data elements to be processed by compute kernels, which are sequences of instructions applied to each element in a stream.

Locality can be maximized because during a kernel's execution, all data accesses can be served by local memory storage (maximizing kernel locality) and because results produced by one kernel are quickly consumed by the next (maximizing producer-consumer locality).

Given the necessary computational resources, multiple kernels can operate simultaneously in a pipeline, exposing thread-level parallelism. For each thread and within a kernel, independent instructions can operate at the same time, exposing instruction-level parallelism. A particular instruction could be vectorized and applied to many elements of the data stream using SIMD hardware, exposing data-level parallelism [7,8].

### 2.1    Stream Applications, Languages, and Compilers

To quickly process high definition images or video sequences, data should be locally available to computational units. For large images, a common approach is to partition the data, effectively maintain intermediate results in low-latency memory, and continuously process the resulting subimages. This fundamental streaming nature is apparent in a number of applications and modern graphics processing units (GPUs) are designed around a stream model both in their hardware [9] and software [10] implementations. A number of languages and compilers have been developed including StreamIT [11], Stream-C and Kernel-C [12].

### 2.2    Stream Architectures

The rising demand for media processing has motivated the development of a number of architectures and re-examination of existing architectures to work with a stream model. Processors like Imagine [13,14], Merrimac [15], and Stream Processors Inc.'s Storm-1 [16] have been developed to exploit the stream model. To support diverse, dynamic applications, architectures that can be reconfigured to execute efficiently for many classes of applications have been introduced. Architectures such as TRIPS [17] and RAW [18] can be described as polymorphous - that is, they can morph between a number of operating modes, each capturing some class of applications.

Researchers have even explored using the stream paradigm on existing general-purpose processors [19]. By using L2 cache as local storage, and multithreading for parallelism, scientific applications can achieve moderate speedups (27%). But cache overhead limits the effectiveness of this approach. For architectures which support L2 SRAM acting more like scratchpad memory (common in many embedded processors, e.g., the ADI Blackfin), there is potential for higher performance.

## 3  Blackfin Processor

The Blackfin is an embedded architecture based on the MicroSignal Architecture developed jointly by ADI and Intel [20]. It supports 8, 16, and 32-bit arithmetic operations, but is optimized for 16-bit operations. The Blackfin reduces power and part cost by integrating RISC and DSP processor capabilities into a single chip. But rather than fusing two cores together, the Blackfin ISA was designed from the beginning with this duality in mind. The 32-bit RISC instruction set is variable-length and supports Single Instruction, Multiple Data (SIMD) operations. As shown in Fig 1, the DSP instruction set makes use of dual 16-bit multiply-accumulate (MAC) units. Additionally, a video pixel instruction set supports four 8-bit video ALUs which can be utilized with vector instructions for addition, multiplication, averaging, and sum of-absolute-differences calculations [21].

The BF561 processor is a Blackfin derivative with two cores, clocked at up to 600 MHz. The BF561 has 128 KB on-chip L2 SRAM, clocked at 300 MHz, and 100 KB in-core L1 SRAM, which is split between instruction, data, and scratch-pad memories.

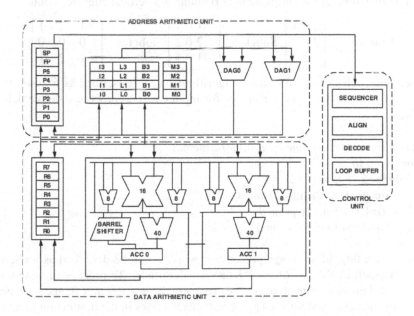

**Fig. 1.** The ADI Blackfin processor core

L1 can be configured as either SRAM or cache. The BF561's L2 memory can not be configured as cache [22], but the programmer is able to map data into regions in L2. Without the turn-key solution of using L2 as cache and given the limitations of cache for image and video processing discussed in the introduction, we examine the use of L2 as a local store in the stream paradigm.

## 4    Implementation

Many image processing algorithms are made up of a sequence of convolutions, which transform images using a set of kernel matrices. To avoid confusion with the computational kernels used in the stream model, we refer to kernel matrices as "masks." For example, an image represented by the 2D matrix $\mathbf{F} := (f_{x,y})_{m \times n}$ can be transformed into another image represented by the matrix $\mathbf{G}$ by convolving $\mathbf{F}$ with a mask, denoted $\mathbf{H}$, by the 2D convolution equation:

$$g_{x,y} = \sum_{i=-1}^{1} \sum_{j=-1}^{1} h_{j+2,i+2} \times f_{x-j,y-i}$$

Such convolutions are frequently used to update pixel values based on neighborhood operations. For example, for images which contain noise, averaging a pixel based on its neighborhood can reduce the intensity of the noise, thus smoothing or blurring the image. In order to determine edges in an image, approximations of the first and second derivative can be used as masks to determine if the intensity level for a pixel neighborhood is uniform or changes (implying an edge). A Gaussian mask implements noise reduction; two Sobel masks implement horizontal and vertical edge detection:

$$\mathbf{Gauss} = \tfrac{1}{16} \begin{bmatrix} 1 & 2 & 1 \\ 2 & 4 & 2 \\ 1 & 2 & 1 \end{bmatrix} \quad \mathbf{Sobel_x} = \begin{bmatrix} -1 & 0 & 1 \\ -2 & 0 & 2 \\ -1 & 0 & 1 \end{bmatrix} \quad \mathbf{Sobel_y} = \begin{bmatrix} 1 & 2 & 1 \\ 0 & 0 & 0 \\ -1 & -2 & -1 \end{bmatrix}$$

In general such image convolution algorithms can be described as follows, where $mem_i$ and $mem_o$ are data sets in memory for input data and processed output data, respectively:

```
IMAGEPROCKERNEL (mem_i, m, n, mask, mem_o)
1    for y ← 0 to m − 1
2        do for x ← 0 to n − 1
3            do p = GETPIXEL(x, y, mem_i)
4            2D CONVOLVE( p, mask )
5            SETPIXEL(p, y, x, mem_o)
```

The control flow of an image processing program can be described as a sequence of kernels (such as the IMAGEPROCKERNEL algorithm). To process an image, each $kernel_i$ would execute, convolving every pixel $p$ in the $m \times n$ source image $src$ with the convolution mask(s), and setting appropriate pixel values in the destination image $dst$. Performance can be increased by ensuring calls to GETPIXEL and SETPIXEL access low-latency memory.

PROCESSIMAGE

```
1   foreach kernel_i in Control Flow
2       RUN(kernel_i (src, m, n, mask, dst))
```

We examine an edge detection program using a Gaussian blur convolution to reduce noise and a Sobel gradient-operator convolution to highlight both horizontal and vertical edges in a high-definition image. The resolution used is 1920x1080 (WxH) which requires 2,073,600 pixels to be convolved. For a 3x3 mask, this requires 9 multiplications and 8 additions per pixel. Therefore, a single convolution would require about 18.7 MMACs. Our program uses three such convolutions, and therefore the ideal is about 56 MMACs.

The actual benchmark code used is taken from existing codebases [23] and from the ADI Blackfin SDK [24]. We examine the assembly-level optimizations given in the SDK code to reduce the execution time on each core, and then attempt to optimize the use of both cores to reduce overall execution time. The computational optimizations underscore the need for efficient memory usage.

### 4.1   Assembly Optimizations

As discussed in section 3, the Blackfin has a dual-MAC architecture: to carry out convolutions, two pixels can be convolved at once. By pushing the unique values of a mask onto the stack and popping them when needed, the program can quickly fetch $h_{x,y}$ mask values. Using parallel-issue instructions, the Blackfin can execute two MAC operations to set two $g_{x,y}$ pixel values while fetching the next $f_{x,y}$ pixel and $h_{x,y}$ mask values in the same clock cycle. This technique allows the 56 MMACS to require only 28 Mcycles, which running on a 600 MHz core clock is less than 0.05 sec. This runtime is the theoretical lower limit for the convolutions alone, and the delay added due to memory latency is substantial - emphasizing the need for efficient memory use.

### 4.2   Dual-Core Utilization

A natural approach to utilize symmetric cores is to divide the image into partitions, giving each core its own portion of the data. This can be described as partitioning the data-flow of the program and has also ben called the "homogenous model" [25]. Another approach is to partition the compute kernels and give each core some set of kernels to perform; the resulting data would flow from one core into the next. This approach can be described as partitioning the control-flow of the program, and embodies some of the characteristics of the stream model.

In order to add more kernels to the stream, we utilize C data structures representing kernels, which include pointers to the input/output records and a callback for the kernel's function, and the three routines discussed below:

- ADDKERNEL - adds a kernel to a linked list representing the program's control flow
- NEWSTREAMREC - allocates memory for input/output records of a kernel
- MAPSTREAM - maps existing records for a kernel

At initialization, we use the above routines to set up the control flow of a program. Following initialization, we call each kernel as specified. To implement other image processing programs using our method, the addition of new kernels or stream mappings only requires a new initialization for each core, and does not require a specialized stream compiler.

To use the two symmetric cores on the BF561, we examined both approaches discussed above. For data-flow partitioning, each core processes half the image. For control-flow partitioning, each core processes half of the computational kernels. This approach is viable for our two convolution kernels, but for programs that lack a balanced set of computational kernels, a heuristic approach may be needed.

### 4.3  Memory Hierarchy Utilization

In order to make use of the BF561's L2 SRAM as local storage memory, we examined two approaches. The first uses regions of L2 SRAM on a per-kernel basis. It copies subimages into input records associated with a computational kernel (denoted $kernel_i.in$), runs the kernel, saves results into output records (denoted $kernel_i.out$), and saves these records back to SDRAM after computation completes; this process is then repeated for the next kernel in the control flow of the program. A side-effect of this approach is that the results of each kernel can be saved, but at the cost of increased memory access for each kernel. This approach is summarized in the following pseudocode:

PER-KERNEL CONVOLUTION
1   **foreach** $kernel_i$ **in** Control Flow
2     **do foreach** $SUBIMAGE$ **in** $IMAGE$
3       **do** COPY($SUBIMAGE, kernel_i.in$)
4         RUN ($kernel_i(kernel_i.in, m, n, kernel_i.out)$)
5         COPY($kernel_i.out, SUBIMAGE$)

The second approach uses the stream processing paradigm. Under this model, SDRAM is only accessed for compulsory reads or completion writes (i.e., only after all $k$ kernels in the control flow have been processed). This approach is summarized in the following pseudocode:

STREAM CONVOLUTION
1   **foreach** $SUBIMAGE$ **in** $IMAGE$
2     **do** COPY($SUBIMAGE, kernel_1.in$)
3     **foreach** $kernel_i$ **in** Control Flow
4         **do** RUN($kernel_i(kernel_i.in, m, n, kernel_{i+1}.in)$)
5     COPY($kernel_k.out, SUBIMAGE$)

Unlike the previous approach, the results of each kernel are not saved - only the final results after every kernel has been run is saved to SDRAM. But for programs where the intermediate results are not important, reducing the number of main memory accesses provides higher performance.

# 5   Results

We produce the following results on a live Analog Devices BF561 system. Figures 2 and 3 show the results using hardware counters.

Figure 2 shows how the different methods reduce the cycle count. For the single-core (SC) case, the use of L2 in the partitioned data-flow method reduces the runtime by nearly half. The use of a second core is effective only when the cores are not waiting for data (i.e., when data is stored in on-chip memory). Ideally, using the second core would half the runtime, but when SDRAM is used the additional core only provides a 27% increase in performance. Only when the latency penalty of SDRAM access is minimized by using L2 do we achieve a 2X speedup due to the second core.

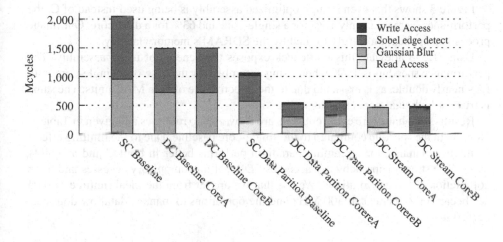

**Fig. 2.** C implementations for single-core (SC) and dual-core (DC) approaches

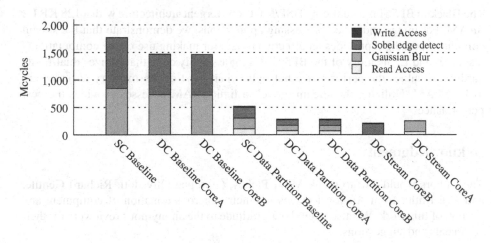

**Fig. 3.** Assembly implementation of the 3x3 convolution program

**Table 1.** Runtimes using single and dual-core, using different memory management approaches, and comparing C and ASM implementations

|  | C | ASM |
|---|---|---|
|  | Runtime (Speedup) in secs. | Runtime (Speedup) in secs. |
| Single-core baseline approach | 3.99 (1.0) | 3.64 (1.10) |
| Dual-core split data | 3.15 (1.27) | 2.45 (1.63) |
| Single-core with L2 | 1.80 (2.22) | 1.08 (3.69) |
| Dual-core split data with L2 | 0.92 (4.34) | 0.44 (9.07) |
| Dual-core streamed approach | 0.80 (4.99) | 0.42 (9.50) |

Figure 3 shows that even though optimized assembly is being used instead of C, the performance increase is only 10% for a single-core and 63% for a dual-core. Our image processing application is truly limited by the SDRAM's memory latency.

Using L2 to alleviate this bottleneck exposes the benefits of using assembly. The performance speedup is 1.7X when using assembly for the case of a single-core with L2 - nearly double, as is expected due to the effective use of both MAC units. The same is true for both dual-core cases as well.

Results from hardware cycle counters are converted to runtimes and given in Table 1, along with the speedup compared to the single-core baseline. Due to the limiting effects of memory latency, the streaming paradigm performs better in both C and assembly cases. The stream approach only accesses SDRAM on compulsory accesses and upon completion of the convolutions. We see that we are far from the ideal runtime of 0.05 sec because L2 operates at 300 MHz and the operations to manage dataflow dominate performance.

## 6    Conclusion

The Blackfin BF561 is a dual-core DSP/MCU convergent architecture with a 128 KB L2 SRAM. For image and video processing applications, we demonstrate that the stream computing paradigm provides an effective model for making use of the computational resources and L2 memory of the BF561. Using assembly code that utilizes dual-MAC hardware doubles the performance but only when most of the memory accesses are to L2 SRAM. Utilizing the stream model to limit SRAM accesses provides the best performance.

## Acknowledgment

The authors would like to thank Mimi Pichey, Giuseppe Olivadoti, Richard Gentile, and Ken Butler from Analog Devices for their generous donation of equipment and support of this work. We also extend our gratitude to the anonymous reviewers for their comments and suggestions.

# References

1. Wulf, W.A., McKee, S.A.: Hitting the Memory Wall: Implications of the Obvious. SIGARCH Computer Architecture News 23, 20–24 (1995)
2. Cucchiara, R., Massimo Piccardi, A.P.: Exploiting Cache in Multimedia. In: Proc. of Int'l Conference on Multimedia Computing and Systems, vol. 1, pp. 345–350 (1999)
3. Pati, A.: Exploring Multimedia Applications Locality to Improve Cache Performance. In: Proc. of 8th Int'l Conference on Multimedia, pp. 509–510 (2000)
4. Naz, A., Kavi, K., Sweany, P., Rezaei, M.: A Study of Separate Array and Scalar Caches. In: Proc. of the 18th Int'l Symposium on High Performance Computing Systems and Applications, pp. 157–164 (2004)
5. Naz, A., Rezaei, M., Kavi, K., Sweany, P.: Improving Data Cache Performance with Integrated Use of Split Caches, Victim Cache and Stream Buffers. In: Proc. of the 2004 Workshop on Memory Performance: Dealing with Applications, Systems and Architecture, pp. 41–48 (2004)
6. Banakar, R., Steinke, S., Lee, B.-S., Balakrishnan, M., Marwedel, P.: Scratchpad Memory: A Design Alternative for Cache On-chip memory in Embedded Systems. In: Proc. of the 10th Int'l Symposium on Hardware/Software Codesign, pp. 73–78 (2002)
7. Dally, W.J., Kapasi, U.J., Khailany, B., Ahn, J.H., Das, A.: Stream Processors: Programmability and Efficiency. ACM Queue 2, 52–52 (2004)
8. Kapasi, U.J., Rixner, S., Dally, W.J., Khailany, B., Ahn, J.H., Mattso, P., Owen, J.D.: Programmable Stream Processors. ACM Computer 8, 54–62 (2003)
9. Venkatasubramanian, S.: The Graphics Card as a Stream Computer. In: Workshop on Management and Processing of Data Streams (2003)
10. Buck, I., Foley, T., Horn, D., Sugerman, J., Fatahalian, K., Houston, M., Hanrahan, P.: Brook for GPUs: Stream Computing on Graphics Hardware. ACM Transactions on Graphics 23, 777–786 (2004)
11. Gordon, M.I., Thies, W., Karczmarek, M., Lin, J., Meli, A.S., Lamb, A.A., Leger, C., Wong, J., Hoffmann, H., Maze, D., Amarasinghe, S.: A Stream Compiler for Communication-Exposed Architectures. SIGPLAN Not. 10, 291–303 (2002)
12. Mattson, P.: A Programming System for the Imagine Media Processor. PhD thesis, Stanford University (2001)
13. Rixner, S., Dally, W.J., Kapasi, U.J., Khailany, B., Lopez-Lagunas, A., Mattson, P.R., Owens, J.D.: A Bandwidth-Efficient Architecture for Media Processing. In: Proc. of the 31th Int'l Symposium on Microarchitecture, pp. 3–13 (1998)
14. Khailany, B., Dally, W.J., Kapasi, U.J., Mattson, P., Namkoong, J., Owens, J.D., Towles, B., Chang, A., Rixner, S.: Imagine: Media Processing with Streams. IEEE Micro 21, 35–46 (2001)
15. Dally, W.J.: Merrimac: Supercomputing with Streams. In: Proc. of the Conference on Supercomputing (2003)
16. Stream Processing: Enabling a New Class of Easy to Use, High-Performance Parallel DSPs. White Paper 1.9, Stream Processors Inc. 455 DeGuigne Drive Sunnyvale, CA 94085, USA (2007)
17. Sankaralingam, K., Nagarajan, R., Liu, H., Kim, C., Huh, J., Ranganathan, N., Burger, D., Keckler, S.W., McDonald, R.G., Moore, C.R.: TRIPS: A Polymorphous Architecture for Exploiting ILP, TLP, and DLP. ACM Transactions on Architecture and Code Optimization 1, 62–93 (2004)
18. Waingold, E., Taylor, M., Srikrishna, D., Sarkar, V., Lee, W., Lee, V., Kim, J., Frank, M., Finch, P., Barua, R., Babb, J., Amarasinghe, S., Agarwal, A.: Baring It All to Software: RAW Machines. Computer 30, 86–93 (1997)

158     M.G. Benjamin and D. Kaeli

19. Gummaraju, J., Rosenblum, M.: Stream Programming on General-Purpose Processors. In: Proc. of the 38th Int'l Symposium on Microarchitecture, Washington, DC, USA, pp. 343–354. IEEE Computer Society Press, Los Alamitos (2005)
20. Kolagotla, R.K., Fridman, J., Aldrich, B.C., Hoffman, M.M., Anderson, W.C., Allen, M.S., Witt, D.B., Dunton, R.R., Booth, L.A.J: High Performance Dual-MAC DSP Architecture. IEEE Signal Processing 19, 42–43 (2002)
21. Analog Devices, Inc. One Technology Way, Norwood, MA 02062, USA: ADSP-BF53x/BF56x Blackfin Processor Programming Reference. 1.0 edn. (2005)
22. Analog Devices, Inc. One Technology Way, Norwood, MA 02062, USA: ADSP-BF561 Blackfin Processor Hardware Reference. 1.0 edn. (2005)
23. Green, B.: Edge Detection Tutorial (2002), http://www.pages.drexel.edu/~weg22/edge.html
24. Analog.com: Software Development Kit (SDK) Downloads (2007), http://www.analog.com/processors/platforms/sdk.html
25. Ning, K., Yi, G., Gentile, R.: Single-chip Dual-core Embedded Programming Models for Multimedia Applications (2005), http://www.ecnmag.com/article/CA502854.html

# MORA: A New Coarse-Grain Reconfigurable Array for High Throughput Multimedia Processing

Marco Lanuzza, Stefania Perri, and Pasquale Corsonello

Department of Electronics, Computer Science and Systems
University of Calabria, Arcavacata di Rende - 87036 - Rende (CS), Italy
{lanuzza, perri}@deis.unical.it, p.corsonello@unical.it

**Abstract.** This paper presents a new coarse-grain reconfigurable array optimized for multimedia processing. The system has been designed to provide a dense support for arithmetic operations, wide internal data bandwidth and efficiently distributed memory resources. All these characteristics are combined into a cohesive structure that efficiently supports a block-level pipelined dataflow, which is particularly suitable for stream oriented applications. Moreover, the new reconfigurable architecture is highly flexible and easily scalable. Thanks to all these features, the proposed architecture can be drastically more speed- and area-efficient than a state of the art FPGA in executing multimedia oriented applications.

**Keywords:** Reconfigurable systems, coarse-grain array, multimedia applications.

## 1 Introduction

Modern multimedia applications, including image processing, digital signal processing, video stream operations and others, demand high-performance computations alongside the capability of matching the rapid evolution of the algorithms. The simultaneous demand for high computational speed and flexibility makes reconfigurable architectures attractive solutions. In fact, they provide performances similar to Application Specific Integrated Circuits (ASICs), with maintaining a level of flexibility not available with more traditional custom circuitry.

In reconfigurable computing, a key role is covered by fine-grained Field-Programmable Gate Arrays (FPGAs). Commercially available FPGAs consist of a matrix of reconfigurable logic cells, with bit-level granularity, interacting through a very flexible programmable routing network. Thanks to this structure, FPGAs offer a high degree of on-chip parallelism; user control over low-level resources definition and allocation; and user-defined data format represented efficiently in hardware. As a drawback, owing to bit-level granularity, many resources have to be used to support multi-bit operations. This leads to a large routing overhead and to a low silicon area efficiency of FPGA-based computing solutions. Another disadvantage of the FPGAs is the large amount of configuration data needed for configuring logic cells and routing switches. This is particularly limiting in terms of required reconfiguration

S. Vassiliadis et al. (Eds.): SAMOS 2007, LNCS 4599, pp. 159–168, 2007.

time and power dissipation especially when multiple hardware reconfigurations are needed an application process [1]. Such characteristics make FPGAs too expensive or not efficient enough when supporting multimedia applications.

In order to overcome the above drawbacks, Coarse-Grain Reconfigurable Architectures (CGRAs) use multiple-bit (typically 8/16-bits) wide arithmetic-oriented processing elements (PEs) in conjunction with faster and more area- and power-efficient routing structures [1-2]. As a consequence, greater efficiency is achieved in executing arithmetic-dominant applications (such as multimedia applications) at lower power, area, and configuration time with respect to FPGAs [3]. From an architectural point of view, CGRAs can be classified as systems based on a linear array or on 2D mesh-based architectures [1]. Linear array based architectures, such as Piperench [4] and RaPiD [5], aim to speed-up highly regular computation-intensive applications by deep data-level pipelines. Their 1D architectural organization is particularly efficient for computations that can be easily linear pipelined. On the contrary, it appears inappropriate to support block-based applications [6], which are very common in multimedia processing. Because of the greater flexibility, 2D mesh-based architectures [6-13] have received more success at both commercial and academic levels. All these systems are based on a 2D array of arithmetic-oriented functional unit, but differ often greatly in the special features provided to enhance the execution of computing intensive-applications.

In this paper a novel 2D coarse-grain reconfigurable array, called MORA (Multimedia Oriented Reconfigurable Array), is proposed. The new architecture merges some promising characteristics of the previously proposed reconfigurable systems with a block-level pipelined computational data flow resulting in a very efficient platform to support the target applications.

The remainder of the paper is organized as follows: in Section 2, an architectural overview of the new CGRA is presented; afterwards, the supported computational models are described in Section 3; examples of applications mapping are presented and compared to FPGA implementations in Section 4; finally, conclusions are given in Section 5.

## 2   Overview of the Proposed Architecture

As shown in Figure 1, the workhorse of the proposed architecture consists of a scalable 2D array of identical Reconfigurable Cells (RCs) organized in 4X4 quadrants and connected through a hierarchical reconfigurable network. In order to simplify the diagram, the interconnection scheme is not drawn. However, the interconnections topology will be detailed in Section 2.2.

Differently from many competitors, such as [6] and [8], the proposed architecture does not use a centralized RAM system. Storage for data is partitioned among the RCs by providing each of them with an internal data memory. This solution supplies a high memory access bandwidth to efficiently support massively-parallel computations, while maintaining both generality and scalability.

The external data exchange is managed in a centralized way by an *I/O Data Controller*, which can access the memory space of the RCs by using standard memory interface functions (i.e. performing read and write operations), whereas internal data flow is controlled in a distributed manner through a handshaking mechanism which drives the interactions between the RCs.

Finally, the integration with external and/or embedded microprocessors and systems is guaranteed by a general I/O system interface including a *Host Interface* and an *External Memory Interface*. The former is used to manage the device configuration and I/O data transfer, whereas the latter is provided to supplement the on chip memory (when needed).

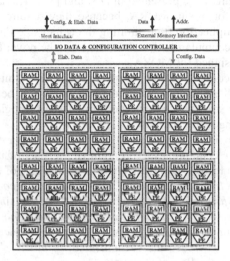

**Fig. 1.** The top level architecture

## 2.1 The Reconfigurable Cell

The block diagram of the RC is depicted in Figure 2.

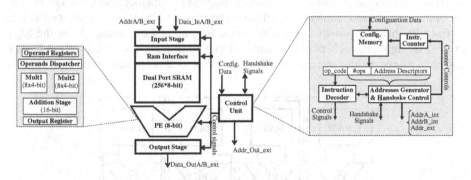

**Fig. 2.** The Reconfigurable Cell

The I/O interface includes two pairs of data/address input ports, two output data ports, a single output address port, a configuration port, and additional interface signals needed to synchronize communication between the RCs. As visible in Figure 2, the main building elements of the circuit are: a 256*8-bit *SRAM* acting as an internal data buffer; an 8-bit Processing Element (*PE*); and a *Control Unit* incorporating the *Configuration Memory*.

As explained above, MORA is proposed to efficiently support high-throughput multimedia applications, in which the most frequently required operations are addition, subtraction, accumulation, multiplication and multiply-accumulation. Possible low-area and low-power architectures of PEs able to support some of these arithmetic operations are those presented in [14] and [15]. The latter do not appear as the most appropriate for use in MORA, because they require two clock cycles for performing a 8x8 multiplication (thus limiting the achievable throughput), and do not support the multiply accumulation. For these reasons, the novel PE depicted in Figure 2 has been purpose-designed for MORA.

The proposed *PE* consists of I/O registers, two 8x4-bit multipliers, an addition stage and some auxiliary logic needed for data exchange between the arithmetic blocks. This simple structure allows performance of single clock cycle 8-bit operations by exploiting hardware reuse.

The *Control Unit* is responsible of all the RC operations. It includes a *Configuration Memory* containing the program (it consists of up to 16 vector/block instructions, which are loaded during the configuration phase of the system) to control the RC elaboration, an *Instruction Counter*, an *Instruction Decoder*, and a *Handshake Control Logic*. The *Instruction Counter* is used to sequentially step through the configured instructions. The *Instruction Decoder* generates the configuration signals for the *PE* at run-time. The *Addresses Generator* produces input and output addressing patterns, whereas the *Handshake Control Logic* manages the communication between the RCs of the array.

Each configured instruction defines the execution of vector/block operations on a large data stream. In order to enable this feature, the instructions consist of different fields: the *op_code* specifies the operation code; the *#ops* specifies the number of the operations to be performed in the current instruction; the *address descriptors* specify the operands organization in the memory. The *address descriptors* are used by the *Internal Address Generator* to establish the appropriate memory addresses to be used for both operands and results during the execution of a given vector/block instruction.

Each RC has two possible operative states: loading and executing. When the RC is in the loading state, packets of data can be inputted through one or both input ports to and then stored in the internal *SRAM*. The latter is dual-ported, thus enabling two

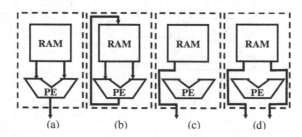

(a)          (b)          (c)          (d)

**Fig. 3.** Functionality of the reconfigurable cell: a) feed-forward mode; b) feed-back mode; c) route-through mode; d) route-through mode (double throughput)

independent write or read operations per clock cycle. Only when all the required operands are available, the RC switches to the executing state.

As illustrated in Figure 3, when the generic RC is in the executing state, it can operate in four different modes. In the feed-forward mode, the packets of data coming from the internal memory are elaborated by the PE and produced results are dispatched to one or more RCs using one or both the output data ports. In the feed-back mode, elaboration results are internally stored to be used by the same cell for future computations. Note that, each *RC* can be used also as a route-through cell. This operation mode is particularly useful to simplify the application mapping process.

The designed RC has some aspects in common with the MATRIX Basic Functional Unit [7], mostly concerning the top-level organization. On the contrary, the circuital implementation and the controlling strategy are quite different. Anyway, the proposed system strongly differs from MATRIX [7] from an architectural point of view, especially considering the array organization and the interconnection topology.

## 2.2 The Interconnections Topology

In order to allow the greatest applicability and the expandability of the new reconfigurable array, a custom interconnection network has been designed. As shown later, the interconnection structure is highly flexible and easily scalable. Similar to commercial FPGAs, all routing resources are static, thus the communications between the RCs are determined during the "configuration phase" of the system and cannot be changed at run-time. This choice does not require a centralized routing controller with benefits in terms of performance and area.

The proposed interconnection scheme consists of a hierarchical reconfigurable network organized on two levels, each routing 8-bit data and address buses plus the needed synchronization signals.

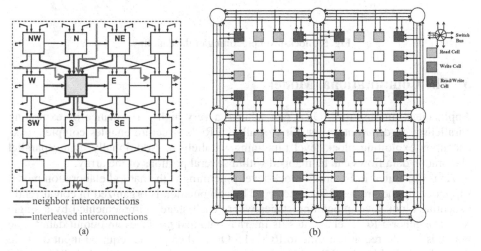

**Fig. 4.** Interconnections topology: a) the level 1 interconnection scheme; b) the level 2 interconnection scheme

The level 1 interconnections are used within each 4x4 quadrant. As depicted in Figure 4a, these interconnections provide nearest neighbours with horizontal, vertical and diagonal connectivity. Interleaved horizontal and vertical connectivity with length two is also furnished. However, each RC can receive input data from at most two cells (one for each input port) and it can send output data to at most four cells (two for each output port). Although bidirectional communication is more flexible, a unidirectional (with cyclic continuation at borders) approach has been used to reduce area occupancy and power consumption.

Data and controls exchange between the quadrants is guaranteed by the level 2 interconnections scheme that, as depicted in Figure 4b, is a combination of long unidirectional buses and *Programmable Bus Switches*. Note that access to global buses is allowed only to peripheral cells of the quadrants. This greatly simplifies the structure of the communication network inside the quadrants with consequent advantages in terms of occupied area and power dissipation.

It is worth noting that the adopted interconnection strategy makes the reconfigurable array easily scalable by hierarchical extending the level 2 interconnection scheme, thus remaining still cost- and power-efficient.

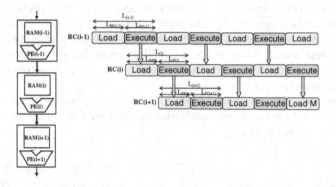

**Fig. 5.** Block-level pipelining of the data flow

# 3   The Computational Model

Applications running on MORA can achieve a very high performance by exploiting parallelism on different levels. First of all, the RC's structure enables complex tasks execution exploiting block level pipelining parallelism. Additionally, many parallel elaboration data flows can be mapped within several portions of the array.

As is illustrated in Figure 5, block-level pipelining is the natural elaboration model supported by the proposed architecture. The computation is organized in concurrently executing block-level pipelining stages where each stage is implemented by a single RC. The generic RC(i) elaborates its internal data and produces an output data frame which is transferred at run-time to RC(i+1). Only when all the required input data are internally available, the RC(i+1) can start its execution phase producing data for the subsequent processing stage. Note that RC(i)'s elaboration and RC(i+1)'s data loading are always overlapped. As a consequence, the latency $L_{M(i+1)}$ due to the data loading into the memory space of RC(i+1) is always hidden by the processing latency $L_{P(i)}$ of the previous cell. It is important to point out that, through the block level pipelining, three key objectives are achieved. First, it is possible to maintain concurrency of each processing stage while providing correct synchronization in data exchange between the RCs; second, since control signals and elaboration data become local, higher performances can be achieved by minimizing routing; third, thanks to the data storage distribution, a high memory bandwidth is also guaranteed.

Another important feature of the proposed architecture is the flexibility offered in balancing the computational load of the RCs involved in the elaboration.

As illustrated in Figure 6, two strategies can be exploited (also simultaneously) to balance the computational load of a given RC: spatial computational load balancing achieved via data parallelism; temporal computational load balancing achieved by increasing the number of block pipelining stages.

Note that increasing the number of block-level pipelining stages introduces an additional latency $L_T$ due to the transfer of unprocessed data. This technique is always applicable whereas exploiting spatial computational parallelism is constrained by the viable input/output cell ports (two only input/output ports are available per cell).

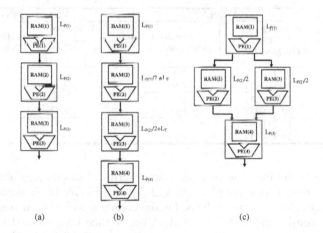

(a)                    (b)                              (c)

**Fig. 6.** Examples of computational load balancing on the application basis where $L_{P(2)}/2 \gg L_{P(1)}$, $L_{P(3)}$ a) Straightforward application mapping (throughput=$L_{P(2)}$, app. latency= $L_{P(1)} + L_{P(2)} + L_{P(3)}$ ) b) Temporal computational load balancing (throughput=$L_{P(2)}/2+L_T$, app. latency= $L_{P(1)} + L_{P(2)} + L_{P(3)} +2L_T$) c) Spatial computational load balancing (throughput=$L_{P(2)}/2$, app. latency= $L_{P(1)} + L_{P(2)}/2 + L_{P(3)}$ )

## 4  Application Mapping Results

In order to validate the proposed architecture, a parametrical software circuit emulator was designed. As a benchmark, three computationally demanding tasks belonging to our target application domain were considered. The first one is the YCrCb to RGB color space conversion necessary in many video applications. The second task is a 2D separable filtering with many applications in medical imaging systems. Finally, the third application is the 2D-DCT which is extensively used for image and video compression purposes. For each of the considered applications, two solutions were evaluated. The first one leads to a low-area implementation, whereas the second one is optimized for high throughput elaboration. In the following they are labeled as LA and HT, respectively. However, owing to the high flexibility offered by the new architecture in balancing the computational load of a given elaboration, some other mappings are possible to achieve the targeted resource-performance trade-off.

LA and HT implementations carried out using MORA were compared to core generated circuits optimized for the XILINX Virtex-4 devices family [16]. Implementations within a XILINX XC4VLSX200 device with -11 speed grade were analyzed using the Integrated Software Environment (ISE) 7.1. Throughputs and occupied resources are summarized in Table 1. Considering that the CORE Generated circuits often offer the best achievable area-speed trade-off, comparison results demonstrate that MORA is very competitive. In fact, for all the evaluated benchmarks, MORA can always reach throughput higher than its counterpart.

**Table 1.** Resources usage/performance trade-off comparisons: MORA to Virtex-4 FPGA

| Algorithm | MORA | | Virtex-4 FPGA | | |
|---|---|---|---|---|---|
| | Reconfigurable Cells (#PEs/Mem.[Kbit]) | Throughput [Samples/cycle] | Resources | | Throughput [Samples/cycle] |
| | | | #Slices | #Block Rams | |
| Color Space Conversion | 7/14 (LA) 16/32 (HT) | 0.32 0.95 | 436 | 2 (36 kbit) | 0.85 |
| 2D separable 4x4 FIR | 12/24 (LA) 20/40 (HT) | 0.60 0.90 | 440 | 2 (36 kbit) | 0.64 |
| 2D-DCT (8x8) | 15/30 (LA) 25/50 (HT) | 0.57 0.92 | 786 | 3 (54 kbit) | 0.85 |

Comparisons with FPGAs were made also in terms of silicon area occupancy and computational time. Clock speeds achieved by the FPGA implementations were evaluated through static timing analysis. On the contrary, their silicon area occupancy was evaluated considering that the generic Virtex4 slice implemented with a 90nm CMOS technology process occupies about 3442 $\mu m^2$ [17]. The silicon area occupied by the generic 18Kb block RAM in the referenced FPGA device was also measured. To this aim, a 18Kb memory module was purpose-implemented with the commercial ST 90nm CMOS technology. It was found that the generic block RAM occupies a silicon area of about 71356 $\mu m^2$. Also the generic RC used in MORA has been implemented using the ST 90nm CMOS technology. A critical path delay of about 1.5 ns and area occupancy of 37900 $\mu m^2$ were measured by Synopsys Design Compiler.

Figure 7 demonstrates that MORA always exhibits silicon area occupancy lower than FPGAs. This advantage comes from the use of high silicon-efficient domain-specific data-paths and small distributed memories, instead of fine-grained logic and relatively large embedded block memories. It is worth underlining that, data reported in Figure 7 do not include the area occupancy due to routing resources. However, as discussed in Section 3.2, MORA uses much less complex interconnections schemes than FPGAs. Therefore, it can be expected that for FPGAs the area overhead owing to routing resources is much higher than MORA.

Figure 8 shows that the proposed HT implementations always outperform the optimized FPGA circuits. In particular, for color space conversion, 2D separable FIR and 2D-DCT algorithms the circuits realized with MORA are about 6, 7 and 4.6 times faster, respectively, than their FPGA counterparts. Also the LA implementations are up to 4.6 times faster than FPGAs.

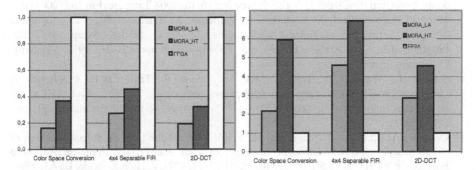

**Fig. 7.** Normalized Area Comparison        **Fig. 8.** Normalized Performance Comparison

Figure 9 shows a comparison in terms of performance per area. The HT implementation reaches the best performance-area trade-off for color space conversion, whereas the LA implementations exhibit the best performance-area trade-off for the other two considered applications.

The high-level evaluations discussed above demonstrate potential significant advantages over commercial FPGAs. Even larger benefits are expected once the new architecture is fully implemented.

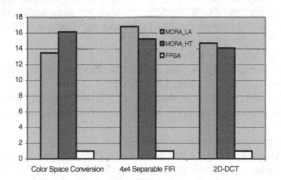

**Fig. 9.** Normalized Performance/Area Comparison

## 5  Conclusions

In this paper a new coarse-grain reconfigurable array for high-throughput multimedia processing has been presented. The architecture has been evaluated in terms of performance and area occupancy for several image processing algorithms. Results demonstrate impressive advantages with respect to conventional FPGA implementations.

# References

1. Hartenstein, R.: A Decade of Reconfigurable Computing: a Visionary Retrospective. In: Proc. of Design, Automation and Test in Europe (DATE), pp. 642–649, March 13-16, 2001 Munich, Germany (2001)
2. Ristimaki, T., Nurmi, J.: Reconfigurable IP blocks: a survey. In: Proc. of Int. Symp. on System-on-Chip (SoC), pp. 117–122, November 16-18, 2004 Tampere, Finland (2004)
3. Marshall, A., Stansfield, T., Kostarnov, I., Vuillemin, J., Hutchings, B.: A reconfigurable arithmetic array for multimedia applications. In: Proc. of Int. Symp. on Field-Programmable Gate Arrays (FPGA), pp. 135–143, February 21-23, 1999 Monterey, California, USA (1999)
4. Schmit, H., Whelihan, D., Tsai, A., Moe, M., Levine, B., Taylor, R R.: PipeRench: A virtualized programmable datapath in 0.18 micron technology. In: Proc. of the IEEE Conf. on Custom Integrated Circuits (CICC), pp. 63–66, May 12-15, 2002 Orlando, Florida, USA (2002)
5. Cronquist, D.C., Fisher, C., Figueroa, M., Franklin, P., Ebeling, C.: Architecture design of reconfigurable pipelined datapaths. In: Proc. of 20th Anniversary Conf. on Advanced Research in VLSI (ARVLSI), pp. 23–40, March 21-24, 1999, Atlanta, Georgia, USA (1999)
6. Singh, H., Lee, M.-H., Lu, G., Kurdahi, F.J., Bagherzadeh, N., Filho, C.: MorphoSys: an integrated reconfigurable system for data-parallel and computation-intensive applications. IEEE Transactions on Computers 49(5), 465–481 (2000)
7. Mirsky, E., DeHon, A.: MATRIX: A Reconfigurable Computing Architecture with Configurable Instruction Distribution and Deployable Resources. In: Proc. of the IEEE Symp. on FPGAs for Custom-Computing Machines (FCCM), Napa, California, USA, April 17-19, 1996, pp. 157–166 (1996)
8. Miyamori, T., Olukotun, K.: A Quantitative Analysis of Reconfigurable Coprocessors for Multimedia Applications. In: Proc. of the IEEE Symp. On FPGAs for Custom-Computing Machines (FCCM), Napa, California, USA, April 14-17, 1998, pp. 2–11 (1998)
9. Veredas, F.J., Scheppler, M., Moffat, W., Bingfeng, M.: Custom implementation of the coarse-grained reconfigurable ADRES architecture for multimedia purposes. In: Proc. of 15th Int. Conf. on Field Programmable Logic and Applications (FPL), Tampere, Finland, August 24-26, 2005, pp. 24–26 (2005)
10. Elixent Ltd. http://www.elixent.com
11. Motomura, M., Dynamically, A.: Reconfigurable Processor Architecture, Microprocessor Forum, October 10,2002, California, USA (2002)
12. Baumgarte, V., Ehlers, G., May, F., Nuckel, A., Vorbach, M., Weinhardt, M.: PCT-XPP A Self-Reconfigurable Data Processing Architecture. The Journal of Supercomputing 26(2), 167–184 (2003)
13. MathStar™, http://www.mathstar.com/products.html
14. Lanuzza, M., Perri, S., Margala, M., Corsonello, P.: Low-cost fully reconfigurable data-path for FPGA-based multimedia processor. In: Proc. of 15th Int. Conf. on Field Programmable Logic and Applications (FPL), Tampere, Finland, August 24-26, 2005, pp. 13–18 (2005)
15. Lanuzza, M., Margala, M., Corsonello, P.: Cost-effective low-power processor-in-memory-based reconfigurable datapath for multimedia applications. In: Proc. of Int.l Symp. on Low Power Electronics and Design (ISLPED), San Diego, California, USA, August 8-10, 2005, pp. 161–166 (2005)
16. Virtex-4 User Guide, http://www.xilinx.com
17. Ebeling, C., Fisher, C., Guanbin, X., Manyuan, S., Liu, H.: Implementing an OFDM receiver on the RaPiD reconfigurable architecture. IEEE Transactions on Computers 53(11), 1436–1448 (2004)

# FPGA Design Methodology for a Wavelet-Based Scalable Video Decoder

Hendrik Eeckhaut, Harald Devos, Philippe Faes,
Mark Christiaens, and Dirk Stroobandt

Ghent University, ELIS, Parallel Information Systems
Sint-Pietersnieuwstraat 41, 9000 Ghent, Belgium
Hendrik.Eeckhaut@elis.UGent.be

**Abstract.** Client-side diversification led the video-coding community to develop scalable video-codecs supporting efficient decoding at varying quality levels. This scalability has a lot of advantages but the corresponding decoding algorithm is complex and really stresses the system bandwidth as it replaces the block-based DCT-approach with frame-based wavelets. This has a tremendous impact on the hardware architecture. We present the implementation of the RESUME decoder using reconfigurable hardware designed through the use of state-of-the-art HW/SW-codesign techniques These techniques were augmented with automatic loop transformations and regression testing. Our efforts resulted in a design capable of decoding more than 25 frames per second at lossless CIF resolution.

## 1 Introduction

The RESUME[1] project [1] explores the benefits of using reconfigurable hardware for the implementation of scalable multimedia applications by building an FPGA implementation of a scalable, wavelet-based video decoder. The term 'scalable video' refers to a coding scheme that can easily accommodate changes in a QoS-level (Quality Of Service) with minimal computational overhead. A scalable video stream can be decoded at varying frame rates, resolutions and image quality by skipping redundant parts in the video stream, only decoding those parts that will contribute to the displayed video.

In SAMOS-IV [10] we explored the performance and resource requirements of RESUME's scalable wavelet-based video decoder through analytical means. We predicted that modern FPGAs would offer enough computational power but managing the memory bandwidth would be really challenging. In this paper we present the applied design methodology and the actual implementation results.

In the remainder of this paper we present an overview of the scalable video coding algorithm and the system specification for the decoder in Section 2. We elaborate on our design methodology, architecture, software and decisions in Section 3. We emphasize the importance of testing in Section 4 and illustrate the magnitude and complexity of our design by enumerating the applied design automation tools in Section 5. Finally, Section 6 summarizes the implementation results and Section 7 concludes this paper.

---

[1] Reconfigurable Embedded Systems for Use in Scalable Multimedia Environments.

S. Vassiliadis et al. (Eds.): SAMOS 2007, LNCS 4599, pp. 169–178, 2007.

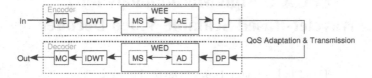

**Fig. 1.** High-level overview of the video encoder and decoder

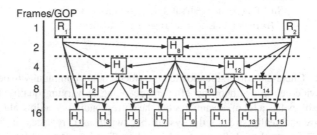

**Fig. 2.** Temporal scalability. Motion estimation processes one GoP (Group of Pictures) consisting of 16 consecutive frames. The arrows illustrate which frames are used as a first approximation of the intermediate frames at lower compositional levels. $R_1$ is the reference frame of this GoP, $R_2$ is the reference frame of the next GoP and the $H_i$ are the intermediate frames.

## 2   System Overview and Specifications

The algorithmic structure of the RESUME scalable video encoder is shown at the top of Figure 1 and is described in [6,10]. The encoder consists of the following parts:

**ME:** "Motion Estimation" [8] exploits the temporal redundancy in the video stream by looking for similarities between adjacent frames. To obtain *temporal scalability* (i.e. adjustable frame rate), motion is estimated in a hierarchical way as illustrated in Figure 2. This dyadic temporal decomposition enables decoding of the video stream at different frame rates. The decoder can choose up to which (temporal) level the stream is decoded. Each extra level doubles the frame rate.

An intermediate frame is predicted from its reference frames by dividing it into macroblocks and comparing each macroblock to macroblocks in the reference frames. The relative positions of the macroblocks in the reference frames with respect to the intermediate frame are stored as motion vectors. The difference between the predicted and the original frame is called an "error frame".

**DWT:** The "Discrete Wavelet Transform" takes a reference or error frame and separates the low-pass and high-pass components of the 2D image. Each LL-subband is a low resolution version of the original frame. The inverse wavelet transform (IDWT) in the decoder can stop at an arbitrary level, resulting in *resolution scalability*.

**WEE:** The "Wavelet Entropy Encoder" [6] is responsible for entropy encoding the wavelet transformed frames. The frames are encoded bit layer by bit layer (from most significant to least significant), yielding progressive accuracy of the wavelet coefficients

**Fig. 3.** Quality scalability: the wavelet transformed frames are displayed as height fields (height= absolute value of the wavelet coefficient). Decoding more bit layers gives a more accurate wavelet-transformed frame. The different subbands are illustrated for the lowest quality wavelet image. The distortions of the decoded images are slightly exaggerated for visual clarity.

(Figure 3) which results in *quality scalability*. The WEE itself consists of two main parts: the "Model Selector" (MS) and the "Arithmetic Encoder" (AE). The MS provides the AE with continuous guidance about what type of data is to be encoded by selecting an appropriate statistical model for the symbol (a bit) that has to be encoded next. It exploits the correlation between neighbouring coefficients in different contexts. Finally the AE performs the actual compression of the symbol stream.

**P:** The "Packetizer" packs all encoded parts of the video together in one bit stream representing the compressed video.

Scalability in color depth is obtained by encoding luminance and chrominance information in three different channels in the YUV 4:2:0 format. Omitting the chrominance channels yields a grayscale version of the sequence, allocating more bits to these channels increases the color depth. Motion estimation is computed from luminance information only, but is also applied to the chrominance channels. In the other parts of the algorithm the channels are processed totally independently.

By inverting the encoding operations we obtain the scalable video *decoder* illustrated at the bottom of Figure 1. It consists of three major blocks: a WED (Wavelet Entropy Decoder), an IDWT (Inverse Discrete Wavelet Transform) and a MC (Motion Compensator). Similar to the WEE, the WED consists of a MS and an AD (Arithmetic Decoder). This paper focuses on the hardware implementation of the decoder.

The design goals of our implementation were real-time, lossless decoding of CIF-sequences ($352 \times 288$ pixels) at 25 frames per second. The available hardware platform was an Altera PCI high-speed development board [2] equipped with a Stratix S60 FPGA plugged into a standard PC with two monitors, one dedicated to displaying the decoded video, the other to interact with the system.

## 3   Implementation

This section elaborates on the implementation of our design. First it gives an overview of our design methodology. Next it presents an overview of the architecture (both in hardware and in software). Finally, it illustrates some trade-offs we made and explains our clocking scheme.

## 3.1 Methodology

Implementing a complete video decoder is a complex undertaking that requires careful planning. The following methodology was applied to the project. As a first step, the entire code base was cleaned-up and we made sure that the algorithms used were properly understood. At this point, it was clear to us that the entire decoder was too complex to completely implement in reconfigurable hardware. As a consequence, we chose to use a HW/SW-codesign approach leaving as much of the algorithm as possible in SW running on a CPU while implementing the time-critical parts in reconfigurable HW.

Locating the time-critical parts was performed through extensive profiling. The resulting HW/SW-partitioning was evaluated further: since the design would need to fit on a PCI-plugin board, it was crucial that the bandwidth requirements over the PCI-bus between the HW and the SW could be met. This led us to the decision to move additional functionality from SW to HW so that in essence the partially decoded video stream (which constitutes the bulk of the data bandwidth) could stay on the PCI-card and did not need to cross the PCI-bus.

Having established a HW/SW-partitioning, we encapsulated the HW parts into SystemC blocks. The data structures used in these blocks had a number of drawbacks: substantial amounts of floating-point code was used and certain data structures where too irregular for efficient hardware implementation.

Prior experience taught us that too many resources would be required for floating-point computation. SystemC support for the use of fixed-point arithmetic (with controllable accuracy) was used to replace all floating-point arithmetic and to establish the required accuracy. It turned out that moderate accuracy (e.g., 18 bit for the representation of the wavelet coefficients) would suffice to reach perfect decoding performance.

Next we converted the C-code of the decoder to Java. The reason for this is that Java tools provide excellent support for the substantial refactoring we foresaw in order to cleanly encapsulate the HW components from the rest of the code. We developed a library (called `mmregion`) and a communication protocol for performing communication between the SW and HW parts of the design. This library functions as an abstraction layer between HW and SW (*bridge pattern*). The advantage is that SW and HW can be interchanged readily. As such, different implementations of the HW functionality can be interchanged as the need arises: high-level SW mock-ups, RTL-VHDL version in co-simulation or direct communication with live hardware are all supported.

We built VHDL Avalon components for the use in Altera's SOPC (System-On-a-Programmable-Chip) framework for each of the components. Once these components passed the tests in simulation, we moved to actual hardware.

When the individual components passed the HW tests, we developed an SOPC design containing all HW components. In addition, we replaced the mock-up objects in the control SW by code that directly drives the HW design resulting (after many hours of careful debugging) in a working decoder.

## 3.2 Architecture

In order to move from a pure software version of the video decoder to a hardware accelerated HW/SW-codesign, we refined the basic structure at the bottom of Figure 1 to the architecture shown in Figure 4.

The main control over the decoder still resides in the CPU. It drives an Altera Stratix development board that is connected to the PCI bus. The development board is equipped (among others) with an Altera Stratix S60 FPGA and 256 MiB of DDR SDRAM memory. On the FPGA, the entire decoding pipeline is implemented. The pipeline is fed by the CPU who copies coded video data into the DDR memory where it is consumed by the decoding pipeline. The pipeline consists of a WED, an AS (ASsembler), an IDWT, a MC and a CC (Color Convertor). After decoding the video, the resulting data is transferred from the on-board DDR to an NVidia GeForce 5200 VGA card on the PCI bus.

As can be seen in Figure 4, the software architecture (Figure 1) was substantially modified. For example the entropy decoder was split into three main components: MS, AD and AS. The partitioning into MS and AD was performed to keep the design manageable. In addition the MS and AD no longer produce ready-made wavelet frames but instead they construct individual bit layers of the wavelet frames. The AS was introduced to reconstruct the wavelet frames from the individual bit layers produced by the MS and AD. The use of the AS substantially improves the memory bandwidth.

Functionally, the IDWT and the MC are identical to their software counterparts. The frames produced by the MC are in YUV format and the visualization of the frames occurs in RGB mode. Therefore, the frames need to be converted from the YUV to the RGB color space. This is the responsibility of the CC.

Another notable difference in the hardware architecture is that communication between the components of the decoding pipeline occurs explicitly through the use of DDR SDRAM. This is caused by the fact that the S60 FPGA does not house sufficient memory to buffer the intermediate results of the decoding process, forcing off-chip buffering. Of course, this results in large bandwidth requirements between the DDR and the FPGA. To alleviate this problem, much of this communication occurs through the use of DMA transfers in efficient burst mode. In Figure 4 dashed arrows indicate that the communication goes via the DMA engine, the continuous arrows indicate direct communication between the component and the DDR.

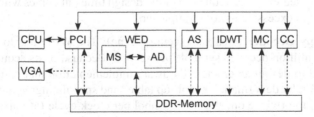

**Fig. 4.** Overview of hardware architecture of the RESUME coder. Continuous lines indicate direct (master) write transfers, dashed lines indicate DMA (slave) transfers.

## 3.3  Control Software

RESUME's control software was written using Java. Although somewhat uncommon, the choice for Java for hardware development has a substantial advantage (on top of the classical advantages for software development). When developing a complex hardware application, a large fraction of the effort is located in refactoring the code: cleaning up, encapsulating components, modifying data types, ... Modern Java development tools provide excellent support for this process through extensive refactoring capabilities.

Since the control software did not constitute our core business, its main design criteria were correctness and simplicity. The basic design of the control software is a processing pipeline consisting of control objects and FIFOs. The control objects are responsible for sending commands to the corresponding hardware components and to process their results. They communicate with each other through the use of FIFOs.

The control object at the head of the pipeline is responsible for parsing the basic structure of the coded video stream and submits jobs, based on the stream, into the FIFO of the next component which processes the job and so on. The FIFOs are responsible for flow-control between the components of the pipeline. All communication between control objects and hardware occurs asynchronously. When a control object has no more work to do it simply passes control (through a priority-based round-robin scheduler) to the next control object. An improvement to the design might be to use interrupts instead of polling, but currently the decoder performs sufficiently well.

## 3.4  Trade-Offs

As in all designs some trade-offs had to be made.

**Line-Based IDWT** (area vs. design time): Initially, a manual design of a Row-Column-based IDWT was made, but its bandwidth requirements could not be met. Therefore, loop transformations to improve the data locality were performed on the original algorithm using the WRaP-IT/URUK tool set [4]. We wrote CLooGVHDL, a back-end to this tool [5], to generate control hardware from the internal polyhedral representation used by this tool set. Currently, only parallelism within statements is supported. The data path was generated semi-automatically as it does not depend on the transformations. After comparing several generated variants, one was selected to be extended with a memory hierarchy and integrated in the decoder. The semi-automatic generation of the hardware resulted in a huge reduction of the design time but comes with a large area cost, mainly due to excessive use of multiplexers.

**Wavelet Entropy Decoder** (area vs. execution time): The WED has to produce approximately 50 million decoded symbols per second. Because of its sequential nature it was very hard to design an efficient hardware implementation that could reach this decoding rate. But by denormalizing look-up tables and speculating on multiple levels, we managed [6] to produce one decoded symbol per clock cycle (at max. 60 MHz on the S60). This way we use some extra memory and logic in exchange for throughput, small latency and predictability.

**Memory Alignment** (memory space vs. bandwidth): To fully exploit the bandwidth boost of using DMA for DDR-memory transfers, we sacrificed some memory as padding to align all data objects to 128-bit addresses. Since we have more than enough DDR-memory available (256 MiB), this was a very straightforward decision to make.

### 3.5 Clocking Scheme

With such a diverse set of hardware components in the design, some components differ substantially from others with respect to their maximum clocking frequency. In order to accommodate this, the design is subdivided into multiple clock domains. The PCI-core runs partially with an external clock at 66 MHz, the DDR core at 65 MHz and each of the hardware components in the video pipeline can run at its own clock speed. Thanks to the use of SOPC Builder this can be achieved fairly easily by assigning different clocks to each of the Avalon components.

In addition, many of the hardware components use DMA to transfer large blocks of data between the DDR memory and local dual-port memories. Using DMA has the advantage that burst transfers are enabled and that there are fewer masters communicating with the DDR which is beneficial to the clock speed. The DMA engine transfers data to and from the dual-port memories using one access port while the hardware component uses the other. After some experimenting, we noticed that it is highly beneficial to have the two memories involved in the DMA transfer run at the same clock speed. Therefore, hardware components that use DMA are subdivided into two clock domains. The DMA side of the dual-port memories runs at the DDR clock speed while the rest of the component runs at its own optimal speed. Clock boundary crossing is then performed partly by the SOPC infrastructure and partly by the dual-port memories.

## 4  Testing

Thanks to our software engineering background we avoided the traditional approach of using tailored scripts and ad-hoc solutions for building and testing our design. Instead we made use of existing software engineering methods such as test driven development, code reuse, regression testing and continuous integration. As explained in Section 3.1 we used the bridge pattern to extensively test our components using the same infrastructure (mmregion) during the entire journey from algorithm to RTL SOPC-component. By using the same infrastructure at the various levels of abstraction, we prevented the error-prone process of writing multiple test benches; we only had to scale the length of our test vectors to accommodate the simulation time span.

In order to automate building and testing, we used the popular Java project management tool Maven (2.0) from the Apache Software Foundation. This tool can compile, test and deploy Java projects. Additionally it tightly integrates with our version control system, Subversion. We extended Maven with a plug-in to support hardware projects in the same way as Java projects. A hardware design project describes an entire (FPGA) chip configuration. The compilation of a hardware design yields an FPGA bit stream, which is used to configure an FPGA. These projects depend on hardware components, which they glue together on the FPGA chip. Hardware components are in turn Maven projects which contain HDL code. Using Maven not only saved us considerable time, it also made the build process more reliable and reproducible.

We also adopted *continuous integration* [7,9] to ensure a continuous quality of the entire hardware project, in particular the quality of the reusable components. During the lifetime of a component, many enhancements occurred such as introduction of additional features or performance enhancements. While each of these enhancements may consist of a small incremental change, the cumulation of all enhancements is very large. Likewise the odds of introducing a bug during one modification may be small, but the odds of introducing a bug over many modifications in the lifetime of a hardware component are close to 100%. While the component designer could run regression tests manually after each code change, we side with the ever increasing number of software programmers advocating the use of a continuous testing server. The server makes sure no code change is ever left untested, and it keeps track of failed and succeeded tests. It makes it easy to confirm whether (and when) a component gets broken. We used Maven and Continuum for the continuous integration of our designs. Every time a designer checks in a code change in our version control system, the Continuum server invokes Maven to rerun all relevant tests. These tests are kept as fast as possible to provide fast feedback to the designer. Every night, a heavier set of regression tests is applied to the changed code. These tests may include a full system synthesis and a thorough HW/SW co-simulation. If a nightly test breaks, the responsible designers find an automated e-mail in their in-box.

In addition to our automated and continuous tests which tested functional correctness of the design, we also had to check the real-time requirements and test performance. To that end, the control software and the hardware components were instrumented to provide profiling information on the run-time behavior of the video decoder. The control software keeps statistics about the execution times of each of the hardware components and about the amount of memory allocated at any time to each of the steps in the processing pipeline. In addition, each of the hardware components was equipped with a performance counter, counting the number of clock ticks required to finish a command. Using this profiling infrastructure, execution times of the hardware, communication overhead and memory consumption can be measured.

## 5    Design Automation Tools

For our design we used a very wide spectrum of design automation tools. During the exploration of the decoder algorithm we used SystemC to determine the required accuracy for the floating-point to fixed-point transition. The original C-specification of the decoding algorithm was converted to Java so that we could use the powerful refactoring tools available for the Java language (e.g., Eclipse, Netbeans ... ). This enabled automatic code transformations that were not feasible to do manually. Furthermore Java facilitates the use of Apache Continuum. Continuous integration ensured the health of our code base by building and testing our code on a daily basis. Because the software blocks were seamlessly replaced by their hardware counterparts, this same infrastructure could be used during the entire design process. To track our code we used the version control system Subversion.

For the RTL-description of our design, we used VHDL. All VHDL-code was custom-built. For the line-based implementation of the inverse discrete wavelet transform we used the WRaP-IT/URUK tool set to perform loop transformations and the CLooG-VHDL back-end to generate VHDL-code from the internal polyhedral representation. All HDL-code (and also some timing annotated net lists) was simulated with Mentor Graphics ModelSim. The different steps of the decoding pipeline were designed as custom SOPC-components for Altera's SOPC Builder tool. SOPC Builder facilitated system integration although a number of uncovered problems needed to be circumvented. For synthesis, place and route of our HDL-code we used Altera Quartus II 6.1. For hardware debugging we used Altera's SignalTap II for on-chip logic analysis but also some traditional logic analyzers and oscilloscopes.

# 6 Implementation Results

The results of synthesizing the design with Quartus 6.1 are described in Table 1. As a point of reference, a 8-bit, 16-tap parallel FIR filter uses 58 LEs, four $9\times9$-multipliers and can be clocked at 133 MHz [3].

Table 1. Resource consumption of the video decoder

| Component | #LE | #9×9 | #18×18 | #Regs | Mem | Clk |
|---|---|---|---|---|---|---|
| IDWT | 19733 | 0 | 9 | 1978 | 395752 | 54 |
| PCI | 4284 | 0 | 0 | 1816 | 23568 | 65(&66) |
| WED | 4133 | 1 | 0 | 1716 | 107392 | 59 |
| AS | 2894 | 0 | 2 | 1402 | 65024 | 65 |
| MC | 2115 | 0 | 0 | 1112 | 25344 | 65 |
| CC | 1315 | 0 | 0 | 500 | 36894 | 65 |
| DDR | 1356 | 0 | 0 | 978 | 4608 | 65 |
| DMA | 767 | 0 | 0 | 313 | 16384 | 65 |
| Others | 7161 | 0 | 0 | 3448 | 0 | 65 |
| **Total** | **43758** | **1** | **11** | **13263** | **674966** | |

**#LE**: number of logic elements, **#9×9**: number of 9-bit multipliers, **#18×18**: number of 18-bit multipliers, **#Regs**: number of 1-bit registers, **Mem**: bits of on-chip RAM, **Clk**: the clock frequency of the component (in MHz).

The substantial system resource usage of the IDWT is a direct consequence of its automatic generation [5]. Although its external memory behavior is near optimal, its internal structure is not. In a second iteration of the design, this will be improved. This component also contains the critical path of the design. The last line of the table, *Others*, consists mostly of the Avalon Switch Fabric (Altera SOPC Builder) that interconnects the different steps of the decoder and takes care of clock domain crossings. In the design, four clock domains are used: one for the IDWT, one for the WED and one for the rest of the design. The fourth clock rate is dictated by the PCI bus. More clock domains are possible but would not contribute to a global higher frame rate since the IDWT is currently the bottleneck.

With the clock settings of Table 1, the design decodes 26.5 lossless CIF-frames per second. The maximum usage of the on-board DDR memory is less than 16 MiB. The largest part (8 MiB) is occupied for buffering the error frames.

# 7  Conclusions

In the scope of the RESUME project we developed a wavelet-based, scalable video decoder on a Stratix PCI development board. The design is clocked at multiple clocks (54-65 MHz) and decodes more than the required 25 lossless CIF frames per second. Our approach was unique due to the large number of advanced tools and methods we combined. We adopted a write-tests-first strategy and used well founded engineering techniques as code reuse, refactoring, regression testing and continuous integration. We implemented a very high-speed WED capable of decoding one symbol per clock cycle and added an AS component to resolve bandwidth congestion. We automatically generated a line-based IDWT using a polyhedral representation of its iteration structure to tailor the wavelet processing to the specific access pattern of the external on-board DDR-memory.

## Acknowledgment

This research is supported by the I.W.T. Vlaanderen, grant 020174, the F.W.O., grant G.0021.03 and by GOA project 12.51B.02 of Ghent University. Altera provided development boards and tools through the Altera university program. Philippe Faes is supported by a PhD grant from the I.W.T. Vlaanderen.

## References

1. The RESUME: project: Reconfigurable Embedded Systems for Use in Scalable Multimedia Environments, http://www.elis.UGent.be/resume
2. Altera: PCI Hight-Speed Development Kit, Stratix Pro Edition, 1.1.0 edn. (October 2005)
3. Altera: Stratix Device Handbook (January 2006)
4. Cohen, A., Girbal, S., Parello, D., Sigler, M., Temam, O., Vasilache, N.: Facilitating the search for compositions of program transformations. In: ACM International Conference on Supercomputing (June 2005)
5. Devos, H., Beyls, K., Christiaens, M., Van Campenhout, J., D'Hollander, E.H., Stroobandt, D.: Finding and applying loop transformations for generating optimized FPGA implementations. Transactions on HiPEAC 1(1), 151–170 (2007)
6. Eeckhaut, H., Christiaens, M., Devos, H., Stroobandt, D.: Implementing a hardware-friendly wavelet entropy codec for scalable video. In: Proceedings of SPIE: Wavelet Applications in Industrial Processing III, vol. 6001, pp. 169–179, Boston (October 2005)
7. Fowler, M., Foemmel, M.: Continuous integration (2000) Online at http://www.martinfowler.com/articles/continuousIntegration.html
8. Munteanu, A., Andreopoulos, Y., van der Schaar, M., Schelkens, P., Cornelis, J.: Control of the distortion variation in video coding systems based on motion compensated temporal filtering. In: Proceedings. International Conference on Image Processing, IEEE Computer Society Press, Los Alamitos (2003)
9. Smith, E.: Continuous Testing. In: Proceedings of the 17th International Conference on Testing Computer Software (2000)
10. Stroobandt, D., Eeckhaut, H., Devos, H., Christiaens, M., Verdicchio, F., Schelkens, P.: Reconfigurable hardware for a scalable wavelet video decoder and its performance requirements. Computer Systems: Architectures, Modeling, and Simulation 3133, 203–212 (2004)

# Evaluating Large System-on-Chip on Multi-FPGA Platform

Ari Kulmala, Erno Salminen, and Timo D. Hämäläinen

Tampere University of Technology, Institute of Digital and Computer Systems,
P.O. Box 553, Korkeakoulunkatu 1, FI-33101 Tampere, Finland
ari.kulmala@tut.fi

**Abstract.** This paper presents a configurable base architecture tailorable for different applications. It allows simple and rapid way to evaluate and prototype large Multi-Processor System-on-Chip architectures on multiple FPGAs with support to Globally Asynchronous Locally Synchronous scheme. It allows early hardware/software co-verification and optimization. The architecture abstracts the underlying hardware details from the processors so that knowledge about the exact locations of individual components are not required for communication. Implemented example architecture contains 58 IP blocks, including 35 Nios II soft processors. As a proof of concept, a MPEG-4 video encoder is run on the example architecture.

## 1 Introduction

The contemporary FPGA chips are large enough to hold complete System-on-Chips (SoCs). However, architectures that contain tens of processors and other Intellectual Property (IP) blocks are still too large for a single FPGA. Therefore, a logically single SoC architecture may need to be divided to several chips for prototyping and to enable early start in software development.

Traditionally, multiple FPGAs have been utilized in emulators as in [1]. Typical emulators are expensive and require special synthesis and partitioning tools. In [2], an industrial example of mapping multi-million gate SoCs on FPGAs is given. The point of view in that paper is slightly different than in this since the multi-FPGA platform is used much like an emulator: functional verification and software development.

Table 1 lists few recent publications on FPGA SoC architectures utilizing multiple processors and possibly multiple FPGAs. The Xilinx FPGA is used in other works than in this. The notation 3+1 means that there are 3 processors in one board and 1 in another. The proposed scalable architectures have usually been evaluated using only a few CPUs. Device and platform independency of the inter-FPGA links with rapid and effortless adoption have not been considered. For example, using MGT links between boards means that all FPGAs must have this capability.

This paper shows our scalable, vendor-independent SoC architecture design method. In particular, we concentrate on how the architecture can be rapidly divided across several FPGAs for prototyping. The multi-FPGA architecture can be prototyped with the exactly same program code as the final product and there are only

S. Vassiliadis et al. (Eds.): SAMOS 2007, LNCS 4599, pp. 179–189, 2007.

**Table 1.** Recent related work on Multiprocessor SoCs on FPGA(s)

| Ref | # CPUs | CPU type | #IPs | MHz | Net. | Inter-FPGA link | Application |
|-----|--------|----------|------|-----|------|-----------------|-------------|
| [3] | 4 | μBlaze | 1 | 80? | Shared bus | No | DWT |
| [4] | 4 | μBlaze | - | 100 | p2p | No | Img. filter |
| [5] | 14 | μBlaze | - | 100 | p2p | No | IPv4 fwd |
| [6] | 3+1 | μBlaze | - | n/a | p2p | MGT integrated | Molec. dyn. |
| [7] | 2+2 | N-core | - | 12.5 | Mesh | No details, globally synchronous | - |
| This | 12+11 +12 | Nios II | 7+9 +7 | 50 | Hier. bus | Synthesizable, asynchronous | MPEG-4 |

*μBlaze = Xilinx Micro Blaze,     p2p = Point-to-Point interconnect,     MGT = Multi-Gigabit Transceivers*

minor additions to the hardware. Thus, also the code development can be started in early phase along with co-verification and optimization. As a proof of concept, we implemented a Multi-Processor SoC (MP-SoC) MPEG-4 video encoder distributed to three FPGA boards, comprising 58 IPs, including 35 synthesizable Nios II processors in three FPGAs. The architecture size and complexity is significantly larger than typical architectures found in related work. In addition, we performed a study on the MPEG-4 video encoder architecture communication details.

This paper is structured as follows. The Section 2 reviews our SoC Architecture design method. An example architecture using this method is illustrated in Section 3 and the hardware is discussed. In Section 4, results are shown and Section 5 concludes the paper.

## 2   SoC Architecture Design Method

The base of our architecture design method is that the architecture should support many applications, be scalable, vendor-independent, rapidly upgradeable, and allow quick prototyping and evaluation. To cope with continuously increasing complexity, the architecture separates computation from communication and supports Globally Asynchronous Locally Synchronous (GALS) scheme with arbitrary number of independent clocks. Software design is simple because the underlying physical hardware is abstracted so that the IP blocks can view the whole architecture logically as just one big chip. The communication procedure is always similar no matter how many boards are utilized, and whether the IPs are on the same board or not. The mapping of the components to FPGAs is arbitrary and based on designer's decisions.

The simplified design flow is demonstrated in Fig. 1. In this paper, we follow the *a*-branch, prototype design. Most importantly, the design process goes exactly alike until the platform analysis. Several FPGAs are needed if the prototype of the design cannot fit to a single FPGA. However, we can use the same configurable architecture to implement these chips. Only a few parameters need to be set individually to the boards, such as the bridge configuration. Also, we are not tied to any existing prototyping platform since the implementation is device independent. The scalability of the architecture and software can be simply and rapidly evaluated as well as, for example, different memory configurations, different amounts of IP blocks, or

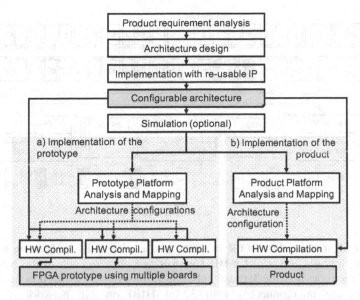

**Fig. 1.** The simplified flow of product design using our design method

parallelization schemes. The device-independency and configurability of the architecture allows comprehensive analysis of the architecture. These are the main benefits in addition to the practical methods presented in [2].

It is possible to analyze and measure the performance limiting factors with real platform and application, even if the architecture does not currently fit into a single FPGA and ASIC has not been produced yet. Arbitrary large designs can be evaluated rapidly because the number of connected FPGA devices is not limited. In comparison to emulators, our method is cheaper and more flexible (device-independent, thus not bounded by platform restrictions because the platform can be easily changed). By changing the clock frequencies of the components of the architecture, the performance limits can be identified. For example, one may run IP blocks at 1 MHz and the interconnection at 100 MHz to approximate the system performance with (nearly) ideal interconnection. This approach can be used to individually evaluate the IP blocks so that the optimization efforts can be targeted optimally.

## 3 Studied Example Hardware Architecture

In order to test our design method, example SoC architecture was developed. First, it was specified that the scalability and feasibility of our design method will be evaluated with very large architecture. A test case application is MPEG-4 encoder [10]. The MP-SoC architecture contains single master processor (M), 34 slave processors (S), one SDRAM control (SD), one resource manager (RM), 1 HIBI network monitor (HM), 9 full-pixel motion estimators (ME), and 9 IPs (DQ) that perform four functions: DCT, Inverse DCT, Quantization, and Inverse Quantization.

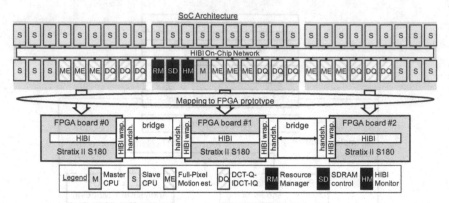

**Fig. 2.** The studied architecture

That totals 56 separate IPs. In the mapping phase, also HIBI bridges are added. For evaluation purposes, we added a HIBI network monitor to each of the buses so the amount of monitors became 3, thus total of 58 IP blocks were utilized in three boards.

The IPs are interconnected with 32-bit HIBI on-chip network [8] but the methodology is also generalizable. The architecture is depicted in Fig. 2. After designing this architecture, the platform was analyzed and mapping of the IP blocks to FPGA boards was done by the procedure shown in Fig. 3. The memory amount in each FPGA device was the limiting factor so three FPGA boards were required to implement this architecture. The chosen criterion of distribution was to balance the amount of processors and accelerators in each board. The shared memory controller and RM were located in the board #1.

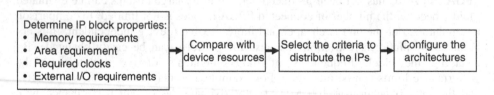

**Fig. 3.** The process to determine the initial mapping to multiple FPGAs

It should be noted that no video application specific mapping optimizations were made because the performance optimizations of the prototype are out of the scope of this paper.

The used external chips (e.g. memories) and processor configurations are omitted from Fig. 2 for simplicity. The FPGA board #1 contains also access to the external peripherals. SDRAM memory is used as shared picture memory. The Ethernet is used to download frames to be encoded and to upload encoded frames.

Master processor uses external instruction memory and the slave processors are programmed using Single Program Multiple Data paradigm so they can share identical memories. Thus, in each board, slaves share a dual-port 128KB on-chip instruction memory. The processors also have 8KB instruction caches to alleviate the shared memory contention and 64 KB local data memory. The CPUs use DMA to transfer the data over HIBI. Also, the SDRAM control contains a special SDRAM DMA unit to improve the efficiency of memory accesses.

CPUs may request certain functionality via resource manager that selects and reserves a free hardware accelerator for the requester. This simplifies scaling as the number of accelerators can be easily modified without affecting the software. Currently, the location of the accelerator is not considered at the selection. The used FPGA boards are Altera's DSP Development Kit Professional Editions, utilizing Stratix 2S180 FPGA. The architecture is run at 50MHz.

## 3.1 HIBI Bridge

All agents connect to the bus network by using a synthesizable HIBI wrapper. A bus bridge is basically constructed from two wrappers. There is fully synchronous (mainly for on-chip) and an asynchronous bridge that is also suitable for connecting FPGA boards together. This paper uses the asynchronous one since there is no global clock. The bridge communication protocol between bridge halves is delay-insensitive so that totally asynchronous (unrelated) clocks can be used on the connected boards if required. The synthesizable synchronization technique is presented in [9].

We utilize 10 pin prototyping header connectors available in the FPGA board. The HIBI bridge properties are summarized in Table 2. The maximum throughput with data with $n=6$ bits is 43 Mbits/s for the bridge whereas 32-bit on-chip HIBI achieves 1.6 Gbits/s at 50 MHz. The data that is sent over the bridge includes the 32 bit bus data and 4 control bits. With six data pins (n=6), 36 bits is chopped to 6 transmissions of 6 bits each. One transfer takes 6 cycles (36 cycles for 32+4 bit transfer) when the boards have the same frequency but possibly different clock phases.

**Table 2.** HIBI Bridge essential properties

| Property | Value(s) |
|---|---|
| Control signals | 2: request and acknowledge |
| Signal lines | Uni-directional |
| Protocol | Transition-encoded |
| Data width | $n$, serial or parallel, compile-time adjustable |
| Clocking | Fully Asynchronous, 2 DFF synchronization |
| HDL Description | RT-level |
| Timing Constrains | Data lines cannot have delay over 2x of control lines |
| Max. throughput (50 MHz, n=6) | 43 Mbits/s |

## 4  Results

As a proof of concept, a parallel, highly scalable MPEG-4 video encoder [10] was run on the platform. Then, the communication of the architecture was studied. A photo of the platform used is shown in the Fig. 4. It contains the architecture as depicted in Fig. 2 and the corresponding FPGA boards are marked in the photo.

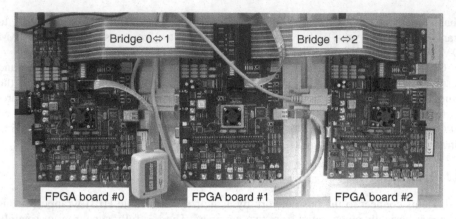

**Fig. 4.** A photo of the platform used with necessary cabling

## 4.1 MPEG-4 Video Encoder

A standard CIF sequence *salesman* (352x288) was used in the measurements. It was run 10 times for 10 frames for each configuration and the averages were counted. The encoder works so that the master CPU orders slaves to encode an evenly sized slice of the current frame. Master does not encode. The image slices are distributed with macroblock (MB) granularity. A CIF frame has 396 MBs. With high number of processors (> 22), the parallelization efficiency gets limited due to unbalanced number of macroblocks per processor.

Fig. 5 shows encoding time of one frame as a function of slave processors. First, 10 slaves in board #1 are utilized, then 12 slaves in board #0, and at last, 12 slaves in board #2. In the benchmarks, only the three MEs and three DQs residing in board #1 have been utilized. The encoding time gets worse when the number of slaves increases over 10, just when the first processor on the other board is taken into use. This clearly indicates that the communication over the bridge becomes a bottleneck.

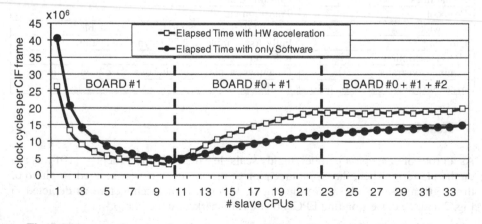

**Fig. 5.** Video encoding time for one frame using HW accelerators and with only software

Adding the third board's processors does improve the performance (22 to 23 slaves) slightly with HW acceleration. That is because the traffic over the bridge between boards #1 and #2 is reduced.

HW accelerators drastically increase the bus utilization (totaling up to 30%) due to increased data fetches to SDRAM. Therefore, software only (utilization max. 9%) is better than the one with hardware accelerators with multiple boards because the traffic over the bridges is smaller and the SDRAM is also less utilized.

As of particular interest, we also obtained the HIBI bus usage statistics for each of the buses (one per board). Due to space limitations, Fig. 6 shows only to segments in configuration which utilized hardware accelerators. HIBI #1 is the segment where the master CPU is. In the figure, payload is the necessary application data and control. Overhead consists of the information that is required to route the data. In HIBI, overhead consists of an address sent before an arbitrarily long data transfer. Retries happen when the receiver has been unable to accept data and the previous transfer had to be interrupted. They are mostly caused by the bridges. Fig. 6 shows how the amount of retries rapidly increases when the traffic over bridge starts (first time with 11 slaves). The amount of data in HIBI #1 does not decrease because the shared image memory is in that board. HIBI #0 has higher addressing overhead because the slow bridge splits the transfers coming from HIBI #1 into short bursts each requiring an address.

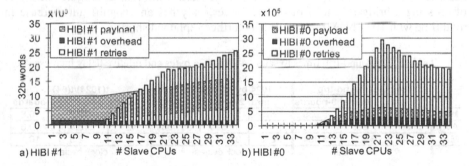

**Fig. 6.** HIBI on-chip bus usage statistics per frame with video encoder using HW acceleration. A) HIBI #1 (master), b) HIBI #0.

Overall, we were able to rapidly distribute and evaluate the application and hardware architecture on multiple FPGAs. Only a few person-days of work was required to implement the architecture on multiple FPGAs after the initial architecture was designed, taking into account the 6-hour hardware compilation time per iteration. Also, we were able to test the functionality of the video encoder in reasonable speed.

## 4.2 Detailed Analysis of the Communication

To evaluate the communication in the architecture, we performed a data transfer round-trip time testing. Fig. 7 shows the arrangements to measure round-trip time with software timers. The software was compiled with highest optimization level. It

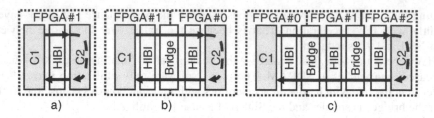

a)                    b)                              c)

**Fig. 7.** Round-trip time measuring arrangements. A) Within one board (1-board), b) with two boards (2-boards), c) with three boards (3-boards).

performs no computation on the received data and the data it sent back was from a pre-defined constant table, thus the time spent in SW is minimal. The purpose is to break the communication time into individual components. The bus, DMA, bridge, and CPU IRQ response times were measured using a clock-cycle-accurate logic analyzer.

The average round-trip times (calculated from 10 000 iterations) are summarized in Table 3. For 64 bytes, the 1-board (Fig. 7a) is 4.1x faster than the 2-board (Fig. 7b), and 5.4x faster than 3-board (Fig. 7c) configuration. With 1024 bytes, the 1-board configuration is 23.4x-24x faster than 2-board or 3-board setups. The bridge crossing has remarkable effect on performance and it increases with transfer length. The effect of crossing 2 bridges instead of one, however, only has an insignificant increase in total time with 1024 byte transfer. This is further explained shortly.

**Table 3.** The round-trip times to send 64 and 1024 bytes and relative delay increase

|  | 64 bytes round-trip | | | 1024 bytes round-trip | | | t(1024)/t(64) | | |
|---|---|---|---|---|---|---|---|---|---|
|  | 1-board | 2-boards | 3-boards | 1-board | 2-boards | 3-boards | 1-board | 2-boards | 3-boards |
| Min | 657 | 2 774 | 3 539 | 1 579 | 37 324 | 38 174 | 2.4 | 13.5 | 10.8 |
| Avg | 680 | 2 800 | 3 640 | 1 600 | 37 520 | 38 456 | 2.4 | 13.4 | 10.6 |
| Max | 746 | 3 029 | 3 854 | 1 673 | 37 974 | 39 084 | 2.2 | 12.5 | 10.1 |
|  | clock cycles | | | clock cycles | | | clock cycles | | |

Fig. 8 shows the round-trip time breakdown for all the configurations. The whole round-trip is the time elapsing when CPU1 starts to the time when it receives the last datum back from CPU2. In all the cases, the CPU processing time stays constant. Total time spent on software (SW), Tx1+Irq2+Tx2+Irq1, is in all cases 605 clock cycles. For clarity, latency caused by DMA (Tx+Rx totaling about 8 clock cycles) is added to the bus time. Time spent on hardware (HW), however, varies greatly: from 75 cycles in 1-board case to 2182 and 3026 cycles spent on 2 and 3-board setup, respectively. In 3-board setup, all the buses and bridges can work in parallel, which somewhat reduces the total latency.

Fig. 9 shows a detailed, cycle-accurate breakdown of the component activity when sending 64 bytes forth and back with 3-board configuration. The communication bottlenecks, namely the bridges, are marked to the figure as limiting. When the bridge utilization reaches (nearly) 100%, it stalls the bus and DMA transfers repeatedly.

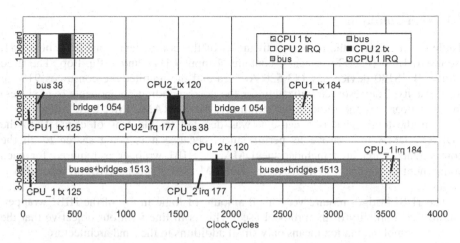

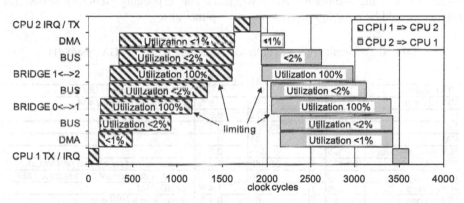

**Fig. 8.** Breakdown of sending 64 bytes forth and back in configuration 1-board (top), 2-boards (middle), and 3-boards (bottom)

**Fig. 9.** Detailed breakdown of sending 64 bytes in 3-board configuration forth and back with two CPUs. The bars show how long the component is active.

Therefore, buses and DMAs are active so long although the optimum case takes only 38 clock cycles in one direction. The bus, however, is not reserved all the time during the transfer. The utilization of bus is under 2% and the remaining bandwidth can be used for other transfers. DMA finishes faster than bus since the DMA fills up the 20-byte transmit buffers at the bus wrapper although the data is not right away sent over to the bridge. The bridge also buffers 20 bytes of the incoming data from the bus in the same board, so the bus transfer stops before the bridge.

These observations encourage to speed-up the bridge communications. For example, investigations on increasing the clock frequency of the bridges, using more pins for data transferring, and opting burst transfers are under way.

### 4.3 Area Utilization

Table 4 summarizes the resource utilization of the components on FPGA board #1. Adaptive LUT (ALUT) basically contains 4-input LUTs and a flip-flop. The used Stratix II 2S180 device has 143 520 ALUTs and the architecture consumes 91% of the capacity. The resource utilization for the corresponding components (e.g. slaves) in other boards is the same. Most strikingly, the SDRAM DMA logic utilization is 26% of the total. That is because it was decided to add tens of channels to the SDRAM DMA to improve its performance, because it is being shared to all the components. CPU area includes the DMA. A HIBI wrapper is required for each component to connect to HIBI. Again, SDRAM uses a special HIBI wrapper that is larger.

The HIBI bridges require very small amount of logic in top of the HIBI wrapper, due to the simplicity of the protocol used. This is in line with our objective that the prototype implementation means only small additions to the final architecture.

Practically all of the available memory of the architecture is dedicated to the CPUs. Therefore, all the internal FIFO buffers, for example, have been implemented in logic instead of utilizing memories. HIBI wrappers and especially SDRAM DMA, for instance, would be notable smaller with on-chip memories.

**Table 4.** The architecture area utilization in Stratix II S180 FPGA (board #1)

| | ALUTs | # | Total ALUTs | % of Total | Note. |
|---|---|---|---|---|---|
| CPU, Master | 5 143 | 1 | 5 143 | 4.0 % | Includes 13-channel DMA |
| CPU, Slave | 4 398 | 10 | 43 980 | 33.8 % | Includes 12-channel DMA |
| DQ | 2 691 | 3 | 8 072 | 6.2 % | |
| ME | 4 502 | 3 | 13 505 | 10.4 % | |
| RM | 545 | 1 | 545 | 0.4 % | |
| SDRAM controller | 395 | 1 | 395 | 0.3 % | |
| SDRAM DMA | 33 485 | 1 | 33 485 | 25.7 % | Parameterized for highest performance |
| HIBI Wrapper a) | 840 | 21 | 17 630 | 13.6 % | For each component to connect to HIBI |
| HIBI Wrapper b) | 1 858 | 1 | 1 858 | 1.4 % | For SDRAM |
| HIBI Bridge | 83 | 2 | 166 | 0.1 % | Needs also a HIBI wrapper |
| HIBI Monitor | 5 280 | 1 | 5 280 | 4.1 % | |
| Total (Architecture) | - | - | 130 059 | 100.0 % | 2S180 has 143 520 ALUTs |

## 5  Conclusions

An efficient and rapid method to prototype and evaluate large MP-SoC architectures has been presented. The method is based on re-usable, flexible, and scalable hardware architecture. The architecture allows large architecture prototypes that do not fit into single FPGAs to be easily distributed over to several chips in a device-independent and platform-independent way. A MPEG-4 video encoder with tens of processors and other IPs was successfully prototyped using the presented method.

The proposed design method allows using the exactly same software as in the final product to be used also in the prototype, thus allowing an early start in the software development. The architecture for the prototype includes only minor additions compared to the final architecture. Therefore, the evaluation of different configurations and functionality verification is simple, reliable, and fast. It also allows testing of different hardware configurations straightforwardly. When combined with ability to control the clocking of individual components, this configuration allows analysis of the software and hardware, their co-optimization and co-verification in early phases of the development.

In the future, the bridge latency will be optimized (wider data, wave-pipelining etc.) and true GALS (different clocks for boards) operation will be evaluated. In addition, other applications will be evaluated as well.

# References

1. Chang, C., Kuusilinna, K., Richards, B., Brodersen, R.W.: Implementation of BEE: a Real-time Large-scale Hardware Emulation Engine. In: Proc. FPGA'03, Monterey, California, pp. 91–99. ACM Press, New York (2003)
2. Krupnova, H.: Mapping Multi-Million Gate SoCs on FPGAs: Industrial Methodology and Experience. In: Proc. DATE, France, vol. 2, pages 6. IEEE Computer Society Press, Los Alamitos (2004)
3. Borgio, S., et al.: Hardware DWT accelerator for MultiProcessor System-on-Chip on FPGA. In: Proc. SAMOS, Samos, pp. 107–114. IEEE Computer Society Press, Los Alamitos (2006)
4. Mouhoub, R.B., Hammami, O.: System-level design methodology with direct execution for multiprocessors on SoPC. In: Proc. ISQED, Paris, France, IEEE Computer Society Press, Los Alamitos (2006)
5. Ravindran, K., Satish, N., Jin, Y., Keutzer, K.: An FPGA-based soft multiprocessor system for IPv4 packet forwarding. In: Proc. FPL, Tampere, Finland, pp. 487–492. IEEE Computer Society Press, Los Alamitos (2005)
6. Patel, A., et al.: A Scalable FPGA-based Multiprocessor. In: Proc. FCCM, Napa, California, pp. 111–120. IEEE Computer Society Press, Los Alamitos (2006)
7. Niemann, J.-G., Porrmann, M., Ruckert, U.: A scalable parallel SoC architecture for network processors. In: Proc. VLSI, pp. 311–313. IEEE Computer Society Press, Los Alamitos (2005)
8. Salminen, E., et al.: HIBI Communication Network for System-on-Chip. Journal of VLSI Signal Processing-Systems for Signal, Image, and Video Technology, vol. 43(2-3), pp. 185–205. Springer, Heidelberg (2006)
9. Kulmala, A., Hämäläinen, T.D., Hännikäinen, M.: Reliable GALS Implementation of MPEG-4 Encoder with Mixed Clock FIFO on Standard FPGA. In: Proc. FPL, Spain, pp. 495–500. IEEE Computer Society Press, Los Alamitos (2006)
10. Kulmala, A., Lehtoranta, O., Hämäläinen, T.D., Hännikäinen, M.: Scalable MPEG-4 Encoder on FPGA Multiprocessor SOC. EURASIP Journal on Embedded Systems 2006, 15 pages (2006)

# Efficiency Measures for Multimedia SOCs

Hartwig Jeschke

Institut für Mikroelektronische Systeme,
Gottfried Wilhelm Leibniz Universität Hannover,
Appelstr. 4, 30167 Hannover, Germany
jeschke@ims.uni-hannover.de

**Abstract.** This paper discusses efficiency measures for the evaluation of high performance multimedia systems on a chip *(SOC)*, considering a throughput rate $R$, chip size $A$, power dissipation $P$, and a flexibility criterion $F$. Based on the analysis of recently published multimedia chips, the paper shows equivalences between the ratio of $R$ over $AP$, a weighted sum on $1/R$, $A$, $P$, and a fuzzy multicriteria analysis on $R$, $A$, $P$. The paper indicates the fuzzy multicriteria analysis as generalization of the other efficiency measures, which can be easily applied to multiple cost and performance criteria. Because of the application of fuzzy set theory, the multicriteria approach supports quantitative criteria with a physical background as well as qualitative criteria by linguistic variables.

## 1 Introduction

Advances in semiconductor technology enable a wide field for the implementation of complex multimedia systems on a single chip. Because of the high data volume of continuously processed image sequences (high throughput rate), the video signal processing part of multimedia applications requires most of the computational performance. Hence the design of systems on a chip *(SOC)* for multimedia frequently must focus on high performance architectures, which support the specific requirements of video signal processing at reasonable costs of silicon.

Depending on the specific target application, the best tradeoff on conflicting design objectives must be found, such as low power, low cost, high computational performance, high quality of implemented signal processing algorithms and a high flexibility for processing of different applications on the same hardware. Mobile communication prefers for low power implementations and low device costs rather than a high quality by a computation intensive implementation of all possible features of a video coding standard. Because of highest quality requirements, video coding of *HDTV* results in a feature rich implementation of the processed video coding standard. The complexity of the processed video coding algorithms and real-time processing of high data volumes result in highest performance requirements for *HDTV*, while low power and low cost are less important. Additional video signal processing applications may emphasize more on the flexibility for processing of different applications on the same hardware.

S. Vassiliadis et al. (Eds.): SAMOS 2007, LNCS 4599, pp. 190–199, 2007.

Problems at early conceptual phases of a new $SOC$ design are the selection of the most appropriate architecture, e. g. the best matching $IP$ cores, as well as the parameter optimization of the envisaged target architecture. The selection of $IP$ cores as well as the optimization of their parameters need a figure of merit for the evaluation of alternatives, which considers performance criteria, such as throughput rate $R$, and multiple cost criteria, such as silicon area of the $SOC$ modules $A$, power dissipation $P$, and others.

This paper addresses efficiency measures for $SOC$ designs, which are based on $R$, $A$, $P$ and more qualitative performance criteria. These efficiency measures are the ratio of the throughput rate $R$ to the product of silicon area and power dissipation $R/(AP)$, a weighted sum of $R$, $A$ and $P$, and a fuzzy multicriteria analysis $(MCA)$ on $R$, $A$, $P$ and as an example for other qualitative performance criteria, a flexibility measure $F$. The proposed efficiency measures are discussed with respect to their common features, their limitations, their advantages, and their disadvantages. The paper is organized as follows. Section 2 introduces specifications of the proposed efficiency measures. Based on recently published video signal processor designs, in section 3 the efficiency measures are analyzed with respect to their equivalences. Section 4 discusses the extension of the fuzzy multicriteria analysis $(MCA)$ for the inclusion of qualitative performance criteria.

# 2   Specification of Efficiency Measures

## 2.1   *AT-Product* and Its Extensions

The evaluation of alternative $IP$ cores for a system on a chip $(SOC)$, the selection of $VLSI$ processors, and the optimization of new processor designs need a figure of merit, which helps to find the best tradeoff on cost and performance criteria for a specific application. Traditionally the *AT-Product* of silicon area $A$ and processing time $T$ is a well established efficiency measure for the local module selection or the optimization of arithmetic modules. A small processing time $T$ is a necessary condition for high performance. Because of the manufacturing yield, a small silicon area $A$ indicates to low costs. The most efficient solution of a set of architectural alternatives is represented by the minimum *AT-Product*.

In the case of pipelined arithmetic modules, such as *adders, multipliers, ALUs,* and *MACs,* $T$ can be derived from the period length of the clock of a synchronous design. As pipelined arithmetic modules continuously process a stream of data samples, their clock rate $(1/T)$ is the same as the throughput rate $(R)$. Considering modern processor designs with parallel processing and with processing of sequences of different tasks at different times under software control, the clock rate is no longer a sufficient performance indicator. The throughput rate of a signal processing system $(R)$ is a preferable performance criterion, to be maximized. Similar to the locally applied *AT-Product*, efficiency at the global processor level can be defined by the ratio of $A/R$ [1], which has to be minimized. Alternatively the ratio of $R/A$ can be used [2], which must be maximized with respect to the most efficient solution.

An important problem of efficiency measures in product or quotient form is their limited extensibility to more cost and performance criteria. In the case of power dissipation *(P)*, the extension to a product of *ATP* or *R/(AP)* may be frequently justified. Additionally the importance of $A, T, P$ can be considered by individual weighting exponents for each criterion ($A^{w_A} T^{w_T} P^{w_P}$). The importance of the silicon area $A$ may be reduced for some deep submicron designs, if the *PAD* cells dominate the lower bounds of *SOC* chip sizes *(PAD limited designs)*. On the other hand, leakage currents and highest clock rates raise the importance of the power dissipation $P$. Hence a *power delay product* has been recently proposed as an efficiency measure for *deep submicron SOC* designs [3] as a special case of $A^{w_A} T^{w_T} P^{w_P}$ with $w_A = 0$.

Within the $A^{w_A} T^{w_T} P^{w_P}$-*Product*, the investigated criteria are inherently compensatory. A small *SOC* with a low throughput rate may be rated equivalent to a large *SOC* with a high throughput rate. Only if an application allows to choose either numerous small chips or a few large chips at a comparable overall system performance, the compensation of $A$ and $T$ may be well reasoned.

In real situations, hard cost or performance constraints, such as a maximum power dissipation for mobile applications, limit the design space. Hence the compensation of multiple criteria is restricted by constraints, too. An extension of *ATP* to a general efficiency measure with multiple and arbitrary cost and performance criteria is not useful.

## 2.2 Weighted Sum

An improved extensibility can be realized by a weighted sum *(S)* of multiple cost and performance criteria, which is to be minimized:

$$S = w_{s_A} \cdot A + w_{s_R} \cdot 1/R + w_{s_P} \cdot P \tag{1}$$

As an advantage, the weighted sum can be used for optimization in a linear programming environment for task mapping and scheduling as well as for optimization of architectural parameters [4]. $S$ inherently compensates the investigated cost and performance criteria. As an advantage constraints on cost and performance can be separately considered within a linear programming environment. As a disadvantage, it is difficult to motivate an extension of the weighted sum to less quantitative but more qualitative criteria, such as the flexibility of an architecture for processing of different applications.

## 2.3 Fuzzy Multicriteria Analysis (*MCA*)

Considering constrained compensatory and non-compensatory cost and performance criteria as well as qualitative criteria, a fuzzy multicriteria analysis *(MCA)* has been proposed as an efficiency measure for *VLSI* architectures [5],[6]. This section first introduces fuzzy numbers, which support the specification of design objectives as well as uncertainty in modeling problems. Then a fuzzy multicriteria approach *(MCA)* is introduced, which is based on fuzzy numbers.

**The application of fuzzy numbers as a measure of possibility.** Modeling values $x$ of $X$ with $\mu_A(x) = 1$ are members of fuzzy set $A$ and may represent realization values, which are certainly possible for a $SOC$ implementation. Parameter values $x$ of $X$ with $\mu_A(x) = 0$ are **not** members of Set $A$ and may represent realization values, which certainly can **not** be realized in a later $SOC$ design. Other values are more or less members of the Set $A$. Using the trapezoidal shape (Fig. 1), a fuzzy set can be specified by four parameters $[m_1, m_2, a, b]$. A fuzzy set with trapezoidal shape can be interpreted as a fuzzy number and can be used for fuzzy arithmetic as an extension to arithmetic with real numbers as well as an extension to classical interval arithmetic [6].

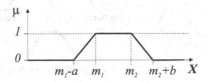

**Fig. 1.** *Fuzzy Number* $X = [m_1, m_2, a, b]$ with trapezoidal shape

In this paper, the discussion of fuzzy sets is focused on the specification of design objectives (Fig. 2). The most feasible values of the realization criteria of throughput rate $R$, silicon area $A$, and the power dissipation $P$ may certainly be members of their related fuzzy set. The degree of membership is $\mu = 1$. Infeasible values, which are excluded by constraints, do not to belong to the related fuzzy set. Their degree of membership is $\mu = 0$. All other parameter values are more or less feasible candidates for an envisaged design. Their feasibility increases according to their degree of membership. Hence various kinds of design objectives can be easily specified by fuzzy sets.

Fig. 2 shows a design objective of a throughput rate $R$, to be *as much as possible*, where $R_{max}$ may characterize the largest known image size and its video format. The design objective of the chip size $A$ represents *as small as possible* and *never more than* $A_{max}$. The design objective of the power dissipation $P$ represents *as low as possible* and *never more than* $P_{max}$. A design objective for a flexibility measure can be specified as *as much as possible*.

Once a known or an estimated criterion on cost or performance *(R, A, P)* is specified by a fuzzy number, a degree of fulfillment of the related design objective $\mu_f$ can be defined [5]. First the intersection of the fuzzy sets of the criterion and its design objectives is derived from the minimum of both shapes (Fig. 3). $\mu_f$

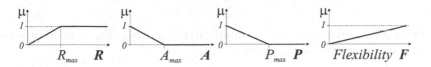

**Fig. 2.** Design objectives specified by fuzzy numbers with trapezoidal shape

can be calculated from the ratio of the *area under the intersection* over the *area under the criterion* and ranges from 0 to 1 (Eq. 2).

$$\mu_f = \frac{Area(design\ objective \cap criterion)}{Area(criterion)} \tag{2}$$

In the case of a real (in terms of fuzzy sets: *crisp*) criterion, the trapezoidal shape reduces to a vertical line. Then $\mu_f$ is directly represented by the degree of membership of the design objective at the value of the criterion.

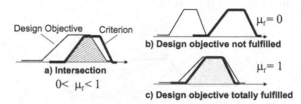

**Fig. 3.** Intersection of a cost or performance criterion with its design objective

**The aggregation of multiple cost and performance criteria.** Yager [7] has proposed a method, which results in an overall degree of fulfillment of multiple design objectives $\mu_{MCA}$. Eq. 3 shows this overall degree of fulfillment for the introduced cost and performance criteria $R, A, P$ and a flexibility measure $F$. Each individual degree of fulfillment $\mu_f$, with $f \in \{A, R, P, F\}$, is weighted by an exponent, which is related to the importance of the criterion.

$$\mu_{MCA} = \mu_R^{w_{\mu_R}} \cdot \mu_A^{w_{\mu_A}} \cdot \mu_P^{w_{\mu_P}} \cdot \mu_F^{w_{\mu_F}} \tag{3}$$

According to the values of the single criteria, $\mu_{MCA}$ ranges from 0 to 1. In the case of $\mu_{MCA} = 0$, the design objectives are not fulfilled. In the case of $\mu_{MCA} = 1$, the design objectives are completely fulfilled.

**The weighting exponents.** A method for the derivation of the weighting exponents has been proposed by Saaty [8]. He suggests a pair wise comparison of the importance $i$ of each two criteria. The ratios of the pair wise comparisons are written in a matrix $M$ (Eq. 4), which is shown for the proposed criteria $R$, $A$, $P$, $F$.

$$M = \begin{pmatrix} 1 & \frac{i_R}{i_A} & \frac{i_R}{i_P} & \frac{i_R}{i_F} \\ \frac{i_A}{i_R} & 1 & \frac{i_A}{i_P} & \frac{i_A}{i_F} \\ \frac{i_P}{i_R} & \frac{i_P}{i_A} & 1 & \frac{i_P}{i_F} \\ \frac{i_F}{i_R} & \frac{i_F}{i_A} & \frac{i_F}{i_P} & 1 \end{pmatrix} \tag{4}$$

The weighting exponents for the multicriteria analysis (Eq. 3) are represented by the components of the eigenvector of $M$.

# 3   Equivalence of the Different Efficiency Measures

In this section the three efficiency measures $R/(AP)$, $S$ and $MCA$ are compared with respect to their equivalences. In the case of $MCA$, the flexibility measure $F$ is not considered ($w_{\mu_F} = 0$), because the other approaches have no corresponding criterion. The design objectives are for $A$ $[0,0,0,100]mm^2$ (*as small as possible and smaller than* $100mm^2$), for $R$ $[120,120,120,0]Mpixel/s$ (*as fast as possible*), and for $P$ $[0,0,0,10000]mW$ (*as low as possible*).

The following comparison is based on recently published *VLSIs* for multimedia and video signal processing. These *VLSIs* have been designed in different technologies from $0.09\mu m$ to $0.18\mu m$. They are motivation examples for the discussion of the proposed efficiency measures. The design of new architectural concepts as well as *IP* core selection need the unified evaluation of architectural alternatives in one target technology. Table 1 shows the characteristic realization data and a ranking of the *VLSIs* with respect to the $R/(AP)$ efficiency measure. The best solution is a processor, which operates up to VGA resolution [9]. At the last position is a programmable multimedia processor, capable of processing of TV formats [10]. These examples are analyzed with the three efficiency measures $R/(AP)$, $S$, and $MCA$.

**Table 1.** Realization data of multimedia *VLSIs* and ranking by $R/(AP)$ (1: best value)

| Processor | Technology ($\mu m$) | R ($Mpixel/s$) | A ($mm^2$) | P ($mW$) | Flexibility for Processing of different Applications | Ranking by $R/(AP)$ |
|---|---|---|---|---|---|---|
| TV [10] | 0.18 | 10.4 | 82 | 4300 | High | 8 |
| HDTV [11] | 0.18 | 27.7 | 32 | 785 | Medium | 6 |
| VGA [12] | 0.09 | 9.2 | 33 | 90 | Medium | 5 |
| HDTV [13] | 0.13 | 27.7 | 31 | 120 | Low | 4 |
| Mobile [14] | 0.13 | 3.0 | 80 | 120 | High | 7 |
| TV [15] | 0.18 | 10.4 | 15 | 12 | Low | 2 |
| HDTV [16] | 0.13 | 62.2 | 8 | 320 | Low | 3 |
| VGA [9] | 0.18 | 9.2 | 3 | 18 | Low | 1 |

One problem is the comparison of the efficiency measures. They are basically used for comparison of different solutions, which can be represented by ranking of the investigated *VLSIs*. In the case of identical rankings for the different efficiency measures, they are equivalent for the considered examples. Another problem is caused by the undetermined weights in $S$ ($w_{s_R}, w_{s_A}, w_{P_A}$) and $MCA$ ($w_{\mu_R}, w_{\mu_A}, w_{\mu_P}$). Hence, only if suitable weights can be found, an equivalence of the discussed measures can be indicated.

Fig.4 shows a strategy for the comparison. In a first step the figures of merit are calculated for the three efficiency measures, starting with arbitrary values of the weights. In a next steps a ranking of the examples is performed for each efficiency measure. The results of the rankings with $S$ and $MCA$ are compared to the ranking of $R/(AP)$, which is used as a reference. The number of differences in the ranking positions are individually counted. In the case of differences, the values of the weights are varied and the calculation is performed again until the best match of the models (minimum of ranking differences) is found. The parameter search has been performed by a genetic optimization algorithm. The

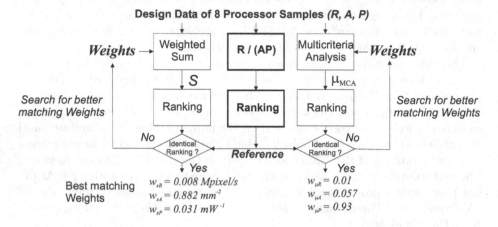

**Fig. 4.** Search strategy for best matching weights for $S$ and $MCA$

optimized weights are shown Fig. 4. They result in an identical ranking of the analyzed processor examples, as shown in the last column of Table 1. Hence, this result indicates a strong relationship between the investigated efficiency measures.

## 4   Extension of the Multicriteria Analysis with a Flexibility Criterion

The previous section has indicated a relationship between the three efficiency measures $R/(AP)$, the weighted sum $S$, and the multicriteria analysis $MCA$. Hence, the $MCA$ can perform as other measures do. First the $MCA$ has a higher flexibility in the specification of the design objectives. Their trapezoidal shapes specify, whether a criterion must be minimized or maximized. Additionally hard constraints are considered by their shape, too ($\mu = 0$).

Another advantage of the $MCA$ is a better expandability to multiple evaluation criteria, which may be independent to a physical background, such as qualitative measures. In fuzzy set theory so called *lingustic variables* are discussed. In the context of the investigated *VLSI* examples, such a qualitative measure could be the flexibility for processing of different applications on the same hardware. An architecture with dedicated modules for the most computation intensive parts of multimedia applications will have a low flexibility. Architectures with a standard *RISC* core and additional extensions for multimedia may have a medium flexibility. *VLIW* architectures with parallelism at the instruction level offer a high flexibility. Table 1 shows a qualitative characterization

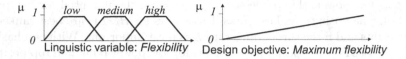

**Fig. 5.** Linguistic variable *flexibility* and a design objective *maximum flexibility*

of the analyzed architectures with respect to their flexibility. Fig. 5 shows the specification of a linguistic fuzzy variable on flexibility. *Low flexibility* is specified as $[10, 30, 10, 10]$, *medium flexibility* is defined as $[40, 60, 10, 10]$, and *high flexibility* is defined as $[70, 90, 10, 10]$. A design objective *maximum flexibility* can be specified as $[100, 100, 100, 0]$.

In the following an example for a multicriteria analysis is performed for design objectives for $A$ with $[0, 0, 0, 100]mm^2$ (*as small as possible* and *smaller than* $100mm^2$), for $R$ with $[120, 120, 120, 0]Mpixel/s$ (*as fast as possible*), for $P$ with $[0, 0, 0, 10000]mW$ (*as low as possible*), and a *maximum flexibility*. The $MCA$ starts with equally weighted criteria ($w_{\mu R} = w_{\mu A} = w_{\mu P} = 1$). A next step investigates, whether an increased importance for a single criterion results in a feasible ranking result. For each criterion a multicriteria analysis is performed, where this criterion is arbitrarily considered as 10 times more important than the others. According to the eigenvalue approach [8] the resulting weights are shown in Table 2. Table 3 shows the results of the multicriteria analyses. If flexibility is most important, a *VLIW* multimedia processor [10] is best rated. A mobile processor [14] with 3 *RISC* cores and a programmable DSP follows. With

**Table 2.** Weighting exponents: One criterion is 10 times more important than others

| 10 x important | $w_{\mu R}$ | $w_{\mu A}$ | $w_{\mu P}$ | $w_{\mu F}$ |
|---|---|---|---|---|
| R | 0.769 | 0.077 | 0.077 | 0.077 |
| A | 0.077 | 0.769 | 0.077 | 0.077 |
| P | 0.077 | 0.077 | 0.769 | 0.077 |
| F | 0.077 | 0.077 | 0.077 | 0.769 |

**Table 3.** Ranking results for *MCA* for each criterion weighted 10 times higher than others

| | Equal weights | Throughput rate $R$ | Chip size $A$ | Power dissipation $P$ | Flexibility $F$ |
|---|---|---|---|---|---|
| TV [10] | 7 | 6 | 8 | 8 | 1 |
| HDTV [11] | 3 | 3 | 5 | 6 | 6 |
| VGA [12] | 4 | 5 | 6 | 3 | 3 |
| HDTV [13] | 2 | 2 | 4 | 2 | 5 |
| Mobile [14] | 8 | 8 | 7 | 7 | 2 |
| TV [15] | 6 | 4 | 3 | 5 | 8 |
| HDTV [16] | 1 | 1 | 1 | 1 | 4 |
| VGA [9] | 5 | 7 | 2 | 4 | 7 |

respect to low power, this processor loses, because the potential for low power is limited, when using standard cores. Processors for *HDTV* are best ranked for equal weights and if the throughput rate $R$ is most important. With emphasis on $P$, *HDTV VLSIs* with special mechanisms for low power remain in top positions [13],[16] while [11] loses in its ranking position. The *HDTV* chips lose in their ranking position, if flexibility counts more. Their performance $R$ is gained from dedicated (less flexible) processing units. The overall result of the rankings with emphasis on each of the criteria $R,A,P,F$ seems to be plausible.

# 5   Conclusion

This paper has discussed three different efficiency measures for the evaluation of multimedia systems on a chip. The efficiency measures are based on the throughput rate $R$, chip size $A$, power dissipation $P$, and a flexibility criterion $F$. The paper has shown for recently published multimedia *VLSIs*, that equivalences can be found for the $R/(AP)$-measure, a weighted sum $S$ of $R,A,P$, and a fuzzy multicriteria analysis *MCA* on $R,A,P$. The paper has indicated, that *MCA* can be considered as an extendable generalization of the other efficiency measures.

# References

1. Jeschke, H., Gaedke, K., Pirsch, P.: Multiprocessor Performance for Real-Time Processing of Video Coding Applications. IEEE Transactions on Circuits and Systems for Video Technology 2(2), 221–230 (1992) Special Issue On: VLSI Circuits And Systems for Video Applications
2. Pirsch, P., Demassieux, N., Gehrke, W.: VLSI architectures for video compression-a survey. In: Proceedings of the IEEE. 83(2), pp. 220–246. IEEE Computer Society Press, Los Alamitos (1995)
3. Sengupta, D., Saleh, R.: Generalized Power-Delay Metrics in Deep Submicron CMOS Design. IEEE Transactions on Computer-Aided Design of Integrated Circuits and Systems 26(1), 183–189 (2002)
4. Schwiegershausen, M.: Ein Verfahren zur Optimierung heterogener Multiprozessorsysteme mittels linearer Programmierung. In: Ph.D. Thesis, Fachbereich Elektrotechnik und Informationstechnik, Universität Hannover (1997)
5. Jeschke, H.: Fuzzy Multiobjective Decision Making On Modeled Architectural Concepts. In: Proceedings of the IEEE International Symposium on Circuits and Systems (ISCAS 1998), vol. 6, pp. 151–154. IEEE Computer Society Press, Los Alamitos (1998)
6. Jeschke, H.: Kosten- und Performance-Modellierung applikationsspezifischer VLSI-Architekturen. In: Ph.D. Thesis, Fakultät für Elektrotechnik und Informatik, Universität Hannover (2005)
7. Yager, R.: Fuzzy Decision Making Including Unequal Objectives. In: Fuzzy Sets and Systems, vol. 1, pp. 87–95. North-Holland, Amsterdam (1978)
8. Saaty, T.L.: Exploring the Interface Betweeen Hierarchies, Multiple Objectives and Fuzzy Sets. In: Fuzzy Sets and Systems, vol. 1, pp. 57–68. North-Holland, Amsterdam (1978)

9. Lin, C.-P., Tseng, P.-C., Chiu, Y.-T., Lin, S.-S., Cheng, C.-C., Fang, H.-C.: A 5mW MPEG4 SP encoder with 2D bandwidth-sharing motion estimation for mobile applications. In: Digest of Technical Papers of the 2005 IEEE International Solid-State Circuits Conference, pp. 1626–1635. IEEE Computer Society Press, Los Alamitos (2006)

10. Stolberg, H.-J., Moch, S., Friebe, L., Dehnhardt, A., Kulaczewski, M.B., Berekovic, M., Pirsch, P.: An SoC with two multimedia DSPs and a RISC core for video compression applications. In: Digest of Technical Papers of the 2004 IEEE International Solid-State Circuits Conference, pp. 330–340. IEEE Computer Society Press, Los Alamitos (2004)

11. Huang, Y.-W., Chen, T.-C., Tsai, C.-H., Chen, C.-Y., Chen, T.-W., Chen, C.-S., Shen, C.-F., Ma, S.-Y., Wang, T.-C., Hsieh, B.-Y., Fang, H.-C., Chen, L.-G.: A 1.3TOPS H.264/AVC single-chip encoder for HDTV applications. In: Digest of Technical Papers of the 2005 IEEE International Solid-State Circuits Conference, pp. 128–588. IEEE Computer Society Press, Los Alamitos (2005)

12. Fujiyoshi, T., Shiratake, S., Nomura, S., Nishikawa, T., Kitasho, Y., Arakida, H., Okuda, Y., Tsuboi, Y., Hamada, M., Hara, H., Fujita, T., Hatori, F., Shimazawa, T., Yahagi, K., Takeda, H., Murakata, M., Minami, F., Kawabe, N., Kitahara, T., Seta, K., Takahashi, M., Oowaki, Y.: An H.264/MPEG-4 audio/visual CODEC LSI with module-wise dynamic voltage/frequency scalings. In: Digest of Technical Papers of the 2005 IEEE International Solid-State Circuits Conference, pp. 128–588. IEEE Computer Society Press, Los Alamitos (2005)

13. Yamauchi, H., Okada, S., Watanabe, T., Matsuo, Y., Suzuki, M., Ishii, Y., Mori, T., Matsushita, Y.: An 81 MHz, 1280 × 720pixels × 30frames/s MPEG-4 video/audio CODEC processor. In: Digest of Technical Papers of the 2005 IEEE International Solid-State Circuits Conference, pp. 130–589. IEEE Computer Society Press, Los Alamitos (2005)

14. Torii, S., Suzuki, S., Tomonaga, H., Tokue, T., Sakai, J., Suzuki, N., Murakami, K., Hiraga, T., Shigemoto, K., Tatebe, Y., Ohbuchi, E., Kayama, N., Edahiro, M., Kusano, T., Nishi, N.: A 600MIPS 120mW 70 $\mu/A$ leakage triple-CPU mobile application processor chip. In: Digest of Technical Papers of the 2005 IEEE International Solid-State Circuits Conference, pp. 130–589. IEEE Computer Society Press, Los Alamitos (2005)

15. Liu, T.-M., Lin, T.-A., Wang, S.-Z., Lee, W.-P., Hou, K.-C., Yang, J.-Y., Lee, C.-Y.: A 125 $\mu$w, fully scalable MPEG-2 and H.264/AVC video decoder for mobile applications. In: Digest of Technical Papers of the 2005 IEEE International Solid-State Circuits Conference, pp. 1576–1585. IEEE Computer Society Press, Los Alamitos (2006)

16. Lin, C.C., Guo, J.I., Chang, H.C., Yang, Y.C., Chen, J.W., Tsai, M.C., Wang, J.S.: A 160kgate 4.5kB SRAM H.264 Video Decoder for HDTV applications. In: Digest of Technical Papers of the 2005 IEEE International Solid-State Circuits Conference, pp. 1596–1605. IEEE Computer Society Press, Los Alamitos (2006)

# On-Chip Bus Modeling for Power and Performance Estimation

Je-Hoon Lee[1], Young-Shin Cho[2], Seok-Man Kim[3], and Kyoung-Rok Cho[3]

[1] CBNU BK21 Chungbuk Information Technology Center, Rep. of Korea
leejh@hbt.cbnu.ac.kr
[2] PDP development team, Samsung SDI, 508, Sungsung-dong, Cheonan, Korea
[3] CCNS Lab., San 12, Gaeshin-dong, Cheongju, Chugnbuk, Rep. of Korea

**Abstract.** This paper presented a latency and power model to determine the bus configuration of a target SoC system at its early design stage. The latency model analyzed the latencies of an on-chip bus and provided throughput reflecting the bus configuration. The power model provided power estimation based on the pre-determined bus architecture. This paper showed new parameters to devise the proposed models such as bus usage, active bridge ratio, etc. Moreover, we evaluated the throughput of the bus and compared this with the required throughput of the target SoC, including a number of real IPs. This target SoC was configured based on the estimation results obtained from the proposed bus model. This estimation were compared with the simulation results of target SoC design for verifying the accuracy of the proposed model. The evaluation showed that the accuracies of the proposed model for the latency and the power model were over 85% and 92%, respectively. This result set the standard for an efficient bus structure for a SoC design.

**Keywords:** SoC, on-chip bus, bus modeling, bus latency.

## 1 Introduction

The platform-based SoC (system on a chip) design was proposed to save design time and to integrate the more complex system in a chip [1-2]. As reusable IP libraries are becoming increasingly feature packed, on-chip bus architecture becomes a relatively significant design issue, especially with respect to the performance and power consumption. The more we know precise bus latency and power consumption of on-chip bus in its early design stage, the more we have chance to design SoC system efficiently with respect to the performance and power consumption.

The research shows that the power consumed by an on-chip bus, accounted for 15% of the total power consumed in a SoC [3]. This is comparable in magnitude to well-known primary power consumption such as a processor. The increasing number of IPs induces a slow down in operation speed, caused by the competition for getting ownership of the bus, and it thereby becomes a bottleneck, limiting system performance. A substantial number of research results, such as

S. Vassiliadis et al. (Eds.): SAMOS 2007, LNCS 4599, pp. 200–210, 2007.
© Springer-Verlag Berlin Heidelberg 2007

the AMBA, Coreconnect and WishBone, have been proposed to resolve these problems [4-6]. However, it is difficult to estimate the required bus throughput and power consumption. This results in difficulty determining the bus configuration at its early design stage.

The following design issues must be considered in its early design stages. First, the bus configuration is an important design issue. The single shared bus architecture suffers from limited bandwidth. Complex SoC needs wider bandwidth to transfer data on time. If the required bandwidth exceeds the allowable bandwidth, this results in a bottleneck [7]. This problem is solved by a bus hierarchy with multiple bus layers [8-10]. This bus hierarchy partitions a whole bus system into several layers. When IPs through the same layer communicates, each layer works independently. The bandwidth increases in proportion to the number of layers. However, this makes the system bus more complicated.

Second, the bus logic is important to analyze the bus. A state-of-art on-chip bus contains multiple bus layers comprising several components, such as an arbiter, a multiplexer, and a decoder. A bridge is used to connect two different bus layers. A transaction across more than one layer is split into the corresponding number of transactions. It needs more cycles compared with a single shared bus. K. Lahiri claimed that the power consumed by the bus lines represents only 14% of the total power consumed by the system bus architecture [3]. In contrast, the total power consumed by the logic components constitutes approximately 51%. We need to analyze the correlation between the SoC system performance and the system power consumption, and find the trade-off between them.

Finally, the transfer mode is important in analyzing the bus performance. Most on-chip buses provide the variable transferring options such as burst and single transaction. Pipelining overlaps the address phase and the data phase for high performance. A burst transaction is defined as one or more data transactions, initiated by a bus master, which has a consistent width of transaction to an incremental region of address space. It reduces the wastage of bandwidth. This method makes the bus master hand over at the end of a burst transfer.

This paper presents a multi-layer system bus modeling method. The proposed latency model is to estimate the performance according to the architectural configuration. The proposed power model comprises two parts: the power estimation over bus lines, and the power estimation for logic components. We measure the power consumption of each component after a system synthesis. The accuracy is verified through an example of SoC.

## 2    Bus Modeling Environment

The overall bus system model is depicted in Figure 1. All IPs are allocated to a corresponding layer. Each layer contains logic components such as read/write multiplexers, arbiters, and address decoders. In this figure, $i$, $j$, and $k$ IP modules are connected to the first, second, and $N_{th}$ bus layer, respectively. $(N-1)$ bridges and $N$ bus logics are needed to connect $N$ layers. $N_M$ and $N_L$ represent the number of master IPs and the number of layers, respectively.

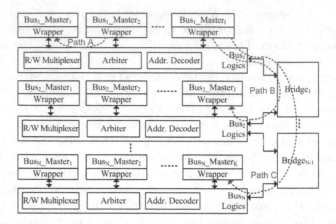

**Fig. 1.** The architecture of a multi-layer on-chip bus

**Table 1.** Definitions of parameters

| Parameter | Definition |
|-----------|------------|
| $L_{Bus}$ | Latency of a shared-bus |
| $N_M$ | Number of masters |
| $N_L$ | Number of layers |
| $N_D$ | Number of data |
| $S$ | Single transfer ratio |
| $B$ | Burst size |
| $U$ | Usage of bus |
| $A$ | Active bridge ratio |
| $\alpha$ | Bridge factor |
| $\beta$ | Number of datapaths in the same bridge |
| $\gamma$ | Number of total datapaths using a bridge |

The presented bus model supports a pipelined and burst transfer. A burst mode needs only one arbitration to transfer one more data words consecutively. A pipeline mode is used to reduce the input latency for each master IP. Both of them are used to enhance the performance of a bus system. In general, there are two kinds of data transfer mode; single transfer and burst one. A single transfer ratio $S$ means the proportion of the single transfer to the total one. The burst transfer ratio can be represented as $1-S$. The burst size $B$ represents the number of data transferred during one burst mode transaction.

Figure 1 shows three kinds of datapaths in a multi-layer bus. The number of active bridges is determined by the required datapath. Path A includes no bridge for datapath. In addition, each layer operates independently. Path B and Path C need one and two activated bridges, respectively. We define parameters with respect to the bridge. The bridge factor $\alpha$ is the latency overhead caused by the datapath, and including the active bridge. The parameter $\beta$ is the number of datapath making the bridge active, and $\gamma$ represents the total number of datapath including an active bridge. Table 1 shows definitions of the parameters used in this paper. This paper assumes the IS (ideal-slave) model, which disregards the state of slave IPs on a bus and makes bus modeling simple. It assumes that slave IPs have no wait-state in response to the master IPs. A slave IP always responds to the master's request without delay. Also, we assume the bridge can always acquire a grant to make our model simple.

## 3    Latency Model for an On-Chip Bus

The bandwidth and latency determine the throughput of an on-chip bus. The latency depends on the bus configuration and the transfer mode. This section presents a latency model reflecting various bus architectures.

A single-layer bus allows only one master to transfer data over the bus at a time. It supports a single transfer and a burst one. An address and a data phase can be overlapped to improve the throughput. The latency of a single layer bus can be calculated by Eq. 1. The bus can support the pipelining operation in a burst mode. The first term is the latency to transfer data using the single transfer mode. The second term is the number of cycles to control the burst mode. The third term is the latency during the pipelined burst mode. Eq. 1 can be written as Eq. 2 when this bus can support a pipelined single transfer mode as well as a pipelined burst transfer mode. The first term is the only difference of both equations. We will now define a bus usage. It increases when transactions occur frequently by different master IPs. The bus usage is defined the ratio of a required bus bandwidth in an available bandwidth. It is easy to get the required bus bandwidth because the system designer can easily estimate the required data rate for each IP and get the summation of all required bus bandwidth.

$$L_{Bus\_B\_Pipeline} = 3N_D \times S + \lceil \frac{N_D \times (1 - S)}{B} \rceil + N_D \times (1 - S) \qquad (1)$$

$$L_{Bus\_S/B\_Pipeline} = (3 - 2U)N_D S + \lceil \frac{N_D(1 - S)}{B} \rceil + N_D(1 - S) \qquad (2)$$

Here $N_D$ is the number of transferring data, $S$ is the proportion of the single transfer, $B$ ($0 \leq B \leq 1$) is the size of a burst, and $U$ ($0 \leq U \leq 1$) is the usage of the bus. $L_{bus}$ means the total number of cycles to transfer entire data $N_D$. The multi-layer bus needs additional parameters: the number of layers and the number of active bridges. Eq. 3 defines the latency of a multi-layer bus reflecting the number of active bridges and the number of layers. The latency decreases along with the number of layers, $N_L$. This equation includes the active bridge ratio $A$ ($0 \leq A \leq 1$) and the bridge factor $\alpha$.

The parameter $A$ is the probability that a datapath would be established including the active bridges. Table 2 shows the possible datapaths and patterns of active bridge on the 3-layer on-chip bus. It needs two bus bridge to connect each layer. in this case, there are three different kinds of possible datapath combination. The longest datapath is the communication between the IP on the *layer0* and the IP on the *layer2*. It needs two activated bus bridges. The shortest datapath is the communication between the IPs on the same layer. It does not need

**Table 2.** Datapath patterns and number of active bridges due to number of bus layes

| Number of layers \ Number of active birdges | 1 bridge | 2 bridges |
|---|---|---|
| 2 layers | L0 ↔ L1 | |
| 3 layers | L0 ↔ L1<br>L1 ↔ L2 | L0 ↔ L2 |

to activate the bus bridge. The other case need only one active bus bridge for communication. Parameter $A$ is obtained by dividing all datapaths in the layers by the number of active bridges. Thus, this division ratio is the proportional of the datapath using the same bridge over the total datapath. The bus latency is inversely proportional to the number of layers and it is proportional to the bridge usage. The first and second terms represent the latency with and without bridge connections, respectively.

$$L_{Multi\_layer} = \frac{N_M}{N_L} \times L_{Bus} \times (1 - A) + \alpha \times A \qquad (3)$$

The bridge factor $\alpha$ is the latency overhead due to the bridge usage. The bandwidth varies according to the number of active bridges. $\beta$ is the number of datapaths using the same number of bridges. Factor $i$ represents the number of bridges used in a datapath. That is, $\beta$ means the summation of datapaths using the same bridge. $\gamma$ is the total number of datapaths using the active bridges. Consequently, $\gamma$ is bigger than $\beta$. The latency overhead due to bridges can be derived from Eq. 5.

$$\alpha = \sum_{i=1}^{N_D-1} (\frac{\beta}{\gamma} \times \frac{N_M}{N_L - i} \times L_{Bus}), \beta = C_i^{N_L-1}, \gamma = \sum_{j=1}^{N_L-1} \times C_j^{N_L-1} \qquad (4)$$

$$L_{Multi\_layer} = \frac{N_M}{N_L} L_{Bus}(1 - A) + \sum_{i=1}^{N_D-1} (\frac{\beta}{\gamma} \times \frac{N_M}{N_L - i} \times L_{Bus})A \qquad (5)$$

Equation 5 shows the latency model for a multi-layer bus. To make it simple, we are not concerned about a request-grant model through layers. We assume the bridge can always acquire a grant without an additional cycle although every change of layer requires re-acquiring a grant by a bridge. The bus latency of the system can be improved based on these factors. The bus latency can be reduced by means of estimation on the bandwidth of IPs and a datapath between IPs.

Figure 2 shows a distribution of the active bridge ratio $A$. This parameter is obtained by dividing all datapaths reflecting the number of active bridges. It is the proportion of datapaths using the same bridge over the total number of datapaths. The throughput increases in proportional to the number of layers, $N_L$, with the same active bridge ratio, $A$. This throughput decreases as $A$ increases. The bus latency is inversely proportional to $N_L$ and proportional to $A$.

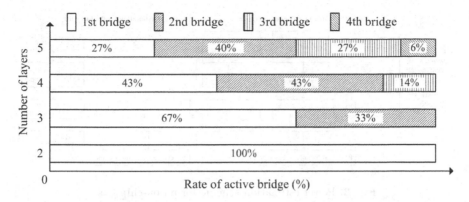

**Fig. 2.** The portion of parameter A on the multi-layer shared bus

The proposed latency model depends on the bus configuration, the transfer mode, and the communication channel. The bus configuration decides the number of IPs, layers, and bridges. The transfer mode decides the single transfer ratio, the burst size, and the number of transferring data. All of these factors can be easily estimated in the early design stage except for the usage of a bus, $U$; and an active bridge ratio, $A$. The proposed latency model can be used to design the bus reflecting the effect caused by the varying bus usage and the active bridge ratio.

## 4   The Proposed Power Model

This section describes the proposed power estimation model as shown in Fig. 3. The power consumed by a system bus is the sum of power consumed by all bus components and the power consumed by signal transition over the bus wire. It is possible to get the power consumed by the bus logics using the commercial design tools like a NanoSim [11]. We generated a synthesizable RT-level description of those bus logics. We set the number of IPs and layers according to the bus system configuration and the constant bus width. Some physical parameters like a wire length and capacitance can be obtained from the specific CMOS process. We can measure an average power of those logics through a simulation after precise post-layout extractions.

We use a transaction model to estimate the power consumed by a bus line. We analyze the impact of varying traffic characteristics, as well as the impact of varying SoC complexity, based on the proposed latency model. One way to estimate the power consumption of an on-chip bus depends on the number of switching such as Eq. 6 [12]. We employ the trace block for bus transaction to obtain the hamming distance for transferring data. Figure 3 shows how to trace the bus and how to merge the hamming distance into the SoC simulator, MaxSim [13]. We add additional functions for the bus tracing and power estimation to the transactor in order to trace the bus transaction. The transactor links and

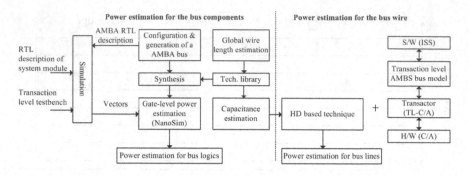

**Fig. 3.** Power estimation scheme for an on-chip bus

converts signal levels between an accurate level of a cycle and a transaction level
in the SoC simulator.

$$C_W = N_{BA} \times C_{phy} \times \sum_{i=1}^{n} P_i(0 \to 1) = HD_W \times C_{phy} \tag{6}$$

$C_{phy}$ is the physical capacitance of wires, and $P_i(0 \to 1)$ is the average probability
of a zero to one transition between two successive samples in the data stream for
the bit $i$. $N_{BA}$ and $P_i(0 \to 1)$ can be replaced $HD_W$. Here $HD_W$ is a hamming
distance on a bus line. The power consumed by the bus wire is represented by

$$P_w = \sum_{i=1}^{N_D}(P_{arb} + P_{addr} + P_{data}) = \frac{V_{dd}^2 f}{2} \sum_{i=1}^{N_D}(C_{arb} + C_{phy} + (HD_{addr} + HD_{data})) \tag{7}$$

$C_{arb}$ is the load capacitance for arbitration. $HD_{addr}$ and $HD_{data}$ are the hamming distance of the address line and data line, respectively. Each term represents
the power consumed to transfer signals. $P_{arb}$ is a power consumed by the control signal transfer, request and grant. $P_{addr}$ is a power consumed by the address
transfer. $P_{data}$ is a power consumed on a data line. The power consumed by each
bus layer, $P_{Layer}$ during the burst mode with a pipelining can be represented by
Eq. 8.

Consequently, the power consumed by the multi-layer bus can be represented
as Eq. 9. $N_{active\_bridge}$ is the number of active bridges and $P_{bridge}$ is the power
consumed by the bridge. The sum of power consumption of each part is the total
power consumed by the on-chip bus. This equation is based on the proposed
latency model. It is used to estimate the power consumption of an on-chip bus
in its early design stage.

$$P_{Layer} = \sum_{i=1}^{N_D S}(P_{arb} + P_{addr} + P_{data}) + P_{arb}\lceil\frac{N_D(1-S)}{B}\rceil + \sum_{j=1}^{B\lceil\frac{N_D(1-S)}{B}\rceil}(P_{addr} + P_{data}) \tag{8}$$

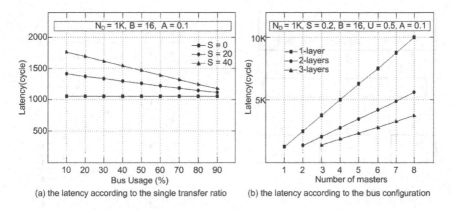

**Fig. 4.** The comparison results of the latencies

$$P_{Bus} = \sum_{i=1}^{N_{active\_layer}} P_{wire\_i} + N_{active\_bridge} P_{bridge} \qquad (9)$$

## 5  Simulation Results

This section presents simulation results based on the proposed bus models. The simulation results are compared with the results from MaxSim tool [13].

Figure 4a shows the comparison results according to the data transfer type and bus usage during transferring 1,000 words. The latency increases when either the single mode transfer ratio or the bus usage becomes higher. The effect of a single transfer is only 10%, compared to a burst transfer when the bus usage exceeds 90%. The latency reflecting a burst transfer is independent of the bus usage. Figure 4b shows the latency according to the number of layers and IPs. The latencies of the 2–layer and the 3–layer cases are reduced by 45% and 63%, respectively, compared to the single-layer case. Although the bus usage changes the latency, the reduction rate remains the same since the parameter A remains the same.

An MPEG encoder SoC is used to decide the number of layers. Figure 5a shows a simple procedure of a video processing, which shows the data flow of compressing and displaying of an image. The color VGA displays at 30 frames/s. The same throughput is required at each stage 1, 2, 3 and 5. The total required system bus bandwidth is 110.6 MBps. In other case, when this system connected to the USB 2.0, it must have a 60 MBps bus bandwidth because USB 2.0 interface provides a transmission rate of 60 MBps. The analysis assumes a bus frequency of 100 MHz and a channel width of 4 bytes for the proposed multi-layer latency model as shown in Fig. 5b. These curves are from the proposed latency model. From these results, a MPEG encoder SoC can have five master IPs in the two layers. The results of Okada's work have three layers and are similar to the simulation result as shown in Fig. 5b.

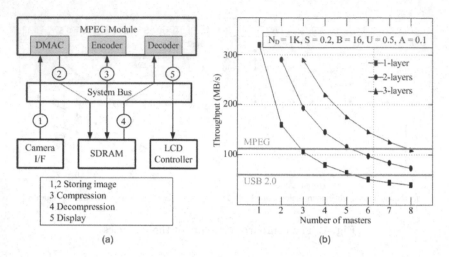

**Fig. 5.** The architecture of a MPEG SoC and the simulation results: (a) An example of a MPEG SoC; (b) The expected throughput of each shared-bus according to the number of layers

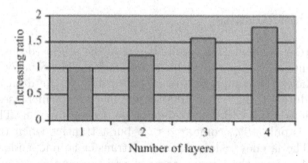

**Fig. 6.** Average power of a multi-layer bus

The multi-layer bus comprises the multiple layer carrying similar logic components. If each layer works in parallel, the power consumed by the bus logic increases two times as the number of layer increases by two times. However, all layers do not work in parallel in a real bus system. We get the power consumption based on the active bus usage as shown in Fig. 2 for fair comparison. The average power consumption reflecting the increase of the bus layer is shown in Fig. 6. It shows a linear increase in the power consumption. However, it does not increase as a multiple of the power consumed by a single layer. The bus has 4 layers consumed 14% more power than the bus with 3 layers. The latencies of the 2-layer and the 3-layer cases are reduced by 45% and 63%, respectively, compared to the single-layer case as shown in Fig. 6b. However, the powers of 2-layer and 3-layer cases are increased by 25% and 56%, respectively. It proves that the increasing the number of layer is more efficient reflecting the power and latency of an on-chip bus. The comparison results are shown in Table 3 for the

**Table 3.** Accuracy of average power estimations

| $N_{activity}$ | Measured power using NanoSim[11] $P_{avg}$ (μW) | Estimated power using the proposed model $P_{avg}$ (μW) | Error rate (%) |
|---|---|---|---|
| 5,000 | 8,663 | 8,598 | 0.74% |
| 10,000 | 12,758 | 12,897 | 1.09% |
| 15,000 | 15,176 | 15,477 | 1.98% |
| 20,000 | 15,980 | 17,197 | 7.62% |

proposed power estimation scheme based on Eq. 9 and the results obtained from the power simulation tool, NanoSim [11]. We use Synopsys Design Compiler and the Hynix 0.35-μm CMOS process to design AMBA bus model for simulation NanoSim from Synopsys is used to estimate the power consumption of the bus. Table 3 shows the comparison of the total average power with respect to the proposed technique. The proposed method has an accuracy of 92.4% comparing to the simulation result using NanoSim.

## 6 Conclusion

This paper presented a latency model that can be used to efficiently design the bus architecture on a SoC platform. The latency model focuses on a shared bus architecture consisting of multiple bus layers. Latencies of shared bus on a SoC were analyzed using the model. The throughput of an example bus design was evaluated for a SoC platform including IPs such as MPEG and USB 2.0. The latency result of the proposed model was compared with the simulation result from MaxSim tool for verification purposes. The proposed latency model makes a way of a power estimation of bus lines. Our evaluations show that the accuracies of the proposed model for the latency and the power are over 85% and 92%, respectively. The proposed latency and power model can be useful in the early phases of SoC design, to estimate the performance and power consumption of bus architecture.

## Acknowledgments

This research was partially supported by the center of SoC design technology (CoSoC) which was conducted by the Ministry of Commerce, Industry and Energy of the Korean Government.

## References

1. Cesario, W.O., Lyonnard, D., Nicolescu, G., Paviot, Y., Yoo, S., Jerraya, A.A., Gauthier, L., Diaz-Nava, M.: Multiprocessor SoC platforms:a component-based design approach. In: Design and Test of Computers, December 2002, vol. 19(6), pp. 52–63. IEEE Computer Society Press, Los Alamitos (2002)

2. Li, L., Gao, M., Cheng, Z., Zhang, D., He, S.: A new platform-based orthogonal SoC design methodology. In: Proc. 5th ASIC 2003, vol. 1(3) pp. 428–432 (2003)
3. Lahiri, K., Raghunathan, A.: Power analysis of system-level on-chip communication archi-tectures. In: Proc. Of CODES+ISSS'04, pp. 236–241 (September 2004)
4. AMBA Specification Rev2.0, ARM co. (May 1999)
5. CoreConnect Bus Architecture, IBM Co. (1999)
6. Peterson, W.: WISHBONE: SoC Architecture Specification, Revision B.2, Silicore Co. (2001)
7. Lee, S.H., Lee, C.H., Lee, H.J.: A new multi-channel on-chip-bus architecture for system-on-chips. In: Proc. of IEEE International SOC Conference, pp. 305–308 (September 2004)
8. Ryu, K.K., Shin, E., Mooney, V.J.: A comparison of five different multiprocessor SoC bus architecture. In: Proc. of Euromicro Symposium on Digital Systems Design, pp. 202–209 (September 2001)
9. Okada, S., Takada, N., Miura, H., Asaeda, T.: System-on-a-chip for digital still camera with VGA-size clip shooting. IEEE Trans. On Consumer Electronics 46(3), 622–627 (2000)
10. Srinvasan, S., Li, L., Vijaykrishnan, N.: Simultaneous partitioning and frequency assign-ment for on-chip bus architecture. In: Proc. Design, Automation and Test in Europe, March 2005, vol. 1, pp. 213–218 (2005)
11. http://www.synopsys.com/product/mixedsignal/nanosim/
12. Zhang, Y., Ye, W., Irwin, M.J.: An alternative architecture for on-chip global intercon-nect: segmented bus power modeling. In: Proc. on ACSSC1998, vol. 2, pp. 1062–1065 (November 1998)
13. MaxSim developer suite user's guide Ver 5.0, AXYS Design Automation Inc. (March 2004)

# A Framework Introducing Model Reversibility in SoC Design Space Exploration

Alexis Vander Biest, Alienor Richard, Dragomir Milojevic, and Frederic Robert

BEAMS Department, Université Libre de Bruxelles, Belgium

**Abstract.** In this paper we present a general framework for the support of flexible models representation and execution in the context of SoC design space exploration. Coming as a C++ library, it allows the user to gather models from its own and existing models into larger and more complete models. Compared to existing modeling systems we introduce the notion of *model reversibility* that allows the user to turn any parameter appearing in a model into the output : it increases the model flexibility and enables its reuse in very different problems. Aside from providing specification and execution support, the framework also permits dynamic model sensitivity analysis and efficient parameter sensitivity analysis for closed-formed models. Through this paper we explain our original 3-level hierarchical representation of model and explain meanwhile how it offers flexibility and model robustness using a XML schema grammar.

## 1 Introduction

Nowadays designing a system-on-chip requires many different and antagonist constraints to be satisfied in terms of silicon area, power consumption, reliability, computation power. Apart from these requirements related to the chip performance, additional economical parameters need to be taken into account like yield, production and design cost, time-to-market and so on. In such a context where many compromises are possible between all the preceding criteria, the need for efficient design space exploration as early as possible in the design flow becomes highly critical to find a solution that fits the requirements [1]. In order to perform this exploration efficiently one have to take both exploration time and accuracy into account : while synthesis tools can lead to very accurate performance estimation results at the expense of the time devoted to the estimation of one solution, simplified models trade accuracy for estimation speed [2] : this last solution is more efficient for the exploration of heterogeneous, complex and large systems like SoCs [3]. In this context we have developed a framework providing support for the specification and execution of flexible performance models. By allowing the user to associate multiple expressions to a model so that inputs and outputs can be reversed, models become reusable in different contexts.

The remainder of the paper is divided as follows : section 2 defines how we use the vast term *model* in the scope of this paper by presenting some model taxonomies and reviews some existing modeling systems for performance prediction. In section 3 we describe the hierarchical model structure of our framework while

S. Vassiliadis et al. (Eds.): SAMOS 2007, LNCS 4599, pp. 211–221, 2007.

highlighting its features and present in section 4 our implementation choices and XML based models grammar. Finally we conclude in section 5.

## 2    State of the Art

Many performance prediction systems have already been defined in the literature but many of them are hard-coded and models remain most of the time hidden to the user. However models in themselves are the cornerstone of performance estimation and often need to be compared in order to find the best suited model for a given problem : this is called *model sensitivity analysis*. Before presenting these systems we will first define our notion of a model to avoid any ambiguity in the following sections.

### 2.1    Model Taxonomy and Definition

Basically a model could be defined as a simplified representation of a "real" and measurable phenomenon in order to capture its main effects[4].

Below we list some interesting model taxonomies trying to gather model classification criteria :

- VSIA defined in 2001 a model taxonomy capturing the behaviour of numerical systems [5] . This classification consists in *five* axes namely the temporal, the data, the functional, the structural and the software programming resolutions each one defined with its own specific metrics. A model of a system is defined by its value on all these axes (further details can be found in the very comprehensive [6]).
- The model of computation is also a precious information for classifying models (Petri Nets, Finite State Machines, Data Flow Graphs...) and refers to the type of building blocks and their interaction mechanisms. Most of these models of computation can be found in the Ptolemy II framework [7].
- In the field of analog systems, the SAE published the J2546 Model Specification Process Standard [8] proposing a classification in eight levels of model completeness based on criteria like the presence of a textual description of the model, its accuracy, execution capability, interface, time representation (static or dynamic) [9] ...

By mixing all these criteria it is possible to find a more general model classification although the usefulness of such a vast model space taxonomy remains highly dependent on the context in which the model is used. For the purpose of our talk we will thus characterize a model by its interface, execution capability (whatever its semantics of execution), having a certain accuracy and defined by its building assumptions.

### 2.2    Modeling with GTX

Many models targeting fast performance estimation exist and it should barely be impossible to enumerate all of them. However some systems devoted to processor performance estimation developed during the last ten years deserve some special attention (like GENESYS[10], RIPE[11], BACPAC[12]). They permit the evaluation of important parameters like power consumption, maximum clock frequency and wire related performance metrics. However all of these tools are using hard-coded models preventing the user from making them evolve over time and make easy model comparison. To cope with these limitations, a very interesting model-centric framework called GTX [13] has been developed by the GSRC. It was also meant to be used as a base for online model repository but never achieved in the success it deserved.

GTX defines three objects : parameters, rules, rule chains.

- *Parameters* represent all the physical data that have to be considered in the model (for instance power consumption, wire resistivity, technology node. . . ).
- *Rules* represent the model and describe how the parameters are related. For instance the dynamic power consumption depends on the capacitance to switch, the operational clock frequency and the supply voltage as follows :

$$P_{dyn} = C_{switch} * f_{clock} * V_{dd}^2 \qquad (1)$$

Different types of rules can be used like hard-coded, ASCII closed-formed expressions and tables.
- *Rule chains* are formed by the gathering of rules allowing the user to build larger models based on several sub-models. For instance if we have at disposal a rule of the total capacitance based on technological parameters, we can use it as an input for the dynamic power.

Rule chains are the cornerstone of GTX giving the framework a lot of flexibility and enabling model-sensitivity analysis. However it suffers from some limitations:

- Each rule is defined in a such a way that it defines one parameter as the output, the other ones being implicitly defined as inputs : GTX then automatically composes the resulting rule chain. Depending on the context of use, we however may want to turn some inputs of the model into outputs and inversely. For instance, all the microprocessor systems presented above estimate the clock frequency based on the technological parameters but it may sometimes be much more useful for a designer to express that same clock frequency as a model input rather than an output so that he can fix constraints on it and find the resulting possibilities for the technological parameters.
- Parameter sensitivity is supported in GTX at the expense of evaluating several times the same rule chain while varying each input parameter value around its nominal value. This leads unavoidably to multiply the number of experiments hence the time required to carry them out and is not very efficient in the context of finding extrema for the output parameters values.
- GTX relies on ASCII textual files to specify rules and their meta-information. Mechanisms to manage rules storage, parameters and rules name uniqueness and a grammar to specify studies were never implemented.

In this paper we present principles that we did implement in our framework to respectively overcome the above limitations :

- By introducing a three-level hierarchical model description we remove input/output reversibility limitations both at rules and rule chains levels.
- Closed-formed expressions may be represented by trees composed out of basic operations allowing both dynamic model execution and faster evaluation of output parameter extrema based on input constraints values.
- The underlying framework grammar for models and parameters is entirely specified by XML schemas to offer automatic verification along with powerful elements constraint mechanisms.

Oppositely to GTX appearing as a standalone tool with its GUI, our framework comes as an easy-to-use C++ library that was originally meant to suit our own needs but may finally be interesting to share. The main functionalities of this library are the following :

- Construction and grammatical verification of user defined models
- Composition of larger models based on the gathering of smaller models
- Single execution of models and parameter sweeps
- Fast evaluation of output parameters extrema for closed-formed expressions
- Easy model sensitivity analysis

In the coming section we detail the general principles listed above.

## 3 Framework Description

### 3.1 Hierarchy

In our representation, models are described in a hierarchical way : each level of abstraction exchange information through *parameters* i.e. the data on which models operate. The parameters are characterized by a unique name and a value (or a list of values).

The three types of entities used for our model description are the following :

- *Generic rules* are equivalent to rules in GTX except that they do not assume any underlying semantics of execution but only requires execution capability.
- A *Relation* is a logical link between $n$ parameters meaning that they are not independent so that we can only fix the $n\text{-}1$ parameters values among the $n$ possible. A relation encompasses generic rules associated to parameters in order to make the relation executable.
- A *behaviour* is a complete model with several input and output parameters and is based on a network of relations.

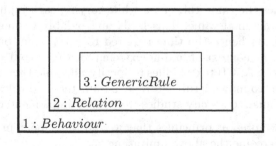

The improved flexibility and context adaptability of our models precisely relies on the introduction of the *relation* and *behaviour* levels in our model representation. Let us now have a closer look at these three levels.

## 3.2   Generic Rules

A generic rule is an executable model as it has been defined in 2.1 for a given output and its corresponding input parameters.

The generic rule for equation 1 is represented as follows :

$$P_{dyn} = GR_1(C_{switch}, f_{clock}, V_{dd}) \tag{2}$$

Examples of generic rules are to be found everywhere like wire delay models based on technological inputs [14] (inter-wire dielectric value, wire resistivity, wire pitch...), any hard-coded model or any algorithm linking the output parameter value with its input value. Each particular model class inherits from the properties of the generic rule definition so that it is easy to derive new model classes. However, we provided special support for analytical closed-formed rules in order to enlarge the framework features to include :

- A well-defined representation of closed-formed expressions
- An efficient parametric sensitivity estimation method based on input parameters value constraints

**Closed-formed tree representation** To allow the user to choose among rules interactively at run-time, we need to find an adequate way to represent closed-formed expression. In order to turn a textual closed-formed expression into a dynamically executable model, we used the Dijkstra shunting yard algorithm [15] to translate it into a tree. Each vertex represents a parameter, each directed edge a basic operation pointing to the vertex that is the output parameter of this basic relation.

$$D = (\log(A) + \frac{C}{2}) * B \tag{3}$$

For instance, the closed-fromed expression 3 is represented by the following graph:

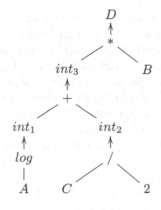

As we can see, intermediate parameters are added resulting from some basic operations : there have no significant meaning but are necessary to ensure the executability of the generic rules. Only input and output parameters are terminal vertices hence are the only visible parameters outside the rule.

Each basic operation, apart from its pure functionality, derives from a more general operation type characterized by its number of required input parameters, its execution associativity and priority. Thus it is very easy to add basic operations without any change in the shunting yard algorithm. The basic operations supported actually are multiplication, division, addition, subtraction, logarithm and power operator. With this basic set of operation and the use of parenthesis to force execution priority, we can already represent a lot of closed-formed model.

**Fast extrema evaluation.** Parametric sensitivity analysis can become highly time-consuming when the number of parameters and values per parameter to sweep increases. If the purpose of this study is to find out the statistical distribution of the output parameter, the time devoted to the study cannot be reduced because all solutions need to be explored. But when it comes to find out extremum values, our representation can save a lot of time. Indeed if we consider any of the previously defined basic operations, it is easy to find out the minimum and maximum output values knowing the input value bounds.

For instance, if we proceed to a parameter sensitivity analysis for two parameters $a$ and $b$ by fixing their respective bounds between $[min_a, max_a]$ and $[min_b, max_b]$ then we can compute the minimum and maximum values for the $+$ operator as being respectively $[min_a + min_b, max_a + max_b]$. Using a depth-first algorithm, we can easily compute the output extrema of the leaves and propagate it to the root. Hence only a sole tree evaluation is needed to get output extrema values (algorithm complexity of $O(1)$) compared to hard-coded rules for which the spanning of all possible input values within the defined bounds would require much more time (algorithm complexity of $O(M * N)$ where $M$ is the number of relations and $N$ the number of values per parameters to explore).

## 3.3  Relations

A relation is a logical dependence between a set of parameters : it expresses that they are related in a certain way and that their value cannot be fixed arbitrarily. The exact dependence is precisely specified by one generic rule defining a parameter as being the output, the others becoming inputs. So if a relation links $n$ parameters together, each parameter may be *associated* with a generic rule (regardless to its exact nature) so that the value of the other $n - 1$ parameters is sufficient to determine the output value. This mechanism of association relates to the reversibility property of some models : based on the knowledge of one generic rule associated with one specific parameter, it may be possible to derive the generic rules for the other parameters. For instance if we take back equation 1 we can easily associate a new generic rule (either manually either automatically using a solver) to $C_{dyn}$, $f_{clock}$ and $V_{dd}$ defining the following relation:

$$GR_1 : P_{dyn} = C_{switch} * f_{clock} * V_{dd}^2$$

$$Rel_{dynPow}(P_{dyn}, C_{switch}, f_{clock}, V_{dd}) \longrightarrow GR_2 : C_{switch} = \frac{P_{dyn}}{f_{clock} * V_{dd}^2}$$

$$GR_3 : f_{clock} = \frac{P_{dyn}}{C_{switch} * V_{dd}^2}$$

$$GR_4 : V_{dd} = \sqrt{\frac{P_{dyn}}{C_{switch} * f_{clock}}}$$

It is important to note that not all generic rules may be inverted (like algorithmic based rules) : in that case, the corresponding association may remain empty. For closed-formed rules using our graph based representation, a simple algorithm can automatically associate all the parameters from a single rule.

### 3.4  Behaviours

A *behaviour* gathers relations to make a complete model without any restriction on the number of outputs and inputs. Starting from a collection of relations, an adequate representation of the relations has to be used in order for the behaviour to be executable.

**Graph representation of behaviours.** Again we used a graph-based representation of the relations :

- Each *relation* is represented by a multi-edge
- Each *parameter* is represented by a vertex
- The parameters (identified by their name) shared by several relations form in turn a whole graph expressing their mutual dependences.

Here is a simple example of a behaviour composed out of four relations and expressed as a system of four equations :

$$Rel_1(A, C, D, E) \qquad Rel_2(B, E, H) \qquad Rel_3(D, F, G) \qquad Rel_4(E, G, H)$$

The number of degrees of freedom of the resulting behaviour equals $\#parameters - \#relations$ and represents the number of parameter values we have to fix in order for the equation system to be completely specified.

Translated in our non-oriented graph representation, this behaviour expresses as the following (all the vertices linked to a same *Rel* vertex belong to the same relation) :

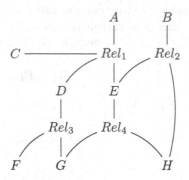

**Behaviour association.** In order for the behaviour to be executable, we have to specify which are the input and the output parameters i.e. associate each relation with an output parameter (which corresponds to orientate the graph). If the maximum combination number equals $\prod_{i=1}^{\#relations} \#parametersInRelation_i$, all these solutions are not leading to directly executable behaviours. To illustrate that, let us take back our previous system of four equations (relations) and choose a rule association for each of them.

$$E = GR_{Rel_1}(A, C, D) \quad E = GR_{Rel_2}(B, H)$$

$$D = GR_{Rel_3}(F, G) \quad G = GR_{Rel_4}(E, H)$$

Looking at these associations we can notice two important things about the way the equation system is formed:

- First, $E$ is the result of two different rules which has no sense at all as it can only have a single value.
- Second, if we try to solve this system by a simple substitution of rules $GR_{Rel_1}$, $GR_{Rel_3}$ and $GR_{Rel_4}$ we get the following result :

$$E = GR_{Rel_1}(A, C, GR_{Rel_3}(F, GR_{Rel_4}(E, H))) \tag{4}$$

As we can see, this equation is not explicit because the parameter $E$ appears in both members. This directly implies that it prevents the equation from being evaluated without using a numerical solver.

Coming back to our behaviour graph representation, these two considerations involve two rules that an oriented graph should respect in order to be valid and executable:

- Each vertex of the oriented graph should have one and only one edge pointing to it
- The graph must be acyclic (in other words, starting from a vertex, there should be no path of consecutive oriented edges that could lead the same vertex).

The following figure shows two valid graphs for our studied behaviour : compared to non-oriented graphs, each relation gets one oriented edge and output parameters are surrounded by boxes while input parameters are surrounded by dashed boxes :

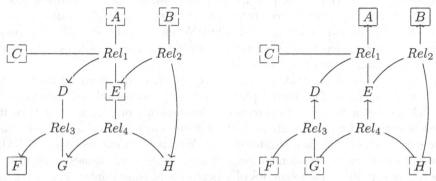

As we can see a same non oriented graph may lead to oriented graphs with different number of outputs : these different behaviour orientations can in turn be used to solve different problems while still using the same underlying models. To find all the rule association combinations that satisfy both previous conditions for the behaviour, we developed a simple algorithm based on a backtracking method. Starting from the graph, the main steps are the following:

1. Gather all the relations into a *unexplored relations list* using a depth-first search algorithm
2. Check the *unexplored relations list*:
   - If the *unexplored relations list* isn't empty select the next relation of the *unexplored relations list*. We go on to point 3.
   - If it is empty, it means that we have explored the whole graph without violating any of our two rules for each of them : this behaviour is valid and all relation associations are memorized. We restore the context (lists states) of the next association to check and go back to point 2.
3. Test the next available association for the current relation :
   - If the relation adjunction to the graph does satisfy both *non acyclic graph* and *one output per vertex* conditions, move the relation from the *unexplored relations list* to the *explored relations list* and go back to point 2 to associate the next relation.
   - If it doesn't, retry another association for the relation as long as there are any : otherwise go to point 2 to try another relation.

This algorithm explores all possible associations while eliminating all associations that do not satisfy both rules for the graph. To keep track of the state of the graph (associations of the relations and lists) along the algorithm execution, we used an incremental context saving mechanism so that only elements that have been modified since the last valid possibility need to be restored saving both memory and computation time. When a partial association of the graph violates one of the conditions, all subsequent associations are not explored as they will unavoidably lead to non-valid solutions.

# 4   Implementation Choices

## 4.1   XML Model Grammar

As explained in section 2, despite its very interesting engine regarding model estimation GTX offers only a relatively partial support for model grammar specification and parameter naming constraints. When it comes to verify that users have correctly encoded rules or chosen parameters names, problems may occur if no strict grammar has been defined.

To provide our framework with a strict yet easy to modify grammar, we decided to use XML for storing parameters and models related information. The XML schema grammar used respects the structure of *generic rules* (and its different derivated types), *relations* and *behaviours* as described in section 3 and defines for each of them a separate schema. We made an extensive use of XML schema features regarding element occurrence and value uniqueness constraints. Practically here are some examples of schema based constraints :

- Restrictions to a defined subset of possible basic operations for closed-formed generic rules
- Relations having from one to $n$ parameter association (with $n$ being the number of parameters in the relation) each one corresponding to a unique parameter name defined in the relation
- Name uniqueness guarantee for all parameters occurring in the behaviour

Any XML parser can check a behaviour, a relation or a generic rule XML instance and *automatically* verify if it is well-formed and valid against the corresponding schema, requiring no additional programming to perform this verification even if the grammar is modified later.

Additionally XML is a good choice in a possible perspective of an online model repository because stylesheets provide a direct way to convert XML files into browsable documents.

## 4.2   Framework Engine

The framework engine is actually being written in C++ (its different functionalities can be found at the end of section 2.2). Its object structure also follows our hierarchical based model representation so that we can easily switch from the XML model representation to the C++ object structure and inversely offering a very convenient way of loading/storing models.

The framework comes as a simple library allowing the user either to compose a behaviour with existing or new relations or to use already existing behaviours. The output parameters values estimation is based on XML input files describing the type of analysis desired by the user (single fixed input values, sweeps or input sensitivity) or can be defined at run-time by passing input values to the behaviour.

# 5    Conclusions

To cope with new VLSI designs complexity, model-based methodologies become crucial to cover the vast design spaces and ensure design flow convergence. As a contribution to that effort, we proposed in this paper a framework for performance model execution and specification. The most important features are flexible association for model reusability in different problems, improved model and parameter sensitivity analysis and strict model grammar for easy verification user-based relations.

# References

1. Vincentelli, A.S.: Defining platform-based design. EEDesign of EETimes (2002)
2. Bossuet, L., Gogniat, G., Philippe, J.: Fast design space exploration method for reconfigurable architectures (2003)
3. Kahng, A.B.: Design technology productivity in the dsm era. In: Proc. Asia and South Pacific Design Automation Conf., pp. 443–448 (2001)
4. Robert, F.: How do we learn models? introducing the supposed range vs real range hypothesis. International Journal of Emerging Technologies in Learning 2(1) (2007)
5. VSIA: Vsia system level design model taxonomy document (2001)
6. Panagopoulos, I.: Models, specification languages and their interrelationship models, specification languages and their interrelationship for system level design. Technical report, HPCL,The George Washington University (2002)
7. Eker, J., Janneck, J.W., Lee, E.A., Liu, J., Liu, X., Ludvig, J., Neuendorffer, S., Sachs, S., Xiong, Y.: Taming heterogeneity - the ptolemy approach. Proceedings of the IEEE 91(1), 127–144 (2003)
8. SAE: Sae model specification process standard (2002)
9. Vachoux, A.: Méthodes et outils pour la modélisation de soc-ams. Technical report, EPFL, Lausanne (2002)
10. Codrescu, L., Nugent, S., Meindl, J., Wills, D.S.: Modeling technology impact on cluster microprocessor performance. IEEE Trans. Very Large Scale Integr. Syst. 11(5), 909–920 (2003)
11. Mangaser, R., Rose, K.: Facilitating interconnect-based vlsi design. In: MSE '97. Proceedings of the 1997 International Conference on Microelectronics Systems Education, Washington, DC, p. 139. IEEE Computer Society Press, Los Alamitos (1997)
12. Sylvester, D., Keutzer, K.: System-level performance modeling with bacpac – berkeley advanced chip performance calculator (1999)
13. Caldwell, A.E., Cao, Y., Kahng, A.B., Koushanfar, F., Lu, H., Markov, I.L., Oliver, M., Stroobandt, D., Sylvester, D.: GTX: the MARCO GSRC technology extrapolation system. In: Design Automation Conference, pp. 693–698 (2000)
14. Sylvester, D., Keutzer, K.: Getting to the bottom of deep submicron ii: A global wiring paradigm (1999)
15. Redziejowski, R.R.: On arithmetic expressions and trees. Commun. ACM 12(2), 81–84 (1969)

# Towards Multi-application Workload Modeling in Sesame for System-Level Design Space Exploration

Mark Thompson and Andy D. Pimentel

Computer Systems Architecture group, Informatics Institute
University of Amsterdam, The Netherlands
{thompson,andy}@science.uva.nl

**Abstract.** The Sesame modeling and simulation framework aims at early and thus efficient system-level design space exploration of embedded multimedia system architectures. So far, Sesame only supported performance evaluation when mapping a single application onto a (multi-processor) architecture at the time. But since modern multimedia embedded systems are increasingly multi-tasking, we need to address the modeling of effects of executing multiple applications concurrently in our system-level performance models. To this end, this paper conceptually describes two multi-application workload modeling techniques for the Sesame framework. One technique is based on the use of synthetic application workloads while the second technique deploys only real application workloads to model concurrent execution of applications. For illustrative purposes, we also present a preliminary case study in which a Motion-JPEG encoder application is executed concurrently with a small synthetic producer-consumer application.

## 1 Introduction

The increasing complexity of modern embedded systems has led to the emergence of system-level design [1]. A key ingredient of system-level design is the notion of high-level modeling and simulation in which the models allow for capturing the behavior of system components and their interactions at a high level of abstraction. As these high-level models minimize the modeling effort and are optimized for execution speed, they can be applied at the very early design stages to perform, for example, architectural design space exploration. Such early design space exploration is of eminent importance as early design choices heavily influence the success or failure of the final product.

In recent years, a fair number of system-level simulation-based exploration environments have been proposed, such as Metropolis [2], GRACE++ [3], Koski [4], and our own Sesame [5] framework. The Sesame modeling and simulation framework aims at efficient system-level design space exploration of embedded multimedia systems, allowing rapid performance evaluation of different architecture designs, application to architecture mappings, and hardware/software partitionings. Moreover, it does so at multiple levels of abstraction. Key to this flexibility is the separation of application and architecture models, together with an explicit mapping step to map an application model onto an architecture model.

So far, Sesame has only supported the mapping of a single application onto an architecture model at the time. But since modern multimedia embedded systems are

S. Vassiliadis et al. (Eds.): SAMOS 2007, LNCS 4599, pp. 222–232, 2007.

increasingly multi-tasking, we need to address the modeling of effects of executing multiple applications concurrently in our system-level architecture models. To this end, this paper presents two multi-application workload modeling techniques. One technique is based on the use of synthetic application workloads while the second technique deploys only real application workloads to model concurrent execution of applications. The presented techniques are currently being implemented in our Sesame framework. This implies that this paper mostly discusses concepts while detailed results will be published in a follow-up paper. However, for illustration purposes, we do present a preliminary case study in which a Motion-JPEG encoder application is executed concurrently with a small synthetic producer-consumer application.

The remainder of the paper is organized as follows. The next section provides an introduction to the Sesame modeling and simulation framework. Section 3 presents the two proposed multi-application workload modeling techniques for Sesame. This section also contains a discussion on how these workload modeling techniques can be used for the modeling of reactive application behavior. In Section 4, we present a small case study in which we model the concurrent execution of two applications. Section 5 describes related work, after which Section 6 concludes the paper.

# 2  Sesame

The Sesame modeling and simulation environment [5], illustrated in Figure 1, addresses the performance analysis of embedded multimedia system architectures. To this end, it recognizes separate application and architecture models, where an application model describes the functional behavior of an application and the architecture model defines architecture resources and captures their performance constraints. After explicitly mapping an application model onto an architecture model, they are co-simulated via trace-driven simulation. This allows for evaluation of the system performance of a particular application, mapping, and underlying architecture. Such an explicit separation between application and architecture opens up many possibilities for model re-use. For example, a single application model can be used to exercise different hardware/software partitionings or can be mapped onto a range of different architecture models.

For application modeling, Sesame uses the Kahn Process Network (KPN) model of computation [6], which nicely fits the targeted multimedia application domain [7]. KPNs are structured as a network of concurrent communicating processes, connected via unbounded FIFO channels. Reading from these channels is done in a blocking manner, while writing is non-blocking. The computational behavior of an application is captured by instrumenting the code of each Kahn process with annotations that describe the application's computational actions. The reading from and writing to Kahn channels represent the communication behavior of a process within the application model. By executing the Kahn model, each process records its computational and communication actions to generate its own trace of *application events*, which is necessary for driving an architecture model. There are three types of application events: the communication events READ and WRITE and the computational event EX(ECUTE). These application events typically are coarse grained, such as EX(*DCT*) or READ(*channel_id,pixel-block*).

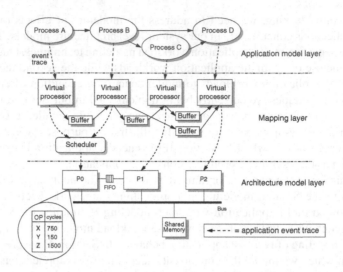

**Fig. 1.** The three layers in Sesame's modeling and simulation infrastructure

An architecture model simulates the performance consequences of the computation and communication events generated by an application model. To this end, each architecture model component is parameterized with a table of operation latencies (illustrated for Processor 0 in Figure 1). The table entries could, for example, specify the latency of an Ex(*DCT*) event, or the latency of a memory access in the case of a memory component.

To map Kahn processes from an application model onto architecture model components and to support the scheduling of application events when multiple Kahn processes are mapped onto a single architecture component (e.g., a programmable processor), Sesame provides an intermediate *mapping layer*. This layer consists of virtual processor components and FIFO buffers for communication between the virtual processors. There is a one-to-one relationship between the Kahn processes in the application model and the virtual processors in the mapping layer. This is also true for the Kahn channels and the FIFO buffers in the mapping layer, except for the fact that the latter are limited in size. Their size is parameterized and dependent on the modeled architecture. A virtual processor in the mapping layer reads in an application trace from a Kahn process and dispatches the events to a processing component in the architecture model. Communication channels – i.e., the buffers in the mapping layer – are also mapped onto the architecture model. In Figure 1, for example, buffers can be placed in shared memory or can use the point-to-point FIFO channel between processors 0 and 1. Accordingly, the architecture model accounts for modeling the communication (and contention) behavior at transaction level, including arbitration, transfer latencies and so on.

The mechanism used to dispatch application events from a virtual processor to an architecture model component guarantees deadlock-free scheduling of the application events from different event traces [5]. In this mechanism, Ex(ecute) events are always immediately dispatched by a virtual processor to the architecture model component that models their timing consequences. Scheduler components in the mapping layer (see Figure 1) allow for scheduling the dispatched application events from different virtual processors that are destined for the same (shared) architecture model resource. Communication events, however, are not immediately dispatched to the underlying architecture model. Instead, a virtual processor that receives a communication event first consults the appropriate buffer at the mapping layer to check whether or not the communication is safe to take place so that no deadlock can occur. Only if it is found to be safe (i.e., for read events the data should be available and for write events there should be room in the target buffer), then communication events may be dispatched. As long as a communication event cannot be dispatched, the virtual processor blocks. This is possible because the mapping layer executes in the same simulation as the architecture model. Therefore, both the mapping layer and the architecture model share the same simulation-time domain. This also implies that each time a virtual processor dispatches an application event (either computation or communication) to a component in the architecture model, the virtual processor is blocked in simulated time until the event's latency has been simulated by the architecture model.

Essentially, the mapping layer can be considered as an *abstract RTOS model*, in which the virtual processors are abstract representations of application processes that are executing, ready for execution or blocked for communication. Here, the scheduler components in the mapping layer provide the scheduling functionality of the RTOS.

## 3   Multi-application Workload Modeling

As mentioned before, Sesame has up to now only supported the mapping of a single application onto an architecture model at the time. Modern multimedia embedded systems are however increasingly multi-tasking. Therefore, we need to address the modeling of effects of executing multiple applications concurrently in our system-level architecture models. To this end, we propose two multi-application workload modeling techniques. One technique, which we will discuss first, is based on the use of synthetic application workloads while the second technique deploys only real application workloads to model concurrent execution of applications.

### 3.1   Synthetic Multi-application Workload Modeling

Multi-application modeling using synthetic application workloads is illustrated in Figure 2. Note that the FIFO buffers between virtual processors are not depicted in Figure 2 for the sake of simplicity. On the left-hand side, a Sesame system-level model with a single, primary application is shown. The three processes in this application are mapped onto two processing cores (P0 and P1) in the underlying architecture. Since processes A and B are mapped onto the same resource, a scheduler named Local-Scheduler (or L-Scheduler) is used for scheduling the workloads (i.e., application events) from both processes. However, a second level of scheduling hierarchy is added by introducing so-called Global-Schedulers (or G-Schedulers). These global schedulers are basically equivalent to local schedulers in terms of functionality but instead of intra-application events they schedule application events from different applications. Evidently, the local and global schedulers can also deploy different scheduling policies. When, for example, the interleaving of processes inside an application is statically determined at compile time, the local scheduler can model this by 'merging' the events from the event traces according to this given static schedule. At the same time, the global scheduler can schedule application events from different applications in a dynamic fashion based on, for example, time slices, priorities, or a combination of these two. Here, we would like to note that although the schedulers support preemptive scheduling, this can only be done at the granularity of application events. The simulation of a single application event is atomic and thus cannot be preemted in Sesame. Furthermore, we currently do not model any overheads caused by the context switching itself (e.g., OS overhead, cache misses, etc.). This is considered as future work.

In synthetic multi-application modeling, the application events external to the primary application (see Figure 2) are generated by a stochastic event generator. Hence, this event generator mimics the concurrent execution of one or more application(s) besides the primary application. Based on a stochastic application description, which will be discussed later on, the application generator generates traces of Ex(ecute), READ and WRITE application events and issues these event traces to special virtual processors, indicated by $VP_S$ in Figure 2. Multiple instances of these event generators, each with their own stochastic application description, can be used

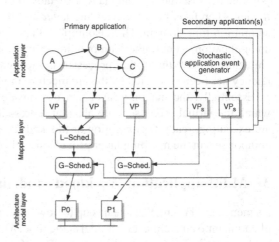

**Fig. 2.** Multi-application modeling using synthetic application workloads

to model concurrent execution of more than two applications.

The virtual processors ($VP_S$) used for the trace events from the stochastic event generator are special in the sense that they, unlike normal virtual processors, are not connected to each other according to the application topology (see Section 2). Rather than explicitly modeling communication synchronizations, a $VP_S$ models synchronization behavior stochastically. To illustrate the interactions between the event generator, a $VP_S$ and a global scheduler of a system-level model, consider Figure 3. The figure shows these interactions in the case an "Ex(A) , Ex(B) , READ , WRITE " event sequence is generated by the event generator. At (simulation) time $t_0$, the Ex(A) event is consumed by the $VP_S$. The $VP_S$ immediately forwards this event to the global scheduler it is connected to, and waits for an acknowledgment from the scheduler. After the Ex(A) event has been scheduled for execution on the architectural resource (taking T(sched) time units) and the actual execution (taking T(A) time units), control is returned to the $VP_S$ by sending it an acknowledgment. Hereafter, the $VP_S$ can consume another application event again. In the case of the example in Figure 3, the $VP_S$ now consumes the Ex(B) event which is handled in an identical fashion as the Ex(A) event. However, $VP_S$ handles the READ and WRITE events, which are consumed at times $t_2$ and $t_3$ respectively, in a slightly different way. Instead of directly forwarding these events to the

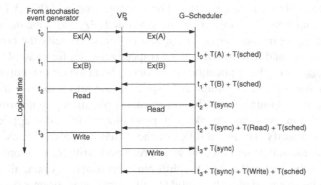

**Fig. 3.** Interaction between Virtual Processor ($VP_S$) and G(lobal)-Scheduler in synthetic multi-application modeling

global scheduler, like is done with Ex events, $VP_S$ now first models a synchronization latency. This latency refers to the time the read and write transactions need to wait for data or room in the buffer from/to which is read/written. The synchronization latency, indicated by T(sync) in Figure 3, is a stochastic parameter of $VP_S$, as discussed below.

Table 1 lists the parameters used by the stochastic event generator as well as a $VP_S$. These parameters can be specified both globally – describing the behavior for all traces (for the event generator) or ports (for a $VP_S$) – and on a per-trace/per-port basis. Descriptions on a per-trace/per-port basis overrule global descriptions, in the case there is an overlap of both types of descriptions. The parameter $A_{Ex}$ specifies the set of

**Table 1.** Parameters for the synthetic application workload generation

| Stochastic event generator parameter | Description |
| --- | --- |
| $A_{Ex}$ | Set of possible Ex(ecute) application events |
| $P_{Ex_i}$, with $\sum_{i \in A_{Ex}} P_{Ex_i} = 1$ | Probabilities of the different events in $A_{Ex}$ |
| $r_{comp} : r_{comm}$ | Computation to communication ratio |
| $r_{read} : r_{write}$ | Read to write ratio |
| M | Set of possible message sizes |
| $P_{M_i}$, with $\sum_{i \in M} P_{M_i} = 1$ | Probabilities of the different message sizes |
| NP | Number of communication ports |
| $P_{port_i}$, with $\sum_{i=0}^{NP} P_{port_i} = 1$ | Probabilities of the different port usages |
| **$VP_S$ parameter** | **Description** |
| $Sync_{Read}$ | Mean synchronization latency for reads |
| $\sigma_{Read}$ | Standard deviation of read latencies |
| $Sync_{Write}$ | Mean synchronization latency for writes |
| $\sigma_{Write}$ | Standard deviation of write latencies |

possible Ex events that can be generated. For example, $A_{Ex} = \{DCT, VLE\}$ specifies that Ex(DCT) and Ex(VLE) events can be generated. $P_{Ex_i}$ describe the probabilities of the events in $A_{Ex}$. The ratio's $r_{comp}:r_{comm}$ and $r_{read}:r_{write}$ specify the computation to communication ratio and read to write ratio, respectively. So, for example, by increasing the $r_{comp}:r_{comm}$ ratio, the application behavior can be made more computationally or communication intensive. The parameter M specifies the set of possible message sizes that can be used in communications. In multimedia applications, application data is often communicated in fixed data chunks (e.g. pixel blocks) from one application phase to the other. $P_{M_i}$ specify the probabilities of the different message sizes. NP denotes the number of communication ports for which read and write transactions can be generated. $P_{port_i}$ are the probabilities of the different port usages. Again, all of the above parameters can be specified globally (valid for all event traces) or on a per-trace basis.

The $VP_S$ parameters $Sync_{Read}$ and $Sync_{Write}$ specify the mean synchronization latency for read and write transactions, respectively. $\sigma_{Read}$ and $\sigma_{Write}$ contain the standard deviations of the two aforementioned means. By default, a $VP_S$ uses an Erlang distribution to determine synchronization latencies. These $VP_S$ parameters can again be specified globally (valid for all communication ports of a $VP_S$) or on a per-port basis.

## 3.2  Realistic Multi-application Workload Modeling

In our second multi-application workload modeling technique, we realistically model the concurrent execution of multiple applications. That is, multiple Kahn application models are actually executed concurrently, as shown in Figure 4, and produce realistic event traces that are again scheduled on the underlying architectural resources using the global schedulers. In contrast to synthetic workload modeling, the secondary KPNs use normal virtual processors in the mapping layer. Hence, synchronization behavior in the parallel applications is modeled explicitly for all participating KPN applications (i.e., there is no difference between primary and secondary applications). This implies

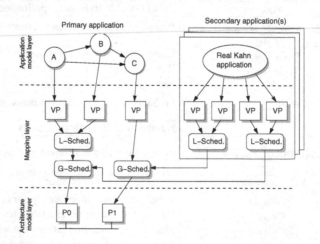

**Fig. 4.** Multi-application modeling using realistic application workloads

that, when considering Figure 3, the T(sync) now refers to the actual synchronization times between application processes. Moreover, the secondary KPNs also require L-schedulers to 'merge' (i.e. schedule) event traces when multiple application tasks are mapped onto a single architecture resource. Naturally, the policies of the L-schedulers can vary between the different KPN applications taking part in the system simulation. When considering Figure 3, we now have T(sched) = T(L-sched) + T(G-sched) for all participating KPNs.

### 3.3 Modeling Reactive Behavior

Because of its deterministic behavior, the KPN model of computation is relatively un-suited for modeling reactive application behavior, such as the occurrence of interrupts (e.g., a user presses a button on the TV's remote control after which teletext is started as a picture-in-picture application on the screen). Several researchers have proposed extensions to the KPN model of computation to resolve this [7,8,9]. Our two multi-application workload modeling techniques support the modeling of reactive behavior *between applications*, which could each be specified as a regular KPN. This can be achieved in a transparent manner by adding a 'SLEEP(N)' application event, which ba-sically indicates that an application process is not active during a period of N time units. More specifically, a SLEEP event causes a virtual processor to sleep (i.e. block in vir-tual time) for the specified period. This event would not be simulated by the underlying architecture model. Evidently, the SLEEP events provide the opportunity to freeze the issuing of application events for a while, which basically mimics sporadic or periodic execution behavior of applications. To give an example in the case of synthetic multi-application modeling, the (stochastic) application event generator could model periods of inactivity (i.e., generating SLEEP events for all application processes) alternated with periods of application activity (i.e., generating EX, READ , and WRITE events). Clearly, this approach would allow us to assess a variety of different scenarios or use cases [10]. However, further research is needed to gain more insight about the qualitative and quan-titative aspects of this modeling mechanism.

## 4   A Preliminary Case Study

For illustrative purposes, we performed a small experiment using the multi-application workload modeling support that has already been realized in Sesame. More specif-ically, we modeled two Kahn applications that execute concurrently. The first (and primary) application is a Motion-JPEG (M-JPEG) encoder, and the other one is a syn-thetic 'producer-consumer' application transferring data from producer to consumer. The M-JPEG application encodes 8 consecutive 128x128 resolution frames, while the producer-consumer application is parameterizable in both computational and commu-nication load. That is, the producer iteratively models a parameterizable computing latency after which it sends a parameterizable chunk of data to the consumer. In our system-level model, both applications are mapped onto a multi-processor SoC, contain-ing 4 processors with distributed memory and connected through a crossbar switch. We applied a simple round-robin policy for scheduling tasks from both applications at the G-schedulers (see Section 3.2).

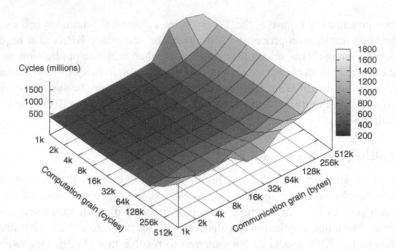

**Fig. 5.** Estimated execution times of concurrent execution of M-JPEG and producer-consumer applications. The latter is parameterized in both computation and communication grainsize.

Figure 5 shows the estimated system-level execution times (combined for both applications) when varying the computation and communication grainsizes of the producer-consumer application. As can be seen from Figure 5, the results show a quite predictable behavior, which helps to gain trust in our multi-application modeling method. That is, the system performance is only marginally affected for small computation and communication grains of the producer-consumer application. But after a certain threshold, the producer-consumer application starts to dominate the system performance (computation-wise, communication-wise, or both). As a next step, we plan to actually validate these results using the ESPAM system-level synthesis framework [11], which would allow us to compare our simulation results against an actual system implementation.

## 5    Related Work

The modeling of (parallel) workloads for the purpose of performance analysis is a well-established research domain, both in terms of realistic and synthetic workload modeling (see e.g. [12,13,14]). A recent focus area is, for example, statistical simulation for micro-architectural evaluation [15]. In this technique, a stochastic program description, which is a collection of distributions of important program characteristics derived from execution profiles, is used to generate synthetic instruction traces. These synthetic traces are subsequently used in trace-driven processor and/or memory-hierarchy simulations. Another area in which synthetic workload modeling has recently received a lot of attention is network workload modeling for network-on-chip simulations [16,17,18].

In [19,20], multimedia application workloads are described and characterized analytically using so-called variability characterization curves (VCCs) for system-level performance analysis of multi-processor systems-on-chip. These VCCs allow for capturing the high degree of variability in execution requirements that is often present in multimedia applications.

A fair number of research efforts addressed the high-level modeling of a RTOS to be used in system-level models for early design space exploration [21,22,23]. Rather than focusing on how to model multi-application workloads, these efforts mainly address abstract modeling of RTOS functionality, efficient simulation of this functionality, and refinement of these abstract RTOS models towards the implementation level.

# 6  Conclusions

In this paper, we addressed the extension of our Sesame modeling and simulation framework to support the modeling of multi-tasking between applications for the purpose of system-level performance analysis. To this end, we proposed two mechanisms for modeling multi-application workload behavior: one based on synthetic workload modeling and the other using only real application workloads. In addition, we indicated how reactive behavior at application granularity could be modeled. All presented methods are currently being implemented in Sesame. Using a small preliminary case study, however, we were already able to show an example of multi-application workload modeling using two applications. Future work needs to study the scope of application scenarios or use cases that can be modeled with these techniques. For example, it should be investigated to what extent the synthetic workload modeling technique allows for capturing the variability in execution requirements that is typically present in multimedia applications. Possibly, this technique could be extended with variability characterization curves such as proposed in [19,20].

# References

1. Keutzer, K., et al.: System level design: Orthogonalization of concerns and platform-based design. IEEE Trans. on CAD of Integrated Circuits and Systems 19 (2000)
2. Balarin, F., et al.: Metropolis: An integrated electronic system design environment. IEEE Computer 36 (2003)
3. Kogel, T., et al.: Virtual architecture mapping: A SystemC based methodology for architectural exploration of system-on-chip designs. In: SAMOS. Proc. of the Int. workshop on Systems, Architectures, Modeling and Simulation, pp. 138–148 (2003)
4. Kangas, T., et al.: UML-based multi-processor SoC design framework. ACM Trans. on Embedded Computing Systems 5, 281–320 (2006)
5. Pimentel, A.D., Erbas, C., Polstra, S.: A systematic approach to exploring embedded system architectures at multiple abstraction levels. IEEE Trans. on Computers 55, 99–112 (2006)
6. Kahn, G.: The semantics of a simple language for parallel programming. In: Proc. of the IFIP Congress 74 (1974)
7. de Kock, E.A., et al.: Yapi: Application modeling for signal processing systems. In: DAC. Proc. of the Design Automation Conference, pp. 402–405 (2000)
8. Geilen, M., Basten, T.: Reactive process networks. In: EMSOFT. Proc. of the 4th ACM International Conference on Embedded Software, pp. 137–146. ACM Press, New York (2004)
9. Dijk, H.W.v., Sips, H.J., Deprettere, E.F.: Context-aware process networks. In: ASAP. Proc. of the Int. Conf. on Application-specific Systems, Architectures, and Processors, pp. 6–16 (2003)

10. Gheorghita, S.V., Basten, T., Corporaal, H.: Application scenarios in streaming-oriented embedded system design. In: Proc. of the Int. Symposium in System-on-Chip (2006)
11. Nikolov, H., Stefanov, T., Deprettere, E.: Multi-processor system design with ESPAM. In: CODES-ISSS'06. Proc. of the Int. Conf. on HW/SW Codesign and System Synthesis, pp. 211–216 (2006)
12. Kotsis, G.: A systematic approach for workload modeling for parallel processing systems. Parallel Computing 22, 1771–1787 (1997)
13. Feitelson, D.: Workload modeling for performance evaluation. In: Calzarossa, M.C., Tucci, S. (eds.) Performance 2002. LNCS, vol. 2459, pp. 114–141. Springer, Heidelberg (2002)
14. Skadron, K., Martonosi, M., August, D.I., Hill, M.D., Lilja, D.J., Pai, V.S.: Challenges in computer architecture evaluation. Computer 36, 30–36 (2003)
15. Eeckhout, L., Nussbaum, S., Smith, J., De Bosschere, K.: Statistical simulation: Adding efficiency to the computer designer's toolbox. IEEE Micro 23, 26–38 (2003)
16. Varatkar, G., Marculescu, R.: On-chip traffic modeling and synthesis for MPEG-2 video applications. IEEE Trans. on Very Large Scale Integration Systems 12, 108–119 (2004)
17. Thid, R., Sander, I., Jantsch, A.: Flexible bus and NoC performance analysis with configurable synthetic workloads. In: Proc. of the Conference on Digital System Design, pp. 681–688 (2006)
18. Mahadevan, S., Angiolini, F., Storgaard, M., Olsen, R.G., Sparso, J., Madsen, J.: A network traffic generator model for fast network-on-chip simulation. In: DATE. Proc. of the Conference on Design, Automation and Test in Europe, pp. 780–785 (2005)
19. Liu, Y., Chakraborty, S., Ooi, W.T.: Approximate VCCs: a new characterization of multimedia workloads for system-level MpSoC design. In: DAC. Proc. of the conference on Design Automation, pp. 248–253 (2005)
20. Maxiaguine, A., Zhu, Y., Chakraborty, S., Wong, W-F.: Tuning SoC platforms for multimedia processing: identifying limits and tradeoffs. In: CODES-ISSS. Proc. of the Int. conference on Hardware/software codesign and system synthesis, pp. 128–133 (2004)
21. Gerstlauer, A., Yu, H., Gajski, D.D.: RTOS modeling for system level design. In: DATE. Proc. of the Conference on Design, Automation and Test in Europe, 10130 (2003)
22. Hessel, F., da Rosa, V.M., Reis, I.M., Planner, R., Marcon, C.A.M., Susin, A.A.: Abstract RTOS modeling for embedded systems. In: RSP'04. Proc. of the 15th IEEE International Workshop on Rapid System Prototyping, pp. 210–216. IEEE Computer Society Press, Los Alamitos (2004)
23. Lavagno, L., et al.: A time slice based scheduler model for system level design. In: DATE. Proc. of the Conference on Design, Automation and Test in Europe, pp. 378–383 (2005)

# Resource Conflict Detection in Simulation of Function Unit Pipelines

Pekka Jääskeläinen, Vladimír Guzma, and Jarmo Takala

Department of Information Technology
Tampere University of Technology
P.O. Box 553
FIN-33101 Tampere
Finland
{pekka.jaaskelainen,vladimir.guzma,jarmo.takala}@tut.fi

**Abstract.** Processor simulators are important parts of processor design toolsets in which they are used to verify and evaluate the properties of the designed processors. While simulating architectures with independent function unit pipelines using simulation techniques that avoid the overhead of instruction bit-string interpretation, such as compiled simulation, the simulation of function unit pipelines can become one of the new bottlenecks for simulation speed.

This paper evaluates commonly used models for function unit pipeline resource conflict detection in processor simulation: a resource vector based-model, and an finite state automata (FSA) based model. In addition, an improvement to the simulation initialization time by means of lazy initialization of states in the FSA-based approach is proposed. The resulting model is faster to initialize and provides equal simulation speed when compared to the actively initialized FSA. Our benchmarks show at best 23 percent improvement to the initialization time.

## 1 Introduction

Processor simulators possess different level of accuracy depending on their purpose. Instruction set simulation is mainly used for program verification and development in cases which do not require detailed modeling of timing. More accurate cycle-based simulators can produce cycle counts and utilization statistics for directing processor design space exploration – a process of finding the most suitable processor architecture for the applications at hand. In automated design space exploration of application-specific processors, the number of examined candidate architectures can reach thousands, thus the time it takes to produce the utilization data and cycle counts for each explored architecture can affect the total exploration time dramatically.

Structural hazards are situations in which multiple operations or instructions try to use the same processor resource simultaneously. Commonly, structural hazards result in processor stall cycles in which the processor waits mostly idle for the hazard to resolve. Cycle-accurate simulators detect these stall cycles and model them accurately. At minimum, the stall cycles should be counted and added to the total cycle count. On the other hand, some architectures, such as the Transport Triggered Architectures (TTA) [1] do not provide hardware locking support in case of structural hazards. In this

S. Vassiliadis et al. (Eds.): SAMOS 2007, LNCS 4599, pp. 233–240, 2007.

case, the detection of structural hazards during simulation is a fundamental part of the program verification process.

Simulation of statically scheduled architectures with relatively simple control logic, such as VLIWs and TTAs, concentrates on simulating the data transports between function units and register files, the functionality of operations in function units, and the function unit latencies. In this type of simulators, especially if the simulation overhead of instruction decoding phase is avoided, simulating the function units and their pipelines can become the new bottleneck for simulation speed.

This paper evaluates models to detect function unit pipeline resource conflicts in cycle-accurate simulation: a resource vector based-model and an finite state automata (FSA) based model. Finally, an improvement to the simulation initialization time by means of lazy initialization of states in the FSA-based approach is proposed and evaluated. Using this model, our benchmarks show that up to 23 percent improvement to the simulation initialization time can be achieved.

The rest of paper is organised as follows. Section 2 analyses existing solutions for improving processor simulation speed. Section 3 gives brief overview of common book keeping methods for structural hazard detection during instruction scheduling and simulation. Section 4 describes our test setup, followed by Section 5 with results from the performed experiments. Section 6 concludes the work and outlines future research directions.

## 2   Related Work

Several research papers discuss the techniques to avoid the instruction bit string interpretation overhead during simulation. These techniques are commonly referred to as "compiled simulation". For example, Shade is a simulator which includes a technique for translating the simulated instructions dynamically to host instructions during simulation and caching the translated instructions for later execution [2]. However, the presented work is a simulator with functional accuracy, as detecting structural hazards and other microarchitectural details required for cycle-accuracy are not discussed.

JIT-CCS technique applies just-in-time (JIT) compilation, common in Java virtual machines, to instruction set simulation. This technique removes the limitation of translating simulator not capable of simulating self-modifying code [3]. Use of JIT techniques for simulation is explored also in DynamoSim, which improves the simulator flexibility by combining interpretive and compiled techniques by compiling only parts of the simulation that benefit the most [4]. The paper also extends the scope of the simulation compilation from basic blocks to traces to exploit better the instruction-level parallelism capabilities of the host processor.

FastSim uses the idea of compiled simulation in detailed out-of-order microarchitectural simulation [5]. The main contribution of the paper is a technique to "memoize" microarchitectural configurations and "fast-forward" the actions to the processor state when the simulation enters a previously executed microarchitectural configuration. The idea is extended in [6] with a language for easy implementation of this type of "fast-forwarding" simulators.

Pees, Hoffman, and Meyr present an architecture description language LISA, which allows generating compiled processor simulators for several architectures automatically [7,8]. The resulting simulators are cycle-accurate thanks to the capabilities of the language to allow detailed modeling of pipeline resources used by the instructions. Similar work is presented in [9] in which ANSI C is used to model the instructions to avoid a new modeling language.

An interesting simulation speedup technique worth noting is "token-level simulation" [10] and "evaluation reuse" [11]. The principle of these techniques is to simulate the program first in functional level for obtaining the basic block traces. Using the basic block traces, the accurate cycle count is produced by evaluating the effects of each basic block to the processor pipeline state but without simulating the actual functionality again since it has already been performed in the previous faster pass. This technique seems very promising for speeding up the collection of the total cycle counts but does not produce cycle-accurate simulation for exact timing or debugging features such as cycle-stepping, due to the separation of the functional and timing simulation.

Literature covering techniques for speeding up processor simulation, in general, is widely available. However, avoiding the bottlenecks in simulation of architectures with independent function unit pipelines is rarely discussed. This paper considers in particular the bottlenecks in simulating such architectures.

## 3   Structural Hazard Detection in Simulation

This section gives a brief overview of the most common methods for keeping book of structural hazards during simulation or instruction scheduling.

### 3.1   Resource Vectors

Reservation table is a two-dimensional (2D) table with one dimension representing the machine resources and the other one representing the latency cycles [12,13]. A resource usage is marked by placing 'X' in the table cell at the position of the cycle and the resource. The same information can be represented in a 1D structure called *resource vector*. A column in this vector lists all resources that are reserved at a cycle [14].

When using this table for resource modeling, the simulator keeps book of the occupied resources at each cycle of the simulation in a *composite resource vector*. Before an operation or instruction is to be executed in the simulator, conflicts are detected by comparing the composite resource vector to the resource usage of the candidate operation. In case there are overlapping resource usages between the candidate operation's resource vector and the composite vector, a structural hazard is detected. Otherwise, the composite vector is updated to reflect the resources occupied by the started operation.

### 3.2   Finite State Automata

The resource vector based structural hazard detection scheme can be refined to a more advanced version by exploiting a Finite State Automaton (FSA) [15] for representing all the legal state transitions in the processor.

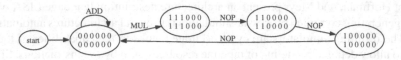

**Fig. 1.** Resources modeled with a finite state automaton

In the FSA-based approach, each state is represented by a collision matrix, a 2D table $S$, which contains rows for each operation and as many cycle columns as the longest latency operation or instruction requires. The element $S[o,t]$ is 0 only if operation $o$ does not "collide" when issued $t$ cycles later after entering the state. That is, if $S[o,1] = 0$, the operation $o$ can be issued at the next cycle after entering state $S$, resulting in a transition to state $S'$. The collision matrix of the target state is computed by shifting the collision matrix of the starting state to the left (which simulates a cycle advance) and ORing it with the issued operation's collision matrix. [12]

Figure 1 illustrates an example automaton for a function unit with two operations: ADD and MUL. The FSA can be used to quickly detect the legal operation sequences that can be executed by the function unit. For example, in the automaton, it is easy to notice that after executing ADD, it is possible to execute both ADD and MUL but, after executing MUL, three cycles are needed (issue NOPs or stall the processor) before issuing new operations.

The FSA-based conflict detection models are known to be very fast, but their initialization time can be long due to large number of states in the automaton that need to be built based on the operation resource usage patterns. This leads to an optimization to the FSA-based approach which is also evaluated in this paper. One of the evaluated models is an FSA-based model in which the states are built "lazily" the first time they are entered, hoping to reduce the initialization time to a minimum. The optimization is derived from the observation that in many cases only the minority of the states are visited by the simulated program, thus, the construction time for the unused states is wasted.

## 4    Test Setup

We evaluated different models for function unit resource conflict detection during simulation by implementing them in our TTA simulator [16] and executing synthetic simulations of function units using these models.

The initialization times were evaluated by initializing each model 100 000 times in a row and the total time was measured.

The simulation speed of each model was measured by simulating sequences of operations and by measuring the total real time it took to simulate the operation sequence. Each operation in each function unit was executed in round-robin fashion in successive cycles with total of 10 000 000 operation executions. All resource conflicts reported by the models were caught and ignored.

The measurements were made in a Pentium 4 CPU with 3.4 GHz clock and 1 GB of RAM. The operating system was Ubuntu Linux 6.10, with GNU GCC compiler version

| | 0 | 1 | 2 |
|-----|---|---|-----|
| MUL | R | A | A+W |

**Fig. 2.** Resource vector for multiplication with three resources R, A and W

4.1.1-13ubuntu5. The compiler optimization switch used to compile the models was '-O3'. All the tests were executed under equal overall system load after a fresh boot. Each test was run three times in a row and the best result was picked. Picking the best result instead of, for example, the average, allowed us to evaluate the peak speed each model can reach. However, the differences between the results were negligible.

The following conflict detection models were evaluated:

**none.** A model without conflict detection. This model simulates only the operation latency, but does not detect if there are conflicting pipeline resource usages between started operations. This model could be used in quick design space exploration.

**vectors.** The traditional resource vector-based approach for conflict detection. It maintains the composite vector and checks resource conflicts against the composite vector each time an operation is started.

**active FSA.** Uses an FSA for conflict detection. FSA is fully constructed before starting the simulation. The used construction algorithm is similar to the one presented in [17].

In this model, the automaton is fully constructed before starting the simulation. Therefore, in case of function units with complicated pipeline resource usage patterns, an "state explosion" can happen, which lengthens the simulation initialization. The simulation itself should be very fast as conflicts are detected with a single table lookup.

**lazy FSA.** Like "active FSA", but the FSA is not fully constructed before starting the simulation. Instead, only the start state is created and other states are created when they are visited for the first time during simulation.

Our hypothesis is that this model should improve startup time when compared to the active FSA model, but the simulation itself might be slower due to the need of checking whether a required state exists and building one if the transition is valid.

Models were evaluated with the following function unit resource usage patterns trying to cover the wide range of function units used in processors.

**ALU.** Arithmetic-logic unit with 18 integer operations. Latency of each operation is one cycle.

**MUL.** A single-operation function unit that implements integer multiplication with latency of 3. The operation uses three pipeline resources (symbols R, A, and W) as illustrated in Fig. 2.

**FPU.** Function unit that models a floating-point unit. Its pipeline matches the one of MIPS R4000 floating-point unit, as described in [18]. The unit includes floating-point operations that share eight different pipeline stages. The double precision floating-point operations range from a simple "absolute value" operation (latency of two) to a long latency operation "square root" (latency of 112).

**Table 1.** Count of created states in the active FSA model

| FU  | states |
|-----|--------|
| MUL | 3      |
| ALU | 2      |
| FPU | 258    |

The count of states in FSA affects the initialization time for the actively initialized FSA-based simulation model. State counts for each function unit pipeline model are listed in Table 1.

## 5   Results

Table 2 lists the startup times for each of the models and Table 3 shows the simulation times. The simulation times do not include the model initialization time, but they do include the time to simulate the actual functionality of the operation.

The startup and simulation times are compared to the model "none" to indicate the slowdown compared to no conflict detection at all. This "baseline" represents an ideal model without any conflict detection overhead.

The results show that the simplest conflict detection model using resource vectors is relatively fast to initialize (still measured a slowdown of 32 to 45 percent), but its simulation speed is at worst about 7.6 times slower than the FSA-based approaches. The FSA-based conflict detection slowed the simulation down about 32 to 59 percent, compared to the model with no conflict detection, while with resource vectors, the slowdown was more drastic, from 736 to 1065 percent. The simulation results for lazy FSA were identical to those of active FSA.

The lazy initialization of the FSA seemed to be a profitable optimization as it reduced the overhead of building the states during initialization from 9 to 23 percent when compared to the active FSA, while still providing equal simulation speed to the active FSA.

**Table 2.** Simulation startup times

|     | none          | vectors        | active FSA     | lazy FSA       |
|-----|---------------|----------------|----------------|----------------|
| MUL | 1.00 (5.7 s)  | 1.32 (7.5 s)   | 1.72 (9.8 s)   | 1.56 (8.9 s)   |
| ALU | 1.00 (38.3 s) | 1.45 (55.5 s)  | 3.24 (124.4 s) | 2.66 (101.8 s) |
| FPU | 1.00 (116.0 s)| 1.35 (157.0 s) | 3.27 (379.4 s) | 2.51 (290.6 s) |

**Table 3.** Simulation times

|     | none         | vectors         | active FSA   | lazy FSA     |
|-----|--------------|-----------------|--------------|--------------|
| MUL | 1.00 (2.0 s) | 10.65 (21.3 s)  | 1.40 (2.8 s) | 1.40 (2.8 s) |
| ALU | 1.00 (2.2 s) | 7.36 (16.2 s)   | 1.32 (2.9 s) | 1.32 (2.9 s) |
| FPU | 1.00 (5.8 s) | 9.66 (56.2 s)   | 1.59 (9.2 s) | 1.59 (9.2 s) |

Low initialization time is important especially during a processor design space exploration with smaller test programs during which frequent short simulations of evaluated architecture variations is usual.

# 6 Conclusion

In this paper, simulation models for detecting function unit pipeline resource conflicts in simulation of architectures with independent function unit pipelines were evaluated. The evaluated models included the traditional resource vector based approach, and an approach that uses an finite state automaton (FSA) to detect resource conflicts quickly.

Additionally, an improvement to the FSA-based approach was proposed. In this "lazy FSA" model, the states are not constructed at simulation initialization time, but at the time they are used the first time, thus reducing the simulation initialization time in case of complex resource usage patterns in the simulated function unit.

The different models were implemented and benchmarked using three different test function units with resource usage patterns of varying complexity and with operations with both short and long latencies. The conclusion from the benchmarks is that the proposed "lazy FSA" approach, due to its reasonable initialization time combined with good simulation speed, is a suitable default model for function unit simulation in a processor simulator.

In the future, we plan to evaluate more techniques for speeding up the simulation of statically scheduled architectures with simplified control logic, like VLIWs and TTAs. Producing a very fast simulator especially for TTAs is quite challenging as it is not a traditional instruction set architecture, thus cannot be easily mapped to the host instruction set by means of compiled simulation. In addition, its architecture is very close to its microarchitecture, thus, even a functional simulation is forced to model quite low level details. However, techniques like combining speed of functional simulation with accuracy of cycle-level simulation or the use of techniques such as "memoization" could be interesting to adapt for our case [10,5].

# Acknowledgement

This work has been supported in part by the Academy of Finland under project 205743 and the Finnish Funding Agency for Technology and Innovation under research funding decision 40441/05.

# References

1. Corporaal, H.: Microprocessor Architectures: from VLIW to TTA. John Wiley & Sons, Chichester (1997)
2. Cmelik, B., Keppel, D.: Shade: a fast instruction-set simulator for execution profiling. In: Proc. SIGMETRICS '94, Nashville, Tennessee, May 1994, pp. 128–137. ACM Press, New York (1994)
3. Nohl, A., Braun, G., Schliebusch, O., Leupers, R., Meyr, H., Hoffmann, A.: A universal technique for fast and flexible instruction-set architecture simulation. In: Proc. DAC '02, New Orleans, Louisiana, June 2002, pp. 22–27. ACM Press, New York (2002)

4. Poncino, M., Zhu, J.: Dynamosim: a trace-based dynamically compiled instruction set simulator. In: Proc. ICCAD '04, San Jose, CA, November 2004, pp. 131–136. IEEE/ACM Press, New York (2004)
5. Schnarr, E., Larus, J.R.: Fast out-of-order processor simulation using memoization. In: Proc. ASPLOS-VIII, San Jose, California, October 1998, pp. 283–294. ACM Press, New York (1998), doi:10.1145/291069.291063
6. Schnarr, E.C., Hill, M.D., Larus, J.R.: Facile: a language and compiler for high-performance processor simulators. In: Proc. PLDI '01, Snowbird, Utah, June 2001, pp. 321–331. ACM Press, New York (2001)
7. Pees, S., Hoffmann, A., Meyr, H.: Retargeting of compiled simulators for digital signal processors using a machine description language. In: Proc. DATE '00, Paris, France, March 2000, pp. 669–673. ACM Press, New York (2000)
8. Pees, S., Hoffmann, A., Meyr, H.: Retargetable compiled simulation of embedded processors using a machine description language. ACM T. Des. Autom. Electron. Syst. 5(4), 815–834 (2000)
9. Engel, F., Nührenberg, J., Fettweis, G.P.: A generic tool set for application specific processor architectures. In: Proc. CODES '00, San Diego, CA, pp. 126–130. ACM Press, New York (2000)
10. Kim, J.K., Kim, T.G.: Trace-driven rapid pipeline architecture evaluation scheme for asip design. In: Proc. ASPDAC '03, Kitakyushu, Japan, pp. 129–134. ACM Press, New York (2003)
11. Kim, H.Y., Kim, T.G.: Performance simulation modeling for fast evaluation of pipelined scalar processor by evaluation reuse. In: Proc. DAC '05, San Diego, CA, June 2005, pp. 341–344. ACM Press, New York (2005)
12. Davidson, E.S., Shar, L.E., Thomas, A.T., Fatel, J.H.: Effective control for pipelined computers. In: COMPCON75 Digest of Papers, February 1975, pp. 181–184. IEEE Computer Society Press, Los Alamitos (1975)
13. Faraboschi, P., Fisher, J.A., Young, C.: Instruction scheduling for instruction level parallel processors. In: Proc. IEEE, Washington, DC, vol. 89, pp. 1638–1659. IEEE Computer Society Press, Los Alamitos (2001)
14. Bradlee, D.G., Henry, R.R., Eggers, S.J.: The marion system for retargetable instruction scheduling. In: Proc. PLDI '91, Toronto, Ontario, Canada, June 1991, pp. 229–240. ACM Press, New York (1991)
15. Cormen, T.H., Leiserson, C.E., R.L.R.: Introduction to Algorithms. The MIT Press, Cambridge, Massachusetts (1999)
16. Jääskeläinen, P.: Instruction Set Simulator for Transport Triggered Architectures. Master's thesis, Department of Information Technology, Tampere University of Technology, Tampere, Finland, P.O.Box 553, FIN-33101 Tampere, Finland (Sepember 2005), See http://tce.cs.tut.fi/
17. Bala, V., Rubin, N.: Efficient instruction scheduling using finite state automata. Int. Journal of Parallel Programming 25(2), 53–82 (1997)
18. Hennessy, J.L., Patterson, D.A.: Computer Architecture: A Quantitative Approach, 3rd edn. Morgan Kaufmann Publishers, San Francisco (2003)

# A Modular Coprocessor Architecture for Embedded Real-Time Image and Video Signal Processing

Holger Flatt, Sebastian Hesselbarth, Sebastian Flügel, and Peter Pirsch

Institut für Mikroelektronische Systeme,
Gottfried Wilhelm Leibniz Universität Hannover,
Appelstr. 4, 30167 Hannover, Germany
{flatt,hesselbarth,fluegel,pirsch}@ims.uni-hannover.de

**Abstract.** This paper presents a modular coprocessor architecture for embedded real-time image and video signal processing. Applications are separated into high-level and low-level algorithms and mapped onto a RISC and a coprocessor, respectively. The coprocessor comprises an optimized system bus, different application specific processing elements and I/O interfaces. For low volume production or prototyping, the architecture can be mapped onto FPGAs, which allows flexible extension or adaption of the architecture. Depending on the complexity of the coprocessor data paths, frequencies up to 150 MHz have been achieved on a Virtex II-Pro FPGA. Compared to a RISC processor, the performance gain for an SSD algorithm is more than factor 70.

## 1 Introduction

In recent years, integration of smart image and video processing algorithms in sensor devices increased. Applications like object detection, tracking, and classification demand high computing performance. It is desirable to have embedded signal processing integrated in the sensor, e.g. video cameras, to perform image or video compression, filtering, and data reduction techniques. Moreover, flexibility is mandatory where new applications have to be supported or existing code needs to be modified.

General purpose processors can be used as a first approach for embedded real-time image and video signal processing. They comprise instruction set extensions like SSE, which allow SIMD operations [1], but efficiency of execution units remains low [2]. Moreover, due to their high power consumption, they are not suitable for embedded systems.

As an alternative to general purpose processors, digital signal processors (DSP) provide high performance at low power consumption. While exploiting the inherent parallelism of algorithms, they are inferior to application specific arithmetic cores [3].

Dedicated arithmetic cores provide highest optimization potential for a specific application, but lack flexibility if support to different applications is required.

S. Vassiliadis et al. (Eds.): SAMOS 2007, LNCS 4599, pp. 241–250, 2007.

Design and modification of dedicated units are time-consuming, while their reusability is low.

The analysis of the algorithmic hierarchy of image and video processing applications yields three layers of hardware abstraction [4]. It is advantageous if the hardware architecture combines processing cores that are optimized for the execution of algorithms associated to one of the layers. High-level algorithms (HLA) consist of data depended decisions and control operations. They require high flexibility. A RISC processor supports mapping of complex HLAs with low development effort if a compiler is available. Low-level algorithms (LLA) comprise simple computing operations that need high processing power. They are regular and have high potential for parallel execution. A coprocessor that is optimized for processing of low-level algorithms is superior to a RISC. Medium-level algorithms (MLA) are situated between HLAs and LLAs. Depending on their complexity, they can be executed either on a RISC or on a coprocessor.

In [5] a special programmable coprocessor was combined with a RISC. This coprocessor is optimized for processing of low-level algorithms. Due to its complexity, adaptations and extensions of the architecture are time-consuming.

In this paper, a modular coprocessor architecture for a generic embedded system is proposed, which can be easily modified or extended for different applications. This embedded system shown in figure 1 comprises a RISC core, a reconfigurable coprocessor, data I/O, debug, and memory interfaces.

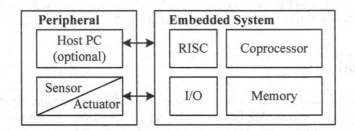

**Fig. 1.** Embedded architecture and peripheral units

The architecture is designed for accelerating different image and video signal processing algorithms. The combination of RISC and coprocessor considers algorithmic complexity of embedded applications [6]. While dedicated processing elements inside the coprocessor compute time-consuming low-level operations, irregular high-level parts of the application are executed on a RISC core.

Commonly used and feature-rich, commercial system-on-chip bus systems like AMBA AHB [7] require complex finite state machines for master units. To reduce modularization efforts for peripheral and coprocessor units, a simplified multi-layer communication bus is introduced.

Due to their reconfigurability, the focus is on FPGA implementations, although the architecture is also suitable for ASIC implementation. Actual FPGAs allow real-time signal processing of sophisticated algorithms. They provide high speed communication interfaces, internal memories and arithmetic cores [8] [9]. Moreover, some FPGAs contain embedded RISC processors [10]. These embedded cores allow the integration of a RISC with a coprocessor in one device [11].

This paper is organized as follows. Chapter 2 gives a brief description of the proposed coprocessor architecture and the communication approach. Chapter 3 shows an application example and the design flow for dedicated processing elements. Subsequently, chapter 4 presents verification and results. Conclusions and an outlook to future work are given in chapter 5.

## 2  Embedded Coprocessor Architecture

### 2.1  Communication Approach

In order to utilize dedicated hardware acceleration units, a sufficient communication structure between RISC and coprocessor is needed. If the processes on the RISC and the coprocessor are frequently synchronized, communication latencies result in a high performance reduction. Aiming at a lower synchronization rate, an hierarchical control approach reduces the communication overhead [12]. Instead of calling and synchronizing single coprocessor micro instructions, e. g. multiply-accumulate, the RISC calls and synchronizes low-level algorithms that consist of a set of micro instructions.

Figure 2 shows the structure of the proposed communication scheme, which includes a *Dynamic Resource Scheduler* for converting medium-level function calls (MLA) into a set of low-level function calls (LLA).

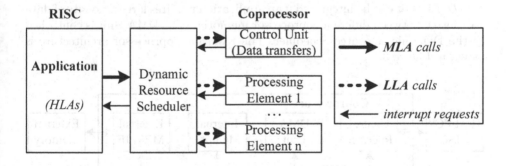

**Fig. 2.** RISC/coprocessor communication approach with Dynamic Resource Scheduler

The RISC transfers MLA function calls to the Dynamic Resource Scheduler. The Scheduler creates a list of LLA function calls and forwards them to the associated *Processing Elements*. Different Processing Elements can work in parallel if no data and resource conflicts occur. The Processing Elements send interrupt requests to the Scheduler after finishing their computation. After a MLA function call has been processed, the Scheduler signals the application through interrupt request.

The Dynamic Resource Scheduler can be implemented in software if saving of hardware resources is intended, or in hardware if reduction of communication cost between RISC and coprocessor is highly important. In this work, a software approach is used.

## 2.2   Architecture Overview

The coprocessor carries out LLAs computations. The proposed modular approach currently supports several dedicated *Processing Elements* executing different LLAs [11]. These autonomous working units are compact and have high potential for optimization. Replacement and extension of PEs demand low development effort. Function calls and data transfers are performed via a central system bus. Synchronization of PEs is managed by a Dynamic Resource Scheduler instead of using semaphores [13].

A *Control Interface* connects the RISC to the system bus of the coprocessor to allow access to all resources. For the current design exploration phase, the RISC has been supplemented by a Host PC, which is attached to an FPGA-based emulation system. This allows HW/SW co-emulation during initial phases of application development to evaluate HLAs, LLAs, and bus communication in detail.

On-chip *memories* can be used to reduce data transfer latencies. Memory modules have been implemented for the proposed system bus with configurable data and address widths prior to logic synthesis. Additionally, external memories like DDR-SDRAM can be accessed through external memory interface modules.

A *DMA Unit* can be integrated if an application requires large amounts of data transferred between different coprocessor memories. The DMA Unit is controlled by the Dynamic Resource Scheduler. The resulting coprocessor architecture is shown in Figure 3.

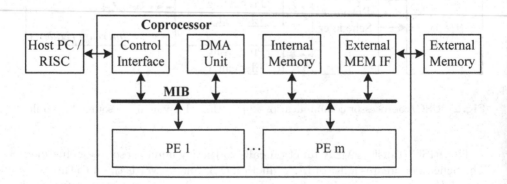

**Fig. 3.** Modular coprocessor architecture

## 2.3   Module Interconnect Bus (MIB)

A key component in any System-on-Chip (SoC) design is the interconnection structure, which is used for inter-module communication . The bus architecture is the most popular integration choice for SoC designs today. The main advantages of buses are flexibility and extensibility [14].

Commercial bus systems allow high speed communication between different units. Common SoC busses like AMBA AHB Bus [7] and Processor Local Bus (PLB) [15] are powerful. But both have multi-state protocols, which result in complex development and integration of new bus modules.

Moreover, the majority of applications only requires a small subset of the specified bus features [16]. If full compatibility to the bus protocol is needed, hardware overhead is unavoidable. For the modular coprocessor architecture approach, these commercial bus systems are not suitable.

Therefore, a small, flexible, and powerful bus system called *Module Interconnect Bus* (MIB) was developed. It allows rapid development of new bus components. Timing conditions of the bus protocol are simple. The communication protocol of the MIB is based upon synchronous transmission with double handshake mechanism. Valid bus transfers occur at every rising clock edge if the sending module asserts a *valid* signal and the receiving module is responding with an *accept* signal.

Two temporally independent sub-busses are used for data transmission. Read requests and write operations are transmitted through a *Request/Write Bus*. Data read operations are sent over a *Read Bus*. All transfers are initiated by master modules while slave modules receive transfer requests. Both sub-busses allow multiple layers to provide independent parallel transfers. Control and data flow is managed by two bus arbiters.

A slave may induce any arbitrary delay to a read operation as long as correct sequential order of responses is sustained. This decoupling allows integration of pipeline stages in both sub-busses, which is very suitable for complex SoCs running at high clock frequencies. A *Reorder Scheduler* on the *Read Bus* is used to keep in-order data delivery from slaves with different latencies. Figure 4 shows the structure of the Module Interconnect Bus.

# 3   Processing Element Design

## 3.1   PE Example Application

An exemplary processing element for implementation of an image classification algorithm based on a support vector machine (SVM) [17] is described in order to demonstrate the modular coprocessor architecture. The purpose of this algorithm is to classify a test image to a given set of classes.

A main processing task of the algorithm is to compare the test image $\mathbf{x}$ with all reference images $\mathbf{y}_j$. Input images of 64x64 pixels with 16 bit fix-point values per pixel are used and a total of 2520 reference images are available.

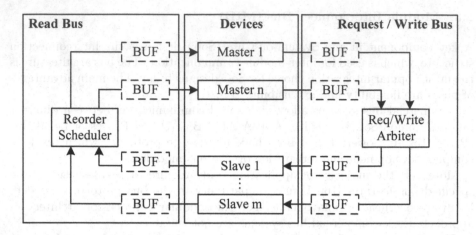

**Fig. 4.** Module Interconnect Bus architecture

The analysis of the algorithm has shown that most of computation time is needed for calculating the sum of square differences function $\mathbf{ssd}_j$.

$$ssd_j = \sum_i (x_i - y_{j,i})^2$$

Figure 5 shows pseudo assembler code of the SSD function for an unoptimized RISC core. After initializing the loop counters, the core operations are executed in lines 5-8. Assuming one cycle per operation, this pseudo code yields four cycles per loop. Considering loop unrolling, only every fourth branch operation is counted. For the given example of 2520 reference images with 64x64 pixels, the code would take roughly 47M cycles to finish.

```
 1: MOV    Rj, #2520
 2: ssdj_loop:
 3: MOV    Ri, #4096
 4: ssdi_loop:
 5: LD     Rx, (Ax+)  ⎤
 6: LD     Ry, (Ay+)  ⎥ x4
 7: SUB    Rx, Rx, Ry ⎥
 8: MAC    Ra, Rx, Rx ⎦
    ...
21: SUB    Ri, Ri, #4
22: BNZ    ssdi_loop
23: ST     (Ar+), Ra
24: DEC    Rj
25: BNZ    ssdj_loop
```

**Fig. 5.** Pseudo RISC code of SSD

## 3.2   SSD Data Path Architecture

Processing Elements carry out the LLA computations in the coprocessor. Figure 6 shows a generic architecture of an autonomous PE. It comprises an *MIB Slave Interface*, a *Control Unit*, an *MIB Master Interface* for accessing external data, and a *Data Path* for performing computations. An *Internal Memory* can be integrated into the PE when needed.

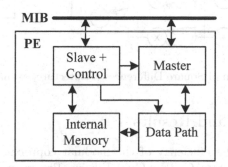

**Fig. 6.** Generic Architecture of a Processing Element

Performing a computation task requires that the Dynamic Resource Scheduler transfers function calls to the processing element via the MIB Slave Interface first. A function call comprises data memory addresses and defines function specific parameters. Afterwards the PE starts processing. Source data is taken from external memories via the MIB bus or directly from internal memories if available. After finishing computations, the PE sends an interrupt request to the Dynamic Resource Scheduler.

For the exemplary algorithm, dedicated hardware can reduce number of clock cycles as follows. The test image $x$ is compared with each reference picture $y_j$. Loading from external memory is necessary only once if the image fits in internal memory. Reference image data is loaded via the MIB Master Interface and is processed by the PE as soon as available.

Data parallelism is exploited in order to increase the computation performance. The level of maximal concurrency is limited by the data bus width of both external memory and system bus.

Figure 7 shows the architecture approach. For this 64 bit example, four 16 bit pixels from a reference image are loaded in parallel. These pixels are subtracted from the corresponding pixels of the test image and squared afterwards. The results are added by a tree of adders and accumulated in the last step. After computing the whole sum of square differences, it is stored into internal memory. To further increase hardware performance, a pipeline stage is inserted after each operation.

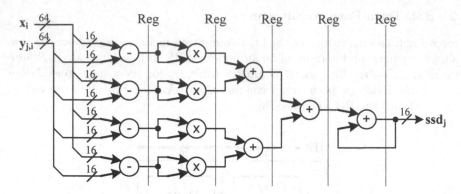

**Fig. 7.** Sum of Square Differences architecture, example 64 bit

## 4   Verification and Results

For demonstrating the efficiency of the modular coprocessor architecture, the ASIC verification system CHIPit Gold Edition Pro from ProDesign [18] was used. CHIPit is used for emulation only. Real embedded processing demands a more area and energy efficient platform. Figure 8 shows the system architecture.

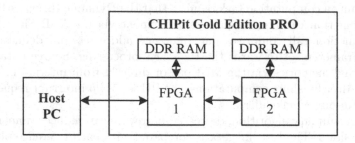

**Fig. 8.** CHIPit Gold Edition Pro architecture

The CHIPit system comprises two *Virtex II Pro XC2VP100-6 FPGAs*. Each of them is connected to *256 MB DDR RAM*. User software running on an *Host PC* can be used for executing high level algorithms and controlling the hardware mapped on the FPGAs. A 528 Mbps connection is provided for communication between Host PC and FPGAs.

In order to use both DDR RAMs, the coprocessor architecture was partioned and mapped onto both FPGAs. The data width of the MIB was adjusted to 128 bit. Using two independent DDR RAMs allows simultaneous data transfers for two Processing Elements.

Table 1 shows the synthesis results for coprocessors with different complexity. Frequency decreases with increasing number of processing elements due to the more complex place-and-route process for the 128 bit multilayer bus system.

**Table 1.** Synthesis Results after Place and Route using one XC2VP100-6 FPGA

| #SSD PEs | Frequency | Slices | Block RAMs | Multipliers |
|---|---|---|---|---|
| 0 | 156 MHz | 5581 | 23 | 0 |
| 1 | 151 MHz | 8173 | 35 | 8 |
| 2 | 147 MHz | 9930 | 47 | 16 |
| 3 | 133 MHz | 12936 | 59 | 24 |
| 4 | 125 MHz | 14785 | 71 | 32 |
| 5 | 119 MHz | 16449 | 83 | 40 |

Computing the SSD application example involves loading of all reference data from external memory. Therefore, maximum processing performance is limited by the available external memory bandwidth [19]. The memory hierarchy of the demonstration system supports memory transfers of 256 bit per cycle, which is equal to SSD processing of sixteen 16 bit pixel per clock cycle. Table 2 shows the processing performance running the SSD algorithm on a RISC and a coprocessor containing two PEs, respectively. Compared to the RISC, the coprocessor needs 1/72 of the RISC clock frequency to achieve the same performance.

According to Amdahl's law, speedup for the whole application is approximately 5 if 20% of the high level computations are remaining on the RISC.

**Table 2.** Performance for 2520 SSD computations with 4096 pixels (16 bit) per image

| Platform | Cycles | Pixels / cycle |
|---|---|---|
| RISC | 47M | 0.222 |
| 2x 128 bit SSD PEs | 645k | 16 |

## 5 Conclusion

In this paper, a modular coprocessor platform is presented, which is easy to extend or modify to support a large range of applications. It allows adding support for new applications without re-implementing all modules from scratch and can be used as a framework for dedicated hardware architectures. The architecture reaches feasible speed even on FPGAs with frequencies up to 150 MHz on a Xilinx Virtex II-Pro.

The architecture approach is optimized for integration of dedicated application specific processing elements. If several irregular low-level algorithms like image warping must be processed by different PEs, a full programmable solution might require less area.

Currently, the coprocessor is only accessible by a Host PC. Future work will be focused on interfacing an external RISC with the coprocessor architecture. To show the capabilities of the embedded architecture, more complex algorithms and processing engines will be implemented.

# References

1. Lee, R.: Multimedia extensions for general-purpose processors. In: IEEE Workshop on Signal Processing Systems SiPS97 Design and Implementation, pp. 9–23. IEEE Computer Society Press, Los Alamitos (1997)
2. Talla, D., John, L., Burger, D.: Bottlenecks in multimedia processing with SIMD style extensions and architectural enhancements. IEEE Transactions on Computers 52, 1015–1031 (2003)
3. Vejanovski, R., Singh, J., Faulkner, M.: ASIC and DSP implementation of channel filter for 3G wireless TDD system. In: 14th Annual IEEE International ASIC/SOC Conference, Proceedings, pp. 47–51. IEEE Computer Society Press, Los Alamitos (2001)
4. Pirsch, P., Stolberg, H.J.: VLSI implementations of image and video multimedia processing systems. IEEE Transactions on Circuits and Systems for Video Technology 8, 878–891 (1998)
5. Jachalsky, J., Wahle, M., Pirsch, P., Capperon, S., Gehrke, W., Kruijtzer, W., Nuñez, A.: A core for ambient and mobile intelligent imaging applications. In: IEEE International Conference on Multimedia & Expo (ICME), Proceedings, IEEE Computer Society Press, Los Alamitos, CDROM (2003)
6. Paulin, P., Liem, C., Cornero, M., Nacabal, F., Goossens, G.: Embedded software in real-time signal processing systems: application and architecture trends. In: Proceedings of the IEEE, vol. 85, pp. 419–435. IEEE Computer Society Press, Los Alamitos (1997)
7. ARM: AMBA specification (rev. 2.0) (1999)
8. Xilinx: Xilinx website, http://www.xilinx.com
9. Altera: Altera website, http://www.altera.com
10. Xilinx: Virtex-II Pro and Virtex-II Pro X platform FPGAs: Complete data sheet (2005)
11. Stechele, W., Herrmann, S.: Reconfigurable hardware acceleration for video-based driver assistance. In: Workshop on Hardware for Visual Computing, Tübingen (2005)
12. Jachalsky, J., Wahle, M., Pirsch, P., Gehrke, W., Hinz, T.: A coprocessor for intelligent image and video processing in the automotive and mobile communication domain. In: IEEE International Symposium on Consumer Electronics, Proceedings, pp. 142–145. IEEE Computer Society Press, Los Alamitos (2004)
13. Dejnožková, E., Dokládal, P.: Embedded real-time architecture for level-set-based active contours. EURASIP Journal on Applied Signal Processing 2005, 2788–2803 (2005)
14. Lee, A., Bergmann, N.: On-chip communication architectures for reconfigurable system-on-chip. In: IEEE International Conference on Field-Programmable Technology, Proceedings, pp. 332–335. IEEE Computer Society Press, Los Alamitos (2003)
15. IBM: 64-bit processor local bus architecture specifications, version 3.5 (2001)
16. Cyr, G., Bois, G., Aboulhamid, M.: Generation of processor interface for SoC using standard communication protocol. IEE Proceedings - Computers and Digital Techniques 151, 367–376 (2004)
17. Schölkopf, B., Smola, A.: Learning with Kernels. MIT Press, Cambridge (2002)
18. ProDesign: CHIPit Gold Edition Pro, http://www.uchipit.com
19. Ding, C., Kennedy, K.: The memory bandwidth bottleneck and its amelioration by a compiler. In: 14th International Symposium on Parallel and Distributed Processing (IPDPS), Proceedings, Washington, DC, USA, p. 181. IEEE Computer Society, Los Alamitos (2000)

# High-Bandwidth Address Generation Unit

Humberto Calderón, Carlo Galuzzi,
Georgi Gaydadjiev, and Stamatis Vassiliadis

Computer Engineering Laboratory,
Electrical Engineering Dept., EEMCS, TU Delft, The Netherlands
{H.Calderon,C.Galuzzi,G.N.Gaydadjiev,S.Vassiliadis}@ewi.tudelft.nl
http://ce.et.tudelft.nl

**Abstract.** In this paper we describe an efficient data fetch circuitry
for retrieving several operands from a n-bank interleaved memory system in a single machine cycle. The proposed address generation (AGEN)
unit operates with a modified version of the low-order-interleaved memory access approach. Our design supports data structures with arbitrary
lengths and different (odd) strides. A detailed discussion of the 32-bit
AGEN design aimed at multiple-operand functional units is presented.
The experimental results indicate that our AGEN is capable of producing 8 x 32-bit addresses every 6 ns for different stride cases when
implemented on VIRTEX-II PRO xc2vp30-7ff1696 FPGA device using
trivial hardware resources.

## 1 Introduction

Nowadays, performance gains in computing systems are achieved by using techniques such us pipelining, optimized memory hierarchies [1], customized functional units [2], instruction level parallelism support (e.g. VLIW, Superscalar)
and thread level parallelism [3] to name a few. These time and space parallel
techniques require the design of optimized address generation units [4,5,6,7] capable to deal with higher issue and execution rates, larger number of memory
references, and demanding memory-bandwidth requirements [8]. Traditionally,
high-bandwidth main memory hierarchies are based on parallel or interleaved
memories. Interleaved memories are constructed using several modules or banks.
Such structures allow distinct banks access in a pipelined manner [9]. In this paper we propose an AGEN for efficient utilization of n-way-interleaved main memory containing vector data, e.g. supporting kernels like SAD (sum of absolute
differences) and MVM (matrix-vector multiply) operations. More specifically,
the main contributions of this paper are:

- An AGEN design capable of generating 8 x 32-bit address in a single cycle. In addition, arbitrary memory sequences are supported using only one
  instruction.
- An organization that uses optimized Boolean equations to generate the 8
  offsets instead of an additional adders stage.

S. Vassiliadis et al. (Eds.): SAMOS 2007, LNCS 4599, pp. 251–262, 2007.
© Springer-Verlag Berlin Heidelberg 2007

– An FPGA implementation of the proposed design able to fetch 1.33 Giga operands per second from an 8-way-interleaved memory system using only 3% of the targeted device.

The remainder of this paper is organized as follows. Section 2 outlines the necessary background on interleaved-memory systems. Section 3, presents the considered vector architecture, the memory interleaving mechanism and the design of the AGEN Unit. In Section 4, we discuss the experimental results in terms of used area and latency. Finally, in Section 5 conclusions and future work are presented.

## 2    Background

The use of multiple memory banks for providing sufficient memory bandwidth is the key element when memory system performance is evaluated [10]. The accessing of consecutive data elements separated by a fixed addressing distance is called a stride. The stride describes the relationship between the operands and their addressing structure. A memory organized with several banks which store elements in a stride manner is called an interleaved memory [11,12].

Given that an n-bit address memory field can be divided into 1) memory-unit-number and 2) address in memory unit (memory-address), two main addressing techniques arise from this basic address division as depicted on Figure 1.

(a) *High interleaved* addressing mapping utilizes the low address bits $v$   as memory-address in the unit, while the higher bits $u$ represent the memory-unit-number. This technique is used by the traditional scalar processors with multiple memory pages.

(b) *Low interleaved* memory mapping use the low address bits $u$ to point out the memory-unit-number, while the higher memory bits $v$   are the memory-address.

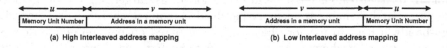

(a) High Interleaved address mapping          (b) Low Interleaved address mapping

**Fig. 1.** Interleave memory formats

The data in low-interleaved-address mapping is distributed in a round-robin like fashion among the memory banks. For example, in the memory system with 8 banks and data structure with stride =1, as presented in Figure 2, word 0 is stored in bank 0, word 1 is stored in bank 1. In general, word $x$ is located in bank $x\ MOD\ 8$. In this figure, one *Major Cycle* (memory latency) is subdivided in 8 *Minor Cycles*. The retrieving of 8 consecutive elements will take one *Major Cycle* and 7 additional *Minor Cycles*. This is due to the fact that the eight consecutive elements from the memory banks are retrieved in parallel. Those read values are stored in intermediate data registers from which are issued to the functional units in a pipelined manner (using 7 additional *Minor Cycles*). With this memory architecture the retrieving of $x$ single-word elements will take *Major Cycle* $+ (x - 1)$ *Minor Cycles*.

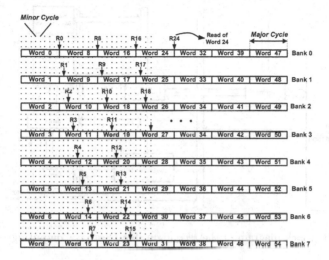

**Fig. 2.** Interleaved memory pipelined access to memory

# 3   AGEN Unit Design

We consider a vector co-processor consisting of a group of reconfigurable functional units [13,14] coupled to a core processor. Figure 3 presents this organization. An arbiter is used to distribute the instructions between the vector unit and the scalar processor following the paradigm proposed in [15]. Please note that many current platforms implement similar approaches, e.g. the Fast Simplex Link interface and the Auxiliary Processor Unit (APU) controller for MicroBlaze and PowerPC IP cores [16]. The memory banks presented in Figure 3 are built using dual ported memories, e.g. BRAMs [17] in case of FPGA implementation, shared by both processors, the scalar and the vector. One port of the BRAM is used by the scalar processor as a linear array memory organization with *high interleaved* address mapping. The second port is used by the vector unit. The memory access from the vector processor side requires dedicated AGEN unit (different from the one embedded into the core processor) that generates the addresses for the 8-way interleaved memory organization in the correct sequence order. The vector data is distributed in an interleaved-way, scattered by the stride values, that requires 8 different addresses for each memory access. The AGEN unit is configured to work with single or multiple groups (with the same stride) of streamed data using a single instruction. The AGEN special instruction configures the base addresses, the stride and the length of the particular streaming data format. The memory accesses can be performed in parallel with the execution phase of a previous iteration using the decoupled approach as presented in [2].

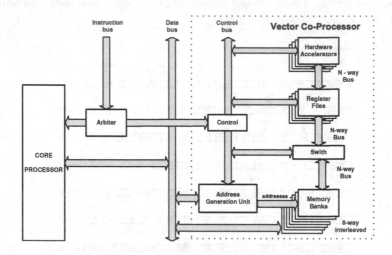

**Fig. 3.** Block diagram of the reconfigurable Custom Computing Unit

## 3.1   Memory-Interleaving Mechanism

In this paragraph the mechanism to retrieve $n$ data elements in parallel is presented. Figure 4, shows eight different stride cases, with odd strides $\leq 15$ for eight memory banks. For example, the stride shown in case $(b)$, is three. One can see, that in all of the cases the data is uniformly distributed in the memory banks. This fact suggests the feasibility of an AGU capable to generate the effective addresses of $n$ data elements every major cycle. This can be formally stated as follows:

> *$n$ data elements stored in $n$ memory banks can be retrieved in a single major cycle if the stride is an odd integer and $n$ is a power of two.*

Otherwise stated this can be extended as follows:

> *$n$ data elements stored in $n$ memory banks can be retrieved in a single major cycle if $gcd(n, Stride)=1$.*

The notation $gcd(a, b)$ is used for the greatest common divisor. Two integers $a, b$ are relatively prime if they share no common positive factors (divisors) except of 1, e.g $gcd(a, b) = 1$.

**Extension to the general case:** Let's consider $n$ banks of memory each holding $m$ memory cells. The $m \times n$ memory array can be represented as a matrix $[m \times n]$ where each column corresponds to a memory bank. In addition, the cell $i$ of the memory bank $j$ corresponds to the matrix element with indexes $(i, j)$. We denote

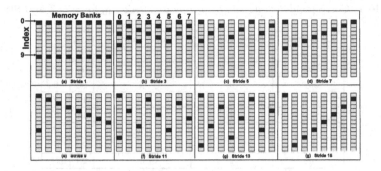

**Fig. 4.** Example of 8-way interleaved memory banks with odd strides $\leq 15$

this matrix as $A$ and consider $n = 2^h$ and $m$ for its dimensions, with $h, m \in \mathbb{N}$. In addition, the stride of the data structures stored on the memory is an integer $Str = 2q + 1, q \in \mathbb{N}$.

From now on, the data stored in the memory banks will be considered as matrix A elements. Let the $n$ consecutive data elements placed in different memory banks be denoted by:

$$a_0, ..., a_{n-1} \tag{1}$$

**Remark 1.** Every element $a_\alpha$, with $\alpha = 0, ..., n - 1$, is identified in the matrix by its row-index $i$, with $i = 0, 1, ..., m - 1$, and its column-index $j$, with $j = 0, 1, ..., n - 1$. This means that there exists a one-to-one relation among $a_\alpha$ and the indexes couple $(i_\alpha, j_\alpha)$. Additionally, the couple $(i_\alpha, j_\alpha)$ can be used to represent $a_\alpha$ as a number in base $n$, obtainable as juxtaposition of $i_\alpha$ as most significant digit and $j_\alpha$ as least significant digit. The two indexes can also be used in a base 10 representation. Therefore, we have the following chain of equivalent representations for $a_\alpha$:

$$a_\alpha \leftrightarrow (i_\alpha, j_\alpha) \leftrightarrow (i_\alpha j_\alpha)_{|n} \leftrightarrow (n i_\alpha + j_\alpha)_{|10}. \tag{2}$$

As an example, Table 1 shows the chain of representations as defined in (2) for a case where $n = 8$ and $Str = 3$.

**Remark 2.** Without loss of generality, we can assume that the first element $a_0$ stored in the matrix remains at position $(i_0, j_0) = (0, 0)$.

**Lemma 1.** The number of rows necessary to hold $n$ elements with stride $Str = 2q + 1, q \in \mathbb{N}$ is $Str$.

**Proof.** The number of cells ($\sharp_{cell}$) necessary to store $n$ elements with stride $Str$ is $\sharp_{cell} = n + (Str - 1) n = n(2q + 1)$. Therefore, the number of rows is

$$\sharp_{cell} \mod n = n(Str) \mod n = Str. \tag{3}$$

□

**Table 1.** Correspondence $a_\alpha \leftrightarrow (i_\alpha, j_\alpha) \leftrightarrow a_{\alpha|n} \leftrightarrow a_{\alpha|10}$ for $n = 8$ and $\mathrm{Str} = 3$

| Element $a_\alpha$ | Row-Index $i_\alpha$ | Column-Index $j_\alpha$ | $a_{\alpha|8}$ | $a_{\alpha|10}$ |
|---|---|---|---|---|
| $a_0$ | 0 | 0 | 00 | 0 |
| $a_1$ | 0 | 3 | 03 | 3 |
| $a_2$ | 0 | 6 | 06 | 6 |
| $a_3$ | 1 | 1 | 11 | 9 |
| $a_4$ | 1 | 4 | 14 | 12 |
| $a_5$ | 1 | 7 | 17 | 15 |
| $a_6$ | 2 | 2 | 22 | 18 |
| $a_7$ | 2 | 5 | 25 | 21 |

Remark 2 and Lemma 1 imply that the necessary rows to store the $n$ elements with stride Str are:

$$\{0, 1, ..., \mathrm{Str} - 1\} \tag{4}$$

The $n$ data $a_\alpha$ can be defined recursively. If $a_0 = (i_0, j_0)$ the elements $a_2, ...,$ $a_{n-1}$ can be recursively defined as follows:

$$a_\alpha = a_{\alpha-1} + \mathrm{Str}. \tag{5}$$

**Theorem 1.** Let $n$ be the number of elements $a_\alpha$, with $\alpha = 0..n - 1$, stored in a matrix A, $m \times n$, with $n = 2^h$. Let the stride be the integer $\mathrm{Str} \in \mathbb{N}$. If $(i_\alpha, j_\alpha)$ and $(i_\beta, j_\beta)$ are the couples of indexes identifying $a_\alpha$ and $a_\beta$ in the matrix and $gcd(n, \mathrm{Str}) = 1$, we have:

$$j_\alpha \neq j_\beta \ \forall \alpha, \beta \in [0, ..., n - 1]. \tag{6}$$

**Proof.** Without loss of generality, by Remark 2, we can assume $(i_0, j_0) = (0, 0)$. By contradiction let $j_\alpha = j_\beta$. We have two possible cases: (1) $i_\alpha = i_\beta$ and (2) $i_\alpha \neq i_\beta$.

The first case is not possible: more precisely, if $i_\alpha = i_\beta$ will lead to $a_\alpha = a_\beta$ since $j_\alpha = j_\beta$ (see Remark 1).

In the second case: $i_\alpha \neq i_\beta$. Firstly, by (4), it follows:

$$i_\beta - i_\alpha \in [0, \mathrm{Str} - 1]. \tag{7}$$

Without loss of generality we can assume $\beta > \alpha$. By (5) we have:

$$a_\beta = a_{\beta-1} + \mathrm{Str} = a_{\beta-2} + 2\mathrm{Str} = ... = a_\alpha + x\mathrm{Str}, \tag{8}$$

with $x \in \mathbb{N}$ and $x < n$; it is straightforward to show that $x = \beta - \alpha$. By using the representations in base 10 of $a_\alpha$ and $a_\beta$ (see (2)), the equation (8) becomes:

$$ni_\beta + j_\beta = ni_\alpha + j_\alpha + x\mathrm{Str}, \tag{9}$$

taking into account the assumption $j_\alpha = j_\beta$ we can rewrite (9) as

$$n(i_\beta - i_\alpha) = x \ \mathrm{Str}. \tag{10}$$

Since $gcd(n, Str) = 1$ and $n$ divides the product $x$ Str, it follows that $n$ is a divisor of $x$. This implies that: $x = r\, n$, with $r \in \mathbb{N}$. Therefore $x > n$ which contradicts the original hypothesis. As a consequence, it must be that $j_\alpha \neq j_\beta$, for all $\alpha, \beta \in [0, ..., n-1]$. $\qquad\qquad\qquad\qquad\qquad\qquad\qquad\qquad\qquad\qquad\qquad\qquad$ $\square$

**Remark 3.** The previous theorem can be reformulated saying that *if n data elements are stored in **n** memory banks with a fixed stride Str and the gcd(n, Str) = 1, each data element is stored in a different memory bank.*

**Corollary 1.** By Theorem 1 it follows that the data are stored in different memory banks if $n = 2^h$ and Str is an odd integer and viceversa if $n$ is an odd integer and Str $= 2^h$.

**Example:** Let's consider the case (b) presented in Figure 4. In this example, $n = 8$, the Str$= 3$. This is also the case considered in Table 1. Column 3 of Table 1, shows that each element of this data structure belongs to a different column and therefore to a different memory bank. This follows by Theorem 1. If there exist two elements $a_\alpha, a_\beta$ with the same column index then there exists $x < 8$ such that: $n(i_\beta - i_\alpha) = x(2q + 1)$ ($q = 1$ in this case). Considering that $n = 8$ in our example, $n(i_\beta - i_\alpha)$ can be either 8 or 16. The difference cannot be 0 since in that case $i_\alpha = i_\beta$ and therefore $a_\alpha = a_\beta$. As a consequence, we have two cases $8 = 3x$ or $16 = 3r$ and both equations don't have an integer solution for $x$.

## 3.2   The AGEN Design

As stated in [18] effective address computation is performance-critical. The AGEN unit described in this section generates **eight** addresses for fetching data elements simultaneously from an 8-way interleaved memory system at high speed. The AGEN is designed to work with multi-operand units [13,14] and uses a special-purpose-instruction such as the ones presented in [19]. In Figure 5 an example of such instruction is presented. The multiple base addresses in this instruction are necessary for cases with multiple indices such as SAD and MVM operations.

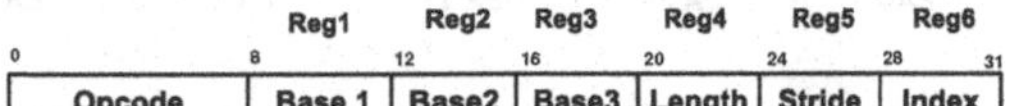

| | Reg1 | Reg2 | Reg3 | Reg4 | Reg5 | Reg6 |
|---|---|---|---|---|---|---|
| 0 | 8 | 12 | 16 | 20 | 24 | 28    31 |
| Opcode | Base 1 | Base2 | Base3 | Length | Stride | Index |

**Fig. 5.** Compound Instruction

The 4-bit instruction fields depicted in Figure 5, define the registers containing the addresses and/or the length and the stride parameters of the data structure to be accessed. More precisely they are:

- $Base_i (i = 1, 2, 3)$. These registers contain the memory addresses that point to the first elements of an data arrays to read or write in the interleaved memory organization. For example, the minuend and subtrahend in the sum of absolute differences (SAD) instruction or multiplicand, multiplier and addendum in multiply-accumulate (MAC) operations.

- *Length.* This register holds the number of $n$-tuples (cycles) needed to gather $y$-elements from the memory. For example, when length value is 10 and $n = 8$, 80 elements will be retrieved in 10 memory accesses.
- *Stride.* This register holds the distance between two consecutive data elements in an $n$-way interleaved memory. In our case the possible strides are odd numbers in the range between 1 and 15. Thus, strides are expressed as $2q + 1$, with $0 \leq q \leq 7$. In our design, these eight possible stride values are encoded using three bits.
- *Index.* The address stored in this register has two uses:
  - The register contains the vertical distance between two consecutive groups of $n$ elements. For example, Figure 4 (a) presents the index (also referred as vertical stride) that is equal to 9.
  - Sometimes the AGEN can be used to retrieve a single data word. In this case the register value is used as an offset address.

Equation (11) describes the effective address (EA) computation. EA is obtained by the addition of a pre-computed base-stride (BS) value, the index (IX) value and the memory-bank offsets represented by $Ai(0...3)$. Figure 6(e) depicts the 8 x EA generators for the targeted 8-way interleaved memory system.

$$EA_i = BS + Ai(0...3) + IX \quad \forall \; 0 \leq i \leq 7 \wedge RES \geq 0 \tag{11}$$

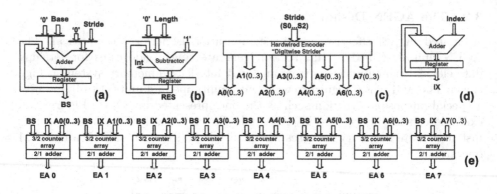

**Fig. 6.** Address Generation Unit: (a) Accumulator for BS computing, (b) Accumulator for loop control, (c) Hardwired encoder, (d) Index Accumulator, (e) Final addition Effective Address computing

The first addendum term ($BS$) of equation(11) is computed using the following relation: $BS = Base + k.Stride$. During the first cycle, BS is equal to the base address, therefore a 0 value is used for the second term. Thereafter, the stride offset is added for each $k$ iteration. Note that the stride value is equal to the offset between two consecutive data elements in the same column (see also Figure 4). In Figure 6(b) the subtractor used for counting the number of memory accesses is presented. In each clock cycle, e.g. equivalent to 8 iterations of an unrolled loop, the subtractor value is decremented by one until it reaches zero. A negative value of the subtractor result (underflow) asserts the "Int" flag, indicating the end of address generation process. Figure 6(c) represents the hardwired logic for computing the offset-value $Ai(0...3)$ which will be discussed in address transformation subsection in more details. Finally, Figure 6(d) shows the IX computation.

The accumulator structure presented in Figure 6 (a) is composed by two stages partially (4-bits only) shown in Figure 7. The first stage consists of an 4/2 counter which receives the SUM and the Carry signals of the previously computed value. The other two inputs (shown left on the figure) receive the mux-es outcomes used to select the appropriate operands (base and stride values) as explained above. The second stage consist of a 2/1 adder that produces the BS values.

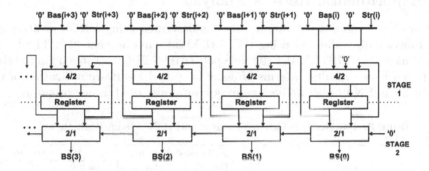

**Fig. 7.** Main accumulator circuitry

**Table 2.** Hardwired Encoder - Set up Table of Equations

| Bank | $A_0$ | $A_1$ | $A_2$ | $A_3$ |
|------|-------|-------|-------|-------|
| 0 | 0 | 0 | 0 | 0 |
| 1 | $S_2 \cdot \overline{S_1} \cdot \overline{S_0} + \overline{S_2} \cdot \overline{S_1} \cdot S_0 +$ $S_2 \cdot S_1 \cdot S_0 + \overline{S_2} \cdot S_1 \cdot \overline{S_0}$ | $S_2 \cdot \overline{S_1}$ | $S_2 \cdot S_0 + S_1 \cdot S_2$ | $S_2 \cdot S_1$ |
| 2 | $S_1$ | $\overline{S_2} \cdot \overline{S_1} \cdot S_0 + S_2 \cdot \overline{S_0} +$ $S_2 \cdot S_1$ | $\overline{S_2} \cdot S_1 \cdot S_0$ | $S_2 \cdot S_0$ |
| 3 | $S_2$ | $S_2 \cdot \overline{S_0}$ | $\overline{S_2} \cdot S_1$ | $S_2 \cdot S_1$ |
| 4 | $S_0$ | $S_1$ | $S_2$ | 0 |
| 5 | $S_2$ | $\overline{S_2} \cdot S_0$ | $S_2 \cdot \overline{S_1} \cdot \overline{S_0} + S_2 \cdot S_1 \cdot S_0$ | $S_2 \cdot \overline{S_1} \cdot S_0$ |
| 6 | $S_1$ | $S_2 \cdot S_1 + S_2 \cdot S_0 +$ $\overline{S_2} \cdot S_1 \cdot \overline{S_0}$ | $S_2 \cdot \overline{S_1} \cdot \overline{S_0}$ | $S_2 S_1 \overline{S_0}$ |
| 7 | $S_2 \cdot \overline{S_1} \cdot \overline{S_0} + S_2 \cdot S_1 \cdot S_0 +$ $\overline{S_2} \cdot S_1 \cdot \overline{S_0}$ | $S_2 \cdot \overline{S_1}$ | $S_2 \cdot \overline{S_1} + S_2 \cdot S_0$ | 0 |

e.g. the address bit $A_2$ for bank 1 will be: $A_2 = S_2 \cdot S_0 + S_1 \cdot S_2$.
This value (offset) is added to the current Base address value for obtain EA.

**Address transformation:** The stride values supported by our implementation are encoded using 3 bits represented by $S_2S_1S_0$. The pattern range $000_2..111_2$ encodes the $2q+1$ stride values with $0 \leq q \leq 7$. A hardwired logic is used to transform the encoded stride values into the corresponding $A0_{(0...3)}, ..., A7_{(0...3)}$ address offsets using a memory-bank-wise operation. A "memory-bank-wise" address is created based on the stride value. For example, consider Figure 4 (c) that presents the case for stride = 5. In this case, concerning banks 1 and 4 offset values of 3 and 2 are required. These correct memory-bank-wise values are generated by our hardwired logic. Please note that our approach supports all possible odd stride values in the range between 1 and 15. The exact transformations are presented as a set of equations in Table 2.

## 4  Experimental Results Analysis

The proposed address generation unit was described using VHDL, synthesized and functionally validated using ISE 7.1i Xilinx environment [20]. The target device used was VIRTEX-II PRO xc2vp30-7ff1696 FPGA. Table 3 summarizes the performance results in terms of delay time and hardware utilization of the complete AGEN unit as well as the major sub-units used in our proposal.

**Table 3.** The Address Generation unit and embedded arithmetic units

| Unit | Time delay (ns) | | | Hardware used | |
|---|---|---|---|---|---|
| | Logic Delay | Wire Delay | Total Delay | Slices | LUTs |
| Address Generation Unit | 4.5 | 1.4 | 6.0 | 673 | 1072 |
| Hardwired encoder (Digitwise) ‡ | 0.3 | - | 0.3 | 9 | 16 |
| 4:2 counter ‡ | 0.5 | 0.5 | 1.0 | 72 | 126 |
| 3:2 counter ‡ | 0.3 | - | 0.3 | 37 | 64 |
| 32-bit CPA (2/1) adder ‡ | 2.2 | 0.7 | 2.9 | 54 | 99 |

‡: Embedded circuitry into AGEN unit. Those are presented without I/O buffers delays.

From Table 3 it can be seen that the 32-bit CPA adder used is the most expensive component in terms of delay. The latency of this adder can be additionally improved using a deeper pipeline of the CPA as shown in [21]. This will improve the overall performance of the proposed unit but will require a deeper pipelined organization. The last is important for technologies with lower memory latency like the Virtex 4 and Virtex 5 devices [22]. The AGEN unit proposed here uses 3 stage pipeline. The first two pipeline stages correspond to the accumulator for BS computation (Figure 6(a)) and the third one to the 3/2 counter array and the final 2/1 adder. The latter forms the critical path for our implementation.

The proposed AGEN reaches an operation frequency of 166 MHz. Otherwise stated, our proposal is capable to generate 1.33 Giga addresses of 32-bits (totaling 43.5 Gbps) from an 8-way interleaved memory. Concerning the silicon area used by the proposed AGEN, the total unit uses only 3 % and 4 % of the targeted device in terms of slices and LUTs respectively.

# 5 Conclusions

A detailed description of an efficient vector address generation circuitry for retrieving several operands from an $n$-bank interleaved memory system in a single machine cycle was presented. The proposal is based on a modified version of the low-order-interleaved memory approach. The theoretical foundation of the proposed approach that guarantees the trivial indexing structure was also presented. Moreover, a new AGEN unit capable to work with dedicated multi-operand instruction that describes inner loops was introduced. An analysis of the latency of the proposed unit indicates that it is capable to generate 8 x 32 bit addresses every 6 ns. In addition, our design uses only 3 % of the hardware resources of the targeted FPGA device.

Our future work will focus on defining the complete ISA for the embedded functional units as well as the design of a more efficient reconfigurable interconnect switch with the aim of diminishing the latency and area cost of our implementation. We are also considering the design and analysis of the complete vector facility.

# References

1. Corbal, J., Espasa, R., Valero, M.: Three-Dimensional Memory Vectorization for High Bandwidth Media Memory Systems. In: Proceedings of the 35th Annual IEEE/ACM International Symposium on Microarchitecture, 2002 (MICRO-35), pp. 149–160. IEEE/ACM Press, New York (November 2002)
2. Espasa, R., Valero, M.: Exploiting instruction- and data-level parallelism. IEEE Micro, 20–27 (September 1997)
3. Mamidi, S., Blem, E.R., Schulte, M., Glossner, C.J., Iancu, D., Iancu, A., Moudgill, M., JinturkarRoesler, S., Nelson, B.: Instruction Set Extensions for Software Defined Radio on a Multithreaded Processor. In: Proceedings of the 2005 international conference on Compilers, architectures and synthesis for embedded systems, pp. 266–273 (September 2005)
4. Wijeratne, S.B., Siddaiah, N., Mathew, S.K., Anders, M.A., Krishnamurthy, R.K., Anderson, J., Ernest, M., Nardin, M.: A 9-GHz 65-nm Intel® Pentium 4 Processor Integer Execution Unit. IEEE Journal of Solid-State Circuits, 26–37 (January 2007)
5. Mathew, S., Anders, M., Krishnamurthy, R., Borkar, S.: A 4-GHz 130-nm address generation unit with 32-bit sparse-tree adder core. IEEE Journal of Solid-State Circuits, 689–695 (May 2003)
6. Kim, J., Sunwoo, M.: Design of address generation unit for audio DSP. In: Proceedings of 2004 International Symposium on Intelligent Signal Processing and Communication Systems, 2004. ISPACS 2004, pp. 616–619 (November 2004)
7. Cho, J., Chang, H., Sung, W.: An FPGA based SIMD processor with a vector memory unit. In: Proceedings of the 2006 IEEE International Symposium on Circuits and Systems, 2006. ISCAS 2006, pp. 525–528 (May 2006)
8. Hirano, K., Ono, T., Kurino, H., Koyanagi, M.: A New Multiport Memory for High Performance Parallel Processor System with Shared Memory. In: Proceedings of the Design Automation Conference ASP-DAC '98, pp. 333–334 (February 1998)
9. Postula, A., Chen, S., Jozwiak, L., Abramson, D.: Automated Synthesis of Interleaved Memory Systems for Custom Computing Machines. In: Proceedings of the 24th Euromicro Conference, pp. 115–122 (August 1998)

10. Sohi, G.: High-bandwidth Interleaved Memories for Vector Processors- a Simulation Study. IEEE Transactions on Computers, 34–44 (January 1993)
11. Hwang, K., Briggs, F.: Computer Architecture and Parallel Processing. McGraw-Hill, New York (1984)
12. Seznec, A., Lenfant, J.: Interleaved parallel schemes. IEEE Transactions on Parallel and Distributed Systems, 1329–1334 (December 1994)
13. Calderón, H., Vassiliadis, S.: Reconfigurable Multiple Operation Array. In: Hämäläinen, T.D., Pimentel, A.D., Takala, J., Vassiliadis, S. (eds.) SAMOS 2005. LNCS, vol. 3553, pp. 22–31. Springer, Heidelberg (2005)
14. Calderón, H., Vassiliadis, S.: Reconfigurable Fixed Point Dense and Sparse Matrix-Vector Multiply/Add Unit. In: Proceedings of the IEEE International Conference on Application-Specific Systems, Architectures, and Processors (ASAP 06), pp. 311–316. IEEE Computer Society Press, Los Alamitos (2006)
15. Vassiliadis, S., Wong, S., Gaydadjiev, G., Bertels, K., Kuzmanov, G., Panainte, E.: The MOLEN Polymorphic Processor. IEEE Transactions on Computers 53(11), 1363–1375 (2004)
16. Inc. XILINX: (2007), http://www.xilinx.com/ipcenter/
17. XILINX-LogiCore: Dual-Port Block Memory v7.0 - Product Specification. DS235 Xilinx (December 2003)
18. Sanu, M., Mark, A., Ram, K., Shekhar, B.: A 4GHz 130nm Address Generation Unit with 32-bit sparse-tree adder core. In: The 11th IEEE International Parallel Processing Symposium (IPPS 97), pp. 310–314. IEEE Computer Society Press, Los Alamitos (April 1997)
19. Juurlink, B., Cheresiz, D., Vassiliadis, S., Wijshoff, H.A.G.: Implementation and Evaluation of the Complex Streamed Instruction Set. In: Malyshkin, V. (ed.) PaCT 2001. LNCS, vol. 2127, pp. 73–82. Springer, Heidelberg (2001)
20. Inc. XILINX: The XILINX Software Manuals, XILINX 7.1i (2005), http://www.xilinx.com/support/sw_manuals/xilinx7/
21. XILINX-LogiCore: Adder/Subtracter v7.0 - Product Specification. DS214 Xilinx (December 2003)
22. Inc. XILINX: Memory Solutions (2007), http://www.xilinx.com/products/ design_resources/mem_corner/

# An IP Core for Embedded Java Systems

Sascha Uhrig, Jörg Mische, and Theo Ungerer

Institute of Computer Science
University of Augsburg
86159 Augsburg
Germany
Tel.: +498215982353
Fax: +498215982359
{uhrig, mische, ungerer}@informatik.uni-augsburg.de

**Abstract.** This paper proposes a multithreaded Java processor as an IP core for Altera's System-on-Programmable-Chip environment. The processor core is an enhancement of the earlier developed multithreaded Java processor named Komodo. It features a real-time capable garbage collection and integrated real-time scheduling schemes. Hence, it is suitable for embedded hard, soft, and non real-time systems. The facts that the processor is designed as an IP core and that it is a special Java processor makes both easier: hardware design and software development.

**Keywords:** Implantable Systems, Embedded System-on-a-Chip Implementations, Multithreaded Processors, Embedded Operating Systems, Real-time Embedded Systems, Java Processor.

## 1 Introduction

Software for embedded systems is getting more and more complex. As a result, not only the effort for software development and maintenance is increasing but also software becomes error-prone. To counteract these problems, developers of embedded systems switched from pure assembler programming to C/C++ several years ago. This step was quite necessary as well as sufficient at that time. But in the past years, Java entered the market of embedded systems, too.

One problem of Java in embedded systems is the need of a suitable run-time system, a Java Virtual Machine (JVM). In most cases, the JVM is a software solution which requires significant resources in terms of memory and computing power (see sec. 2). An additional operation system is responsible for resource management and hardware support. Overall, it is hard to use Java in an embedded system.

A further problem of several embedded systems is the need for real-time capabilities. In fact, a real-time JVM is defined by the Real-Time Specifications for Java (RTSJ) but it only takes care of rudimental real-time requirements, e.g. only a fixed priority scheduling is supported. Additionally, objects must be statically located in an immortal memory area or they must be self-managed in a so-called scoped memory [1].

We present a Java framework which deals with both topics: an easy hardware design and a familiar software environment. Additionally, our solution is fully capable

S. Vassiliadis et al. (Eds.): SAMOS 2007, LNCS 4599, pp. 263–272, 2007.

for real-time requirements and small embedded systems. The developed processor is a multithreaded core which executes most Java bytecodes directly in hardware (see [2]). Hence, we eliminate the operation system layer and thus its overhead. Additionally, we save the need of a (JIT) compiler or interpreter. Both circumstances lead to a system which works with limited hardware resources.

The performance of the proposed Java system is mainly influenced by the throughput of the memory interface of the IP core. Because of the restricted capacity of this interface, we integrated a built-in scratch RAM for frequently used JVM code and an instruction cache for general application code. A proper WCET analysis of real-time threads can be reached by switching off the cache for these threads. In this case, the cache is only available for the non real-time threads. A vice versa scenario is also possible: the cache is only available for the real-time thread. We evaluated the performance of the processor with different configurations at the memory interface. Furthermore, we analyze the impact of the garbage collection to the main application thread. The garbage collection runs as helper thread in parallel to the application.

The paper is organized as follows: In section 2 we describe several related Java environments. Section 3 presents the two tool chains for hardware resp. software development. Our Komodo processor IP core and the corresponding JVM are described in sections 4 and 5. The evaluations are shown in section 6 before section 7 concludes the paper.

## 2   State-of-the-Art Embedded Java System Design

Currently, Java is established in embedded systems. Nevertheless, using Java in embedded systems requires enhanced resources compared to conventional embedded systems using only a *small* microcontroller. The *Jamaica*VM from Aicas for example supports processors like ARM, Blackfin, PowerPC, XScale and x86 (among others [3]). As operating system, several real-time and non real-time systems are supported: Linux, Linux/RT, MacOS, WinCE, VxWorks and others.

Furthermore Sun offers an implementation of the RTSJ, the *Java SE Real-Time* [4]. The main drawback of this JVM is that it targets especially at dual core processors. It also runs on a single core but with a noticeable performance loss.

The mentioned solutions require at least a general purpose processor, a large amount of memory and an operating system with drivers for several peripheral components, i.e. they require a dedicated hardware and software development phase.

Another approach, especially for embedded systems, is the Java Optimized Processor (*JOP*). It is designed as an IP core for Altera and Xilinx FPGAs with very low hardware requirements [5]. JOP runs at 100MHz and provides a predictable timing behavior. Currently, it supports only the integer instruction set of Java. Besides a real-time capable scheduling [6], JOP also offers a real-time garbage collection [7].

An interpreter-based Java solution for very small systems is called JControl [8]. It requires only an 8- or 16-bit microcontroller and about 50kBytes of memory. As Java API, JControl supports a small subset of the Java standard classes based on the *integer* data type.

# 3   Hardware Design and Software Tool Chain

The development of a new embedded system involves two design steps: hardware design and software development. The presented IP core takes both parts into account.

## 3.1   Hardware Design

The Komodo processor core exits as an IP core (a component) for Altera's SoPC Builder with two standard Avalon bus master interfaces. Hence, it can easily be combined with other Altera, third party, or customer-made components to a System-on-Programmable-Chip. Figure 1 illustrates an example system architecture.

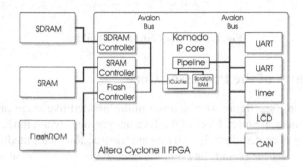

**Fig. 1.** Architecture of an SoPC (Example)

In figure 2 a snapshot of the SoPC builder from Altera is shown. Here, the processor core as well as the peripheral components can be connected by drag-and-drop. After that, the SoPC builder automatically generates a module which can be connected via a schematic to the pins of an FPGA. Besides the selection of the components and the connections to the desired Avalon bus, the address and interrupt mapping is done within the SoPC builder.

## 3.2   Software Tool Chain

For software development any Java tool chain can be used. In addition to an editor and a Java compiler, which can be found in any IDE, a so called *mapper* is required. Starting from the necessary Java class files, the mapper generates a memory image for the Komodo IP core. Figure 3 shows a snapshot of the mapper, the so-called *boot file generator*. The memory image contains the whole code of all required class files including class and method tables, information for garbage collection, and for dynamic class loading. In addition, all trap routines are located within the memory image.

The usage of Java as programming language allows the easy reuse of software written for other platforms. Additionally, it enables third-party IP core developers to distribute drivers and libraries only as class files without source code.

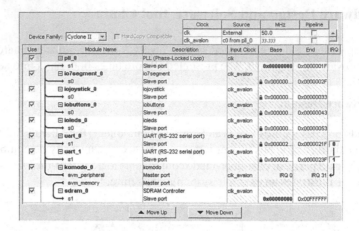

**Fig. 2.** Snapshot of the SoPC builder

# 4   Architecture of the Processor Core

The processor core (see figure 4) contains a multithreaded five stage pipeline with an integrated real-time scheduler. Most of the Java integer and several long, float, and double bytecodes are executed directly in hardware. Instructions with medium complexity are realized by microcodes and the complex operations, such as *new* and most floating point commands, call trap routines. As operand stack, a 2k-entry stack cache is integrated within the pipeline which is shared between the hardware thread slots. During the initialization phase, different portions of the stack cache can be assigned to the thread slots so that one thread entirely works on the stack cache while the data of other threads has to be swapped in and out.

Each thread slot possesses an instruction window in which up to six bytecodes can be prefetched. The instruction windows decouple fetching and decoding of the bytecodes. Instructions can be fetched from three different sources which are evaluated in section 6:

**External memory:** The external memory is connected via a standard Avalon bus master interface. Hence it is possible to use different types of memory with varying timing behavior.
**Instruction cache:** The instruction cache is a direct mapped cache which is shared by all thread slots. For better real-time predictability, it is possible to deactivate cache line replacement for each thread separately.
**Internal scratch RAM:** The scratch RAM is the fastest of the three available instruction memory types. During initialization, the most frequently called trap routines are copied to that memory. Additionally, the garbage collection could be fetched from the scratch RAM.

As interfaces to components outside the pipeline, two Avalon bus master interfaces with dedicated tasks are present. The separation into two busses improves processor throughput and decouples fast instruction fetching from possibly slow peripheral accesses:

**Memory bus:** The first interface is responsible for memory accesses. Only one additional component should be connected to this bus, e.g. a SRAM or a SDRAM controller. All kinds of memory accesses are managed by this bus.

**Peripheral bus:** The second bus master coordinates accesses to the peripheral modules. Here several miscellaneous components like UARTs, PWM modules, timers, CAN controllers, and $I^2C$ interfaces are possible. Only special extended bytecodes allow the access to this bus.

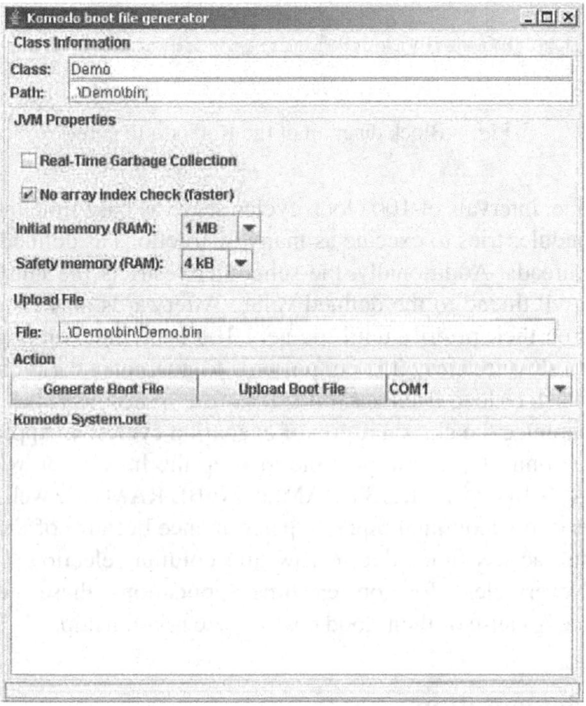

**Fig. 3.** Snapshot of the boot file generator

The integrated real-time scheduler supports two scheduling schemes: a simple fixed priority preemptive (FPP) scheduling and the so-called guaranteed percentage (GP [9]) scheduling scheme. Each hardware thread slot is assigned to one of these scheduling schemes. For the FPP scheduling a priority in the range from 0 to #threadslots − 1 and for GP a percentage between 0 to 100 is required. Both parameters can be set by a special extended bytecode.

The responsibility of the real-time scheduler is to guarantee a predefined ration of computing power to several hardware threads. For this purpose, it issues one instruction out of the instruction window of the most urgent thread to the decode unit each cycle. The urgency of the threads depends on the selected scheduling scheme and the current state of the threads, i.e. latencies, activity, already executed instruction, and the fill level of the corresponding instruction window.

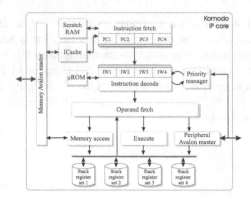

**Fig. 4.** Block diagram of the Komodo IP core

During run-time, intervals of 100 clock cycles serve as base timelines. Within these intervals, the scheduler tries to execute as many instructions as defined by the percentage for the GP threads. Additionally, the scheduler restricts the number of executed instructions of a GP thread to the defined value. Afterwards all FPP threads are executed depending on their priority until the next 100 cycle interval begins. If the code is fetched out of a slow memory it is not possible to guarantee the required throughput because of long fetch or load latencies.

In order to guarantee the chosen ration of execution cycles, an appropriate program memory must be connected to the pipeline to keep the instruction window as full as possible. Fast RAMs like SRAM, ZBT RAM, or NoBL RAMs are well suited. DRAMs and SDRAMs lead to suboptimal pipeline performance because of the long latencies, the indeterministic access times due to row and column selection, and the required refresh cycles. Nevertheless, for non-real-time applications, these memory types are also a good choice because of their good cost-to-size relationship.

## 5   JVM Implementation

Currently, the presented embedded Java system implements the CLDC 1.1 (*Connected Limited Device Configuration*) standard. The only exceptions are the *double* data type and the number of Java threads which is restricted to the amount of hardware thread slots at present.

Several complex instructions as e.g. *invoke*, *new*, and *athrow* are realized as trap routines. The most often used trap routines will be located within the pipeline-internal scratch memory for a fast access. Also the garbage collection will be moved into the scratch RAM with the objective to speedup the collection of unused objects. Hence the garbage collection is able to run during the memory and branch latencies of the main threads. Additionally, the garbage collection thread gets a minimum execution percentage to guarantee an advancing garbage collection.

Presently, only the so-called `HardwareThread` as a subclass of the `Thread` class is supported. It extends the `Thread` class by the parameters required by the hardware scheduler. Each instance of `HardwareThread` represents one hardware thread slot.

Hence, it is possible to create only as much `HardwareThreads` as thread slots are available. Further creations result in an `VirtualMachineError`.

An `OutOfMemoryError` can be handled with a dedicated event handler. Therefore, a special memory area can be preallocated which allows a safe shutdown of the system or a memory defragmentation where applicable.

# 6  Evaluation

Our evaluations concentrate on the performance of the whole Java system versus resource requirements. Additionally, we analyze the impact of the garbage collection to the application threads. All measurements are made with a pipeline frequency of 33Mhz. The basic SoPC contains a four threaded Komodo pipeline and a UART which deals as standard output (*System.out*). The main memory is a state-of-the-art 32-Bit SDRAM running at the same frequency as the processor core.

In comparison to the basic version, a Komodo pipeline without cache and scratch RAM, we evaluated three variations of the pipeline with different instruction fetch capabilities. Insufficient instruction fetch capabilities reduce pipeline utilization and hence the performance of the processor.

**Scratch RAM:** An integrated scratch RAM holds the most important trap routines. All other instructions are fetched out of the memory.

**ICache:** The pure pipeline (without scratch RAM) is extended by a small 128 byte direct mapped instruction cache. All instructions including the trap routines are fetched out of the SDRAM or the cache.

**Combined:** The SoPC contains both, a scratch RAM for the traps and an ICache (128 byte) for the application. The traps inside the scratch RAM are not cacheable. Hence, they do not pollute the cache.

Table 1 shows the hardware effort of the four variations of the whole Komodo SoPC. These values are obtained by a synthesis of the SoPC for Altera's Cyclone II FPGA, an EP2C35F484C7. We used the Quartus II 6.0 Web Edition for the synthesis.

**Table 1.** Hardware effort for different variations of Komodo

|             | Logic Cells | memory blocks (M4Ks) | DSP Elements | max. Frequency |
|-------------|-------------|----------------------|--------------|----------------|
| Basic       | 8329        | 18                   | 6            | 39.55          |
| Scratch RAM | 8329        | 34                   | 6            | 39.55          |
| ICache      | 10777       | 18                   | 6            | 35.70          |
| Combined    | 10777       | 34                   | 6            | 35.70          |

Because the cache is realized as logic cells, the used internal memory blocks (M4Ks) depends only on the scratch RAM. The amount of logic cells does not change between the basic and the scratch RAM version because a small scratch RAM is always required for the boot routine. As can be seen, the cache is a frequency restricting factor; integrating a bigger cache would lead to a frequency less than the aimed 33Mhz.

In the next step, we measured the pipeline utilization using the different instruction fetch capabilities. Therefore, we evaluated the utilization with a different amount of active thread slots. As benchmark we used the KFL benchmark of the JOP processor which can be downloaded at [10]. For the multithreaded benchmark, we executed it several times in parallel. We run our benchmarks ten times and calculated the average values. Figure 5 shows the results with one to four active threads which are scheduled using FPP scheduling.

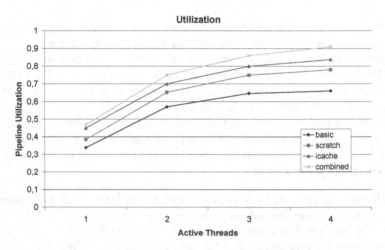

**Fig. 5.** Pipeline utilization with different fetch capabilities and different number of active threads

The reason for the low utilization in single threaded mode is the slow SDRAM. A 32 bit read access to the SDRAM in average takes about 6 cycles including instruction window management. Due to the mean bytecode length of 1.9 byte, the theoretical maximum pipeline utilization is about 35%. The circumstance that on the one hand several bytecodes are realized as microcode (and therefore need no fetch accesses) and on the other hand branch and memory latencies occur, the pipeline utilization varies from the theoretical value. With increasing thread number, the latencies can be bridged by the execution of instructions out of the instruction windows of other threads and during microcode execution, instructions of other threads can be fetched into the corresponding instruction window. The instruction windows deal as buffers to decouple fetch and execution phase and, hence, it is possible to execute instructions although it is currently not possible to fetch new ones (e.g. because of another memory access). This leads to a higher utilization of the basic pipeline. The instruction cache and the scratch RAM increase fetch throughput which results in a higher overall utilization independent of the number of running threads.

In a final step, we evaluated the impact of the running garbage collection (gc) to the application thread. In a former study (see [11,12]) we found out that a percentage of about 5-20% of computing power is enough for a sufficient garbage collection and an average application. These evaluations were made with a perfect instruction cache capability (simulation). Hence, a 100% utilization of the pipeline was possible and the performance of the application thread was harmed by the garbage collection in the corresponding amount. In the current implementation, the application thread cannot reach a pipeline utilization of 100% because of the long fetch latencies. That circumstance leads to the question, at which percentage the garbage collection influences the application and at which quantity.

For the evaluation, we used the KFL benchmark of the JOP processor again which uses no dynamic objects, i.e. there are no synchronization points between the application and the garbage collection. In parallel to the benchmark, we run the garbage collection with different percentages of computing power. Figure 6 shows the overall utilization of the pipeline and the impact of the garbage collection to the results of the benchmark. The measurements are made with active instruction cache for the application and the garbage collection running out of the scratch RAM. So, using GP scheduling is possible because the scheduler can guarantee the assigned percentage of computing power to the garbage collection.

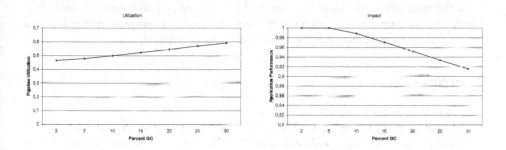

**Fig. 6.** Pipeline utilization and impact of GC to the application

As can be seen in the right diagram of figure 6, the impact of the garbage collection to the application is much less than the computing power assigned to it. Using up to 5% of the theoretical performance of the Komodo pipeline for gc has no effect to the running application. A value of about 15% gc which is enough for almost all applications, reduces the performance of the application only by 3%. The highest value of 30% gc is only required for applications that frequently allocate new objects and free old ones.

## 7   Conclusions and Future Work

We presented a highly integrated and user-friendly Java environment for embedded systems. The environment consists of a multithreaded processor IP core which executes native Java bytecode, a nearly complete implementation of the CLDC 1.1 JVM, and a tool for generating a boot file for the processor core. A processor integrated real-time scheduler and a dedicated design of the JVM allow the useability in real-time systems. The processor core is realized as an IP core for the Altera SoPC builder toolkit.

The main performance restricting topic is the instruction fetch procedure. We equipped the processor core with an instruction cache, a scratch RAM, and a combination of both. Our evaluations showed that the pipeline utilization of the basic version in single threaded mode is extremely low (33%) due to the fetch latencies. It could be raised to 67% running four threads and it could be further increased to the top utilization of 92% using an instruction cache and a scratch RAM.

Additionally, we evaluated the impact of a garbage collection running as helper thread in its own thread slot. The maximum impact of the garbage collection running with 30% of the total computing power to the application is about 8%. A feasible value of 10% garbage collection harms the application only by 1.5%.

In the future, we will redesign and enlarge the instruction cache because its speedup was very promising. Therefor we will use the integrated memory blocks as cache memory which allows a bigger cache without restricting clock frequency in the mentioned way. But, as a drawback, an additional cycle for the cache access has to be added. This cycle is not required for the currently implemented cache within the logic cells.

Besides the improvement of the pipeline utilization by the cache enhancement, we will try to increase the clock frequency. Without a frequency-restricting cache, the scheduler is the bottleneck which we have to optimize for a better performance.

Furthermore, the entire CDC standard will be realized and all bytecodes (including *double*) will be implemented. As a result, we want to offer a complete embedded Java environment for application in SoPCs with real-time requirements.

# References

1. RTSJ: http://www.rtsj.org/
2. Kreuzinger, J., Brinkschulte, U., Pfeffer, M., Uhrig, S., Ungerer, T.: Real-time Event-handling and Scheduling on a Multithreaded Java Microcontroller. Microprocessors and Microsystems 27, 19–31 (2003)
3. aicas: http://www.aicas.com/platforms.html
4. Sun: http://java.sun.com/javase/technologies/realtime.jsp#what
5. Schoberl, M.: JOP, http://www.jopdesign.com/
6. Schoeberl, M.: Real-time scheduling on a Java processor. In: Proceedings of the 10th International Conference on Real-Time and Embedded Computing Systems and Applications (RTCSA 2004), Gothenburg, Sweden (2004)
7. Schoeberl, M.: Real-time garbage collection for Java. In: Proceedings of the 9th IEEE International Symposium on Object and Component-Oriented Real-Time Distributed Computing (ISORC 2006), Gyeongju, Korea, pp. 424–432. IEEE Computer Society Press, Los Alamitos (2006)
8. Böhme, H.: JControl, http://www.jcontrol.org/
9. Kreuzinger, J., Schulz, A., Pfeffer, M., Ungerer, T., Brinkschulte, U., Krakowski, C.: Real-time Scheduling on Multithreaded Processors. In: 7th International Conference on Real-Time Computing Systems and Applications (RTCSA 2000), Cheju Island, South Korea, pp. 155–159 (2000)
10. Schoberl, M.: JavaBenchEmbedded V1.0, http://www.jopdesign.com/perf.jsp
11. Pfeffer, M.: Ein echtzeitfähiges Java-System für einen mehrfädigen Java-Mikrocontroller. PhD thesis, Faculty of Applied Informatics, University of Augsburg (2004)
12. Fuhrmann, S., Pfeffer, M., Kreuzinger, J., Ungerer, T., Brinkschulte, U.: Real-time Garbage Collection for a Multithreaded Java Microcontroller. In: Int. Symposium on Object-Oriented Real-Time Distributed Computing (ISORC 2001), Magdeburg, Germany, pp. 69–76 (2001)

# Parallel Memory Architecture for TTA Processor

Jarno K. Tanskanen[1], Teemu Pitkänen[1], Risto Mäkinen[2], and Jarmo Takala[1]

[1] Tampere University of Technology, P.O. Box 553, FIN-33101 Tampere, Finland
jarno.tanskanen@tut.fi, teemu.pitkanen@tut.fi, jarmo.takala@tut.fi
[2] Plenware Oy, P.O. Box 13, FIN-33201 Tampere, Finland
risto.makinen@plenware.fi

**Abstract.** A conflict resolving parallel data memory system for Transport Triggered Architecture (TTA) is described. The architecture is generic and reusable to support various application specific designs. With parallel memory, more area and power consuming multi-port memory can be replaced with single-port memory modules. Number of ports can be increased over what is available on a design library for multi-port memories. In an FFT TTA example, dual-port data memory was replaced by the proposed architecture. To avoid memory conflicts, the original code was rescheduled and the TTA core was regenerated for the new schedule. The original memory required an area higher by a factor of 3.38 and energy higher by a factor of 1.70. In this case, the energy consumption of the processor core increased so that system energy consumption remained about the same. However, the original system required an area higher by a factor of 1.89.

## 1 Introduction

TTA [1] belongs to a class of statically scheduled processors exploiting instruction level parallelism and resembles VLIW architecture. TTA framework can be efficiently used to generate optimized application specific cores, e.g., to DSP, telecommunication, and multimedia fields. Several applications from these fields contain well exploitable parallelism which can be used by increasing processing resources. As a result, higher performance can be obtained or power consumption could be decreased if the processing requirements are met with a lower clock frequency. Increasing the processing resources leads often also to the higher data bandwidth need which can be provided by multiple data memory ports. Multi-port memories have higher power consumption, require larger area, and longer access time than equally sized single-port memories. To avoid the cost of actual multi-port memory structure, the following different methods have been used in multiple-issue processors [2,3,4]. To provide $n$-port functionality, $n$ single port memory modules with the same data content could be employed. A write operation is always sent to all the memory modules to maintain the data coherence. As a drawback, the memory must be replicated $n$ times and no other accesses can be made during a write operation. A single port memory can be also accessed with a higher frequency than the processing frequency. However, this solution might not scale to higher port numbers. Finally, $n$ single port memories having total size of multi-port memory can be used to emulate the multi-port memory. Additional permutation and address computation circuitry is needed. Also, memory conflicts may exist. This is referred as parallel memory architecture. More recent multi-port memories have been presented in

S. Vassiliadis et al. (Eds.): SAMOS 2007, LNCS 4599, pp. 273–282, 2007.
© Springer-Verlag Berlin Heidelberg 2007

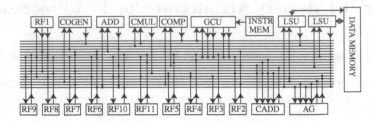

**Fig. 1.** Architecture of the FFTTA processor. ADD: Real adder. AG: Data address generator. CADD: Complex adder. CMUL: Complex multiplier. COGEN: Coefficient generator. COMP: Comparator unit. GCU: Global control unit. LSU: Load-store unit. RFx: Register files, containing total of 23 general purpose registers.

[5,6,7,8]. The parallel memory approach is the most promising to us since the application specific designs may have regular and predictable memory access patterns and the existing parallel memory theory can be used to construct specific storage schemes to avoid or significantly reduce the memory conflicts. Furthermore, the permutation and address computation circuitry might be fitted in the existing pipeline structure of the processor without lowering the clock frequency or increasing the number of pipeline stages. Often, the designs which consider conflict resolving multi-port memory architecture, employ some form of a simple low-order interleaving scheme [2,4,6,8]. On the other hand, new storage scheme proposals, like the one in [9] employed in this paper, concentrate to conflict-free, complex memory storage and rarely consider conflict resolving support. This paper presents a hardware in detail for dynamic conflict resolving. The proposed parallel memory architecture supports also alternative storage schemes.

## 2   TTA Processor Architecture

In the TTA programming model, the program specifies only the data transports to be performed by the interconnection network and operations occur as "side-effect" of data transports [1]. Operands to a function unit are input through ports and one of the ports is dedicated to be a trigger. When data is moved to the trigger port, execution of an operation is initiated. A TTA processor consists of a set of function units and register files of general-purpose registers. These structures are connected to an interconnection network, which connects the input and output ports of the resources. The architecture can be modified by adding or removing resources. Furthermore, special function units with user-defined functionality can be easily included. The structural VHDL description of the TTA core can be obtained using the processor generator of the TCE framework [10]. As an example, the FFTTA core [11,12] employed in Sec. 6 is illustrated in Fig. 1.

## 3   Parallel Memory

In a parallel memory system, a module assignment function $S(i)$ is a function of the incoming address $i$ from the LSU and determines the index of the memory module MM

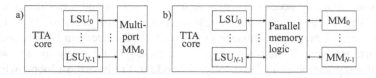

**Fig. 2.** Different data memory configurations: a) multi-port memory and b) single-port memories with parallel memory logic

where the data is located. The address for $MM_{S(i)}$ is determined by the address assignment function $a(i)$. If the parallel memory logic has $N$ LSUs, then $N$ module $S(i_k)$ and address $a(i_k)$ assignment functions are computed simultaneously, when $i_k$ refers to an address from $LSU_k$, $0 \le k < N$. Basically, $S(i)$ determines, how well the memory performs for a given parallel address trace. The most simple and well-known module assignment functions are low-order and high-order interleaving functions. Low-order interleaving, $S(i) = i \bmod N$, $a(i) = i/N$, is efficient for parallel access of successive array elements. High-order interleaving, $S(i) = i/(a_{max} + 1)$, $a(i) = i \bmod (a_{max} + 1)$, performs well when several different arrays are accessed in parallel. The term $(a_{max} + 1)$ is simply a constant telling the number of locations in each MM. In many cases, the operands for parallel processing can be stored so that conflict-free access to certain patterns is possible, e.g., rows, columns, blocks, forward- and backward-diagonals [13,14]. These are called the access formats. In general, the module assignment functions used for this purpose are linear [13] or so called XOR-schemes [15,16]. Multi-skewing scheme [17] provides versatile access formats. Storage schemes supporting stride accesses are presented in [18,19]. A brief overview of storage schemes is provided in [20]. For an FFT we employ a generic FFT parallel memory scheme proposed in [9].

## 4  Parallel Memory in a System

As shown in Fig. 2, the parallel memory logic is designed to locate between the load-store units (LSUs) and synchronous single-port memory modules (MMs). Parallel memory non-optimally emulates multi-port memory. Unlike in multi-port memories, in parallel memories there can be memory conflicts, i.e., one or more single port MMs are tried to be accessed more than once during a single cycle parallel memory access. It is not possible to find a generic storage scheme that is conflict-free for all address traces. In the case of memory conflict, parallel memory hardware recognizes the conflict, locks the processor by sending a lock request to the global control unit (GCU) of the TTA, performs conflicting accesses sequentially (requiring more cycles), and releases the lock. No modifications to software are required for correct functionality. Because of this locking behavior, the software does not know whether multi-port or parallel memory system is employed. However, possible conflicts increase the cycle count.

A multi-port memory can be replaced by a parallel memory architecture after the application code has been written. In this case, the software has been likely developed assuming an ideal multi-port memory and no attention is paid into the addresses of simultaneous memory accesses. It can be possible not to find a conflict-free parallel memory storage scheme since the address traces can be irregular, not fitting to typical access formats. A better performance in terms of clock cycles can be obtained when a conflict-free storage scheme is found for application specific access formats which are used in the application code. Especially, the code of the innermost loops, where typically the most of the execution time is spent, should be written so that the addresses of simultaneous memory accesses would not cause memory module access conflicts. This may require manual assembler optimization and regeneration of the hardware for the TTA core. However, as will be seen in Sec. 6, care must be taken since the modifications can increase the power consumption of the core.

The proposed parallel memory design is generic and re-usable. Application specific memory functions can be fitted in and generics are employed in the VHDL design so that several parallel memory components with different parameters (buswidths, number of ports, and memory functions) could be fitted in the same design. Parallel memory logic provides the needed address computation, interconnection, and conflict resolving logic. This is a matched memory system, i.e., the number of load store units (LSUs) and memory modules (MMs) is the same $N$. Often power-of-two $N$ is preferred.

## 5 Conflict Resolving Parallel Memory Architecture

Depending on the address $i_k$ and the module assignment function $S(i_k)$, the load or store operation from $LSU_k$ may refer to any MM. For this reason, crossbars are needed to route the MM input signals from the LSUs to the MMs. A crossbar is also needed to route the read (load) data from the MMs back to the LSUs, which made the corresponding load requests. These crossbars, related to read and write operations, are illustrated in Fig. 3 for $N = 4$. The read data from the MM needs to be saved to Rlatch registers at the correct moment when several accesses are made to the same MM during the conflict resolving. Rlatches are controlled by simple state machines.

For each $LSU_k$ and $MM_k$ pair, there is a control unit which correctly enables the $MM_k$ and drives the crossbar mux controls for the address (AddrMuxCtrl$_k$), read data (RdMuxCtrl$_k$), and write data (WrMuxCtrl$_k$) crossbar muxes related to $MM_k$. This control unit circuitry is shown in Fig. 5. The module assignment functions $S(i_k), 0 \le k < N$ are solved in parallel. They can be used to control read data crossbar so that $S(i_k)$ drives RdMuxCtrl$_k$ (connected to RdMux$_k$ in Fig. 3) at the correct moment. For various other control purposes, $S(i_k)$ indices are binary decoded and used to construct a binary control matrix. This is shown in Fig. 5, where a decoder produces a single control matrix row, CtrlMatrixRow$_k$. An example matrix is shown in Fig. 4a for $N = 4$. It can be seen that $LSU_0$ and $LSU_3$ are accessing $MM_3$, and $LSU_1$ and $LSU_2$ are accessing $MM_2$.

Each control unit needs to know which LSUs will access their memory module. This is obtained by transposing the control matrix. A transposed control matrix is shown in Fig. 4b. The $k$th row of the transposed matrix is delivered for the $k$th control unit. In Fig. 5, the control matrix composed from CtrlMatrixRows from all the control units is transposed and TCtrlMatrixRow$_k$ is obtained for each control unit $k$. If there are more than one '1' bits on any TCtrlMatrixRow of the transposed matrix, then there are corresponding number of memory conflicts. Parallel control units make always as

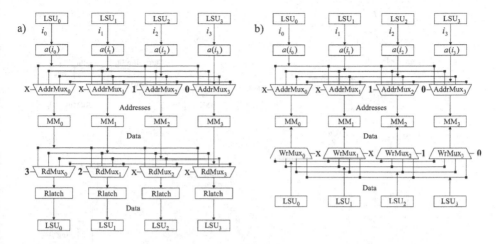

**Fig. 3.** Parallel data memory a) read (load) and b) write (store) operation examples and related address, read data, and write data crossbars. The fixed control signals for the muxes refer to the example case from the next page.

**a) Control matrix.**

| $MM_k$ | 0 | 1 | 2 | 3 | |
|--------|---|---|---|---|---|
| $LSU_0$ | 0 | 0 | 0 | 1 | $S(i_0)$ |
| $LSU_1$ | 0 | 0 | 1 | 0 | $S(i_1)$ |
| $LSU_2$ | 0 | 0 | 1 | 0 | $S(i_2)$ |
| $LSU_3$ | 0 | 0 | 0 | 1 | $S(i_3)$ |

**b) Transposed control matrix.**

| $LSU_k$ | 0 | 1 | 2 | 3 |
|---------|---|---|---|---|
| $MM_0$ | 0 | 0 | 0 | 0 |
| $MM_1$ | 0 | 0 | 0 | 0 |
| $MM_2$ | 0 | 1 | 1 | 0 |
| $MM_3$ | 1 | 0 | 0 | 1 |

**c) '1' bits served in the first cycle.**

| $LSU_k$ | 0 | 1 | 2 | 3 |
|---------|---|---|---|---|
| $MM_0$ | 0 | 0 | 0 | 0 |
| $MM_1$ | 0 | 0 | 0 | 0 |
| $MM_2$ | 0 | 0 | 1 | 0 |
| $MM_3$ | 0 | 0 | 0 | 1 |

**d) '1' bits served in the second cycle.**

| $LSU_k$ | 0 | 1 | 2 | 3 |
|---------|---|---|---|---|
| $MM_0$ | 0 | 0 | 0 | 0 |
| $MM_1$ | 0 | 0 | 0 | 0 |
| $MM_2$ | 0 | 1 | 0 | 0 |
| $MM_3$ | 1 | 0 | 0 | 0 |

**Fig. 4.** An example control matrix

many parallel accesses as possible. If there is a conflict, a priority encoder (PriEncoder) of the control unit $k$ selects the rightmost bit (LSU) on the TCtrlMatrixRow$_k$ in the first cycle, the next rightmost bit in the second cycle, and so on, until all the '1' bits on the row are served. '1' bits are reduced one by one with the XOR-ports producing NewTCtrlMatrixRow$_k$ in Fig. 5. This loop is enabled by the multiplexer controlled by LockrqReg signal. All the rows of the transposed control matrix are processed in parallel by the control units.

Each priority encoder has MoreToCome signal which tells if there are more '1' bits left. As is shown in Fig. 5, these MoreToCome signals are combined from each control unit to a single bit using an OR-tree. After registering, this bit becomes the lock request signal (LockrqReg) to be send to the processor. CurrLsu signal of the control unit tells the index of the LSU which is to be currently served by the memory module. The same position CurrLsu signal bits have been combined by $N$ OR-trees shown in Fig. 5. The resulted CurrLsuEnBits are used to control the state machines and RdMuxCtrl signals.

The transposed control matrices for the first and second memory cycles of the example are shown in Figs. 4c and 4d, respectively. The rows of these matrices are used

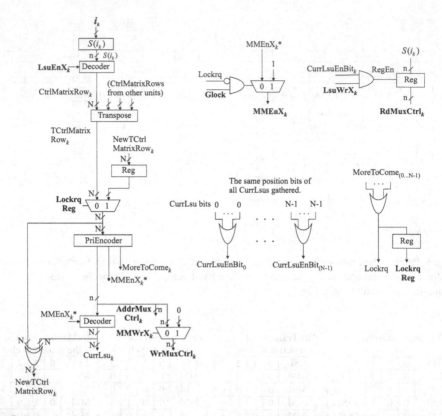

**Fig. 5.** Control unit logic. There is one control unit circuit for each LSU$_k$ and MM$_k$ pair. OR-trees producing CurrLsuEnBit and Lockrq signals combine the data from all the control units. $N$ refers to the number of memory ports and $n$ is the bit width of $N$. Block input and output signals are written in bold. LsuEnX$_k$, LsuWrX$_k$, and $i_k$ are coming from LSU$_k$. MMEnX$_k$ and MMWrX$_k$ are enable and R/W signals for MM$_k$. (With true multi-port memory, we would simply have LsuEnX$_k$ = MMEnX$_k$ and LsuWrX$_k$ = MMWrX$_k$.) Glock refers to the global lock signal coming from the processor core.

to control the corresponding muxes of the address (AddrMuxCtrl), write data (WrMux-Ctrl), (write mask), and write signal crossbars. The crossbar mux control signals for the control matrix given in Fig. 4 would be the following (x refers to don't care condition):

When all the accesses are load operations, the mux controls are:

Cycle 1: AddrMuxCtrl$_{0...3}$ = $\{x,x,2,3\}$, RdMuxCtrl$_{0...3}$ = $\{x,x,2,3\}$.
Cycle 2: AddrMuxCtrl$_{0...3}$ = $\{x,x,1,0\}$, RdMuxCtrl$_{0...3}$ = $\{3,2,x,x\}$.

When all the accesses are store operations, the mux controls are:

Cycle 1: AddrMuxCtrl$_{0...3}$ = WrMuxCtrl$_{0...3}$ = $\{x,x,2,3\}$.
Cycle 2: AddrMuxCtrl$_{0...3}$ = WrMuxCtrl$_{0...3}$ = $\{x,x,1,0\}$.

The cases for cycle 2 are shown with a simplified architecture in Fig. 3. In practice, of course, a parallel memory access may consist of both load and store operations. The main benefit of using the control matrix is that any kind of module assignment function, $S(i)$, can be included and used to construct the rows of the control matrix. After that, all the memory module and crossbar controls can be obtained automatically.

The lock request signal (LockrqReg) from the parallel memory logic is registered, and thus, the previous input values have to be saved to registers (i.e., addresses ($i_k$), memory enables (LsuEnX$_k$), write enables (LsuWrX$_k$), write data, and possible write masks), because otherwise they would be overwritten by new values. A simple state machine controls the saving of this data at the correct moment. The saving is not shown in the figures. The previous input values caused memory conflict(s) and the lock request and thus, they are needed to resolve the conflict(s) sequentially.

## 5.1 Scalable Hardware Modules

The design contains numerous scalable components including crossbars, OR-trees, decoders, and priority encoders:

- Three crossbars, one for addresses $a(i_k)$, read data, and write data. (When LSUs with subword support are used, an additional crossbar is needed for the write mask.) Each crossbar has $N$ input and output busses with corresponding bus widths. In addition, one smaller crossbar for single-bit memory write signals is needed.
- $(N + 1)$ OR-trees (each OR-tree merges an $N$-bit input into a single bit).
- $N$ priority encoders (each with an $N$-bit input).
- $2N$ decoders (each with a $log_2N$ bit input).

When the number of ports $N$ is increased, crossbars become more and more expensive, especially in terms of power and area, but also in delay. OR-trees, priority encoders, and decoders mainly affect the delay of the critical path of the design. The cost of the crossbars can be reduced by replacing one large parallel memory design with a couple of smaller designs. In that case, the LSUs would have access only to the MMs connected to their own parallel memory.

## 5.2 Pipelining

No new stages are added in the original system. The number of the LSU unit pipeline stages stays in three with the parallel memory architecture: the LSU signals going to and coming from the MMs are registered requiring two clock cycles, and the memory access itself requires one clock cycle. The input signals for the synchronous MMs (i.e., address, enable, write enable, write data (and write mask)) are read in the rising clock edge. Thus, because there is not much logic between the registered LSUs and input/output ports of the MMs, there is time available in the timing budget. The parallel memory logic between the LSU input and output registers (not shown) for read and write operations are illustrated in Fig. 6. The control logic, address crossbar, and write crossbar are located in the 1st cycle slot between the LSUs and MMs. The read crossbar is connected between the outputs of the MMs and LSUs. During a read clock cycle, the data appears to the MM data output bus after a related memory access delay. After that, the data goes through the read crossbar to the data input registers of the LSUs.

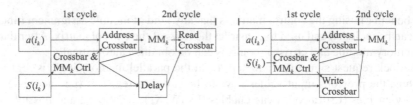

**Fig. 6.** Parallel memory pipelines: read on the left and write on the right

# 6   Experiments

In [11,12], a TTA processor for radix-4 1024-point FFT using a dual-port data memory is presented. To test the proposed parallel memory, the multi-port $2048 \times 32$ bits data memory was replaced with the parallel memory logic and two $1024 \times 32$-bit single-port MMs. A general form of the used storage scheme for FFT processors was presented in [9]. In our case $N = 2$ and the scheme reduces to a parity bit computation of an address $i_k$ from the $LSU_k$. The computed bit $S(i_k)$ defines which one of the MMs should be accessed. An address for the module $S(i_k)$ is simply defined by $a(i_k) = i_k/N$. Due to memory access conflicts, the execution time was much longer with the FFT parallel memory scheme (7775 vs. 5234 cycles). (The low- and high-order schemes required 7775 and 9293 cycles, respectively.) The FFT memory scheme would be conflict-free if the parallel accesses would always consist of two subsequent input operand loads or alternatively, two subsequent result stores. However, in the original, manually written code, the first access of the parallel memory access always loads an input operand and the second access stores a result. Because of the in-place implementation, the result address trace starts to follow the input operand address trace after 10 clock cycles (excluding the first stage). This disturbs the regularity of the parallel address trace.

For conflict-free data accesses, the original code was now manually rescheduled and the hardware was reconfigured. The FFTTA was synthesized to a 130nm, 1.5V CMOS standard cell ASIC technology with Synopsys Design Compiler. This was followed by a gate level simulation at 250 MHz. Synopsys Power Compiler was used for the power analysis.

Table 1 provides various data for the considered implementations. The proposed double load/double store approach (C,D in Table 1) does not fit to the system so well as the original code (A,B), because now there is parallel operand access but not parallel function units to directly consume the operands (or produce the results). As a result, the core for the new schedule (C,D) required additional resources in terms of busses, registers, and register ports. The power consumption of the core increased significantly and the total energy consumption of the system remained about the same (A vs. D). However, the original system (A) required an area higher by a factor of 1.89 than the system with parallel memory (D). As expected, the data memory results were improved and the original data memory (A) required an area higher by a factor of 3.38 and an energy higher by a factor of 1.70 than the parallel memory (D).

The synthesis results for the parallel memory architecture only, with $N = 2, 4, 8$ ports (or MMs) are shown in Table 2. The size of a single-port MM was kept constant in $1024 \times 32$ bits. The related $S(i)$ and $a(i)$ were derived from the FFT storage scheme in

**Table 1.** Radix-4 1024-point FFT implementation on TTA

|   |   |   | Area/kgates | Energy/$\mu$J | Power/mW | Clock cycles |
|---|---|---|---|---|---|---|
| A | Original | DP Data Mem | 102.4 | 0.56 | 27.0 | |
|   | Schedule | Core + others | 37.6 | 0.98 | 46.6 | |
|   |   | *Total* | 140.0 | 1.54 | 73.6 | 5234 |
| B | Original | Par Data Mem | 30.2 | 0.36 | 11.7 | |
|   | Schedule | Core + others | 37.7 | 1.01 | 32.5 | |
|   |   | *Total* | 67.9 | 1.37 | 44.2 | 7775 |
| C | Modified | DP Data Mem | 102.4 | 0.57 | 27.2 | |
|   | Schedule | Core + others | 43.2 | 1.20 | 57.7 | |
|   |   | *Total* | 145.6 | 1.77 | 84.9 | 5208 |
| D | Modified | Par Data Mem | 30.3 | 0.33 | 16.1 | |
|   | Schedule | Core + others | 43.7 | 1.21 | 58.2 | |
|   |   | *Total* | 74.0 | 1.55 | 74.3 | 5208 |

**Table 2.** Demonstration of the scalability of the parallel memory implementation

|   |   | $N = 2$ | $N = 4$ | $N = 8$ |
|---|---|---|---|---|
| Total memory size/32-bit words | | 2048 | 4096 | 8192 |
| Area/kgates | Control logic | 0.2 | 0.8 | 2.9 |
|   | Crossbars | 1.9 | 6.1 | 16.7 |
|   | Memory | 27.8 | 55.7 | 111.4 |
|   | *Total* | 29.9 | 62.6 | 131.0 |
| Clock period/ns | | 4.0 | 5.1 | 6.3 |

[9]. Note that the dual-port memory of size 2048 × 32 in Table 1 requires an area higher by a factor of 1.64 than the parallel memory of size 4096 × 32 with four ports.

## 7  Conclusion

A conflict resolving parallel data memory for TTA was proposed. With a parallel memory, more area and power consuming multi-port memory module can be replaced with single-port memory modules. For an application specific processor the address trace can be highly regular and predictable, and there can be a good change to find well performing storage scheme. The existing parallel memory theory can be used to construct application specific storage schemes. In an FFT TTA example, a dual-port data memory was replaced by the proposed architecture. To avoid memory conflicts, the original code was rescheduled and the TTA core was regenerated for the new schedule. Care must be taken in this approach since, e.g., in this specific case, the power consumption of the core increased enough to consume the power savings from the data memory. As a benefit, the area was divided by 1.89 compared to the original system.

# References

1. Corporaal, H.: Microprocessor Architectures: From VLIW to TTA. John Wiley & Sons, Chichester, UK (1997)
2. Sohi, G.S., Franklin, M.: High-bandwidth data memory systems for superscalar processors. In: Proc. 4th Int. Conf. Architectural Support for Programming Languages and Operating Systems, Santa Clara, CA, U.S.A., pp. 53–62 (April 8-11, 1991)
3. Juan, T., Navarro, J.J., Temam, O.: Data caches for superscalar processors. In: Proc. 11th Int. Conf. Supercomputing, Vienna, Austria, pp. 60–67 (July 7-11, 1997)
4. Rivers, J.A., Tyson, G.S., Davidson, E.S., Austin, T.M.: On high-bandwidth data cache design for multi-issue processors. In: Proc. 30th Ann. ACM/IEEE Int. Symp. Microarchitecture, pp. 46–56. Research Triangle Park, NC, U.S.A (December 1-3, 1997)
5. Sawyer, N., Defossez, M.: Quad-port memories in Virtex devices. Xilinx application note, XAPP228 (v1.0) (September 24, 2002)
6. Zhu, Z., Johguchi, K., Mattausch, H.J., Koide, T., Hirakawa, T., Hironaka, T.: A novel hierarchical multi-port cache. In: Proc. 29th European Solid-State Circuits Conf., Estoril, Portugal, pp. 405–408 (September 16-18, 2003)
7. Patel, K., Macii, E., Poncino, M.: Energy-performance tradeoffs for the shared memory in multi-processor systems-on-chip. In: Proc. IEEE Int. Symp. Circuits and Systems, Vancouver, British Columbia, Canada, May 23-26, 2004, vol. 2, pp. 361–364. IEEE Computer Society Press, Los Alamitos (2004)
8. Ang, S.S., Constantinides, G., Cheung, P., Luk, W.: A flexible multi-port caching scheme for reconfigurable platforms. In: Bertels, K., Cardoso, J.M.P., Vassiliadis, S. (eds.) ARC 2006. LNCS, vol. 3985, pp. 205–216. Springer, Heidelberg (2006)
9. Takala, J.H., Järvinen, T.S., Sorokin, H.T.: Conflict-free parallel memory access scheme for FFT processors. In: Proc. IEEE Int. Symp. Circuits and Systems, Bangkok, Thailand, May 25-28, 2003, vol. 4, pp. 524–527. IEEE Computer Society Press, Los Alamitos (2003)
10. Jääskeläinen, P., Guzma, V., Cilio, A., Takala, J.: Codesign toolset for application-specific instruction-set processors. In: Proc. SPIE - Multimedia on Mobile Devices (2007)
11. Mäkinen, R.: Fast Fourier transform on transport triggered architectures. M.Sc. Thesis, Tampere University of Technology, Tampere, Finland (October 2005)
12. Pitkänen, T., Mäkinen, R., Heikkinen, J., Partanen, T., Takala, J.: Low-power, high-performance TTA processor for 1024-point Fast Fourier transform. In: Vassiliadis, S., Wong, S., Hämäläinen, T.D. (eds.) SAMOS 2006. LNCS, vol. 4017, pp. 227–236. Springer, Heidelberg (2006)
13. Budnik, P., Kuck, D.J.: The organization and use of parallel memories. IEEE Trans. Comput. C-20(12), 1566–1569 (1971)
14. Kim, K., Prasanna, V.K.: Latin squares for parallel array access. IEEE Trans. Parallel and Distrib. Syst. 4(4), 361–370 (1993)
15. Frailong, J.M., Jalby, W., Lenfant, J.: XOR-schemes: a flexible data organization in parallel memories. In: Proc. Int. Conf. Parallel Processing, pp. 276–283 (August 20-23, 1985)
16. Liu, Z., Li, X.: XOR storage schemes for frequently used data patterns. Journal of Parallel and Distributed Computing 25(2), 162–173 (1995)
17. Deb, A.: Multiskewing – a novel technique for optimal parallel memory access. IEEE Trans. Parallel and Distrib. Syst. 7(6), 595–604 (1996)
18. Rau, B.R.: Pseudo-randomly interleaved memory. In: Proc. 18th Ann. Int. Symp. Computer Architecture, Toronto, Ontario, Canada, pp. 74–83 (May 27-30, 1991)
19. Seznec, A., Lenfant, J.: Odd memory systems: a new approach. Journal of Parallel and Distributed Computing 26(2), 248–256 (1995)
20. Tanskanen, J.K., Creutzburg, R., Niittylahti, J.T.: On design of parallel memory access schemes for video coding. J. VLSI Signal Processing 40(2), 215–237 (2005)

# A Linear Complexity Algorithm for the Generation of Multiple Input Single Output Instructions of Variable Size*

Carlo Galuzzi, Koen Bertels, and Stamatis Vassiliadis

Computer Engineering, EEMCS
TU Delft
{C.Galuzzi, K.L.M.Bertels, S.Vassiliadis}@ewi.tudelft.nl

**Abstract.** The Instruction-Set extension problem has been one of the major topics in the last years and it is the addition of a set of new complex instructions to a given Instruction-Set. This problem in its general formulation requires an exhaustive search of the design space to identify the candidate instructions. This search turns into an exponential complexity of the solution. In this paper we propose an algorithm for the generation of Multiple Input Single Output instructions of variable size which can be directly selected or combined for Instruction-Set extension. Additionally, the algorithm is suitable for inclusion in a design flow for automatic generation of MIMO instructions. The proposed algorithm is not restricted to basic block level and has linear complexity with the number of processed elements.

## 1 Introduction

The use of electronic devices has became a routine in our everyday life. Just consider the devices we are using in the daily basis such as mobile phones, digital cameras, electronic protection systems in the cars, etc. This great variety of devices can be implemented using different approaches and technologies. Usually these functionalities are implemented using either *General Purpose Processors* (GPPs), or *Application-Specific Integrated Circuits* (ASICs), or *Application-Specific Instruction-Set Processors* (ASIPs). GPPs can be used in many different applications in contrast to ASICs which are processors designed for a specific application such as the processor in a TV set top box.

Last years, processors with a customizable architecture, also known as *Application-Specific Instruction-Set Processors* (ASIPs), have became more and more popular. ASIPs are situated in between GPPs and ASICs: they have a *partially customizable Instruction Set* and perform only a limited number of tasks so giving a tradeoff between flexibility, performance and cost. Although performance of an ASIP is usually lower than an ASIC, the design time and non-recurring engineering costs (the one-time charge for photomask development, test, prototype

---

* This work was supported by the European Union in the context of the MORPHEUS project Num. 027342.

S. Vassiliadis et al. (Eds.): SAMOS 2007, LNCS 4599, pp. 283–293, 2007.

tooling, and associated engineering costs) can be amortized with the multiple addressable applications tuning the processor characteristics toward the requirements of the specific application.

Maximizing the performance of the ASIP is crucial. One of the key issues involves the choice of an *optimal* instruction-set for the specific application given. Optimality can refer to power consumption, chip area, code size, cycle count and/or operating frequency. A computable solution is not always feasible due to many subproblems such as design space exploration or combinatorial problems. In those cases heuristics are used to find a *close-to-optimal* solution.

Basically there are two types of Instruction-Set customizations which can be pursued: the first and most radical one is to generate a complete instruction set for the specific applications [1,2,3]. The second and less drastic one extends an existing instruction set with instructions specialized for a given domain [4,5,6,7]. In both cases the goal is to design an instruction set containing the most important operations needed by the application to maximize the performance.

The first step in this process is the identification of the operations that should be implemented in hardware and the ones that will be executed in software. The operations implemented in hardware are implemented as peripheral devices or they can be incorporated in the processor as new instructions and/or special functional units integrated on the processor.

In this paper we present a linear complexity algorithm for the generation of Multiple Input Single Output (MISO) instructions which can directly undergo a selection process for hardware-software partitioning or can be clustered with different policies for the generation of MIMO instructions [7,8]. More specifically, the main contributions of this paper are:

- an overall linear complexity of the proposed algorithm. The generation of complex instructions is a well known NP problem and its solution requires, in the worst case, an exhaustive search of the design space which turns into an exponential complexity of the solution. Our algorithms generate MISO instructions of variable size suitable for inclusion in a design flow for automatic generation of MIMO instructions as the ones proposed in [7,8]. Our approach springs from the notion of MAXMISO introduced by [9] and, in a similar way, it requires linear complexity in the number of processed elements as proven in Section 4.
- the proposed approach is not restricted to basic-block level analysis and can be applied directly to large kernels.

The paper is structured as follows. In Section 2, background information and related works are provided. In Section 3 and 4, the basic definitions and the algorithm for MISO instruction generation are presented. Concluding remarks and an outline of research conducted are given in Section 5.

## 2   Background and Related Works

The algorithms for Instruction Set Extensions usually select clusters of operations which can be implemented in hardware as single instructions while providing maximal performance improvement. Basically, there are two types of clusters that can be selected, based on the number of output values: MISO or MIMO. Accordingly, there are two types of algorithms for Instruction Set Extensions that are briefly presented in this section.

Concerning the first category, a representative example is introduced in [9] which addresses the generation of MISO instructions of maximal size, called MAXMISO. The proposed algorithm exhaustively enumerates all MAXMISOs. Its complexity is linear with the number of nodes. The reported performance improvement is of few processor cycles per newly added instruction. The approach presented in [10] targets the generation of general MISO instructions. The exponential number of candidate instructions turns into an exponential complexity of the solution in the general case. As a consequence, heuristic and additional area constraints are introduced to allow an efficient generation. The difference between the complexity of the two approaches is due to the properties of MISOs and MAXMISOs: while the enumeration of the first is similar to the subgraph enumeration problem (which is exponential) the intersection of MAXMISOs is empty and then once a MAXMISO is identified, its nodes are removed from the set of nodes that have to be successively analyzed. In this way the MAXMISOs are enumerated with linear complexity in the number of nodes.

The algorithms included in the second category are more general and provide more significant performance improvement. However, they have exponential complexity. For example, in [5] the identification algorithm detects optimal convex MIMO subgraphs but the computational complexity is exponential. A similar approach described in [11] proposes the enumeration of all the instructions based on the number of inputs, outputs, area and convexity. The selection problem is not addressed. In [6] the authors target the identification of convex clusters of operations under given input and output constraints. The clusters are identified with a ILP based methodology similar to the one proposed in [7]. The main difference is that in [6] the authors iteratively solve ILP problems for each basic block, while in [7] the authors have one global ILP problem for the entire procedure. Additionally, the convexity is addressed differently: in [6], the convexity is verified at each iteration, while in [7] it is guaranteed by construction. Other approaches cluster operations by considering the frequency of execution or the occurrence of specific nodes [4,12] or regularity [13]. Still others impose limitation on the number of operands [14,15,16,17] and use heuristics to generate sets of custom instructions which therefore can not be globally optimal.

In this paper we propose a linear complexity algorithm based on the notion of MAXMISO introduced by [9]. Although the algorithm for the generation of MAXMISOs instructions requires linear complexity in the number of processed elements, it is not always possible to implement MAXMISOs directly in hardware due to a relatively high number of inputs. A way to address this problem is the use of the MAXMISO algorithm for the generation of MISO instructions of reduced size as described in Section 4. Moreover the generated instructions can be directly selected for hardware implementation as well as clustered with different policies for the generation of MIMO instructions [7,8].

# 3   Theoretical Background

## 3.1   MISO and MIMO Graphs

In order to formally present the approach previously presented, we first introduce the necessary definitions and the theoretical foundation of our solution. We
assume that the input dataflow graph is a DAG $G = (V, E)$, where $V$ is the set
of nodes and $E$ is the set of edges. The nodes represent primitive operations,
more specifically assembler-like operations, and the edges represent the data dependencies. The nodes can have two inputs at most and their single output can
be input to multiple nodes.

Basically, there are two types of subgraphs that can be identified inside a
graph: Multiple Input Single Output (MISO) and Multiple Input Multiple Output (MIMO).

**Definition 1.** *Let $G^* \subseteq G$ be a subgraph of $G$ with $V^* \subseteq V$ set of nodes and
$E^* \subseteq E$ set of edges. $G^*$ is a MISO of root $r \in V^*$ provided that $\forall\, v_i \in V^*$ there
exists a path[1] $[v_i \to r]$, and every path $[v_i \to r]$ is entirely contained in $G^*$.*

By Definition 1, A MISO is a connected graph. A MIMO, defined as the union of
$m \geq 1$ MISOs can be either connected or disconnected. Let $G_{MISO}$ and $G_{MIMO}$
be the sets of subgraphs of $G$ containing all MISOs and MIMOs respectively.
An exhaustive enumeration of the MISOs contained in $G$ gives all the necessary
building blocks to generate all possible MIMOs. This faces with the exponential
order of $G_{MISO}$, and since $G_{MISO} \subset G_{MIMO}$[2], of $G_{MIMO}$. A reduction of the
number of the building blocks reduces the total number of MIMOs which it is
possible to generate. Anyhow, it can *drastically reduces* the overall complexity
of the generation process as well. A trade-off between complexity and quality of
the solution can be achieved considering MISO graphs with specific properties.

## 3.2   MAXMISO and SUBMAXMISO

**Definition 2.** *A MISO $G^*(V^*, E^*) \subset G(V, E)$ is a MAXMISO (MM) if $\forall v_i \in
V \backslash V^*$, $G^+(V^* \cup \{v_i\}, E^+)$ is not a MISO.*

It is known from the set-theory that each MISO is either maximal (a MAX-
MISO) or there exists a maximal element containing it [8,9]. [9] observed that if
$A, B$ are two MAXMISOs, then $A \cap B = \emptyset$. This implies that the MAXMISOs
contained in a graph can be enumerated with *linear complexity in the number
of its nodes* (see. [9,7,8]).

Let $v \in V$ be a node of $G$ and let $\text{LEV} : V \to \mathbb{N}$ be the integer function which
associates a level to each node, defined as follows:

– $\text{LEV}(v) = 0$, if $v$ is an input node of $G$;

---

[1] A path is a sequence of nodes and edges, where the vertices are all distinct.
[2] $G_{MISO} = \{G^* \subset G, \ s.t. \ N_{Out} = 1\} \subset \{G^* \subset G, \ s.t. \ N_{Out} \geq 1\} = G_{MIMO}$.

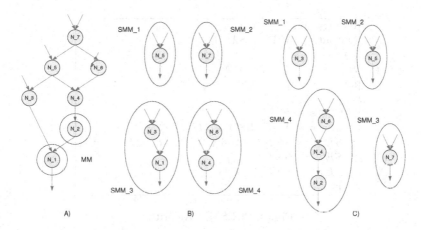

**Fig. 1.** SMMs of a MAXMISO with different nodes removed: $a$) a MAXMISO MM, $b$) SMMs of $MM \setminus \{N_2\}$, $c$) SMMs of $MM \setminus \{N_1\}$

- $\text{LEV}(v) = \alpha > 0$, if there are $\alpha$ nodes on the longest path from $v$ and the level 0 of the input nodes.

Clearly $\text{LEV}(\cdot) \in [0, +\infty)$ and the maximum level $d \in \mathbb{N}$ of its nodes is called the **depth** of the graph.

**Definition 3.** *The level of a MAXMISO $MM_i \in G$ is defined as follows:*

$$\text{LEV}(MM_i) = \text{LEV}(f(MM_i)). \tag{1}$$

*where $f : G \rightarrow \hat{G}$ is the collapsing function, the function which collapses the MAXMISOs of $G$ in nodes of the graph $\hat{G}$ (see [8]).*

Let's consider a $MAXMISO$ $MM_i$. Each node $v_j \in MM_i$ belongs to level $\text{LEV}(v_j)$. Let $\overline{v} \in MM_i$, with $0 \neq \text{LEV}(\overline{v}) \leq d$. If we apply the MAXMISO algorithm to $MM_i \setminus \{\overline{v}\}$, each MAXMISO identified in the graph is called a SUBMAXMISO (SMM) of $MM_i \setminus \{\overline{v}\}$ (or, shortly, of $MM_i$). Clearly the set of the SMMs tightly depends on the choice of $\overline{v}$ (see Figure 1). For example $\overline{v}$ can be either an exit node (Figure 1c), or an inner node randomly chosen (Figure 1b) or a node with specific properties like area or power consumption below or above a certain threshold previously defined.

The definition of level of a SMM is the obvious extension to SMM of the definition of level of a MAXMISO.

## 4    The Algorithm for MISO Instruction Generation

In Figure 2 and 3 we present the FIX SMM algorithm and the VARIABLE SMM algorithm respectively. The main difference between the two algorithms is represented by the choice of the node selected for the generation of the SUB-MAXMISOs, as outlined in Section 3.2.

```
Input:= MM₁, ..., MMₙ
Output:= SMM₁, ...SMMₖ
─
SET₁, SET₂, SET₃ = ∅
for i = 1..n do
  {
  Choose v̄ᵢ ∈ MMᵢ
  Generate MAXMISO of MMᵢ \ {v̄ᵢ}
  SET₁ := SET₁ ∪ {MAXMISOs of MMᵢ \ {v̄ᵢ}}
  SET₂ := SET₂ ∪ {v̄ᵢ}
  SET₃ := SET₁ ∪ SET₂
  }
```

**Fig. 2.** FIX SMM Algorithm

## a) FIX SMM Algorithm

The main steps of this algorithm are described in Figure 2 and depicted in Figure 4:

*a)* Given the DAG $G$ of an application, the graph is partitioned in MAXMISOs;
*b)* For each MAXMISO $MM_i$ we select a node $\bar{v}_i \in MM_i$;
*c)* $MM_i \setminus \bar{v}_i$ is partitioned in MAXMISOs;
*d)* Generate the set $SET_1$ of the SMMs, the set $SET_2$ of the nodes selected and the set $SET_3$ union of $SET_1$ and $SET_2$.

We have the following property:

*Property 1. The complexity of the algorithm is linear in the number of node analyzed.*

*Proof.* This follows from the empty intersection of two MAXMISOs. Let $A$ and $B$ two MAXMISOs, and $\bar{v}_1 \in A$ and $\bar{v}_2 \in B$. Therefore $A \cap B = \emptyset$. This means that:

$$\forall \, MM_i \in A \setminus \bar{v}_1 \text{ and } \forall \, MM_j \in B \setminus \bar{v}_2, \quad MM_i \cap MM_j = \emptyset. \tag{2}$$

∎

## b) VARIABLE SMM Algorithm

The main steps of this algorithm are described in Figure 2 and depicted in Figure 4:

*a)* Given the DAG $G$ of an application, the graph is partitioned in MAXMISOs;
*b)* For each MAXMISO $MM_i$ a node $\bar{v}_i \in MM_i$ is selected;
*c)* $MM_i \setminus \bar{v}_i$ is partitioned in MAXMISOs. If the set of SMMs does not satisfy a specific property $P_i$ a different node is selected and the SMMs are regenerated till the property is satisfied.

```
Input:= MM₁, ..., MMₙ
Input:= Properties P₁, ..., Pₙ
Output:= SMM₁, ...SMMₖ
—
SET₁, SET₂, SET₃ = ∅
for i = 1..n do
  {
    repeat
    {
      Choose v̄ᵢ ∈ MMᵢ
      Generate MAXMISO of MMᵢ \ {v̄ᵢ}
    }
    until Pᵢ is satisfied
    SET₁ := SET₁ ∪ {MAXMISOs of MMᵢ \ {v̄ᵢ}}
    SET₂ := SET₂ ∪ {v̄ᵢ}
    SET₃ := SET₁ ∪ SET₂
  }
```

**Fig. 3.** VARIABLE SMM Algorithm

d) The set $SET_1$ of the SMMs, the set $SET_2$ of the nodes selected and the set $SET_3$ union of $SET_1$ and $SET_2$ are generated.

We have the following properties:

*Property 2.* The complexity of the algorithm is linear in the number of nodes analyzed (as well as for the FIX SMM algorithm as a consequence of the properties of the MAXMISOs).

*Property 3.* The maximum number of iterations of the algorithm is less than or equal to the order of $G^3$.

*Proof.* This follows by the fact that the MAXMISOs are a partition of the graph. For each MAXMISO $MM_i$ is therefore possible to select $n_i$ different nodes. Independently by the value of $n_i$ we have that $\Sigma_i n_i = n$. ∎

*Remark 1.* The algorithm presented in this paper in its two versions, namely FIX SMM, and VARIABLE SMM, is suitable for an iterative process for the generation of MISO instructions of relatively smaller size, when severe input constraints are applied. This can be obtained using as input of the algorithm(s), instead of the set of MAXMISOs $MM_1, ..., MM_n$, the final set $SET_1$ as described in Section 4.

### 4.1   Application

In [7,8] we presented two methods for the automatic generation of convex MIMO instructions based on the following result:

---

[3] The order of a graph $G(V, E)$ with $V$ set of nodes and $E$ set of edges is the order of $V$.

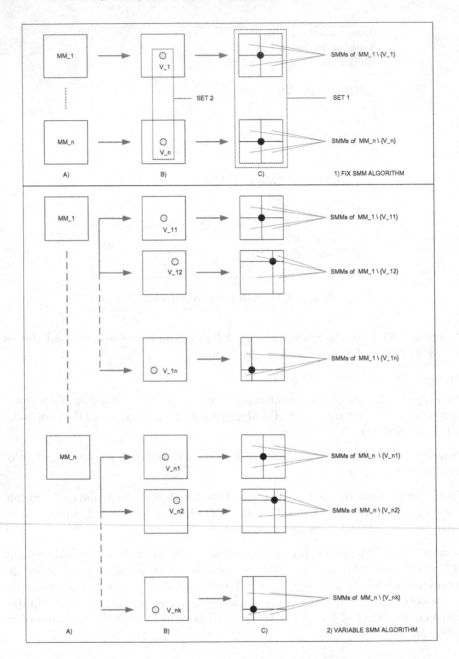

**Fig. 4.** Description of the main steps required by the algorithms for the generation of the SMMs: 1) FIX SMM algorithm and 2) VARIABLE SMM algorithm. The main steps are A) MM generation, B) selection of the node to remove, and C) SMM generation. (NB In the figure, each MAXMISO is partitioned in 4 SMMs of random size for explanatory reasons. As we have seen in Figure 1 the SMMs depend on the node chosen.)

**Theorem 1.** *Let $G$ be a DAG and $A, B \subset G$ two MAXMISOs. Let $\mathrm{LEV}(A) \geq \mathrm{LEV}(B)$ be the levels of $A$ and $B$ respectively. Let $C = A \cup B$. If*

$$\mathrm{LEV}(A) - \mathrm{LEV}(B) \in \{0, 1\} \tag{3}$$

*then $C$ is a convex MIMO. Moreover*

- *$C$ is disconnected if the difference is 0.*
- *Any combination of MAXMISOs at the same level or at two consecutive levels is a convex MIMO.*

We note that a subgraph $G^* \subset G$ is convex if there exists no path between two nodes of $G^*$ which involves a node of $G \backslash G^*$. Convexity guarantees a proper and feasible scheduling of the new instructions which respects the dependencies.

This theorem can be extended to SMMs.

**Corollary 1.** *Any combination of SMMs at the same level or at two consecutive levels is a convex MIMO.*

*Proof.* This follows by the definition of SMM: given a graph $G$, a MAXMISO $MM \subset G$ and a node $\bar{v} \in MM$ the SMMs of $MM$ are the MAXMISOs of $G \backslash \bar{v}$. This means that if $A$ and $B$ are SMMs, then $A \cap B = \emptyset$. Therefore all the hypothesis of Theorem 1 are satisfied. ∎

Basically the two approaches cluster optimally MAXMISOs at the same level [7], or heuristically at different levels [8], in convex MIMOs to implement in hardware reducing the execution time. Both approaches target the Molen organization [18] which allows for a virtually unlimited number of new instructions to be executed on the reconfigurable hardware, without limiting the number of input/output values.

Although the speed-up achieved by the two approaches is similar to the speed-up achieved for state-of-the-art algorithms for automatic instruction-set extension, the main limitation is represented by the MAXMISOs. The MAXMISOs are used as building block to generate convex MIMO instructions since they can be enumerated linearly with the number of nodes and they represent a trade off between quality of the solution and complexity of the approach. Nevertheless the speed-up is limited by a high number of inputs and outputs, on average, of the clusters selected for hardware implementation.

Every time a cluster undergoes a check to verify if a specific property is verified, the complexity of the approach increases. A limitation on the number of inputs and outputs of the clusters keeping a linear complexity, can then be obtained using SMMs instead of MMs. By Property 1 and 2 we know that SMMs can be enumerated with linear complexity in the number of nodes. *This means that the complexity of the two approaches does not increase if we use SMMs instead of MMs as building blocks to generate convex MIMO instructions.*

We can observe the following:

*Remark 2.* The partitioning of a graph in MAXMISOs generate a MMs-cover of the graph. Since every SUBMAXMISO is contained in a MAXMISO the

SMMs-cover is a refinement of the MMs-cover[4] [19]. This implies that the number of convex MIMO instructions which is possible to generate increases. More detailed, if there are $n_1$ MAXMISOs and $n_2$ SUBMAXMISOs with $n_2 = n_1 + \alpha$ and $\alpha > 0$, the additional MIMOs that is possible to generate are:

$$2^{n_1}(2^\alpha - 1). \tag{4}$$

## 5  Conclusions

In this paper, we have introduced an algorithm which enumerates with linear complexity in the number of processed elements, MISO instructions of variable size, and more specifically SUBMAXMISOs. These instructions can directly undergo a selection process for hardware-software partitioning or can be clustered with different policies for the generation of MIMO instructions. The algorithms can be included in an automatic design flow for the automatic generation of MIMO instructions as the ones proposed in [7,8]. In our future work we intend to verify with experimental results the benefit of the insertion of the SUB-MAXMISOs generation algorithm in such a design flow. Moreover we aim to design and test additional algorithms for the generation of (convex) MIMO instructions.

## References

1. Holmer, B.: Automatic Design of Computer Instruction Sets. PhD thesis, University of California, Berkeley (1993)
2. Huang, I., Despain, A.: Generating instruction sets and microarchitectures from applications. In: Proceedings of ICCAD '94 (1994)
3. Van Praet, J., Goossens, G., Lanneer, D., Man, H.D.: Instruction set definition and instruction selection for asips. In: Proceedings of ISSS '94 (1994)
4. Kastner, R., Kaplan, A., Memik, S.O., Bozorgzadeh, E.: Instruction generation for hybrid reconfigurable systems. ACM Trans. Des. Autom. Electron. Syst. 7(4), 605–627 (2002)
5. Atasu, K., Pozzi, L., Ienne, P.: Automatic application-specific instruction-set extensions under microarchitectural constraints. In: Proceedings of DAC '03 (2003)
6. Atasu, K., Dündar, G., Özturan, C.: An integer linear programming approach for identifying instruction-set extensions. In: Proceedings of CODES+ISSS '05 (2005)
7. Galuzzi, C., Panainte, E.M., Yankova, Y., Bertels, K., Vassiliadis, S.: Automatic selection of application-specific instruction-set extensions. In: Proceedings of CODES+ISSS '06 (2006)
8. Galuzzi, C., Bertels, K., Vassiliadis, S.: A linear complexity algorithm for the automatic generation of convex multiple input multiple output instructions. In: Proceedings of ARC 2007 (March 27-29, 2007)
9. Alippi, C., Fornaciari, W., Pozzi, L., Sami, M.: A dag-based design approach for reconfigurable vliw processors. In: Proceedings of DATE '99 (1999)

---

[4] A refinement of a cover C of X is a new cover D of X such that every set in D is contained in some set in C.

10. Cong, J., Fan, Y., Han, G., Zhang, Z.: Application-specific instruction generation for configurable processor architectures. In: Proceedings of FPGA '04 (2004)
11. Yu, P., Mitra, T.: Scalable custom instructions identification for instruction-set extensible processors. In: Proceedings of CASES '04 (2004)
12. Sun, F., Ravi, S., Raghunathan, A., Jha, N.K.: Synthesis of custom processors based on extensible platforms. In: Proceedings of ICCAD '02 (2002)
13. Brisk, P., Kaplan, A., Kastner, R., Sarrafzadeh, M.: Instruction generation and regularity extraction for reconfigurable processors. In: Proceedings of CASES '02 (2002)
14. Goodwin, D., Petkov, D.: Automatic generation of application specific processors. In: Proceedings of CASES '03 (2003)
15. Choi, H., Hwang, S.H., Kyung, C.M., Park, I.C.: Synthesis of application specific instructions for embedded dsp software. In: Proceedings of ICCAD '98 (1998)
16. Baleani, M., Gennari, F., Jiang, Y., Patel, Y., Brayton, R.K., Sangiovanni-Vincentelli, A.: Hw/sw partitioning and code generation of embedded control applications on a reconfigurable architecture platform. In: Proceedings of CODES '02 (2002)
17. Clark, N., Zhong, H., Mahlke, S.: Processor acceleration through automated instruction set customization. In: Proceedings of MICRO 36
18. Vassiliadis, S., Wong, S., Gaydadjiev, G., Bertels, K., Kuzmanov, G., Panainte, E.M.: The molen polymorphic processor. IEEE Trans. Comput. 53(11), 1363–1375 (2004)
19. Kosniowski, C.: A First Course in Algebraic Topology. Cambridge University Press, Cambridge (1980)

# Automated Power Gating of Registers Using CoDeL and FSM Branch Prediction

Nainesh Agarwal and Nikitas J. Dimopoulos

Department of Electrical and Computer Engineering
University of Victoria
Victoria, B.C., Canada
{nagarwal,nikitas}@ece.uvic.ca

**Abstract.** In this paper, we use the CoDeL hardware design platform to analyze the potential and performance impact of power gating individual registers. For each register, we examine the percentage of clock cycles for which they can be powered off, and the loss of performance incurred as a result of waiting for the power to be restored. We propose a static gating method, with very low area overhead, which uses the information available to the CoDeL compiler to predict, at compile time, when the registers can be powered off and when they can be powered on. Static branch prediction is used in the compiler to more intelligently traverse the finite state machine description of the circuit to discover gating opportunities. We compare this static CoDeL based gating method to a dynamic, time-based technique. Using the DSPstone benchmark circuits for evaluation, we find that CoDeL with backward branch prediction gives the best overall combination of gating potential and performance, resulting in 22% bit cycles saved at a performance loss of 1.3%. Compared to the dynamic time-based technique, this method gives 52% more power gated bit cycles, without any additional performance loss.

## 1 Introduction

To keep up with the requirements of miniaturization and long battery life for portable devices, it is essential to reduce power consumption in the VLSI circuit components of such devices. To reach this objective, the most effective method is to lower the supply voltage. As the voltage is reduced, by scaling the CMOS technology past sub 100nm, an exponential growth in subthreshold leakage current is seen [1]. As this trend continues, the leakage current will become the dominant source of total power dissipation in CMOS circuits.

To reduce leakage, power gating has been shown to be an effective technique [2]. Power gating relies on the detection of idle periods in the circuit. During these idle periods, the supply voltage can be switched off to the appropriate circuit component to conserve leakage power. At the end of the idle period, the supply voltage is restored to resume normal operation. Power gating approaches rely on trying to predict idle periods for either storage structures (SRAMs, registers) [3, 4] or functional units [5, 6].

S. Vassiliadis et al. (Eds.): SAMOS 2007, LNCS 4599, pp. 294–303, 2007.

Here we examine how power gating techniques can also be used effectively for the reduction of leakage power in low level design. To allow us to efficiently detect and utilize idle periods we use the CoDeL design platform. CoDeL (Controller Description Language) [7, 8] is a rapid hardware design platform that allows circuit description at the algorithmic level. Since CoDeL implements a design as a state machine it has sufficient information on the usage of registers and functional units to predict idle times and allow efficient power gating.

In [9] we examine the potential of power gating registers using a time-based technique and show that a CoDeL assisted technique can significantly increase gating efficiency. However, a CoDeL assisted time-based technique can be expensive in terms of logic area. In the work reported here, we explore a set of purely static gating techniques, which require very little area overhead. These techniques use static branch prediction to increase gating efficiency by reducing mispredictions of future register usage. In addition, here we use CoDeL to predict when a "wakeup" is needed, reducing the performance penalty incurred while waiting for the supply voltage to be restored to a register.

## 2    Power Gating

Power gating of a circuit block is performed by using an appropriate header or footer transistor [6]. To begin power gating, a "sleep" signal is applied to the gate of this transistor to turn off the supply voltage to the circuit block. To revive the block for use, the "sleep" signal is de-asserted and power is restored.

In the case of memory elements, such as registers, multi-threshold CMOS (MTCMOS) [10] retention registers can be used (see figure 1). During normal operation, there is no loss in performance and during power-down mode the register state is saved to a "balloon" latch, which has a high voltage threshold resulting in minimal leakage. Using a MTCMOS register, all reads can be performed from the balloon latch. It is only when a write is necessary that we need to power up the high-performance low-threshold flip-flop.

In figure 2 we present the supply voltage and the various phases of a circuit component as it is power gated[1]. From time $T_0$ to $T_1$ the circuit component is busy and thus can not be gated. This period is $T_{busy}$. At time $T_1$, the component becomes idle. It takes the control logic from $T_1$ to $T_2$ ($T_{idledetect}$) to make the decision to engage gating. From $T_2$ the supply voltage begins to drop. At $T_3$ the aggregate leakage power savings equals the overhead of switching the header transistor on and off. The period, $T_{breakeven}$, from $T_2$ to $T_3$, is the minimum power gating duration to achieve net leakage power savings. During the period $T_{sleep}$, from $T_3$ to $T_4$ the device is asleep and we accumulate net power savings. At $T_4$ the control logic needs to reactivate the component. From $T_4$ to $T_5$ the voltage rises. During this period, $T_{wakeup}$, a performance penalty may be incurred if the pending operation needs to wait for the power to be restored. Finally, at $T_5$ the power is fully restored and the circuit can resume normal operation.

---

[1] Our model here follows the description presented in [6].

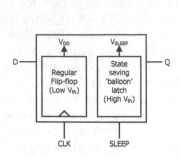

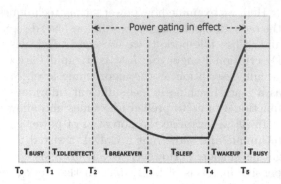

**Fig. 1.** MTCMOS register          **Fig. 2.** Voltage during power gating phases

# 3    Gating Methods

## 3.1    Time-Based Power Gating

A simple technique to power gate circuit components is to dynamically observe their state and initiate power gating when a sufficient number of idle cycles are detected. Techniques such as this have been used for cache memories [3] and show significant leakage savings with minimal performance impact.

To implement this technique, each circuit component needs to have state machine logic similar to the one shown in figure 3. Normally the component is in the IDLE_DETECT or BUSY state. As long as the component is being used, the state remains BUSY. Once the component becomes idle we enter the IDLE_DETECT state. When the consecutive idle cycle count increases beyond $T_{idledetect}$, the component enters the POWER_DOWN state. Here it waits for period $T_{breakeven}$ to allow for the voltage supply to reduce. If at any time the component is needed, a signal is generated causing the component to enter the WAKEUP state. Otherwise, after $T_{breakeven}$ cycles, the SLEEP state is entered. When the circuit component is next needed, the WAKEUP state is entered where a waiting period of $T_{wakeup}$ cycles is required to restore the supply voltage. Once the component is powered up, the BUSY state is entered. When the circuit prematurely goes from the POWER_DOWN state to the WAKEUP state, the component may not be fully powered down. Thus, for restoring the power it will not take the full $T_{wakeup}$ cycles. However, we conservatively penalize the full $T_{wakeup}$ cycles in this case. Further, we only consider the savings while in the SLEEP state. There may be some additional power savings in the WAKEUP state, which we conservatively do not include.

According to this framework, we see that our results are dependent on three parameters: $T_{idledetect}$, $T_{breakeven}$, and $T_{wakeup}$. $T_{breakeven}$ is the time it takes to overcome the energy overhead of gating a unit. $T_{wakeup}$ is the overhead of restoring the power to a unit. The parameters $T_{breakeven}$ and $T_{wakeup}$ are a function of the VLSI technology and thus can not be controlled by circuit design.

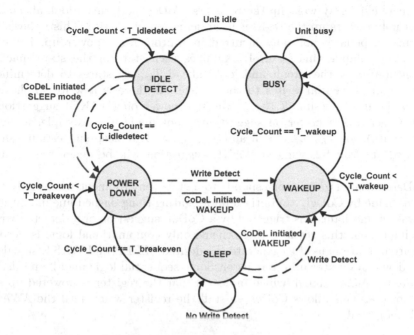

**Fig. 3.** Gating logic. The short dashed line is used for time-based gating. The long dashed transition line is used for CoDeL initiated power gating. Both dashed lines are used for CoDeL assisted time-based gating.

The $T_{idledetect}$ parameter, however, can be controlled to effect the aggressiveness of the power gating mechanism.

To implement this scheme each register would require a controller to count the idle cycles, and logic to detect a new value being written to the register. This logic is expensive in terms of area and power, and therefore motivates an alternative method of initiating power gating.

## 3.2 CoDeL Initiated Power Gating

The CoDeL platform [8] uses a sequential machine to determine the sequence of operations and data transfers in and out of registers. Because of this sequential machine, we know the exact time of the events, and we can anticipate them. For each register, at compile time, CoDeL iterates through each state of the state machine implementation of the circuit and looks ahead $T_{idledetect}$ states to determine if there are any potential writes to the register. If there is no write to the register in the next possible $T_{idledetect}$ states, a power off (SLEEP) suggestion is noted for the gating control logic. If during the next $T_{idledetect}$ possible states the register is written, a power off suggestion is not made. As with the time-based technique, the $T_{idledetect}$ parameter is chosen a priori, and is the same for all registers of the circuit under design.

To more efficiently wake up the registers, CoDeL performs a look ahead and prematurely powers up the register in anticipation of a write. This reduces the performance penalty normally incurred in waiting for a power up. For each register, at compile time, CoDeL examines each state of the state machine implementation of the circuit and looks ahead $T_{wakeup}$ states to determine if there are any potential writes to the register. If there is a write to the register in the next possible $T_{wakeup}$ states, a power on (WAKE) suggestion is noted. Otherwise, a power on suggestion is not made. For example, referring to figure 4(a), for $T_{idledetect} = 3$ and $T_{wakeup} = 1$, a sleep suggestion will be generated at state S2, while a WAKE suggestion will be generated at state S10.

CoDeL initiated gating corresponds to a static environment where only suggestions made by CoDeL can initiate power gating (long dashed line in figure 3). The wakeup mechanism is triggered by a CoDeL suggestion or a detected write.

To implement this static gating scheme only combinational logic is needed. The current state is used to generate the desired SLEEP and WAKE signals to power down and power up the register. Some sequential logic may be needed to generate the AWAKE signal, which indicates that the register is powered up and ready for use. This allows CoDeL to stall the register write until the AWAKE signal is asserted.

### 3.3   CoDeL Assisted Time-Based Power Gating

In CoDeL assisted time-based gating, the decision to initiate gating is still dependent on a streak of idle cycles as in the time-based technique (short dashed line in figure 3). In many cases, however, based on CoDeL's suggestion (long dashed line in figure 3), gating can be initiated prematurely without waiting for the full $T_{idledetect}$ cycles[2]. Also, based on CoDeL's suggestion, wakeups are initiated in anticipation of a register write to reduce the performance penalty.

The implementation of this gating scheme is the most complex as it requires the circuit features of the static and dynamic gating methods.

## 4   FSM Branch Prediction

CoDeL's gating and wakeup suggestions are dependent on a look-ahead search of the FSM description of the circuit to determine whether a register write is performed in the next $T_{idledetect}$ or $T_{wakeup}$ possible states. In performing this search, branches in the state machine are handled in three different ways. The first method uses no branch prediction (figure 4(a)), and therefore searches all possible state paths. The second method uses static forward branch prediction and assumes that a branch to the furthest state forward is taken (figure 4(b)). The third method uses static backward branch prediction and assumes that a branch to the furthest state backward is taken (figure 4(c)).

---

[2] The value of $T_{idledetect}$ used for the CoDeL and time-based parts is the same.

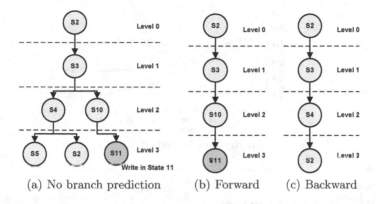

(a) No branch prediction    (b) Forward    (c) Backward

**Fig. 4.** States look-ahead to determine possible writes. $T_{idledetect} = 3$.

## 5   Evaluation Framework

To evaluate the power gating methods we use the the DSP kernel benchmarks from the DSPstone suite [11]. All kernels from the suite are implemented using CoDeL and compiled to generate synthesizable VHDL. To perform the required arithmetic operations, we have used a single cycle 16 bit fixed point unit (FXU) written in VHDL using the fixed point package obtained from [12]. It is interfaced by the CoDeL implemented kernels to perform the required arithmetic operations. For data storage, a single port memory is implemented in VHDL for simulation. Any registers in the FXU or the memory are not gated. All clock cycle results presented are based on trace data obtained from VHDL simulation of the kernel circuits.

## 6   Results

We examine the effects of $T_{idledetect}$, $T_{breakeven}$ and $T_{wakeup}$ on the power gating ability and performance of the circuit. The power gating effectiveness is determined by the percentage of bit cycles in the SLEEP state. It is computed as

$$\frac{\sum_{i=0}^{N} \text{len}(R_i) \cdot (\text{cycles in SLEEP state})_i}{\text{total cycles executed} \cdot \sum_{i=0}^{N} \text{len}(R_i)} \cdot 100\%, \tag{1}$$

where $N$ is the number of registers, $R_i$ is the $i$th register and $\text{len}(R_i)$ is the bit width of the $i$th register. The performance impact of gating is computed as the number of additional clock cycles needed when power gating is introduced. This is computed as

$$\frac{\text{total cycles executed without gating}}{\text{total cycles executed with gating}} \cdot 100\%. \tag{2}$$

The results presented here are an arithmetic average of the results obtained for the 14 DSPstone kernels.

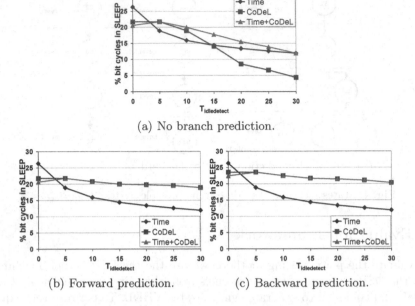

(a) No branch prediction.

(b) Forward prediction.  (c) Backward prediction.

**Fig. 5.** Gating effectiveness with $T_{wakeup} = 2$. Results averaged over $T_{breakeven} = 5, 10, 15, 20$.

Figure 5 presents the gating effectiveness using the three methods presented and the different branch prediction schemes. From figure 5(a) we see that when no branch prediction is used, the CoDeL based gating schemes perform poorly for larger values of $T_{idledetect}$. This is because since all possible branches are searched to find a write, many more writes are predicted than actually occurring resulting in missed gating opportunities. This is exacerbated in the case of only CoDeL initiated gating, since there is no help from time-based gating to reclaim some of the lost gating opportunities.

Examining the branch prediction schemes (figures 5(b) and 5(c)) we see that the CoDeL based and the CoDeL assisted time-based schemes significantly outperform the time-based technique. For $T_{idledetect} = 30$, the CoDeL schemes provide 59% more gated bit cycles than the time-based technique. It is interesting to note that for $T_{idledetect} \geq 5$, both CoDeL based schemes exhibit the same savings. This means that the dynamic decision criteria in the CoDeL assisted time-based technique presents no new gating opportunities in comparison to the purely static CoDeL scheme.

Comparing the forward and backward branch prediction schemes we find that the backward prediction results in more gating opportunities resulting in 8% more gated bit cycles. This means that more backward branches are taken in our designs than the forward branches.

Figure 6 shows the performance impact for different values of $T_{wakeup}$. Backward branch prediction is used here for the CoDeL schemes since it provides

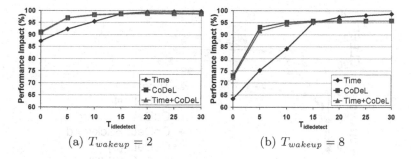

(a) $T_{wakeup} = 2$              (b) $T_{wakeup} = 8$

**Fig. 6.** Performance impact (see equation 2). Backward branch prediction used for CoDeL schemes. Results averaged over $T_{breakeven} = 5, 10, 15, 20$.

the best gating potential as compared to forward and no branch prediction. In all cases, we see that the CoDeL schemes outperform the time-based technique for lower values of $T_{idledetect}$ (less than 15), while for larger $T_{idledetect}$, the time-based technique dominates. This is because the time-based technique gates registers less frequently for larger $T_{idledetect}$, and thus results in fewer wakeup procedures resulting in lower performance loss. Even for these larger $T_{idledetect}$ values, however, the difference in performance for the time-based and CoDeL schemes is very small (less than 3%). But the number of sleep cycles gained with the CoDeL method far exceeds those of the time-based method by more than 60%. Comparing the two CoDeL schemes we see they provide roughly the same performance. Expectedly, as the value of $T_{wakeup}$ increases, performance decreases as more cycles are spent in waiting for the power to be restored.

In figure 7 we are able to more clearly see the entire design space consisting of the various techniques. We have also included the CoDeL based scheme used in [9] for comparison. The solid curves indicate results using a static gating method where the area overhead is extremely low. The dashed curves are for methods which employ a dynamic scheme resulting in significant overhead.

Common in all performance results, we see that lower values of $T_{idledetect}$ cause significant performance loss. This means that although there are a large number of short idle periods which can benefit from gating, the performance degrades since this causes a large increase in the number of cases where the circuit needs to wait for a power up to occur.

We see that the time-based technique provides very poor overall gating effectiveness and performance. Comparing the branch prediction schemes, we see that the performance loss of the CoDeL scheme with no branch prediction is the lowest, but it also results in the poor gating potential. The backward branch prediction provides better performance than the forward branch prediction since it is more accurately able to predict wakeups.

We find that CoDeL, with backward branch prediction, is able to provide an excellent compromise of high gating effectiveness and low performance loss. For $T_{idledetect} = 15$ we find that the CoDeL scheme with backward branch prediction provides 52% more bit cycles in SLEEP mode than the time-based technique for

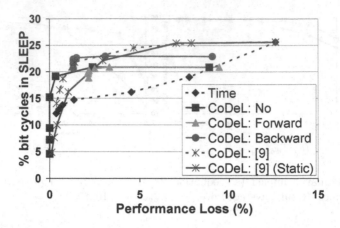

**Fig. 7.** Gating effectiveness vs performance loss for $T_{breakeven} = 10$ and $T_{wakeup} = 2$. $T_{idledetect}$ varies from 30 to 0 from left to right.

the same approximate performance loss of 1.3%. CoDeL with forward branch prediction provides a relatively poor combination of gating effectiveness and performance. This is due to the high rate of misprediction with this method. CoDeL with no branch prediction provides lower gating effectiveness but provides excellent performance for larger values of $T_{idledetect}$, and thus may be useful in cases where high performance is critical.

In figure 7 we provide two results based on the CoDeL scheme presented in [9]. The dynamic scheme ("CoDeL: [9]") is a CoDeL assisted time-based technique with no branch prediction and no "wakeup" prediction. Since we have not factored in overhead, we see that it performs quite well. Due to the dynamic nature of this method, however, it entails significant overhead. Assuming a three bit counter to count the elapsed idle cycles, our preliminary results suggest that the overhead reduces the SLEEP mode bit cycles by 18% (below what is indicated in figure 7). This overhead considerably reduces the apparent effectiveness of all dynamic techniques presented (dashed curves). The static version of this scheme ("CoDeL: [9] (Static)") is a modified version of the method presented in [9]. This method is the same as the "CoDeL: No" method without "wakeup" prediction. We see that the lack of "wakeup" prediction causes increased performance loss.

## 7   Conclusion

Test circuits, implemented using the CoDeL platform, were examined to determine the expected savings that can be achieved from power gating individual registers, and the associated performance impact. It was found that a CoDeL initiated power gating scheme with static backward branch prediction provides an overall superior combination of high gating effectiveness and low performance loss. For high performance applications, CoDeL with no branch prediction (full state space exploration) is the best choice. In both these methods, since the gating decisions are made at compile time, there is very little circuit area overhead. We are currently investigating other branch prediction schemes (including dynamic prediction) which may help in further reducing mispredictions, and thus improve performance without degrading gating effectiveness.

Here, we have introduced a methodology for implementing efficient power gating using the CoDeL platform. Using the ideas presented we hope to enhance the CoDeL design environment and fully automate the process of power gating in VLSI circuits. We are also working on more accurately defining the power gating overhead needed. This will allow more accurate break even analysis, and thus allow us to determine the minimum register size that should be power gated.

# References

1. Kim, N.S., Austin, T., Blaauw, D., Mudge, T., Flautner, K., Hu, J.S., Irwin, M.J., Kandemir, M., Narayanan, V.: Leakage current: Moore's law meets static power. Computer 36(12), 68–75 (2003)
2. Powell, M., Yang, S.H., Falsafi, B., Roy, K., Vijaykumar, T.N.: Gated-vdd: a circuit technique to reduce leakage in deep-submicron cache memories. In: ISLPED 2000, pp. 90–95. ACM Press, New York (2000)
3. Flautner, K., Kim, N.S., Martin, S., Blaauw, D., Mudge, T.: Drowsy caches: simple techniques for reducing leakage power. In: ISCA 2002, pp. 148–157. IEEE Computer Society Press, Los Alamitos (2002)
4. Liao, W., Basile, J.M., He, L.: Microarchitecture level leakage reduction with data retention. IEEE Transactions on VLSI Systems 13(11), 1324–1328 (2005)
5. Rele, S., Pande, S., Onder, S., Gupta, R.: Optimizing static power dissipation by functional units in superscalar processors. In: Horspool, R.N. (ed.) CC 2002 and ETAPS 2002. LNCS, vol. 2304, pp. 261–275. Springer, Heidelberg (2002)
6. Hu, Z., Buyuktosunoglu, A., Srinivasan, V., Zyuban, V., Jacobson, H., Bose, P.: Microarchitectural techniques for power gating of execution units. In: ISLPED '04, pp. 32–37. ACM Press, New York (2004)
7. Sivakumar, R., Dimakopoulos, V., Dimopoulos, N.: CoDeL: A rapid prototyping environment for the specification and automatic synthesis of controllers for multi-processor interconnection networks. In: SAMOS III, pp. 58–63 (July 2003)
8. Agarwal, N., Dimopoulos, N.: Power efficient rapid hardware development using CoDeL and automated clock gating. In: ISCAS 2006 (May 2006)
9. Agarwal, N., Dimopoulos, N.: Towards automated power gating of registers using CoDeL. In: ISCAS 2007 (May 2007)
10. Mutoh, S., Douseki, T., Matsuya, Y., Aoki, T., Shigematsu, S., Yamada, J.: 1-v power supply high-speed digital circuit technology with multithreshold-voltage cmos. IEEE Journal of Solid-State Circuits 30(8), 847–854 (1995)
11. Zivojnovic, V., Martinez, J., Schläger, C., Meyr, H.: DSPstone: A DSP-oriented benchmarking methodology. In: ICSPAT 1994 (October 1994)
12. Bromley, J.: Synthesizable vhdl fixed point arithmetic package (2006), http://www.doulos.com/knowhow/vhdl_designers_guide/models/fp_arith/

# A Study of Energy Saving in Customizable Processors

Paolo Bonzini[1], Dilek Harmanci[2], and Laura Pozzi[1]

[1] University of Lugano
Faculty of Informatics
Switzerland
paolo.bonzini@lu.unisi.ch, laura.pozzi@unisi.ch
[2] University of Lugano
Advanced Learning and Research Institute
Switzerland
dilek.tekbas@alari.ch

**Abstract.** Embedded systems are special purpose systems which perform pre-defined tasks with very specific requirements like high performance, low volume or low power. Most of the time, using a general purpose processor for such systems results in a design which is poor to meet the application specific requirement. On the other hand, ASIC design cycle is too costly and too slow for the embedded application market. Recent development in configurable processors significantly improved the performance metrics of a general purpose processor by coupling it with an application specific hardware. Although there has been a large amount of work in the literature to improve the performance and automation of such designs, little has been done to examine the power consumption of a system coupled with an application specific functional unit. Monitoring this power behavior may provide new directions in the ASIP design. We augmented *wattch* (a power simulator based on SimpleScalar) with a model of the power consumption of functional units (using a combination of RTL- and gate-level power modeling). Our results show that a well-designed custom instruction set may reduce register and memory accesses, and hence the overall power consumption of an embedded system.

## 1 Introduction

Embedded systems are special purpose systems which perform pre-defined tasks with very specific requirements in terms of high performance, low noise or low power consumption. Most of the time, using a general purpose processor for such systems results in a design which is poor to meet the application specific requirement. On the other hand, ASIC design cycle is too costly and too slow for the embedded application market. Recent development in configurable processors significantly improved the performance metrics of a general purpose processor by coupling it with an application specific hardware.

Several companies (Tensilica [1], ARC [2], ST [3], MIPS [4]) provide configurable cores and effective design tools to implement application specific hardware in the market. As a result, in the last few years, research focused on automated HW/SW partitioning and accelerator design. However, studies of the power consumption of a system coupled with an application specific functional unit, are still rare.

S. Vassiliadis et al. (Eds.): SAMOS 2007, LNCS 4599, pp. 304–312, 2007.

Likewise, existing tools provide a way to easily describe custom instructions, and include simulators to evaluate performance improvements, but they lack support for power analysis of the application-specific functional units (AFUs) and the rest of the processor.

Power analysis of AFUs, however, is very important as it can suggest new directions in ASIP design. For example, performing fewer accesses to the register file or to the memory is an important source for power reduction. Evaluation of this behavior will show whether instruction-set extension can be a means to reduce power demands.

In this paper we aim at analyzing power consumption during design space exploration. Therefore, empirical methods for power measurement are not applicable. Likewise, hardware power estimation after place & route [5][6] is not practical since the RTL level description of the base processor may not be available to the designer. Therefore, our approach is to build an RTL-level model of the functional unit, and to compute switching power using gate-level models of 1-bit cells. The result is a fast and automated architectural level power estimation tool for ASIPs based on *wattch* [7].

The remainder of the paper is organized as follows. Section 2 presents related work on power modeling for customized processors. Section 3 details how we construct functional and power models of the custom instructions. Section 4 presents our toolchain, which integrates the techniques described in this paper, and the evaluation environment we used; experimental results are shown in section 5. Finally, section 6 concludes the paper and describe possible future work in this area.

## 2   Related Work

In [6], Biswas at al. study the performance and power benefits of instruction set extensions, using a Xilinx Multimedia Board (which includes a Virtex II FPGA) equipped with a Microblaze soft-core. Since there is no direct way to measure power of a running system on the FPGA fabric, they obtain a structural model, as well as timing and routing information, from the results of place-and-route. Using a cycle-accurate hardware simulator, they generate a Value Change Dump (VCD) of all the signals in the structural netlist. Finally, the routing information and VCD information are used by a power simulator to compute the dynamic power consumed. In this work, the availability of a soft core is exploited to directly use an RTL or gate level power simulator; unfortunately, this is often not possible in practice. Also, the process applied is a manual work which has to be performed again for every different ISE defined. Our method uses an automated toolchain that automatically provides the power consumption of a given configuration and ISE set.

In [8], Fei at al. propose a hybrid energy estimation technique for extensible processors. They define a macro-modeling procedure to obtain energy coefficients of a processor configuration and custom instruction. This macro model is then used to estimate the energy consumption of the system with different selections of custom instructions. Their methodology characterizes instruction level parameters (dynamic execution trace of a program and the base processor micro-architecture) and structural level parameters (energy effect of instructions on the custom hardware) and uses linear regression on a set of test programs to model the energy consumption of both the base processor and the custom instructions. This statistical modeling phase also relies on a synthesized hardware description of the processor; a power simulator is used to run a set of test programs, and statistical analyses are performed to derive the coefficients of the model. Energy estimates for extension instructions are based on these coefficients and on the result of bitwidth analysis on the extensions' operands. The relationship to the bit width is linear for components like adders (+, -), comparators ($<$, $>$ etc.), bitwise logic ($\hat{\ }$, &, |   etc.), shifters ($\gg$, $\ll$) and latches, while it is quadratic for multiplications.

Fei et al's work does have a few similarities to the approach we present in this paper. For example, the library of components is similar to the one we use. We also base our models on the results of a power simulator; however, instead of doing this for full test programs, we only run power simulations on the basic cells in our library, for which we used a gate-level model. Another important difference between this work and ours is that we use a synthesizable RTL model of the functional units, while Fei starts from a C description. For this reason, our technique does not need a statistical modeling phase.

In [5], Cheung at al. go one step further and propose a methodology to generate battery-aware instruction set extensions. When the selected extension is long enough, they observed that the current supplied to run the extension can be lowered by separating the extension into smaller instructions and applying clock gating to each of them. Furthermore, the slack time of each extension can then be used to synthesize slower but less power consuming hardware. Again, to estimate the power consumption of the extension, they produce Verilog implementations of the extension instructions and then apply Synopsys Design Compiler. In our work, we propose to extend an architecture-level power simulator, so that power consumption of extensible processors can be monitored. Our power simulator could also provide a platform to experiment with optimization algorithms such as the one evaluated by Cheung.

As the model of the underlying processor we chose *wattch* [7], an architectural simulator that collects resource usage counts in a cycle-accurate simulator, and uses them to estimate overall CPU power consumption. In general, this approach is more flexible, and more suitable to design space exploration, than instruction-level power models such as [9], [10], [11].

## 3   Methodology

An instruction set extension consists of a group of instructions that will be executed in a special hardware coupled with the processor. Our aim is to estimate the power consumed both by the special hardware and the processor in a fully automated fashion, and without going through the place-and-route process.

In order to fulfill these requirements, the compiler (which is responsible for selecting profitable custom instructions in the user program) must be enhanced to construct power models too. To do this, the compiler will use a standard library of components, comprising every operation that can potentially be included in a special instruction.

Power consumption in the basic components varies for different transitions on the input. For the implementation of the models to be fast, one can prepare look-up tables of the equivalent capacitance of the circuit, which are indexed on the previous and next states of the inputs [12]. The equivalent capacitance includes both switching and leakage capacitance; it is possible to split these two components if, for example, one wants to use a more precise model for leakage, or to analyze the influence of temperature on power consumption.

It is of course infeasible to use such a technique for all but the smallest cells: the transition space for an $n$-cell input would consist of $2^{2n}$ possible transitions, and this would be hard to store and very expensive to compute off-line. Therefore, our component library is built as a hierarchy of models (see figure 1). Together, these models cover all the operations that the compiler can extract into an extended instruction. The models for the custom instructions will use these components and logically sit at the top of the hierarchy.

Leaf components use gate-level models, where the switching capacitance is obtained using Synopsis Power Compiler. Power models of basic operations (see figure 2) have been obtained by using Synopsys Power Compiler based on the switching activity of the circuits at the RTL level. These operations have 4 or fewer bits of input, so the number of possible input transitions is at most 256. We compiled VHDL descriptions of each basic operation to estimate the power consumption of every possible case based on the Artisan 180u technology library. The power consumption is then kept in a look-up table.

Higher-level models, instead, are RTL-level models that express the circuit in terms of the lower level cells—possibly also modeled as RTL.

The total dissipated power is then computed by adding up the power consumed in each basic operation. The ROM cell is an exception, as we used a probabilistic model assuming that the possible inputs are uniformly distributed.

For the components listed in figure 2, the inputs to the operations can be either both variable, or one variable and one constant. Some operations can be implemented simply as wires in the latter case (e.g. bitwise AND, rotates or shifts); if this is not the case, the power consumption will still be different[1], so we implemented two different models for the operation. Furthermore, the models can be parameterized on the width of the operands.

We provide one implementation for every component: for example, in the case of the adder, we use a carry-select design which provides a good balance between speed and area. It is possible however to extend this library with multiple models, in order to satisfy the latency, area or power requirements for the extended instruction.

# 4 Experimental Setup

We implemented the power modeling tool as an extension to an ASIP code generation toolchain, also used in [13]. This toolchain includes the instruction set extension selection algorithm proposed, and modified GCC and SimpleScalar to respectively compile and simulate an ARM-like processor with an extensible instruction set. The processor can be extended with up to seven new instructions, each with at most four input and two outputs.

The toolchain described in this paper automatically generates instruction set extensions, performance and power simulation results, given an application source code in

---

[1] If one input of an adder is constant, for example, each full adder can be replaced with two gates. This obviously consumes less power than a full adder.

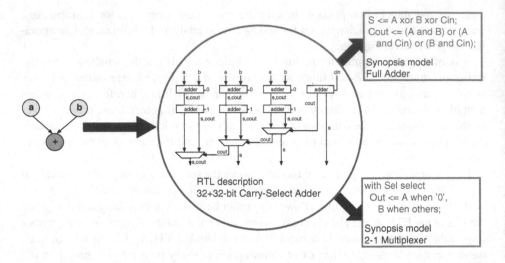

S <= A xor B xor Cin;
Cout <= (A and B) or (A and Cin) or (B and Cin);

Synopsis model
Full Adder

RTL description
32+32-bit Carry-Select Adder

with Sel select
Out <= A when '0',
B when others;

Synopsis model
2-1 Multiplexer

**Fig. 1.** Composing the library components hierarchically

C and the configuration of target processor's micro-architecture. The new toolchain (shown in figure 3) uses *wattch* instead of plain SimpleScalar, in order to gather power simulation of the system from the timing information. *wattch* was also modified to include the power consumption of the custom functional units.

Power models for the basic operations of figure 2 were obtained with Synopsys Power Compiler, based on VHDL descriptions of each cell. The descriptions were compiled using the Artisan 180 *nm* technology library, and simulations were run for every possible transition of the input values.

Glue code to access the resulting look-up tables, as well as the implementation of the RTL models, was written in C. The compiler-generated C code for the power models augments these basic models and is dynamically linked into the simulator.

## 5   Experimental Results

We measured the speed up and energy gain obtained by applying AFUs to eight benchmarks; seven of these are taken from MiBench, while the eighth (*aes*) is an implementation of AES that does not use precomputed tables to speed up its software operation (this style of implementation is closer to the design of cryptographic hardware, and proves to be extremely apt to instruction set customization).

Results for speedup and energy gain are shown in figure 4. One interesting point is that the energy gain always exceeds the speedup offered by custom instructions. This result is worth noting, because it shows that the total energy consumed is not only lower because of a decrease in execution cycles; instead, the average power consumption decreases too.

There are a number of reasons for this behavior. First, the circuitry for the newly introduced functional units is simpler than that of an ALU. The custom instructions,

| Gate-level models | RTL-level models |
|---|---|
| inverter | logic operations (AND/OR/XOR/XNOR/NOT) |
| 2- and 4-input AND gate | 2-1 multiplexer |
| 2- and 4-input OR gate | left/right/arithmetic right shift |
| 2-input NAND gate | left/right rotate |
| 2-input NOR gate | adder |
| 2-input XOR gate | subtractor |
| 2-input XNOR gate | multiplier |
| 2-1 multiplexer | signed/unsigned comparator |
| full adder | signed/unsigned maximum/minimum |
| full subtractor | ROM |

**Fig. 2.** List of components in the library

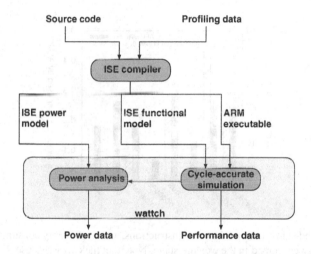

**Fig. 3.** Structure of the toolchain

in fact, include only the hardware needed to perform the requested operations, instead of supporting addition/subtraction, logical operations, updating the flags, and so on. In addition the implementation of custom instructions can use simpler circuits when the operands have a reduced bitwidth, for example, or are constant.

Power was reduced, that is energy gain is higher than the speedup, whenever the compiler could place read-only arrays in the AFUs. This happens in *aes, des, rawcaudio, rawdaudio*. In these cases, small constant tables are inserted in the AFUs, and all cache accesses for these tables are removed. Apart from saving execution cycles for address generation, the use of small tagless memories in the AFUs reduces power.

A second interesting result can be gathered by observing figure 5. Here it can be seen that, for many benchmarks, 30% or more of the executed instructions are ISE; yet the energy consumed by the ISE is only a very small fraction (less than 0.5%) of the total energy consumed by the *Execute* phase of the pipeline.

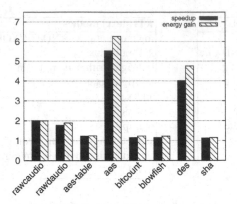

**Fig. 4.** Comparing the improvement offered by customized instruction sets, in terms of speed and consumed energy

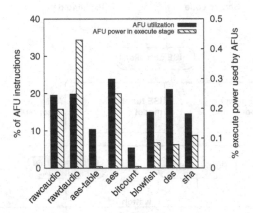

**Fig. 5.** % of extended instructions out of all instructions, and % of energy consumed by AFUs out of the total energy consumed in the execute stage. Note that the two series use different scales.

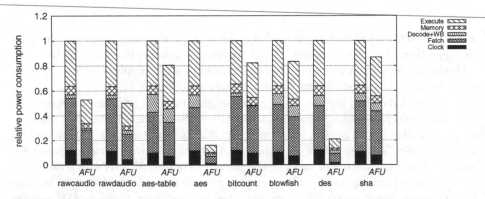

**Fig. 6.** Break up of consumed energy for clock and the different pipeline stages. The first bar refers to a non-customizable processor, while the second bar adds up to seven customizable instructions.

In figure 6, energy consumption is broken up according to pipeline stages, so that differences between stages can be appreciated. The behavior can be very different for the various benchmarks. For example, the memory cost[2] is vastly improved for the aforementioned benchmarks *aes* and *des*, as well as for *rawcaudio* and *rawdaudio*. Instead, it remains the same for *aes-table* or *blowfish*, where the AFUs mostly generate addresses to access tables stored in RAM.

Finally, the cost of the fetch phase, which includes branch prediction, is improved when AFUs include multiple unrolled copies of a loop, and when the compiler can apply if-conversion to generate AFUs that include a multiplexer [13]. If-conversion happens *rawcaudio* and *rawdaudio*; unrolling happens for all the other benchmarks.

## 6 Conclusion

In this paper, we proposed a micro-architectural power estimation tool for customizable processors. We implemented a library to characterize the power consumption of a set of standard cells, and used this library to build power models of extended instructions in a structural way. Unlike existing techniques to estimate the energy consumption of an ASIP, our methodology automates the construction of the extension's power model and eliminates the need to perform place-and-route prior to the power simulation.

We used this technique to monitor the performance and power benefits which can be obtained using an automated instruction selection algorithm. We found that customizable instructions enable energy saving thanks to the usage of simpler circuits within the application-specific functional units. In addition, putting local memory elements inside instruction set extensions reduces the access to the memory elements in the system and hence enables higher power savings.

Our experiments show performance improvements up to 5.6x and energy gains up to 6.2x. Therefore, customizable processors also provide a way to limit the power consumed by the processor.

## References

1. Halfhill, T.R.: Tensilica's software makes hardware. Microprocessor Report (2003)
2. Halfhill, T.R.: ARC Cores encourages "plug-ins". Microprocessor Report (2000)
3. Faraboschi, P., Brown, G., Fisher, J.A., Desoli, G., Homewood, F.: Lx: A technology platform for customizable VLIW embedded processing. In: Proceedings of the 27th Annual International Symposium on Computer Architecture, pp. 203–213 (2000)
4. Halfhill, T.R.: MIPS embraces configurable technology. Microprocessor Report (2003)
5. Cheung, N., Parameswaran, S., Henkel, J.: A quantitative study and estimation models for extensible instructions in embedded processors. In: Proceedings of the International Conference on Computer Aided Design, San Jose, Calif, pp. 183–189 (2004)
6. Biswas, P., Banerjee, S., Dutt, N., Ienne, P., Pozzi, L.: Performance and energy benefits of instruction set extensions in an FPGA soft core. In: Proceedings of the 19th International Conference on VLSI Design, Hyderabad, India, pp. 651–656 (2006)

---

[2] I-cache cost, which is almost linear in the speedup, is part of the fetch phase rather than the memory phase. The memory phase only includes data accesses.

7. Brooks, D., Tiwari, V., Martonosi, M.: Wattch: a framework for architectural-level power analysis and optimizations. In: Proceedings of the 27th Annual International Symposium on Computer Architecture, pp. 83–94 (2000)
8. Fei, Y., Ravi, S., Raghunathan, A., Jha, N.K.: Energy estimation for extensible processors. In: Proceedings of the Design, Automation and Test in Europe Conference and Exhibition, pp. 682–687 (2004)
9. Tiwari, V., Malik, S., Wolfe, A.: Power analysis of embedded software: A first step towards software power minimization. IEEE Transactions on Very Large Scale Integration (VLSI) Systems VLSI-2, 437–445 (1994)
10. Simunic, T., Benini, L., Micheli, G.D.: Cycle-accurate simulation of energy consuption in embedded systems. In: Proceedings of the 36th Design Automation Conference, New Orleans, La, pp. 867–872 (1999)
11. Wan, M., Ichikawa, Y., Lidsky, D., Rabaey, J.: An energy conscious methodology for early design exploration of heterogeneous DSPs. In: Proceedings of the IEEE Custom Integrated Circuit Conference—CICC 1998, Santa Clara, Calif., pp. 111–117. IEEE Computer Society Press, Los Alamitos (1998)
12. Ye, W., Vijaykrishnan, N., Kandemir, M.T., Irwin, M.J.: The design and use of SimplePower: a cycle-accurate energy estimation tool. In: Proceedings of the 37th Design Automation Conference, Los Angeles, Calif., pp. 340–345 (2000)
13. Bonzini, P., Pozzi, L.: Code transformation strategies for extensible embedded processors. In: Proceedings of the International Conference on Compilers, Architectures, and Synthesis for Embedded Systems, Seoul, South Korea, pp. 242–252 (2006)

# Trends in Low Power Handset Software Defined Radio

John Glossner[1,3], Daniel Iancu[1], Mayan Moudgill[1], Michael Schulte[2],
and Stamatis Vassiliadis[3]

[1] Sandbridge Technologies, 1 N. Lexington Ave., White Plains, NY 10601
[2] UW Madison, Dept. of EECS, Madison, Wisconsin
[3] Delft University of Technology, EEMCS, Delft, The Netherlands
jglossner@sandbridgetech.com

**Abstract.** This paper presents an overview of trends in low power handset SDR implementations. With the market for SDR-enabled handsets expected to grow to 200M units by 2014, the barriers to efficient handset implementations – both hardware and software – have been removed based on new and innovative architectures. We describe advances in DSP architectures and compilers that are enabling SDR handset implementations and present some results for a specific SDR design.

**Keywords:** Software Defined Radio, SDR, DSP, Multithreaded processors.

## 1 Introduction

Spectrum is scarce with precious little available for future technologies. Most of the world's available frequencies have already been allocated to specific services. What precious little remains is auctioned by government agencies typically for billions of dollars.

From a mobile operator's perspective delivering services to customers is dependent upon network capacity and coverage. Capacity is concerned with allowing more non-interfering users within a basestation cell or providing higher bandwidth to users within range of a basestation. Each new generation of communications systems designs attempts to provide additional capacity based on technological advances in the field. Recently MIMO-OFDM systems have been proposed [1] .

Coverage is concerned with providing voice and data services over large distances – with quality of service. In the future, data services may be the focus of cellular operators. Generally as a user moves farther away from a particular base station or service area the data speeds available to a user decreases. Additionally, cost is a concern. Providing high-speed cellular connections may be expensive. A common scenario proposed is providing wireless LAN hotspot coverage over a few hundred feet, WiMax coverage over a few miles, and cellular coverage (HSxPA, 1xEVDO) everywhere else.

Fig. 1 shows that the situation is actually more complicated than the above discussion. There are in fact multiple standards world-wide. Interestingly, the same is true of multimedia, location-based services, and user interfaces.

S. Vassiliadis et al. (Eds.): SAMOS 2007, LNCS 4599, pp. 313–321, 2007.

Software Defined Radio (SDR) has been proposed as a solution to providing better coverage. The SDR Forum [2] defines five tiers of solutions. Tier-0 is a traditional radio implementation in hardware. Tier-1, Software Controlled Radio (SCR), implements the control features for multiple hardware elements in software. Tier-2, Software Defined Radio (SDR), implements modulation and baseband processing in software but allows for multiple frequency fixed function RF hardware. Tier-3, Ideal Software Radio (ISR), extends programmability through the RF with analog conversion at the antenna. Tier-4, Ultimate Software Radio (USR), provides for fast (millisecond) transitions between communications protocols in addition to digital processing capability. This is an underlying technology necessary to realize cognitive radios.

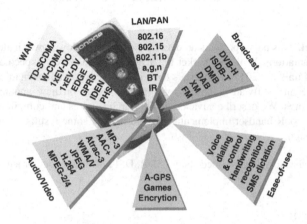

**Fig. 1.** Competing and Complementary Technologies

The advantages of reconfigurable SDR solutions versus hardware solutions are significant. First, reconfigurable solutions are more flexible allowing multiple communication protocols to dynamically execute on the same transistors thereby reducing hardware costs. Specific functions such as filters, modulation schemes, encoders/decoders etc., can be reconfigured adaptively at run time. Second, several communication protocols can be efficiently stored in memory and coexist or execute concurrently. This significantly reduces the cost of the system for both the end user and the service provider. Third, remotely reconfigurable protocols provide simple and inexpensive software version control and feature upgrades. This allows service providers to differentiate products after the product is deployed. Fourth, the development time of new and existing communications protocols is significantly reduced providing an accelerated time to market. Development cycles are not limited by long and laborious hardware design cycles. With SDR, new protocols are quickly added as soon as the software is available for deployment. Fifth, SDR provides an attractive method of dealing with new standards releases while assuring backward compatibility with existing standards.

SDR enabling technologies also have significant advantages from the consumer perspective. First, mobile terminal independence with the ability to "choose" desired feature sets is provided. Second, global connectivity with the ability to roam across operators using different communications protocols is enabled. Third, future scalability and upgradeability provide for longer handset lifetimes.

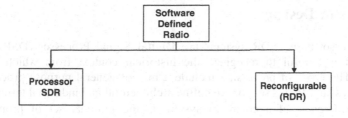

**Fig. 2.** SDR Variants

Fig. 2 shows two variants of Tier-2 SDR systems. Reconfigurable Digital Radio (RDR) platforms are generally FPGA-based with millisecond or longer reconfiguration times between communications systems. Of key importance is that RDRs generally follow a hardware design methodology. Processor SDR systems are instruction set computers. They follow a software design methodology and generally can be reconfigured in nanosecond timeframes. Historically, processor-based SDRs have not had enough performance to implement modern communications systems. Recently processor-based solutions with sufficient processing power have appeared [8] [9] [10] [11] [12] [13] [14] [15] [16] [17] [18] [19] . The remainder of this paper focuses on processor-based SDR solutions.

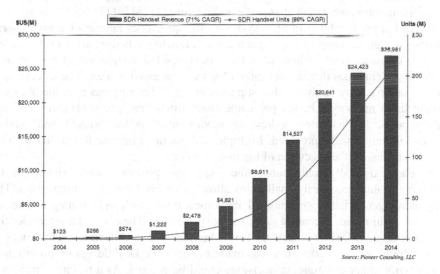

**Fig. 3.** SDR Handset Market (source: Pioneer Consulting, LLC)

Fig. 3 shows the growth in the SDR handset time both in terms of money value and unit shipments. We are now at the beginning of SDR-based handset deployments. In Section 2 we discuss processor related design issues both in terms of real-time parallel systems implementation and low-power. In Section 3 we discuss programmability and applications development for SDR solutions. In Section 4 we make concluding remarks on the future of SDR systems.

## 2  Processor Design

Since processor-based SDR systems are Digital Signal Processor (DSP) computer systems, it is helpful to recognize the historical context from which they have emerged. The types of processing include a mix of general purpose processing and signal processing. In this section we define architectural and industrial terms.

The *architecture* of a computer system is the minimal set of properties that determine what programs will run and what results they will produce [3] . It is the contract between the programmer and the hardware. Every computer is an interpreter of its *machine language* – that representation of programs that resides in memory and is interpreted (executed) directly by the (host) hardware.

The logical organization of a computer's dataflow and controls is called the *implementation or microarchitecture*. The physical structure embodying the implementation is called the *realization*. The architecture describes what happens while the implementation describes how it is made to happen. Programs of the same architecture should run unchanged on different implementations. An architectural function is *transparent* if its implementation does not produce any architecturally visible side effects. An example of a non-transparent function is the load delay slot made visible due to pipeline effects. Generally, it is desirable to have transparent implementations. Most DSP and VLIW implementations are not transparent and therefore the implementation affects the architecture [4] [5] [6] [7] .

Execution predictability in SDR systems often precludes the use of many general-purpose design techniques (e.g. speculation, branch prediction, data caches, etc.). Instead, classical DSP architectures have developed a unique set of performance enhancing techniques that are optimized for their intended market. These techniques are characterized by hardware that supports efficient filtering, such as the ability to sustain three memory accesses per cycle (one instruction, one coefficient, and one data access). Sophisticated addressing modes such as bit-reversed and modulo addressing may also be provided. Multiple address units operate in parallel with the datapath to sustain the execution of the inner kernel.

In classical DSP architectures, the execution pipelines were visible to the programmer and necessarily shallow to allow assembly language optimization. This programming restriction encumbered implementations with tight timing constraints for both arithmetic execution and memory access. The key characteristic that separates modern DSP architectures from classical DSP architectures is the focus on compilability. Once the decision was made to focus the DSP design on programmer productivity, other constraining decisions could be relaxed. As a result, significantly longer pipelines with multiple cycles to access memory and multiple cycles to compute arithmetic operations could be utilized. This has yielded higher clock frequencies and higher performance DSPs.

In an attempt to exploit instruction level parallelism inherent in DSP applications, modern DSPs tend to use VLIW-like execution packets. This is partly driven by real-time requirements which require the worst-case execution time to be minimized. This is in contrast with general purpose CPUs which tend to minimize average execution times. With long pipelines and multiple instruction issue, the difficulties of attempting assembly language programming become apparent. Controlling instruction dependencies between upwards of 100 in-flight instructions is a non-trivial task for a programmer. This is exactly the area where a compiler excels.

A challenge of using VLIW processors includes large program executables (code bloat) that result from independently specifying every operation with a single instruction. As an example, a VLIW processor with a 32-bit basic instruction width requires 4 instructions, 128 bits, to specify 4 operations. A vector encoding may compute many more operations in as little as 21 bits (for example – multiply two 4-element vectors, saturate, accumulate, and saturate).

Another challenge of VLIW implementations is that they may require excessive write ports on register files. Because each instruction may specify a unique destination address and all the instructions are independent, a separate port must be provided for the target of each instruction. This can result in high power dissipation, which is unacceptable for handset applications.

A challenge of visible pipeline machines (e.g. most DSPs and VLIW processors) is interrupt response latency. Visible memory pipeline effects in highly parallel inner loops (e.g. a load instruction followed by another load instruction) are not typically interruptible because the processor state cannot be restored. This requires programmers to break apart loops so that worst case timings and maximum system latencies may be acceptable.

Signal processing applications often require a mix of computational calculations and control processing. Control processing is often amenable to RISC-style architectures and is typically compiled directly from C code. Signal processing computations are characterized by multiply-accumulate intensive functions executed on fixed point vectors of moderate length. Therefore, a DSP requires support for such fixed point saturating computations. This has traditionally been implemented as one or more multiply accumulate (MAC) units. In addition, as the saturating arithmetic is non-associative, parallel execution of multiple data elements may result in different results from serial execution. This creates a challenge for high-level language implementations that specify integer modulo arithmetic. Therefore, most DSPs have been programmed using assembly language.

The problems associated with previous approaches require a new architecture to facilitate efficient convergence applications processing. An SDR architecture must allow for real-time execution, be highly parallel, and provide exceptionally low latency interrupt response times. Sandbridge Technologies has designed a processor with these characteristics. It is a multithreaded vector machine with multiple cores on a single die. The simplicity of VLIW implementations is embodied in the design with multithreading overcoming the limitations [20] .

## 3  Software Design

Obtaining full utilization of parallel processor resources has historically been a difficult challenge. Much of the programming effort can be spent determining which processors should receive data from other processors. Often execution cycles may be wasted for data transfers. Statically scheduled machines such as Very Long

Instruction Word architectures and visible pipeline machines with wide execution resources complicate programmer productivity by requiring manual tracking of up to 100 in-flight instruction dependencies. When non-associative DSP arithmetic is present, nearly all compilers are ineffective and the resulting burden falls upon the assembly language programmer. A number of these issues have been discussed in [21] .

A good programming model should adequately abstract most of the programming complexity so that 20% of the effort may result in 80% of the platform utilization [22] [23] . While there are still some objections to a multithreaded programming model [24] , to-date it is widely adopted particularly with the introduction of the Java programming language [23] [25] .

With hardware that is multithreaded with concurrent execution and adopting a multithreaded software programming model, it is possible for a kernel to be developed that automatically schedules software threads onto hardware threads. It should be noted that while the hardware scheduling may be fixed, the software should be free to use any scheduling policy desired [26] . The POSIX pthreads open standard [27] provides cross platform capability as the library is compilable across a number of systems including Unix, Linux, and Windows.

There are many challenges faced when trying to develop efficient compilers for parallel DSP technologies. First and foremost, the Sandblaster processor is transparent in the architectural sense. This proscribes that there are no visible implementation effects for the programmer or compiler to deal with [3] . This is in distinct contrast with VLIW designs where the implementation strongly influences the architecture. A benefit of a true architecture approach is that object code will execute unmodified (e.g. without any translation required) on any Sandblaster compliant implementation.

If a SIMD datapath to implement vector operations is utilized, the compiler must vectorize C code to exploit the data level parallelism inherent in signal processing applications and then generates the appropriate vector instructions. The compiler must also handle the difficult problem of outer loop vectorization.

Since saturating arithmetic is non-associative, out-of-order execution may produce different bit results. In some wireless systems this is not permissible [28] . By architecting parallel saturating arithmetic (i.e. vector multiply and accumulate with saturation), a compiler is able to generate code with the understanding that the hardware will properly produce bit-exact results. A compiler algorithm used to accomplish this is described in [29] . Some hardware techniques to implement this are described in [30] .

In multithreaded processors compilers should also automatically generate software threads. If the same pthreads mechanism for thread generation in the compiler is used as the programmer who specifies them manually, many economies of scale can be achieved. For most signal processing loops it is not a problem to generate threads and a compiler will automatically produce code for correct synchronization.

Fig. 4 shows the results of a number of communications systems as a percentage utilization of a 4-core 600MHz Sandbridge SB3011 platform. Particularly, WiFi 802.11b, GPS, AM/FM radio, Analog NTSC Video TV, Bluetooth, GSM/GPRS, UMTS WCDMA, WiMax, CDMA, and DVB-H. A notable point is that all these communications systems are written in generic C code with no hardware acceleration required. It is also notable that performance, accuracy, and concurrency can be dynamically adjusted based on the mix of tasks desired. For most of the systems, the values are measured on hardware from digitized RF signals that have been converted in real-time.

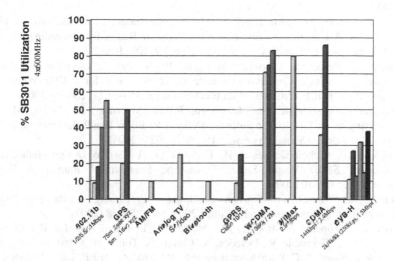

**Fig. 4.** Communication Systems Results as a Percentage of Utilization (4 cores at 600MHz)

## 4 Conclusions

The market for SDR-enabled handsets is expected to grow significantly over the next few years. This has been brought about by advances in low power DSP designs, improved software design methodologies, and a market demand for multimode multimedia devices. Such devices allow for improved carrier coverage over increasingly limited spectrum ranges. The result of SDR devices is improved coverage areas by means of dynamically reconfigurable radios.

## References

[1] Stuber, G., Mclaughlin, S., Ingram, M., Pratt, T.: Broadband MIMO-OFDM Wireless Communications. Proceedings of the IEEE 92(2), 271–294 (2004)
[2] http://www.sdrforum.org
[3] Blaauw, G., Brooks Jr., F.: Computer Architecture: Concepts and Evolution. Addison-Wesley, Reading, MA (1997)
[4] Case, B.: Philips Hopes to Displace DSPs with VLIW. Microprocessor Report, pp. 12–15 (December 1997)
[5] Wolf, O., Bier, J.: StarCore Launches First Architecture. Microprocessor Report 12(14), 1–4 (1998)

[6]  Fridman, J., Greenfield, Z.: The TigerSHARC DSP Architecture. IEEE Micro 20, 66–76 (2000)
[7]  Turley, J., Hakkarainen, H.: TI's New 'C6x DSP Screams at 1,600 MIPS. Microprocessor Report 11(2), 1–4 (1997)
[8]  Glossner, J., Iancu, D., Lu, J., Hokenek, E., Moudgill, M.: A Software Defined Communications Baseband Design. IEEE Communications Magazine 41(1), 120–128 (2003)
[9]  Lin, Y., Lee, H., Woh, M., Harel, Y., Mahlke, S., Mudge, T., Chakrabarti, C., Flautner, K.: SODA: A Low-power Architecture For Software Radio. In: Proceedings of the 33rd Intl. Symposium on Computer Architecture, pp. 89–100 (June 2006)
[10] Kneip, J., Weiss, M., Drwscher, W., Aue, V., Strobel, J., Oberthür, T., Bolle, M., Fettweis, G.: Single Chip Programmable Baseband ASSP for 5 GHz Wireless LAN Applications. IEICE Transactions on Electronics, pp. 359–367 (February 2002)
[11] van Berkel, C., Heinle, F., Meuwissen, P.P.E., Moerman, K., Weiss, M.: Vector Processing as an Enabler for Software-Defined Radio in Handheld Devices. EURASIP Journal on Applied Signal Processing 16, 2613–2625 (2005)
[12] Robelly, J.P., Cichon, G., Seidel, H., Fettweis, G.: A HW/SW Design Methodology for Embedded SIMD Vector Signal Processors. International Journal of Embedded Systems 1(11), 2–10 (2005)
[13] Duller, A., Panesar, G., Towner, D.: Parallel Processing — the picoChip Way! Communicating Processing Architectures 2003, pp. 125–138 (2003)
[14] Lodi, A., Cappelli, A., Bocchi, M., Mucci, C., Innocenti, M., De Bartolomeis, C., Ciccarelli, L., Giansante, R., Deledda, A., Campi, F., Toma, M., Guerrieri, R.: XiSystem: A XiRisc-Based SoC With Reconfigurable IO Module. IEEE Journal of Solid-State Circuits 41(1), 85–96 (2006)
[15] Mohebbi, B., Filho, E.C., Maestre, R., Davies, M., Kurdahi, F.J.: A Case Study of Mapping a Software-Defined Radio (SDR) Application on a Reconfigurable DSP Core. In: Proceedings of the International Conference on Codesign and System Synthesis, p. 103 (2003)
[16] Ungerer, T., Robič, B., Šilc, J.: A Survey of Processors with Explicit Multithreading. ACM Computing Surveys 35(1), 29–63 (2003)
[17] Smith, B.J.: The Architecture of HEP. In: Kowalik, J.S. (ed.) Parallel MIMD Computation: HEP Supercomputer and Its Applications, pp. 41–55. MIT Press, Cambridge, MA (1985)
[18] Mankovic, T.E., Popescu, V., Sullivan, H.: CHoPP priciples of operations. In: Proceedings of the 2nd International Supercomputer Conference, pp. 2–10 (1987)
[19] Tullsen, D.M., Eggers, S.J., Levy, H.M.: Simultaneous Multithreading: Maximizing on-chip Parallelism. In: Proceedings of the 22nd Annual International Symposium on Computer Architecture, pp. 392–403 (June 1995)
[20] Glossner, J., Iancu, D.: The Sandbridge SB3011 SDR Platform. In: Proceedings of the Symposium on Trends in Communications (SympoTIC'06), Bratislava, Slovakia (June 24-26, 2006)
[21] Glossner, J., Schulte, M., Moudgill, M., Iancu, D., Jinturkar, S., Raja, T., Nacer, G., Vassiliadis, S.: Sandblaster Low-Power Multithreaded SDR Baseband Processor. In: Proceedings of the 3rd Workshop on Applications Specific Processors (WASP'04), Stockholm, Sweden, pp. 53–58 (September 7, 2004)
[22] Goering, Richard: Platform-based design: A choice, not a panacea. EE Times (September 11, 2002), Available at http://www.eetimes.com/story/OEG20020911S0061

[23] Silvén, O., Jyrkkä, K.: Observations on Power-Efficiency Trends in Mobile Communication Devices. In: Hämäläinen, T.D., Pimentel, A.D., Takala, J., Vassiliadis, S. (eds.) SAMOS 2005. LNCS, vol. 3553, pp. 142–151. Springer, Heidelberg (2005)

[24] Lee, E.: The Problem with Threads. Computer Magazine, IEEE Press (May 2006)

[25] Gosling, J., McGilton, H.: The Java Language Environment: A White Paper. Sun Microsystems Press (October 1995)

[26] Schulte, M.J., Glossner, J., Mamidi, S., Moudgill, M., Vassiliadis, S.: A Low-Power Multithreaded Processor for Baseband Communication Systems. In: Pimentel, A.D., Vassiliadis, S. (eds.) SAMOS 2004. LNCS, vol. 3133, pp. 393–402. Springer, Heidelberg (2004)

[27] Nichols, B., Buttlar, D., Farrell, J.: Pthreads Programming: A POSIX Standard for Better Multiprocessing, O'Reilly Nutshell Series, Sebastopol, CA (September 1996)

[28] Jarvinen, K., et al.: GSM Enhanced Full Rate Speech Codec. In: IEEE International Conference on Acoustics, Speech, and Signal Processing, pp. 771–774 (1997)

[29] Kotlyar, V., Moudgill, M.: Detecting Overflow Detection. In: Proceedings of the 2004 CODES+ISSS International Conference on Hardware/Software Codesign and System Synthesis, Stockholm, Sweden, pp. 36–41 (September 8-10, 2004)

[30] Balzola, P., Schulte, M., Ruan, J., Glossner, J., Hokenek, E.: Design Alternatives for Parallel Saturating Multioperand Adders. In: Proceedings of the International Conference on Computer Design, pp. 172–177 (September 2001)

# Design of a Low Power Pre-synchronization ASIP for Multimode SDR Terminals

Thomas Schuster, Bruno Bougard, Praveen Raghavan, Robert Priewasser,
David Novo, Liesbet Van der Perre, and Francky Catthoor

IMEC
Kapeldreef 75
3000 Leuven, Belgium
{schuster,bougardb,ragha,priewasr,novo,vdperre,catthoor}@imec.be

**Abstract.** SDR enables cost-effective multi-mode terminals but still suffers from significant energy penalty when compared to dedicated hardware solutions. At system level, this energy bottleneck can be leveraged capitalizing on heterogeneous MPSOC platforms where specific engines are dedicated to classes of functions with similar computation characteristics and duty cycle. In burst-based communication as in IEEE802.11 or IEEE802.16, burst detection functions have high duty cycle and hence need an ultra low power implementation. Besides, programmability must be preserved to support multiple modes. A low-power pre-synchronization ASIP is designed targeting the IEEE802.11a/g/n and IEEE802.16e synchronization at 20MHz input rate. Power simulations at gate-level show that an IEEE802.16e synchronization (20MHz) can be carried out with an average power of 15.86mW. This corresponds to an effective energy efficiency of 115.89MOPS/mW (32-bit equivalent operations).

## 1 Introduction

The combination of the continuously growing variety of wireless standards and the increasing costs related to IC design and handset integration make implementation of wireless standards on reconfigurable radio platforms the only viable option in the near future. The Software Defined Radio (SDR) paradigm, according to which digital radio functionality is executed on widely reusable programmable platforms, is an effective way to provide the therefore necessary performance and flexibility.

If programmable from a high-level language (such as C), SDR enables cost-effective multi-mode terminals but still suffers from a significant energy penalty compared to dedicated hardware solutions. Hence, programmability and energy efficiency must be carefully balanced. To maintain energy efficiency at the level required for mobile device integration, abstraction may only be introduced where its impact on the total average power is sufficiently low or at those places where the resulting extra flexibility can be exploited by improved energy management (Targeted Flexibility, [5]). Many different architecture styles have already been proposed for SDR. Most of them are designed keeping in mind the important

S. Vassiliadis et al. (Eds.): SAMOS 2007, LNCS 4599, pp. 322–332, 2007.

characteristics of wireless physical layer processing: high data level parallelism (DLP) and data flow dominance [11,14,18]. Targeted Flexibility and the fact that in wireless systems area can partly be traded for energy efficiency ask for heterogeneous MPSOC architectures [6,9], in which the different tasks of a transmission scheme are implemented on specific engines providing just the necessary performance at minimum cost.

In practice, a radio standard implementation contains, next to modulation and demodulation, functionality for Medium Access Control (MAC) and, in case of burst-based communication, signal detection and time synchronization. The high DLP does not hold for the MAC processing which is, by definition, control dominated and should be implemented separately (e.g. on a RISC). Moreover, packet detection and coarse time synchronization have a significantly higher duty cycle than packet modulation and demodulation. They, therefore require a different flexibility/efficiency tradeoff.

In this work, we develop an instruction set processor specialized for signal detection and coarse time synchronization that will be part of a heterogeneous MPSOC platform for SDR [6]. We focus on the IEEE 802.11a/g/n and IEEE 802.16e standards, where packet-based radio transmission is implemented based on Orthogonal Frequency Division Multiplexing or Multiple-Access (OFDM(A)). The main design target is energy efficiency. Performance must be just sufficient to enable real time processing at the rates defined by the standards. In our reference implementations, packet detection and coarse synchronization account for less than 5% of the total code size. Hence, the effort for assembly programming is reasonable and compiler support not critical.

The remainder of the paper is structured as follows. In section 2, we analyze the targeted functionality and define the processor architecture. Section 3 focuses on design flow and implementation. Conclusions are drawn in section 5.

# 2    Architecture Definition

Specific target applications for our design are signal detection and time synchronizations for IEEE 802.11a/g/n and IEEE 802.16e. Reason is that those functions have the highest duty cycle and dominate the standby power consumption.

Because one also wants to take provision for future standards such as 3GPP-LTE, an Application Specific Instruction-set Processor (ASIP) approach is preferred [12,14]. For energy-aware implementation, special attention must be paid to the selection of the instruction-set, parallelization, storage elements (register files, memories) and interconnect. In this section, the most important architectural decisions are motivated.

## 2.1    Instruction-Set Selection

Usually, ASIP design starts with a careful analysis of the targeted algorithms. We applied a flow where profiling is performed on the application to obtain the parts of the data flow graph which are activated often [4,19]. Therefore, code for

```
/* loop 1 – correlate */
for i = START_IDX : END_IDX
begin
    sample = indata[i];
    sample16 = indata[i-16];
    sample32 = indata[i-32];
    sum = sample16 + sample32;
    prod = sum * conj(sample);
    corr[i] = accumulate(prod);
end

/* loop 2 – normalize */
for i = START_IDX:END_IDX
begin
    sample = indata[i];
    power = sample * conj(sample);
    power_accu = accumulate(power);
    power_corr = corr[i]*conj(corr[i]);
    corr_normal = power_corr / power_accu;
end

/* loop 3 – detect */
for i = START_IDX : END_IDX
begin
    if (corr_normal[i] > max) and (corr_normal[i] > THRESHOLD) then
        max = corr_normal[i];
        pos = i;
    end
    if (corr_normal[i] < max) and (i==pos+TRAILINGSMALLER) then
        return(pos);
    end
end
```

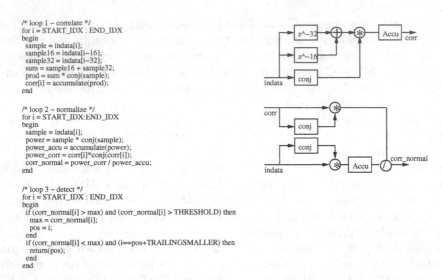

**Fig. 1.** Pseudo-code and data-flow in 802.11a synchronization

the targeted modes was written in Matlab and evaluated. Figure 1 illustrates the typical structure of a synchronization algorithm on the example of IEEE802.11a.

The code mainly consists of three loops. In the first two of them, the correlation in the input signal is explored. Here significant DLP is present that can be efficiently exploited by vector machines. In the third loop, one scans for a peak in the correlation result and compares it to a threshold. This is a more control oriented task. It can also be seen that a number of input samples (correlation window) needs to be stored in memory.

The code for IEEE802.16e, shows very similar characteristics. Moreover, many common computational primitives can be identified, which suits the followed ASIP approach. However, compared to the IEEE802.11a synchronization, the algorithms for IEEE802.16e are far more computationally intensive (191 op/sample in average vs. 82 op/sample for IEEE802.11a). In terms of throughput, both applications are very demanding (up to 20Msamples/s). Throughput will be even higher for the multi-antenna operations in IEEE802.11n. Here it is intended to use 1 processor per antenna tile.

Fixed-point refinement shows that all computations for IEEE802.11a and IEEE802.16e can be done within 16bit signed precision. Moreover, all divisions can be removed by algorithmic transformations. The code has been optimized, including merging of the kernels into a single loop to improve data locality and reduce control. Afterwards, the code was vectorized and mapped to a number of pragmatically selected primitives.

Table 1 shows the derived instruction set and the instruction count breakdown for the computations on a single input vector in our IEEE802.11a and IEEE802.16e detection loop. Vector size is a parameter. The number of vector operations per iteration is independent of the vector size. Bigger vectors will just reduce the number of iterations needed to process the whole input stream.

**Table 1.** Instruction-set and Statistic Coarse Time Synchronization

| vector operation | description | 11a/g/n | 16e |
|---|---|---|---|
| vmov | fill vector with immediate | 0 | 0 |
| vcmul | complex vector multiplication | 5 | 16 |
| vadd,vsub | vector add, sub | 2 | 9 |
| vasr,vlsl | shift vector elements right, left | 1 | 0 |
| vand,vor | and, or vectors | 0 | 0 |
| vtriang | accumulate across vector | 2 | 5 |
| vlevel | fill vector with vector element | 2 | 5 |
| vrotX | rotate vectors X positions | 0 | 2 |
| vcon | conjugate complex vector | 2 | 9 |
| vreal/vimag | real/imag vector components | 0 | 0 |

| generate vector | description | 11a/g/n | 16e |
|---|---|---|---|
| spread | fill vector with scalar elements | 1 | 4 |
| vload | load vector from address | 2 | 5 |
| pinld | load vector from i/o interface | 1 | 1 |

| evaluate vector | description | 11a/g/n | 16e |
|---|---|---|---|
| rgrep/igrep | extract real/imag value from vec | 1 | 3 |
| rmax/imax | max in real/imag vec elements | 1 | 1 |
| vstore | store vector to address | 1 | 1 |

| scalar operation | description | 11a/g/n | 16e |
|---|---|---|---|
| mov | move scalar register | 2 | 5 |
| mul | scalar multiplication | 0 | 0 |
| add, sub | scalar add, sub | 4 | 1 |
| lsl,asr | shift left, right | 1 | 0 |
| and,or,xor | and, or, xor scalar values | 6 | 4 |
| modi | modulo index calculation | 0 | 0 |
| pinst | write value to i/o interface | 0 | 0 |
| branch,jump | cond., uncond. branch | 3 | 3 |

The behavior of the derived instructions is widely self-explaining (see description column in Table 1). Instructions with zero operation count are used in other kernels or glue-code. Because all computations are done on complex samples, we decided to implement complex arithmetic in hardware. This has already been proven efficient for SDR processing [17]. The biggest challenge was the development of a mechanism for vector accumulation. The detection of the synchronization peak must be sample accurate. Hence, all correlation outputs need to be evaluated. We therefore introduced a scheme that preserves the intermediate results of a vector accumulation (vtriang, vlevel - fig. 2) and instructions to extract maxima from vectors (rmax/imax).

## 2.2   Parallel Processing

It has already been demonstrated that in-order VLIW machines with capabilities for vector processing are most energy efficient for SDR [18]. Following this

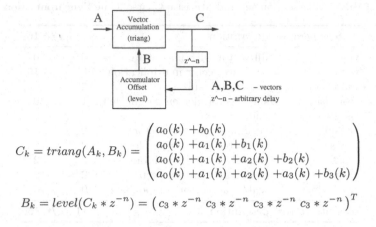

$$C_k = triang(A_k, B_k) = \begin{pmatrix} a_0(k) +b_0(k) \\ a_0(k) +a_1(k) +b_1(k) \\ a_0(k) +a_1(k) +a_2(k) +b_2(k) \\ a_0(k) +a_1(k) +a_2(k) +a_3(k) +b_3(k) \end{pmatrix}$$

$$B_k = level(C_k * z^{-n}) = \begin{pmatrix} c_3 * z^{-n} & c_3 * z^{-n} & c_3 * z^{-n} & c_3 * z^{-n} \end{pmatrix}^T$$

**Fig. 2.** Vector accumulation concept

approach, after the instruction set definition, one has to decide about the amount of parallel processing that is needed to guarantee real-time performance at minimum energy cost.

We first derive a target clock. The maximum achievable clock rate is limited to 200MHz by the available low power memories, which we intend to read and write without multi-cycle access or stalling the processor. Next, instruction and data-level parallelism are analyzed. From the application, it is observed that control and data processing can easily be parallelized. This yields separate scalar and vector slots. Since DLP is largely present in the considered algorithms, the amount of vectorization is decided first. Assuming a processor with a single vector slot and a clock rate of 200MHz, we would need a vectorization factor of at least 4.5 to process a zero-slack schedule of our most demanding application real-time (IEEE802.16e at 20MHz input rate). Realistic (close to zero-slack) schedule for a vectorization factor of 4 is made possible by using multiple vector slots with orthogonal instruction set. This also guarantees maximum utilization of the operators [13]. The ratio of vector operations to scalar operations is 46/28 in the IEEE802.16e and 23/16 in the IEEE802.11a kernel (Tab. 1). Accordingly, the target architecture should ideally be able to process 3 vector and 2 scalar operations in parallel. The design is therefore partitioned in three vector and two scalar instruction slots.

Figure 3 shows the derived processor micro-architecture and the distribution of the instruction set. The instructions in the scalar slots operate on 16bit signed operands, the instructions in the vector slots on 4 complex samples in parallel (128bit). It is intuitive that further vectorization (256-bit or 512-bit) will lead to larger complexity in the interconnection network and hence is not considered [7]. Register file organization and interconnect will be discussed next.

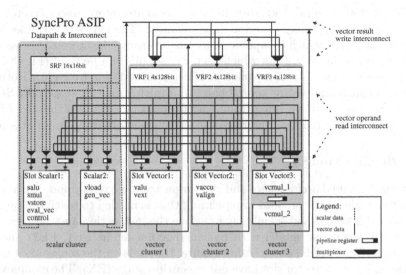

**Fig. 3.** SyncPro Vector Processor

## 2.3 Clustered Registerfiles and Interconnect

A shared multiported register files is typically a scalability bottleneck in VLIW structures and also one of the highest power consumers. Therefore, a clustered register file implementation is preferred.

We decided to implement 4 general purpose register files (Fig. 3). The scalar register file (SRF) contains 16 registers of 16 bit and has 4 read and 2 write ports. Because of its small word-width, the costs of sharing it amongst the functional units (FUs) in the two scalar slots is rather low [15]. The vector side of the processor is fully clustered. Each of the three vector register files (VRF), holds 4 registers of 128 bit and has 3 read and 1 write port. Two of the read ports are dedicated to the FUs in a particular vector slot. The third one, is used for operand broadcasting (intercluster read) and can be accessed from all the other FUs in non-local issue slots and slot scalar1 (vector evaluation, vector store). Because each VRF has only one broadcast port, only one intercluster read per VRF can be carried out per cycle. Routing the vector operands is done via a *vector operand read interconnect*. Respectively, the *vector result write interconnect* is used to route computation results to the write ports of the VRFs. Each VRF write port can be written from all vector slots and from FUs in slot scalar2 (generate vector, vector load). The programmer is responsible to avoid access conflicts. The selected interconnect provides almost as much flexibility as a central register file, but at a lower energy cost [16].

## 2.4 Memory and I/O

For all targeted modes, at least the correlation distance of the input signal needs to be buffered in memory. We therefore implemented a data scratchpad with a capacity of 256 vectors (4 kByte). In order to share interconnect, vector load and vector store are implemented in different units. The load FU is connected to the first scalar slot, which is capable of writing vectors. The store FU is assigned to the second scalar slot, from which vector operands can be read (Fig. 3). The L1 program memory has a capacity of 256 words of 96bit (3kByte). Both, L1 program memory and vector scratchpad are implemented as single port SRAM macros. To ease platform integration, the processor provides a number of I/O ports, specifically a blocking interface for reading vectors from an input stream.

## 2.5   Pipeline Model

Given the described architecture and the target technology in mind, it is now required to decide on the amount of pipelining that is needed to reach the targeted clock rate of 200MHz and seamlessly interface the instruction and data memory. We derived a pipeline model with two instruction fetch (FE1, FE2) and one instruction decode (DE) stage. Additionally, the units in the scalar slots and in the first and second vector slot have one execution stage (EX). The complex vector multplier FU, in the third vector slot, has two execution stages (EX, EX2). The FE1 stage implements the addressing phase of the program memory. The instruction word is read in FE2. In stage DE, the instruction is decoded and the data memory is addressed. The decoder decides, which register file ports need to be accessed. Routing, forwarding and chaining of source operands are fully software controlled. Source operands are saved in pipeline registers at the end of DE and consumed by the activated FUs in the following cycle. Register files are written at the end of EX (or EX2).

# 3   Implementation

The proposed processor architecture has been implemented in a 90nm CMOS technology. Therefore, three major steps have been carried out. First, the processor was modelled in LISA (Language for Instruction-Set Architecture), capitalizing on the Processor Designer$^{TM}$ toolsuite from Coware [2]. Then, RTL code was generated, synthesized and profiled in a gate-level power simulation. Finally, a backend experiment was carried out to ensure timing closure.

## 3.1   Instruction-Set Architecture Modelling

Coware Processor Designer is a tool-suite for automated embedded processor design [8,10]. Our motivation for using it is that it enables the generation of software development tools, such as assembler, linker and instruction-set simulator very early in the design process. So that, the processor micro-architecture can be co-optimized with the kernel software. Moreover, the tools offer strong support for platform integration (by generating wrapper for SystemC-based virtual platform modeling) and good-quality automated RTL code generation. Figure 4 illustrates the mentioned co-optimization strategy.

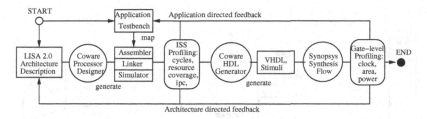

**Fig. 4.** Optimization methodology

We start with describing the instruction-set architecture in LISA. The resulting model is then iteratively refined into a pipelined micro-architecture representation, from which RTL code can be generated. Software and hardware are developed in parallel. The tools offer profiling functions, enabling fast application and architecture directed feedback, based on information about cycle count, instruction per cycle (IPC), code coverage and resource utilization. As soon the targets on those high level figures are met, the exploration is extended to architecture implementation level.

### 3.2  Logic Synthesis and Power Estimation

Implementation cost assessment requires the knowledge of silicon area, achievable clock rate and power consumption. Therefore, VHDL is generated from Processor Designer (HDL Generator - fig. 4) and synthesized using a mainly Synopsys based tool-chain (fig. 5) [3].

Following the depicted flow, the design was synthesized for a 90nm general purpose process with a standard cell library for nominal $V_t$. We target a clock rate of 200MHz under worst case operating conditions ($V_{DD} = 0.9V$, $T = 125C$).

Power estimation based on gate-level activity has been done utilizing Synopsys PrimePower$^{TM}$. Therefore, the automatically generated netlist, after preliminary placement and physical synthesis, was simulated with stimuli from the

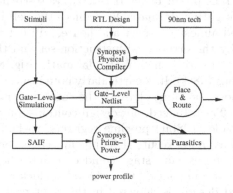

**Fig. 5.** Power Estimation Flow          **Fig. 6.** Chip Layout

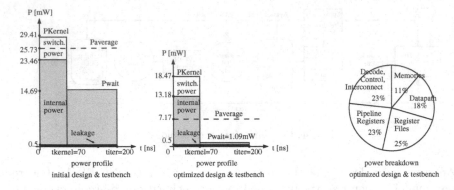

**Fig. 7.** Power Profile          **Fig. 8.** Power Breakdown

IEEE802.11a synchronization kernel. The left plot in figure 7 shows the power profile $(VDD = 1V, T = 25C)$ for a typical kernel iteration. The instruction- and data-dependent instantaneous power variation is averaged out since non-significant. The example refers to an input sample rate of 20MHz (5M vector/s with 4x vectorization) and a clock rate of 200MHz. The profile is characteritic for the processing of a real-time stream. At $0ns$, the first vector is read from the input interface. Consequently, the processor starts operating and consumes maximum power $(P_{kernel})$. After all necessary computations are done $(t_{kernel})$, the processor goes back to halt mode, waiting for new data $(t_{iter})$ to arrive. In this state, far less power is consumed $(P_{wait})$.

During micro-architecture design and software development, reduction of the surface (energy) in this power profile has been our major concern. To further reduce power consumption on implementation level two experiments have been carried out: operand isolation and clock gating. While the first optimization is supposed to cancel superfluous toggeling of operators, the latter aims on the re-duction of the power dissipated within the boundaries of standard cells (internal power).

By introducing clock gating the average power in the IEEE802.11a testbench could be reduced by 64%. While clock gating dramatically reduces the cell in-ternal power, operand isolation showed almost no effect and hence, will not be implemented. This can be explained by the orthogonal instruction-set and the fact that only 18% of the total power are consumed in the datapath (Fig. 8). Biggest power consumer are the flip-flops (48%). It is particularly noted that the pipeline registers (23%) consume almost the same share of the total power as the four general purpose register files (25%). Indeed, our design contains a high number of frequently accessed very wide (128bit) pipeline registers, to buffer source operands between the decode (DE) and execute (EX) pipeline stage (Sec. 2.5). Moving the register file read in the execute stage could eliminate those registers. However, it would have dramatic impact on the achievable clock rate.

The power profile for the optimized design, is depicted in the right part of figure 7. The energy spend for the processing of one input vector of four complex samples could be reduced from $3.97nJ$ to $1.43nJ$. First power simulations for the IEEE802.16e synchronization show very similar results for $P_{kernel}$ and $P_{wait}$. However, for the most demanding mode with 20MHz input rate, we estimate a duty cycle of 85%. Under this assumption, the energy for the computations on one input vector is 3.17 nJ.

### 3.3  Backend Experiment

For a first place, route and clock tree insertion, we utilized SOCEncounter$^{TM}$ from Cadence [1]. Post-Layout back-annotation was only performed for verification and to ensure timing closure. The final processor will be taped out as an integrated part of a MPSOC platform [6]. Our results show that the targeted clock rate of 200MHz can be easily met. Assuming 9 layers of metal, the layout footprint is $0.8mm^2$, including 3KB program memory ($0.06mm^2$) and 4KB data memory ($0.07mm^2$) (fig. 6).

## 4  Conclusion

Heterogeneous MPSOC platforms are considered to enable SDR implementation competitive in energy efficiency with dedicated hardware solutions. In such platforms, specific engines execute classes of functions that relate in their computation characteristics and duty cycle. In burst-based communication, signal detection functions have high duty cycle and hence need ultra low power implementation. Besides, programmability must be preserved to support the implementation of multiple modes. Therefore, a low-power pre-synchronization ASIP is designed targeting IEEE802.11a/g/n and IEEE802.16e. The processor delivers a theoretical maximum performance of 5 GOPS (32bit equivalent) at a peak power of 25 mW. Energy efficiency is hence 200 MOPS/mW (fully loaded). An IEEE802.11a synchronization (20 MHz) requires only 630 MOPS. The processor consumes 7.17 mW when executing this kernel (79.5 MOPS/mW). The more demanding IEEE802.16e synchronization (20MHz) requires 1838 MOPS. For this kernel the estimated average power is 15.86 mW (115.89 MOPS/mW). The achieved energy efficiency is 2-4 times higher than in typical SDR baseband processors. Our ASIP can therefore be used to implement low power packet detection, enabling energy aware multi-processor SDR platforms.

## References

1. Cadence, http://www.cadence.com/
2. Coware inc., http://www.coware.com/
3. Synopsys, http://www.synopsys.com/
4. Biswas, P., Choudhary, V., Atasu, K., Pozzi, L., Ienne, P., Dutt, N.: Introduction of local memory elements in instruction set extensions. In: DAC '04. Proceedings of the 41st annual conference on Design automation, pp. 729–734 (2004)

5. Bougard, B., Hollevoet, L., Naessens, F., Ng, A., Schuster, T., Van der Perre, L.: A low power signal detection and pre-synchronization engine for energy-aware software defined radio. In: SDRForum, November 2006 (2006)
6. Bougard, B., Novo, D., Naessens, F., Hollevoet, L., Schuster, T., Glassee, M., Dejonghe, A., Van der Perre, L.: A scalable programmable baseband platform for energy-efficient reactive software-defined-radio. In: CrownCom, June 2006 (2006)
7. DeMan, H.: Ambient intelligence: Giga-scale dreams and nano-scale realities. In: Proc of ISSCC, Keynote Speech (February 2005)
8. Gloeckner, T., Hoffmann, A., Meyr, H.: Methodical low-power asip design space exploration. In: Journal of VLSI Signal Processing 33 (2003)
9. Glossner, J., Moudgill, M., Iancu, D.: The sandbridge sdr communication platform. In: SympoTIC, October 2004 (2004)
10. Hoffmann, A., Meyr, H., Leupers, R.: Architecture exploration for embedded processors with LISA. Kluwer Academic Publishers, Dordrecht (2002)
11. Hosemann, M., Cichon, G., Robelly, P., Seidel, H., Draeger, T., Richter, T., Bronzel, M., Fettweis, G.: Implementing a receiver for terrestrial digital video broadcasting in software on an application-specific dsp. In: SIPS (2004)
12. Ienne, P., Leupers, R.: Customizable Embedded Processors: Design Technologies and Applications. Morgan Kauffman, San Francisco (2006)
13. Jacome, M.F., de Veciana, G., Lapinskii, V.: Exploring performance tradeoffs for clustered VLIW ASIPs. In: Proc. of ICCAD, November 2000 (2000)
14. Lin, Y., Lee, H., Woh, M., Harel, Y., Mahlke, S., Mudge, T., Chakrabarti, C., Flautner, K.: SODA: A low-power architecture for software radio. In: Proc of ISCA (2006)
15. Raghavan, P., Lambrechts, A., Jayapala, M., Catthoor, F., Verkest, D.: Empirical power model for register files. In: Workshop on Media and Streaming Processors (with MICRO-38) (November 2005)
16. Rixner, S., Dally, W.J., Khailany, B., Mattson, P.R., Kapasi, U.J., Owens, J.D.: Register organization for media processing. In: HPCA, January 2000, pp. 375–386 (2000)
17. Rounioja, K., Puusaari, K.: Implementation of an hsdpa receiver with a customized vector processor. In: SoC2006 (November 2006)
18. van Berkel, K., Heinle, F., Meuwissen, P., Moermann, K., Weiss, M.: Vector processing as an enabler for software-defined radio in handsets from 3g+ wlan onwards. In: SDR Technical Conference (2004)
19. Yu, P., Mitra, T.: Characterizing embedded applications for instruction-set extensible processors. In: DAC '04. Proceedings of the 41st annual conference on Design automation, pp. 723–728 (2004)

# Area Efficient Fully Programmable Baseband Processors

Anders Nilsson and Dake Liu

Division of Computer Engineering at Department of Electrical Engineering,
Linköping University, Linköping, Sweden
{andni,dake}@isy.liu.se

**Abstract.** Multi-mode wireless devices and the ever changing wireless standards have increased the popularity and the use of programmable baseband processors. A large portion of the power consumption in programmable baseband processors arises from memory accesses and control-path overhead. It is for that reason crucial to reduce the control-path overhead and the amount of memory accesses by using efficient yet flexible execution units in the processor. By utilizing the vector nature of most baseband processing algorithms it is possible to achieve multi-GIPS processing performance with a limited power budget. In this paper we present an architecture that uses the vector property to provide a good trade-off between the flexibility of VLIW processors and the efficiency of SIMD processors. Our DSP is based on the Single Instruction stream Multiple Tasks (SIMT) architecture which allows concurrent tasks to be executed on the processor controlled by only a single instruction stream

The SIMT architecture is demonstrated by the BBP2 processor which has been fabricated using the ST 0.12μm process. The BBP2 processor is designed for supporting DVB-T/H, WCDMA, Wireless LAN and WiMAX.

## 1 Introduction

Efficient programmable baseband processors are important to enable true multi-standard radio platforms as convergence of mobile communication devices and systems require multi-standard processing devices. The processors do not only need the capability to handle differences in a single standard, often there is a need to cover several completely different modulation methods such as OFDM and CDMA with the same processing device.

Programmability can also be used to quickly adapt to new and updated standards within the ever changing wireless network industry in situations where a pure ASIC solution will not be flexible enough. ASIC solutions for multi-standard baseband processing are also less area efficient than their programmable counterparts since processing resources cannot be efficiently shared between different operations.

However, as baseband processing is computationally demanding, traditional DSP architectures cannot be used due to their limited computing capacity. Instead VLIW- and SIMD-based processors are used to provide enough computing capacity for baseband applications.

The drawback of VLIW-based DSPs is their low power efficiency due to the wide instructions that need to be fetched every clock cycle and their control-path overhead.

S. Vassiliadis et al. (Eds.): SAMOS 2007, LNCS 4599, pp. 333–342, 2007.

On the other hand, pure SIMD-based DSPs lack the possibility to perform different concurrent operations. Since memory access power is the dominating part of the power consumption in a processor [1], other alternatives should be investigated.

Instead of designing a processor based on traditional architectures, this project has started from the application requirements and designed a processor with a new architecture to meet the requirements with efficiency in mind. The architecture is named "Single Instruction stream Multiple Tasks", SIMT in short. The SIMT architecture uses the vector nature of most baseband programs to provide a good trade-off between the flexibility of a VLIW processor and the processing efficiency of a SIMD processor.

Compared to other promising projects such as the OnDSP [2] or EVP16 [3] from Philips/NXP and Sandblaster [4] from Sandbridge, the SIMT architecture proves competitive. Even compared with the most efficient code compaction scheme for VLIW, the code size is reduced by approximately a factor of two. In this paper we first present the SIMT architecture. Secondly we present the BBP2 processor which demonstrates the SIMT architecture.

## 2    Baseband Properties

Analysis of baseband processing applications reveals that most baseband processing tasks can be divided into one of the following three categories:

- Front-end processing and filtering
- Modem processing
- Forward error correction

In order to ensure high computing efficiency, the processing resources used by each category of tasks should be optimized for the tasks. If an operation is performed on every sample in one or many standards it should be considered for acceleration. For example, it is not justified to use generic computing resources to perform front-end filtering, decimation and I/Q-mismatch compensation since these operations are used by all standards and are performed on every received sample. Accordingly the data-type should be selected with the operations performed in mind. In the presented architecture, configurable accelerators are used to provide efficient yet flexible front-end and forward error correction support.

Since the modem processing stage is the stage where the diversity among standards and implementations differ the most, it is important to provide most flexibility here.

### 2.1    Task Level Pipelines

Further analysis of signal processing operations within the modem stage shows that most operations operate on large *vectors* of data such as convolution, FFT or dot-product. Since there is no or little backward data dependencies within a block of data, *task level pipelines* can be used. Task level pipelining is a method of increasing the processing parallelism by running several independent tasks simultaneously and passing data between the tasks at specific times. Task level parallelism is illustrated in Figure 1.

This technique is also used to store incoming and outgoing samples in one memory while other execution units operate concurrently. When a processing task is finished the

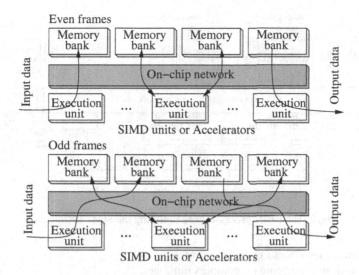

**Fig. 1.** Illustration of the concept of task level parallelism. The vector property of baseband modem processing allows parallelization of processing tasks. Data are handed over between tasks at distinct time intervals.

memory banks are reconnected so that the output memory buffer from one execution unit is connected to the input port of the next execution unit in the processing pipeline. This memory arrangement allows the processor to perform most reception and transmission tasks without moving any data between memories.

## 3   SIMT Architecture

The SIMT architecture utilizes the vector property described earlier to provide an trade-off between the flexibility of a VLIW processor and the efficiency of SIMD processors.

As detailed application benchmarking shows that most operations in a baseband processor are performed on vectors of complex data, the SIMT architecture uses *vector instructions*. Vector instructions operate on a large set of data, such as a 256 point complex dot-product or one layer of an FFT. The vector instructions execute on one of several heterogenous complex valued SIMD clusters attached to an on-chip network. Typical SIMD clusters include Complex MAC (CMAC) units and Complex ALUs (CALU).

An example of a SIMT processor architecture, the BBP2 processor is shown in Figure 2.

### 3.1   Instruction Set

The instruction set architecture (ISA) of a SIMT processor consists of three classes of compound instructions.

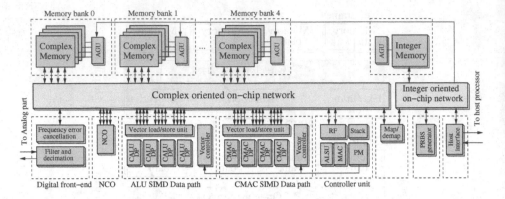

**Fig. 2.** The BBP2 processor; exemplifying the SIMT architecture

**RISC instructions** operating on 16 bit integers.
**DSP instructions** operating on complex numbers.
**Vector instructions** executing vector operations on a particular SIMD-cluster.

All instructions are narrow, typically 16-24 bit. The RISC-instruction class contains most control oriented instructions and this instruction class is executed on the controller unit of the processor. The DSP-instructions operate on complex-valued data and are executed on one of the SIMD units. Vector instructions are extensions of the DSP instructions since they operate on large data-sets and utilize advanced addressing modes.

### 3.2   SIMT - Instruction Issue

The key idea in the SIMT architecture is to *issue* only one instruction each clock cycle while letting several operations execute in parallel as vector instructions may run for several clock cycles on the SIMD units. This approach results in a degree of parallelism equivalent to a VLIW processor without the need for the large control-path overhead. This is illustrated in Figure 3.

In this way the vector property of baseband processing can be utilized to reduce the complexity and thus the power and the area of the processor. For example the integer data-path could execute operating system tasks while the CMAC performs one layer of an FFT and the CALU performs DC-offset cancellation.

To be able to take full advantage of the SIMT architecture, several key components are necessary: efficient vector execution units, a corresponding memory system and a controller core capable of managing several threads efficiently.

### 3.3   SIMD Processing Clusters

The SIMT processor architecture contains one or several SIMD execution clusters, accelerators and a controller unit. Common to the SIMD execution units are the vector controller and vector load/store unit (VLU/VSU). The VLU is the interface towards the memory blocks and the on-chip network (crossbar switch). The purpose of the VLU is to relax the memory access rate and reduce the number of memory data fetches.

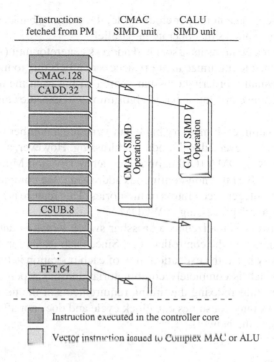

Fig. 3. SIMT - Single issue. Vector instructions are issued to the corresponding SIMD cluster and will execute for a number of clock cycles thus enabling processing parallelism with only a narrow instruction flow.

The VLU can load data in two different ways. In the first mode, multiple data items are loaded from a bank of memories. In the second mode, data are loaded one data item at a time and then distributed to the SIMD-data paths in the cluster. This later mode is used to reduce the number of memory accesses when consecutive data are processed by the SIMD cluster. If consecutive data are processed, the load unit can reduce the number of memory fetches by 3/4 in a 4-way execution unit. The VSU is used to create local feedback between data-paths within the execution unit. This is used to post process data in the accumulator registers without having to move data to a memory for intermediate storage.

Control signals for memory read and write operations are generated locally in the SIMD unit by the vector controller, while addressing support is provided by the memory bank.

### 3.4 Memory System and On-Chip Network

Efficient memory management is essential in order to efficiently use SIMD data-paths. To provide enough memory bandwidth to the SIMD data-paths and accelerators, a number of memory banks are used. The memory banks are then connected to the execution units via an on-chip network. Since each data-path within a SIMD execution unit requires one or several data items per clock cycle, the memory banks are partitioned as several small memory blocks that operate in parallel.

Each memory bank contains its associated address generator unit (AGU). The memory system is designed to minimize memory access conflicts due to memory block collisions by using a small reordering crossbar switch within each memory bank. In this way, radix-2/4 FFT and convolution based algorithms will execute completely collision free.

The AGU unit within each memory bank can generate a number of addressing patterns such as linear, bit-reversed and modulo addressing. However, as modern modulation schemes such as OFDMA (Orthogonal Frequency Division Multiple Access) and pilot extraction in DVB-H use non-continuous addressing, the complex memory banks can be addressed by integer accelerators or memories. This feature is also used to create buffers for "Rake finger" processing in WCDMA.

The on-chip network is realized as a crossbar switch which is under direct control of the software running on the controller core. Since each execution unit get "private" access to the memory bank, the execution time of each operation is fully predictable.

The crossbar switch is completely combinatorial and has pipeline registers at the edge of the network thus relaxing the timing requirements of the network. Reconfiguration of the network only consumes one clock cycle and does not affect other communications occurring in the network.

## 4  The BBP2 Processor

The BBP2 processor has been designed to demonstrate the SIMT concept by supporting symbol processing in the following diverse wireless standards:

- DVB-T and DVB-H
- WiMAX, IEEE 802.16d,e
- Wireless LAN, IEEE 802.11a,b,g
- WCDMA R6, including HSDPA

To support these standards the BBP2 processor is equipped with the following core components:

- Five complex valued memory banks organized as four banks of 8k complex words (16+16 bit) and one larger bank of 10k complex words. Each bank is divided into four memory blocks enabling read and write of four consecutive complex values each clock cycle.
- One integer memory of 4k × 16 bit used for data buffering between the Media Access Control layer and the processor.
- A controller core using 24 bit instructions with multi-context support, real valued multiplier and a 512 byte integer stack.
- A 4-Way Complex Multiply-accumulate SIMD unit capable of performing one radix-4 FFT butterfly per clock cycle.
- A 4-Way Complex ALU SIMD unit capable of performing multi-code de-spread in WCDMA.

The following functionality is accelerated using configurable accelerators:

- Digital front-end functionality such as filtering, decimation, sample-rate conversion and I/Q mismatch compensation. The digital front-end also contains a packet detector to wake up the processor core when a packet arrives.
- A 4-way Numerically Controlled Oscillator (NCO) used to provide coefficients for the CMAC unit during phase error correction calculations.
- A map/demap unit capable of automatically map/demap vector data.
- A PRBS generator used to index pilot tones in OFDM symbols.

Accelerators are selected according to the methodology presented in [5].

### 4.1 SIMD Execution Units and Accelerators

**Vector CMAC Unit.** The Complex MAC execution unit is capable of performing a number of different operations on its 4 Complex MAC lanes. The unit can execute a radix-4 butterfly or two parallel radix-2 operations per clock cycle in addition to vector multiplication and similar operations. The execution unit also supports Modified Walsh Transforms (MWT) and DCT. Each data-path within the unit uses $14 \times 14$ bit complex multipliers and has eight $2 \times 40$ bit accumulator registers.

**Vector ALU Unit.** The complex ALU unit is similar to the CMAC unit except for the multipliers that are replaced by a "short" complex multiplier [6] capable of only multiplying by $\{0, \pm 1; 0, \pm i\}$. Along with address and code generators, this unit can efficiently be used to perform Rake finger processing and de-spread in WCDMA and DSSS. By implementing a 4-way complex ALU unit with accumulator, the processor can perform either four parallel correlations or de-spread of four different codes at the same time in addition to normal add/subtract operations. The short complex multiplier can be controlled from either the instruction word, a de-scrambling code generator or from a OVSF code generator. All subunits are controlled from a vector controller which manages load and store order and hardware loop counting.

### 4.2 Benchmarking

To illustrate the effectiveness of the SIMT architecture kernel benchmarks of the BBP2 processor are presented in Table 1.

**Table 1.** Kernel benchmarks on the BBP2 processor. The presented cycle cost includes all set-up costs for memory addressing.

| Operation | Clock cycles |
|---|---|
| 4k point FFT | 6186 |
| 4k sample vector multiplication | 1027 |
| 32 sample dot product | 11 |
| 256 sample correlation | 4288 |

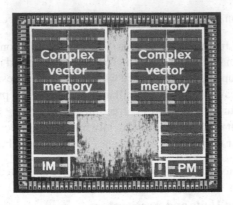

**Fig. 4.** Layout snapshot of the BBP2 processor. IM denotes the integer memory. Note the size of the Program Memory (PM) which is enough for managing Wireless LAN and DVB at the same time. The core area including memories is 11 mm$^2$ in a 0.12 μm process.

Since each vector operation only requires one 24 bit instruction word, the code density is very high. A complete 8192 sample FFT routine requires only 12 assembly instructions. A complex dot-product or vector multiplication can be performed using only one instruction word. Processing efficiency is further improved by the SIMT concept since multiple (up to two in BBP2) vector operations can be executed in parallel.

The resulting code size for the BBP2 processor is reduced by approximately a factor of two compared to the state-of the art VLIW processors [3] with code compaction for a comparable case of flexibility and parallelism.

## 5  Implementation

The BBP2 processor was taped-out in a ST 0.12 μm process early 2007. A layout snapshot is presented in Figure 4.

The main features of the BBP2 processor are:

- 1.92 G complex OP/s, @ 240 MHz (Complex MAC, Complex Arithmetics).
- Memory bandwidth of 153.6 Gbit/s @ 240 MHz.
- 24 bit instructions.
- 200k NAND2 equivalent gates.
- One 4-way CMAC unit with 14 × 14 bit multipliers and
- One 4-way complex ALU.
- Five complex valued memory banks of total 1.37 Mbit memory.
- 2k words of program memory. This is enough to hold a complete IEEE 802.11g (both OFDM and DSSS/CCK) software stack together with a DVB-receiver stack in RAM at the same time.
- 158 instructions divided among:
  - 92 RISC instructions
  - 22 Complex ALU instructions
  - 30 Complex MAC instructions
  - 14 Load / Store instructions

## 5.1  Cell Area of Individual Components

The cell area of each individual core component is presented in Table 2. Worth noticing is the low complexity of the controller core and the low percentage of the total cell area used for on-chip interconnect. In total, only 4.3 % of all gates are located in the crossbar switch.

**Table 2.** Gate count and relative area of BBP2 core components

| Unit | Area [kGates] | Relative area [%] |
|---|---|---|
| Controller core | 26.84 | 13.1 |
| Complex ALU SIMD unit | 20.01 | 9.8 |
| Complex MAC SIMD unit | 61.29 | 29.8 |
| Complex memory AGU | $5 \times 2.53$ | $5 \times 1.7$ |
| Integer memory AGU | 0.22 | 0.1 |
| Complex network | 8.61 | 4.2 |
| Integer network | 1.02 | 0.1 |
| NCO | 3.74 | 1.8 |
| Map/Demap | 2.35 | 1.1 |
| Front-end, filter | 6.12 | 3.0 |
| Front-end, farrow | 20.05 | 9.8 |
| Front-end, misc. | 33.99 | 16.5 |
| Host interface | 1.64 | 0.8 |
| PRBS Address generator | 2.38 | 1.2 |
| Total | 200.91 kGates (NAND2) | 100 % |

## 5.2  Clock and Power Gating

The SIMT architecture provides excellent opportunities for both clock and power gating at the boundary of the on-chip network. Since the network and execution units are under strict program control, clock and power gating can easily be applied. However, due to lack of proper back-end tool support for clock and power gating, these techniques were not implemented in the test chip.

# 6  Software

The availability of software tools is as important as a low silicon area for programmable baseband processors. The SIMT architecture is compiler friendly due to the straightforward issue of SIMD instructions. Scheduling is simplified since the runtime and resource usage is known for all instructions. Currently a C-compiler and a task scheduler are under development.

# 7  Conclusion

Programmability is essential for multi-standard baseband processors. For efficient support of multiple standards within a processing device, new architectures are necessary.

As a response to this, we have presented the SIMT architecture, a SIMD based architecture utilizing the vector property of baseband processing tasks to reduce the control overhead and the amount of memory accesses. We have also presented the BBP2 processor which is a versatile and area efficient processor capable of efficiently supporting a broad range of wireless standards.

To conclude, the SIMT architecture provides a flexible yet efficient platform for multi-standard baseband processing combining benefits from both VLIW- and SIMD-based DSPs. Relying on the large fraction of vector based processing in baseband processing, it achieves a high degree of parallelism combined with low control overhead and compact programs by using SIMT technology, enabling future efficient multi-standard wireless terminals.

**Acknowledgments.** Back-end, verification and design support from Coresonic AB, especially Dr Eric Tell and Erik Alfredsson are gratefully acknowledged. This work was supported by the STRINGENT research center at Linköping University and the Swedish Foundation for Strategic Research.

# References

1. Lidsky, D.B., Rabaey, J.: Low-power design of memory intensive functions. In: IEEE Symposium on Low Power Electronics, October 1994, pp. 16–17. IEEE Computer Society Press, Los Alamitos (1994)
2. Kneip, J., Weiss, M., Drescher, W., Aue, V., Strobel, J., Bolle, M., Fettweis, G.: Hipersonic: Single-chip programmable baseband assp for 5 GHz wireless lan applications. In: Cool Chips IV, Tokyo, April 2001, pp. 359–367 (2001)
3. van Berkel, K., Heinle, F., Meuwissen, P.P.E., Moerman, K., Weiss, M.: Vector processing as an enabler for software-defined radio in handheld devices. EURASIP Journal on Applied Signal Processing 16, 2613–2632 (2005)
4. Glossner, J., Iancu, D., Lu, J., Hokenek, E., Moudgill, M.: A software-defined communications baseband chip. IEEE Communications Magazine (January 2003)
5. Nilsson, A., Tell, E., Liu, D.: An accelerator structure for programmable multi-standard baseband processors. In: International conference of Wireless Networks and Emerging Technologies, Banff, AB, Canada (July 2004)
6. Nilsson, A., Tell, E., Liu, D.: A programmable simd-based multi-standard rake receiver architecture. In: European Signal Processing Conference, Antalya, Turkey (September 2005)

# The Next Generation Challenge for Software Defined Radio

Mark Woh[1], Sangwon Seo[1], Hyunseok Lee[1], Yuan Lin[1], Scott Mahlke[1], Trevor Mudge[1], Chaitali Chakrabarti[2], and Krisztian Flautner[3]

[1] University of Michigan - Ann Arbor, Ann Arbor MI, USA
[2] Arizona State University, Tempe, AZ, USA
[3] ARM Ltd., Cambridge, UK

**Abstract.** Wireless communication for mobile terminals has been a high performance computing challenge. It requires almost super computer performance while consuming very little power. This requirement is being made even more challenging with the move to Fourth Generation (4G) wireless communication. It is projected that by 2010, 4G will be available with data rates from 100Mbps to 1Gbps. These data rates are orders of magnitude greater than current 3G technology and, consequently, will require orders of magnitude more computation power. Leading forerunners for this technology are protocols like 802.16e (mobile WiMAX) and 3GPP LTE.

This paper presents an analysis of the major algorithms that comprise these 4G technologies and describes their computational characteristics. We identify the major bottlenecks that need to be overcome in order to meet the requirements of this new technology. In particular, we show that technology scaling alone of current Software Defined Radio architectures will not be able to meet these requirements. Finally, we will discuss techniques that may make it possible to meet the power/performance requirements without giving up programmability.

## 1 Introduction

The Third Generation Wireless age (3G) has provided an increase in data rate to the user which allows them to experience more than just voice over the air. Fourth Generation (4G) wireless networks is aimed at increasing that data rate by an order of magnitude in order to allow for users to experience richer content and get true mobility, freeing themselves from the need for wires or WiFi networks. The International Telecommunications Union (ITU) released a recommendation ITU-R M.1645 which sets data rate goals for 4G. They proposed a maximum data rate of 100Mbps for high mobility situations and 1Gbps for stationary and low mobility situations like hot spots. These targets are being used by most research on 4G today. It is also envisioned that 4G will include earlier standards and their protocols, and that they will work harmoniously together. SDR solutions can help reduce the cost of systems, which are required to support such a wide range of existing wireless technologies.

S. Vassiliadis et al. (Eds.): SAMOS 2007, LNCS 4599, pp. 343–354, 2007.

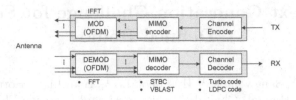

**Fig. 1.** The physical layer for a 4G terminal

Previous papers have characterized the computational requirments of 3G [1]. There have been several proposals for SDR architectures capable of supporting 3G W-CDMA and 802.11 physical layers. Examples are Sandbridge's Sandblaster [2] and SODA [3]. But these architectures are not able to handle the almost 10-1000x increase in throughput required for 4G systems. This paper outlines the 4G physical layer. The aim is to show the requirements that are needed to process the new 4G physical layer and also to identify computational patterns that might suggest an architecture that can support 4G.

The 4G system we will study is based on orthogonal frequency division multiplexing (OFDM) that uses a 1024-point FFT/IFFT, a 4x4 16QAM multiple input multiple output (MIMO) antenna system, and a low density parity (LDPC) encoder and decoder. Detailed analysis of the major algorithms that make up these components and their computational characteristics show the following repeated computational pattern: load data from a memory element (initially this is the received data), permuting that data, performing one or two ALU operations, and storing the processed data back to memory. These patterns are similar to those found in 3G kernels. The architectures that are designed to support them, such as SODA, will not be able to meet the 4G requirements through technology scaling alone. As we will show, other techniques will have to be enlisted such as wider SIMD engines, special purpose functional units, and special memory systems.

This paper is organized as follows. In the next section, we begin by presenting a simplified 4G system and by describing some of major kernels: an OFDM modulator/demodulator, a MIMO modulator/demodulator, and a channel decoder for LDPC. In section 3, we give a brief overview of SODA and use it as a baseline to identify the dominate workload profiles and common computational patterns of the kernels. In section 4, we present programmable hardware support for implementing these kernels efficiently to meet the high throughput required for 4G. The summary and concluding remarks are given in section 5.

## 2   4G Physical Layer

Figure 1 shows a 4G wireless terminal. Like other wireless communication system, its major blocks are a channel encoder/decoder and a modulator/demodulator. The role of the channel encoder is forward error correction that enables receivers to correct errors without retransmission. Modulation maps input data sequence onto signal waveforms which are specifically designed for the wireless channel. Demodulation estimates the transmitted data sequence from

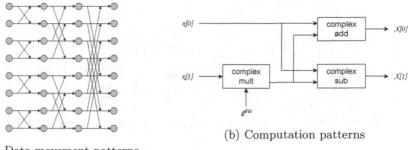

(a) Data movement patterns

(b) Computation patterns

**Fig. 2.** The data movement of an 8 point FFT and the computations in a 2 point FFT

the received waveform, which have been corrupted by noise and interference when they traversed the wireless channel.

In order to satisfy the gigabit level throughput requirement, 4G systems employ three techniques not found together in 3G: 1) orthogonal frequency division multiple access (OFDMA); 2) MIMO to support multiple antennas; and 3) LDPC codes for the channel encoder/decoder.

## 2.1 OFDMA

OFDMA is a modulation scheme which transmits input signals over multiple narrow sub-channels. Both modulation and demodulation in OFDMA systems can be implemented with fast fourier transforms (FFT). Although additional synchronization procedures are required in OFDMA receivers, we can ignore them because their contribution is small.

**FFT.** As shown in Figure 1, the transmitter uses an inverse FFT (IFFT) for modulation and the receiver uses an FFT for demodulation. Because FFT and IFFT are almost identical, we will just analyze the FFT.

The FFT operation consists of a data movement followed by multiplication and addition on a complex number. If we assume an N point FFT, it consists of $\log_2 N$ stages. As an example, Figure 2.1 shows the data movement pattern of an 8 point FFT. It consists of 3 stages. Each stage shows a different but regular data movement pattern. The operation of each stage can be divided into several 2 point FFT operation as depicted in Figure 2.1.

The FFT allows wide data level parallelism because all 2 point FFT operations required for proceeding from one stage to the next can be done in parallel. It is important to exploit this type of data level parallelism to meet power and performance requirements of 4G system, because the FFT width of 4G systems can be as large as 2048.

## 2.2 MIMO

MIMO is a technique that uses multiple antennas both for the transmission and reception. It can be used for two purposes: signal quality enhancement by

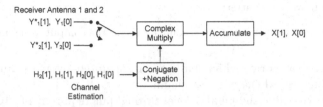

(a) Transmission Matrix—the * indicates complex conjugate.

(b) Computation patterns of an STBC encoder

(c) Computation pattern of an STBC decoder

**Fig. 3.** Transmission code matrix and computation patterns of the Alamouti 2x2 STBC

transmitting identical signal through multiple antennas and channel capacity enhancement by transmitting different signals on multiple antennas. Space time block codes (STBC) is a popular MIMO technique for the signal quality enhancement and the vertical Bell Laboratories layered space-time (V-BLAST) technique is popular for channel capacity enhancement.

**STBC.** This is used to increase the signal quality by transmitting the same signal multiple times through different antennas. Signal quality is increased by receiving those redundant copies of the same signal and using the information from each receiver to optimally combine them to produce a better signal. The implementation we used is based on Alamouti's 2x2 scheme [4], which uses 2 transmit and 2 receive antennas.

*STBC Encoder.* The encoder orders and transmits data based on the transmission matrix shown in figure 3(a). The operation consists of transmitting two different symbols at the first time instance, then transmitting the conjugate of the same two symbols with antennas switched (see the matrix in figure 3(a)). Figure 3(b) shows the computation needed to perform this operation. First the data is sent to each modulator and then the conjugate and negation are performed. This corresponds to a simple predication operation to obtain the real and imaginary values. This is highly parallelizable, and a 1024 point FFT could be run in parallel on a 1024 wide SIMD (Single Instruction, Multiple Data) processor.

*STBC Decoder.* The decoder takes the transmitted data from both time instances and combines them together to create the original two symbols. The decoder operation consists of performing complex multiplications between each of the received signals and the channel estimation for each antenna and then summing the values. Figure 3(c) shows this operation pattern. Calculating both symbols can be done at the same time with the least amount of data movement. Once again, because subcarriers are totally independent, this algorithm is highly data parallel, and a 1024 point FFT could be run in parallel on a 1024 wide SIMD.

**V-BLAST.** This is one of the spatial multiplexing schemes that improves multiplexing gain by transmitting independent data streams over different antennas. This technique combines multipath signals to obtains higher data rate compared to STBC. The V-BLAST algorithm that was used was based on work from [5] which reduces the computational complexity of V-BLAST.

*V-BLAST encoder.* The V-BLAST encoder is similar to the STBC encoder. It also uses a transmission matrix to decide ordering, conjugating and negating for a block of data. Therefore, the pattern of required operations is: load the real and imaginary received data, permute the data based on the transmission matrix, then negate and store the result before sending it to the OFDM modulators associated with the multiple antennas. The computation pattern would be the same as figure 3(b) except the matrix for V-BLAST is 4x4.

*V-BLAST decoder.* The decoding process of V-BLAST consists of two major steps: channel estimation and signal detection. The channel matrix is estimated based on pre-defined training symbols. The operations for channel estimation are relatively simple with shift and sign-change operations. Once the channel matrix has been estimated, the detection order is determined. The detection order is based on signal strength found among all the signals received. The strongest signal is selected and extracted from the received signal. This process is repeated for the remaining signals. This process is iterative and is referred to as successive interference cancelation. The signal detecting operations can be described by the following steps: 1) load the received signal; 2) vector multiplication for obtaining the stongest signal; 3) vector multiplication and subtraction for canceling the strongest signal; and 4) repeat.

## 2.3   Channel Encoder/Decoder

4G systems are expected to use both Turbo codes and LDPC codes as channel coding schemes. We limit our discussion to the characteristics of the LDPC codes in this section, because Turbo codes have already been used in 3G systems and their characteristics have been well documented elsewhere [6] [7].

**LDPC.** Figure 1 shows the channel encoder and decoder for LDPC. It is currently used in IEEE 802.16e and 802.11n. The encoder for LDPC is trivial in the sense that for each LDPC code there are a set of codewords available. For

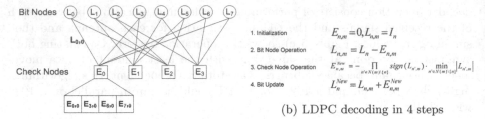

(a) Graphical representation of LDPC code

(b) LDPC decoding in 4 steps

**Fig. 4.** LDPC graphical representation and decoding operations

different data rates there are different number of codewords. In order to transmit data a codeword is picked and sent through the transmitter. Because the operation is fairly simple we will only discuss the LDPC decoding operation.

Decoding is based on an architecturally aware design for LDPC codes given in [8]. The code rates and the block sizes used were based on the IEEE 802.16e standard [9] and picked in order to meet the 100Mbps and 1Gbps target data rate.

The graphical representation of LDPC is shown in figure 4(a). The check nodes represents the number of rows in the parity check code and the bit nodes represent the number of columns. The edges connecting the check nodes and bit nodes are the 1's in the parity check code matrix—all other values are 0. The LDPC decoding operation is broken down into 4 stages as shown in figure 4(b). These four stages are the Initialization, Bit Node, Check Node, and Bit Update operation. This implementation is based on the Min-Sum algorithm.

The major operation in the implementation of LDPC is to first load the $L_n$ and $E_{n,m}$ values. The next step is to permute the $L_n$'s so they align with the $E_{n,m}$ values. Then it is possible to compute $L_{n,m}$ by performing an subtraction. Finally we do a compare and select to find the first and second minimum. This operation performs the Bit Node operation and the Check Node operation. The Bit Update operation first loads the $L_n$, then it does a comparison to determine whether the location of the minimum $E_{n,m}$ is the same as the $L_n$ position. If it is not, then it will use the first minimum as the minimum $E_{n,m}$. Otherwise it will use the second minimum. Finally, it adds the new $E_{n,m}$ value to $L_n$ , updating the $L_n$ value. This operation is done for each block row of the code. After all block rows have been updated an iteration is complete.

LDPC exhibits considerable data level parallelism. For each $E_{n,m}$ we process one $L_n$ at a time. Potentially we can do an N SIMD wide operation for the Bit Node and Check Node operation where N is the number of Check Nodes.

## 3   Computational Analysis

### 3.1   Baseline Architecture

In order to calculate the workload characteristic we took an existing architecture for 3G and programmed the 4G algorithms onto it. The architecture we used is

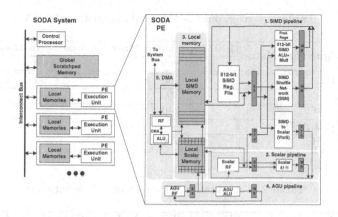

**Fig. 5.** SODA Architecture for SDR

SODA. The SODA multiprocessor architecture is shown in Figure 5. It consists of multiple processing elements (PEs), a scalar control processor, and global scratchpad memory, all connected through a shared bus. Each SODA PE consists of 5 major components: 1) an SIMD pipeline for supporting vector operations; 2) a scalar pipeline for sequential operations; 3) two local scratchpad memories for the SIMD pipeline and the scalar pipeline; 4) an AGU (address generation unit) pipeline for providing the addresses for local memory access; and 5) a programmable DMA unit to transfer data between memories and interface with the outside system. The SIMD pipeline, scalar pipeline and the AGU pipeline execute in VLIW-styled lock-step, controlled with one program counter.

The SIMD pipeline consists of a 32-way 16-bit datapath, with 32 arithmetic units working in lock-step. It is designed to handle computationally intensive DSP algorithms. Each datapath includes a 2 read-port, 1 write-port 16 entry register file, and one 16-bit ALU with multiplier. The multiplier takes two execution cycles when running at the targeted 400MHZ. Intra-processor data movements are supported through the SSN (SIMD Shuffle Network). The SIMD pipeline can also take one of its source operands from the scalar pipeline. There are also several SIMD reduction operations that are supported, including vector summation, finding the minimum and the maximum.

## 3.2  Workload Profile

The breakdown of the major algorithms in our 4G protocol is listed in table 1. This analysis is based on the algorithms as they would be programmed for the SODA architecture. We calculated the number of cycles per second needed to support the data rate shown. Referring back to the system diagram in figure 1: for the 100Mbps rate we assume the STBC algorithm based on the Alamouti scheme which uses 2 transmit and 2 receive paths; and for the 1Gbps rate we assume a 4 transmitter and 4 receiver multiplexing diversity scheme based on V-BLAST. In the STBC algorithm we require that each receiver performs one FFT but only one STBC decoder for all the receivers. Each receiver is independent

**Table 1.** Cycle Count of Major 4G Kernels on SODA

| Algorithm Name | 100Mbps Data Rate MCycle/s | 1Gbps Data Rate MCycle/s |
|---|---|---|
| FFT | 360 | 360 |
| IFFT | 360 | 360 |
| STBC | 240 | - |
| V-BLAST | - | 1900 |
| LDPC | 7700 | 18500 |

**Table 2.** Computational Pattern of 4G algorithms

| Algorithm Name | Load | Permute | First ALU Op | Secondary Op | Store |
|---|---|---|---|---|---|
| FFT | X | X | X | | X |
| IFFT | X | X | X | | X |
| STBC | X | X | X | X | X |
| V-BLAST | X | X | X | X | X |
| LDPC | X | X | X | X | X |

of the other's operation so both FFTs can run on separate processors. For the multiplexing diversity scheme each receiver processes separate data. That means that for the 1Gbps data rate we have 4 independent streams of 250Mbps being processed, but still only one V-BLAST decoder has to be performed.

From the table we can see that the channel coding algorithm is the dominate workload. Assuming we were processing each multiplexing diversity stream on one processor it would require us to run SODA at more than 10GHz for the 100Mbps case and almost 30Ghz for the 1Gbps case. An alternative approach would be to have one processor for each kernel. This would mean we would need the maximum frequency of SODA to be 8GHZ and 20Ghz for the 100Mbps and 1Gbps cases respectively. Though it may seem that the FFT, IFFT, STBC and V-BLAST algorithms are somewhat negligible compared to the channel coding we should not forget that the workload of channel coding is related to the data rate. As the data rate decreases the workload of the channel coding also decreases but the other kernels do not. At low data rates the other algorithms become comparable in cycle count and the optimization for these algorithms will then be key to an efficient design.

### 3.3 Computational Patterns

Analysis of each algorithm reveals that there is a consistent computational pattern. Table 2 shows each kernel's inner loop broken down into simpler operations. The pattern of loading the received data, permuting the data, performing an ALU operation, then a secondary ALU operation and finally storing the result back is very common to all the algorithms. These patterns make up the majority of the cycle time and are repeated for all the data being streamed in.

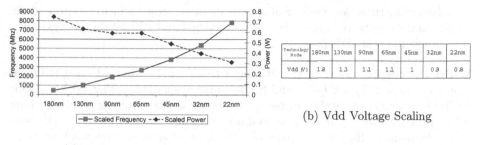

(a) Technology Scaled SODA

(b) Vdd Voltage Scaling

**Fig. 6.** Technology scaling from 180nm to 22nm with respect to Frequency, Power, Vdd on SODA for 4G

Another point to the note is that the data is streamed through the operations. Once the data is consumed we do not refer back to it until the next iteration, or a summation, or a max/min is performed. Often sequences of operations are performed before having to store results. This suggests that there is little temporal locality of the data. Once the data is consumed we do not expect it to be used again. This is true for most DSP applications [10].

Data alignment is a key problem in each of the algorithms. Each algorithm has to align data before any computation can be performed. In the SODA architecture we use the SSN which includes a perfect shuffle network to perform this operation.

## 4   Architectural Implications

The frequency that the SODA processor would need to operate at in order to processes 4G was estimated at 20Ghz. Based on data from the ITRS roadmap [11] and [12] we show in figure 6(a) that technology scaling will still leave us a factor of 3x behind in frequency for a given power budget at 22nm. The power budget was set at $3W/mm^2$ combined for all cores. It is set by limitations of cooling and packaging based on data from ITRS. At 22nm this would be around 1W. Until recently technology scaling has also been accompanied by a scaling in supply voltage. As we get to smaller technology nodes this is no longer the case and the supply voltage is not scalling as much [13]. Figure 6(b) shows the decrease in supply voltage with technology node. The table shows that power consumption will be decreasing more slowly and also that frequency scaling and voltage scaling will be less effective in terms of power reduction.

From the figure we see that at 22nm we could support the 100Mbps data rate on SODA and still meet the power requirement. The 100Mbps solution would require 2 SODA processors running at 10Ghz. If our projections are correct, this is a possible future solution, because the 22nm technology node is expected to be in production in 2011 [14] which coincides with when ITU expects 4G networks to be deployed. This still does not leave us with any solution for the 1Gbps data rate. However, there are many features of the algorithms which we can exploit architecturally to help us reach the goal of 1Gbps and still retain the flexibility of a programmable SDR processor.

**Multi-Processor.** Most of the 4G algorithms can be divided onto multiple processors especially for FFT, and STBC, and even LDPC. The workload can be divided evenly among the processors. However, as we subdivide the algorithms across processes we get an increase in data communication. Although each stage of an algorithm is highly data parallel, stages requires data movement between different subcarriers in the FFT and between different check nodes in the LDPC. As we subdivide the algorithms, communication will increase, but, because the operations of each stage are streamed, we may be able to hide the latency of this communication under the computations itself. This would require an efficient routing and interconnect network and also scheduling that would be able to meet the constraints of data communication when multiple processors are used.

By dividing the workload across multiple processors we would be able to meet the frequency target for the 4G 1Gbps workload but we would still be 3x off the power budget. Multicore designs themselves cannot solve the problem of meeting the 4G requirement.

**Wider SIMD.** Increasing the SIMD width of the processors takes advantage of the highly data parallel nature of the algorithms. Based on historical transistor growth, at the 22nm node we can expect to grow from a 32 wide SIMD to a 2048 wide SIMD machine. This assumes a fixed area constraint. This increase in width would allow us to reduce the cycle count to compute any size FFT as long as N is greater than or equal to the SIMD width. For FFT, the data movement can be accomplished by the SSN shuffle network.

For LDPC this increase in SIMD would also be beneficial because we can process more parity check nodes for LDPC at once. LDPC though would not gain the same data movement advantages as FFT, because it needs to align the check nodes and the bit nodes. However, this would not increase the amount of data movement dramatically.

STBC would also benefit, because it would be possible to process more subcarriers at one time. Because there is little data movement within the STBC we can expect gains equal to the increase in width.

**Special Purpose Functional Units.** Currently in SODA the operations are RISC like in that after every instruction is simple and then writes back to the register file. This can be costly in terms of power and latency, because, as we stated earlier, the algorithms are streaming in nature. Writing back the data may not be very efficient. This suggests that functional units that chain operations will be beneficial not only in performance but also power. There has been work [15] that shows that using special functional units to streamline common operational patterns may not only increase performance but also will be more area and energy-efficient.

LDPC would also benefit from having special minimum and maximum registers embedded into the ALU. For each row operation of the parity check matrix that is performed the result will be compared with the current state of the register and swapped if the condition is met. In comparison with SODA, by implementing this special functional unit, LDPC can be reduce in cycle count by about 30 percent.

**Memory System.** Most of the algorithms like LDPC, FFT and STBC all treat each row of the SIMD as independent. The data is loaded from memory then permuted and stored back. There is no instance in those algorithms where two rows have to access the same data at the same time. This suggests that the memory system does not have to be a large global shared memory. Instead it can be divided into banks. Banking the memory as much as possible will reduce the cost of reading and writing data into a large global memory. Banking will allow us to reduce the size of each memory, increase the speed, and lower power of the memory system. In algorithms like LDPC, which may need block sizes that are larger than currently used, we would be able to efficiently scale the size of the memories too.

Algorithms would also benefit from a smarter memory systems that support flexible gather/scatter accesses. Currently many cycles are wasted in LDPC aligning the check nodes and bit nodes. V-BLAST would also benefit, because the algorithm has to read and write back data in changing orders.

## 5   Conclusion

The power/performance requirements for 4G presents a significant challenge for computer architects, especially if some degree of programmability is to be retained. Currently technology is not capable of processing a 4G system on a single processor. In this paper we have analyzed a 4G system in the context of the SODA architecture and have shown that 3G solutions cannot meet the performance of 4G even if technology scaling is taken into account. We have presented architectural options that can improve the performance and reduce the power consumption of 4G solutions. We have argued that one solution to the power/performance challenge for 4G will increase the number of cores, and that each core will include a very wide SIMD processor with special purpose function units and highly banked memories.

## References

1. Lee, H., Lin, Y., Harel, Y., Woh, M., Mahlke, S.A., Mudge, T.N., Flautner, K.: Software defined radio - a high performance embedded challenge. In: Conte, T., Navarro, N., Hwu, W.-m.W., Valero, M., Ungerer, T. (eds.) HiPEAC 2005. LNCS, vol. 3793, pp. 6–26. Springer, Heidelberg (2005)
2. Schulte, M., Glossner, J., Jinturkar, S., Moudgill, M., Mamidi, S., Vassiliadis, S.: A low-power multithreaded processor for software defined radio. J. VLSI Signal Process. Syst. 43, 143–159 (2006)

3. Lin, Y., Lee, H., Woh, M., Harel, Y., Mahlke, S.A., Mudge, T.N., Chakrabarti, C., Flautner, K.: Soda: A low-power architecture for software radio. In: ISCA, pp. 89–101. IEEE Computer Society Press, Los Alamitos (2006)
4. Alamouti, S.M.: A simple transmit diversity technique for wireless communications. IEEE J. on Select Areas in Communications 16, 1451–1458 (1998)
5. Guo, Z., Nilsson, P.: A vlsi architecture of the square root algorithm for v-blast detection. J. VLSI Signal Process. Syst. 44, 219–230 (2006)
6. Lin, Y., Mahlke, S., Mudge, T., Chakrabarti, C., Reid, A., Flautner, K.: Design and implementation of turbo decoders for software defined radio. In: SiPS, IEEE Computer Society Press, Los Alamitos (2006)
7. Lee, S.-J., Shanbhag, N.R., Singer, A.C.: A low-power vlsi architecture for turbo decoding. In: ISLPED '03. Proceedings of the 2003 international symposium on Low power electronics and design, pp. 366–371. ACM Press, New York (2003)
8. Zhu, Y., Chakrabarti, C.: Architecture-aware ldpc code design for software defined radio. IEEE Workshop on Signal Processing Systems (2006)
9. http://www.ieee802.org/16/pubs/80216e.html
10. Robelly, J.P., Seidel, H., Chen, K.C., Fettweis, G.: Energy efficiency vs. programmability trade-off: architectures and design principles. In: DATE '06. Proceedings of the conference on Design, automation and test in Europe, Leuven, Belgium. European Design and Automation Association, vol. 3001, pp. 587–592 (2006)
11. http://public.itrs.net
12. Rodriguez, S., Jacob, B.: Energy/power breakdown of pipelined nanometer caches (90nm/65nm/45nm/32nm). In: ISLPED '06. Proceedings of the 2006 international symposium on Low power electronics and design, pp. 25–30. ACM Press, New York (2006)
13. McPherson, J.W.: Reliability challenges for 45nm and beyond. In: DAC '06. Proceedings of the 43rd annual conference on Design automation, pp. 176–181. ACM Press, New York (2006)
14. Chau, R., Doyle, B., Doczy, M., Datta, S., Hareland, S., Jin, B., Kavalieros, J., Metz, M.: Silicon nano-transistors and breaking the 10 nm physical gate length barrier. In: Device Research Conference, pp. 23–25 (2003)
15. Karnik, T., Borkar, S., De, V.: Sub-90nm technologies: challenges and opportunities for cad. In: ICCAD '02. Proceedings of the 2002 IEEE/ACM international conference on Computer-aided design, pp. 203–206. ACM Press, New York (2002)

# Design Methodology for Software Radio Systems

Chia-han Lee and Wayne Wolf

Princeton University
Princeton, New Jersey, USA
{chial, wolf}@princeton.edu

**Abstract.** The design of software radio systems faces many challenges due to demands on high bandwidth processing. In order for system designers to tackle the problems more easily, we propose a complete, efficient, and flexible design methodology. The proposed method not only considers software radios from front-ends to baseband but also includes the performance and power models. This methodology is efficient in the way that the whole system and constraints are described by mathematical equations and inequalities such that it becomes an optimization problem which is easier to solve. By replacing the equations and with different combination of the models, various architectures can be simulated. In this paper, design considerations and procedure for software radios are described, and the constraints are formulated in the form of equations and inequalities. Examples are also given to demonstrate the methodology.

**Keywords:** Software radio, methodology, front-ends, RF, ADC, baseband, convex optimization.

## 1 Introduction

The design of software radio systems [1] is a challenging interdisciplinary work involving the knowledge of analog and digital circuits, front-end and baseband architectures. Due to inherently demanding high bandwidth processing, it requires high performance ADC and high speed baseaband processing, resulting in significant power consumption [2]. To alleviate required ADC sampling rate and resolution while introducing minimal noise, novel front-end architectures are required. Several design methodologies were proposed to accommodate an easy environment for software radio designers. However, either does it lack the front-end and power consumption model [3], [4], or it relies on Matlab models and lacks flexibility [5]. That motivates us to propose an efficient, flexible, and complete design methodology for software radios. "Efficient" means the design time is short and the simulation result is informative. We use mathematical equations and inequalities to describe the functions and constraints, so it is much faster than probabilistic approaches. "Flexible" means that this methodology is able to model different hardware architectures. It is also "complete" because the design methodology considers the whole system, from front-ends to baseband, and includes models of processing speed, error rate performance, and power consumption. At the end, we model this as an optimization problem, which can be solved efficiently with handy tools.

S. Vassiliadis et al. (Eds.): SAMOS 2007, LNCS 4599, pp. 355–364, 2007.

## 2  Software Radio Systems and the Challenges

The concept of software radio was proposed by J. Mitola in 1992 [1]. It originated from the need to detect and access various frequency bands and recognize different modulation signals using one single transceiver. The idea of software radio is to place the ADC as close as possible to the antenna, ideally right after the low noise amplifier (LNA) and bandpass filter (BPF), thus the remaining RF/IF functions can be performed digitally on the general purpose processors (GPP) to provide the full advantages of reconfigurability. To achieve this, software radio needs to deal with wideband signals so, according to the Nyquist sampling criterion, high speed processing is unavoidable. Performing high-frequency and high-data rate functions in software requires large amounts of computation, so various software radio front-end architectures have been proposed in the last few years.

### 2.1  RF Front-End Architectures

Traditional analog radios use heterodyne or superheterodyne architectures for the front-end, but it is hard to fulfill the need of software radio systems. Among the proposed front-end software radio architectures are direct conversion (zero-IF), six-port architecture, low-IF, wideband IF double conversion, and bandpass sampling. Different architectures require different sampling rates and generate different kinds of noise, such as DC offset caused by I/Q mismatch, LO leakage, flicker noise, and aliasing. Different filter coefficients result in different distortion, and RF circuits usually exists mismatch and nonlinearity distortion problems. Those noise and distortion are reflected in the noise figure (NF), which describes noise generated by receiver circuits and noise due to images. Other than noises, ADC sampling rate and resolution are two important parameters need to be determined. Sampling rate is dependent on the chosen front-end architecture, and the resolution depends mainly on the signal bandwidth, although it also depends on the architecture. Besides, the cost and the chip area depend on the number of components, which and the easiness of implementation are the two main concerns to pick a front-end architecture.

### 2.2  ADC

To process very wideband signals, it requires not only high sampling rate according to Nyquist sampling criterion but also large dynamic range due to aliasing problems. The dynamic range is determined by the resolution, i.e., how many bits in an ADC. Unfortunately, it is usually hard to achieve high sampling rate and high resolution at the same time, and the power consumption is very high [6]. Currently available high-speed and high-resolution ADC structures are Sigma-Delta ADC, interleaved ADC, and polyphase filter banks. Sigma-Delta ADCs are well-known for their high resolution performance, but the oversampling may become an issue when dealing with already high sampling rate. Interleaved ADCs have high sampling speed but the mismatch in gain, offset, and clock skew results in linearity problem, causing the degradation in SFDR [7]. Calibration has to be employed to alleviate those problems.

## 2.3 Baseband Architectures

Many efforts have been spent on building baseband architectures for high speed signal processing purposes. The ideal software radio uses single processor, but currently available processor is unable to handle such huge amount of information generated by software radio front-ends, and the power consumption is usually unacceptable. The combination of DSP, GPP, and FPGA in a heterogeneous multiprocessor platform provides a balance between flexibility, processing capability, and power consumption [2]. The decision of which baseband architecture to follow is truly a trade-off of the reconfigurability, processing speed, and power consumption. Sample rate conversion, channelization, and digital filtering are basic software radio functions which have to run on baseband processors. After the front-end architecture is chosen, the noise compensation scheme, such as I/Q compensation for direct downconversion receiver, must also be implemented in digital domain. For bandpass sampling architecture, baseband needs to run an algorithm to find the ADC sampling rate. Compensation for ADC distortion, such as using calibration techniques, also needs to be included. In addition, the baseband processors have to deal with traditional time and frequency synchronization, channel coding, and source coding.

## 3 Optimization

Optimization, especially convex optimization, has been developed for decades and recently reaches its maturity. Convex optimization has already been applied to various areas, including wireless communications and networks [8]. The strength of convex optimization is that many tools are available and efficient methods have been developed. To form an optimization problem, functions have to be rewritten as standard form. The standard form of an optimization problem is [9]

$$
\begin{aligned}
\min \quad & f_0(x) \\
\text{subject to} \quad & f_i(x) \le 0, \quad i = 1, \dots, m, \\
& h_i(x) = 0, \quad i = 1, \dots, p
\end{aligned}
\tag{1}
$$

where $f_0(x)$ is called objective function or cost function, $f_i(x)$ are inequality constraint functions, and $h_i(x)$ are equality constraint functions. Predetermined parameters are regarded as constants and the others become variables to be decided through the optimization process. According to the type of the object and constraint functions, an optimization problem can be categorized into linear programming (LP), quadratic programming (QP), second-order cone programming (SOCP), geometric programming (GP), or semidefinite programming (SDP) problem [9]. After finding out what type of optimization it belongs to, commercial tools or free tools available to download from the internet, such as MOSEK [10], will take care of the rest work. It may happen that some problems are very difficult to solve and approximations need to be applied. Another scenario is to handle uncertainties. Noise is uncertain for sure, but even models can be inaccurate to some extent. Robust optimization provides a way to take uncertainties into account. The underline is to leave a margin at the constraint functions and the details can be found in [9]. A variant of optimization problem is called feasibility problem. This is useful when we want to find out whether a particular target is achievable or not. A feasibility problem is formulated like this

$$find \qquad\qquad x$$
$$subject\ to \quad f_i(x) \le 0, \quad i = 1,...,m \qquad\qquad (2)$$
$$h_i(x) = 0, \quad i = 1,...,p$$

# 4  Methodology

Our design methodology is based on several building blocks, as shown in Fig. 1. A software radio system has three main parts, namely front-ends, ADC, and baseband. The performance and power consumption of the described architecture is evaluated using models in the form of sets of equations. The design must satisfy a bunch of constraints, categorized as either performance-related or power-related constraints. Since it is desirable to implement software radio systems on portable devices, the battery model is also included to give an accurate description of the battery usage.

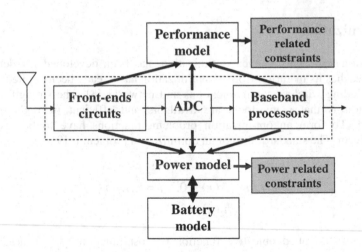

**Fig. 1.** Overall model for software radio design process

## 4.1  Design Process and Constraints

The design flow of a software radio system is (1) Pick and determine parameters of front-end architecture. (2) Choose ADC architecture according to the parameters of the front-end. (3) Apply noise reduction schemes in digital domain according to the front-end architecture. (4) Choose a baseband architecture based on the work load. (5) Formulate power consumption models of front-ends, ADC, and baseband processors. (6) Formulate performance model considering bit-error-rate caused by circuit noise and distortion generated by front-ends and ADC. (7) Write power consumption, performance, and constraint equations and inequalities into standard form of optimization problem, and then use optimization tools to solve the problem.

**Table 1.** Design constraint parameters

| Constraint | Symbol | Unit | Constraint | Symbol | Unit |
|---|---|---|---|---|---|
| Highest frequency | $f_H$ | Hz | Battery power | $E_{Bat}$ | Joule |
| Lowest frequency | $f_L$ | Hz | Data rate | $R$ | Bit/Second |
| Signal bandwidth | $BW$ | Hz | Transmitter latency | $\tau_{TX}$ | Second |
| Total noise figure | $NF$ | None | Receiver latency | $\tau_{RX}$ | Second |
| Channel noise | $N_0$ | Walt/Hz | FEC code rate | $R_C$ | None |

Design parameters and constraints are summarized in Table 1 and Table 2, and the constraints are listed below.

*Latency constraints*: The total latency of front-end, ADC, and baseband has to smaller than the specified value.

$$\tau_{RF} + \tau_{ADC} + \tau_{BB,RX} \le \tau_{RX}$$

$$\tau_{BB,TX} + \tau_{DAC} + \tau_{PA} \le \tau_{TX}$$

(3)

*Power dissipation constraints*: The total power consumption of front-end, ADC, and baseband processing has to smaller than the designed value.

$$P_{TX,total} = P_{BB,TX} + P_{DAC} + P_{PA} \le P_{TX}$$

$$P_{RX,total} = P_{RF} + P_{ADC} + P_{BB,RX} \le P_{RX}$$

(4)

*Data rate and error rate (noise) constraints*: The system data rate cannot be smaller than the system specification. The data rate is dependent on the error rate, which is affected by the circuit noise figure [11].

$$\eta_{BW} \cdot BW \cdot \frac{N_{Data}}{N_{Packet}} \cdot R_C \cdot \left(1 - \varepsilon_{DET} \cdot \varepsilon_{DEC,D}\right) \ge R$$

$$\varepsilon_{DET} \cdot \varepsilon_{DEC,U} \le \varepsilon$$

(5)

$$NF_{total} = NF_{RF} \cdot NF_{ADC} \cdot C_{RF} \cdot C_{ADC} \le NF$$

*ADC constraints*: The ADC sampling rate needs to be fast enough in order not to lose signal information.

$$f_{ADC} \ge 2\alpha \cdot BW_{signal}$$

$$f_{ADC} \cdot b_{ADC} \le R_{BB}$$

(6)

In the first equation, $\alpha$ is the oversampling ratio and $BW_{signal}$ depends on the front-end architecture. The second equation states that the output from the ADC must be lower than the processing rate that the baseband processor can support.

*Battery constraints*: The operation time of portable devices are usually limited by the battery power, so the total energy has to lower than the battery capacity.

$$P_{RX,Total} \cdot T_{RX} + P_{TX,Total} \cdot T_{TX} \le E_{Bat} \tag{7}$$

*Baseband constraints*: The baseband constraints depend on the specific structure of the baseband processors. Two basic constraints are that the tasks must be done by a specified time and the total power consumption has to be limited.

**Table 2.** Design parameters

| Parameter | Symbol | Unit | Parameter | Symbol | Unit |
|---|---|---|---|---|---|
| Receiver RF power dissipation | $P_{RF}$ | Walt | Receiver baseband latency | $\tau_{BB,RX}$ | Second |
| Receiver ADC power dissipation | $P_{ADC}$ | Walt | Transmitter output latency | $\tau_{PA}$ | Second |
| Receiver baseband power dissipation | $P_{BB,RX}$ | Walt | Transmitter DAC latency | $\tau_{DAC}$ | Second |
| Transmitter DAC power dissipation | $P_{DAC}$ | Walt | Transmitter baseband latency | $\tau_{BB,TX}$ | Second |
| Transmitter baseband power dissipation | $P_{BB,TX}$ | Walt | Received power (signal strength) | $S$ | Walt |
| Total noise figure | $NF_{Total}$ | None | Probability of detection error | $\varepsilon_{DET}$ | None |
| RF noise figure | $NF_{RF}$ | None | Probability of detected decoding error | $\varepsilon_{DEC,D}$ | None |
| ADC noise figure | $NF_{ADC}$ | None | Probability of undetected decoding error | $\varepsilon_{DEC,U}$ | None |
| RF noise and distortion compensation | $C_{RF}$ | None | Bandwidth efficiency | $\eta_{BW}$ | None |
| ADC noise and distortion compensation | $C_{ADC}$ | None | Data length | $N_{Data}$ | Byte |
| ADC sampling rate | $f_{ADC}$ | Hz | Packet length | $N_{Packet}$ | Byte |
| ADC resolution | $b_{ADC}$ | Bit | Total receiver power consumption | $P_{RX,Total}$ | Walt |
| Baseband processor rate | $R_{BB}$ | Bit/Sec | Total transmitter power consumption | $P_{TX,Total}$ | Walt |
| Receiver RF latency | $\tau_{RF}$ | Second | Supply voltage | $V_{dd}$ | Volt |
| Receiver ADC latency | $\tau_{ADC}$ | Second | | | |

## 4.2  Front-End Model

In order to evaluate the system performance, it is necessary to build hardware models. The front-ends can be viewed as a set of functional blocks, in which signals go through sequentially. This simplifies the modeling process, meaning that each block can be modeled separately. Therefore, the total response is simply the convolution of all the responses in time domain, or multiplication in frequency domain as

$$H = H_1 * H_2 * \cdots * H_n .$$ (8)

Receiver circuit models include LNA, filter, mixer, PLL, VCO, ADC, and baseband amplifier. The transmitter circuit models contains DAC and power amplifier. Since the total power consumption is the summation of power consumption of each block, we can build the power models individually. The total power is then

$$P = P_1 + P_2 + \cdots + P_M .$$ (9)

With different combination of the equations for circuit blocks, power consumption of various architectures can be modeled.

### 4.3 Baseband Processor Model

The baseband model could be more challenging than front-end and ADC model. In order to process significant amount of software radio data, the baseband architecture is usually quite complicated. Different number and combination of GPP, DSP, and FPGA might be used. Even if a single processor is used, that processor might employ complicated parallel processing architectures and specialized circuits for specific functions, increasing the difficulty of modeling. Therefore, the best (and maybe the only) strategy is to use the models or simulation tools provided by the baseband designers Parameters extracted from the data sheets or the simulation results are then be plugged back into the system model to check whether design constraints are satisfied or not. In the single processor case, if the processor detail is known, processor architectural-level simulation tools like Wattch [12] can be used. For multi-processor cases, the hierarchical modeling approach [13] is available to tackle this problem.

### 4.4 Design Optimization by Performance and Power Evaluation

Performance of RF front-ends is reflected in two aspects- bit error rate and power consumption. Bit error rate performance can be estimated by modeling and simulating the front-end architecture. This model includes down-conversion circuits and ADC. The RF front-end model also includes the impairments such as I/Q imbalance, DC offset, and modulation image which affect bit error rate performance. The power consumption of front-end circuits can also be simulated and modeled in equations. After gathering all the equations of constraints and models, a feasibility or optimization problem is formed and then can be solved efficiently.

## 5 Design Example

### 5.1 Front-End Model Example

Namgoong proposed a hardware model for direct conversion receiver (DCR) [14]. To avoid DC offset problem, he used an AC-coupled version DCR. Through this model, we are able to simulate the performance (distortion, nonlinearity, and etc.) of a direct conversion front-end architecture. Usually a receiver has two paths, i.e., in-phase and quadrature-phase channels, so the signal right before ADC can be described as

$$z(t) = \sum_k x_k p_1(t - kT_{sym}) + \sum_k x_k^* p_2(t - kT_{sym}) + n_{eq}(t) \tag{10}$$

where $p_1(t)$ and $p_2(t)$ are convolution of RF time response $h_{RF}$, in-phase channel response $h_I(t)$, and quadrature-phase channel response $h_Q(t)$. The ADC error model can be built using equations derived in [7]. Those equations can then be used to derive the ADC noise figure. As to power model, Li *et al.* proposed a comprehensive energy model for wireless transceiver front-ends [15]. These power models are functions of gain ($G$), quality factor ($Q$), capacitance ($C$), resistance ($R$), center frequency ($\omega_0$), reference ($f_{ref}$) and LO frequency ($f_{LO}$), supply voltage ($V_{dd}$), bandwidth ($B$), noise figure ($NF$), antenna gain ($A$), driving current ($I$), signal-to-noise ratio ($SNR$), symbol error rate ($SER$), peak-to-average ratio ($PAR$), and path loss ($Lp$).

**Table 3.** Power models

| Component | Power model |
|---|---|
| LNA | $P_{LNA} = G_{LNA} A / NF_{LNA}$ |
| Mixer | $P_{mixer} = G_{mixer} \cdot K / NF_{mixer}$ |
| Analog filter | $P_{filter} = n \cdot kT \cdot Q \cdot f_0 \cdot SNR^2$ |
| Phase-locked loop | $P_{PLL} = b_1 \cdot C_1 \cdot V_{dd}^2 \cdot f_{LO} + b_2 \cdot C_2 \cdot V_{dd}^2 \cdot f_{ref}$ |
| Voltage-controlled oscillator | $P_{VCO} = C \dfrac{R}{L} V_{dd}^2 = RC^2 \omega_0^2 V_{dd}^2 = \dfrac{R}{L^2 \omega_0^2} V_{dd}^2$ |
| ADC | $P_{ADC} = \dfrac{V_{dd}^2 \cdot L_{min} \cdot (f_{sample} + f_{signal})}{10^{(-0.1525 N_1 + 4.838)}}$ |
| DAC (current-steering) | $P_{DAC} = 0.5 \cdot V_{dd} \cdot I_0 \left( 2^{SNR + PAR - 4.77\,dB\,/\,6.02} - 1 \right)$ |
| Power amplifier | $P_{PA} = \dfrac{16\pi^2 d^2 L_p}{3 G_r G_t \lambda^2 K} \cdot (2^b - 1) \cdot N \cdot \left( Q^{-1} \left( \dfrac{1}{4} \left( 1 - \dfrac{1}{2^{k/2}} \right)^{-1} SER \right) \right)^2 PAR$ |

## 5.2 Baseband Model Example

The example baseband model is SODA [16], which focuses on low power baseband architecture. Power consumption of a processing element (PE) $P_{PE}$ is the product of frequency $f_{BB}$ and $E_{PE}$, the energy consumption of one cycle of PE operation.

$$P_{PE} = E_{PE} \cdot f_{BB}$$

$$E_{PE} = C + w(L_e I + R_e U_r + A_e U_a) + M_e U_m + S_e U_s + D_e U_d \tag{11}$$

## 5.3 Example of Optimization Problem

To give a quick example, we consider a simple feasibility problem. The object function is ADC sampling rate, and the subjects are a set of equations and inequalities stating the power consumption constraints related to ADC sampling rate. For simplicity, we do not consider the battery model. The baseband model is based on SODA architecture.

$$
\begin{aligned}
&find && f_{ADC} \\
&s.t. && 2 \cdot BW_{signal} - f_{ADC} \leq 0 && P_{PE} - E_{PE} \cdot f_{BB} = 0 \\
& && f_{ADC} \cdot b_{ADC} - f_{BB} \cdot w \leq 0 && P_{BB,TX} + P_{DAC} + P_{PA} - P_{TX,total} = 0 \\
& && P_{TX,total} - P_{TX} \leq 0 && P_{total} - P_{TX,total} - P_{RX,total} = 0 \\
& && P_{RX,total} - P_{RX} \leq 0 && P_{ADC} - \dfrac{V_{dd}^2 \cdot L_{min} \cdot (f_{sample} + f_{signal})}{10^{(-0.1525 \cdot N_1 + 4.838)}} = 0 \\
& && && P_{LNA} + P_{mixer} + P_{filter} + P_{PLL} + P_{VCO} \\
& && && \qquad + P_{ADC} + P_{BA} + P_{BB,RX} - P_{RX,total} = 0
\end{aligned}
\tag{12}
$$

A more complicated but interesting case is to maximize the ratio of data processing rate over total power consumption. In this case, $R_i(x)$, $R_j(x)$, $P_i(x)$, and $P_j(x)$ are inequalities and equations for data rate and power consumption models.

$$
\begin{aligned}
&max && \dfrac{R_{overall}}{P_{total}} \\
&subject\ to && R_i(x) \leq 0, \quad i = 1, \ldots, m \\
& && R_j(x) = 0, \quad j = 1, \ldots, n \\
& && P_i(x) \leq 0, \quad i = 1, \ldots, p \\
& && P_j(x) = 0, \quad j = 1, \ldots, q
\end{aligned}
\tag{13}
$$

# 6  Conclusions and Future Works

To solve the design challenges of software radio due to large signal bandwidth and high computational rate, we have given comprehensive design considerations and proposed a systematic, complete, flexible, and efficient design methodology. We have shown how to build and describe models and constraints for software radio systems using equations and inequalities. In addition, examples were given to show the modeling of performance and power consumption of the direct downconversion architecture and the formation of optimization problem. This paper shows the idea of using optimization methods to solve the completely-modeled software radio system design problem. Our future work is to provide more concrete examples, solutions, and results to this methodology.

# References

1. Mitola III, J.: Software radios-survey, critical evaluation and future directions. In: National Telesystems Conference, May 19-20, 1992, vol. 13, pp. 15–23 (1992)
2. Lee, C.-H., Wolf, W.: Architectures and platforms of software (defined) radio systems. Int'l Journal of Computers and Their Applications 13(3), 106–117 (2006)
3. Dorie, L., Le Nours, S., Pasquier, O., Diouris, J.F.: A system level model for software defined radio design. In: IEEE Radio and Wireless Symposium, pp. 463–466 (2006)
4. Vasilko, M., Machacek, L., Matej, M., Stepien, P., Holloway, S.: A rapid prototyping methodology and platform for seamless communication systems. In: 12th International Workshop on Rapid System Prototyping, June 25-27, 2001, pp. 70–76 (2001)
5. Agnelli, F., Albasini, G., Bietti, I., Gnudi, A., Lacaita, A., Manstretta, D., Rovatti, R., Sacchi, E., Savazzi, P., Svelto, F., Temporiti, E., Vitali, S., Castello, R.: Wireless multi-standard terminals: system analysis and design of a reconfigurable RF front-end. IEEE Circuits and Systems Magazine 6(1), 38–59 (2006)
6. Kenington, P.B., Astier, L.: Power consumption of A/D converters for software radio applications. IEEE Tran. on Vehicular Tech. 49(2), 643–650 (2000)
7. Walden, R.H.: Analog-to-digital converter survey and analysis. IEEE Journal on Selected Areas in Communications 17(4), 539–550 (1999)
8. Eisenblatter, A., Geerd, H.-F.: Wireless network design: solution-oriented modeling and mathematical optimization. IEEE Wireless Comm. 13(6), 8–14 (2006)
9. Boyd, S., Vandenberghe, L.: Convex Optimization. Cambridge University Press, Cambridge (2004)
10. The MOSEK optimization sofeware, http://www.mosek.com/
11. Bose, V., Hu, R., Morris, R.: Dynamic physical layers for wireless networks using software radio. In: ICASSPP, Salt Lake City, UT (May 2001)
12. Brooks, D., Tiwari, V., Martonosi, M.: Wattch: a framework for architectural-level power analysis and optimizations. In: ISCA, June 10-14, 2000, pp. 83–94 (2000)
13. Delahaye, J.P., Palicot, J., Leray, P.: A hierarchical modeling approach in software defined radio system design. In: IEEE SiPS, November 2-4, 2005, pp. 42–47. IEEE Computer Society Press, Los Alamitos (2005)
14. Namgoong, W.: Modeling and analysis of nonlinearities and mismatches in AC-coupled direct-conversion receiver. IEEE Trans. on Wireless Comm. 4, 163–173 (2005)
15. Li, Y., Bakkaloglu, B., Chakrabarti, C.: A comprehensive energy model and energy-quality evaluation of wireless transceiver front-ends. In: IEEE SiPS, November 2-4, 2005, pp. 262–267 (2005)
16. Lin, Y., Lee, H., Woh, M., Harel, Y., Mahlke, S., Mudge, T., Chakrabarti, C., Flautner, K.: SODA: A low-power architecture for software radio. In: ISCA, June 17-21, 2006, pp. 89–101 (2006)

# Power Efficient Co-simulation Framework for a Wireless Application Using Platform Based SoC

Tseesuren Batsuuri[1], Je-Hoon Lee[2], and Kyoung-Rok Cho[1]

[1] CCNS Lab., San 12, Gaeshin-dong, Cheongju, Chugnbuk, Rep. of Korea
tslee@hbt.cbnu.ac.kr
[2] CBNU BK21 Chungbuk Information Technology Center, Rep. of Korea
leejh@hbt.cbnu.ac.kr, krcho@cbu.ac.kr

**Abstract.** This paper presents a new co-simulation framework supporting system level power estimation. The goal of this work is to support precise power estimation in the early design stage. The proposed co-simulation provides a guideline to reduce the power dissipation for a SoC design. This approach resulted in energy saving of 61% for redesigned medium access control processors while code size increased by 14%. The accuracy of the power estimation obtained from the proposed framework was around 94.9%. The contribution of the proposed framework was a straightforward method to merge system level power estimation techniques into the system level design environment.

**Keywords:** Platform based SoC, verification, HW/SW co-simulation.

## 1 Introduction

To yield large-power saving of a target SoC, the designer should make analysis and optimization for power consumption in its early design stage. It can lead to fewer and faster design iterations with aggressive power consumption constraints. Reducing design turn-around-time while better exploring system-level constrains requires efficient and accurate analysis tools. These tools should be compliant with the de facto system level design strategy such as platform/IP based design methodology.

Our survey covers two research domains, including a survey on system level power estimation techniques and a survey on efficient methods to combine these power estimation techniques with a system level design environment. The power estimation for software design can be classified into structural and instruction level techniques. The structural techniques use a RTL description to collect dynamic activity information for each architectural block [1]. The RTL description is not always available to a designer. The instruction-level techniques compute the energy consumption of a program based on its instruction profile. It is a viable approach in practice [2].

The power estimation for hardware designs also can be classified into information theoretic approaches and macro modeling techniques. Nemani and Najm [3] proposed an information theoretic approach employing an entropy function of

S. Vassiliadis et al. (Eds.): SAMOS 2007, LNCS 4599, pp. 365–374, 2007.

input/output signals to predict area complexity and average transition density in a logic circuit. The power macro modeling is a promising approach. A key idea of power macro modeling is to generate a mapping table between power dissipation of a circuit that is obtained by low level power simulation and certain statistics of its input-output signals such as the average signal probability or average transition density [4]. The mapping process is a one time process. Once the mapping is executed, the power estimation uses the mapping results instead of using expensive low level power estimation. Many power macro models have been proposed using different mapping approaches. An effective lookup table (LUT) based approach was introduced in Gupta's paper [5].

There has been some work focused on the use of these power estimation techniques in a co-simulation environment. Lajolo et al. [6] proposed a co-simulation based power estimation for on chip hardware/software system designs. This system-level co-simulation actually involves integration between heterogeneous simulation tools that operate at different design levels such as gate or circuit level. This approach is computationally expensive and inefficient, although it can result in high accuracy.

Talarico et al. [7] proposed a new power estimation framework for a system level design. He used some power estimation techniques for hardware and software designs. There was no obvious method of how he merged it into a system level design environment. Lidsky and Rabaey [8] proposed a power estimation framework reporting estimation results as a datasheet for web applications. A drawback is its power estimation techniques aiming at computing average power consumption, rather than generating power profiles.

We propose a co-simulation framework enhancing some efficient system level power estimation techniques for all major components in SoC. This framework shows a very straightforward method, based on XML, to merge power estimation techniques into a co-simulation environment. The rest of paper is organized as follows. Chapter 3 describes the proposed co-simulation framework. Chapter 4 presents a demonstration of the proposed idea through case study. Finally, Chapter 5 provides the conclusion.

## 2   Proposed Co-simulation Environment

This chapter presents the proposed co-simulation framework and its power estimation techniques in detail. The proposed co-simulation environment is illustrated in Fig 1. We extended the conventional co-simulation environment by adding power estimation techniques. The conventional co-simulation environment uses a cycle accurate (C/A in Fig.1) simulator for hardware design, an ISS (instruction set simulator) for software design and a TL (transaction level) model for an on-chip bus.

It includes some additional models. For example, it includes an interface between processor and software code. A transactor is used to connect different simulators and models operating at different signal levels (TL$\longleftrightarrow$C/A). The ISS for a target processor is to simulate the software component while the hardware

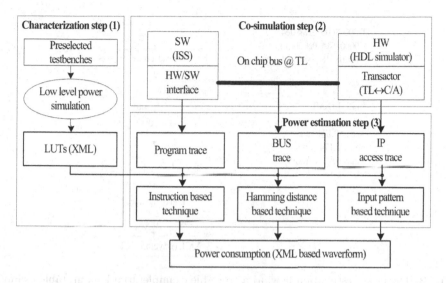

**Fig. 1.** Proposed co-simulation framework

component is simulated on a HDL simulator [9-11]. The proposed environment provides monitoring and power estimation functions. The monitor probes a datapath needed to characterize the component's behavior. The power estimation function then computes an accurate cycle or average power and total energy consumption using the trace. This power estimation process, however, actually proceeds in three steps.

The first step is the characterization of a component, which is a one-time process. The characterization step is a low-level circuit simulation for a pre-designed circuit. Pre-selected test benches are used to construct a lookup table since promising power estimation techniques, used in the proposed framework, are based on the lookup table. The lookup table contains power dissipation data of a circuit and its corresponding input/output signals.

The next step is a hardware/software co-simulation for probing execution traces of components. The final step is power estimation using the probed traces and power estimation functions to derive the power from the lookup table. A notable feature of the proposed environment is its XML based configuration. All of the data extracted at the characterization step are stored in a lookup table in XML format. The results of power estimation and output profiling are also stored in XML format. Figure 2 shows in detail an estimation flow of the power estimation technique for software. We have adopted an instruction level technique. This power estimation technique is originally from Sinha et al [3]. It is given by equation (1)

$$E_{total} = \sum V_{dd} I_{ins} \Delta t \tag{1}$$

Here $V_{dd}$ is a supply voltage, $I_{ins}$ is current consumption for an instruction of a processor, and $\Delta t$ is instruction execution time. In the proposed framework, all current consumptions of the instructions, which were measured at a circuit

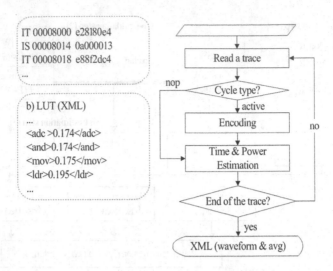

**Fig. 2.** The power estimation flow, a) a trace file example; b) a look up table example

level, are stored in a file in XML format as shown in Fig. 2b. The tool reads the file and software's execution trace file probed in the co-simulation step for an estimation of the given soft-ware, as shown in Fig. 2a. There are two ways to get the programming trace: using ISS or probing data on a system bus. The format has three columns: an instruction type, an address and an operation code. The instruction type is set to 'IT' (instruction taken) when the processor normally executes the instruction. Otherwise it is set to 'IS' (instruction skipped) indicating cache misses. If an instruction type is 'IT', the corresponding instruction is encoded by an operation code. The power and timing values are subsequently estimated. For the instruction type 'IS', power and timing values of the NOP instruction are used.

The power consumption of the bus is another sizeable component. The total energy dissipation of a bus increases linearly when the hamming distance in two consecutive data increases. It means that the hamming distance based approach is useful for power estimation of the on-chip bus at a system level. The linear relation between the ham-ming distance and the power dissipation implies that power consumption on the bus is a first order function of the hamming distance, which can be written as,

$$P_{cycle} = V_{dd}^2 \cdot f \cdot (C_{eff} + C_{switch} \cdot HD(d_i, d_{i+1})) \qquad (2)$$

Here $V_{dd}$ is a supply voltage, $f$ is a clock frequency. $C_{eff}$ is an effective capacitance, $C_{switch}$ is the switching capacitance and $HD$ is the hamming distance between 2 consecutive data $d_i$ and $d_i + 1$. Figure 3 shows a transactor for the bus tracing and power estimation. The power consumption of a hardware design as an IP is discussed next. However it is not easy to find out a technique for power estimation for all IPs. At a minimum, we need the details of IPs'. But sometimes this detail is not available to a designer. We have brought in a

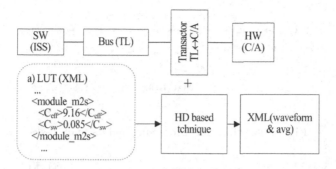

**Fig. 3.** A power estimation scheme for the bus, a) lookup table example

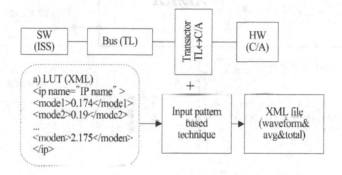

**Fig. 4.** A power estimation scheme for the hardware, a) a lookup table example

simple LUT that contains all input signal patterns and the corresponding average power consumption for an IP. The designer builds the LUT using low level power estimation tools.

We use the same method used to merge the hamming distance based technique into the co-simulation environment for this approach, as shown in Fig 4. The transactor is used to probe input signals of the hardware design. The probed input signals are used as an address of the lookup table to get the corresponding average power.

## 3   Case Study

In the case study, we try to reduce power consumption of a software part after analyzing its power consumption using the proposed framework. The experimental design is a modem chip complying with the IEEE 802.11a standard, and includes a baseband and a MAC processor. The entire MAC was implemented with C/C++, and the baseband processor was implemented with HDL.

We focused on reducing the MAC design's power. The 802.11a MAC handles a set of communicating tasks. Figure 5 shows the MAC operations for outgoing frames. The LLC (Logical Link Control Layer) receives data frames and stores

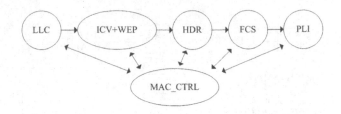

**Fig. 5.** 802.11a MAC processing and its main tasks

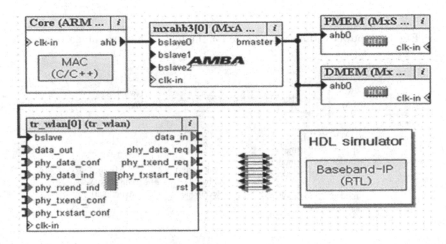

**Fig. 6.** An experimental co-simulation framework

them in system memory. The ICV task then computes an integrity checksum vector. The WEP task encrypts the frame data using the RC4 stream cipher. Then, the HDR task generates a MAC header and adds this to the start of a frame. The FCS task computes a CRC-32 checksum over the encrypted frame and its header. The MAC_CTRL controls all other tasks and transmits the frame data according to the CSMA/CA algorithm. The PLI (Physical Layer Interface) task retrieves encrypted frames from the MAC memory and sends them to the baseband processor [12]. Figure 6 shows an experimental framework for a SoC platform, comprising ARM processor and AMBA bus. For this task, we used commercial simulators MaxSim and ModelSim [13].

The MAC and a testbench are simulated on an ISS of the target ARM processor. The baseband processor is connected to the AMBA AHB bus as a slave element. There is a transactor, called "tr_wlan," which is used to connect two simulators and is also extended by the proposed power estimation functions. In a simulation, 1950 byte frame data is sent through the MAC and AMBA bus to the baseband processor.

A simulation result is summarized in Table 1. The rows 1-4 show energy dissipations of MAC functions. The rows 5, 6 show the total energy for the MAC software and corresponding bus energy consumption, respectively. The

**Table 1.** Power estimation and accuracy

|  | Proposed (uJ) | JouleTrack (uJ) | NanoSim (uJ) | Error(%) |
|---|---|---|---|---|
| WEP | 335.8 | 340.3 | - | 1.3 |
| FCS&ICV | 878.9 | 892.6 | - | 1.5 |
| Others | 111.1 | 112.9 | - | 1.6 |
| Total | 1325.8 | 1345.8 | - | 1.5 |
| Bus | 120.4 | - | 126.9 | 5.1 |

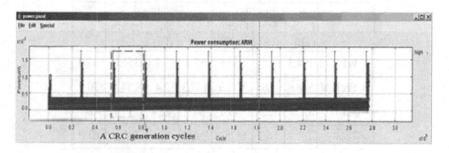

**Fig. 7.** Power profiling of the CRC implemented using a bitwise algorithm

column 2 shows a power estimation of the proposed tool and column 3 is power estimation with Joule-Track which has been developed by Sinha et al [3]. The column 4 shows power estimation by Nanosim from Synopsys for the bus. The bus has been implemented with Verilog-HDL. The Synopsys Design Compiler was used for circuit synthesis based on the Hynix $0.35\mu m$ CMOS process. The power estimation error for the software is less than 2% compared to the results from JouleTrack. The power estimation for the bus has an error of about 5.1%, compared to the results from Nanosim. In the simulation results in Table 1, the CRC function, called in the FCS and ICV tasks, consumes the greatest amount of energy. The CRC32 function was implemented using a bitwise algorithm [14].

Figure 7 shows power profiling of the CRC function. The function is called 10 times in a simulation. It generates a 256 byte CRC code. A part framed by the dotted line in Fig. 7 shows power profiling of CRC generation. The function was re-implemented by the LUT based approach [14]. Figure 8 shows power profiling of the new CRC function. The LUT initialization takes many cycles, and consumes most of the power. However, CRC generation process takes very few cycles and consumes less power than the previous design. If we call the CRC function 10 times, the new one's energy is increased by just 15% and the bitwise based CRC function's energy is increased by 88.9%.

In such a way, we chose an efficient algorithm. Once the algorithm is selected, the source code level optimization is also effective. For example, 'for' loop coded

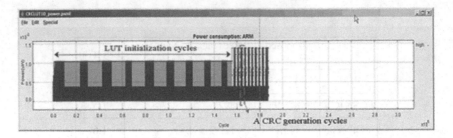

**Fig. 8.** Power profiling of the CRC implemented using a LUT algorithm

**Table 2.** Percentage change by power reduction technique

|  | Origianl | | | Optimized | | | Save (%) |
|---|---|---|---|---|---|---|---|
|  | Cycle (x10³) | Size (kb) | Energy (uJ) | Cycle (x10³) | Size (kb) | Energy (uJ) |  |
| WEP | 194.3 | 2.5 | 335.8 | 87.3 | 3.7 | 151.0 | 55.0 |
| FCS&ICV | 508.6 | 0.9 | 878.9 | 147.3 | 2.4 | 254.6 | 70.9 |
| Others | 64.3 | 12.9 | 111.1 | 64.3 | 12.9 | 111.1 | 0.0 |
| Total | 767.1 | 16.3 | 1325.8 | 298.9 | 19.1 | 516.7 | 61.0 |

as 'for (i = 1; i ≤ max; i++)' can be replaced by for (i = max ; i>0 ; i- -). The latter style is more efficient, since no register is required for saving max. Another approach is to use an inline function. A program normally contains a number of subroutines. Calling a subroutine is always associated with stacking and unstacking overhead. In Fig. 7 and 8, ten peaks appear in every start of the CRC generation due to this overhead.

Because the stacking and un-stacking often involves load and store instructions that consume more power than typical data processing instructions. This overhead can be eliminated if the function is coded inline. The other efficient power reduction techniques refer the ARM application note [15]. Table 2 shows the performance, size and energy consumption for the original and the optimized function. The row 1 shows the WEP functions. The re-designed WEP function uses 55% less energy. The row 2 shows the FCS, ICV functions employing CRC32. The re-designed CRC implementation uses up to 71% less energy. The row 3 shows the other functions that are not able to use power reduction techniques. The row 4 summarizes the total results for the MAC design. The power reduction techniques yield an energy saving of 61%, while its code size increases by 14%.

## 4   Conclusion

This paper proposes a co-simulation framework supporting power estimation at the system level. It helps to reduce power consumption of an embedded design.

For demonstration, we estimated power consumption of a modem chip complying with the IEEE 802.11a standard. The range of power estimation error is around 5.1% based on the evaluating results from commercial software including Nanosim, JouleTrack. The MAC was designed again to reduce power yielding energy saving by 61%, while its code size increased by 14%. This paper provides a method to merge the power estimation techniques into a system level design environment using XML.

## Acknowledgments

This work was supported by the Regional Research Centers Program of the Ministry of Education & Human Resources Development in Korea. And Dr. J. H. Lee participated in this work is supported by the Second Phase of the Brain Korea 21 Project at Chungbuk National University.

## References

1. Hsieh, C.T., Pedram, M.: Microprocessor power estimation using profile–driven program synthesis. IEEE Trans. Computer–Aided Design of Integrated Circuits and Systems 17(11), 1080–1089 (1998)
2. Sinha, A., Ickes, N., Chandrakasan, A.P.: Instruction level and operating system profiling for energy exposed software. IEEE Trans Very Large Scale Integration (VLSI) Systems 11(6), 1044–1057 (2003)
3. Nemani, M., Najm, F.N.: Towards a high–level power estimation capability. IEEE Trans. Computer–Aided Design of Integrated Circuits and Systems 15(6), 588–598 (1996)
4. Wu, Q., Qiu, Q., Pedram, M., Ding, C.S.: Cycle–accurate macro–models for RT–Level power analysis. IEEE Trans. Very Large Scale Integration Systems 6(4), 520–528 (1998)
5. Gupta, S., Najm, F.N.: Power modeling for high–level power estimation. Very Large Scale Integration Systems 8(1), 18–29 (2000)
6. Lajolo, M., Raghunathan, A., Dey, S., Lavagno, L.: Co–simulation-based power estimation for system–on–chip design. IEEE Trans. Very Large Scale Integration Systems 10(3), 253–256 (2002)
7. Talarico, C., Rozenblit, J.W., Malhotra, V., Stritter, A.: A framework for power estimation of embedded systems. IEEE Trans. Computer 38(2), 71–78 (2005)
8. Lidsky, D., Rabaey, J.M.: Early power exploration – a world wide web application. In: Proc, DAC Conf., pp. 27–32 (1996)
9. Yoo, S., Jerraya, A.A.: HW/SW co–simulation from inter face perspective," Proc. IEE Computer and Digital Techniques. Proc. IEE Computer and Digital Techniques 152(3), 369–379 (2005)
10. Chung, S.K., Kyung, C.M.: Enhancing performance of HW/SW co–simulation and co–emulation by reducing communication overhead. IEEE Trans. Computers 55(2), 125–136 (2006)
11. Chung, M.K., Yang, S., Lee, S.H., Kyung, C.M.: System–level HW/SW co–simulation framework for multiprocessor and multithread SoC. In: Proc. VLSI-TSA Design, Automation, and Test Conf., pp. 177–179 (2005)

12. emphISO/IEC, Wireless LAN MAC and PHY Specifications – High–Speed Physical Layer in the 5 GHz Band, ISO/IEC 8802–11:1999(E)/Amd 1:2000(E), New York IEEE (2000)
13. MaxSim Developer Suite User's Guide ver 5.0, AXYS Design Automation Inc. (March 2004)
14. Ramabadran, T.V., Gaitonde, S.S.: A tutorial on CRC computations. IEEE Trans., Micro 8(4), 62–75 (1988)
15. Writting Efficient C for ARM, ARM Application Note 34, ARM Corporation (1998)

# A Comparative Study of Different FFT Architectures for Software Defined Radio

Shashank Mittal, Md. Zafar Ali Khan, and M.B. Srinivas

Center for VLSI and Embedded System Technologies
International Institute of Information Technology, Gachibowli, Hyderabad,
INDIA-500032
shashankmittal@research.iiit.ac.in,{zafar, srinivas}@iiit.ac.in

**Abstract.** Fast Fourier Transform (FFT) is the most basic and essential operation performed in Software Defined Radio (SDR). Thus designing regular, reconfigurable, modular, low hardware and timing-complexity FFT computation block is very important. A single FFT block should be configurable for varying length FFT computation and also for computation of different transforms like Discrete cosine/sine transform (DCT/DST) etc. In this paper, the authors analyze area, timing complexity and noise to signal Ratio (NSR) of Bruun's FFT w.r.t. classical FFT from a SDR perspective. It is shown that architecture of Bruun's FFT is ideally suited for SDR and may be used in preference over classical FFT for most practical cases. A detailed comparison of Bruun's and classical FFT hardware architectures for same NSR is carried out and results of FPGA implementation are discussed.

## 1 Introduction

The concept of SDR was first introduced in by Mitola [1] and Tuttlebee [2]. SDR refers to a converged system or hardware which can be reconfigured easily to support all wireless communication standards. This device should provide backward support and capability to adapt to future communication standards without any changes in hardware. Thus there is a need for converged and reconfigurable hardware architectures to perform various signal processing functions.

In order to effectively utilize the services provided by different wireless communication standards, especially those with high bandwidth, devices such as mobile phones should also support various multimedia standards which require computation of different transforms like FFT, DCT etc. Here baseband and multimedia operations are on different parts of the chip and different multimedia standards themselves require different transforms for their computations. Further, these computational blocks should be able to operate at varying computational (word or bit) lengths [3]. These converged architectures should have properties like regularity, reconfigurability, low hardware complexity, low timing complexity and low NSR.

Recent research related to FFT computation for SDR applications has dealt mainly with two issues, viz., i) variable length FFT computation architectures

S. Vassiliadis et al. (Eds.): SAMOS 2007, LNCS 4599, pp. 375–384, 2007.

[4-5] that focus on how one can utilize a 16-point or smaller length FFT for 32 or higher length FFT computation and vice-versa. ii) universal computational FFT architectures [6-7] in which a single FFT structure can compute different transforms like decimation in time/frequency (DIT/DIF) FFT, DCT, DST etc.

Bruun's FFT [8] can be considered to be an ideal candidate for SDR since its architecture has low computational complexity and can also be configured to compute FFT, DCT and DST [8]. However it suffers from high NSR [9] for a given fixed point implementation and because of this, is not generally used in practice. In this paper, the authors compare the hardware and timing complexity of Bruun's and DIT/DIF FFT for same NSR. It is shown that Bruun's FFT has less hardware complexity than that of DIT/DIF FFT for a given NSR, in most cases practical for SDR.

The rest of the paper is organized as follows: Section 2 describes the basic FFT computation algorithm while Bruun's FFT architecture is described in section 3. In section 4 we analyze and compare various FFT architectures for SDR. Results of hardware implementation are provided in section 5 and a detailed comparison is carried out. Finally, conclusions are drawn in section 6.

## 2  Basic FFT Computation Algorithm

A DFT of length $N$ is defined as

$$X(k) = \sum_{i=0}^{N-1} x(i) \cdot W_N^{ik}, 0 \le k \le N - 1 \tag{1}$$

where $W$ denotes the $N$th root of unity, with its exponent evaluated modulo $N$. Among the many possible ways, DFT can also be implemented by using transversal filters [8]. This filter structure has N, Z-transform based transfer functions, one at each output node of FFT, of the form

$$F_n(z) = z^{-(N-1)} + W^{-1.n}z^{-(N-2)} + \cdots$$

$$+ \cdots W^{-k.n}z^{-(N-k-1)} + \cdots W^{-(N-1).n} \tag{2}$$

Equation (2) can be factored using repeated application of

$$F_n(z) = (z^{-(N/2)} + W^{-(N/2).n})(z^{-((N/2)-1)}$$

$$+ W^{-n.1}z^{-((N/2)-2)} + \cdots + \cdots + W^{-((N/2)-1).n}$$

so that (2),

$$F_n(z) = \prod_{t=1}^{log_2 N} (z^{-(N/v)} + W^{-(N/v).n}) \tag{3}$$

Where, $v = 2^t$ and $Z^{-1} * x(0) = x(1)$. This transfer function can also be represented as a tree structure after decomposition [8], which results in a classical FFT structure.

## 3  Bruun's FFT Algorithm

Bruun's algorithm [8] is a very promising method for computation of different discrete transforms, particularly FFT. It utilizes the fact that (2) can also be factored using the following equation (4)

$$1 + aZ^{2q} + Z^{4q} = (1 + \sqrt{2-a}Z^q + Z^{2q})(1 - \sqrt{2-a}Z^q + Z^{2q}) \qquad (4)$$

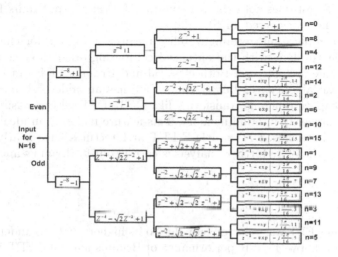

**Fig. 1.** Bruun's FFT Computation Architecture for length N=16 [8]

This factorization has a nice property that all the coefficients are real except in the last stage. Equation (4) replaces complex multiplications with real ones by requiring only real coefficients to be multiplied with complex inputs which needs only two real multipliers instead of four in a complex multiplication. This re-composition reduce the area required by corresponding hardware implementation to a significant extent. An example architecture of this is given in Fig. 1 [8].

Bruun's algorithm not only reduces the number of computations, which is same as that for a split-radix algorithm, but also maintains the regularity in the structure which is a primary requirement for hardware realization of a reconfigurable system like SDR. It also allows computation of cos/sin transform of an input signal with small changes at the last stage [8], which is essential for universal transform computation.

## 4  Comparison of Different FFT Architectures for Software Defined Radio

SDR requires flexible DSP algorithms which can be implemented effectively as/on a reconfigurable hardware like FPGAs. Main disadvantages of a reconfigurable system, however include extra hardware required for providing reconfigurability and features like dynamic and partial reconfiguration, etc. One more disadvantage is that reconfigurable systems tend to be slower than dedicated systems due to extra switches/multiplexers and long interconnect lengths in the critical path of computation. This requires them to operate at higher frequencies which in turn increase the power consumption of the system.

Further, regular architectures can be partitioned easily in to sub-blocks and both classical and Bruun's FFT exhibit regularity in their architecture. In contrast, split-radix algorithm has low computational complexity, same as that of Bruun's FFT, but does not exhibit regularity. Therefore, split-radix FFT architectures are not considered for SDR [3].

In FFT computation, reconfigurability means a provision for change in operational length along with the option of computing other discrete transforms using the same architecture. Both classical and Bruun's FFT can be made to operate at variable lengths but Bruun's FFT has an added advantage that it can also compute different transforms like DCT, DST [8] etc. easily and with minimum changes in internal memory. This feature makes it an ideal candidate for converged systems. DIT and DIF FFT architectures have nearly the same performance, therefore further analysis is carried out for Bruun's and DIT FFT only.

## 4.1   NSR

In [9], Bruun's FFT was rejected only due to its higher NSR. To understand this, a comparison between NSR performance of Brunn's and DIT FFT is provided in this subsection. Signal power followed by noise power calculations for these FFT algorithms are explained below.

If an overall scaling factor $1/k$ is used, then the output signal power (SP) is given by [9]

$$SP = N/(3K^2)$$

Classical complex FFT has scaling factor $k = N$, whereas Bruun's FFT has scaling factor $k = N^2/8$ for $N > 8$ [9]. For a complex input sequence, the output signal power for both FFT algorithms is as follows:

i) Signal power for classical FFT ($SP_{cfft}$)

$$SP_{cfft} = 1/(3N) \tag{5}$$

ii) Signal power for Bruun's FFT ($SP_{bfft}$)

$$SP_{bfft} = 64/(3N^3) \tag{6}$$

The reduction in signal power with $(1/N^3)$ in Bruun's FFT as compared to $(1/N)$ in classical FFT is a significant disadvantage for the Bruun's algorithm. Noise power introduced due to '$b$' bit quantization at the output of a real multiplier is $\sigma_e^2 = 2^{-2b}/12$. Total output noise at each output node is equal to the sum of the noise propagated to that node with scaling which is done on per stage basis in FFT. This attenuates noise introduced at early stages by scaling introduced in later stages. Scaling is performed by shifters and because of truncation they also contribute noise in the computation.

i)Noise power in classical FFT $(NP_{cfft})$

$$NP_{cfft} = (4/3) \cdot 2^{-2b} \quad [10] \tag{7}$$

From (5) and (7) NSR value for classical FFT $(NSR_{cfft})$ can be written as:

$$NSR_{cfft} = 4N \cdot 2^{-2b} \tag{8}$$

ii) Bruun's FFT

In Bruun's FFT, first stage requires scaling by $(1/2)$ while all the middle stages need scaling by $(1/4)$ and no scaling is required for the last stage of computation.Due to this unequal scaling requirement, noise power is calculated as follows:

a) O/P noise power due to noise sources of first stage $(NP_1)$:
A FFT computation consists of $v = \log_2 N$ stages. Using the procedure in [10],

$$NP_1 = (1/3) \cdot 2^{-2b} \cdot (1/2)^{(3v-7)} \tag{9}$$

Note that $2^v$ noise sources at first stage are connected to one particular output node of FFT.

b) O/P noise power due to noise sources in middle stages $(NP_2)$:
Number of noise contributing butterflies and therefore noise sources contributing to overall noise at a particular output node decreases by 2 per stage as the computation progresses from one stage to the next stage. $(NP_2)$ is given by,

$$NP_2 = (32/21) \cdot 2^{-2b} \tag{10}$$

c) O/P noise power due to noise sources at last stage $(NP_3)$:

$$NP_3 = (1/3) \cdot 2^{-2b} \tag{11}$$

Total noise power for Bruun's FFT $(NP_{bfft})$ is

$$NP_{bfft} = NP_1 + NP_2 + NP_3$$

In this calculation we can neglect $NP_1$ for $v \geq 3$, so equation (10) and (11) gives,

$$NP_{bfft} = (39/21) \cdot 2^{-2b} \tag{12}$$

From (6) and (12), NSR value for Bruun's FFT $(NSR_{bfft})$ can be written as:

$$NSR_{bfft} = \frac{39}{448} \cdot 2^{-2b} \cdot N^3 \tag{13}$$

In this paper, a simplified noise analysis has been done for complex input sequence-based Bruun's FFT using a general procedure given in [10] as compared to that in [9]. From (8) and (12), we see that for the same bit width '$b$' the NSR of Bruun's FFT increases in proportion to $N^3$ while that of DIT FFT is proportional to $N$. However this comparison is not fair as the hardware requirement of the two architectures is different.

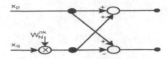

**Fig. 2.** Butterfly structure for Classical FFT computation

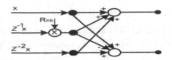

**Fig. 3.** Butterfly structure for Bruun's FFT computation

## 4.2   Hardware Complexity

Butterfly architectures used in classical and Bruun's FFT computation are shown in Figs 2 and 3 respectively. Here $W_N^{nk}$ and $R_{nk}$ represents complex and real valued coefficients for classical and Bruun's FFT butterflies respectively. A classical FFT butterfly require complex multiplication which is equivalent to four real multiplications and two real additions. Overall it requires 4 real multiplications and 6 real additions. Similarly a Bruun's FFT butterfly require to multiply a complex input with a real coefficient and therefore needs only two real multiplications. It overall needs two real multiplications and six real additions to get it's output. Now it is clear from Figs. 3 and 4 that Bruun's FFT will reduce the number of multiplications by half without adding any extra arithmetic block. Since an N point FFT consists of N/2 butterflies per stage, hardware complexity for different FFT algorithms is as follows:

i) Classical FFT

$$C_{cfft}^m = 2Nlog_2N, \quad C_{cfft}^a = 3Nlog_2N \tag{14}$$

ii) Bruun's FFT
In Bruun's computation, last stage consists of classical butterflies, therefore complexity will be given by,

$$C_{bfft}^m = Nlog_2N + N, \quad C_{bfft}^a = 3Nlog_2N \tag{15}$$

Here $C^m$ and $C^a$ represent the cost function for real multipliers, adders in FFT computation and subscripts $cfft$, $bfft$ represent classical and Bruun's FFT respectively.

In literature, complexity of a single multiplier is assumed to be 6-8 times the complexity of an adder [11]. In this analysis, authors assumed this number to be 5 based on their experiments. Bruun's FFT also uses classical butterfly at the last stage which has the complexity of $13N$ and is different from it's regular butterfly. Therefore, total hardware complexity for classical and Bruun's FFT in terms of real adders ($C_{cfft}$) and ($C_{bfft}$) using (14) and (15) is

$$C_{cfft} = 5 \cdot 2N \cdot \log_2 N + 3N \cdot \log_2 N \Rightarrow 13N \log_2 N \qquad (16)$$

$$C_{bfft} = 5N(\log_2 N - 1) + 3N(\log_2 N - 1) + 13N \Rightarrow 8N \log_2 N + 5N \qquad (17)$$

### 4.3 Comparison Between Hardware Complexity of Different FFT Architectures for Same NSR

In this subsection we first find the bit widths required by Bruun's FFT to get same NSR as DIT FFT. Let b1 denote the bit width required by Bruun's FFT to obtain the same NSR as that of DIT FFT for bit width b. Equating the NSR's of both FFTs and using (8) and (13) we have,

$$NSR_{cfft} = NSR_{bfft}$$

which simplifies as,

$$b1 = b + \log_2 N - 3 \qquad (18)$$

Equation (18) indicates that for 8 $(= 2^3)$ point Bruun's FFT, no extra bit is required for equal NSR. But Bruun's FFT requires 3 extra bits for 64-point FFT to achieve same NSR as classical FFT. In general hardware complexity of an adder increases linearly with the number of bits [12], for example, as in high speed parallel-prefix adders. In order that classical FFT will have more hardware complexity compared to Bruun's FFT the following condition must be satisfied: using equation (16), (17) and (18)

$$13N \log_2 N \cdot b \geq (8N \log_2 N + 5N) \cdot b1$$

$$13 \log_2 N \cdot b \geq (8 \log_2 N + 5) \cdot (b + \log_2 N - 3)$$

by simplifying above equation,

$$8(\log_2 N)^2 - (5b + 19) \log_2 N + (5b - 15) \leq 0$$

$$\log_2 N = \frac{(5b + 19) \pm \sqrt{(5b + 19)^2 - 32(5b - 15)}}{16} \qquad (19)$$

for $b = 8$,

$$N \leq 2^{6.92} \Rightarrow N \leq 121$$

Usually in wireless communication applications, bit sizes of 10-16 or more have been used. As an example, using b=12 in (19) gives

$$N \leq 2^{9.26} \quad \Rightarrow \quad N \leq 613$$

This shows that up to 613≃512 point FFT with bit width b=12, Bruun's FFT will provide less hardware complexity than DIT FFT for same NSR. Therefore, Bruun's FFT can be used with higher bit length operations for compensating the high NSR value while maintaining it's low hardware complexity.

### 4.4  Timing Complexity

Timing complexity for Bruun's and classical FFT can be realized from the butterfly structures shown in Figs. 2 and 3. In Fig. 2, critical path delay is the summation of delays offered by one real multiplier $(T_m)$ and two real adders $(T_a)$ for a particular stage of classical FFT. Therefore, $\log_2 N$ stages in FFT structure will make total delay for DIT FFT $(T_{cfft})$ to be

$$T_{cfft} = (T_m + 2T_a)log_2 N$$

In Bruun's FFT, critical path delay per stage is sum of delays offered by one real multiplier and one real adder, so total delay $T_{bfft}$ is given by

$$T_{bfft} = (T_m + T_a)log_2 N,$$

which is less than the critical path delay of classical FFT.

In Bruun's FFT, operations will be done with higher bit length for same NSR but that will add just one more level of basic gate computation in delay of adders/multipliers. But a new adder attached sequentially in classical FFT's critical path will increase the delay to at least 5-7 levels of basic gates computation [12]. Therefore Bruun's FFT has less computational delay as compared to classical FFT which reduces linearly with the number of stages. Thus it may be claimed that Bruun's FFT architecture is an optimal FFT architecture for reconfigurable and converged hardware systems like SDR.

## 5  Hardware Implementation Results for Different FFT Architectures and Comparisons

Both classical and Bruun's FFT architectures have been coded in Verilog HDL, simulated and synthesized on Virtex series FPGA, v50bg256 (speed grade -6) from Xilinx using Mentor's Leonardo Spectrum. Butterflies in Fig. 2 and 3 are basic components of FFT and they determine the hardware requirement and also the critical path delay of the design. Therefore we have implemented and compared hardware architecture of these butterflies for different bit lengths. Coefficient length is fixed for a constant NSR and only precision of arithmetic operations needs to be changed. Thus one operand in multiplier will have constant bit length.

Table 1 provides a comparison of area and delay performance of classical and Bruun's butterfly architectures. It can be seen from the table that Bruun's butterfly consumes less number of LUTs (and therefore less area) for 10 bit operation as compared to 6 bit operation in classical butterfly, for a comparable NSR. This is due to the fact that two 2-bit functions will take 2 LUTS while a single function with 4 bits takes only one LUT to implement. Table 1 also shows that delay in Bruun's butterfly is very less compared to classical butterfly for reasonable bit lengths which is due to reasons explained in subsection 4.4. This reduction in delay allows designer to operate FFT with lower frequency which reduces the dynamic power consumption.

**Table 1.** A Comparison of Hardware and Timing performance of Butterfly Architectures for different bit lengths

| Synthesis Device | Parameters of comparison | Classical Butterfly | | Bruun's Butterfly | | | |
|---|---|---|---|---|---|---|---|
| | | 6 bits | 8 bits | 6 bits | 8 bits | 10 bits | 11 bits |
| FPGA | Area(LUTs) | 134 | 258 | 76 | 88 | 116 | 138 |
| (Virtex) | Time(ns) | 12.1 | 12.5 | 10.5 | 10.7 | 10.9 | 11.1 |

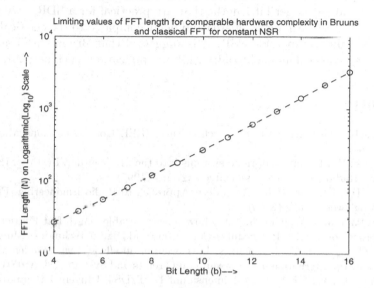

**Fig. 4.** Limiting values of FFT length N ($\log_{10}$ scale) for comparable hardware complexity and constant NSR in Bruun's and classical FFT, according to equation (19)

In Fig. 4 straight line shows the limiting values of FFT length $(N)$ on $\log_{10}$ scale for which classical FFT will have more hardware complexity as compared to Bruun's FFT for a particular bit length $(b)$ and same NSR according to (19). Bruun's FFT will have more hardware complexity for values of $N$ greater than or equal to the limiting values for maintaining same NSR. This clearly shows that for practical operational bit lengths in FFT computation, $N$ should be high to invert the low hardware complexity advantage offered by Bruun's algorithm.

A programmable shifter at the output will adjust the final output bit length according to requirement of next computing block's input in the system. Bit length adjustment adds to reconfigurability in SDR as different modules may require different bit lengths for their operation. This block can also perform re-ordering of FFT outputs and also helps in increasing the SNR value at the output by doing appropriate shifting. Moreover, it can be well adjusted with Bruun's FFT due to it's low hardware and timing complexity.

Our analysis covers nearly all basic and important properties required for SDR. VLSI implementation results show that Bruun's FFT requires less area and also has less delay which in turn reduce both static and dynamic power

384     S. Mittal, M.Z. Ali Khan, and M.B. Srinivas

consumption. Thus it may be suggested that Bruun's FFT provides a better modular and universal architecture.

## 6  Conclusion

This paper provides an insight in to an important problem of finding and analyzing optimal FFT architectures for SDR. The authors have shown that Bruun's FFT can operate at larger bit lengths that are practical for a SDR, give better hardware performance in terms of area and delay compared to the classical FFT, while maintaining comparable NSR. It is suggested that Bruun's FFT may be preferred over classical and split-radix FFT in applications such as SDR.

## References

1. Mitola, J.: The Software Radio Architecture. IEEE Communications Magazine, 26–38 (May 1995)
2. Tuttlebee, W.: Evolution of radio systems into the 21st century. In: Proc. IEE Int. conf. on Radio receivers an associated systems (1995)
3. Reed, J.H.: Software Radio: A Modern Approach to Radio Engineering. Prentice Hall, Englewood Cliffs (2000)
4. Lin, Y.T., Tsai, P.Y., Chiueh, T.D.: Low-power variable-length fast Fourier transform processor. In: IEE Proceedings-Computers and Digital Techniques (July 2005)
5. Hung, C.-P., Chen, S.-G., Chen, K.-L.: Design of an efficient variable-length FFT processor. In: International Symposium on Circuits and Systems(ISCAS)'04 (2004)
6. Britanak, V., Rao, K.R.: Two-Dimensional DCT/DST Universal Computational Structure for 2m X 2n Block Sizes. IEEE Transaction on Signal Processing 48(11), 3250–3255 (2000)
7. Tell, E., Seger, O., Liu, D.: A converged hardware solution for FFT, DCT and Walsh transform. In: Seventh International symposium on Signal Processing and Its Applications, pp. 609–612 (2003)
8. Bruun, G.: Z-Transform DFT filters and FFT's. IEEE Trans.Acoust. Speech, Signal Processing ASSP-26, 56–63 (1978)
9. Storn, R.: Some Results in Fixed Point Error Analysis of the Bruun-FFT Algorithm. IEEE Transaction on Signal Processing. 41(7) (1993)
10. Oppenheim, A.V., Schafer, R.: Digital Signal Processing.Pearson Education (2004)
11. Parhami, B.: Computer Arithmetic: Algorithms and Hardwrae Designs. Oxford University Press, New York (2000)
12. Zimmermann, R.: Binary Adder Architectures for Cell-Based VLSI and their Synthesis, PhD thesis, Swiss Federal Institute of Technology (ETH) Zurich, Hartung-Gorre Verlag (1998)

# Design of 100 µW Wireless Sensor Nodes on Energy Scavengers for Biomedical Monitoring

Lennart Yseboodt[1], Michael De Nil[1], Jos Huisken[2], Mladen Berekovic[3], Qin Zhao[3], Frank Bouwens[3], and Jef Van Meerbergen[1,4]

[1] Eindhoven University of Technology Den Dolech 2
5612 AZ Eindhoven, Netherlands
lennart@belf.be, michael@flex-it.be
[2] Silicon Hive High Tech Campus 45 5656 AA Eindhoven, Netherlands
jos.huisken@philips.com
[3] Holst-centre High Tech Campus 48 5656 AA Eindhoven, Netherlands
mladen.berekovic@imec-nl.nl, frank.bouwens@imec-nl.nl,
qin.zhao@imec-nl.nl
[4] Philips Research Eindhoven High Tech Campus 5
5656 AA Eindhoven, Netherlands
jef.van.meerbergen@philips.com

**Abstract.** Wireless sensor nodes span a wide range of applications. This paper focuses on the biomedical area, more specifically on healthcare monitoring applications. Power dissipation is the dominant design constraint in this domain. This paper shows the different steps to develop a digital signal processing architecture for a single channel electrocardiogram application, which is used as an application example. We aim for less than 100µW power consumption as that is the power energy scavengers can deliver.

We follow a bottleneck-driven approach, the following steps are applied: first the algorithm is tuned to the target processor, then coarse grained clock-gating is applied, next the static as well as the dynamic dissipation of the digital processor is reduced by tuning the core to the target domain. The impact of each step is quantified. A solution of around 11µW is possible for both radio and DSP with the electrocardiogram algorithm.

## 1 Introduction

A new generation of biomedical monitoring devices is emerging. The main challenge for this kind of devices is low power dissipation. In this context a power budget of only 100µW is available for the whole system including radio, digital processing and memories. This power is taken from extremely small batteries or energy scavengers. To reduce the power dissipation of the radio data compression or feature extraction is used to reduce the number of bits that must be transmitted. Thus the bottleneck shifts towards the digital part which is the focus of this paper.

S. Vassiliadis et al. (Eds.): SAMOS 2007, LNCS 4599, pp. 385–395, 2007.

The goal of our work is to create a low-power C-programmable DSP, optimized for the application domain via hardware support for application specific instructions. As starting point a reconfigurable processor from Philips' technology incubator Silicon Hive [4] is selected. This technology includes a retargetable C compiler making code development and portability for these processors easy. This programmability is important because of the wide range of applications that can run on the nodes. Programmable nodes allow a lower non recurring engineering cost for the software and the hardware.

We differentiate between static and dynamic power dissipation. The dynamic power is the power consumed due to switching and the internal power, which is the power used inside the cells due to short-circuits and all the power used in the internal nets. It includes the functional units, memories, controller and clock. Current CMOS technology trends indicate that leakage is becoming more dominant with every new process generation. In our experiments leakage power soon turns out to be an important factor, up to 100μWof leakage was measured. Our focus has gone both into reducing static as in reducing dynamic power by minimizing the time the processor is active. As a case study we examined an ECG algorithm running on the proposed platform, what we learned from this example led to more general system level conclusions.

## 2   System Level Architecture

A generic sensor node consists of several subsystems as depicted in Fig. 1. There is a digital processing subsystem with level 1 local memory, a level 2 memory subsystem, including RAM and non-volatile memories, an array of sensors and possibly actuators, a radio system and a power subsystem including a source and powermanager, which is responsible for waking up various parts of the node when needed. This conceptual model holds independent of specific chip or die boundaries and leaves open several packaging technologies. If level 2 memories are kept off-die then multiple instances of the sensor node can be made without having to create a new chip.

In current systems the power is supplied by a small battery or from energy scavengers. Battery powered nodes have the disadvantage of requiring maintenance. Different forms of energy scavenging are possible but in this paper we assume a power budget of around 100μW [5]. This number includes power consumed by the radio and the sensors, it is the global power budget of the entire sensor node.

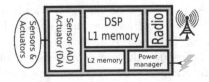

**Fig. 1.** Overview of the architecture of a wireless sensor node

The digital subsystem must be programmable in order to be able to run different algorithms such as ECG or EEG analysis, or altogether new algorithms from the biomedical domain. Furthermore real time constraints must be met especially when actuators are involved.

From a power dissipation point of view the most important consumers are the radio, the memory and the digital subsystem. Commercially available radios consume 150nJ/bit [7] and as a consequence the transmission of raw data can be expensive. An algorithm to reduce the amount of data via compression or feature extraction usually is a better compromise between computation and communication. In addition to the radio most subsystems exploit duty cycling and sleep modes to reduce the dissipation. Next the DSP must be tuned to the application. Also the memory subsystem can dissipate a lot of power. What is needed is a hierarchical memory subsystem optimized for power dissipation by reducing the size of the lowest level memories. These design principles will now be discussed in more detail and illustrated with an example, which is explained first.

## 3   Application

The electrocardiogram is a well studied topic, several interesting algorithms exist. One of the simplistic functions such an algorithm can offer is the detection for the ventricular contraction, when the heart pumps blood to the lungs and the body. In an ECG we call this event the R peak, situated in the QRS complex (Fig. 2). The algorithm we use as a testcase is based on the opensource ECG detection program from EP Limited [3].

The algorithm uses the Pan-Tomkins [1] method for R peak detection. The Pan-Tomkins method is a filtering based method to detect the frequency that is unique to the steeper R peak.

This algorithm extracts the key features reducing the amount of transmitted bits by 100x. The minimum frequency for ECG analysis is 200Hz, with a 16 bit sample width. Indeed sending raw data requires $200 * 16b = 400B/s$. Assuming 150 nJ/ bit the dissipation is 480µW which is higher than the available budget. The Pan-Tomkins method reduces this to 4B/s or 4.8 µW. The 4 bytes can hold all the information that can be extracted by this algorithm: the time between R peaks, the height of the R peak and the baseline drift.

## 4   Optimization DSP

After removing the radio bottleneck the problem shifts towards the DSP. Therefore we have chosen an ASIP (Application Specific Instruction set processor [12]) approach which allows to tune the core to the application domain. First we describe the reference core followed by the power optimizations.

### 4.1   Reference Core

Because of flexibility (easy to modify) a PearlRay processor from Silicon Hive [6] was selected. The processor is reconfigurable, i.e. there exists a parameterizable

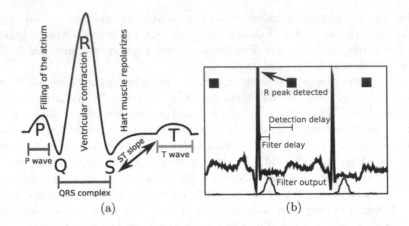

(a)                                      (b)

Fig. 2. The QRS complex and the detection of beats

description of the architecture and a C-compiler that can generate code for any possible architecture instance. The top level configuration file controls certain aspects of the processor: data widths, functional unit placement, custom functional units, configurations of the issue slots... We generated a default configuration with 32kB of data memory and 32kB of program memory. The processor is a VLIW with three issue slots, 128 bit wide instructions and is synthesized for a speed of 100MHz. This speed is the 'sweet spot' for this design. Synthesizing the core for several clock frequencies shows that speeds above 100MHz make the design grow exponentially in area and leakage as depicted in Fig. 3.

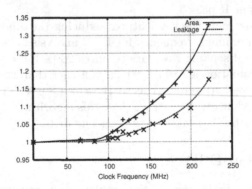

Fig. 3. Clock frequency vs. Area & Leakage

The algorithm was optimized by recoding the filters in such a way that their behavior was largely unaffected, when several expensive divisions were replaced by shifts. The PearlRay does not have a hardware divider and relies on a software divider taking 25 cycles per division. After these optimizations the cost of analyzing one sample of ECG data at a 200Hz sampling frequency was 250 cycles, however when a beat is detected this number is higher: 1200 cycles. A detection of a beat occurs only once or twice every second so on average it takes $198 \cdot 250 + 2 \cdot 1200 = 51900$ cycles per second. If the PearlRay is running at 100MHz the duty cycle is $51900/100 \cdot 10^6 = 0.05\%$.

Power figures for the processors, as seen in Table 2, were obtained using Synopsys PrimePower with layout extracted capacitances. As input a vector file from a netlist simulation was used, which was generated using Cadence Ncsim. Simulations were based on the processor netlist after layout on a 90nm CMOS process.

The power dissipation of the PearlRay was analyzed first. Three modes are identified: active, idle and sleep. In active mode the processor is running a program and processing samples. In idle mode the clock is still running. In sleep mode the only dissipation is due to leakage.

Graphically sketched this is visible in Fig. 4. In this diagram the $x$ axis is the time that elapses, while the $y$ axis represents the power consumption at that time. The area of the bars represents the energy consumed. The lightest bars represent the active energy, which can vary dependent on the input sample. We also observed this behavior in our ECG software. The middle bar is the idle energy and the darkest block is the ever present leakage energy.

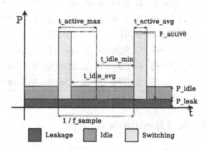

**Fig. 4.** Causes of power consumption over the time domain

$$P_{\text{Tot}} = P_{\text{Leak}} + f_{\text{sample}}\left( (P_{\text{Act}} \cdot t_{\text{Act\_avg}}) + (P_{\text{Idle}} \cdot t_{\text{Idle\_avg}}) \right)$$

The ECG application is an example of an algorithm that does not require a large portion of the processing power that a typical DSP offers. The developed processor is optimized for algorithms with a low duty cycle. Table 1 shows the power characteristics of the standard version of the PearlRay, which is used as a reference. At first glance the active power is dominant, but since the processor is only 'active' for a small fraction of the time, the actual energy usage attributed to active mode constitutes only to 0.4% of the total energy consumption. The power used in idle mode is the dominant factor here.

**Table 1.** Standard version of the PearlRay used as a reference. The last column shows the energy for one input sample and one ECG computation.

| Source | Power | Duration | Mean Power |
|--------|-------|----------|------------|
| Active | 6.87mW | 496µs | 3.41µW |
| Idle | 0.76mW | 1s−496µs | 758µW |
| Leak | 100µW | 1s | 100µW |
| Total power 861.4µW | | | |

**Table 2.** PrimePower output results for reference PearlRay while active. The `coreio` contains the data memory.

|  | P_Switch | P_Int | P_Leak | P_Total | % |
|--|----------|-------|--------|---------|---|
| imec_ref | 1.46e-3 | 5.41e-3 | 1.00e-4 | 6.97e-3 | 100% |
| core | 9.11e-4 | 7.78e-4 | 9.53e-6 | 1.70e-3 | 24.4% |
| dec | 3.86e-5 | 1.75e-4 | 2.34e-7 | 2.13e-4 | 3.1% |
| is_I0 | 1.00e-4 | 4.21e-5 | 9.67e-7 | 1.44e-4 | 2.1% |
| is_I1 | 2.71e-4 | 1.56e-4 | 2.80e-6 | 4.30e-4 | 6.2% |
| is_I2 | 8.96e-5 | 5.64e-5 | 9.61e-7 | 1.47e-4 | 2.1% |
| rf_I0 | 4.69e-5 | 9.61e-5 | 1.35e-6 | 1.44e-4 | 2.1% |
| rf_I1 | 1.03e-4 | 8.30e-5 | 2.07e-6 | 1.88e-4 | 2.7% |
| rf_I2 | 3.24e-5 | 5.32e-5 | 8.07e-7 | 8.65e-5 | 1.2% |
| coreio | 2.21e-4 | 1.11e-3 | 5.01e-5 | 1.38e-3 | 19.8% |
| genI1 | 2.69e-6 | 3.45e-5 | 7.15e-7 | 3.79e-5 | 0.5% |
| genI2 | 3.54e-5 | 5.92e-5 | 2.69e-7 | 9.49e-5 | 1.4% |
| genI3 | 1.47e-6 | 6.69e-5 | 1.38e-6 | 6.98e-5 | 1.0% |
| pmem | 4.14e-5 | 3.37e-3 | 3.90e-5 | 3.45e-3 | 49% |

## 4.2 Reduce Idle Mode Dissipation

To counter the effects of idle energy we use coarse grained clockgating. The PearlRay reference core was already using fine grained low-level clock gates but the top level clock gate was not implemented. The top level clock gate disconnects the clock from the entire clocktree, meaning that when this gate is open no switching will occur in the processor. As a consequence an external piece of circuitry must revive the processor when this is required. Such a clock gate was very important as shown by the results in Table 3. After this optimization the dominant energy component is leakage (96%).

## 4.3 Reducing Leakage

Now we are faced with dominant leakage power so we analyze in which part of the processor the leakage occurs. Our total leakage is 100µW, of which 50µW is caused by the data memory, 40µW by the program memory and 10µW by the processor itself. The large majority of the leakage is in the memories. We tried four things to improve this leakage.

- Reduce the size of that data memory to 2kB. Since the ECG program only requires 1.2kB and 120 bytes of stack this was possible. This reduced the leakage to 65.6 µW, a 34.5% improvement.
- By removing one of the three issue slots in the PearlRay processor and reducing the size of the immediates, the width of the program memory could be reduced from 128b to 64b. Due to the decrease of parallelism the instruction count was increased with 27%, but the instruction width was reduced by 50%, allowing us to reduce the program memory from 32kB to 16kB. This resulted in a reduction of leakage power to 82µW, a 18% improvement.
- The use of memory modules designed in a technology with a high threshold option (High$V_t$). This drastically reduces the leakage of the memories. They will become slower but speed was not really a constraint and the memories still operated on 100MHz. Using these memories leakage was reduced to 16.2µW, a 84% improvement.
- Reduce the datapath from 32 bit to 16 bit. As the samples are only 16 bit wide and all operations occur on them, it is optimal to scale the core to this width. This gave a moderate improvement in leakage to 94.7µW, or 5.3%.

When combining these techniques together with floorplan optimizations, the results shown in Table 4 were obtained, which reduced the leakage of the original PearlRay processor to 5.45µW, a 94.5% improvement. Furthermore scaling down the datapath to 16 bit also contributed to reduce the dissipation of the active mode.

**Table 3.** Power results with a top level clockgate installed

| Source | Power | Duration | Mean Power |
|--------|-------|----------|------------|
| Active | 6.87mW | 496µs | 3.41µW |
| Idle | 0W | 1s−496µs | 0W |
| Leak | 100µW | 1s | 100µW |
| Total power 103.41µW | | | |

**Table 4.** Power result with anti-leakage techniques combined

| Source | Power | Duration | Mean Power |
|--------|-------|----------|------------|
| Active | 4.7mW | 628µs | 2.95µW |
| Idle | 0W | 1s−628µs | 0 W |
| Leak | 5.45µW | 1s | 5.45µW |
| Total power 8.4µW | | | |

## 5  System Level Optimization

In this section we describe system level optimizations that are a work in progress. We are currently experimenting with power gating and level 2 memories that can be used to save the state and shutdown the core.

## 5.1    Power Down the Core

From Table 4 we conclude that the leakage is still dominant. Therefore an interesting option is to power down the core and to save the state to level 2 memory and restore it when the next batch of samples have to be processed. There are positive and negative contributions to the power dissipation. In those circumstances where the final net result is positive this is an interesting option. It means a hierarchical memory subsystem: small level 1 memories with a high number of accesses and larger level 2 memories with a very limited number of accesses. This is similar to a memory hierarchy in computer architectures but optimized for power dissipation instead of performance. Level 2 memory (or part of it) is also used for other purposes, e.g. to collect the samples that arrive while the core is down or to store multiple applications, which are not active simultaneously.

Let's apply this to the ECG example. The state includes not only data (1.2kB) but also the program (16kB). This data is used to retain the state of the filters and for several other variables such as the baseline drift. An important decision is the granularity of switching between modes. If we do this at a sample basis this can become quite expensive. Assuming a low power (level 2) SRAM memory in a 90 nm process and a size of 32kB the cost of an access is 0.875 pJ/B and the leakage equals 2.5µW. If the processor is powered down after every sample the cost is 28.8µW, the calculation is detailed in Table 5. This can be improved by grouping the samples in groups of 50, then the cost of saving and restoring is also reduced by a factor 50 which translates into an acceptable level of 3.0µW. This can even be further improved to 0.5 by using a non-volatile memory (flash).

The swapping between level 2 and level 1 memories can be done for complete applications but also for parts of an application. The Pan-Tomkins algorithm for ECG is a good example. As mentioned above it consists of 2 parts: the filtering and the feature extraction. Both parts have similar code size. The filtering is executed for every sample but the feature extraction is executed with a low probability (0.5%), i.e. only when a beat is detected, which is about once per second. Therefore it is possible to reduce the level 1 code memory by a factor of 2, which reduces the access energy. The consequence is that the programmer or the compiler must be aware of this, e.g. to insert statements for code swapping.

## 5.2    Results

Table 6 shows a system level overview of the different components of the power consumption in µW. Furthermore the application scope is widened. The first four rows show an ECG application with different assumptions. The first row shows the simple baseline ECG case with 1 channel as discussed above. The second row assumes 3 channels. The next one is again 1 channel but now a more complex algorithm for a more extensive analysis including extra parameters (such as Q&S peaks and average beat rate). The fourth one is the same as the previous one but now for 3 channels. The last two rows show FFT analysis on 1 and 10 channel(s) respectively. The different columns represent the different contributions to the power dissipation in µW. A 90 nm process is assumed.

**Table 5.** Level 1 to level 2 state save calculation

| Cause | Calculation | Result |
|-------|-------------|--------|
| | *Granularity: 1 sample* | |
| Leak | | 2.5µW |
| $R_{pm}$[a] | $16kB \cdot 8192 \cdot 0.875pJ \cdot 200/s$ | 22.94µW |
| $W_{st}$[b] | $1200B \cdot 8 \cdot 0.875pJ \cdot 200/s$ | 1.68µW |
| $R_{st}$[c] | $1200B \cdot 8 \cdot 0.875pJ \cdot 200/s$ | 1.68µW |
| | **Total:** | 28.8µW |
| | *Granularity: 50 samples* | |
| Leak | | 2.5µW |
| $R_{pm}$ | $16kB \cdot 8192 \cdot 0.875pJ \cdot 4/s$ | 0.46µW |
| $W_{st}$ | $1200B \cdot 8 \cdot 0.875pJ \cdot 4/s$ | 0.03µW |
| $R_{st}$ | $1200B \cdot 8 \cdot 0.875pJ \cdot 4/s$ | 0.03µW |
| | **Total:** | 3.02µW |

[a] Read program memory
[b] Write state
[c] Read state

**Table 6.** Power consumption with different assumptions, all numbers represent micro watts

| | $P_{radio}$ | $P_{active}$ | $P_{idle}$ | $P_{state}$ | $P_{tot\ L1}$ | $P_{tot\ L1\ L2}$ |
|------|------|------|-----|-----|------|------|
| 1ch | 4.8 | 3.3 | 5.5 | 3.0 | 13.5 | 11.0 |
| 3ch | 4.8 | 9.8 | 5.5 | 3.1 | 20 | 17.6 |
| 1ch+ | 9.6 | 4.6 | 5.5 | 3.3 | 19.6 | 17.5 |
| 3ch+ | 9.6 | 13.7 | 5.5 | 3.6 | 28.7 | 26.8 |
| eeg1 | 2.16 | 2.1 | 5.5 | 3.0 | 9.8 | 7.3 |
| eeg10 | 21.6 | 21.3 | 5.5 | 3.0 | 48.4 | 45.9 |

The second column represents the radio power assuming 150 nJ/bit. Columns 3 and 4 are related to the processor and show the dissipation when active and the leakage. The next column shows the dissipation due to state-saving and restoring in a 32 KB level 2 SRAM memory. The last 2 columns show the total dissipation for 2 different scenarios. The last column assumes level 2 memory is used and the processor put in power down mode. The previous column assumes the opposite.

We conclude for various use scenarios different components can have the largest contribution in power consumption. Therefore it is not easy to predict and a careful analysis is needed for each situation. The data in Section 4 shows that the average power consumption constraint of 100µW is feasible.

# 6  Conclusion

Power dissipation is the most important constraint for wireless sensor nodes for healthcare applications. This paper describes the different steps in the development of an architecture using a single channel ECG application as an example. It shows that a 100μW solution is feasible.

For minimum power dissipation there is an optimum balance between computation and communication. Transmitting raw data is usually not optimal. A significant reduction in the amount of transmitted bits is obtained via compression or feature extraction. As a consequence the bottleneck shifts towards the DSP. Static as well as dynamic dissipation must be tackled. Both components are reduced by tuning the core to the target domain (application specific instructions, proper memory sizes, etc.) In an optimized architecture the level 1 memories have a limited size due to the high number of accesses in active mode. When the processor is inactive it can be powered down while the state is saved in level 2 memory. This requires that the granularity is carefully chosen. Analyzing different ECG applications it is shown that optimizing the digital processing technology is important.

Therefore this is chosen as the focus of this paper. Using ECG as a driver and adopting a bottleneck-driven step-by-step approach a factor of 100 reduction of power dissipation of the DSP core was measured via simulations. This is a result of the following actions that span the different design levels.

- Algorithm level: optimization and simplification of the code.
- Architecture level: e.g. level 1 memory size reduction by a factor of 2 for instructions and a factor of 16 for data
- Gate level: e.g. clock gating.
- Technology with High$V_t$.

# References

1. Rangayyan, R.: Biomedical Signal Analysis. USA: Wiley ©2002
2. Pan, J., Tompkins, W.J.: A Real-Time QRS Detection Algorithm. IEEE Transactions Biomedical Engineering BME-32(3), 230–236 (1985)
3. EP Limited http://www.eplimited.com
4. Silicon Hive http://www.siliconhive.com
5. Bert Gyselinckx. Human[++]: emerging technology for body area networks
6. Halfhill, T.R.: Silicon Hive Breaks Out. December 1, 2003 Microprocessor Report (2003), www.MPRonline.com
7. True System-on-Chip with Low Power RF Transceiver and 8051 MCU, TI Datasheet CC, SWRS033A 1110
8. Low power DSP, TI MSP430F149, http://www.ti.com
9. Coolflux DSP, www.coolfluxdsp.com

10. Ekanayake, V.N., IV Kelly, C., Manohar, R.: BitSNAP: Dynamic Significance Compression For a Low-Energy Sensor Network Asynchronous Processor. In: Proc. ASYNC, pp.144–154 (March 2005)
11. Warneke, B.A., Pister, K.S.J.: An Ultra-Low Energy Microcontroller for SmartDust Wireless Sensor Networks. In: Proc.ISSCC, (February 2004)
12. Meyr, H.: System-on-chip for communications: The dawn of ASIPs and the dusk of ASICs. In: Proc. IEEE Workshop on Signal Processing Systems (SIPS'03), Seoul, Korea (August 2003)

# Tool-Aided Design and Implementation of Indoor Surveillance Wireless Sensor Network

Mauri Kuorilehto, Jukka Suhonen, Marko Hännikäinen, and Timo D. Hämäläinen

Tampere University of Technology, Institute of Digital and Computer Systems
P.O. Box 553, FI-33101 Tampere, Finland
{mauri.kuorilehto, jukka.suhonen, marko.hannikainen,
timo.d.hamalainen}@tut.fi

**Abstract.** This paper presents the design and implementation of an indoor surveillance Wireless Sensor Network (WSN) using tools for hastening and facilitating the different phases in the WSN development. First, the application case is described in WISENES (WIreless SEnsor NEtwork Simulator) framework by four models, which define application, communication, node, and environment. WISENES enables a graphical design of the models combined with accurate simulations for performance evaluation. Next, surveillance application tasks and communication protocols are implemented on node platforms on top of SensorOS Operating System (OS). A congruent programming model of SensorOS allows a straightforward mapping of WISENES models to the final implementation. The evaluation of the indoor surveillance WSN implemented with Tampere University of Technology WSN (TUTWSN) protocols and platforms reaches a lifetime in order of years while still ensuring reactive operation. Further, the results show only 9.5 % and 6.6 % differences in simulated and measured networking delay and power consumption, respectively. Our results indicate that accurate early design phase simulations can relieve the burden of prototyping and low level implementation by a realistic configuration evaluation during design time.

## 1 Introduction

Wireless Sensor Networks (WSN) are an emerging ad hoc networking technology, in which a large number of miniaturized sensor nodes organize and operate autonomously. Communication, computation, energy, and memory capacities of individual nodes are limited, but the overall network capability results from the cooperation of nodes [1].

The envisioned applications for WSNs are diverse in environmental monitoring, home, industry, health care, and military. In spite of the diversity of applications, they possess common domain independent characteristics. A typical application gathers measurement data from different sensors, aggregate them, and route data to a central gathering point, a *sink*. Alternatively, nodes perform in-network data fusion and make either independent or distributed control actions through actuators [2].

The communication in WSNs is controlled by a layered protocol stack. The key layers are Medium Access Control (MAC) that manages channel access and network topology, and routing that creates and maintains multi-hop paths between end points [1]. The communication requirements for a WSN are application-specific, thus a single protocol stack is not suitable for all cases. Yet, the maturity and properties of WSN

S. Vassiliadis et al. (Eds.): SAMOS 2007, LNCS 4599, pp. 396–407, 2007.

protocol stacks are evolving, which allow the optimization of existing protocols and software architectures for a variety of applications through configuration [3].

As the number of design choices and complexity of WSN applications increases, the management of the vast design space and the configuration exploration for an application requires design automation tools. Until recently, design automation has not been considered in WSN community, but the main focus of research has been on energy efficient and scalable protocols [2]. However, considering the rapid evolution, the burden of WSN design without tools will evidently be unbearable. In order to substantially hasten and facilitate WSN development, tools need to support all phases in the WSN design and help the designer to make reasonable the design choices [4].

The WSN design flow used in this paper is presented in Fig. 1. Design dimensions extract the key parameters from the application requirements for steering system design and implementation phases. In the design phase, a system is divided into separate models for *application*, *communication*, *node*, and *environment*. These models are defined, configured, and evaluated to obtain a suitable system composition for hardware and software implementation. The system is evaluated by both simulations and prototyping. In general, simulations reveal possible performance tweaks in large-scale and long-term deployments, while prototyping verifies the operation of the implementation in its final execution environment. Before the final deployment, required phases are iterated until application requirements are met.

In this paper, we present the design and implementation of an indoor surveillance WSN using support tools. For WSN design, our WIreless SEnsor NEtwork Simulator (WISENES) [5] defines methods for the formal description of application and communication model functionality and dependencies. WISENES allows accurate performance evaluation of graphical Specification and Description Language (SDL) models through simulation. For the final deployment, application and communication models are implemented on top of SensorOS [6] Operating System (OS) that offers a congruent interface with WISENES. The indoor surveillance application is designed and implemented with TUTWSN (Tampere University of Technology WSN) node platforms and protocols [7]. The evaluation of the design case shows the feasibility of the tools and their applicability for rapid development of application-specific WSNs.

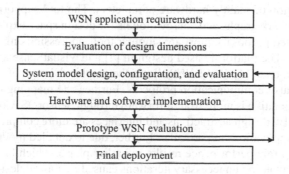

**Fig. 1.** Different phases in the proposed WSN design flow

The rest of the paper is organized as follows. Section 2 discusses related research in area of WSN design. The requirements for the surveillance application, and TUTWSN protocols and platforms are presented in Section 3. Section 4 shows WSN design with WISENES. The prototype implementation of the surveillance WSN on top of SensorOS is presented Section 5. Finally, conclusions are given in Section 6.

## 2   Related Work

While a wide variety of system architectures are proposed for WSNs, TinyOS [8] has gained the most popularity. TinyOS is a component-based OS for event-driven WSNs. TinyOS component development is facilitated by nesC [9] programming language that adopts the TinyOS programming model. TOSSIM [10] implements a simulation environment for large scale WSNs built with TinyOS. For data gathering applications, TinyOS can be supplemented with TinyDB [11] that abstracts WSN as a database.

Several higher abstraction level design tools are also proposed for TinyOS systems. VisualSense [12] extends Ptolemy II with WSN features and allows the development of WSN protocols and applications using different Models-of-Computation (MoC) available in Ptolemy II. Applications developed with VisualSense are integrated to TinyOS and TOSSIM through a Viptos interface. GRATIS [13] introduces a graphical tool for TinyOS component design and management. In [14], the mapping of applications implemented as SDL models to TinyOS components is proposed. A loose relation to TinyOS is present also in Prowler [15] that is a MATLAB-based simulation environment targeted for application algorithm testing and optimization for TinyOS nodes.

A platform based design methodology for WSNs is proposed in [4]. The approach is based on three abstract models for applications, protocols, and hardware platforms. A Rialto tool defines requirements for the protocols by exploring all possible communication combinations of the application model. The protocol stack configuration is optimized to meet application requirements in the constraints set by platform candidates. A quite similar approach is taken in [16], in which communication protocols and platform are abstracted to a virtual architecture for algorithm design and synthesis. The proposed design flow concentrates on the modeling concepts and does not provide tool support. In [17], a system level design methodology is proposed for cost function guided optimization of mainly hardware parameters. The tool supported optimization utilizes static network graphs and energy models for design space exploration.

From the related proposals, most are singular tools addressing only a minor part of the WSN design. The platform based design in [4] and VisualSense are nearest to our approach. Compared to [4], WISENES allows the graphical design of not only application models but also communication protocols. Further, the mapping of the models to the final implementation is more straightforward through SensorOS. Compared to VisualSense, WISENES design abstractions and interfaces are more comprehensive and oriented for WSN applications in particular. Further, due to detailed modeling WISENES outputs more accurate performance results in earlier phase, which hastens the overall development by avoiding unnecessary iterations caused by flawed design choices.

# 3    Indoor Surveillance WSN

An indoor surveillance WSN monitors temperature and detects motion in the public premises of a building. The WSN has three active tasks; motion detection, temperature sensing, and a sink task for data gathering. The relations between tasks together with the basic network architecture are illustrated in Fig. 2a.

The surveillance WSN is designed and implemented with TUTWSN protocols and platforms. In addition to a configurable protocol stack and a family of node platforms, TUTWSN consists of several applications and different monitoring and control User Interfaces (UI) [7]. TUTWSN is accessed through an Application Programming Interface (API) that defines the data interests for the network.

## 3.1    Surveillance WSN Requirements

The motion detection task interfaces a Passive Infra-Red (PIR) sensor for generating movement alerts, which are forwarded to the sink task. The temperature sensing task measures surrounding temperature periodically and sends it to the sink task. Temperature sensing task is activated once per minute in all nodes. The motion detection task is present only on nodes located in public premises, such as isles. The sink task is executed on a gateway that connects WSN to external networks. The sink stores data to a database and forwards alerts to monitoring UIs.

The requirements for the two sensing tasks differ significantly. The motion detection task is event-based and activated by movement. Generated alerts have high priority, are delay critical, and need reliable transmission. Instead, periodic temperature measurements are low priority packets and occasional data losses are acceptable. In order to avoid constant maintenance, the WSN should operate approximately a year without battery replacements.

## 3.2    TUTWSN Protocols

TUTWSN MAC protocol combines slotted-ALOHA and reservation data slots for adaptive and extremely energy efficient operation. The clustered topology is maintained with periodic beacons by cluster *headnodes* that also perform inter-cluster communication by synchronizing to neighbor headnodes. *Subnodes* maintain synchronization and communicate only with their parent headnodes. The MAC protocol provides a reliable data transmission service for upper layers. A bandwidth allocation within a cluster is controlled by an adaptive algorithm that reacts to the communication profile changes.

TUTWSN routing protocol forms routes towards a sink based on cost-gradients. Each node maintains several alternative routes each with a different cost function. Routing selects typically two or three synchronized parents for MAC according to the next hops for routes. The cost function used for application data depends on the traffic class. The cost information is updated in the network maintenance communication, thus additional control communication is needed only for adaptive recovering from link failures.

TUTWSN protocols can be tailored for different kinds of applications with a rich set of configuration parameters during both design and runtime. Design time MAC layer configuration includes e.g. access cycle and network maintenance timing, role selection

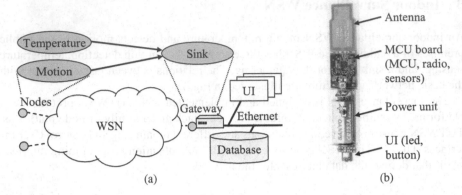

**Fig. 2.** An overview of (a) surveillance WSN architecture and (b) TUTWSN PIC node

directions, intervals for topology control, and bandwidth reservation and usage parameters. Cost function coefficients and protocol reactiveness can be configured for routing at design time. During runtime, MAC layer can be configured by altering number of Time Division Multiple Access (TDMA) slots and node roles, and routing by selecting used cost functions. The applications of a network can be configured by changing the data interests.

### 3.3 TUTWSN Prototype Platform

TUTWSN node platform used in this paper is illustrated in Fig. 2b. The main component is PIC18LF4620 nanowatt series Micro-Controller Unit (MCU) with 64 KB code and 3986 B data memory. MCU contains also an 10-bit integrated Analog-to-Digital Converter (ADC) and 1 KB of EEPROM as a non-volatile data storage. The power unit consists of a MAX1725 regulator with 2.4 V output voltage and a 3 V CR123A lithium battery with 1600 mAh capacity. In addition, a DS620 digital thermometer is integrated to the platform. A PIR-sensor is attached to a connector provided for external sensors. The radio interface on the platform is a 2.4 GHz nRF2401A transceiver unit, which supports 1 Mbit/s data rate and transmit power between -20...0 dBm.

## 4  WSN Design with WISENES

In WISENES [5], protocols and applications are designed in high abstraction level using SDL. SDL components, blocks, can be structured hierarchically in order to clarify the presentation, while the functionality is implemented in processes described as Extended Finite State Machines (EFSM). Processes communicate with signals that initiate state transitions at the recipient processes. Such a programming model is suitable for communication systems and for WSN applications that are typically activated by an event and alter their state and processing depending on the events and their parameters.

WISENES utilizes commercial Telelogic TAU SDL Suite for the graphical design of protocols and applications, and for the code generation of simulation cases. The core functionality, modeling approach, simulation framework, and environment and platform description are independent of the Telelogic tools. The characteristics of the environment and sensor nodes are defined accurately for WISENES in a set of eXtensible Markup Language (XML) configuration files. The detailed parameters and the realistic modeling of wireless transmission medium, physical phenomena, and sensor node hardware capabilities result to accurate performance information of simulated protocols, nodes, and networks. Simulation results are stored to logs for the post-processing of the energy, processing, memory, and sensor usage statistics for individual nodes. Further, networking performance for the whole WSN and for different applications is output in terms of delays, throughput, collisions, and bandwidth utilization.

## 4.1 WISENES Model Abstraction

WISENES incorporates four models defined by a designer. These are *application model*, *communication model*, *node model*, and *environment model*. The hierarchy and main properties of the models are depicted in Fig. 3. The environment model defines the parameters for wireless communication (signal propagation, noise), describes overall characteristics (average values, variation) for different phenomena, and specifies separate target areas (e.g. buildings) and objects (e.g. humans, animals, vehicles). The environment model defines also the mobility of nodes and target objects.

WISENES application model allows a designer to describe the functionality and requirements of an application separately. This eases the exploration of the performance and suitability of application configurations for different kinds of networks and environments. The functionality of an application is divided into tasks that are implemented as SDL statecharts. The operational parameters and requirements of the application are specified in XML configuration files. These parameters define the dependencies between the application tasks, task activation patterns, and Quality of Service (QoS) requirements for the applications. The QoS parameters define task priorities, networking requirements in terms of data reliability and urgency, and an overall network optimization target. The optimization target is used to steer communication model and it can be for example a maximal network lifetime, load balancing, or high performance.

The communication model specifies the networking for WSN applications. The WISENES communication model consists of a protocol stack implemented in SDL and

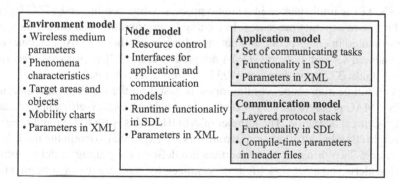

**Fig. 3.** WISENES models for designer and their main characteristics

a set of configuration parameters. Protocol configuration parameters are set at design time, while application-specific requirements, such as network optimization target, are input from the application model during runtime.

The node model describes the characteristics and capabilities of physical node platforms. The node model is implemented by WISENES framework and it is parameterized in XML configuration files that define node resources, peripherals and transceivers. WISENES SDL node model implements an OS type interface to applications and communication protocols for resource management and execution control.

### 4.2 Surveillance WSN Design

In WSN design with WISENES, the initial selection of the communication protocols and their parameters is made by the designer. It is our belief that hands-on knowledge and past experiences always result to a sophisticated selection for a starting point.

**WISENES Model Design.** WSN design in WISENES starts with the definition of models. The environment model is defined in XML. For the indoor surveillance WSN case, it specifies a slightly error-prone communication environment, stationary node locations, typical average values for phenomena, and few target objects with random mobility patterns. A node model is implemented for TUTWSN PIC node by describing its physical characteristics in XML configuration files. The main functionality for the designed WSN is defined in application and communication models.

The application model consists of the three tasks. Their parameters are given in XML configuration files. Fig. 4a shows configuration parameters for the motion detection task. The functionality of tasks is implemented as SDL statecharts. WISENES implementation of the motion detection task is depicted in Fig. 4b. The task is activated by two events; a motion detection event from a PIR-sensor and a timer event for PIR-sensor reactivation. A motion detection event triggers a data transmission and the initialization of a timeout, while a timer event reactivates the PIR-sensor. Timeout is needed to avoid continuous alerts. The periodical sensing task initiates a temperature measurement on a timer event, and sends data and initializes the timer after a sensor event. The sink task stores received data to a database.

The communication model design for TUTWSN consists of five SDL processes. TUTWSN API is implemented in a single process, while routing and MAC layers are divided into two separate processes. In routing layer, topology and route management are implemented in one process, and data handling in another. In MAC, channel access is implemented separately from TDMA adaptation control. The processes incorporate totally 48 states, 372 transitions, and 4937 different execution paths.

The communication model configuration is based on the application requirements. TUTWSN MAC protocol uses 2 s access cycle to balance energy-efficiency, scalability, and delay-critical operation. The number of ALOHA slots is set to four and reservation slots to eight. Bandwidth allocation parameters are explored to obtain the most suitable configuration. Two different cost functions are defined for routing; a delay optimized for motion alerts and a network lifetime optimized for temperature measurements.

**Simulation Results.** The performance of the surveillance WSN with the presented model implementations is evaluated with WISENES simulations. A network of 150

```
<application_model>
  <task id="MOTION">
    <interval ms="0"/>
    <priority level="1"/>
    <sensors>
      <sensor id="PIR"/>
    </sensors>
    <data>
      <target task="SINK"/>
      <priority level="1"/>
      <reliable set="yes"/>
      <urgent set="yes"/>
      <opt target="DELAY"/>
    </data>
  </task>
  <task id="TEMPERATURE">
    ...
  </task>
</application_model>
```

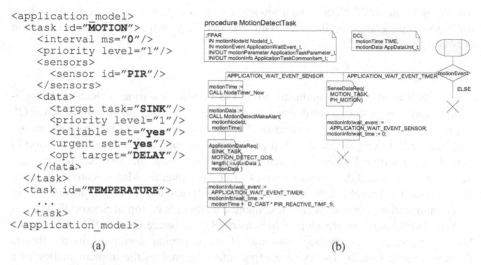

(a)                                    (b)

**Fig. 4.** Example WISENES application model (a) XML parameters and (b) SDL implementation for motion detection task

semi-randomly deployed nodes is simulated for a 24 hour period. 30 nodes include a PIR-sensor and three operate as a sink, while the rest measure temperature and perform data routing. Different configurations are evaluated by parameterizing bandwidth allocation algorithm. A default reservation slot interval ($r$) sets the maximum time between granted reservation slots for a member node. In simulations $r$ is set to 6 and 12 seconds.

Application requirements are verified by monitoring the delay of motion alerts, and node power consumption. The delay of temperature measurements is considered for comparison. Fig. 5a shows the average delays of motion alerts and temperature measurements for different $r$ values as the function of number of hops from a sink node (hop count). As shown, with a same hop count, the alerts experience slightly smaller delay than the temperature measurements, because of the delay optimized routing of alerts. Further, in TUTWSN a delay optimized route has typically less hops, which further improves the performance compared to temperature measurements. The average power consumptions of 10 randomly selected headnodes are $650\,\mu W$ and $635\,\mu W$, and of 10 subnodes with PIR-sensor $434\,\mu W$ and $443\,\mu W$ for $r = 6$, and $r = 12$, respectively.

The simulation results of initial communication model configuration are acceptable. The configuration with $r = 6$ obtains a slightly better performance and balances networking reactiveness and lifetime. Assuming that 90 % of the battery capacity can be exploited, with 1600 mAh CR123A battery the simulated power consumptions indicate lifetimes of 276 and 414 days for TUTWSN headnode and subnode, respectively. By rotating headnode and subnode roles the network can reach a lifetime of a year.

## 5   WSN Prototype Implementation

After the design is validated by simulations, the prototype implementation is made. The application tasks and protocols are implemented manually on top of SensorOS [6] according to the WISENES application and communication models. SensorOS offers a congruent programming interface with WISENES, which makes a fluent transition between phases possible.

### 5.1  SensorOS

SensorOS is a pre-emptive multi-threading OS targeted for time critical WSN applications and very resource constrained nodes. The scheduling algorithm of SensorOS is priority-based, but for less time critical applications SensorOS incorporates an optional more lightweight kernel with a polling run-to-completion scheduler. SensorOS kernel includes Inter-Process Communication (IPC), timing, memory, and power management services and drivers for interrupt-driven peripherals. Mutexes are included to the pre-emptive kernel for the synchronization of thread execution. Application tasks and communication protocols are implemented as threads on top of SensorOS API.

WISENES interfaces are adopted in SensorOS by message-passing IPC and an event waiting interface. The message-passing allows a similar communication between threads as SDL signals. The event waiting interface enables the implementation of a state-based operation similar to WISENES by offering a single function for the waiting of timeouts, external peripheral events, and IPC messages. Further, the power and memory management in SensorOS are identical to those of WISENES node model.

### 5.2  Surveillance WSN Implementation on TUTWSN Prototypes

The prototype implementation of the surveillance WSN is realized in a limited scale with 28 nodes (10 with PIR-sensors) on a realistic deployment environment. The full version of SensorOS is used in nodes equipped with PIR-sensors to guarantee reactiveness, while the rest of the nodes have a lightweight kernel that allows longer packet queues. The topology and environment for the prototyped surveillance WSN is depicted on a TUTWSN UI screen capture in Fig. 6. Arrows in the figure show the latest route.

**Prototype Implementation.** Application tasks are implemented as SensorOS threads. Fig. 7 lists the code of the thread implementing the motion detection task. For

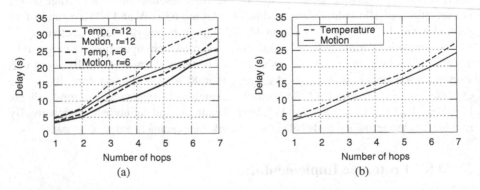

**Fig. 5.** Average (a) simulated and (b) measured (with $r=6$) delays for motion alerts and temperature measurements

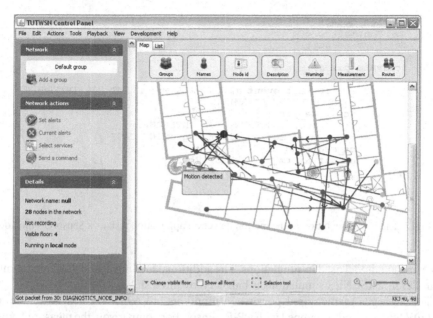

**Fig. 6.** A screen capture from TUTWSN UI illustrating the prototyped surveillance WSN operation

readability, the details of PIR-sensor interfacing and data message construction are left out. Other application tasks are implemented similarly. The TUTWSN protocol stack is implemented in four threads. API, data routing, and MAC channel access are implemented as separate threads similarly to WISENES communication model design, but MAC and routing layer management operations are integrated to a same thread in order to diminish IPC messaging. TUTWSN protocols are parameterized with the values obtained in WISENES design.

The subnode implementation on TUTWSN PIC node with full feature SensorOS consumes 38.1 KB of code and 2253 B of data memory. These are 60 % and 57 % of available memory resources, respectively. The data memory consumption does not include a heap reserved for dynamic memory. The implementation of temperature measurement application and TUTWSN protocols on top of a lightweight SensorOS kernel takes 58.2 KB code and 2658 B data memory, which are 91 % and 67 % of available memory, respectively.

**Prototype Results.** The same performance metrics gathered from WISENES simulations are evaluated also for the prototype implementation in order to verify the accuracy of WISENES models and to validate the implementation for final deployment. The delays of motion alerts and temperature measurement data as the function of hop count are depicted in Fig. 5b. In the prototype implementation $r$ is 6 seconds.

The results correspond closely to those obtained from WISENES, average difference being 8.9 % for motion alerts and 10.2 % for temperature data. The reason for a slightly better performance obtained in WISENES is less retransmissions due to a bit optimistic

```
void motion_detect (void) {
    os_eventmask_t event;
    os_ipc_message_t *msg;

    activate_pir ();
    while (1) {
        event = os_wait_event (EVENT_ALARM | EVENT_PIR_INTERRUPT);
        if (event & EVENT_ALARM) {
            activate_pir ();
        } else if (event & EVENT_PIR_INTERRUPT) {
            msg = make_motion_alert_msg (SINK_TASK);
            os_msg_send (API_PID, msg);
            os_set_alarm (PIR_REACTIVATE_TIMEOUT_MS);
        }
    }
}
```

**Fig. 7.** The implementation of the motion detection application task as a SensorOS thread

environment model used in simulations. The additional loading due to the larger number of nodes in WISENES simulations is balanced by three sinks.

The averages of measured power consumptions are $693\,\mu W$ for a headnode and $467\,\mu W$ for a subnode equipped with a PIR-sensor. For comparison, the measured power consumption of a subnode running a lightweight kernel without a PIR-sensor in the same WSN is $257\,\mu W$. These are also analogous with WISENES results, average difference being 6.2 % for headnodes and 7.0 % for subnodes with PIR-sensor.

## 6  Conclusions

In this paper, we present the design and implementation of an indoor surveillance WSN with WISENES and SensorOS. The high abstraction level models are first designed in graphical environment and then implemented on top of a full feature OS on node platforms. By enabling a realistic evaluation of different configurations during the design phase, the presented tools hasten the WSN development significantly. Further, the congruent programming models make the implementation of applications and protocols on top of SensorOS straightforward according to the WISENES models. The surveillance WSN evaluation proves the accuracy of WISENES simulations and shows the suitability of TUTWSN and SensorOS for the application implementation.

## References

1. Akyildiz, I.F., Su, W., Sankarasubramaniam, Y., Cayirci, E.: A survey on sensor networks. IEEE Communications Magazine 40(8), 102–114 (2002)
2. Akyildiz, I.F., Kasimoglu, I.H.: Wireless sensor and actor networks: research challenges. Elsevier Ad Hoc Networks 2(4), 351–367 (2004)
3. Römer, K., Mattern, F.: The design space of wireless sensor networks. IEEE Wireless Communications 11(6), 54–61 (2004)
4. Bonivento, A., Carloni, L.P., Sangiovanni-Vincentelli, A.: Platform based design for wireless sensor networks. Mobile Networks and Applications 11(4), 469–485 (2006)

5. Kuorilehto, M., Kohvakka, M., Hännikäinen, M., Hämäläinen, T.D.: High level design and implementation framework for wireless sensor networks. In: Proc. Embedded Computer Systems: Architectures, Modeling, and Simulation, Samos, Greece, pp. 384–393 (2005)
6. Kuorilehto, M., Alho, T., Hännikäinen, M., Hämäläinen, T.D.: Sensoros: a new operating system for time critical wsn applications. In: Proc. Embedded Computer Systems: Architectures, Modeling, and Simulation, Samos, Greece (2007)
7. Suhonen, J., Kohvakka, M., Hännikäinen, M., Hämäläinen, T.D.: Design, implementation, and experiments on outdoor deployment of wireless sensor network for environmental monitoring. In: Proc. Embedded Computer Systems: Architectures, Modeling, and Simulation, Samos, Greece, pp. 109–121 (2006)
8. Hill, J., Szewczyk, R., Woo, A., et al.: System architecture directions for networked sensors. In: Proc. 9th ACM International Conference on Architectural Support for Programming Languages and Operating Systems, Cambridge, MA, USA, pp. 94–103 (2000)
9. Gay, D., Levis, P., Behren, R.v., Welsh, M., Brewer, E., Culler, D.: The nesc language: A holistic approach to networked embedded systems. In: Proc. ACM Conference on Programming Language Design and Implementation, San Diego, CA, USA, pp. 1–11 (2003)
10. Levis, P., Lee, N., Welsh, M., Culler, D.: Tossim: accurate and scalable simulation of entire TinyOS applications. In: Proc. 1st ACM Conference on Embedded Networked Sensor Systems, Los Angeles, CA, USA, pp. 126–137 (2003)
11. Madden, S., Franklin, M.J., Hellerstein, J.M., Hong, W.: The design of an acquisitional query processor for sensor networks. In: Proc. ACM International Conference on Management of Data, San Diego, CA, USA, pp. 491–502 (2003)
12. Baldwin, P., Kohli, S., Lee, E.A., Liu, X., Zhao, Y.: Modeling of sensor nets in ptolemy II. In: Proc. 3rd International Symposium on Information Processing in Sensor Networks, Berkeley, CA, USA, pp. 359–368 (2004)
13. Völgyesi, P., Lédeczi, Á.: Component-based development of networked embedded applications. In: Proc. 28th Euromicro Conference, Dortmund, Germany, pp. 68–73 (2002)
14. Dietterle, D., Ryman, J., Dombrowski, K., Kraemer, R.: Mapping of high-level sdl models to efficient implementations for tinyos. In: Proc. Euromicro Symposium on Digital System Design, Rennes, France, pp. 402–406 (2004)
15. Simon, G., Völgyesi, P., Maróti, M., Lédeczi, Á.: Simulation-based optimization of communication protocols for large-scale wireless sensor networks. In: Proc. 2003 IEEE Aerospace Conference. vol. 3., Big Sky, MT, USA pp. 1339–1346 (2003)
16. Bakshi, A., Prasanna, V.K.: Algorithm design and synthesis for wireless sensor networks. In: Proc, International Conference on Parallel Processing, Montreal, Quebec, Canada pp. 423–430 (2004)
17. Shen, C.C., Badr, C., Kordari, K., Bhattacharyya, S.S., Blankenship, G.L., Goldsman, N.: A rapid prototyping methodology for application-specific sensor networks. In: Proc. IEEE International Workshop on Computer Architecture for Machine Perception and Sensing, Montreal, Quebec, Canada (2006)

# System Architecture Modeling of an UWB Receiver for Wireless Sensor Network

Aubin Lecointre, Daniela Dragomirescu, and Robert Plana

LAAS-CNRS
University of Toulouse
7, Av du Colonel Roche
31077 Toulouse cedex 4, France
{alecoint, daniela, plana}@laas.fr

**Abstract.** This paper presents a method for system architecture modeling of an IR-UWB (Impulse Radio Ultra WideBand) receiver for sensors networks applications. We expose the way for designing an FPGA (Field Programmable Gate Array) receiver starting from a previous study based on system modeling on Matlab. The proposed receiver architecture is first designed and validated on Matlab, before being implemented, thanks to VHDL language, on a FPGA. Our study shows the interest and the advantages of co-design Matlab-VHDL. We will propose here different IR-UWB receiver architecture depending on the modulation used. We will also introduce in this paper a data-rate and TH-code reconfigurable receiver. Using co-simulation Matlab-VHDL, we have compared three kind of IR-UWB receiver: TH-PPM, TH-OOK, TH-BPAM, with respect to BER/SNR criteria and in the specific context of wireless sensors networks, at high level (Matlab) and hardware level (FPGA-Xilinx).

## 1 Introduction

We lead our study in the context of wireless sensors networks (WSN). We define WSN as systems having a very large number of nodes on a small area. WSN is a WPAN-like concept (Wireless Personal Area Networks). There are a lot of kinds of applications for this variety of networks; such as: monitoring, military applications, house automation, civil safety applications, etc ... By considering these applications, we could deduce easily that there are some intrinsic constraints for WSN, which are: low cost, low power, simplicity and tiny nodes. Indeed, without theses characteristics none networks could be a viable WSN. Thus all along this paper we keep in mind this context in order to design and compare in an appropriate way the UWB receivers.

The Federal Communications Commission (FCC) defines a radio system to be an UWB system if the -10 dB bandwidth of the signal is at least 500 MHz or the fractional bandwidth is greater than 20% [1].

IR-UWB is a very promising technology for the WSN applications. Let us quote these advantages: 7,5 GHz of free spectrum which could permit to reach high data rate, extremely low transmission energy, extremely difficult to intercept, multi-path immunity, low cost (mostly digital architecture), "Moore's Law Radio" (performances, size, data rate, cost follow Moore's Law), simple CMOS transmitter at

S. Vassiliadis et al. (Eds.): SAMOS 2007, LNCS 4599, pp. 408–420, 2007.

very low power [2]. Among the various families within UWB, we focus on family IR-UWB, Impulse Radio UWB which is appropriate for our context of application: wireless sensor network. The principal modulation techniques we will use are: Time Hopping – Pulse Position Modulation (TH-PPM), Time Hopping – On Off Keying (TH-OOK), and Time Hopping – Binary Pulse Amplitude Modulation (TH-BPAM).

We will study these three major IR-UWB techniques: TH-PPM, TH-OOK, and TH-BPAM [1]. For each of them we will propose one or more schemes of receivers. We will present theirs design and co-simulation using Matlab and ModelSim. Our goal is to develop and validate, at first, the receiver architecture at a high level using MATLAB. Then, we would reach the low-level of hardware simulation and implementation, i.e. the FPGA development.

Finally, we would compare theses different systems, including data rate and TH-code reconfigurable receiver, according to the BER (Bit Error Rate) versus SNR (Signal Noise Ratio) criteria and with respect to the WSN constraints.

This paper is organized as follows: Section II presents the principle of TH-OOK, TH-PPM, and TH-BPAM, as well as theirs high level modeling on Matlab. Section III describes the design and the implementation of the UWB receiver on the FPGA. We will compare TH-PPM, TH-OOK, TH-BPAM architectures and performances in section IV, before conclusion in the section V.

## 2   High Level Modeling of UWB Transceivers

### 2.1   Principle of Pulse Modulation for Time Hopping IR-UWB

TH looks like a dynamic TDMA [3]. TH consists of the sharing of the medium in the frame. Each frame is divided in time slots. TH allows making multi user communications. The repartition of information depends of the time hopping code which is associated with each user. Once slots are defined, we could apply the pulse modulation either PPM or OOK or BPAM.

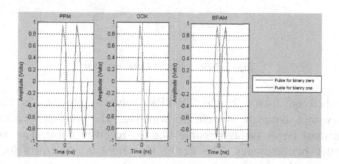

**Fig. 1.** IR-UWB Modulation: PPM, OOK, BPAM

For the PPM, bits are differed by a time shift in each time slot selected by the TH code. Concerning the OOK, we send a pulse in the slot for transmitting a binary one. The binary zero will correspond to an absence of impulsion. For the BPAM, the binary one and the binary zero differ by the phase of the pulse. Thus, the binary zero is represented by the binary one pulse multiplied by minus one (-1 ⇔ 180°) (Fig. 1).

## 2.2 High Level Modeling on Matlab for TH IR-UWB Emitters

The implementation of these three TH systems on Matlab is based on a high-level modeling. We have developed a complete link, from emitter to receiver including channel model. Our Matlab model is parametric, so we can select the kind of IR-UWB we want to study among TH-PPM, TH-OOK, and TH-BPAM. This choice will impact both end (emitter and receiver) of the IR-UWB link.

Thanks to the time domain approach of IR-UWB, emitters are very simple. Indeed, it is enough to implement an UWB pulse generator which is commanded by a binary signal where binary one and binary zero have a specific meaning according to the IR-UWB modulation considered. They impose, for example, the amplitude, or the position of modulated pulse.

At the output of these receivers, the IR-UWB signal is sent over a channel. This latter could be an AWGN (Additive White Gaussian Noise) channel or the IEEE 802.15.4a UWB channel [4], [5]. Receivers follow the channel. There are different receivers in function of the IR-UWB technique employed.

## 2.3 High Level Modeling on Matlab for TH IR-UWB Receivers

For TH-OOK, we propose a non-coherent receiver described in figure 2 [6]. This non coherent architecture is composed of four blocks: a filter on the considered band, a square bloc, an integrator bloc, and a decision bloc. Its principle is energy detection. The received signal is squared before being integrate. Consequently there is no need of synchronization mechanism; this confers the simplicity advantage at this architecture [6]. That's why this receiver is less expensive, simpler, less greedy in power consumption, and it has smaller overall dimensions than the TH-PPM receiver.

**Fig. 2.** Non coherent OOK receiver

As described on figure 3, the TH-PPM coherent receiver is based on the correlation, with a template waveform, principle. The receiver generates a pulse whose form must be as far as possible like the received pulse. This should allow reaching better performances. The nearer the template waveform looks like the received pulse, the better the performances are. Once the template is generated, the correlation between the template and the received pulse is carried out. The concept is to compare the received pulse with the expected pulse corresponding to a "one" or a "zero". The higher the resemblance with a "one" template is, the probability that the received pulse is a one logic, is more important. At the output of the two correlation blocs (one and zero logic), it is enough to place a comparator with two inputs to distinguish, according to the amplitude, one logic from zero logic.

A synchronization bloc is also necessary, in order to provide a synchronous correlation between the received pulse and the template waveform. This function is carried out by a matched filter defined on a known (emitter and receiver side) sequence of pulse [7]. This sequence has a good autocorrelation property. This filter generates a peak in the presence of a synchronization trailer at its input. Thus, we detect the peak, thanks to a comparator, and we have the time arrival of the pulse. As the result we are able to synchronize the receiver. This synchronization is difficult, because of the pulse duration (< 1 ns) and should be the most precise possible, otherwise the correlation output will be always at zero, and so the received bit will be also always at zero.

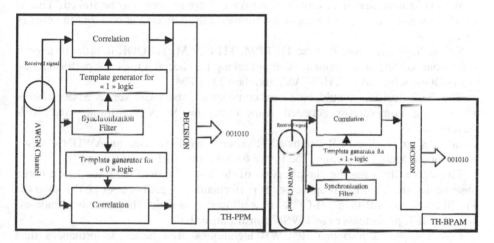

**Fig. 3.** TH-PPM coherent receiver and TH-BPAM coherent receiver

Figure 3 and 4 illustrate the TH-BPAM receiver. Its concept is very similar to the TH-PPM receiver. Indeed, the correlation principle is employed in order to determine the state of received data. As correlation is used, synchronization mechanism is also required.

For TH-BPAM receiver, we propose to use only one correlation with template, instead of two correlation proposed in TH-PPM receiver [1]. Since the BPAM pulse representing the binary one is the inverse of the pulse for the binary zero, if we use only one correlation block, we will have at its output, either a positive squared impulse or a negative squared impulse. This simplifies the decision, because at the output of the correlation block binary one and binary zero could be distinguished by the polarity of the signal.

Compare to TH-PPM and TH-OOK architecture, this one seems to be an intermediate solution. Indeed, thanks to the use of only one correlation block, a simpler decision, this receiver is simpler, cheaper, smaller and have a lower energy consummation than TH-PPM receiver. Nevertheless, the TH-OOK receiver remains the reference concerning the principal WSN constraints (cf. table 1). We will decide, in the next part, between these receivers, according the BER versus SNR criteria.

## 2.4 Comparative Analysis

Table 1 summarizes the behavior of each IR-UWB proposition in the WSN context.

**Table 1.** Comparative analysis of IR-UWB architectures

| Classification | WSN Constraints | | | | |
|---|---|---|---|---|---|
| IR-UWB for WSN | Power | Cost | Simplicity | Size | BER vs SNR |
| TH-PPM | 3 | 3 | 2 | 3 | 1 |
| TH-BPAM | 2 | 2 | 2 | 2 | 2 |
| TH-OOK | 1 | 1 | 1 | 1 | 3 |

We could note that size, cost, and power constraint seems to be linked. This is logic, since the increase in components number will increase the cost and the energy needs.

So, we have three possibilities: TH-PPM, TH-BPAM, TH-OOK in order to answer WSN context. The most adequate, without taking into account the BER performances, is TH-OOK, followed by TH-BPAM, and then TH-PPM.

The final decision should be taken considering, the BER versus SNR criteria. There is a compromise between respect of the WSN constraints and BER performances.

In order to use the BER versus SNR criteria, we have used an AWGN channel model in our Matlab modeling. The figure 6 shows this BER comparison [8].

This curve illustrates the classification of the last column of the table 1. We could observe that the TH-PPM propose better performances, a gain of about 6 dB, than the TH-BPAM and 8 dB than TH-OOK. This allows us to notice that there is a trade-off between BER performances and WSN constraints criteria.

Figure 4 proves also that IR-UWB techniques offer better performances than continuous wave (CW) modulation (FSK, PSK QAM). Indeed, figure 6 permits us to quantify the gain when we use IR-UWB systems instead of CW techniques; its value is about 40 dB.

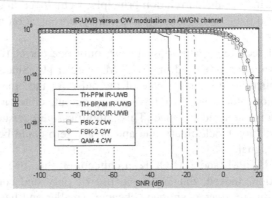

**Fig. 4.** IR-UWB versus continuous wave, according to BER/SNR criteria, on AWGN channel

In order to conclude, we can say that our high level modeling with Matlab shows:

- on one hand that IR-UWB is very interesting in the WSN context, because of its adaptability to the four WSN constraints and its better BER performance than classical CW techniques.
- on the other, our Matlab modeling validates the different architectures in terms of viability for WSN.

As a result, after this essential phase, we could begin the FPGA implementation and simulation, i.e. the hardware-level study.

## 3  FPGA Design of an UWB Receiver

### 3.1  The Low-Level Modeling Context

For implementing an IR-UWB receiver we have decided to use Xilinx Spartan III FPGA, because it is a cheaper and a optimized signal processing solution. We have chosen Xilinx software solution for designing and simulating our receiver. Nevertheless, since we won't set up the emitter on the FPGA, we will use Matlab in order to emulate the comportment of the channel and of the emitter. Moreover we use also the platform to simulate the MAC (Medium Access Control) layer, that is to say the layer which is responsible for piloting the receiver at the PHY (PHYsical) level. Before exposing our low level developing platform, note that we don't consider the RF stage at hardware level. The RF stage, as well as the channel, will be simulated by MATLAB. Thus, as we can see on the figure 7, each element is designed in baseband, behind the ADC for the receiver.

Figure 5 shows the collaboration work between the computer and the FPGA. The computer allow us to develop and program the FPGA, then it is used for emitter plus channel emulation, and finally, it permit to estimate the BER, thanks to received data which come from the FPGA.

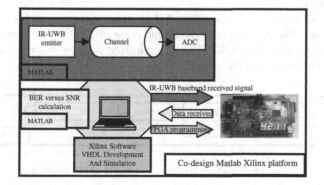

**Fig. 5.** Co-simulation and co-performances analysis Matlab Xilinx Platform

## 3.2 FPGA Implementation with VHDL

VHDL (Very-high-speed integrated circuit Hardware Description Language) is the design programming language we use for digital circuits. We designed our three receivers (TH-OOK, TH-PPM, TH-BPAM) in VHDL according to a modular concept. We designed each of the elementary blocs in charge of elementary receiver function such as multiplication, TH-discrimination, TH code management, decision...

Using this kind of modular design, we can propose easily different versions of each kind of receiver. For each IR-UWB receiver, i.e. TH-PPM, TH-OOK, TH-BPAM, we have created different solutions in order to answer to the four WSN constraints at different levels. For example, one version could be greedier in energy consumption but in return it should have, for example, better BER performance or an additional function. As the opposite, we could imagine some light versions, which could have as goals to offer correct BER performance but especially optimize the four other constraints: power, size, cost, simplicity. Thus we have distinct receiver versions more or less complex, more or less performing, more or less greedy in energy, etc ...

Our panel of receivers is configurable according to four main parameters:

- number of bits used for representing IR-UWB signal,
- number of TH logic channel implemented,
- the presence or not of the localization module,
- the fact that receiver properties are static, or reconfigurable.

Note that we will discuss in the next section (§ 3.3) on the concept of static and reconfigurable properties.

### 3.2.1 TH-OOK Receivers

We have seen in the section II that TH-OOK is the low power, low cost, smallest, and simplest solution among TH-PPM and TH-BPAM. Thus, it seems to be logic to propose an optimized TH-OOK receiver. That's why we have implement on our FPGA a simple solution, whose characteristic are: mono channel reception, absence of localization mechanism, static properties, and 64 bits processing. Let us call this version TH-OOK-v1.

TH-OOK-v2 consists of practically TH-OOK-v1 except that this second version work on 32 bits. Figure 6 exposes the architecture of TH-OOK-v1 and TH-OOK-v2. We can consider that TH-OOK-v2 is an optimized receiver for ultra low cost, ultra low power, ultra small and ultra simple WSN applications.

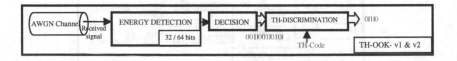

**Fig. 6.** FPGA implementation of TH-OOK receiver

Let us benefit from this illustration (figure 6) to explain the concept of TH-discrimination. Previously, we have introduced the TH concept, by recalling that the channel was divided in frame and time slot. One TH-code is allotted per user or per communication. TH-code defines which time slot will be used by the user or the associated communication. As a result, TH-discrimination consists in extracting the information corresponding to the considerate TH-code among the multi TH-code signal. So, we need a TH-code for the discrimination.

Thanks to this TH-discrimination notion, we could apprehend the mono channel or double channel receiver. Some WSN need an information data channel and a control data channel, or also, multi-user channel. Thus WSN receivers must be able to deal with several "channels". This implies they must be able to extract several TH-channels from a multi-channel flow; so TH discrimination bloc should have as many TH-code entries as there are channels to receive.

### 3.2.2 TH-BPAM Receivers
TH-BPAM receiver versions, TH-BPAM-v1 and TH-BPAM-v2, are represented on figure 7. These two versions allow us to analyze the importance of the blocs' position.

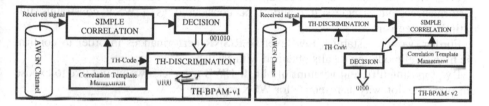

Fig. 7. FPGA implementation of TH-BPAM-v1 and TH-BPAM-v2 receiver

Indeed, we have changed the position of the TH-discrimination bloc in the second version in comparison with the first one. Note that we could easily invert the blocs' positions, thanks to the modularity conception principle. These TH-BPAM receivers, based on the simple correlation concept, are mono channel, static, and work with 32 bits. They don't implement distance estimation and localization.

### 3.2.3 TH-PPM Receivers
We have implemented the distance estimation in one of the TH-PPM FPGA receiver versions. Theirs architectures follow the figure 5, i.e. the Matlab TH-PPM double correlation coherent receiver. We will use four versions:

– TH-PPM-v1: mono channel, static properties, 32 bits, without distance estimation.
– TH-PPM-v2: mono channel, static properties, 32 bits, with distance estimation.
– TH-PPM-v3: mono channel, reconfigurable, 64 bits, without distance estimation.
– TH-PPM-v4: double channel, reconfigurable, 64 bits, without distance estimation.

We have chosen these four versions in order to be able to examine the impact of: size of sample, reconfigurability, distance estimation, and multi channel aspect, on the IR-UWB receiver according to the WSN constraints.

Fig. 8 presents the TH-PPM-v2 receiver architecture with localization mechanism.

Some WSN applications want to be able to geo-localize each node reciprocally to optimize the network routing. To estimate the position of the emitter, the receiver

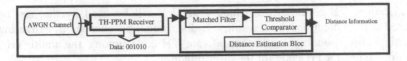

**Fig. 8.** FPGA implementation of TH-PPM-v2 receiver with distance estimation mechanism

must be able to evaluate the time of arrival of the received pulse. Using this information, the receiver could determine the distance separating the emitter from the receiver, since the celerity of the pulse over the air is known. For obtaining this arrival time, we use at the entrance of the receiver, a matched filter (figure 10). Its output is maximal when we are at the time arrival of the pulse [9]. Thus we have just to add a threshold comparator to detect this maximum, for determining the arrival time and consequently the distance.

As the opposite of TH-OOK-v2 receiver, we can say that TH-PPM-v4 is a suitable receiver for the most of WSN applications while offering good BER/SNR performances. Nevertheless it couldn't be considered as a WSN constraints full optimized receiver.

Further, we will establish low level BER/SNR performances in order to confirm the high level modeling results obtained with Matlab.

By proposing different versions of our IR-UWB receivers, we would like to expose our two reflexion way as response for WSN problematic:

– either we create an optimized radio interface for each main category of WSN;
– or we will direct ourselves toward a kind of absolute solution, whose the goal would be to adapt to any WSN applications needs.

This second way is the most innovative way, and it proposes the implementation of reconfigurablity concept inspired from software-defined radio [10].

### 3.3 Data Rate and Time Hopping Code Reconfigurable Receiver

In this part, we will present the reconfigurable aspect of our system. We consider two type of properties receiver reconfigurability

– Static properties: absence of reconfigurability. Receiver characteristics values, such as the TH-frame duration, number of time slots per TH-frame, TH-code, TH-time slot duration, etc … are registered in hard in the VHDL code. Thus for adapting our reception system, we modify the code, and re-download it in the FPGA.
– Reconfigurable properties: it is the most accomplished of our receiver according to the radio reconfigurability concept. Receiver characteristics values are modifiable without re-program the FPGA. We implement that in TH-PPM-v3 and v4 receivers by means of MAC-layer entries. This kind of reconfigurable receiver has many applications in self-organizing WSN where the data rate can be very variable.

Modifying the Time Hopping properties, (number of slot per frame, frame duration, time slot duration), leads to data rate change. Since the data rate, on the whole Time Hopping link (considering all the possible TH-code), depend on the frame duration (Tf), the time slot duration (Tc), and the number of time slot per frame (Nc).

$$D_{total}(bits/s) = N_c / T_f = Nc / ( N_c \times T_c ) = 1 / T_c .$$    (1)

The TH-PPM-v4, mentioned previously, is a data rate reconfigurable receiver.

During a transmission between two nodes of a WSN, one of them decides to change its data rate; the second is able to modify also its data rate, in order to continue the communication. This possibility of data rate modification is an advantage in the concurrent context of channel access in WSN. We will note that it is upper layer protocol, such as MAC layer and applications layers, which are responsible for selecting the best moment to commute the data rate.

Furthermore, in our reconfigurable receiver, we have also implement TH-code reconfiguration. It consists of being able to change the TH-code reception during the communication and consequently the received channel.

In order to set up this reconfiguration concept, we have implanted the reconfigurable parameters as MAC layer entries (fig. 9). The MAC layer emulated by the computer thanks to Matlab, or Xilinx software, is in charge of:

– sending the configurable parameters to the FPGA
– start the reconfiguration by sending a signal, called "reconfiguration signal".

As MAC layer is an intelligent organ we could make the supposition that it sends the "reconfigurable signal" only after correctly place reconfigurable parameters at entries.

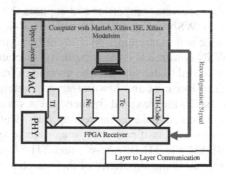

Fig. 9. PHY and MAC Layer interface

Our radio reconfigurability design has some limitations. Indeed, as we use VHDL entity entries for reconfigurability, we undergo theirs limitations. In our example, we choose 8 bits to implement each reconfigurable parameter. It implies that we couldn't reach any kind of data rate in the reconfiguration (without re-programmed the FPGA). Nevertheless, this is true only if we don't take into account the RF limitations (due to RF circuits). In fact, it is this one, which will limit the data rate. Consequently, the VHDL entries limitations sizes (when FPGA is programmed) is not a limit but rather a dimensioning preoccupation. Since, once the FPGA is programmed we would be limited by the defined maximum value of your distinct entries. This dimensioning is important because the number of bits allocated impact the size and consumption of the receiver, which are two important constraints in our WSN context.

In the following part, we will make a comparative analysis of our receivers; we will demonstrate the relation between the number of bits used and the size of the receiver.

## 3.4 FPGA Receiver Performance

In this part, we will compare eight versions of IR-UWB receiver according to the BER versus SNR criteria, and the four WSN constraints: energy consumption, size, cost, and simplicity. Besides, this comparative analysis should highlight the impact of change in VHDL implementation: number of bits for processing, limit size (in bits) for the VHDL variable, presence/absence of distance estimation or radio reconfigurability, and the number of received channel.

**Table 2.** Receivers' Characteristics and receivers' comparison

| Receiver Properties | | | | | | WSN Constraints | | | Performances |
|---|---|---|---|---|---|---|---|---|---|
| VERSION | Receiver Principle | Sample Size | Channel Number | Distance | Radio Reconf | VERSION | Size (in gate) | Max. Frequency | BER/SNR |
| TH-OOK-v1 | Energy Detection | 64 bits | Mono Channel | NO | Static | TH-OOK-v1 | 86 234 + 864 | 89,506 MHz | 8th |
| TH-OOK-v2 | Energy Detection | 32 bits | Mono Channel | NO | Static | TH-OOK-v2 | 68 666 +864 | 111,693 MHz | 7th |
| TH-BPAM-v1 | Simple Correlation | 32 bits | Mono Channel | NO | Static | TH-BPAM-v1 | 68 663 + 864 | 111,693 MHz | 5th |
| TH-BPAM-v2 | Simple Correlation | 32 bits | Mono Channel | NO | Static | TH-BPAM-v2 | 68 716 +864 | 111,693 MHz | 5th |
| TH-PPM-v1 | Double Correlation | 32 bits | Mono Channel | NO | Static | TH-PPM-v1 | 69 674 + 864 | 110,9 MHz | 1st |
| TH-PPM-v2 | Double Correlation | 32 bits | Mono Channel | YES | Static | TH-PPM-v2 | 101 565 + 864 | 66,089 MHz | 1st |
| TH-PPM-v3 | Double Correlation | 64 bits | Mono Channel | NO | Reconfigurable | TH-PPM-v3 | 107 753 + 864 | 72,844 MHz | 3rd |
| TH-PPM-v4 | Double Correlation | 64 bits | Double Channel | NO | Reconfigurable | TH-PPM-v4 | 125 441 + 1056 | 72,844 MHz | 3rd |

Table 2 summarizes the receivers' properties and exposes the architecture receiver comparison according to the WSN constraints and the BER/SNR performances.

In table 2 we expose size and maximum frequency criteria; thanks to them we are able to obtain the four WSN constraints (cost, simplicity, size, energy). Indeed, these four WSN constraints are linked to the size and the maximum frequency of the FPGA circuit. Small circuits mean low cost and low power consumption circuits. The low power property depends also by the maximal frequency. Thus with size and frequency criteria and BER criteria, we could make an interesting classification of receivers.

The "size" column gives us a classification between diverse systems. We will note that TH-OOK-v2, TH-BPAM-v1, TH-BPAM-v2, and TH-PPM-v1 are the smallest receivers. Their common point is the simplicity of theirs architecture and the fact that they use 32 bits for the samples coding. Whereas most of 64 bits architectures TH-PPM-v3 and TH-PPM-v4 are the most cumbersome receiver, in addition with TH-PPM-v2, which implements distance estimation mechanism. In order to conclude, size is function of the complexity (presence of distance estimation, number of channel, double/simple correlation) and the size sample (32/64 bits) of the architecture.

Concerning the maximum frequency criteria, we could notice the classification is approximately the same as for the size criteria. The smaller the architecture is, the faster is. Indeed TH-OOK-v2, TH-BPAM-v1, TH-BPAM-v2, and TH-PPM, which are the smallest architectures, are also the faster receivers (frequency of the clock), while, TH-PPM version 2, 3 and 4, are the bigger and the slower architectures. Thus we could say that use 64 bits sample and set up distance estimation block imply an increase of the receiver size and a decrease of the maximum frequency acceptable.

We point out your attention on the fact that, in Time Hopping IR-UWB architecture, the maximum data rate depends on the maximum frequency. We have demonstrated (1) that data rate is function of the frame duration ($T_f$) and the time slot duration ($T_c$). Consequently, since $T_f$ and $T_c$ are expressed in clock period, data rate depends on the maximum frequency. The higher the max frequency is, the higher the data rate is.

The last column of the table 2, summarizes the BER/SNR performance, by proposing a classification according the BER criteria. We obtained thanks to this low level design and simulation the same BER results that with high level Matlab simulation, i.e. TH-PPM proposed a better BER than TH-BPAM, which is better than TH-OOK.

Now study the impact of the size sample, the number of channel, the distance estimation, the reconfigurable capability, and the block positioning.

TH-BPAM-v1 and TH-BPAM-v2 allow us to analyze the impact of the block position. Indeed, in the TH-BPAM version, only the TH-discrimination block position change. By comparing the capacities of these two architectures, we could note that they are identical, thus blocks position don't impact the receiver properties.

Concerning the size sample, thanks to TH-OOK-v1 and TH-OOK-v2, you could demonstrate that a change in size sample imply a size increase and a clock speed (consequently data rate) decrease.

TH-PPM version 3 and 4, show that the increase of the channel number on the receiver leads to a decrease of the maximum frequency and an increase of the size. We could obtain the same conclusion, thanks to TH-PPM-v1, TH-PPM-v2 and TH-PPM-v3, relevant to the impact of the reconfigurability and distance estimation implementation. Nevertheless, distance estimation impact in a higher way the maximum frequency than the implementation of the reconfigurability or the rise of the number of channel.

In conclusion, the addition of advanced functionality, such as distance estimation, double correlation, multi channel capability leads to size increase and consequently cost and power consumption increase.

This analysis comparative have permitted to deduce some interesting choice in design to optimize the receiver in the WSN context.

# 4 Conclusion

High level and low level modeling, co-design and co-simulation of IR-UWB receiver are presented in this paper. Using Matlab and VHDL software, we could validated, compared, classified distinct receiver architecture in the WSN networks. First, we present TH-PPM, TH-OOK, TH-BPAM IR-UWB concept. Second, we have compared them with respect to the BER versus SNR criteria and WSN constraints at low and high level each time. In particular, our study proves that TH-PPM offers better BER performance than TH-BPAM and TH-OOK systems.

The paper exposes also the impact of the design architecture choice on the respect of the WSN constraints. We introduced the two design way: optimized radio interface versus reconfigurable radio interface. Among our different receiver architecture propositions, we have developed data rate reconfigurable, TH-code reconfigurable and distance estimation capabilities receiver. Each receiver is implemented on FPGA.

The co-design Matlab - VHDL software carried out here, allowed us to propose an software-defined radio PHYsical layer. We have developed here a platform for simulation and modeling (before FPGA implantation) at two levels: system level (our IR-UWB Matlab Model) and PHYsical level. We have shared the work between Matlab and VHDL simulator in order to design and emulate the distinct layers (application layer, MAC layer and PHY layer). This platform allows the system co-design, co-simulation and co-performances analysis.

# References

1. Opperman, I., et al.: UWB theory and applications. Wiley, Chichester (2004)
2. Morche, D., et al.: Vue d'ensemble des architecture RF pour l'UWB, LETI, UWB Summer School, Valence, France à l'ESISAR (October 2006)
3. Win, M.Z., et al.: Impulse radio: how it works. IEEE Communications Letters (1998)
4. Saleh, A., Valenzuela, R.: A statistical model for indoor multipath propagation. IEEE Journal on selected areas in communications (1987)
5. Molisch, A., et al.: IEEE 802.15.4a channel model – final report, IEEE 802.15.4a.
6. Aubert, L.M.: Ph.D. dissertation: Mise en place d'une couche physique pour les futurs systèmes de radiocommunications hauts débits UWB, INSA Rennes, France (2005)
7. Di Benedetto, M.G.: (UWB)$^2$: Uncoordinated, Wireless, Baseborn Medium Access for UWB Communication Networks. Mobile Networks and Applications 10 (2005
8. Lecointre, A.: IR-UWB Receiver Architectures Performances on AWGN Channel for Sensor Network Applications, Master dissertation, University of Toulouse (September 2006)
9. Gezici, S., et al.: Localization via UWB radios. IEEE Signal Processing (2005)
10. Mitola III, J.: Software radio architecture. Wiley, Chichester (2000)

# An Embedded Platform with Duty-Cycled Radio and Processing Subsystems for Wireless Sensor Networks

Zhong-Yi Jin[1], Curt Schurgers[2], and Rajesh Gupta[3]

[1] UCSD Dept. of Computer Science & Eng
zhjin@cs.ucsd.edu
[2] UCSD Dept. of Electrical & Computer Eng
curts@ece.ucsd.edu
[3] UCSD Dept. of Computer Science & Eng
rgupta@cs.ucsd.edu

**Abstract.** Wireless sensor nodes are increasingly being tasked with computation and communication intensive functions while still subject to constraints related to energy availability. On these embedded platforms, once all low power design techniques have been explored, duty-cycling the various subsystems remains the primary option to meet the energy and power constraints. This requires the ability to provide spurts of high MIPS and high bandwidth connections. However, due to the large overheads associated with duty-cycling the computation and communication subsystems, existing high performance sensor platforms are not efficient in supporting such an option. In this paper, we present the design and optimizations taken in a wireless gateway node (WGN) that bridges data from wireless sensor networks to Wi-Fi networks in an on-demand basis. We discuss our strategies to reduce duty-cycling related costs by partitioning the system and by reducing the amount of time required to activate or deactivate the high-powered components. We compare the design choices and performance parameters with those made in the Intel *Stargate* platform to show the effectiveness of duty-cycling on our platform. We have built a working prototype, and the experimental results with two different power management schemes show significant reductions in latency and average power consumption compared to the *Stargate*.

## 1 Introduction

A wireless sensor network (WSN) consists of a collection of wireless sensor nodes which are small embedded devices with on-board sensors and wireless radios. Without wires, sensor nodes either rely on limited energy supply from batteries or harvested energy from intermittent sources like solar or wind. To ensure long lifetimes demanded by the application and deployment scenarios, the sensor nodes have to be very energy efficient. Popular sensor nodes such as the Berkeley Mote [1] address this issue using low power hardware as well as aggressive power management techniques. However, their design choices also make these nodes useful only to applications requiring limited processing power, short communication range and low network bandwidth.

A common WSN architectural solution to these constraints is to deploy within the sensor network a small number of high performance nodes equipped with high powered components like fast processors or high bandwidth radios. As high performance

S. Vassiliadis et al. (Eds.): SAMOS 2007, LNCS 4599, pp. 421–430, 2007.

sensor nodes are usually placed in the same environment as regular sensor nodes, they also rely on limited energy sources. Therefore, energy-efficiency is critical for the high performance nodes to last as long as the rest of the sensor nodes.

There are two observations that we can explore to improve the energy-efficiency of high performance nodes. Firstly, as a general fact, using components with high peak power consumption doesn't necessarily imply high energy consumption. Studies have shown that when a sufficient amount of data need to be processed or transmitted, high performance processors or radios that consume more power than their sensor node counterparts may complete the same amount of work faster and therefore end up using less energy [2,3]. Secondly, in the specific case of sensor networks, those high powered components are not required to be active all the time as sensor networks usually do not generate large amounts of data until certain triggering events are detected. In other words, the node or its components needs to be active only a fraction of the time to achieve application goals. Therefore, duty-cycling based power management techniques such as selectively enabling or disabling components are important in reducing energy consumption for high performance nodes.

A platform needs to meet two requirements to support efficient duty-cycling. One is that it needs to consume very little (or no) power when there are no ongoing activities. While general purpose high performance nodes such as the *Stargate* [4] provide a good balance of performance and power consumption, they are not designed to support efficient power management via duty-cycling. For example, the lowest power consumption of a *Stargate* is 16.2mW in its inactive suspended state [5]. In contrast, a typical sensor node such as the Telos Mote uses only about 10$\mu$W in a similar state [6]. This high standby power consumption significantly limits the effectiveness of duty cycling, making the *Stargate* less energy efficient for very low duty cycle sensor network applications such as environmental monitoring. The other requirement is that a platform needs to be able to activate or deactivate various subsystems with very little overheads according to runtime demands. Existing high performance nodes built around 32-bit embedded processors and embedded versions of traditional desktop Operating Systems (OS), both old [4] and new [7,3], generally take a long time to transit in and out of the suspend or power off states, bringing significant energy and performance overheads to duty-cycling [5,7,3].

In this paper, we describe the design, implementation and evaluation of a wireless gateway node (WGN) that enables efficient power management through duty-cycling. Gateway nodes are often intrinsic parts of sensor networks and are required to bridge data between sensor networks and servers/devices in other networks. Without gateway nodes, data collected by a sensor network are only local to that sensor network and therefore no remote monitoring or interactions can be achieved. The low and bursty traffic load of sensor networks makes the WGN an ideal application of our low power design.

Specifically, we focus on using Wi-Fi (802.11b) radios to interface sensor nodes with devices in other networks because Wi-Fi radios offer higher bandwidth and consume less energy per bit than most existing sensor node radios [8], making them a useful air interface for many sensor network applications. Although our focus is on the gateway nodes, the basic design and techniques can also be applied to any other high performance nodes or used in the context of wakeup radios [9] or any other multiple radio hierarchies [10] to reduce switching overheads with respect to energy and latencies.

## 2 Related Work

To energy efficient design, the importance of separating real-time monitoring functions that have to be optimized for low power from functions invoked with light duty-cycles is first unveiled in the development of the WINS nodes [11]. The WINS node enables continuous sensing over an extend period of time by partitioning the system into a low powered event-detection subsystem and a high powered processing subsystem which can be enabled or disabled on demand.

Our work is directly comparable to the emerging Micro-servers that are being explored to solve a large body of sensor network research problems [12,7]. Triage [7] extends the lifetimes of their Micro-servers by trading latency for power reduction. Its tiered architecture consists of a slightly modified *Stargate* computer and a MicaZ mote, which is used to power on the *Stargate* only when sufficient amount of data are being batched for processing. Due to the large latency in powering on/off the *Stargate*, their platform is not usable for our gateway application in terms of delay and power consumption. The LEAP platform [3] faces similar issues as stated in their future work section. The PASTA platform [13] also uses an Intel PXA255 processor. Since their demonstrated mode of operation is to keep the processor module in sleep state (7.3mW) during periods of inactivity to save power, no experiments and latency numbers are reported for activating this module from power-off state.

## 3 Design Approach

Fig. 1 shows a high-level block diagram of our design. To minimize standby energy consumption, we exploit the low power operation of a sensor node processor and use it for subsystem scheduling and power management. A second, more powerful application processor is used to provide on demand processing capabilities to subcomponents such as the Wi-Fi radio, which are physically connected to the application processor. Power to each individual subcomponent is either controlled directly by the sensor node processor or indirectly by the application processor through the sensor node processor.

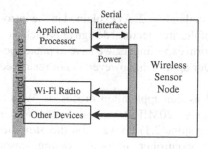

**Fig. 1.** WGN Block Diagram

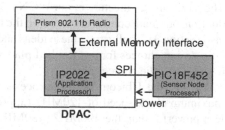

**Fig. 2.** WGN Architecture

We use a serial interface for inter-processor communication because it is supported in various forms by most of the existing sensor node processors.

Unlike the PASTA platform [13] where multiple microcontrollers are used to regulate power to the modules, we have the sensor node processor acting as the "master" device for power management. Our approach simplifies the design while also taking advantage of the fact that the sensor node processor is almost always on for sensing or networking purposes. This enhances the efficiency of running the power management itself. Besides supporting the low-power sleep mode as described in the PASTA paper, we also want to be able put the application processor in and out of power-off mode without introducing significant energy and latency overheads.

In contrast to the low-power sleep mode where a certain amount of power is still consumed by the application processor running in power saving modes, a processor uses no power at all while in power-off mode. However, it generally takes less time to resume a program from low-power mode when the program is either suspended or running at a slower speed than to reload the entire program by powering the application processor back on from power-off mode. While it is clear that having minimal standby power consumption would extend the operation time, some real time applications also have time constraints, as they need to complete certain tasks within a fixed amount of time. Instead of making the power and latency trade off at design time, the sensor node processor needs to be able to put the application processor into either low-power mode or power-off mode at runtime based on application requirements.

To reduce the energy and latency overheads in activating the application processor from power-off mode, we found it is critical to minimize both hardware and software startup time. On the hardware side, commercial microcontrollers for embedded devices are usually designed to support fast startup. On the software side, it is important to minimize the amount of the code that needs to be loaded and executed every time during boot up. This include both OS and application specific code.

For our specific WGN application, we use the power saving mode of the 802.11b protocol [14] to lower the latencies in switching the Wi-Fi radio in and out of low-power mode. We develop techniques to take advantage of certain features of the power saving mode of the 802.11b protocol [14] to further reduce communication and synchronization overheads in terms of energy and latency.

## 4   Platform Implementation

The hardware architecture of our WGN is illustrated in Fig. 2. As explained in the introduction, our main contributions are on the level of the architectural design approach (see also section 3). To illustrate these ideas and perform experiments, we have to make specific design choices for our test bed platform. Our approach, however, is not restricted to these specific choices alone.

We use the Ubicom IP2022 processor [15] as our application processor. With a maximum clock speed of 120MHz (approximately 120MIPS), this 8-bit processor is less powerful than the 400MHz (480MIPS, Dhrystone 2.1) PXA255 on the *Stargate*. However, it is significantly faster than the microcontrollers on most existing sensor nodes and provides sufficient processing capability to our gateway application. With its integrated flash memory and RAM, this processor doesn't need complex external hardware support and thus doesn't incur extra energy and latency overheads. We also find the IP2022 a convenient choice as it is used in the DPAC module [16] with a Wi-Fi radio.

Because of a clear separation of the master (sensor node processor) and the rest of the system on our platform, we can select any existing sensor nodes such as the Berkeley Mote [1] for our power management purposes. Our design only requires that the sensor node processor and the application processor can communicate and wake each other up as necessary. This is easier to implement than those that require external logics or chipset supports as in PC platforms. Commonly used serial interfaces such as the UART, I2C or SPI are sufficient to meet these requirements. We select the SPI as it supports duplex data transfers at a rate of more than 11Mbps, sufficient to sustain the throughput of the Wi-Fi radios.

For evaluation purposes, we use for power management a home grown sensor node equipped with a PIC18F452 microcontroller that consumes about 8mW (3.3V) in full power mode (10MIPS). The hardware SPI on the PIC is still available. The power to the DPAC module is managed by the PIC through a MOSFET switch. Alternatively, we can use an I2C power switch to control additional components. We use Ubicom IPOS, a lightweight OS for the IP2022. The IPOS provides the very basic OS functions and gets compiled with the target application. Our entire gateway application is about 60 Kbytes in uncompressed form.

# 5   Power Management Schemes

We experiment with two different power management schemes for our gateway application to evaluate the platform as well as to understand the power versus latency tradeoffs. We refer to these two schemes broadly as *power-gating* and *power-saving* modes. In the former, the emphasis is on subsystem shutdown for both communication and processing, while the latter seeks to exploit various slowdown modes. In the following subsections, we describe the design choices behind the two schemes.

## 5.1   Power-Gating Scheme

Our *power-gating* scheme saves power by putting the system into *power-gating* mode according to online demands. While in the *power-gating* mode, the Wi-Fi radio and the application processor are powered off and no packets can be sent or received. A successful use of the *power-gating* scheme requires participating gateway nodes and devices in other networks to coordinate their active periods while minimizing the total amount of energy required for such synchronizations [17]. We measure the overheads of such protocols when used with our WGN. The overheads are quantified either as time in seconds or energy in Joules calculated by integrating power over time.

## 5.2   Power-Saving Scheme

Our *power-saving* scheme reduces power consumption by putting the radio in the 802.11b power saving mode [14] while keeping the application processor in various low power modes. Since most Wi-Fi radios natively support the 802.11b power saving mode, it is significantly faster to put the radio in and out of the power saving mode than to suspend and resume the entire radio in each duty cycle. Although the speedup is hardware dependent, it is reported in one case that it is almost 86 times faster to resume from power saving mode than from suspended mode [10].

One challenge in supporting such a scheme is to synchronize power saving states across the processors, the radio and the access point. In the 802.11b power saving mode, a radio wakes up periodically to check for any incoming packets buffered at the AP (Access Point) and the sleep duration is determined by the listen interval. A listen interval is established during the association process and is fixed until new association attempts are made. Since the re-association process involves multiple packet exchanges between the station and the AP, it is expensive to change the listen interval frequently. However, a fixed listen interval is not ideal for most sensor network applications as events occur randomly. Long listen intervals introduce large communication delays while short listen intervals waste energy if there are no events or data to send or receive. Thus, the choice of the listen interval is a matter of design tradeoff between energy savings and latency incurred. Instead of listening at a fixed interval, we use an event-driven approach to transition in and out of the power saving mode as explained in its implementation below.

Our strategy is based on the 802.11b standard [14] that after a station exits power saving mode, the AP should send all buffered packets to that station as if they just arrived. Therefore, if the listen interval is set to an arbitrary large value (up to $2^{16}$ beacon intervals), one can eliminate its effects and dynamically control the packet receiving time by forcing the station out of the 802.11b power saving mode. Although a successful packet exchange is required between the station and the AP to enable or disable the 802.11b power saving mode, this can by done by simply changing the power management bit in the frame control field of any outgoing packets. A potential benefit of this strategy is that with some buffering, sending and receiving can be performed within the same active periods and therefore reduces the total amount of time the radio and the application processor need to be awake. We experiment with this approach on our WGN by sending and receiving 1024 bytes of data in an UDP packet every 6 seconds for a period of 30 minutes and observe no packet loss. We also verify this technique on a Linux laptop with a Netgear WG511 Wireless PC card (V1.0) and latest hostAP driver (V0.5.1) and observe similar results. Note that to avoid overrunning the buffer of the AP, a small packet should be sent to instruct the receiving device running our scheme to wakeup more frequently before transmitting a large amount of data.

### 5.3 Measurements

Power consumption is measured as the product of voltage and current. Our WGN is directly powered by a DC power supply of 3.3V. To measure current, a resistor of 1Ohm is connected in series with the DC power supply. The voltage drop across the resistor is sampled using a National Instrument DAQPad-6020E (12Bit, 100KS/S) and stored in Lab-View spreadsheet format. For simplicity, sensor data are randomly generated by the PIC processor rather than from real sensors or other sensor nodes.

**Table 1.** Latencies and Power consumption

|  | Stargate | | Our WGN | | |
|---|---|---|---|---|---|
|  | Suspend Wi-Fi scheme | Suspend system scheme | Always on scheme | Power gating scheme | Power saving scheme |
| Enable Latency | 0.485s | 3.329s | - | 0.28s | 0.03s |
| Enable Power | 0.751w | 0.155w | - | 0.545w | 0.693w |
| Active Power | 2.009w | 2.009w | 1.419w | 1.419w | 1.419w |
| Disable Latency | 0.313s | 0.757s | - | 0s | 0.003s |
| Disable Power | 1.62w | 1.11w | - | 1.419w | 1.32w |
| Sleep Power | 0.751w | 0.054w | - | 5.13mw | 0.495w |

# 6   Experimental Results and Analysis

Average system power consumption is calculated[1] based on the amount of energy consumed in one working-period, which is defined as the period from the beginning of one active period to the beginning of the next active period. A power managed working-period can be further divided into four sub-periods: a period to enable the system, a period of doing the real work, a period to disable the system and a sleep period. A duty-cycle is calculated as the percentage of the time that a system does real work over an entire working-period. It does not include time spent in enabling or disabling the system. Note that we can maintain a fixed duty cycle by proportionally changing the working time and the duration of the working-period.

Table 1 lists the durations of these periods as well as the corresponding power consumptions in these periods for both the *Stargate* and our system running different power management schemes. We choose to compare our platform with the *Stargate* because it is one of a few gateway nodes commonly used in sensor networks. Other gateway nodes, such as those based on the Soekris board [18], share similar architecture as the *Stargate*.

For our WGN, the enable-power of the *power-gating* scheme is less than that of the *power-saving* scheme because not all components are powered up at the same time. The high sleep-power of our *power-saving* scheme is caused by the limitations of the Intersil chip as reported in [19]. The *Stargate* has very high sleep-power because its PXA255 processor is in charge of power management and can not be powered off completely.

In the remainder of this section, we compare the performance of our power management schemes using the WGN with the performance of the following two commonly used schemes on the *Stargate*:

1. Suspend-Wi-Fi Scheme: Suspend the Wi-Fi radio only.
2. Suspend-System Scheme: Suspend both the Wi-Fi radio and the *Stargate* computer.

The *Stargate* data are based on measurements from [5]. We combine the latencies that are reported separately for the Wi-Fi radio and the PXA255 and compute the average power consumption. Similar to our approach, the authors in [5] measure data

---

[1] $Average\ System\ Power = \dfrac{Total\ energy\ consumed\ in\ one\ working-period}{Duration\ of\ the\ working-period}$

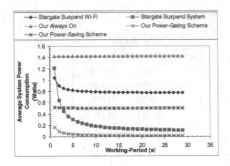 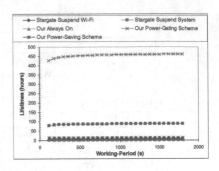

**Fig. 3.** Average system power consumption under various working-periods and at a fixed 1% duty cycle

**Fig. 4.** Lifetimes under various working-periods and at a fixed 1% duty cycle (2200 mAh at 3 volts)

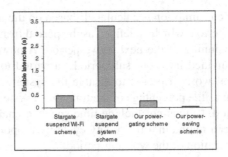

**Fig. 5.** System response time

without sensors attached. Accordingly, we use the "Processor Core Idle" data for the Suspend-Wi-Fi scheme and the "Proc./Radio Core Sleep" data for the Suspend-System scheme. The active power consumption in the active period is based on 50% TX and 50% RX. For our own schemes, the power consumed by the entire WGN is reported. The load on the 1Ohm resistor is included to simulate a real sensor. Our always-on scheme simply keeps the system in maximum power all the time and is used to serve as a baseline. The sleep-power of our *power-gating* scheme is the same as the sleep-power of the attached sensor node.

Fig. 3 shows the average system power consumption of the five schemes running under various working-periods and at a fixed 1% duty cycle, which is very common for sensor networks. With a fixed duty cycle, the time spent doing real work increases in proportion to the duration of the working-period, and therefore the average amount of real work per unit time remains constant. Large duty-cycle latencies mean less sleep time. The WGN running our *power-gating* scheme performs about 6 times better than the *Stargate* running the suspend-system scheme for large working-periods where the active power dominates. For short working-periods where the transition (enable/disable) power becomes dominant, we perform up to 7 times better. This is partially due to the small transition latencies that result from applying the 802.11b based power saving techniques described in section 5.2.

Fig. 4 shows the lifetimes of our WGN and the *Stargate* running the five schemes under various working-periods and at a fixed 1% duty cycle. They are computed based on a power supply of 2200 mAh at 3 volts from a pair of AA batteries. The WGN could last longer with smaller duty cycles because of the extremely low sleep-power.

Although it is possible with some hardware modifications to eliminate the sleep power of the *Stargate* processor by powering it off and to reduce the active-power of the *Stargate* processor by dynamic voltage scaling (DVS) [7,3], our WGN would still perform better because of lower duty-cycle latencies. This is a direct result of the new architecture we propose.

While it seems that the enable/disable latencies are not important in terms of average system power consumption for applications that are dominated either by active or sleep power, they are critical in determining the responsiveness of a system. A large latency in activating a subsystem from low-power or power-off mode would be prohibitive for many sensor network applications to employ duty-cycling, not to mention the energy overhead associated with the delay. Smaller latencies also provide additional space for applications to trade latencies for energy savings. Fig. 5 shows the system response time under different power management schemes. When running power-gating scheme, our WGN is about 12 times better than the *Stargate* running the suspend-system scheme. The WGN running the power-saving scheme is about 16 times better than the *Stargate* running the suspend-Wi-Fi scheme.

## 7   Conclusions and Future Work

In this paper, we present the design and optimizations of a low power wireless gateway node. By introducing a dual-processor hardware architecture and a choice of appropriate duty-cycling of the processing and radio subsystems, we successfully reduce the standby power consumption while also providing support for spurts of high MIPS and high bandwidth connections. We are also able to improve the performance of duty-cycling with respect to energy and latencies by reducing software and networking protocol related overheads and through careful system integration. The result is a platform that supports efficient power management through duty-cycling. We believe our architecture can be useful for building other types of high performance nodes or the emerging Micro-servers.

In our ongoing work, we are exploring ways to optimize the performance of our WGN in sensor networks running various low power MAC protocols or wakeup protocols. We are also planning to replace our PIC based sensor nodes with Telos motes [6] in these experiments for compatibility with existing sensor network applications and for evaluation purposes.

## References

1. Polastre, J., Hill, J., Culler, D.: Versatile low power media access for wireless sensor networks. In: SenSys '04. Proceedings of the 2nd international conference on Embedded networked sensor systems, pp. 95–107. ACM Press, New York, NY, USA (2004)

2. Jejurikar, R., Gupta, R.: Dynamic voltage scaling for systemwide energy minimization in real-time embedded systems. In: ISLPED '04. Proceedings of the 2004 international symposium on Low power electronics and design, pp. 78–81. ACM Press, New York, NY, USA (2004)
3. McIntire, D., Ho, K., Yip, B., Singh, A., Wu, W., Kaiser, W.J.: The low power energy aware processing (leap)embedded networked sensor system. In: the Fifth International Conference on Information Processing in Sensor Networks, Nashville, Tennessee, pp. 449–457. ACM Press, New York 1127846 (2006)
4. Stargate: http://www.xbow.com
5. Margi, C.B., Petkov, V., Obraczka, K., Manduchi, R.: Characterizing energy consumption in a visual sensor network testbed. In: 2nd International IEEE/Create-Net Conference on Testbeds and Research Infrastructures for the Development of Networks and Communities (2006)
6. Polastre, J., Szewczyk, R., Culler, D.: Telos: Enabling ultra-low power wireless research. In: The Fourth International Conference on Information Processing in Sensor Networks (2005)
7. Banerjee, N., Sorber, J., Corner, M.D., Rollins, S., Ganesan, D.: Triage: A power-aware software architecture for tiered microservers. Technical Report 05-22, University of Massachusetts-Amherst (April 2005)
8. Raghunathan, V., Pering, T., Want, R., Nguyen, A., Jensen, P.: Experience with a low power wireless mobile computing platform. In: The 2004 international symposium on Low power electronics and design, Newport Beach, California, pp. 363–368. ACM Press, New York 1013322 (2004)
9. Gu, L., Stankovic, J.: Radio-triggered wake-up capability for sensor networks. In: RTAS 2004. Real-Time and Embedded Technology and Applications Symposium, May 25-28, 2004, pp. 27–36. IEEE Computer Society Press, Los Alamitos (2004)
10. Agarwal, Y., Schurgers, C., Gupta, R.: Dynamic power management using on demand paging for networked embedded systems. In: Asia South Pacific Design Automation Conference (ASP-DAC'05), China, pp. 755–759 (2005)
11. Pottie, G.J., Kaiser, W.J.: Wireless integrated network sensors. Commun. ACM 43(5), 51–58, 332838 (2000)
12. Rahimi, M., Baer, R., Iroezi, O.I., Garcia, J.C., Warrior, J., Estrin, D., Srivastava, M.: Cyclops: in situ image sensing and interpretation in wireless sensor networks. In: SenSys '05. Proceedings of the 3rd international conference on Embedded networked sensor systems, pp. 192–204. ACM Press, New York, NY, USA (2005)
13. Schott, B., Bajura, M., Czarnaski, J., Flidr, J., Tho, T., Wang, L.: A modular power-aware microsensor with >1000x dynamic power range. In: IPSN '05. Proceedings of the 4th international symposium on Information processing in sensor networks, Piscataway, NJ, USA, p. 66. IEEE Press, New York (2005)
14. 802.11b Spec. 1999 edition: http://grouper.ieee.org/groups/802/11
15. Ubicom IP2022: http://www.ubicom.com
16. DPAC www.dpac.com
17. Ye, W., Heidemann, J., Estrin, D.: An energy-efficient mac protocol for wireless sensor networks. In: Infocom '02, New York, NY, pp. 1567–1576 (2002)
18. Hartung, C., Han, R., Seielstad, C., Holbrook, S.: Firewxnet: a multi-tiered portable wireless system for monitoring weather conditions in wildland fire environments. In: MobiSys 2006. Proceedings of the 4th international conference on Mobile systems, applications and services, pp. 28–41. ACM Press, New York, NY, USA (2006)
19. Pering, T., Raghunathan, V., Want, R.: Exploiting radio hierarchies for power-efficient wireless device discovery and connection setup. In: VLSID '05. Proceedings of the 18th International Conference on VLSI Design held jointly with 4th International Conference on Embedded Systems Design, Washington, DC, pp. 774–779. IEEE Computer Society, Los Alamitos (2005)

# SensorOS: A New Operating System for Time Critical WSN Applications

Mauri Kuorilehto[1], Timo Alho [2], Marko Hännikäinen[1], and Timo D. Hämäläinen[1]

[1] Tampere University of Technology, Institute of Digital and Computer Systems
P.O. Box 553, FI-33101 Tampere, Finland
{mauri.kuorilehto, marko.hannikainen, timo.d.hamalainen}@tut.fi
[2] Nokia Technology Platforms, Tampere, Finland
timo.a.alho@nokia.com

**Abstract.** This paper presents design and implementation of a multi-threading Operating System (OS), SensorOS, for resource constrained Wireless Sensor Network (WSN) nodes. Compared to event-handler kernels, such as TinyOS, SensorOS enables coexistence of multiple time critical application tasks. SensorOS supports preemptive priority-based scheduling, very fine-granularity timing, and message passing inter-process communication. SensorOS has been implemented for resource constrained Tampere University of Technology WSN (TUTWSN) nodes. In TUTWSN node platform with 2 MIPS PIC micro-controller unit, SensorOS kernel uses 6964 B code and 115 B data memory. The context swap time is 92 $\mu$s and the variance of timing accuracy for a high priority thread less than 5 $\mu$s. The results show that the realtime coordination of WSN applications and protocols can be managed by a versatile OS even on resource constrained nodes.

## 1 Introduction

Wireless Sensor Networks (WSN) consists of a large number of randomly deployed nodes that self-organize and operate autonomously. A WSN node is characterized by restricted resources in terms of memory, energy, and processing capacity, and by unreliable wireless link with limited bandwidth. While advances in manufacturing technologies have resulted in smaller and cheaper platforms suitable for WSN realizations, the resource constraints persist as the environments become more demanding. Simultaneously, the complexity and number of tasks of WSN applications increases [1].

The key functionalities for the layered WSN protocol stack are the controlling of channel access, network topology creation and maintenance, and route formation. The protocols together with multiple applications comprise an extremely complex system that must be fitted to resource constrained WSN nodes. Further, due to the tight interaction with the real world, realtime requirements are strict. Therefore, realtime communication and coordination are required in both single node and network level [2]. At a single node level, resource usage, timeliness, and peripheral access are managed by an Operating System (OS) [3]. The network level control in WSNs is handled by middleware architectures that perform task allocation and network control [2,4]

This paper presents the design and implementation of SensorOS, a preemptive multi-threading kernel for resources constrained TUTWSN (Tampere University of Technology WSN) nodes [5]. The time sliced Medium Access Control (MAC) protocol of

S. Vassiliadis et al. (Eds.): SAMOS 2007, LNCS 4599, pp. 431–442, 2007.

TUTWSN requires timing accuracy and efficient use of power saving modes. SensorOS guarantees timing with a priority-based realtime scheduler. The evaluation proves SensorOS suitability for WSNs, and shows the feasibility of the simple POSIX-like Application Programming Interface (API). A network level coordination can be incorporated into SensorOS by a distributing middleware for task allocation [6].

## 1.1  Related Work

Embedded Realtime OSs (RTOS), such as OSE, QNX Neutrino, and VxWorks are widely used in industrial and telecommunication systems. However, their memory consumption even in the smallest configurations is too large for resource constrained WSN nodes. Small memory footprint RTOSs, such as FreeRTOS, have a general purpose approach and do not meet the strict timing and energy saving requirements of WSNs.

The most widely known OS for WSNs is TinyOS [7] that uses a component-based event-driven approach for task scheduling. Each component has a separate command handler for upper layer requests and an event handler for lower layer events. The processing is done in an atomic task. SOS [8] adopts the component model from TinyOS but allows dynamic runtime loading and unloading of components. Similar approach without relation to TinyOS is taken in BerthaOS [9]. Event handler kernel of Contiki [10] supports dynamic loading and can be complemented with a library for preemptive multi-threading. In CORMOS [11], all system and application modules consist of handlers that communicate seamlessly with local and remote modules using events.

Preemptive multi-threading for sensor nodes with POSIX API is implemented in MOS [12] and nano-RK [13]. Both support priority-based scheduling and have integrated networking stack and power management features.

Due to run to completion semantics, event handler OSs, such as TinyOS, are poorly suitable for applications with lengthy computation, e.g. cryptographical algorithms. Further, compared to traditional preemptive kernels, their programming paradigm can be difficult to understand. The drawback of preemptive schedulers is the increased data memory consumption as a separate stack is needed for each thread. While Contiki partially solves this, it faces the problems of event-driven OS if multi-threading is not used.

The approach in SensorOS is similar to MOS and nano-RK. Features that put SensorOS apart from these two are very accurate time modeling and energy efficiency. The energy efficiency results from the sophisticated use of advanced power saving modes.

## 1.2  Contents of the Paper

The architecture and design of SensorOS are discussed in Section 2. Section 3 presents TUTWSN platform and environment. The implementation of SensorOS on target platform is presented in Section 4 and evaluation results in Section 5. Finally, conclusions are given in Section 6.

## 2  SensorOS Design

SensorOS design objective is a realtime kernel that supports features required by WSN protocols and applications. WSN protocol and application tasks are executed as separate threads communicating with SensorOS Inter-Process Communication (IPC) methods. The composition of threads implementing protocols and applications is not restricted.

In this paper, a *task* is a functional entity, whereas a *thread* is the OS context, in which a task is executed. A task can be divided into multiple threads, but on the other hand several tasks can be executed within a single thread.

## 2.1  Design Requirements

A WSN protocol stack consists of several functional entities that require cross layer interaction for controlling network operation. Typically, the energy efficiency of a WSN results from the accuracy of MAC protocol timing. Accurate timing allows longer sleep periods since the wake-up can be done just before the active period. In addition, a tight relation to the real world requires reactiveness from applications. As a result, the programming of complex protocols and applications, and the managing of their communication and synchronization are extremely challenging and tedious without OS control.

The requirements for SensorOS derive from the characteristics of WSNs. The main functional requirements are seamless coexistence of multiple tasks, realtime capability, and timing accuracy. Due to limited WSN node capabilities, efficient usage of resources is essential. Portability is required to deal with heterogeneous WSN node platforms. Memory management is needed to allow as many tasks as possible to be located in a node and power management to maximize the lifetime of battery-powered nodes.

More abstract requirements for SensorOS relate to the ease of use and the integration of a distributing middleware. A simple API facilitates application development. The middleware integration is alleviated by using a message passing IPC that can be easily abstracted to network packets.

## 2.2  SensorOS Architecture

The architecture of SensorOS is divided into components as depicted in Fig. 1. Tasks access OS services through API. The main components in the kernel are *scheduler*, *message passing IPC*, *timer*, *synchronization*, *memory* and *power management*. Interrupt-driven device drivers (UART and Analog-to-Digital Converter (ADC) in Fig. 1) are integrated into the kernel, whereas context-related drivers ($I^2C$, radio) are executed in the context of a calling thread without a relation to the OS kernel. In general, devices accessed by a single thread are context-related, while shared devices are included in the kernel. Hardware resources are accessed through a Hardware Abstraction Layer (HAL).

Each thread in SensorOS has a Thread Control Block (TCB) for per threadL information. A thread can be in three different states. When a thread is executed on MCU it is *running*. The state of a thread is *ready* when it is ready for execution but another thread is running, and *wait* when it needs an event to occur before execution.

A thread can be waiting for multiple different type of events in SensorOS. The relation between a running thread, a ready queue, and different wait queues are depicted in Fig. 2. When a thread is created it is put to the ready queue, and it can explicitly exit when running. Threads waiting for a timeout are in timer queues and those waiting for IPC in message set. Synchronization is waited in per mutex queues and a completion of peripheral operation in a peripheral specific item.

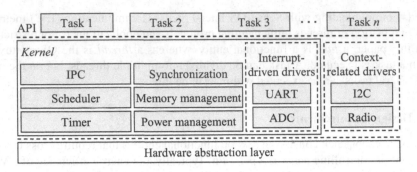

**Fig. 1.** Overview of SensorOS architecture

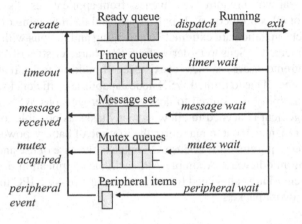

**Fig. 2.** Thread queues and events moving a thread from a queue to another

### 2.3 SensorOS Components

SensorOS components maintain TCBs of threads accessing their services. The inter-relations between components are kept in minimum, but clearly scheduler is dependent on other components.

*Scheduler* – SensorOS incorporates a priority-based preemptive scheduling algorithm. Thus, the highest priority thread ready for execution is always running. Threads at the same priority level are scheduled by a round robin algorithm without a support for time-slicing.

When an event changes a thread to the ready state, the scheduler checks whether it should be dispatched. If it has a higher priority than the running thread, contexts are switched. When the running thread enters to a wait state, the highest priority thread from the ready queue is dispatched. If the ready queue is empty, power saving is activated.

*Timer* – Timer component implements timeout functionality. The local time in SensorOS is microseconds since system reset. Timing is divided into two separate approaches that have their own timer queues. A fine granularity timing provides microsecond accuracy for applications and communication protocols that need exact timestamps. The coarse timing is for tasks that tolerate timeout variations in order of millisecond.

*IPC* – The method for communication between tasks in SensorOS is message-passing IPC. A thread allocates a message envelope and fills it, after which it is sent to the recipient. The message must always be assigned to a certain thread. Broadcast messages can be implemented using multiple unicast messages.

*Synchronization* – Synchronization controls the flow of execution between tasks and access to peripheral devices and other hardware resources. The synchronization is implemented with binary mutexes. A mutex can be waited by several threads, of which the highest priority thread acquires it when released. Each mutex has its own wait queue. Avoiding of priority inversion is not considered but it is left to programmers [3].

*Memory Management* – In SensorOS, dynamic memory management is incorporated for message envelopes and for temporary buffers occasionally needed by tasks. A thread allocates and frees previously reserved blocks from a memory pool.

*Power Management* – Since the activity of WSN nodes is in order of few per cents, power management is crucial. In SensorOS, the power management of peripherals is implemented in the device drivers. The power saving activation of context-related devices is left to the task that controls the device, because the task is aware of the device activation patterns. Instead, the power modes of MCU and integrated peripherals are managed by OS. When there are no threads to schedule, MCU is set to platform dependent power saving mode, of which it is woken up by an external event.

*Peripherals* – The interrupt-driven device drivers integrate peripherals, such as ADC and UART, tightly to SensorOS kernel. They have separate functions for open, close, control, read, and write operations. The read and write operations are controlled by interrupts. A thread can block its execution on such peripheral until the specified number of bytes has been transferred. The context-related device drivers are either non-blocking or can use an external interrupt source for controlling read and write operations.

## 3  TUTWSN Platforms and Protocols

SensorOS is primarily targeted to TUTWSN node platforms and protocols. TUTWSN is an energy efficient WSN framework targeted mainly for monitoring applications. TUTWSN incorporates several different types of node platforms, a configurable protocol stack, and user interfaces for network monitoring and application visualization.

### 3.1  TUTWSN Node Platform

Several different types of node platforms are used in TUTWSN. An outdoor temperature sensing node platform illustrated in Fig. 3 is built from off-the-shelf components. The main component is PIC18LF4620 MCU, which contains a 10-bit integrated ADC and 1 KB of EEPROM as a non-volatile data storage. The power unit consists of a MAX1725 regulator with 2.4 V output voltage and a 3 V CR123A lithium battery. In addition, a DS620 digital thermometer is integrated to the platform. The radio interface

**Fig. 3.** TUTWSN PIC node platform

**Table 1.** TUTWSN PIC node power consumption in different states

| MCU | Radio | Power (mW) |
|---|---|---|
| active | receive | 60.39 |
| active | transmit (0 dBm) | 39.90 |
| active | transmit (-20 dBm) | 26.73 |
| active | active | 3.68 |
| active | off | 3.29 |
| idle | off | 1.27 |
| sleep | off | 0.031 |

on the platform is a 2.4 GHz nRF2401A transceiver unit that supports 1 Mbit/s data rate and transmit power between -20...0 dBm.

MCU has a 64 KB Flash as code memory, each instruction word taking two bytes. Internal SRAM data memory is limited to 3986 B. With internal oscillator the MCU frequency can be either 4 MHz or 8 MHz resulting in 1 MIPS and 2 MIPS, respectively. For power saving, PIC supports idle and sleep modes. The measured power consumptions of TUTWSN node platform in PIC MCU power modes with 4 MHz frequency and different radio activation states are depicted in Table 1. The power consumptions of other, application dependent, peripherals are typically in order of hundreds of $\mu$Ws. The radio power consumption on receive and transmit is dominant.

### 3.2 TUTWSN Protocols

The main protocols in TUTWSN stack are Time Division Multiple Access (TDMA) MAC and gradient-based routing. The MAC protocol creates a clustered network topology and controls wireless channel access. The coordination between clusters is done on a dedicated signaling channel, while each cluster operates on its own frequency channel. The routing protocol creates routes from cluster *headnodes* to a *sink* based on the cost gradient of the route.

The cluster headnode maintains its access cycle by periodic beacons. Neighbor headnodes and *subnodes* associate to the cluster for data communication. The objective of TDMA MAC is to minimize power-hungry radio idle listening, which requires accurate time synchronization among nodes.

## 4    SensorOS Implementation

SensorOS is implemented on TUTWSN PIC nodes. The implementation follows the architecture presented in Section 2. Common functionality is implemented separately, whereas hardware dependent parts are included in HAL in order to facilitate portability. The common functionalities and most of HAL are implemented in ANSI C. Only a small portion of the lowest level HAL, e.g. context switch, is implemented in assembly.

### 4.1   Implementation of Hardware Abstraction Layer

Lowest level context switching, power saving, timer, and peripheral access are detached from SensorOS kernel to the HAL implementation. Internal registers that need to be saved at context switch are MCU dependent. Also power saving modes need low level register access. Each peripheral has a HAL component that implements interface to dedicated I/O ports and interrupt handlers.

Each MCU has an own set of hardware timers and their control registers. HAL timer implementation consists of time concept, interrupt handlers, and time management routines. SensorOS utilizes two different time concepts implemented by HAL; a microsecond resolution timer for accurate timing and a millisecond resolution timer for timeouts. The interrupt handlers update internal time and when a time limit expires indicate this to the OS timer through a callback function. The time management routines are for getting and manipulating internal time, setting of timeout triggers, and atomic spinwait for meeting an exact timeline.

### 4.2   Implementation of SensorOS Components

SensorOS API consists of system calls listed in Table 2. Peripheral system calls are for character devices (e.g. UART) while context-related devices have dedicated interfaces. SensorOS is initialized in *main* -function, which issues *user_main* -function after OS components have been initialized. In user_main, threads for application tasks and required mutexes are initialized. After the user_main returns, scheduling is started.

*Scheduler* – A thread is created with **os_thread_create** that takes the stack and Process IDentifier (PID) as parameters. This simplifies the implementation but prevents runtime creation and deletion of threads. The modification of the kernel for such a support is straightforward. When a thread is created it is inserted to the ready queue but the scheduler is not invoked until the running thread releases processor.

Instead of a completely modular approach, the scheduling decisions are distributed to kernel components. This complicates the changing of scheduling algorithm but improves context switching performance. When an event moves thread(s) to the ready queue, the OS component checks whether one of the threads has a higher priority than the running one. If true, an OS service for swapping threads' contexts is invoked. The context of a thread is stored in its stack. A running thread can release processor with **os_yield** or it can permanently exit. When there are no threads to schedule, an *idle thread* is scheduled for activating MCU sleep mode through HAL.

Event waiting in SensorOS is implemented by a single interface that allows a thread to wait simultaneously for multiple events. The events include timeout, message received, character device read and write, peripheral device, and user generated events. Function **os_poll_event** loops actively while **os_wait_event** blocks the thread until any of the events occur. When an event for a thread is raised, the scheduler checks whether the thread waits for the event and if it does performs scheduling.

***Timer*** – Timer operation is mainly implemented in HAL but API and scheduling on timeouts are provided by the OS component. The system time is obtained with the function **os_get_time**. Accurate timestamps for events are set with **os_get_entryperiod**, which returns the internal time at the moment of the function call. Both utilize microsecond resolution timer.

The accurate microsecond resolution wait is implemented by **os_wait_until**. The thread is blocked until a threshold before the deadline. The atomic spinwait in HAL is used to suspend the operation until the timestamp. In the current implementation, only one thread can issue **os_wait_until** at a time to guarantee accurate timing.

**Table 2.** SensorOS system call interface, categorized by components

| Thread and scheduler management system calls |
|---|
| void **os_thread_create**( os_proc_t *p, os_pid_t pid, os_priority_t pri, char *stack, size_t stackSize, prog_counter_t entry ) |
| void **os_yield**( void ) |
| os_eventmask_t **os_wait_event**( os_eventmask_t events ) |
| os_eventmask_t **os_poll_event**( os_eventmask_t events ) |

| Timer system calls |
|---|
| uint32_t **os_get_time**( void ) |
| os_uperiod_t **os_get_entryperiod**( void ) |
| int8_t **os_wait_until**( os_uperiod_t event ) |
| void **os_set_alarm**( uint16_t timeout ) |

| IPC system calls |
|---|
| os_status_t **os_msg_send**( os_pid_t receiver, os_ipc_msg_t *msg ) |
| os_ipc_msg_t* **os_msg_recv**( void ) |
| int8_t **os_msg_check**( void ) |

| Synchronization system calls |
|---|
| void **os_mutex_init**( os_mutex_t *m ) |
| void **os_mutex_acquire**( os_mutex_t *m ) |
| void **os_mutex_release**( os_mutex_t *m ) |

| Memory management system calls |
|---|
| void* **os_mem_alloc**( size_t nbytes ) |
| void **os_mem_free**( void *ptr ) |

| Character device system calls |
|---|
| os_status_t **os_open**( os_cdev_t dev ) |
| void **os_close**( os_cdev_t dev ) |
| int8_t **os_write**( os_cdev_t dev, const char *buf, uint8_t count ) |
| int8_t **os_read**( os_cdev_t dev, char *buf, uint8_t count ) |
| void **os_close**( os_cdev_t dev ) |

To initialize a millisecond resolution wait, a thread issues **os_set_alarm**. The thread is put to the timer queue that is sorted according to the timeouts. The first item in the queue is passed to HAL in order to trigger a callback function when the timeout expires. The callback function sets the timer event for the first thread in the queue. A zero timeout period can be used with **os_wait_event** to check a status of other events.

*IPC* – The memory allocation for message envelopes and the contents of messages are left to the application. A message is sent with **os_msg_send** that inserts the message to the recipient's queue and sets the message received event. Each thread has an own message queue in its TCB. A thread can check whether its queue is empty with **os_msg_check**. A message is removed from the queue by calling **os_msg_recv**.

*Synchronization* – When a mutex is created with **os_mutex_init**, its wait queue and owner are cleared. If the mutex is blocked by another thread when **os_mutex_acquire** is issued, the calling thread is inserted to the wait queue of the mutex. Otherwise the caller becomes the owner of the mutex. When the owner calls **os_mutex_release** and the wait queue is not empty, the highest priority thread is moved to the ready queue, or scheduled immediately if its priority is higher than that of the running thread.

*Memory Management* – Currently, there are two alternatives for memory management. A *binary buddy* algorithm allows the allocation of different sized blocks, while a more lightweight alternative uses static sized blocks and is mainly targeted to message envelopes. Memory is allocated with **os_mem_alloc** and released with **os_mem_free**.

*Peripherals* – The interrupt-driven character device drivers are opened and closed by **os_open** and **os_close**, respectively. The device handle contains the owner, type, and event information and defines the HAL routines and data pipe for communication between HAL and OS. Data to the device is sent with **os_write** and received with **os_read**. Both return the number of bytes handled. The completion of a pending operation can be waited either by **os_flush** or **os_wait_event**.

# 5 Evaluation

The objectives of SensorOS evaluation are the verification of correct functionality and the measuring of OS resource consumption and performance. A test application, which consisting of three tasks and emulates WSN protocol stack and an application, is implemented for evaluation. *Task1* models TDMA-based WSN MAC protocol, *task2* a routing protocol, and *task3* an WSN application with periodic sensing and processing.

The highest priority thread (*task1*) is activated periodically with a hard deadline. It executes for a short period and sends a message to the next highest priority thread (*task2*) on every tenth activation. *Task2* waits for message and processes it when received. Then it sends a message to the lowest priority thread (*task3*). *Task3* is activated periodically and if it has a message it performs lengthy processing.

## 5.1 Resource Usage

The portable implementation in ANSI C results slightly more inefficient use of resources than an assembly optimized one. The code and static data memory consumption of each OS component are depicted in Table 3. Help routines include implementations for internal OS lists and a small set of library functions.

The code memory usage of SensorOS with static block memory management is 6964 B and with binary buddy 7724 B, which are 10.6 % and 11.8 % of the available memory, respectively. These do not include an optional I/O library that implements *printf* type routines. Static data memory used by SensorOS is 115 B or 118 B, depending on the used memory management. These do not include thread stacks and TCBs. A thread context takes 36 B on average but in interrupts additional 35 B is stored. Since the context is kept in the thread's stack, a typical stack size is 128 B. The size of TCB is 17 B. Thus, over 20 threads can be active simultaneously in TUTWSN PIC platform.

## 5.2 Context Switch Performance

The performance of SensorOS is evaluated by measuring the context switch overhead and the executions times of main kernel operations. These are given in Table 4 with timing accuracy results. MCU is run at 8 MHz and loaded by five threads that have averagely 2 ms activation interval. The results are gathered over 50000 iterations.

Context swap time includes the storing of an old and restoring of a new thread to MCU. The initialization of **os_wait_until** sets a trigger to HAL. The thread is woken up 2 ms before the deadline and after a scheduling delay the rest of the time is spent in spinwait. The time in **os_set_alarm** is consumed in timer queue handling and a trigger setting. The **os_wait_event** time is the delay from a timer interrupt to the scheduling of the thread. The IPC delay is measured from the sending of a message from a lower priority thread to its processing in a higher priority one.

The **os_wait_until** is evaluated by measured the absolute error between the resulted timing and the real world time. The maximum inaccuracy is below 5 $\mu$s and typically the error is less than 2 $\mu$s. The variance is caused by thread atomicity consideration when returning from the spinwait, thus it is affected by MCU clock frequency.

**Table 3.** Code and data memory usage of different SensorOS components

| OS component | Code memory (B) | Data memory (B) |
| --- | --- | --- |
| Scheduler | 728 | 38 |
| Thread | 184 | 0 |
| Event handling | 384 | 1 |
| Timer | 646 | 6 |
| IPC | 248 | 0 |
| Mutex | 428 | 0 |
| Binary buddy memory management | 1048 | 5 |
| Static block memory management | 288 | 2 |
| Character device | 414 | 0 |
| HAL | 2266 | 68 |
| Help routines | 1378 | 0 |
| I/O library | 862 | 16 |

**Table 4.** SensorOS kernel operation times and timing accuracy

| Operation | Time ($\mu s$) | | |
|---|---|---|---|
| | Min | Mean | Max |
| HAL context swap | 92 | 92 | 92 |
| **os_wait_until** timeout initialization | 125 | 125 | 125 |
| **os_wait_until** spinwait time after thread wakeup [1] | 680 | 1110 | 1310 |
| **os_set_alarm** timeout initialization [1] | 222 | 270 | 324 |
| **os_wait_event** context switch from timer interrupt [1] | 486 | 532 | 558 |
| IPC from lower priority thread to higher one | 346 | 346 | 346 |
| **os_wait_until** timing absolute error | 0.0 | 1.8 | 4.2 |

1) The results may vary slightly depending on the number of threads.

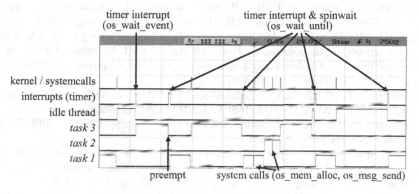

**Fig. 4.** Task and kernel activation in SensorOS

## 5.3   Test Application Operation

The scheduling of tasks and kernel components in the test application is depicted in Fig. 4. MCU preemption on periodic scheduling of *task1* is clearly visible. Kernel is activated when system calls are done for timer wait, messaging, and memory allocation. The idle thread is scheduled to activate power saving when other tasks are inactive.

The lengths of timer interrupt periods show the difference between **os_wait_until** and **os_wait_event** triggered by **os_set_alarm**. As the latter can return immediately after the timeout interrupt, the delay is considerably shorter than in **os_wait_until**.

## 6   Conclusions and Future Work

This paper presents a full functionality OS for resource constrained WSN nodes. Compared to existing WSN OSs, SensorOS implements more accurate time concept and sophisticated power management routines, which are needed by energy efficient and time critical WSN protocols and applications. The portability and conventional API facilitate the implementation of large WSN scenarios with multiple applications. The evaluation shows that SensorOS obtains excellent performance with minimal resources.

Our future work concentrates on implementation and integration of the distributing middleware to OS. Further, we are exploring methods for lightweight dynamic linking of new application threads transferred over wireless link.

# References

1. Akyildiz, I.F., Su, W., Sankarasubramaniam, Y., Cayirci, E.: A survey on sensor networks. IEEE Communications Magazine 40(8), 102–114 (2002)
2. Stankovic, J.A., Abdelzaher, T.F., Lu, C., et al.: Real-time communication and coordination in embedded sensor networks. Proceedings of the IEEE **91**(7) (2003) 1002–1022
3. Stallings, W.: Operating systems internals and design principles, 5th edn. Prentice-Hall, Englewood Cliffs (2005)
4. Kuorilehto, M., Hännikäinen, M., Hämäläinen, T.D.: A survey of application distribution in wireless sensor networks. EURASIP Journal on Wireless Communications and Networking (5), 774–788, Special Issue on Ad Hoc Networks: Cross-Layer Issues (2005)
5. Kohvakka, M., Hännikäinen, M., Hämäläinen, T.D.: Ultra low energy wireless temperature sensor network implementation. In: Proc. 16th Annual IEEE International Symposium on Personal Indoor and Mobile Radio Communications, Berlin, Germany, pp. 801–805. IEEE Computer Society Press, Los Alamitos (2005)
6. Kuorilehto, M., Hännikäinen, M., Hämäläinen, T.D.: A middleware for task allocation in wireless sensor networks. In: Proc. 16th Annual IEEE International Symposium on Personal Indoor and Mobile Radio Communications, Berlin, Germany, pp. 821–826. IEEE Computer Society Press, Los Alamitos (2005)
7. Hill, J., Szewczyk, R., Woo, A., et al.: System architecture directions for networked sensors. In: Proc. 9th ACM International Conference on Architectural Support for Programming Languages and Operating Systems, Cambridge, MA, USA, pp. 94–103 (2000)
8. Han, C.C., Kumar, R., Shea, R., et al.: A dynamic operating system for sensor nodes. In: Proc. 3rd International Conference on Mobile Systems, Applications, and Services, Seattle, WA, USA, pp. 163–176 (2005)
9. Lifton, J., Seetharam, D., Broxton, M., Paradiso, J.: Pushpin computing system overview: a platform for distributed, embedded, ubiquitous sensor networks. In: Proc. 1st International Conference on Pervasive Computing, Zurich, Switzerland, pp. 139–151 (2002)
10. Dunkels, A., Grönvall, B., Voigt, T.: Contiki - a lightweight and flexible operating system for tiny networked sensors. In: Proc. 29th Annual IEEE International Conference on Local Computer Networks, Tampa, FL, USA, pp. 455–462. IEEE Computer Society Press, Los Alamitos (2004)
11. Yannakopoulos, J., Bilas, A.: Cormos: a communication-oriented runtime system for sensor networks. In: Proc. 2nd European Workshop on Wireless Sensor Networks, Istanbul, Turkey, pp. 342–353 (2005)
12. Bhatti, S., Carlson, J., Dai, H.: Mantis os: An embedded multithreaded operating system for wireless micro sensor platforms. Mobile Networks and Applications 10(4), 563–579 (2005)
13. Eswaran, A., Rowe, A., Rajkumar, R.: Nano-rk: An energy-aware resource-centric rtos for sensor networks. In: 26th IEEE International Real-Time Systems Symposium, Miami, FL, pp. 256–265. IEEE Computer Society Press, Los Alamitos (2005)

# Review of Hardware Architectures for Advanced Encryption Standard Implementations Considering Wireless Sensor Networks

Panu Hämäläinen[1], Marko Hännikäinen[2], and Timo D. Hämäläinen[2]

[1] Nokia Technology Platforms, WiWLAN SF
Visiokatu 3, FI-33720 Tampere, Finland
panu.hamalainen@nokia.com
[2] Tampere University of Technology, Institute of Digital and Computer Systems
P.O.Box 553, FI-33101 Tampere, Finland
marko.hannikainen@tut.fi, timo.d.hamalainen@tut.fi
http://www.tkt.cs.tut.fi/research/daci

**Abstract.** Wireless Sensor Networks (WSN) are seen as attractive solutions for various monitoring and controlling applications, a large part of which require cryptographic protection. Due to the strict cost and power consumption requirements, their cryptographic implementations should be compact and energy-efficient. In this paper, we survey hardware architectures proposed for Advanced Encryption Standard (AES) implementations in low cost and low-power devices. The survey considers both dedicated hardware and specialized processor designs. According to our review, currently 8-bit dedicated hardware designs seem to be the most feasible solutions for embedded, low-power WSN nodes. Alternatively, compact special functional units can be used for extending the instruction sets of WSN node processors for efficient AES execution.

## 1 Introduction

Cryptographic algorithms are utilized for security services in various environments in which low cost and low power consumption are key requirements. Wireless Sensor Networks (WSN) [1] constructed of embedded, low-cost, and low-power wireless nodes fall into the class of such technologies [2], ZigBee [3] and TUTWSN [4] as examples. Nodes themselves are independent of each other but they collaborate to serve the application tasks of WSNs by sensing, processing, and exchanging data as well as acting according to the data content [1]. WSNs are envisioned as cost-effective and intelligent solutions for various applications in automation, health care, environmental monitoring, safety, and security. A large part of the applications require protection for the data transfer as well as for the WSN nodes themselves [5]. Even though WSNs can contain devices with varying capabilities, in this paper the term *node* refers to an embedded, highly resource-constrained, low-cost, and low-power WSN device.

Compared to software, significantly higher performance and lower power consumption can be achieved with dedicated hardware and specialized processor architectures

S. Vassiliadis et al. (Eds.): SAMOS 2007, LNCS 4599, pp. 443–453, 2007.

tuned for the execution of security procedures in WSN nodes. A software implementation on a general-purpose processor always contains overhead due to instruction fetch and decode, memory access, and possibly due to an unsuitable instruction set and word size. As Advanced Encryption Standard (AES) [6] is a standardized encryption algorithm and considered secure, it has become the default choice in numerous applications, including the standard WSN technologies IEEE 802.15.4 [7] and ZigBee [3].

In this paper, we review and compare hardware architectures that are potentially suitable for AES implementations in WSN nodes. We have selected the architectures from more than 150 examined research papers, including both dedicated hardware as well as specialized cryptographic processor designs. We believe that the paper is comprehensive as well as valuable for designers evaluating and developing AES implementations for embedded, low-cost, and low-power WSN nodes. The survey focuses on academic research papers as publicly available information on commercial implementations is typically very limited. However, we believe that the reviewed designs comprehensively cover the utilized design choices and trade-offs suited for WSN node implementations.

The paper is organized as follows. Section 2 presents an overview of the AES algorithm, discusses high-level architectural alternatives for its hardware implementation, and argues their suitability for WSN nodes. In Section 3, we survey existing low-cost and potentially low-power AES hardware designs. Section 4 reviews specialized processor architectures proposed for efficient AES implementations in low-cost wireless devices. In this paper, a specialized processor architecture refers to a design that includes support for AES but the design can be capable of executing other tasks as well. A dedicated hardware implementation can only be used for executing AES.

## 2  Overview of AES Algorithm

AES [6] is a symmetric cipher that processes data in 128-bit blocks. It supports key sizes of 128, 192, and 256 bits and consists of 10, 12, or 14 iteration rounds, respectively. Each round mixes the data with a *roundkey*, which is generated from the encryption key.

The encryption round operations are presented in Fig. 1. The cipher maintains an internal, 4-by-4 matrix of bytes, called *State*, on which the operations are performed. Initially State is filled with the input data block and XOR-ed with the encryption key. Regular rounds consist of operations called *SubBytes*, *ShiftRows*, *MixColumns*, and *AddRoundKey*. The last round bypasses MixColumns. Decryption requires inverting these operations.

SubBytes is an invertible, nonlinear transformation. It uses 16 identical 256-byte substitution tables (*S-box*) for independently mapping each byte of State into another byte. S-box entries are generated by computing multiplicative inverses in *Galois Field* GF($2^8$) and applying an affine transformation. SubBytes can be implemented either by computing the substitution [8,9,10,11,12] or using table lookups [10,13,14]. ShiftRows is a cyclic left shift of the second, third, and fourth row of State by one, two, and three bytes, respectively. MixColumns performs a modular polynomial multiplication in GF($2^8$) on each column. Instead of computing separately, SubBytes and MixColumns can also be combined into large Look-Up-Tables (LUT), called *T-boxes* [9,15]. During each round,

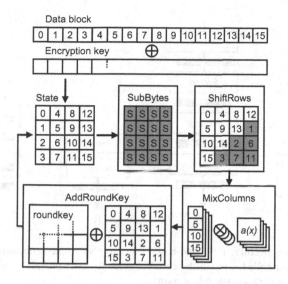

**Fig. 1.** Round operations of AES encryption

AddRoundKey performs XOR with State and the roundkey. Roundkey generation (*key expansion*) includes S-box substitutions, word rotations, and XOR operations performed on the encryption key. For more details on the AES algorithm and its inversion, we refer to [6].

## 2.1  Design Choices for AES Support in Hardware

The basic techniques for implementing a block cipher with rounds, such as AES, are iterated, pipelined, and loop-unrolled architectures [16]. The more advanced structures include partial pipelining and sub-pipelining combined with these basic techniques. The architectures are illustrated in Fig. 2.

The iterated architecture leads to the smallest implementations as it consists of one round component which is fed with its own output until the required number of rounds has been performed. The pipelined architecture contains all the rounds as separate components with registers in between. As a result, it is the fastest (in terms of throughput) and the largest of the basic structures. The loop-unrolled architectures perform two or more rounds per clock cycle and the execution of the cipher is iterated. In a pipelined architecture, unrolling can only decrease the latency of outputting the first block. In sub-pipelining, registers are placed inside the round component in order to increase the maximum clock frequency. In the partial pipelining scheme, the pipeline contains e.g. the half of the rounds with registers in between.

Although pipelined and loop-unrolled architectures enable very high-speed AES implementations, they also imply large area and high power consumption, which makes them unattractive for WSN nodes. Furthermore, they cannot be fully exploited in feed-back modes of operation [9,14]. Feedback modes are often used for security reasons in encryption and for Message Authentication Code (MAC) generation, e.g. as in the

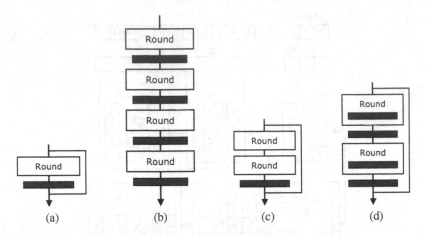

**Fig. 2.** Hardware architectures for round-based block cipher implementations: (a) iterated, (b) pipelined, (c) loop-unrolled, and (d) the combination of partial pipelining and sub-pipelining. The exemplar full cipher consists of four rounds.

security schemes of the standard WSN technologies [7,3]. Iterative architectures enable low-resource implementations with full-speed utilization also in feedback modes. The width of the AES data path can be further reduced to decrease logic area and power [8,9,10,11,12,13,14]. Hence, the review of this paper focuses on AES designs utilizing iterated structures.

In addition to the architectural choices, the design of AES enables a large number of algorithm-specific hardware trade-offs. The trade-offs consist of choosing between memory-based LUTs and combinatorial logic, decreasing the amount of parallelism, transferring the GF computations into another arithmetic domain, choosing between precomputed and on-the-fly key expansion, and sharing resources between encryption, decryption, and key expansion data paths. These aspects and their effects are discussed in the review of the following sections.

## 3   Hardware Implementations of AES

Since the ratification of AES in 2001, a large number of its hardware implementations has appeared. We surveyed more than 100 papers for the review of this section. According to the survey, most AES designs have been targeted at and implemented in Field Programmable Gate Array (FPGA) technologies. Whereas earlier AES designs mainly focused on intensively pipelined, high-speed implementations, the more recent work has concentrated on compactness and lower power consumption. Of all the designs, Table 1 lists the proposals which we have considered to have achieved the most significant results and which are possibly suitable for highly resource-constrained WSN nodes. The table is organized according to the time of publication of the designs, in order to reflect also the evolution in the field. A more comprehensive table, containing the

**Table 1.** Compact hardware implementations of AES

| Design | Tech. | Data width | E/D (1) | Mode (2) | Keys (3) | S-box (4) | Cells (5) | Mem (6) | Lat (7) | Clk [MHz] | Tp [Mbit/s] |
|--------|-------|------------|---------|----------|----------|-----------|-----------|---------|---------|-----------|-------------|
| Ref. [16] | Xilinx | 128 | E | ECB | n/a | logic | 3528 | 0 | 11 | 25 | 294 |
|  | Xilinx | 128 | E | ECB | n/a | logic | 3061 | 0 | 21 | 40 | 492 |
| Ref. [18] | Altera | 16 | E | ECB | n/a | ROM | 1693 | 3 | 80 | n/a | 32 |
|  | Altera | 16 | ED | ECB | n/a | ROM | 3324 | 3 | 80 | n/a | 24 |
| Ref. [19] | Altera | 32 | E | ECB | n/a | ROM | 824 | 10 | 44 | n/a | 115 |
|  | Altera | 32 | ED | ECB | n/a | ROM | 1213 | 10 | 44 | n/a | 115 |
| Ref. [8] | .11 $\mu$m | 32 | ED | ECB | 128 | logic | 5400 | 0 | 54 | 131 | 311 |
|  | .11 $\mu$m | 32 | ED | ECB | 128 | logic | 6300 | 0 | 44 | 138 | 400 |
|  | .11 $\mu$m | 64 | ED | ECB | 128 | logic | 8000 | 0 | 32 | 137 | 549 |
|  | .11 $\mu$m | 128 | ED | ECB | 128 | logic | 12500 | 0 | 11 | 145 | 1691 |
| Ref. [13] | Xilinx | 32 | ED | ECB | 128 | ROM | 222 | 3 | 46 | 60 | 166 |
| Ref. [15] | Xilinx | 32 | ED | ECB | 128 | ROM | 146 | 3 | 46 | 123 | 358 |
| Ref. [10] | .60 $\mu$m | 32 | ED | CBC | all | logic | 8500 | 0 | 92 | 50 | 70 |
|  | Xilinx | mix | ED | CBC | all | ROM | 1125 | 0 | n/a | 161 | 215 |
| Ref. [11] | .35 $\mu$m | 8 | E | ECB | 128 | logic | 3600 | 0 | 1016 | 100 | 13 |
| Ref. [14] | Altera | 32 | E | ECB | 128 | ROM | 512 | 7 | 55 | 116 | 270 |
|  | Altera | 32 | ED | CCM | 128 | ROM | 1434 | 11 | 112 | 78 | 90 |
| Ref. [9] | Xilinx | 8 | ED | ECB | 128 | logic | 124 | 2 | n/a | 67 | 2 |
| Ref. [12] | .35 $\mu$m | 8 | ED | ECB | 128 | logic | 3400 | 0 | 1032 | 80 | 10 |
| Ref. [20] | .13 $\mu$m | 8 | E | ECB | 128 | logic | 3100 | 0 | 160 | 152 | 121 |

(1) Encryption (E) or decryption (D) or both (ED) supported for the mode in (2).
(2) Supported mode of operation by the design.
(3) 'n/a' means no key expansion included, a value refers to the supported keys sizes.
(4) Specifies the technique used for the SybBytes implementation. 'ROM' means memory-based table-lookups and 'logic' combinatorial logic.
(5) Resource consumption of the design. ASICs in gate-equivalents and FPGAs as general-purpose programmable resources: Xilinx *slices* or Altera *Logic Elements* (LE).
(6) Dedicated memory components used from the specific FPGA of the reference.
(7) The number of clock cycles for encrypting a block of data. Latencies caused by precomputed key expansion not included.
'Tp' refers to the encryption throughput in the mode of (2). Latencies caused by precomputed key expansion not included.

highest-speed pipelined implementations as well, can be found in [17]. For the details of Xilinx and Altera FPGA devices, the readers are referred to their specific data sheets.

The references [16,18,19] are included in the table mainly for historical reasons as AES implementations that are better suited for WSNs have appeared later. However, those references were the first most comprehensive implementation studies that proposed compact AES designs as well. Ref. [16] presents a thorough study of AES encryption data path implementations with the different architectural choices described in Section 2.1 but lacks decryption and key expansion logic. The functionalities are also lacking from [18,19]. Nevertheless, [18,19] have been the first to propose *folded* AES designs [13], in which the data path width has been decreased from its native width (128 bits). Later on, folding has successfully been utilized in the most compact and low-power AES implementations discussed below. Direct comparison between [16] and [18,19] is not possible as different FPGA and SubBytes implementation technologies have been used (logic vs. ROM). A Xilinx slice roughly equals to two Altera LEs. As [16] uses the native data width, its latency is lower and throughput higher than in [18,19]. Since [19] utilizes the T-box method, its LE count is lower than that of [18], despite of the wider data path. On the other hand, the method requires larger amount of memory for the LUTs. The folding factor increases the latency as more clock cycles are needed for processing a 128-bit block of data.

A number of iterative Application Specific Integrated Circuit (ASIC) designs with varying data path widths have been reported in [8]. The designs are based on an efficient S-box architecture and include en/decryption for 128-bit keys. Roundkeys are generated on-the-fly, either by sharing S-boxes with the main data path or by dedicating separate S-boxes for key expansion. The smallest version is a 32-bit AES architecture with four shared S-boxes. The results of [8] are still currently relevant: even though the gate counts are not the lowest, according to our knowledge the implementations offer the best area-throughput ratios of existing compact AES implementations.

A 32-bit AES architecture with a precomputed key expansion is developed for FP-GAs in [13]. The design takes advantage of the dedicated memory blocks of FPGAs by implementing S-box as a LUT. The paper proposes a method for arranging the bytes of State so that it can efficiently be stored into memory components or shift registers. The arrangement allows performing ShiftRows with addressing logic. The same method is proposed again in [10]. For decreasing the amount of storage space as well as support-ing various data path widths, we have developed the idea further in [21] without an implementation. In [14], we removed the decryption functionality of [13] and used the core for implementing the security processing of IEEE 802.15.4 [7] and ZigBee [3] in a low-cost FPGA. Ref. [15] improves the FPGA resource consumption of [13] with the T-box method. The design requires equal amount of memory components in the FPGA but uses them more efficiently.

A resource-efficient ASIC design supporting en/decryption is presented in [10]. The on-the-fly roundkey generation shares S-boxes with the main data path. The design is based on a regular architecture that can be scaled for different speed and area require-ments. The smallest ASIC version contains a 32-bit data path. The FPGA design uses varying data widths for different phases of the algorithm. Support for the Cipher Block Chaining (CBC) encryption mode is also included. Compared to the 32-bit implementa-tions of [8], the throughput of the ASIC implementation is lower and area larger. Ref. [10] also uses an older ASIC technology which prevents absolute area comparisons. However, the latencies of [8] are lower, which indicates that its designs are more efficient.

A low-power and compact ASIC core for 128-bit-key AES encryption is reported in [11]. The 8-bit data path is used for the round operations as well as for the on-the-fly key expansion. The data path contains one S-box implemented as combinatorial logic. State and the current roundkey are stored in a $32 \times 8$-bit RAM, which has been imple-mented with registers and multiplexers. The memory is intensively used by cycling each intermediate result through the RAM, increasing the total cycle count of the design. For

MixColumns, the design uses a shift-register-based approach, which is capable of computing the operation in 28 cycles. Decryption functionality is added to the design in [12], which also reports results from a manufactured chip. As stated, an increase in the folding factor increases latency and thus decreases throughput from the designs with wider data paths.

A 8-bit AES processor for FPGAs is designed in [9], capable of 128-bit-key encryption and decryption. The data path consists of an S-box and a GF multiplier/accumulator. The execution is controlled with a program stored in ROM. RAM is used as data memory. The design is fairly inefficient as the cycle count is significantly higher than e.g. in [15] with not much lower FPGA resource consumption.

According to our knowledge, our encryption-only core presented in [20] is the most efficient one of reported 8-bit AES implementations in terms of area-throughput ratio. This is due to the novel data path architecture that is based on the 8-bit permutation structure proposed in [21]. In [9,11,12], the AES round operations as well as the round-key generation operations are performed sequentially. In our design, the operations are performed in parallel (for different 8-bit pieces of data/key), which considerably decreases the total cycle count and increases the throughput. Still, we succeeded in maintaining the hardware area and the power consumption low. The gate area is at the same level with [11,12]. The achieved cycle count of 160 can be seen as the minimum for an iterated 8-bit AES implementation. We have estimated that including the decryption functionality would add about 25% to the total area.

Only [12,20] of the ASIC references include power consumption measures. For [12] the power consumption is 45 $\mu$W/MHz and for the area optimized implementation of [20] 37 $\mu$W/MHz. In [12], the power has been measured from a manufactured chip. However, the higher throughput of [20] potentially results in considerably lower energy consumption per processed block. For achieving equal throughputs, [20] can be run at considerably lower clock frequency.

### 3.1   WSN Suitability of Dedicated Hardware Implementations

According to the survey, the best suited approaches for the hardware implementation of AES in WSN nodes seem to be the 8-bit designs [12,20]. They result in the lowest hardware area (i.e. cost). Their power consumptions are presumably also among the lowest even though power has not been reported for the other designs. Even though [20] includes only encryption functionality, it is still usable in real WSNs: decryption functionality of the AES core itself is not often required in commonly used security processing schemes. For example, this is the case in the standardized WSN technologies [7,3].

In addition to these two 8-bit designs, the 32-bit implementations of [8] can also be suitable for WSN nodes. The hardware areas are low and the area-throughput ratios high. The 32-bit cores can be combined with the encryption-mode wrapper of [14] for efficient security processing in the standard WSN technologies. Considering FPGAs, the T-box method of [13] seems to be the best approach for resource-efficient implementations. However, FPGA technologies are currently not feasible solutions for WSN nodes due to their high power consumption.

## 4   Specialized Processor Architectures for AES

An effective performance-area trade-off between dedicated hardware implementations and general-purpose processors can be achieved with programmable specialized processors. Such Application Specific Instruction set Processors (ASIP) are typically general-purpose but they have also been tailored to support a specific application domain or task. A large part of the proposals in the cryptographic domain have concentrated on maximizing performance and programmability [17], which often results in high power consumption and cost and thus makes the proposals unsuited for WSN nodes. In this section we review processor architectures proposed for efficient AES execution in low-cost devices, shown in Table 2.

The ASIP implementation reported in [22] uses the Xtensa configurable processor architecture from Tensilica. In the paper, the execution of cryptographic algorithms, including AES, is accelerated by extending the instruction set of the processor with algorithm-specific instructions. As a result, the performance is improved by several ten-folds from the original (however, the original implementations are poor). The achieved throughput for AES is 17 Mbit/s at 188 MHz in a 0.18 $\mu$m ASIC technology. Area or power figures have not been reported.

An ASIP architecture based on the 32-bit MIPS processor architecture has been published in [23]. A special unit supporting fast LUT functionality is included for accelerating the RC4 and AES algorithms. The unit consists of two 1024$\times$32-bit RAMs implying large area. For accelerating Data Encryption Standard (DES), [23] proposes a very large configurable permutation unit consisting of 512 32$\times$1-bit multiplexers. The achieved throughput for AES is around 64 Mbit/s at 100 MHz. The size of the processor core is 6.25 mm$^2$ in a 0.18 $\mu$m ASIC technology. The power is approximately 90 mW.

In [26], an instruction set extension has been developed for accelerating AES in 32-bit processors. The custom instruction performs the SubBytes (or its inverse) operation using a special functional unit. The unit has been integrated into a LEON-2 processor prototyped in an FPGA. The resulting encryption speedup is up to 1.43 and the code size reduction 30–40%. The area of the unit is 400 gates in a 0.35 $\mu$m ASIC technology. The absolute value for the throughput and the complete processor size in the ASIC technology have not been reported.

We have utilized a processor architecture called Transport Triggered Architecture (TTA) to develop an area-efficient ASIP design for accelerating the execution of RC4 and AES in [24]. In addition to the standard functional units, the processor includes four 256$\times$8-bit RAM-based LUT units, a 32-bit unit for converting between byte and word

Table 2. Specialized processor architectures for AES execution

| Design | Technology | Area | Clock [MHz] | Throughput [Mbit/s] | Power [mW/MHz] |
|--------|-----------|------|-------------|---------------------|----------------|
| Ref. [22] | .18 $\mu$m | n/a | 188 | 17 | n/a |
| Ref. [23] | .18 $\mu$m | 6.25 mm$^2$ | 100 | 64 | 0.90 |
| Ref. [24] | .13 $\mu$m | 70 kgates | 100 | 68 | n/a |
| Ref. [25] | .18 $\mu$m | 2.25 mm$^2$ | 14 | 1.8 | 1.2 |

representations of the AES State, and a unit for performing a combined 32-bit Mix-Columns and AddRoundKey operation in a single clock cycle. The LUT units eliminate main memory accesses in the same way as the custom instruction of [26]. The size of our TTA processor that supports AES and RC4 is 69.4 kgates in a 0.13 $\mu$m ASIC technology. The throughput is 68.5 Mbit/s for AES using precomputed roundkeys at 100 MHz. Power consumption was not evaluated in this study.

A microcoded cryptoprocessor designed for executing DES, AES, and Elliptic Curve Cryptography (ECC) has been published in [25]. The data path contains an expansion/permutation unit, a shifter, four memory-based LUTs, two logic units, and a register file consisting of sixteen 256-bit registers. The processor can be reconfigured by modifying the microcoded program and the contents of the LUTs. The encryption throughput for AES is 1.83 Mbit/s at 13.56 MHz with on-the-fly key expansion. The hardware area in a 0.18 $\mu$m technology is 2.25 mm$^2$ and the power consumption for AES is 16.3 mW.

### 4.1 WSN Suitability of Specialized Processor Architectures

Compared to the most compact AES hardware implementations of Section 3, the reviewed specialized processor architectures result in significantly larger areas, lower performances, and higher power consumptions. Their benefits are in programmability and/or reconfigurability compared to dedicated hardware and in performance when compared to general-purpose processors of the same application domain.

The cost of the processor presented in [23] is high and thus it is poorly suited for WSN nodes. On the contrary, the special operation units presented in [24,26] can be used for increasing the performances of the main processors in WSN nodes. Whereas [26] dedicates its unit for AES only, the LUT unit of [24] is suited for other tasks as well. The performance results in these two papers are considerably better than in [22]. If a 32-bit general-purpose processor is considered to be used in a WSN node, the complete processor design of [24] with its special support for AES is a feasible solution. Even though the AES performance of [25] is lower than e.g. in [24], the processor can be suitable for WSN nodes which frequently need to perform also ECC computations.

## 5  Conclusions

A large part of WSN applications require cryptographic protection. Due to the constraints of WSN nodes, their cryptographic implementations should be low-cost and energy-efficient. In this paper, we reviewed hardware architectures proposed for AES implementations in such environments. The survey considered both dedicated hardware and specialized processor designs. According to our survey, currently 8-bit dedicated hardware designs seem to be the most feasible solutions for WSN nodes. Alternatively, compact special functional units can be used for extending the instruction sets of WSN node processors for efficient AES execution. The reviewed designs often offer significantly higher throughput at their maximum clock speed than what is actually required for WSN communications. Hence, considerable power savings can be achieved by decreasing the clock speed from its maximum without affecting the wireless data rates of nodes. We believe that the review presented in this paper is valuable for designers evaluating and developing AES implementations for environments in which low cost and low power consumption are key requirements, beyond WSNs as well.

# References

1. Stankovic, J.A., Abdelzaher, T.F., Lu, C., Sha, L., Hou, J.C.: Real-time communication and coordination in embedded sensor networks. Proceedings of the IEEE 91(7), 1002–1022 (2003)
2. Hämäläinen, P., Kuorilehto, M., Alho, T., Hännikäinen, M., Hämäläinen, T.D.: Security in wireless sensor networks: Considerations and experiments. In: Proc. Embedded Computer Systems: Architectures, Modelling, and Simulation (SAMOS VI) Workshop–Special Session on Wireless Sensor Networks, Samos, Greece, pp. 167–177 (July 17-20, 2006)
3. ZigBee Alliance: ZigBee Specification Version 1.0 (December 2004)
4. Suhonen, J., Kohvakka, M., Hännikäinen, M., Hämäläinen, T.D.: Design, implementation, and experiments on outdoor deployment of wireless sensor network for environmental monitoring. In: Proc. Embedded Computer Systems: Architectures, Modelling, and Simulation (SAMOS VI) Workshop–Special Session on Wireless Sensor Networks, Samos, Greece, pp. 109–121 (July 17-20, 2006)
5. Avancha, S., Undercoffer, J., Joshi, A., Pinkston, J.: Security for Wireless Sensor Networks. In: Wireless Sensor Networks, 1st edn. pp. 253–275. Springer, Heidelberg (2004)
6. National Institute of Standards and Technology (NIST): Advanced Encryption Standard (AES), FIPS-197 (2001)
7. IEEE: IEEE Standard for Local and Metropolitan Area Networks—Part 15.4: Wireless Medium Access Control (MAC) and Physical Layer (PHY) Specifications for Low-Rate Wireless Personal Area Networks (LR-WPAN), IEEE Std 802.15.4 (2003)
8. Satoh, A., Morioka, S., Takano, K., Munetoh, S.: A compact Rijndael hardware architecture with S-box optimization. In: Boyd, C. (ed.) ASIACRYPT 2001. LNCS, vol. 2248, pp. 239–254. Springer, Heidelberg (2001)
9. Good, T., Benaissa, M.: AES on FPGA from the fastest to the smallest. In: Rao, J.R., Sunar, B. (eds.) CHES 2005. LNCS, vol. 3659, pp. 427–440. Springer, Heidelberg (2005)
10. Pramstaller, N., Mangard, S., Dominikus, S., Wolkerstorfer, J.: Efficient AES implementations on ASICs and FPGAs. In: Proc. 4th Conf. on the Advanced Encryption Standard (AES 2004), Bonn, Germany, May 10-12, 2005, pp. 98–112 (2005)
11. Feldhofer, M., Dominikus, S., Wolkerstorfer, J.: Strong authentication for RFID systems using the AES algorithm. In: Joye, M., Quisquater, J.-J. (eds.) CHES 2004. LNCS, vol. 3156, pp. 357–370. Springer, Heidelberg (2004)
12. Feldhofer, M., Wolkerstorfer, J., Rijmen, V.: AES implementation on a grain of sand. IEE Proc. Inf. Secur. 152(1), 13–20 (2005)
13. Chodowiec, P., Gaj, K.: Very compact FPGA implementation of the AES algorithm. In: D.Walter, C., Koç, Ç.K., Paar, C. (eds.) CHES 2003. LNCS, vol. 2779, pp. 319–333. Springer, Heidelberg (2003)
14. Hämäläinen, P., Hännikäinen, M., Hämäläinen, T.: Efficient hardware implementation of security processing for IEEE 802.15.4 wireless networks. In: Proc. 48th IEEE Int. Midwest Symp. on Circuits and Systems (MWSCAS 2005), Cincinnati, OH, USA, August 7-10, 2005, pp. 484–487 (2005)
15. Rouvroy, G., Standaert, F.X., Quisquater, J.J., Legat, J.D.: Compact and efficient encryption/decryption module for FPGA implementation of the AES Rijndael very well suited for small embedded applications. In: Proc. IEEE Int. Conf. on Inf. Tech.: Coding and Computing (ITCC 2004), Las Vegas, NV, USA, April 4-6, 2004, vol. 2, pp. 583–587 (2004)

16. Elbirt, A.J., Yip, W., Chetwynd, B., Paar, C.: An FPGA implementation and performance evaluation of the AES block cipher candidate algorithm finalists. In: Proc. 3rd AES Candidate Conf. (AES3), New York, NY, USA, April 13-14, 2000 (2000)
17. Hämäläinen, P.: Cryptographic Security Designs and Hardware Architectures for Wireless Local Area Networks. PhD thesis, Tampere Univ. of Tech. Tampere, Finland, (December 2006), Available online: http://www.tkt.cs.tut.fi/research/daci/phd_hamalainenp_thesis.html
18. Fischer, V.: Realization of the round 2 AES candidates using Altera FPGA. In: Proc. 3rd AES Candidate Conf. (AES3), New York, NY, USA, April 13-14, 2000 (2000)
19. Fischer, V., Drutarovsky, M.: Two methods of Rijndael implementation in reconfigurable hardware. In: Koç, Ç.K., Naccache, D., Paar, C. (eds.) CHES 2001. LNCS, vol. 2162, pp. 77–92. Springer, Heidelberg (2001)
20. Hämäläinen, P., Alho, T., Hännikäinen, M., Hämäläinen, T.D.: Design and implementation of low-area and low-power AES encryption hardware core. In: Proc. 9th Euromicro Conf. Digital System Design (DSD 2006), Cavtat, Croatia (August 30-September 1, 2006), pp. 577–583 (2006)
21. Järvinen, T., Salmela, P., Hämäläinen, P., Takala, J.: Efficient byte permutation realizations for compact AES implementations. In: Proc. 13th European Signal Processing Conf. (EU-SIPCO 2005), Antalya, Turkey, September 4-8, 2005 (2005)
22. Ravi, S., Raghunathan, A., Potlapally, N., Sankaradass, M.: System design methodologies for a wireless security processing platform. In: Proc. 39th Design Automation Conf. New Orleans, LA, USA, June 10-14, 2002, pp. 777–782 (2002)
23. Lewis, M., Simmons, S.: A VLSI implementation of a cryptographic processor. In: Proc. Canadian Conf. Electrical and Computer Engineering (CCECE 2003), Montreal, Canada, May 4-7, 2003, pp. 821–826 (2003)
24. Hämäläinen, P., Heikkinen, J., Hännikäinen, M., Hämäläinen, T.D.: Design of transport triggered architecture processors for wireless encryption. In: Proc. 8th Euromicro Conf. Digital System Design (DSD 2005), Porto, Portugal, August 30-September 3, 2005, pp. 144–152 (2005)
25. Eslami, Y., Sheikholeslami, A., Gulak, P.G., Masui, S., Mukaida, K.: An area-efficient universal cryptography processor for smart cards. IEEE Trans. VLSI Systems 14(1), 43–56 (2006)
26. Tillich, S., Grosschädl, J., Szekely, A.: An instruction set extension for fast and memory-efficient AES implementation. In: Dittmann, J., Katzenbeisser, S., Uhl, A. (eds.) CMS 2005. LNCS, vol. 3677, pp. 11–21. Springer, Heidelberg (2005)

# $k^+$ Neigh: An Energy Efficient Topology Control for Wireless Sensor Networks[*]

Dong-Min Son and Young-Bae Ko

Graduate School of Information and Communication,
Ajou University, Suwon, Republic of Korea
dongmin@uns.ajou.ac.kr, youngko@ajou.ac.kr

**Abstract.** For most applications in wireless sensor networks (WSNs), it is often assumed that the deployment of sensor nodes is unmanaged and random, so the density of local node may vary throughout the network. In high density areas, nodes consume more energy due to frequent packet collisions and retransmissions. One of the ways to alleviate this problem is to adjust the transmission power of each sensor node by means of efficient topology control mechanisms. In this paper, we propose an efficient topology control for energy conservation, named "k+ Neigh." In our scheme, each sensor node reduces its transmission power so that it has minimum number of k neighbor nodes. Later, we will show that the preferred value of the k is 2 by simulation. In the performance evaluation, the proposed scheme can make significant energy saving with such a topology structure, while the network connectivity is guaranteed.

## 1 Introduction

Wireless sensor networks (WSNs) consist of a number of sensors that have responsibility for informing any sensed event to a centralized node (often, called a "sink") via multi-hop wireless transmissions. In general, sensor nodes are randomly deployed, so the local density of each node may vary according to their locations. In highly dense areas, sensor nodes may suffer from more contentions among themselves and a severe interference with their local neighbors. It is not difficult to expect that a high contention increases the possibility of packet collisions and hence retransmissions, resulting in faster energy depletion of sensor nodes. Moreover, it will increase the end-to-end latency of packet transmissions.

One of the solutions to alleviate this problem is to manage the network topology by adjusting a transmission power of each sensor node. An optimally adjusted transmission range of each node can decrease the frequency of packet collisions and improve the network performance with the effect of spatial reuse. However, it is not easy to get this optimal value because the connectivity from the whole network's point of view should be guaranteed, while keeping the transmission range of each

---

[*] This research was supported by the MIC(Ministry of Information and Communication), Korea, under the ITRC(Information Technology Research Center) support program supervised by the IITA(Institute of Information Technology Advancement)" (IITA-2006-(C1090-0602-0011)).

S. Vassiliadis et al. (Eds.): SAMOS 2007, LNCS 4599, pp. 454–463, 2007.
© Springer-Verlag Berlin Heidelberg 2007

node as small as possible. In this paper, we propose an efficient topology control algorithm for energy conservation, named "$k^+$ *Neigh*." In the proposed scheme, a sensor node tries to reduce its transmission power based on the value of $k$ which represents the number of local neighbors of each node that can guarantee the network connectivity as well as energy efficiency. We argue that such a value of $k$ can be utilized for the nodes to control their transmission power (i.e., to adjust its transmission range as optimal as possible). The transmission power control is possible in the real world sensor network. The Mica Mote, which is famous sensor node, can adjust its transmitting power in 255 different levels (e.g., from 0x01 to 0xff) [9]. Mica Mote has been developed at U.C. Berkeley and is now commercially available from Crossbow Inc. It is equipped with a low-power micro processor, 128K of program memory, 4 K of SRAM, and low power transceiver for wireless communication.

The rest of the paper is organized as follows. Related works on topology control schemes are presented in Section 2. Section 3 introduces our proposed scheme followed by simulation results in Section 4. We conclude our paper in Section 5.

## 2 Motivation and Related Work

Our $k^+$ *Neigh* protocol can be said to be motivated from the existing k-NEIGH topology control scheme [3]. The authors of [3] argue that some optimal form of topology can be created by having every node keep their number of neighbors below a specific value of k. The value k is chosen in such a way that the entire network is connected with high probability. The k-NEIGH topology control produces a symmetrically connected graph by addressing technical machinery of [4]. They show that setting k to 9 produces the optimal topology with high connectivity. They also argue this value of k can be minimized to 6 if applications accept weakly connected network topologies.

Now, we want to point out that these values of k (either 6 or 9) in the k-NEIGH protocol look too large to minimize energy consumption and interference among neighboring nodes in WSNs. In addition, we believe that k-NEIGH protocol can cause a severe problem of network partition in some cases. Therefore, we need to develop a better scheme for topology control both in terms of energy efficiency and network connectivity.

In order to guarantee complete network connectivity, each node should guarantee one more link towards the sink. To get the link, we use an Interest Message of the Directed Diffusion [5] with slight modification. The Interest Message has been proposed for data-centric paradigm. In WSNs, every sensing data is always reported to the monitoring terminal (e.g., sink). To make such procedure efficiently, sink names and diffuses its interest, each sensor node then collects and reports the named sensing data. The important feature is that the Interest Message is periodically diffused from the sink to the entire network. The Interest Message contains named task description such as data type, report interval, and task duration. Other than these task descriptions, we will add topology control information on the Interest Message.

One more thing that we consult from Directed Diffusion is data aggregation. The early model of Directed Diffusion provides in-network data aggregation as opportunistic aggregation at intermediate nodes along the established paths. However, the opportunistic path selection only provides chance of aggregation. Therefore greedy aggregation is proposed in [6]. In the greedy approach, path sharing mechanism improves early shared and merged path by using a greedy incremental cost. Similar to the greedy aggregation, we will also use a similar kind of information, named Cost-to-Sink (i.e., cost to reach the sink), to guarantee the path to sink.

## 3   Proposed Scheme: $k^+$ *Neigh Topology Control*

The ultimate goal of our work is to minimize energy consumption and radio interference while maintaining connectivity in wireless sensor networks. To accomplish this goal, we propose to adjust the number of neighbors per node into some optimal value. Such an approach can be thought to be similar to the existing k-NEIGH protocol in [3]. However, we propose a better solution here to resolve some limitations of the k-NEIGH which are already described in the previous section. Thus, we present a novel neighbor-based solution which guarantees the network connectivity with any value of $k$ -- in section 4 we will show setting k to 2 is the optimal choice in terms of energy cost and spatial reuse. The proposed solution for energy efficient topology control is called as "$k^+$ *Neigh*", and consists of two phases: *Neighbor Discovery with MAC-level Beaconing*, and *Topology Control with Interest Message Exchange*. Note that the messages in both phases are periodically issued. The periodic *MAC-level Beaconing* allows to detect node failure, while the periodic *Interest Message* enables reconstruction of the topology without link failure. More details of each phase are described in the following subsections.

### 3.1   Neighbor Discovery Phase

In this phase, each sensor node discovers its neighbors by maintaining a neighbor table that is updated with periodic MAC-level Beaconing of Hello messages. Note that we assume sensor nodes have no or minimal mobility. Each node broadcasts its Hello message, which contains its identification (i.e., each node's ID information). The neighboring nodes obtain this message, and store the identification and the estimated distance to each of their neighbor table. The storing process is done in order of the distance. We assume that several techniques such as Received Signal Strength Intensity (RSSI) [7] or Time of Arrival (ToA) [8] can be used to estimate the distance between each sensor node. These techniques do leave room for criticism, but they can be effective in that they take lower cost than using the Global Position System (GPS). Although, in this paper, we present our scheme by using the distance information, the distance information can be substituted by other routing metrics such as signal strength or air-time cost. Therefore the problems when the distance information is utilized (e.g., multipath propagation, bit error rate) can be relieved by using these metric. For example, the signal strength reveals the radio interference (i.e., the radio interfered node is the actual neighbor node).

### 3.2   Topology Control Phase

After the end of the Neighbor Discovery phase, each sensor node will obtain a sorted neighbor table that contains the ID and the distance information of all of its physical neighbors. To reduce the medium access contention and the transmitting power of the nodes, each node *logically* adjusts the number of its local neighbors by selecting $k$ smallest distanced entries from the original neighbor table. We call this logically selected list as *k-Neighbor List* (k-NL for short). The k-NL is included in the Interest Message that is initially issued by the sink, and it is later continuously modified and forwarded by the intermediate nodes. (We illustrate how an Interest Message looks like, and how it is used for topology control later in this subsection). Based on the information of k-NL, each node can verify which neighbors are symmetric to it. Here, a symmetric neighbor means that any two nodes are included in each other's k-NL that they can have a symmetric link between them. However the verification mechanism causes a problem. A node can have no symmetric neighbor because all of its neighbors may not include this node as their symmetric neighbor. In this case, that node is isolated from the network.

To resolve this problem, we devise the concept of special neighbor node for guaranteeing a link towards the sink. We call this special neighbor node as Node-to-Sink. Once a node sets another node as the Node-to-Sink, the node set as the Node-to-Sink should include that node even if it has more than k symmetric neighbors. To make an energy efficient topology, a node selects Node-to-Sink, which is the shortest distanced neighbor among which that is closer to the sink than the node. The distance from a node to its neighbors can be obtained by using the neighbor list, but the distance from a sink to the node cannot be known.

So we add one more information named Cost-to-Sink. The Cost-to-Sink is the accumulated value of the distance from the sink to the current node with the Interest Message. To get the appropriate accumulated value, the diffusion (message forwarding) sequence of the Interest Message is very important. Fundamentally, the procedure of our Interest Message diffusion is some what similar with the directed diffusion [5] in that the sending of the Interest Message starts from the sink. However, it is unique in that it does not use the random back-off forwarding that is used in the directed diffusion. Instead of the forwarding, we design "Distance-based Forwarding." Further description about this mechanism is given below:

**Distance-Based Forwarding.** Assume that a generic node u sends a message to node v. To forward the message in ascending order of the estimated distance between node v and u, the receiving node v should send a message at time $T_s$ within the sending interval $T_{SI}$. The time is obtained by using the first received message as the standard. The equation of $T_s$ is as follows: (Distance between nodes u and v is denoted by $d_{uv}$, and Maximum transmission range of node is denoted by $R_{MAX}$)

$$T_S = T_{SI} \times \frac{d_{uv}}{R_{MAX}} \qquad (1)$$

Fig. 1 on the next page shows an example of our $k^+$ *neigh* topology control where $k$ is set to 2. Fig. 1(a)-(e) shows the diffusion procedure of Interest Message. In Fig. 1(a), a sink initially transmits Interest Message with three types of information. To fill in the 2-Neighbor List, the sink picks out nodes A and C from its neighbor list. The Cost-to-Sink and Node-to-Sink attributes are set to 0 and none, respectively, as the node itself is the sink. When receiving this Interest Message from the sink, the

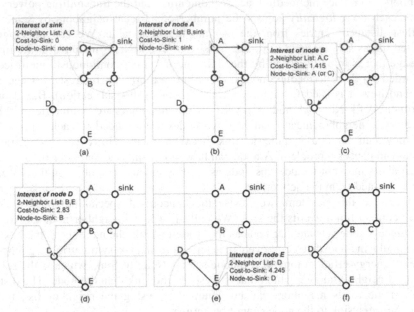

**Fig. 1.** Diffusion process of Interest Message for Topology Control. (a) Initially, sink generates an Interest Message with three types of information, i.e., 2-NL, Cost-to-Sink, and Node-to-Sink. (b) On receiving the Interest Message from the sink, node A modifies and rebroadcasts it. (Node C's transmission is omitted here) (c) After A's forwarding, node B forwards the message as it is farther than node A from the sink. (d) Node D also fills out the three info of Interest Message and forwards it. (e) Finally, node E does the same. (f) Final topology graph, where each node adjusts its power properly.

neighboring nodes A, B, and C are required to update their Cost-to-Sink value. The Cost-to-Sink will be determined by a summation of the value included in the received Interest Message from the sink and the distance between the sink and the receiving node. That is, nodes A, B, and C will set their Cost-to-Sink values into 1, 1.415, and 1, respectively. After this setting, each node then decides when it should forward the modified Interest Message at the specific time, according to Distance-based Forwarding. If the sending interval ($T_{SI}$) is 1 second then node A and C forward the Interest Message at the time of 0.67 (= $1 \times 1 / 1.5$). In this case, although the sending time is same between node A and C, the actual sending time becomes different because the contention at MAC layer. Consequently, the Interest Message is diffused in the sequence of [sink, {A, C}, B, D, and E]. By this mechanism, every node can be assured to obtain the least Cost-to-Sink before forwarding.

Fig. 1(c) and (d) show the construction of the Symmetric Neighbor List (SNL) by exchanging of 2-Neighbor List attribute. In Fig. 1(d), node D includes nodes B and E into its 2-Neighbor List. However, in Fig. 1(c), node B did not include node D in its 2-Neighbor List, thus node D realizes that node B is not a symmetric neighbor. If node D cannot be a neighbor with node B then node D cannot connect to the sink. For this case, the Node-to-Sink attribute is utilized as illustrated in Fig. 1(d). Node D decides to set the Node-to-Sink to node B and includes node B in its Symmetric

Neighbor List. Once node B gets the message that it has been set as the Node-to-Sink, then it has to include the node D to its Symmetric Neighbor List.

After the diffusion of the Interest Message, each node sets its transmission power to the power that is needed to transmit to the farthest node in SNL. Note that we assume the sensor nodes are able to control their transmitting power. Fig. 1(f) shows the resulting topology of our $2^+$ Neigh Topology Control where k is set to 2. At initial time, the power of every node sets 1.5, so that the total energy cost is 9, but after topology control, the total energy cost becomes 7.245, thus we can save the energy amount of 1.755. This example is very simple and uniform. However, in practice, the topology can be untethered and unattended so the energy can be saved much more than this example. The further evaluation for energy cost in the random topology is shown in section 4.

## 4 Performance Evaluation

In this section, we evaluate $k^+$ Neigh using NS-2 [10] simulator. The ultimate goal of simulation is to show that our proposed $k^+$ Neigh topology control protocol contributes to significant improvements of both energy efficiency and network capacity. For the purpose of a comparison, we consider the following two topology control algorithms:

- **Minimum Spanning Tree (MST)**: Euclidian MST algorithm produces the topology which consumes minimum energy in data communication. Basically, MST can not be used easily in practical because it assumes that each node knows the global position of all other nodes in the network.
- **k-NEIGH**: As in the section 2, k-NEIGH algorithm insists that the number of physical neighbors of every node maintains equal to or slightly below a specific value k. We set the k to the value of 6, for small network (e.g., where the total number of nodes is under 100), and generally k is set by 9. We have considered the result of Phase 1 only (i.e., without pruning).

### 4.1 Simulation Environment

In our simulation, a total number of nodes $n$, ranges from 10 to 1000. To decide the network size, we consider the power control capability of Mica Mote series [9] and the empirical transmission range for ensuring connectivity (refer to [2] and [3]). In practice, the Mica Mote is able to adjust the transmission range by at most 150m. According to [2] and [3], when $n$ is equal to 10 the transmission range should be empirically larger than $0.86622 \times r$, where $r$ is a network radius. Thus we set the maximum transmission range to 86m when $r$ is set to 100m. We use the two-ray ground model as a radio propagation model and an omni-directional antenna which having homogeneity gain in the simulation. We measure the following metrics: *energy cost*, and *physical node degree*.

We define the energy cost as the equation shown below:

$$c(PA) = \sum_{i \in N} (PA(i)) \tag{2}$$

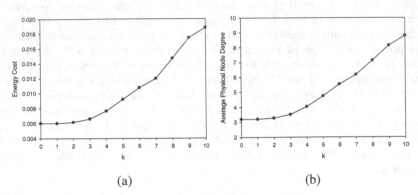

**Fig. 2.** The performance results of k$^+$ Neigh for different values of the number of neighbors (a) Energy cost according to k. (b) Average physical node degree according to k.

where PA is the power assignment which is adjusted at the end of the Topology Control Phase.

In our simulation study, we convert the distance to power according to the Friis free space model [11] and the two-ray ground reflection models [11] that are currently implemented in the well-known network simulator NS-2. The free space propagation model assumes the ideal condition, thus it is useful for short distance. On the other hand, the two-ray ground reflection model considers both the direct path and a ground reflection path. Therefore we consider the crossover point of two models (If the distance is less than 86.14m then the Friis model is applied otherwise the two-ray ground is used [10].)

The physical node degree represents the actual number of interfered neighbors. This notation can be distinguished from logical node degree because the logical degree shows only the number of one-hop symmetric neighbors. Therefore physical node degree is the more meaningful metric than the logical node degree in evaluating the actual contention at the MAC layer. In addition, the low physical node degree increases the spatial reuse, so that the network capacity becomes enhanced.

Before explaining more details of the simulation results, we have studied about the appropriate number of neighbors for energy efficient topology control by means of a simulation-based evaluation. The number of neighbors is denoted by k and indicates the intensity of the contention. Therefore the smallest value of k is recommended for topologies requiring the lowest contention. However if the number of neighbors becomes too few, it may cause instability of the network and cannot work on rigorous environments. Consequently, when adjusting the value of k, the energy cost and physical degree should be carefully considered.

To see the effect of the value k, we measure the energy cost and the physical degree by varying it from 0 to 10. 100 nodes are distributed randomly in the network. In the first experiment, the result of energy cost is shown in Fig. 2(a). The interesting point is that the energy cost is almost the same when k=0 and 1. When k=0, each node can have no symmetric neighbor with an empty k-Neighbor List (i.e., 0-NL), so that a node purely relies on Node-to-Sink to create the symmetric neighbor. The symmetric

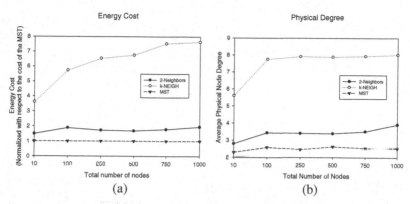

**Fig. 3.** The performance results of 2-Neighbors compared with k-NEIGH and MST. (a) Energy cost according to the network size. The energy cost is normalized with respect to the cost of the MST. (b) Average physical degree according to the network size.

neighbor from Node-to-Sink guarantees a path towards a sink. Likewise, it is difficult to make the symmetric neighbor for the $1^+$ Neigh because it is rare to have each other as 1-NL of two nodes. So $1^+$ Neigh also relies on Node-to-Sink and the result of $1^+$ Neigh is similar with that of $0^+$ Neigh. The $0^+$ Neigh or $1^+$ Neigh can be thought as good for extremely energy sensitive network environments. One more thing to observe is the energy cost of $2^+$ Neigh is almost same as $0^+$ Neigh. As previously stated, the large value of k makes the network stable. Therefore $2^+$ Neigh is recommendable for energy efficient networks. Besides, the MST, which is considered as the optimal network topology scheme, tries to maintain its number of neighbors as two. This is made clearer by Fig. 2(b), which the physical degree values for k=0 and k=3 are shown to be similar. This means, when k is 2 or 3, a topology becomes energy efficient with a low contention while having more stable number of neighbors. Larger values over 4 may be suitable for applications requiring highly stable network environments, but at the cost of energy consumption.

## 4.2 Simulation Results

Performance results of $2^+$ Neigh are reported in Fig. 3 compared with k-NEIGH, and MST. In Fig. 3(a), we show the energy cost which is normalized with respect to the cost of the MST. We can see the energy cost of $2^+$ Neigh is significantly less than k-NEIGH and quite close to that of MST. This result is very meaningful because our scheme requires only 2n message where n is the number of nodes. Moreover the half of the required messages are relatively low cost MAC-level beaconing. We recall that the MST requires global position of every node so that $n^2$ messages should be exchanged. The average physical node degree of $2^+$ Neigh topology control protocol is also reported in Fig. 3(b). The figure shows an evident result that the upper bound (k) of k-NEIGH is still large to reduce the number of physical neighbors. Our protocol achieves 30% lower average physical degree compared to k-NEIGH. For the proposed $2^+$ Neigh protocol, we emphasize that the spatial reuse, which is represented

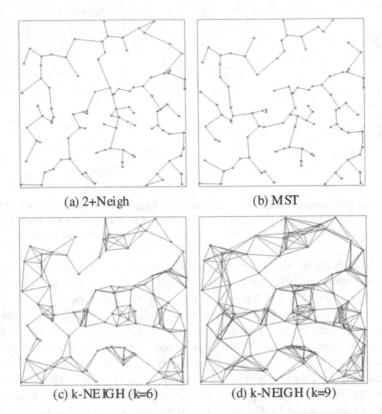

(a) 2+Neigh                    (b) MST

(c) k-NEIGH (k=6)              (d) k-NEIGH (k=9)

**Fig. 4.** Sample topologies produced by k+Neighbors, MST, and k-NEIGH Topology Control when n=100. We call the k+Neighbors where k=2 as "2+ Neigh." Note that $k$ is set to 6 or 9 for the k-NEIGH in (c) and (d) above.

by the physical node degree, is approximated to the sparsest possible topology (MST) while the cost of topology construction is tremendously reduced.

To compare the visual network topologies of $k^+$ Neigh, MST, and k-NEIGH, we use the graph drawing software called Himmeli [12]. The sample topologies generated by the various protocols for n=100 are shown in Fig. 4 on next page. In $k^+$ Neigh Topology Control, we set the value of k to 2, as recommend in section 4.1. Unlike our scheme, in k-NEIGH, the value of k is set to 6 and 9 as suggested in [3]. We recall that our scheme guarantees network connectivity even when k is set to 2. On the other hand, the k-NEIGH causes a severe problem of network partition if k is set to 2. Fig. 4 also shows that our $2^+$ Neigh scheme significantly removes the number of over-connected links from k-NEIGH. Not only the topology of $2^+$ Neigh looks similar to the MST (See Fig. 4(a) and (b), respectively), but $2^+$ Neigh also has some more number of links for connection towards a sink (located in a center of all the figures). In result, our scheme is proved to be efficient in terms of energy cost and to be robust in terms of the available number of paths towards a sink.

# 5  Conclusion

Topology control has been proved to be an efficient method in improving both energy conservation and network capacity [1]. However, previous researches on topology control do not take into account the untethered and unattended sensor networks. For this reason, we proposed a novel topology control for sensor networks.

Our proposed scheme, named $k^+$ *Neigh*, tries to maintain $k$ number of neighbors. This approach seems a bit like k-NEIGH [3] but the possible value of k is different. The k-NEIGH can not prevent network connectivity at a small k value. In contrast, the $k^+$ *Neigh* is connected by any value of the k. Among the values of the k, setting k to 2 is suggested for energy efficiency and network capacity. The $k^+$ *Neigh* defines two phases: Neighbor Discovery and Topology Control. In the Neighbor Discovery phase, each node sends Hello messages periodically and obtains the neighbor entries. In the Topology Control phase, the sink diffuses the Interest Message which contains information for creating the topology. Since the Interest Message is periodically sent, our $k^+$ Neigh topology network can recover and maintain network connectivity.

For further researches, we plan to study the sink mobility issues on the sparsest possible topology and the data aggregation method which can relieve traffic bottleneck. These investigations are expected to enhance $k^+$ *Neigh* Topology Control. We shall also implement our scheme on Mica Mote platform to show that this scheme is effective in the real sensor world.

# References

[1]  Santi, P.: Topology Control in Wireless Ad Hoc and Sensor Networks. ACM Comp. Surveys 37(2), 164–194 (2005)
[2]  Santi, P., Blough, D.M.: The Critical Transmitting Range for Connectivity in Sparse Wireless Ad Hoc Networks. IEEE Trans. 2(1), 1–15 (2003)
[3]  Blough, D.M., Leoncini, M., Resta, G., Santi, P.: The k-Neighbors Approach to Interference Bounded and Symmetric Topology Control in Ad Hoc Networks. IEEE Trans. on Mobile Computing 5(9), 1267–1282 (2006)
[4]  Xue, F., Kumar, P.R.: The Number of Neighbors Needed for Connectivity of Wireless Networks. Wireless Networks 10(2), 169–181 (2004)
[5]  Intanagonwiwat, C., Govindan, R., Estrin, D.: Directed diffusion: A scalable and robust communication paradigm for sensor networks. In: Proc. of the ACM International Conference on Mobile Computing and Networking (MOBICOM), ACM Press, New York (2000)
[6]  Intanagoniwawat, C., Estrin, D., Govindan, R., Heidemann, J.: Impact of Network Density on Data Aggregation in Wireless Sensor Networks. In: Proc. of the International Conference on Distributed Computing Systems (ICDCS) (July 2002)
[7]  Bahl, P., Padmanabhan, V.N.: Radar: An in-building rf-based user location and tracking system. Proc. of the IEEE Infocom 2000 2, 775–784 (2000)
[8]  Girod, L., Estrin, D.: Robust Range Estimation Using Acoustic and Multimodal Sensing. In: Proc. of the IEEE/RSJ International Conference on Intelligent Robots and Systems (2001)
[9]  MPR/MIB User's Manual, Document 7430-0021-03, (August 2003), http://www. xbow.com/
[10]  ns-2 network simulator: http://www.isi.edu/nsnam/ns
[11]  Pahlavan, K., et al.: Principles of Wireless Networks. Prentice Hall, Englewood Cliffs (2002)
[12]  http://www.artemis.kll.helsinki.fi/himmeli/himmeli.html

# Author Index

# Lecture Notes in Computer Science

Sublibrary 1: Theoretical Computer Science and General Issues

For information about Vols. 1– 4488
please contact your bookseller or Springer

Vol. 4641: A.-M. Kermarrec, L. Bougé, T. Priol (Eds.), Euro-Par 2007 Parallel Processing. XXVII, 974 pages. 2007.

Vol. 4639: E. Csuhaj-Varjú, Z. Ésik (Eds.), Fundamentals of Computation Theory. XIV, 508 pages. 2007.

Vol. 4638: T. Stützle, M. Birattari, H. H. Hoos (Eds.), Engineering Stochastic Local Search Algorithms. X, 223 pages. 2007.

Vol. 4630: H.J. van den Herik, P. Ciancarini, J. Donkers (Eds.), Computers and Games. XII, 283 pages. 2007.

Vol. 4628: L.N. de Castro, F.J. Von Zuben, H. Knidel (Eds.), Artificial Immune Systems. XII, 438 pages. 2007.

Vol. 4627: M. Charikar, K. Jansen, O. Reingold, J.D.P. Rolim (Eds.), Approximation, Randomization, and Combinatorial Optimization. XII, 626 pages. 2007.

Vol. 4624: T. Mossakowski, U. Montanari, M. Haveraaen (Eds.), Algebra and Coalgebra in Computer Science. XI, 463 pages. 2007.

Vol. 4623: M. Collard (Ed.), Ontologies-based DataBases and Information Systems. X, 153 pages. 2007.

Vol. 4621: D. Wagner, R. Wattenhofer (Eds.), Algorithms for Sensor and Ad Hoc Networks. XIII, 415 pages. 2007.

Vol. 4619: F. Dehne, J.-R. Sack, N. Zeh (Eds.), Algorithms and Data Structures. XVI, 662 pages. 2007.

Vol. 4618: S.G. Akl, C.S. Calude, M.J. Dinneen, G. Rozenberg, H.T. Wareham (Eds.), Unconventional Computation. X, 243 pages. 2007.

Vol. 4616: A. Dress, Y. Xu, B. Zhu (Eds.), Combinatorial Optimization and Applications. XI, 390 pages. 2007.

Vol. 4614: B. Chen, M.S. Paterson, G. Zhang (Eds.), Combinatorics, Algorithms, Probabilistic and Experimental Methodologies. XII, 530 pages. 2007.

Vol. 4613: F.P. Preparata, Q. Fang (Eds.), Frontiers in Algorithmics. XI, 348 pages. 2007.

Vol. 4600: H. Comon-Lundh, C. Kirchner, H. Kirchner (Eds.), Rewriting, Computation and Proof. XVI, 273 pages. 2007.

Vol. 4599: S. Vassiliadis, M. Bereković, T.D. Hämäläinen (Eds.), Embedded Computer Systems: Architectures, Modeling, and Simulation. XVII, 466 pages. 2007.

Vol. 4598: G. Lin (Ed.), Computing and Combinatorics. XII, 570 pages. 2007.

Vol. 4596: L. Arge, C. Cachin, T. Jurdziński, A. Tarlecki (Eds.), Automata, Languages and Programming. XVII, 953 pages. 2007.

Vol. 4595: D. Bošnački, S. Edelkamp (Eds.), Model Checking Software. X, 285 pages. 2007.

Vol. 4590: W. Damm, H. Hermanns (Eds.), Computer Aided Verification. XV, 562 pages. 2007.

Vol. 4588: T. Harju, J. Karhumäki, A. Lepistö (Eds.), Developments in Language Theory. XI, 423 pages. 2007.

Vol. 4583: S.R. Della Rocca (Ed.), Typed Lambda Calculi and Applications. X, 397 pages. 2007.

Vol. 4580: B. Ma, K. Zhang (Eds.), Combinatorial Pattern Matching. XII, 366 pages. 2007.

Vol. 4576: D. Leivant, R. de Queiroz (Eds.), Logic, Language, Information and Computation. X, 363 pages. 2007.

Vol. 4547: C. Carlet, B. Sunar (Eds.), Arithmetic of Finite Fields. XI, 355 pages. 2007.

Vol. 4546: J. Kleijn, A. Yakovlev (Eds.), Petri Nets and Other Models of Concurrency – ICATPN 2007. XI, 515 pages. 2007.

Vol. 4545: H. Anai, K. Horimoto, T. Kutsia (Eds.), Algebraic Biology. XIII, 379 pages. 2007.

Vol. 4533: F. Baader (Ed.), Term Rewriting and Applications. XII, 419 pages. 2007.

Vol. 4528: J. Mira, J.R. Álvarez (Eds.), Nature Inspired Problem-Solving Methods in Knowledge Engineering, Part II. XXII, 650 pages. 2007.

Vol. 4527: J. Mira, J.R. Álvarez (Eds.), Bio-inspired Modeling of Cognitive Tasks, Part I. XXII, 630 pages. 2007.

Vol. 4525: C. Demetrescu (Ed.), Experimental Algorithms. XIII, 448 pages. 2007.

Vol. 4514: S.N. Artemov, A. Nerode (Eds.), Logical Foundations of Computer Science. XI, 513 pages. 2007.

Vol. 4513: M. Fischetti, D.P. Williamson (Eds.), Integer Programming and Combinatorial Optimization. IX, 500 pages. 2007.

Vol. 4510: P. Van Hentenryck, L.A. Wolsey (Eds.), Integration of AI and OR Techniques in Constraint Programming for Combinatorial Optimization Problems. X, 391 pages. 2007.

Vol. 4507: F. Sandoval, A.G. Prieto, J. Cabestany, M. Graña (Eds.), Computational and Ambient Intelligence. XXVI, 1167 pages. 2007.

Vol. 4502: T. Altenkirch, C. McBride (Eds.), Types for Proofs and Programs. VIII, 269 pages. 2007.

Vol. 4501: J. Marques-Silva, K.A. Sakallah (Eds.), Theory and Applications of Satisfiability Testing – SAT 2007. XI, 384 pages. 2007.

Vol. 4497: S.B. Cooper, B. Löwe, A. Sorbi (Eds.), Computation and Logic in the Real World. XVIII, 826 pages. 2007.

Vol. 4494: H. Jin, O.F. Rana, Y. Pan, V.K. Prasanna (Eds.), Algorithms and Architectures for Parallel Processing. XIV, 508 pages. 2007.

Vol. 4493: D. Liu, S. Fei, Z. Hou, H. Zhang, C. Sun (Eds.), Advances in Neural Networks – ISNN 2007, Part III. XXVI, 1215 pages. 2007.

Vol. 4492: D. Liu, S. Fei, Z. Hou, H. Zhang, C. Sun (Eds.), Advances in Neural Networks – ISNN 2007, Part II. XXVII, 1321 pages. 2007.

Vol. 4491: D. Liu, S. Fei, Z.-G. Hou, H. Zhang, C. Sun (Eds.), Advances in Neural Networks – ISNN 2007, Part I. LIV, 1365 pages. 2007.

Vol. 4490: Y. Shi, G.D. van Albada, J.J. Dongarra, P.M.A. Sloot (Eds.), Computational Science – ICCS 2007, Part IV. XXXVII, 1211 pages. 2007.

Vol. 4489: Y. Shi, G.D. van Albada, J.J. Dongarra, P.M.A. Sloot (Eds.), Computational Science – ICCS 2007, Part III. XXXVII, 1257 pages. 2007.